NUMBER 325

THE ENGLISH
EXPERIENCE

ITS RECORD IN EARLY PRINTED BOOKS
PUBLISHED IN FACSIMILE

JOHN FAVOUR

ANTIQVITIE TRIVMPHING OVER NOVELTIE

LONDON 1619

DA CAPO PRESS
THEATRVM ORBIS TERRARVM LTD.
AMSTERDAM 1971 NEW YORK

The publishers acknowledge their gratitude
to the Curators of the Bodleian Library, Oxford,
for their permission to reproduce
the Library's copy (Shelfmark: 4°.F.10 Th.)
and to the Syndics of the Cambridge University Library
for their permission to reproduce
the leaves $A2^v$,X1,X2,Dd8
from the Library's copy.
(Shelfmark: F.3.137.)

S.T.C. No. 10716
Collation: A-Z ^{8}, Aa-Qq^8.

Published in 1971 by
Theatrum Orbis Terrarum Ltd.,
O.Z. Voorburgwal 85, Amsterdam

&

Da Capo Press
- a division of Plenum Publishing Corporation -
227 West 17th Street, New York, 10011
Printed in the Netherlands
ISBN 90 221 0325 0

ANTIQVITIE
TRIVMPHING
OVER NOVELTIE:

*WHEREBY IT IS PROVED THAT ANTIQVI-
tie is a true and certaine Note of the Christian Catholicke Church
and verity, againſt all new and late vpſtart hereſies, aduancing
themſelues againſt the religious honour of old Rome, whoſe ancient
faith was ſo much commended by* S. Pauls *pen, and after
ſealed with the bloud of many Martyrs and
worthy Biſhops of that Sea.*

With other neceſſarie and important queſtions incident and proper
to the ſame ſubiect:

By Iohn Favovr *Doctor of the Lawes, ſometimes Fellow of New
Colledge in Oxford, now Vicar of Halifax.*

Iob 8. 8.

Inquire I pray thee of the former age, and prepare thy ſelfe to ſearch of their Fathers
(for we are but of yeſterday and know nothing, becauſe our dayes vpon earth are a
ſhadow:) ſhall not they all teach thee, and tell thee, & vtter words out of their hearts?

Hieron. ad Pammach. Epiſt. 5. c. 8.

Aut profer meliores epulas & me conuiuâ vtere, aut qualicunque noſtrâ cœnulâ contentus eſto.

LONDON,
Printed by Richard Field dwelling in Great
Woodſtreete. 1 6 1 9.

TO THE MOST
REVEREND FATHER
IN GOD, *TOBIE*, BY THE PRO-
VIDENCE OF GOD, LORD ARCH-
bifhop of *Yorke* his Grace, Primate of *England* and
*Metropolitan, mine honorable good Lord and
Patron, increafe of grace now, cer-
taintie of glory for euer.*

Moft Reuerend,

I Owe my felfe, and all I haue, vnto
your Grace, much more my feruice, with the labour of my hands,
head and heart, as moft bounden.
Though Truth need no Patron,
being it felfe free, and that which
freeth vs; protected by the God
of truth, preached by him that is
the Way, the Truth and the Life; publifhed, preferued
and infpired by that Comforter that is the Spirit of
truth, and therefore is great, and muft preuaile: yet do
I betake my felfe and my flender endeuours to your
Graces protection, as my chiefe Patron; leauing Gods
truth, which I haue laboured to make manifeft, to his
owne gracious blefling, and the cenfure thereof to

A 2   his,

his moſt Chriſtian, Catholique, and Apoſtolique Church.

Your Grace did not onely by ſpeech moue me to meditate vpon this ſubieɑ, but alſo gaue me great encouragement to proceed, when I preſented vnto you a few ſheets of paper the next morning after your motion, a ſlender modell of one nights framing. Hereunto I was pricked forward by a godly emulation (and it is good to emulate the good euer, yea and not onely the good, but the euill alſo in that which is good, as by the example of the vniuſt ſteward appeares) partly toward thoſe multitudes of Authors, ſacred, profane, old, new, friends and foes, with whoſe works your Graces great and good Library is plentifully furniſhed; deeming it a ſhame to my ſelfe, being then threeſcore yeares old, to dye and ſorrow like *Callicrates*, who as he gaue vp the ghoſt, ſaid, *My death grieueth me not, becauſe I came out of my countrey to dye; but it grieueth me to dye before I giue a wound vnto mine enemie.* So verily it grieueth me not to be old, or to dye; but it would grieue me to dye before I had wounded a head of that beaſt which perſecuteth the Saints of God. Wherefore ſeeing ſo many haue written great and tedious volumes againſt the truth, I would not paſſe like an arrow in the ayre, or a ſhip in the ſea, and leaue no monument behind me, *to put my flocke in mind of thoſe things which I would wiſh to be beleeued after my departure*; as well by my pen, which may haply pierce when I am dead, as by my tongue, which ſhall not ceaſſe (if it pleaſe God) to preach while I liue: and God knoweth I deſire to liue no longer. Yea and not without ſome emulation of your Graces ſelfe, whom I continually obſerue to be

as

as painfull in your ſtudies, as diligent in your preaching; as actiue in your gouernment, as affable
in your entertainment; as iudicious in the obſeruation of all authors as euer : which I haue not onely
conſidered with due admiration, but alſo bene emu-
lous to follow and imitate ſuch a guide, and ſo
good, *quamuis non paſſibus æquis*. Theſe haue bene
my motiues. Such as my poore labours are, I preſent to your Graces feete, as a part of that dutie
which I owe for the great bountie of your more then
liberalitie and continuall fauour extended to me and
mine. Which if they ſhall be vouchſafed your fatherly acceptance, I ſhall ſolace my ſelfe as *Antima-*
chus did, when all his auditors failed ſaue onely *Plato*:
Legam nihilominus: Plato enim vnus mihi inſtar omnium
eſt. So if all my readers ſhould faile me but your Grace,
I would notwithſtanding write; for your Grace vnto
me is in ſtead of all, ſeeing you haue already ſtood me
in more ſtead then all. If theſe obligations of your deſert and worth, were either by my negligence forgotten, or by mine vnthankfulneſſe miſpriſed; yet the very
ſubieċt matter of my book would challenge it for your
Grace before any other, and as ſoone from me as from
any other.

For I writing of *Antiquitie* in mine old age, to whom
ſhould I commit it (for I cannot commend it) but to
an Ancient in Gods Iſrael, who is the ſtaffe and ſtay of
my declining dayes ? And ſeeing I hold, that the moſt
Ancient Religion is the beſt, why ſhould I not offer it to
the moſt ancient Doctor of Diuinitie that I heare of
in this land, and the moſt ancient Biſhop, both for age
and conſecration, that I know in our Church? who hath

not onely read all the *Ancient Fathers* with a diligent eye, but hath alſo noted them with a iudicious pen (as mine owne eyes are witneſſes, and God reward you for ſuch my libertie) and made continuall vſe of them in his Sermons, as any ancient Father in our nation, ſhall I ſay? yea in all Chriſtendome, as I dare ſay, and verily do beleeue: which our aduerſaries howſoeuer they did enuie it, yet in their conſcience could not de-nie it.

Wherefore as *Cicero* wrote his booke *De Seneſtute,* *in ſeneſtute;* made noble *Cato Maior* his obieſt, as the beſt patterne whereto he might conforme his proieſt; and commended it to *Pomponius Atticus* an old man, as the worthieſt Patron of ſuch a ſubieſt: So my poore ſelfe, in theſe mine old yeares (hauing entred my Cli-maſtericke) for the comfort of mine age, haue pen-ned this little paſſage of the oldeſt Religion, and cho-ſen your Grace as the fitteſt and moſt worthie Patron thereof. Not to be tedious or troubleſome to your Grace any farther, I will beg leaue (which your Grace will vouchſafe) to vſurpe in the concluſion of mine Epiſtle, that which your old friend and familiar vſed as the Preface of his booke: *Nunc mihi viſum eſt de* *ſeneſtute (ſiue Antiquitate) ad te ſcribere: hoc e-* *nim onere quod mihi tecum commune eſt, aut iam vr-* *gentis, aut certè aduentantis ſeneſtutis, & te, & me-* *ipſum leuari volo. Etſi te quidem, id modeſtè & ſapien-* *ter ſicut omnia, & ferre & laturum eſſe certò ſcio. Sed* *mihi cùm de ſeneſtute, (id eſt, Antiquitate) vellem ali-* *quid ſcribere, tu occurrebas dignus eo munere, quo* *vterque noſtrûm communitèr vteremur. Mihi quidem* *ita iucunda huius libri confectio fuit, vt non modò abſter-* *ſerit*

Cicero de Se-neſtute.

serit omnes senectutis molestias, sed effecerit mollem e-
tiam & iucundam senectutem. Nunquam igitur satis
laudari (Theologia & Antiquitatis peruestigatio) potest,
cui qui pareat, omne tempus ætatis sine molestia, imò
summa cum lætitia & conscientiæ securitate possit de-
gere.

Your Graces most humble
and bounden Chaplaine,

John Fauour.

A 4   To

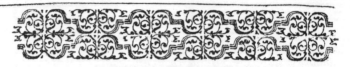

To the Readers.

MY hearts defire and endeuour in this my poore labour, hath bene, and is, to glorifie God, and benefite his Church. What I haue, or fhall attaine vnto, ftandeth and refteth vpon Gods bleffing, and the Chriftian Catholique Churches cenfure. My humbleft prayer to God is, that my heart and worke may be acceptable in his fight, and profitable to his Church. My tender fuite vnto this Church, is, that my paines may reft approued vnto each honeft heart; or that I may receiue brotherly admonition from the learned, for any thing in it which is amiffe. As for them that are without, I fay, Parum eft me à vobis iudicari, aut ab humano die. If thofe which fit in fcorners chaire fhall contemne or condemne me, I will folace my felfe with Seneca, Argumentum eft recti malis difplicere. If my glorious Father and gracious mother iuftifie me, I fhall care litle who condemne me.

Yet becaufe Readers may be of diuers fafhions and factions, fome beneuolent and propitious, fome maleuolent and captious; fome ignorant, though malicious; fome better inftructed, yet humorous; fome pregnant enough to difcerne, yet as peeuifh and peremptorie, either wittily to carpe, or wilfully to mifconfter, or wickedly to peruert and flander what may be miftaken or wrefted; I haue thought good to addreffe a few words, and become an humble fuiter, or an earneft foliciter of all that fhall reade, and will cenfure this my booke. For how many readers, fo many cenfurers I looke to find. To whom I would tender in generall but two requefts : That they would reade this booke with Chriftian humilitie, and cenfure it with brotherly charitie, without preiudice or partialitie. And perhaps it will not be amiffe to reade twice, before they cenfure once.

I was firft moued and led to this labour by the commanding intreatie of my moft reuerend Lord, whom I am bounden to honour

and

and obey whileſt I liue. A long ſickneſſe ſucceeded the firſt motion: yet it being rather tedious by continuance, then vexatious with pain, I made it aduantageable to my purpoſe, ſtole ſo much time for meditation and ſearch, as furniſhed me with more ſpeed to pen it, in that order wherein it is now digeſted.

Wherein notwithſtanding I had many impediments, well knowne vnto the places of my reſidence: as preaching euery Sabbath day, lecturing euery day in the weeke, exerciſing iuſtice in the Commonwealth, practiſing of Phyſicke and Chirurgerie, in the great penurie and neceſſitie thereof in the countrey where I liue, and that onely for Gods ſake, which will eaſily multiply both clients and patients: yet the night hath affoorded me that which the day would not allow me: the ſilence and quiet whereof, hath miniſtred much matter and meanes to further my meditations. The due conſideration whereof, I do not tender as a vaine boaſt, or an excuſe for my ſelfe: but to ſtirre vp the able minds of many that are more learned, and better furniſhed in this kind then I am, who liue either in Cathedrall Churches or Colledges, or are placed ouer ſmall congregations, where they haue more eaſe and leiſure, with fewer diſtractions and impediments then ſuch as my ſelfe haue, to ſet their hands and their hearts with Ezra *and* Nehemiah *to the repaire of Gods Temple and Citie, againſt* Tobiah *and* Sanballat *beyond the riuer, that is, the Pope and the Ieſuites, with other conſpirators, who terrifie the peoples hearts from ſo needfull and gracious a worke as the entertainment of Chriſts truth and Goſpel, to the ſauing of their ſoules. The Pope with Briefe vpon Briefe, Priuiledge vpon Priuiledge, Indulgence vpon Indulgence, encourageth his Ieſuites and other Prieſts, Regulars and Seculars. They like ſwarmes of Locuſts ouerſpread the field where Gods precious ſeed is ſowne, and are not onely diligent and painfull in compaſſing ſea and land to make Proſelytes, the children of hell, ſeuen times worſe then themſelues, but are re dy to aduenture their liues, euen out of their bloud to raiſe a ſeed of ſedition and rebellion to Antichriſt their ſole and ſoueraigne king; whileſt too many amongſt vs are ſo lumpiſh and idle, as if the danger appertained not vnto vs. We haue (bleſſed be the name of God) many vigilant Paſtors and reuerent Doctors, that preach diligently, and write learnedly of all Controuerſies queſtioned in theſe*

euill

euill times, who neither preferre pleaſure nor profit, nor honour, before the aduancement of Gods glorie and the benefite of Chriſts Church ; neither would ſpare their liues for the furtherance of the Goſpell. Yet haue we ſome that are not prouoked by their good example, but propoſe vnto themſelues a more broad, pleaſant and eaſie way, as if the way were not narrow that leadeth to life. Whom I would onely intreate as brethren, ſeriouſly to conſider the improbous labour and inceſſant induſtrie of our aduerſaries, who are ſo captious as to cauill at all we ſay or do, that make mountaines of mole hils, great outcries vpon ſmall occaſions, God knoweth, and are readie to call our vertues vices, and for our ſakes whom they hate, ſpeake euill of the way of truth which we profeſſe, and they know not; and neuer to ſuffer their hypocriſie to outface our ſinceritie, their policy preuent our due circumſpection, their crafty informations outſtrip our plaine and honeſt dealing in the ſight of God or men ; leſt their double diligence in euill, riſe vp in iudgement againſt our negligence in good: or leſt their mouths be vniuſtly opened againſt the truth, for the vnholines of thoſe that preach & profeſſe it. Let vs rather ſtop the mouths of fooliſh and ignorant men by wel doing, and gloriſie God in our holy calling, leſt God require it. O that the careful Gouernors, by the wel eſtabliſhed diſcipline of our Church, would take order to ſtir vp the minds of ſuch Miniſters as are able vnto this work, and ſpur the idle forward, and make them go or bleed; and by due puniſhment chaſtiſe the inſolency of fruitleſſe and careleſſe men, if any ſuch be, to a ſpeedy reformation, or vtter expulſion; that the pleaſant paſture of the laboring oxe, be not deuoured either by lazie aſſes or rauening wolues.

My learned and ſtudious fathers and brethren I would humbly pray, friendly to admoniſh me of any thing in my booke, which an aduerſarie may not onely iuſtly taxe, but probably calumniate ; that I may receiue aduertiſement and admonition from a friend, before a reproofe from an aduerſarie ; that the mouth of reproach may be ſtopped, before it be opened to ſlander the Goſpell for my ſake. If I ſhall haply receiue your approbation, it ſhall ſtand for my reall and comfortable contentment and ſatisfaction. Vpon the ignorant, curious, captious or malicious I repoſe not my credit. For Ea

Cicero.

eſt profectò iucunda laus quæ ab his proficiſcitur qui & ipſi in laude vixerunt. If I haue offended, let the righteous ſmite me;

for

for the ſtripe of a friend is better then the kiſſe of an enemie, when the balme of the wicked may breake my head. If the leud ſhould approue or applaud me, I might fall into Antiſthenes *feare* : O me miſerum, metuo ne in crimen aliquod inciderim.

If any of our aduerſaries ſhall vndertake by writing to anſwer this that I haue publiſhed, I would intreate them alſo that they would write as becometh Diuines, without the ſpirit of Rabſheca *that railed on the liuing God. To auoid all perſonall calumniations, which as they are beſide the cauſe, ſo do they not further the affe-ction of any honeſt mind, and are moſt diſgracefull to them that vſe them.* Michael *gaue not railing words to the Diuell. It pleaſed God himſelfe to viſite and comfort his Prophet in a ſoft and ſtill aire, rather then in fire, tempeſt or earthquake. It was a good mo-tion,* Diſcite à me, quia ego mitis & humilis ſum ; *and as good an example to follow, When he was reuiled, he reuiled not againe. Which I remember the rather, becauſe many of our aduerſaries bookes, wherein they anſwer others on whom they would raile, which mattereth not ſo much where no perſon is touched, are diuulged either without names at all, like ſpeechleſſe idols, or onely with a paire of letters, perhaps truly importing the firſt cha-racters of their names, but for the moſt part tranſpoſed, that* Oedi-pus *himſelfe could not find out the riddle : or a plaine counterfet name, as* Mattheus Tortus *for* Robert Bellarmine, *appearing vnto the world like whifflers at a play, with vizards of diuers ſhapes to terrifie or delude the ſimple, and to abuſe whom they liſt without controlment, while themſelues are vnknowne, as diſguiſed in ſuch hypocriticall and diſſembled attire. Which notwithſtanding is not onely cenſured as a fault in Printers,* qui ſæpe tacito, ſæpe etiam emetito prælo, & quod grauius eſt, ſine nomine authoris im-primunt, *by the Conuenticle of Trent, but alſo by a ſolemne Decree is forbidden for euer hereafter:* Decernit & ſtatuit, vt nulli liceat imprimere, aut imprimi facere, quoſuis libros de rebus ſacris ſine nomine autoris. *Though they haue a crafty cautel following, yet this were a good rule, were it generally obſerued, eſpecially in mat-ters of cotrouerſy, where there may be expectatio of anſwer or reply.*

Finally, I would intreate, that if any anſwer be publiſhed, it be not generall, or at randon, or by ſnatches and peeces, but diſtinct

and

and particular, either by Paragraph and Paragraph, or by Chapter and Chapter, as it ſtandeth in order. Theſe conditions are reaſonable, friendly and Chriſtian, becoming both the cauſe we handle,
and the men we profeſſe our ſelues to be; and ſo let cauſa cum cauſa, ratio cum ratione concertare.

The Lord Ieſus giue a gracious bleſſing vnto theſe my paines in
the worke of my Miniſterie, and that not onely I, but all my brethren may be found faithfull in the fruitfull emploiment of his talents committed vnto vs, vnto the day of the ſtraight reckoning and
account, at that great iudgement, when euery mans worke
ſhall be approued or diſallowed before the feete of that
Lord who ſhall iudge both quicke and
dead at his appearing
in glorie.

THE

THE CONTENTS.

The Contents.

The Contents.

in *so great varietie of opinions as are now ventilated in the Chri-*
stian world, secure himselfe, and haue his conscience satisfied with
comfort, that he is a member of the true, holy, ancient, Catholicke,
and Apostolicke Church.

Chap. XXI.

Seeing our Aduersaries will haue no other witnesses but domesti-
call, against whom we may iustly except: no other Iudge but the Bi-
shop of Rome their obliged friend, our capitall enemie; often igno-
rant, vniust, and wicked, and therefore partiall and incompetent;
we vpon so iust cause appeale, from Babylon to Ierusalem, from
Trent to Nice, from Romes new Consistorie on earth, to Gods Tri-
bunall in heauen; from that pretended Vicar, to God the Father, and
to Iesus Christ his Sonne, the iust Iudge of quicke and dead, with the
holy Ghost the sanctifier of the Elect, for a faithfull and finall sen-
tence, whether Protestants or Papists haue and hold the truth of God
in their Religion.

CHAP.

CHAPTER I.

Nothing is more dangerous to the Chriſtian Catholique Church, then the vſurped pretence of Antiquity, and the falſe imputation of Nouelty, whereby the truth of God is deluded, & error ſupported among the children of vnbeleefe, within the boſome of the ſeeming viſible Church.

NO winde hath bene of ſo great force, to remoue the wauering mindes of vnconſtant men from the grounds of euident truth, as the vaine blaſt of pretended *Antiquitie*. Not becauſe true *Antiquitie* is a vaine blaſt, or ſhould be compared thereunto: but becauſe vaine men, who are altogether *ſet on the loue of vanitie*, puſt Pſal.4.2. vp with the vnconſtant winde of their vaniſhing imaginations, abuſing the name thereof to credit their Nouelties, without the nature and ſubſtance of it, haue withdrawne ignorant ſeduced men from the way of truth; like a ſhooting ſtarre, which being indeed a groſſe Meteor, exhaled from the foggieſt earth in farre diſtance, hath the ſhining and glory of a true fixed ſtarre, and ſo is taken by the rude and ſimple, but the skilfull Aſtronomer can eaſily diſcouer it; yea the moſt rude and ignorant, when they finde it, and feele it, can diſcry it, to be but a ſlimie ſlough, that hath loſt its brightneſſe, and is good for nothing.

2 No terror hath ſo withdrawne men, that are *Children in* 1.Cor.14. 10. *vnderſtanding, though ſtrong in malice,* as the viſard of *Antiquity*; not that true *Antiquity* is a viſard, more then Chriſtian liberty 1.Pet.2. 16. is a *cloake for maliciouſneſſe:* but becauſe the betrayers of truth, abuſe it as a vizard, both to couer the deceipt of their inſoyſted Nouelties, and to obſcure the truth which they trample vnder foote, *as ſwine do do pearles, or dogges holy things.* They Math.76. teach the ignorant to call ſuperſtition the *old Religion,* and the reformed religion the *New learning.* As the brutiſh theeues

in

in the borders were wont to fay, that the commandement of
God, *Thou fhalt not fteale*, was not Gods *Old Law*, but a *New
Law*, of King *Henrie* his making. Or like the Cleargy of
Scotland, in the dayes of their ignorance ; *qui Nouitatis nomine offenfi, contendebant Nouum teftamentum nuper à ᴄMartino
Luthero inuentum, ac Vetus teftamentum repofcebant :* Who offended with the name of Nouelty, contended the *New Teftament* to be of *Martin Luthers* making, and therefore required the *Old teftament.* So ardent were they for *Antiquity*,
againft Noueltie, they would haue the *Old teftament*, but not
the *New.* And that this ignorance may not feeme monftrous,
though it be maruellous, the Bifhop of Dunkelden, *George
Treiton*, who liued about thofe times, profeffed to Deane
Thomas Forret, that he knew neither the *Old teftament*, nor the
New; but his *Portuife* ferued his turne. In fo much that it grew
to a prouerbe, Like the Bifhop of *Dunkelden, that knew, neither
the Old law, nor the New.* And therefore it was no wonder,
that the Cleargy could not diftinguifh the one from the o-
ther, when a Bifhop was fo learned that he knew neither.
About which time there was a great difpute, which troubled
fuch learned BB. long, whether the *Pater nofter* might be fayd
to the B. *Virgin Marie;* when one anfwered perhaps rafhlie,
yet very vnhappily; Let God haue his *Pater nofter*, &c. let our
Lady be contented with her *Aue*, in the diuels name. Yet
perhaps it is not fo barbarous to fay it to the bleffed Virgine,
as to Saint *Barbara* or Saint *Katherine*, in *Bellarmines* conceit.
And left Ierufalem *fhould mocke her fifter Samaria* with this
groffe darkneffe, I could tell of a Doᶜtor in Cambridge, a little before the beginning of King *Edwards* dayes, who finding
a New teftament of *Erafmus* tranflation in a fcholers hand,
tooke and read it a while, and redeliuering it to the owner,
faid, *It was a pretty booke, but he had neuer feene it before. Robert
Stephens* reports alfo of a great *Sorbonift in Paris*, *that fwore
per diem, quod nunquam fciret quid effet nouum teftamentum*, by
the day, he neuer knew what was the New teftament. This
is the leffe ftrange, if we confider that the Scriptures were feldome or neuer read in fchooles, but either *Dionyfius*, or the
Maifter

Marginal notes:

To old M. Gilpin.

Buch. in hift. rerum Scoti-carum, l. 15.

Fox. Aᶜts, & Mon. p. 1266.

Bellar. de San-ᶜtorum Bea-tit. l. 1. c. 16.

Refponf. 1552

Maifter of the Sentences, or *Thomas Aquinas*, or *Bonauenture*, fchooleman vpon fchooleman: but none vpon the old Tefta- ment, or new. And by thefe meanes each tooke of other, at fecond hand, and fo *forfaking the fountaine of liuing waters*, they digged vnto themfelues pits, yea broken pits, that would hold no water. Ier.2.13.

3 Thus either *the blind leading the blind*, or the malicious fub- uerting the wilfull, do either ignorantly pretend, or wicked- ly obtrude the name of *Antiquitie* againft all reformation, as an armour of impregnable proofe ; though they know not what it is, neither can difcerne betweene *New and old*. Yet *Bellarmine* maketh this, euen fuch as it is, the fecond note to proue the certainty of the prefent Romaine Church. Math.15.14.

Bellar.de no- tis Ecclef.

But when the arrowes of Gods, not onely ancient, but e- uerlafting truth, fhall be fhot againft this falfe pretence, *A- dams* fig leaues could as well couer his nakedneffe from the fight of God, or *Goliahs forehead* withftand the ftroke of *Da- uids* fling, as this maske can couer the fhame of Rome, or gainftand the force of Gods eternall truth: though her face were of the mettall of the Giants boots. Gen.3.7. 1.Sam.17.

4 Valiant *Iofuah*, and the fageft elders of *Ifrael* were decei- ued by the *Gibeonites*, fhrowded and fhadowed vnder this veile. They pretended nothing but *Old* clothes, *Old* fhoes, rent bottles, torne bagges, fowre drinke, mouldie bread, all old, and all fo old, that all was naught, and themfelues too: all affected, all diffembled *Antiquity*, neuer a word true; and yet fuch wife, fuch great men, vnder this pretence were de- ceiued. No maruell then if many, neither fo valorous as *Iofuah*, nor fo wife in experiment of policy as the ancients of Ifrael, be fometimes ouertaken with this fleight, while the Gibeonites of Rome bring fuch old ftuffe, moth-eaten and canker-fretted monumēts, that to the fimple may beare a pro- bable fhew of *Antiquity*, but being throughly fifted and feri- oufly examined, they appeare, as indeed they are, meere in- truders vpon the ancient euidences of the Church, which they either falfifie by rafing, or interlining, or make away by imbezeling and purloyning, or fophifticate by glofing, and Iofuah.9.12.

B 2   commen-

commenting, or bring in their roome *New* inuentions vnder the names of old Authors, and so craftily cosin the people of God.

5 There is most danger and cunning in counterfeiting the most precious mettals. To sophisticate base minerals will neuer quite cost. This makes the Romanists so eager and desperate in adulterating of *Antiquity*, because it is a pearle of most esteemed price, which once entertained by them whom they desire to deceiue, is holdē as a *Iewel* of most precious value, but any skilful lapidary can soon espie the Alchumy. It seemeth gold, it is but brandished brasse; it seemeth a rubie, one of the stones in *Aarons* holy attyre, or a foundation of new *Ierusalem*, wherein is admitted no counterfeit; but it is onely a polished Garnet: It beareth resemblance of a Diamond, but it is digged out of Saint *Vincents* rocke, as good as a Saint *Martins* chaine. At one word, many things are offered and vrged for *Antiquitie*, which vpon triall proue meere *Noueltie*, yea and worse then vanitie, a plaine nullity.

Hieron. ad
Trapezitam.

6 When *Constantine* the first constant Christian Emperour came to Bizantium, there came to him certaine Philosophers, and complained that he worshipped not God as he ought to do, and that he practised certaine *Nouelties* in holy things, bringing in a *New* kind of worship into the commonwealth, *Præter ea quæ eius Maioribus visa sunt, & Græcorum Romanorumque Principibus, quos transacta sæcula habuērunt:* Besides, those things which seemed good to his *Ancestors*, and to the Nobles of *Greece*, and *Rome*, who liued in *passed* ages. If this noble and religious Emperour had not bene as an Angell, to discerne truth from error, good from euill, this shadow of *Antiquitie* might haue depriued him of the substance of *verity*. But theirs was *fabulosa Antiquitas*, fabulous *Antiquity*, a bable to please fooles, no solide learning to conuince conscience.

Erasmus in
Paracl. in
Athan.

Epist. Simach.
apud Ambro.
lib. 5. Epist. 30

7 *Simachus* the Prefect of a City, wrote vnto the Emperour *Valentinian*, for the continuance and support of heathenish Idolatry; his greatest inducements were, *Præstate oro vos vt ea quæ pueri suscepimus, senes posteris relinquamus:* I beseech

you

you that what we learned when we were children, that we may leaue in our old age, to our poſterity. And againe, *Si longa ætas authoritatem religionibus faciat, ſeruanda eſt tot ſæculis fides, & ſequendi ſunt nobis parentes, qui ſequuti ſunt fœliciter ſuos.* If old age giue authority to religion, then muſt we preſerue „ the faith of ſo many ages, and our fathers are to be followed „ of vs, who moſt happily ſucceeded theirs. And againe, *Sera* „ *& contumelioſa eſt emendatio ſenectutis.* The reformation of *old* „ *age,* is late and contumelious. What a face of *Antiquity* pre- „ tendeth this deceiued Idolater? I will omit the anſwer, and commit the reader to *Ambroſe* in the next Example, and to *Prudentius* that anſwered the ſame. Therefore *Conſtantine* did wiſely when he publiſhed his edict for the Chriſtian religion, in preuenting this obiection of the heathens, (who euer pre-
tended *Antiquity*) ſaying, *This our religion is neither new nor* Euſeb. in vita *newly inuented, but is as old as we beleeue the creation of the world* Conſt. l. 2. *to be: and which God hath commanded to be celebrated with ſuch myſteries as ſeemed good and pleaſed him: but all liuing men are ly-ers, and are deceiued with diuerſe and ſundry illuſions, &c.* Where-with we may ſtop the mouthes of our Romaine aduerſaries, *Our religion is neither new, nor newly inuented, &.* and theirs is neuer a whit the better for its age, rather pretended then pro-ued, to be old.

8 If ſuch pretended *antiquity* in that good Emperors dayes, had receiued admittance & acceptance, Chriſtian religion had bin diſgraced for the time, if not degraded for euer; This is the very plea of counterfeit Catholiques at this day. *Ignatius* was Ad Philadelp. troubled with ſuch pleaders, and proctors for idolatry. *Audi-ui quoſdam dicentes, niſi Euangelium in Antiquis inuenero, non cre-dam:* I haue heard ſome ſay, except I can find the Goſpell in the *Ancients,* I will not beleeue. To whom not only his an-ſwer would ſerue, *His ego dico, Ieſum Chriſtum mihi pro Archi-uis eſſe cui non parere manifeſtum eſt exitium, & Antiquitas mea Ieſus Chriſtus:* I ſay to theſe, that Ieſus Chriſt is to me a treaſu- „ ry of Charters, to whom not to obey is manifeſt damnation: & „ my *Antiquity* is Ieſus Chriſt: But alſo that if they had grace „ to ſeeke, they might haue found the Goſpell in Paradiſe,

when the promiſe was made that *the ſeed of the woman ſhould*
bruiſe the ſerpents head : with *Abraham, when it was foretold by*
God, that in his ſeed *all the nations of the earth ſhould be bleſſed:*
with many more in the bookes of *Moſes*, whoſe writings
were *Vetuſtiſſima & ante omnes alios ſcriptores,* (as *Euſebius,* from
Ioſephus reporteth,) moſt ancient and before all writers. Thus
the heathen on all hands, contemned the Iewes, and condemned the Chriſtians , vpon this onely ſurmiſe. Wherein they
flattered themſelues, as the pretended Catholiques do at this
day : that they had a certaine *Antiquity of their owne*, and
therefore they would not obey the truth, which they reputed
Nouelty. As the Captaine that perſecuted the Martyr *Ro-*
manus obiected, *Thy crucified Chriſt is but a yeſterdayes God, the*
Gods of the Gentiles were of moſt Antiquity; yet was Chriſt neuer the leſſe the euerlaſting Sonne of his Father, who is God
aboue all to be bleſſed for euer ; was before *Abraham*, and
before the world , which was made by him, without whom
nothing was made.

    9 I thinke Idolaters haue the lucke on't , (as we ſay.) The
Samaritans after *Iſraels* captiuity, *vnto this day they do after the*
old maner ; they neither feared God, neither do after his Ordinan-
ces, nor after his Cuſtomes, nor after the Law, nor after the com-
mandement , which the Lord commanded the children of Iacob,
whom he named Iſrael.— *they obeyed not , but did after their old*
Cuſtome. Theſe were Iſraelites as well as heathen, therefore
they had ordinances and cuſtomes, and a Law from God, *older*
then their old maner, and theſe *old Cuſtomes* which they pretended. Yet ſee how ſtrangely they were withdrawne from the
true ſeruice of God , vnder the ſhew and ſemblance of *Old*
manners, old Cuſtomes: vnto which they ſeemed to be ſo wedded, yea ſo bound, ſo chained, that euen vnto the time of
our Sauiour Chriſts appearing in the fleſh, they would worſhip God where their fathers worſhipped. *Our fathers worſhip-*
ped in this mount. They had an interuenient commandement of
God, *to ſeeke the place which the Lord their God ſhould chuſe out*
of all their tribes, to put his name there, and there to dwell, and thi-
ther ſhould they come, &c. They had the manifeſt teſtimonies
of

Gen.3.15.
Cen.12.3.
22.18.
Euſeb. de
præpar.
Euang.l.10.

Prudentius in
hymmis de

2.Reg.17. 34.

Ver.40.

Iohn 4.20.

Deut.12.5.

of the Prophets: *God refused the tabernacle of Ioseph, & chose not the tribe of Ephraim : but chose the tribe of Iuda and mount Sion* Pſal.78.67. *which he loued : he built his Sanctuary as an high pallace , like the earth which he eſtabliſhed for euer :* And againe , *God laid his* Pſal.87.1. *foundations among the holy mountaines ,The Lord loued the Gates of Sion aboue all the habitations of Iacob.* They had the prayer of *Salomon; That the eyes (of the Lord) may be open toward this houſe,* 1.King. 8.29. *(which he had built in Ieruſalem) night and day , euen toward the place whereof he had ſaid , My name ſhall be there.* They had Gods owne choice , *I haue choſen Ieruſalem. that my name may* 2.Chron.6.5. *be there.* They had Gods owne approbation, and ratification of his choice, yea and his gracious promiſe annexed thereun- 2.Cron.7.12. to, *I haue heard thy prayer, and haue choſen this place for my ſelfe, to be an houſe for ſacrifice.* Yet neither Gods commandement, nor the Prophets teſtimonies, nor *Salomons* prayer, nor Gods choyce, nor confirmation, no nor his promiſe annexed there-unto , could weane the Samaritanes from the place where their fathers worſhipped: So potent, ſo violent, is the perſwa-ſion of *Antiquity* , if it be once faſtened to the hearts of men, eſpecially if it finde either profit, or pleaſure, or eaſe, ioyned therewithall.

10 As the profane *Iſraelites* preferred their *Old* diet of fiſh, Numb.11.15. cucumbers, pepons, leekes, onions, and garlicke in Egypt, whereunto they had bene vſed foure hundred yeares, and which they had for nought, and very good cheape, before the remembrance of the hony, nuts, almonds , and ſpices which Gen.43.11. their fathers had , when they liued in the land of Canaan, yea & before the preſent fruition of Manna , Angels food in the wilderneſſe. So do our Romaine Samaritans, our Iſraelitiſh recuſants at this day. Our Rhemiſts could ſee , I cannot ſay Annot.in a Moate in the Samaritanes eye, but *that beame* in thoſe Ido- Iohn 4.20. latrous eyes, that *they pretended their worſhipping there to be more ancient then the Iewes at Ieruſalem, referring it to Iacob* : yet they cannot ſee a *greater beame in their owne eyes,* who haue not ſo much pretence, nor ſuch probability as the Samaritanes had. For they had the *Antiquity* of Ieruſalem indeed, though the law of God coming after, made that argument of none

effect. But the Romanes haue not their *Antiquitie* beyond
Gods commandements, but after the Gospell was preached;
and therefore cannot so much as in pretence prescribe any
shew of *Antiquitie* beyond that verity which the Gospell of-
Esay.10.9.   fereth. But is not *Calno*, as *Carchamish?* Is not *Hama* as *Arphad?*
Is not *Ierusalem*, as *Samaria?* Aske the Prophet *Ieremie*, who
will not onely tell you, but complaine most grieuously of the
Ierem.44.17.   people in his time, that said, *We will do whatsoeuer thing goeth*
out of our own mouth, as to burne incense to the Queene of Heauen,
& to powre out drink offrings vnto her, as we haue done, both we and
our fathers, our Kings, and our Princes, in the Citties of Iuda, and
in the streets of Ierusalem; for then had we plentie of victuals, and
were well, and felt no euill. Since we left off——We haue had
scarsnesse of all things, and haue bene consumed by the sword and
by the famine. Are not these words, in the whole effect of them,
in the mouthes of all the *old superstitious* people of this land?
And do not the yong learne of the old? *When we prayed to our*
Lady, and offred tapers on Candlemasse day, and heard Masse as we
haue done, both we and our fathers, our Kings and our Princes, in
the Cities of this land, then we had plentie of all things, and were
well, we felt no euill. But since we haue left the religion of our fa-
thers, our kings and our Princes, we haue scarsnesse of all things.

11 The old superstitious people of Christ-Church in
Hampshire, would say, that there came fewer Salmons vp their
Riuer, since the masse went downe : for they were wont to
come vp when they heard the sacring Bell ring; as true as the
fall of Tenterdon steeple, was the cause of Goodwin sands.
Thus do they measure religion by their bellies, by prosperity and aduersity; but the pretence is still, that the former way was the *Old way*, and that *Old way* was the best way.
Ierem 44.21.   But what answereth the Prophet? *Did not the Lord remember*
the incense, that was burnt in the Cities of Iuda; and in the streets
of Ierusalem? You and your fathers, your Kings, and your Princes,
and the people of the land —— the Lord could no longer forbeare be-
cause of the wickednesse of your inuentions ---- therefore your land
shall be desolate, and an astonishment, and a Curse, because you haue
sinned against the Lord, and haue not obeyed the voice of the Lord,
nor

nor walked in his law, nor his statutes, nor in his testimonies, there-
fore is this plague come vpon you, as appeareth this day.

12 If a present spectator of the occurrences in these times, had written a story, of the experimented nature and disposition of our deceiued ignorant people, who are yet euery day taken with this pleasing baite of their fathers dayes; he could not haue more directly & significantly described it, then the Prophet did in that age, when the truth of God, preached and proclaimed by the messengers of God, was vtterly disgraced and abandoned, because the eies of wretched men were blinded, and their hearts misled by this bewitching and out-facing, crooked and misleading Lesbian lyne of pretended *Antiquitie.*

13 When the Prophet *Isaiah* foretold the destruction of *Tyrus*, he vpbraided their obstinacie, with that wherein they most gloried: *Is not this that your glorious Citie? her Antiquitie is* Isay.23.7. *of ancient dayes.* What a brauing style was this? yet euen this their glory was their shame. It seduced them, and hardened their hearts in the dayes of their prosperity, it could not defend them in the day of their destruction.

14 Is not this the very case of Rome at this day? She glorieth in nothing more then in her *Antiquitie. of ancient dayes,* which maketh such a glorious shew, that it vtterly dazeleth bleared and weake eyes, in these flourishing dayes of Antichrist, and misguideth them to the pit of euerlasting perdition.

15 These fetches haue bene obserued of the Popes, by others, before this time, *Non vno loco deprehenditur &c. This is not once found* (only) *that they chiefly ayme at this, that they may* Sleidan de 4. *ad the opinion of Antiquity to their lawes, to acquire more weight* Imperijs.lib. *and authority vnto them.* But this pretence will not serue the 3. turne, when *The Ancient of dayes shall come to iudge and renenge* Dan.7.9. *his owne cause, against the children of disobedience, & that abomination of desolatiō that yet sitteth in the temple:* who vnder this colour, with-hold the *truth of God in vnrighteousnesse, and heape* Rom.1.18. *vnto themselues swift damnation, euen wrath against the day of wrath.* For that *Alpha and Omega, that first and last, which was,*

and

and which is, and which is to come, will bring forth those books of true *Antiquitie in deed, whereby the dead shall be iudged of* those things which are written in those bookes, according to their *Workes*, Then the euidence shall be giuen, the verdict shall be taken, and the sentence pronounced, not according to vnwritten, and therefore vncertaine, but according to written, and therefore most certaine, *Verities*: that is, according to true and vndoubted, not supposed and pretended *Antiquitie*. Which is a matter very remarkable, especially if we consider, how the Romanists equall (if they do not preferre) traditions of men to the Scriptures of God, as hereafter shall be proued. Let him therefore *that hath eares heare what the Spirit saith*, yea what he hath written for our *learning, that through patience and comfort of the Scriptures, we may haue hope*. For this is a *lanterne to our feete and a light vnto our steps*. This is *the rule, after which who so walketh*, shall neuer fall.

Reuel.20,12.

Chap.10.
Reuel.2,11.
Rom.15.4.
Psal.119.105.
Psal.15.vlt.

16 All other *Antiquitie* in comparison hereof, is but Nouelty, and much thereof pretended and obtruded. It obscureth the light of truth, cleane puts out the weake eyes of the simple, misguideth the ignorant, enrageth the desperate, enforceth error, confirmeth heresie, outfaceth grace, abandoneth religion, and like the gust of a whirlewind ouerthroweth, rooteth vp, or like a whirepoole or quickesand, swalloweth downe all arguments neuer so pregnant, certaine, demonstratiue, by what reason or authority soeuer confirmed; and as a floud, and torrent in a tempest, carrieth grauell and dirt before it : so this pretended *Antiquitie* taketh all vnstable and wauering minded men, all dogged and obstinate hearts, al preiudicate and foreprized conceipts, all seared and crusted consciences, in a word, *all that are louers of the world, more then louers of God*, and tumbleth them all on confused heapes, as if in it, and them, were contained all the treasures of truth and pietie.

2.Tim.3.4.

17 If this blast be allayed with the sweet gall of Gods spirit, which as the wind bloweth, so it inspireth whom it listeth: Or with that mighty strong *West winde, which tooke away the grashoppers* out of the land of Egypt, *and violently cast them into*

Iohn 3.8.
Exod.10.19.

to

to the *Redsea*· If this vizard can be pulled off the whore of Babilons face, as *Tamar* put off her harlots *veyle*, our aduersaries Gen.38.19. will proue plaine *Gibeonites*, that whatsoeuer they pretend in shew, they intend nothing but deceipt in proofe ; like the counterfeit of *Tekoa*, who seemed like a woman, *that had* 2.Sam.14.2. *long mourned for the dead*, but was indeed the new consort of *Ioab*, *whose hand was wholy in that matter*. *Ioab* of Rome sendeth forth his seruants to search for such subtill minions, who would perswade, that the Religion, wherwith they beare the world in hand, is as old as *Methuselah*, *and yet* is newer then the prophane *Nouelties of words*, of which Saint *Paule* 1.Tim.6.20. speaketh : but a *Dauids* wife, and vnderstanding heart will easily descry & discouer them: as *Akijah* the Prophet knew the 1.King.14. 6. wife of *Ieroboam* by the inspiration of Gods Spirit, though he was blind, and she was disguised.

18 *Melchior Canus* giues a very good instance and obser- Loc.com.l.11. uation of this passage in *Berosus. Res ita priscas memoria pro-* c.6.fol.327. *dit &c.* He tels things so *old, that though by the conieᶜture of thine owne minde, thou mayst know them to be false, yet by reason of their ouer great Antiquity thou canst not reproue them. For in such matters by how much a man is more impudent, by so much he hath the more liberty to cog. In so much that of bookes and of authors (as Fabius saith) they may lye by authority; for they can neuer be found that neuer were; and in the matters themselues, he may most safely lye, because there can be no witnesses produced, which are not children if they be compared with the most Ancient.* Who is older then this Author ? What is older then his reports ? If old ancient *Antiquity*, with the bare name and title should preiudice truth, why should not he be beleeued that is so old? why should not his reports be receiued, that are so ancient ? yet is he but a *Gibeonite* with clouted shoes. Therefore as all is not gold that glistereth, nor all precious that is so in appearance; so is not all *Antiquity* that hath the shew of old age, nor all truth that beareth the similitude therof. Our aduersaries in this case may be taxed as *Tertullian* censured some in his time, *Vbi reli-* In Apol. *gio? vbi veneratio maioribus debita? Where is religion? where is the reuerence due to our forefathers? In apparell, in diet, in furniture, in*

sense,

sense, yea as in your very speech you renounce your Ancestors; you euer praise Antiquity; and euery day liue after the new fashion. By which it is manifest, that while you depart from the good precepts of your predecessors, you hold and keepe the things you should not, and the things you should, you keepe not. Whereby we may obserue that it is not a new or vnheard of matter to pretend *Antiquity,* and yet to be as far from it, as earth is from heauen, or the Sun-setting from the rising thereof. Whereby how easily may silly people be deceiued? as God knoweth the Christian world hath bene diuers hundred yeares, and is yet among superstitious people.

Cont. Fauft. Manichæ.lib. 15.cap.3.

19 Saint *Augustin* seemes to note some, *Qui legem Dei culpant nomine vetustatis, & errorem suum laudant nomine nouitatis. That did find fault with the law of God vnder the name of Antiquity, and praised their owne error by the name of nouelty; as if all old things were to be abadoned, & all new things to be receiued Wheras the Apostle Iohn, thought the old commandment praiseworthy. And the Apostle Saint Paul chargeth to auoide Nouelty of words.* Thus some preferre new before old, some preferre old before new. As if Gods truth which is as himselfe euerlasting, were to be measured by the line of a few generations passed, and not to be drawne from the Well which God himselfe hath digged; Or as if a new inuention should get preferrence before an old rule, as a new garment is better then an old coate. The

Act.17.21.

simplicity of men may be deluded by both. But as they must not with the *Athenians* gape after newes, so must they take heed that they be not ouertaken by *Gibeonites,* with shew of

Apollinis oracul.

age. Howbeit let them looke that their *Antiquissimum* be *optimum, that their oldest be best,* as the oracle answered; and so can they neuer be deceiued. For *Antiquity* must be obserued in *genere bonorum,* then will it neuer faile. Not but that one good that is later in manifestation then another, may be better in it selfe, as the Gospell is better then the Law, and as eternall life is the last and best good that befalleth man, and Christs last coming shall be more excellent and glorious then his first, as far as possession is better then the title. But because

Iames 1.17.

All good things come from God, as from the fountaine, from
whose

whofe authority whatfoeuer is deriued, it is oldeft, and therefore beft, beft and therefore oldeft; which becaufe the world
hath not perceiued, they haue bene long and many ages deceiued.

20 Many a yong ranke theefe hath robbed with a counterfeit gray beard, and many old letchers haue fophifticated
their withered faces, with new ttimming, or frefh painting.
It behooueth true men to be wel armed with the knowledge
of difcerning fpirits, and to be furnifhed with fufficient 1.Iohn 4.1.
ftrength to hold their owne. For this yong theefe, with his
old fhew, will neuer ceaffe to affaile them. It much concerneth the modeft and chafte, to know their owne fpoufes,
and to hold faft in their firft loue, left the daliance of youth
furprife them, and leade them vnto fpirituall adulterie before
they are aware. Age is often crafty, youth as often witty,
which of them may not deceiue the fimple? The wife hear-
ted will trie both, before they truft either. Old wine is good, Luke 5.39.
an old friend is better, yet Chrifts new commandment is beft Iohn 13.34.
of all. A new *name* is good, a *new man* is better, but the *Anci-* Reuel.2.17.
ent of Dayes is beft of all. If any thing be good, accept it, be Daniel.7.9.
it new or old. If any thing be naught, reiect it, be it old or
new. For it is neither youth nor age that maketh it good
or bad. Be not therefore any longer deceiued by pretences.
It is the truth that is greateft, and fhall preuaile vnto, and in,
the day of Iefus Chrift.

CHAP. II.

It is not onely expedient, but neceffary, that euery Chriftian
Catholicke fhould in his owne particular know, how to
diftinguifh betweene this pretended Antiquity,
and imputed Nouelty.

Very trade hath its myftery. A man muft well
know the thing offered and commended to
fale, how to fearch, to trie and to difcerne it,
before he aduenture to cheapen, much more
to conclude and ftrike a bargaine: fpecially in
the hazard of his ftocke and eftate, where-

on

on dependeth the weale or wo of himſelfe and family du-
1.Tim.3.16.   ring life. So in the *great myſterie* either of *godlineſſe or iniquitie*,
2.Theſſ.2.7. (which are euer in violent oppoſitió) a man muſt be furniſhed
with knowledge and vnderſtanding to diſtinguiſh each from
other, and to conceiue the nature of them both, that he may
1.Pet.3.10.   embrace the *good, and eſchue the euill*; for hereon dependeth
the probation of truth and error, the ſauing or loſing of
Chriſtian ſoules. In which caſe, *Try and then truſt*, *is a good*
1.Iohn 4.1.   *leſſon. Try the ſpirits, whether they be of God or not*, is the Apoſtle
1.Theſſ. 5.21. Saint *Iohns* aduice; and *Try all things, but hold faſt that which is*
good, is the Apoſtle Saint *Paules* counſell, both inſpired *with*
the ſpirit of truth, to ſtand faſt themſelues, and eſtabliſh o-
thers, *againſt* all ſpirits of error and falſhood, which by faire
ſhewes and pretences ſeeke the ruine of the Goſpell and true
religion, and deſtruction of Chriſtian ſoules.

2 Theſe are Apoſtolicall rules to be duly obſerued againſt
all impoſture and ſeduction, vnder what colour ſoeuer : and
that not onely by the learned, but by all Chriſtians, who haue
care of their owne ſaluation, and who are bound *pro toto & in*
ſolid. for themſelues as principall, to anſwer for their owne
faith and obedience vnto the truth of Chriſt. For although
Ezech.3.18.   the bloud of the deceiued, be required at the ſeducers hands,
& ſo their torment double, yet the miſ-led ſhal periſh in their
owne ſinnes, and their bloud ſhall be vpon their owne heads.
And therefore it ſtandeth euery Chriſtian vpon, to be able of
himſelfe to taſte new wine from old, and to diſcerne a new
Eſay. 5.20.   friend from an old, leſt he take *ſowre for ſweet*, euill for good,
fulſome for wholſome, error for truth, death for life, hell for
heauen : that is, counterſaited age, for true *Antiquity* : whereof the one leadeth to health, life, and glory; the other to ſin,
death, ſhame, and finall condemnation.

3 An *Old* Prophet deceiued a yong Prophet. *Old* yeares
1.Kings.13.   were reuerend, gray haires to be reſpected, the very grauity
of an ancient man moueth much : againe, youth ſhould be modeſt and ſhame-faced, yong yeares want experience, therefore ſhould be neither cenſorious, nor cótradictorious in preſence of old age; all which notwithſtanding he was ſlaine by

a Lyon in the way. The seducer liued, the seduced perished; a fearefull example. Pretended *Antiquity* is this old Prophet, which sayth that the Lord hath spoken in it, but if the yong Prophet had the wit to remember, or the heart to consider, or the conscience to performe, what he knew the Lord had said vnto himselfe, he had done Gods will, and had saued his owne life. Happy is he that can profit himselfe by the example of this seduced Prophet.

4 We must not *beleeue all we reade*, much lesse all we heare from the mouthes of partiall speakers. An enlightening spirit is not onely expedient or requisite, but necessary, to find out the secret deceipts of them that couer their actions with darknesse. *It is difficult and troublesome* (saith Saint *Chrysostome*) *to walke from one countrey to another by night; how can it be safe to trauell in the way that leadeth from earth to heauen, if we haue not the light of the Spirit? The true light* (saith *Saint Iohn*) *enlighteneth euery man that cometh into the world.* Not that euery man hath this *light,* but euery one that is enlightened, it is by this true light, which who so hath not, is in darknesse, and may be easily mis-led from the truth. And therefore not onely the *Rabbins,* and great subtill schoolemen, but euery man that hath interest in Christ, is bound to begge that good Spirit of God, whereby he may know that truth by which he must be saued.

Aug. de natura & gratia cont. Pelag. c. 39.

In 1. Thess. 5. 21. hom. 11.

Iohn 1. 9.

5 *He that walketh in darknesse knoweth not whither he goeth.* He knoweth not whether he be going to his owne, or to a strange countrey, to heauen, or to hell. This was the cause that the Romane leaders were euer cautelous that the people should liue without the light of Scriptures, or knowledge of any faithfull *Antiquity*; so might they leade ignorance whither they would. An old stratagem of old theeues: *Latrones lampadem primùm extinguunt, & tum demum latrocinantur.* Theeues first put out the light, and then begin to steale: Take the light of vnderstanding out of the peoples hearts, and what may not be poched into them? what may not be filched and imbezeled out of them?

Iohn 12. 35.

Chrysost. in 1. Thess. 5. hom. 6.

6 What was the reason that *Moses* wished that all the people

people could prophecie, as *Eldad* and *Medad* did? *And that God would giue his Spirit to them all?* *Moſes* right well knew, that if all the people could haue prophecied,& had bene guided by Gods Spirit,there had not bene ſo many *murmurings, inſurrections, rebellions, Idolatries, and other abhominations committed,* to Gods diſhonour, his diſcomfort,the peoples owne deſtruction. It was neuer the poſition of a Patriarch,or Prophet,or Apoſtle, or Euangeliſt, *That ignorance was the mother of deuotion.* The ancient Fathers learning was neuer abuſed to defend vnlearnedneſſe in any of the children of God. They commended lay men, yea women for their skill in the Scriptures. Their exhortations, their homilies, their lectures, their tractates,their ſermons, are as full as the Moone, cleare as the Sunne, with teſtimonies to this purpoſe ; wherein they proclaime to the world that *Ignorance is the mother of errour,* yea of all *errors,* yea of all euils, a brutiſh mother , and turbulent daughter. *The ignorance of the Scriptures is the ignorance of God,* a diſmal,and a deſperate gueſt in a Chriſtian heart,that expelleth God. *He that knoweth not the Lords buſineſſe, ſhall neuer be acknowledged of him.* Better no knowledge then not to know God; better vnknowne to all the world , then to haue God ſay, *Depart from me, I know you not:* If this be true,*To know God, and whom he hath ſent Ieſus Chriſt , is eternall life :* then out of all queſtion not to know God, *and whom he hath ſent Ieſus Chriſt* is eternal death,but the the ignorance of the Scriptures is not onely the ignorance of God, but of Chriſt alſo, as another ſaith. If it be true bleſſedneſſe *to haue delight in the Law of the Lord, and to meditate therein day and night,* then is it curſedneſſe and infelicity in his waies *that taketh no delight therein,* neuer thinketh vpon it,nay is perſwaded that it appertaineth not vnto him; nay, that it is a ſin to reade the euidence of his owne inheritance.

7 Is it not a ſhame a man ſhould be carefull to know what concerneth and conduceth to his bodily health,how to eate, drinke, cloath himſelfe,to take times for reſt, ſleepe,labor,recreation, and to be ignorant of that which may furniſh the ſoule,and further it to happineſſe and glory ? *Quid prodeſt in*
mundanis

Hieron. ad
Paul.&
Euſtoch.

Concil. To-
let. 4.
Chryſoſt. in
Coloſſ. hom.
9.
Gregor. in
Paſtor.

Math.25.12.
Ioh.17.3.

Iunilius Po-
meranus lib.
1.cont.Iul.

mundanis doctrinis proficere, & inanescere in diuinis? caduca sequi Isid.Hispal. de
figmenta, & cœlestia fastidire mysteria? What doth it profit to summobono.
proceed in humane learning, and to be void of diuine? To l.3.c.13.
follow transitory toyes or fables, and to loath heauenly
mysteries? Yea what is it to gaine the whole world, and to Mat.16.26.
lose a mans own soule? as the Son of God himselfe speaketh.

8 Our Saviour makes ignorance of *the Scriptures* the cause Mat.22.
of the *Sadduces* seducing of themselues, and others, about the
resurrection; the occasion of his Apostles vnbeleefe, *and slow-* Iohn 20.4.
nesse of heart, in that they conceiued not, that Christ must
rise againe from the dead. *Irenæus* made this the very foun- Contra heres.
dation of the *Valentinian* heresie, that they were ignorant of l.3. cap 12.
the *Scriptures of God.* Herewith Christ refuted *Scribes*, and Math.4.4.
confounded diuels. The Apostles answered the Priests and
Doctors, taught their hearers & disciples; the ancient Councels reprooued schismatickes, and confuted heretikes. The
old Fathers by preaching and writing preuented and ouerthrew all nouelties, *vanities, yea and villanies* of all that opposed the Christian, Catholike, and orthodoxall faith of the
Sonne of God, yea I say, onely by the Scriptures.

9 Saint *Augustine* reporteth that *Scœuola Pontifex*, an ido- De Ciuit.Dei
latrous Bishop of Rome, in the time of heathennesse, would lib.4.cap.27.
haue the people know *the state of their idolatrous worship of*
false gods, because they thinke them not false, Expedire igitur ex-
istimat falli in religione ciuitates. It was *expedient Cities should be*
deceiued in their religion. And *Varro* doubted not to say the
same. *Præclara religio.* A famous religion (saith the Father)
where the weake shall seeke for his deliuerance: and when he seekes
the truth, by which he should be freed, it is beleeued that it is most
expedient for him to be deceiued. And againe of *Varro*, whom he Id. Ibid. c.31.
calleth *acutissimum & doctissimum*, most acute, most learned, he
affirmeth, that he wrote *de religionibus loquens*, speaking of religions, *multa esse vera*, there were many truths, *which it was*
not onely expedient that the people should know, but also though they
be false, yet the people should not so esteeme them. It was no maruell the Father pitied him, that a man so acute, so learned,
should thus make religion a stage-play: or rather indeed a

C   matter

matter of ſecret policie, to keepe the people in awe, ſo they had any religion, it mattered not what, true, or falſe. The Roman BB. in theſe latter times haue not written with their pennes (that I know) the ſame words, no more then the foole

Pſal 14. 1. hath ſaid with his lips, *There is no God:* but as *the foole hath ſaid in his heart there is no God:* So verily this ignorance of Scriptures is the very heart of Romaine ſuperſtition, at this day, which the ouerlong continued practiſe of that Church hath made manifeſt to the world.

10 Examine the moſt of the vulgar Recuſants, they haue no ſetled grounds of their profeſſion, and (as they glory) their perſecuted Religion. They know neither white from blacke, old from new, Manna from garlicke, nor ſweete from ſowre. Onely theſe are their beſt anſwers: Either, if they be old, they were Chriſtened in that religion, and yet know not what religion is. Or if they are yonger, they will liue and die in the religion of their fathers; and yet neither vnderſtand who thoſe fathers were, beyond one or two generations, nor what religion thoſe fathers profeſſed. Or at the beſt, they will boaſt, they are of the *Old religion,* and will none of

Math. 16. 17. this new learning, and yet conceiue no particular of either. How eaſily may ſuch through the inſtinct and draught of

1. Cor. 2. 14. nature, *which is vncapable of the things which are of God,* and apt vnto the baſeſt idolatry, or through that groſſe and palpable ignorance that is in them, ioyned with a preiudicate conceit, againſt all reaſons and perſwaſions, ſtrengthened with a peruerſe and peremptory ſelfe will, bound vp in a ſeared and obſtinate heart, be led into euery by-path of ſuperſtitious worſhip, & loſt in the Labyrinth of inextricable abſurdities, and palpable Egyptian darkneſſe?

11 This affected ignorance of youth, and either retchleſſe careleſneſſe, or wilfull obſtinacie in old folkes, maketh them both indocible, and intractable, to be better informed in the

Rom, 1. 16. truth of the Goſpell, which would be the *power of God vnto ſaluation,* if they could *beleeue it.* As *Diogenes* found it as eaſie a matter to bring an old dog to his couuples, or cure a dead man, as to teach an old wilfull foole: for he will not ſticke to

ſay,

ſay, *Ne me doceto annoſum,iam & veternoſum,& propterea indo-* Apud The-
cilem, Teach not me an old doting fellow , and therefore in- ognidē.
docible. Wherefore as Saint *Hierome* ſaith,*Pius labor,ſed peri-* S. Hierome.
culoſa præſumptio ſenis linguam erudire: It is a godly labor,yet a
perillous preſumption to teach an old mans tongue.

12 Such as theſe remaine and continue either Semi-fidi- Iohn 4.22.
ans , like the Samaritanes, who worſhipped they knew not
what,or Nulli-fidians like the Athenians,that *ignorantly wor-* Act 17.23.
ſhipped an vnknowne God; or hauing their vnderſtanding darkened, Ephel.4.18.
*and being ſtrangers from the life of God, through the ignorance that
is in them, becauſe of the hardneſſe of their heart :* like very *brute
beaſts giuen vnto ſenſualitie , and made to be taken and deſtroyed,* 2.Pet.2.12.
*ſpeake euill of thoſe things which they know not , and ſhall periſh in
their owne corruption:* Or like the *Iewes,* who being *ignorant of* Rom.10.3.
*the righteouſneſſe of God, and going about to eſtabliſh their owne
righteouſneſſe , haue not ſubmitted themſelues vnto the righteouſneſſe of God.* In which ignorance *they put Chriſt to death* , they Act.3.17.
perſecuted the Saints, as *Saul did before* his conuerſion. Of 1.Tim.1.13.
them all, that fearefull ſentence of the Apoſtle is denounced,
The Lord Ieſus ſhall ſhew himſelfe from heauen , with his mighty 2.Theſ.1.8.
*Angels,in flaming fire,rendring vengeance to them that do not know
God , and which obey not the Goſpell of our Lord Ieſus Chriſt :* to
whom belongeth that dreadfull doome,as it is in the Romiſh
language,and Rhemiſh tranſlation,*qui ignorat,ignorabitur.He* 1.Cor.14.38.
that knoweth not,ſhall not be knowne.

13 All this notwithſtanding, thoſe that ſhould be eyes to
the blind, and feete to them that cannot go, keepe the ignorant people whom they make idiots indeed , in this blind
eſtate wherein they know nothing at all. Of whoſe caſe one
hath ſaid both well and truly, *Olim pueri ſenes, nunc ſenes pueri,
imò bis pueri : The time hath bene when children were old men,*
that is, like them for modeſtie and grauitie : now *old men are
children,* in knowledge and diſcretion ; for they vnderſtand
not the firſt principles of pietie, when they are readie to die.
This certainly is a lamentable caſe , if it be duly conſidered :
yet ſo common as that it carrieth thouſands blindfold into
the pit of euerlaſting perdition, who know not where they

are themfelues, till they be paft all ftay, or hope of recouery.
Howbeit this maketh the cafe moft defperate, and paft feeling, that their very teachers and guides do encourage them
in their blind ignorance, and deterre them from the light of
truth, as if it nothing appertained vnto them, to fearch into
that *great myfterie of godlineffe*, or to find the direct way vnto e-
ternall life. S. *Hierome reporteth* that the Iewes taught their
children the genealogies from *Adam* to *Zorobabel*, the hardeft to remember of the old Teftament, fo exactly, that they
could repeate them by heart, fo perfectly, as that you would
thinke they did but tell their owne names. And another Father, that the ancient Chriftians could fpeake of the myfteries
of the Trinitie, and reafon of them, as they plowed in their
fields and husbanded their grounds. Not onely thefe old
Chriftians, but thefe Iewes alfo fhall rife in iudgement a-
gainft our ignorant negligent Romanifts: and I feare other
too, that take no care to learne, and come to the knowledge
of Gods truth.

 14 But is any man defirous to finde a remedy againft this
malady? Let him take the counfell of him that was verily
perfwaded he had the Spirit of God: *Concerning fpirituall
things, or gifts, (brethren) I would not haue you ignorant*, faith
Saint *Paul to the Corinthians*. And before, *I would not you fhould
be ignorant, that all our fathers were vnder that cloud &c. that
they were all baptized &c. that they all ate the fame fpiritual meate,
and dranke the fame fpirituall drinke &c.* And to the Romanes;
*I would not haue you ignorant of this myfterie or fecret, that partlie
obftinacie is come vpon Ifrael, vntill the fulneffe of the Gentiles be
come in.* And to the *Theffalonians, I would not haue you ignorant
concerning thofe that are afleepe.* From which places if we well
weigh to whom the Apoftle writeth, and of what matters,
we fhall eafily perceiue that he would haue euery Chriftian
to diue into the oldeft, and fecreteft monuments of *Antiquity*,
and not onely the learned. For thefe Epiftles were not written to a *Timothy*, or a *Titus*, but vnto all beleeuers of the
Churches o' *Rome, Corinth,* and *Theffalonica.* The things he
comendeth to fuch vulgar knowledge, are not temporall, but

fpirituall

Margin notes:
1. Tim 3 16.
Hiero in Titu
cap. 3.

Chryfoft.

1. Cor. 7. vlt.
1. Cor. 1 2. 1.

1. Cor. 10. 1;

Rom. 11. 25.

1. Thef. 4. 13.

spirituall things or gifts; not matters of present action, but of great *Antiquity*, the times and acts of *Moses* and the people of God; in a matter of comparison, betweene the shadowes and figures of the old Fathers, with the accomplishment and performance of them by Christ in his person, & in his Sacraments of the new Testament; of the great question of the reiection of the Iewes, and receiuing of the Gentiles; of the resurrection of the dead, and state of the *Saints* after this life, which are of the greatest mysteries of Christianity. But what do I instance in these few particulars?

15 All the Scriptures *were written for our learning*; they are as wel milke for the weake, yea for new borne babes, as they are strong meate for them who are more expert in the word. They are shallow foords where Lambes may wade, as wel as riuers, wherein Elephants may swimme, *Mysteriis prudentes exercet, superficie simplices refouet, &c.* It exerciseth the wise with deepe mysteries, and nourisheth the simple with outward plainnesse; It hath in publike to nourish the little ones, and it keepeth in secret, wherewith to draw the minds of the excellent into admiration. And another saith: *In Scripturis sanctis quasi in montibus excelsis, &c.* In the holy Scriptures as in high mountaines, both the perfect haue matters of high vnderstanding, whereby they may lift vp like Harts, the passage of their vnderstanding; and the simple may find things of plaine meaning, whereunto they may resort in their humility, &c. *Doctrina Apostolica, tam salubris atque vitalis est, vt pro capacitate vtentium, neminem sui relinquat exortem: quia siue paruuli, siue magni, siue infirmi, siue fortes, habēt in ea vnde alantur, vnde satientur.* The Apostolicall doctrine is so wholsome, so vitall, as that for euery ones capacity, it leaues no man without it selfe: for whether little or great, weake or strong, euery one hath wherewith to be nourished, and satisfied.

16 And therefore all the secrets of Gods sanctuary, all the riches of Gods treasury, all the pleasures of Gods paradise, are as obuious and exposed by the disposition of diuine prouidence, to the vnlearned, as to the learned Christian, to high and low, rich and poore, free and bound, who are *all one in*

Rom.15.4.
1.Pet.2.2.
Hebr.5.

Greg.epist. in lib. Iob.c.4.

Isidor. Hispal. de Summo bono l.1.c.18.

In sententijs Augusti 8.

Chriſt Ieſus: For there *is no accepting of perſons with God.* But whereſoeuer and whoſoeuer *feareth him & worketh righteouſneſſe, is accepted of him.* Wherefore all men would be admoniſhed, euery where, to attend the things that concerne their ſaluation, and to vſe the priuiledge of Gods moſt liberall grant, and letters Patent, which are ſealed with the great ſeale of his bleſſed Sonnes bloud; To reade it, peruſe it, examine it, meditate on it, digeſt it, and lay it vp in the high treaſury of the memory, and in the ſecret cloſet of the heart, that it may be euer ready to furniſh vs, to confute aduerſaries, conuince hereſies, withſtand temptations, and to triumph o-

Ex diabolica meditatione. Chryſoſt.In Math. hom. 2.

uer diuels who ſeeke the ſubuerſion of our ſoules, *Hoc eſt quod omnia quaſi vna quadam peſte corrumpit, &c.* This is it, which corrupteth all as with a common plague, that you thinke the reading of the Scriptures appertaineth onely to Monks, whereas it is much more neceſſary for you. Therefore it is a greater ſinne to thinke the word of God ſuperfluous, then not to reade it at all. For to ſay ſo is the diuels leſſon.

Iohn 5.39.

17 Whom did our Sauiour Chriſt charge to ſearch *the Scriptures?* was it not the multitude that followed him? and in them all Chriſtians that beleeue in his name? As if he ſhould ſay, You ſee the Scribes with their learning, the Phariſes with their outward ſhew of holineſſe, the Prieſts with their authority, are all againſt me; they pleade *Antiquity,* and

Iohn 8.33.39. 53.

tell you, *That Abraham is their father, that they are the ſeede of Abraham, that they are Moſes his diſciples,* and aske me, *Art thou greater then our father Abraham which is dead? and the Prophets which are dead? Whom makeſt thou thy ſelfe?* But ſtand not you vpon ſuch pretences of *Antiquitie; I know you are the ſeed of Abraham, but you ſeeke to kill me, becauſe my word hath no place in you; you are of your father the diuell; if you were of Abraham you would do the workes of Abraham.* I appeale to *Moſes* and the Prophets. What *is written in your law?* Therefore *Search the Scriptures, for in them ye hope to haue eternall life, and they are they that teſtifie of me;* Theſe are vnpartiall Iudges, they will neither incline to the right hand, nor decline to the left. Theſe haue written of me, theſe muſt be fulfilled by me. May

not

not this ſtand as a ſufficient anſwer to our pretenders and ob-
truders of *Antiquity* at this day? The ſame obiection may receiue the ſame anſwer. Neuer tell me what the Prophets ſaid,
and what the Apoſtles did, out of incertaine and changeable
Tradition : vpbraide me not with the names and titles of ancient Fathers, and fore-Elders; Let me ſee what they haue
written, or what is written of them in the Scriptures of God;
theſe are they that will not deceiue, nor can be deceiued.
Saint *Paule* made this his chiefeſt plea before *Felix* the Gouernor, *I confeſſe vnto thee, that after the way which they call hære-* A.ct.24.14.
ſie, ſo worſhip I the God of my fathers, beleeuing all things which are
written in the Law and the Prophets. This ſatisfied the heathen
Gouernor, for the preſent, *who knew very well that way.* It will
not ſatisfie an Inquiſitor, to ſay, *I beleeue the Law, the Prophets,*
the new Teſtament and all the Scriptures of God, and all the Creeds
of the Apoſtles and old Councels without impeachment.

18 If euery good Catholike Chriſtian were furniſhed with
this approued & neuer danted weapon, he would be able eaſily to withſtand in all ſpirituall combats, both men, and diuels. And without this ſword *of the ſpirit, which is the word of* Epheſ.6.17.
God, we loſe both *the ſhield of faith, and the breſtplate of righ-*
teouſneſſe, and lie open to all *the fiery darts of Sathan.* We may
be deluded, miſ-led, and drawne from all aſſurance of our
hope, euen from the end of our faith, *which is the ſauing of* 1.Pet.1.9.
our ſoules.

19 O that I might ſpeake theſe things vnto *men of vnder-*
ſtanding, they could iudge what I ſay. But I know not how, the 1.Cor.10.15.
rude vulgar are indocible, either they are not, or will not be
taught. They will be ſtill *children in vnderſtanding, though not* 1.Cor.14.20.
in maliciouſneſſe; they will neuer come to ripe yeares in vnderſtan-
ding of Gods truth. And therefore *I cannot ſpeake vnto them as* 1.Cor.3.1.
vnto ſpirituall men, but as vnto carnall. They muſt haue *milke*
to drinke, and not meate; for they are not able to beare it, becauſe
they are yet carnall: nay I cannot ſpeake vnto them; for our
bookes vnder threat of ſeuere Penance are kept from their
ſight. And whereas in theſe dayes of doubt and ſinne, wherin the world is turmoyled and toſſed, and controuerſies ſo

C 4   eagerly

eagerly on all hands bandied, euery wife and difcreet man
ſhould arme himſelfe to ſtand on his owne guard, and to
defend himſelfe from error, ſuperſtition, and Idolatry : yet
2.Tim.3.7. ſome perhaps are euer *learning, and neuer attaine to the know-*
Heb.5.12. *ledge of the truth.* Others *who concerning the time might be tea-*
chers, yet haue need againe to be taught the firſt Principles of the
Pſal.58.4.5. *word of God,&c.* Others euen *ſtop* their eares *like deafe Adders,*
and will not heare the voice of the Charmer, charme he neuer ſo
Iohn 8.47. *wiſely.* Becauſe they *are not of God, they will not ſo much as heare*
1.Iohn 4.6. *Gods word.* Others *ſpeake euill of that they know not, neither vn-*
1.Tim.1.7. *derſtand what they ſpeake, neither whereof they affirme*: and hate
Eſa.52.7. them *that bring the glad tidings of good things,* and perfecute
Rom.10.15. like *Wolues, the ſheepe* that come to them, to feede them with
their owne fleſh, to cloath them with their *owne Wooll,* that
bring vnto them the Goſpell of the Sonne of God, *which is*
2.Cor.2,16. *the fauour of life vnto them that beleeue it, vnto the ſaluation of*
their ſoules.

Aug.   20 O that they would conſider that in *Schola dominica, qui*
non proficit deficit, In the ſchoole of Chriſt, he that ſwimmeth not
ſinketh, he that profiteth not, doth not onely not proſ-
per, but falleth away. If this be a ſhame euen in this world,
and will be certainely laid vnto your charge in the day of
Eſa.55.6. Chriſt, then *ſeeke the Lord while he may be found, and call vpon*
Heb.12.17. *him while he is neere :* aske mercie before the bleſſing be vnre-
Pſal.24.7. couerable, though you *ſeeke it with teares. Knocke at the euer-*
laſting gates, where *the king of glory is gone in* before you, *that*
Epheſ.6.19. *the doore of knowledge and vtterance may be opened vnto you, that*
Epheſ.3.18. *you may* by your owne ſelues *be able, being rooted and grounded*
in loue, to comprehend with all Saints, what is the length, & breadth,
and depth, and height, and to know the loue of Chriſt which paſſeth
knowledge, that you may be filled with all fulneſſe of God. That
your ſelues not as Iuie on a wall, or as a bryar on a hedge,
Pſal.92. but as *Trees* planted in *or neare the Sanctuarie of God,* that
Ezech. 47.12. are ſtrong with the ſtrength of God; and being coupled together in loue, you may *grow vp in all things in him that is the*
Epheſ.4.13. *head, euen Chriſt. Vntill you be perfect men in him, and attaine vn-*
to the meaſure of the age of the fulneſſe of Chriſt. That henceforth

you

you be no more children, wanering and caried about with euery wind of doctrine by deceit of men, and with craftinesse, whereby they lie in waite to deceiue. For God *would haue all men to be saued, and to* 1.Tim.2.4. *come to the knowledge of his truth;* as if the knowledge of Gods truth were the onely high way to saluation, as indeed it is.

21 Aduenture not your soules vpon pretences, subtilties, vncertainties, things you vnderstand not. What will it aduantage you *To gaine the whole world, and lose your owne soules?* —— Mat. 16.16. *Nunc tua res agitur,* It is euery mans own case, to attend the sauing of his owne soule. Let therfore the *word of God be dearer* Psal. 119.72. *vnto you then thousands of gold & siluer:* It is more precious then gold, *yea then much fine gold; sweeter then the hony and the hony-* Psal. 19.10. *combe. It giueth light to the blind, wisedome to the simple, reioyceth the heart, conuerteth the soule, endureth for euer, and is righteous altogether:* vse it as a *lanterne to your feete, and a light vnto your* Psal. 119.105. *steps. For by it you shall be taught, and in keeping of it, there is great* Psal. 19.11. *reward. By it a young man shall be taught to redresse his waies,* and Psal. 119.9. by learning *it, shall be made wiser then the aged.* It is vnto the hungry, *the bread of life,* it is vnto the thirstie *a well of life,* it is 2.Pet.1.19. vnto the blind, *a light shining in a darke place,* —— *vntill the day* Psal.36.9. *dawne in their hearts, in the light whereof they shall see light.*

22 But the ignorance of the Scriptures is *profundum bara-* Chrysost. de *thrum, a deepe dungeon,* full of fearefull horror and darknesse; Lazaro hom. the neglect of the Scriptures is the very mother of not onely 3. superstition, but infidelitie, it is the ignorance of God. The Hierom. dist. contempt of Gods word, preached by *Noah,* brought the 38 c. Iuxta. deluge or floud vpon the whole world; preached by *Lot,* cal- Gen.7. led for fire and brimstone from heauen vpon *Sodome* and *Go-* 1.Pet.3.20. *morrha.* It caused desolation to the land, captiuity to the peo- Gen.18. ple, ruining of the Citie, profaning of the Sanctuary, burning 2.Per.2.6. and consuming of the Temple, in the dayes of the Prophets Ier.7.14. and Kings, when many of them being righteous men, desired to see *the things that we see, and haue not seene them, and to heare* Mat.13.17. *the things we heare, and haue not heard them.* Whosoeuer is culpable of the same sinne, is obnoxious and lyeth open to the same punishment. And therefore as the armes of the Lord

are

are ſtretched abroad to receiue the penitent conuert, ſo is his *mighty hand ſtretched forth* to take vengeance on the obſtinate and diſobedient, *and he will iudge euery man according to his owne works.* Wherefore as it is neceſſary that euery man in his own particular, know to diſtinguiſh pretended and obtruded *Antiquitie,* from true and reuerend old age; ſo let him beg for the aſſiſting grace of Gods holy Spirit, in frequent and hearty prayers, that he may truly diſcerne vanities from verities, ſhadowes from truth, pretences from pregnant and demonſtratiue proofes.

Rom.2.6.

And for a more certaine, both illuſtration and reſolution, let him take that caueat or admonition of *Chryſoſtome,* who ventilateth all this in one period or ſentence: *Magna aduerſus peccatum munitio eſt Scripturarum lectio. The reading of the Scriptures, it is a great munition or defence againſt ſinne. Magnum præcipitium, a great ſcoute,* or *breaknecke,* a deepe and helliſh dungeon, is the ignorance of the Scriptures. A great perdition of ſaluation to know *nothing of Gods Law:* which want hath brought forth hereſies in doctrine, corruption of life, hath mixed and turned all vpſide downe. *Nam fieri non poteſt, non poteſt inquam fieri, For it cannot be, I ſay it cannot be,* that any man ſhall depart from the diligent and daily reading of the Scriptures without fruite. Nay more, it cannot be without reading them, *vt quiſquam ſalutem conſequatur,* that any man ſhould attaine vnto ſaluation. The ſame Father is full fraught to this purpoſe in many paſſages and diuers Homilies. And therefore I will ſay vnto all, both labourers and loyterers in this vineyard, as an ancient writer ſaith: *In eodem bonitatis gradu perſiſtere impoſſibile eſt, retrocedere periculoſum, procedere fructuoſum; nam quamcunq̃, terrã calcauerit planta pedis veſtri, veſtra erit; igitur ambulate. To ſtand at the ſame ſtay it is impoſſible, to go backe it is dangerous, to go forward is fruitfull;* for whatſoeuer ground the ſole of your foote ſhall tread vpon, it ſhall be yours: therefore go on; we wiſh you proſperitie in the name of the Lord. This promiſe was not made onely to *Moſes* and *Aaron,* or to *Ioſua* and *Caleb:* but to all the people of God, who had for them and their heires, intereſt in that good and pleaſant land. E-

De Lazaro hom.3.

Chryſoſt.in Gen.hom. 35. in 2.Theſ.3. in Ioan.1. hõ. 2.Ad Conſtãt. hom.10.de Pœnitentia hom.22. Beda. Ioſu. 1.3.

Pſal.122.8.

gypt

gypt may be called hell, the land of promise heauen, the wildernesse this life. In this life we cannot liue for euer, hell is
dangerous, heauen is glorious. The way to God by Christ is
faith and obedience; this is taught, and this is commanded in
the Scriptures of God: and certainly no where else.

21 The knowledge wherof is a *medicine to cure euery disease* Remig. Anti-
of the soule: a staffe for the weake, armor for the strong, it preuen- siodorensis in
teth the subtill snares of our enemies, and promiseth euerlasting Psal. 36.
crownes to them that ouercome. It ministreth sharpnesse to the sense, Smarag. in
increaseth vnderstanding, shaketh off sloth, remoueth idlenesse, com- præfat. expla.
poseth the life, correcteth our manners, maketh wholsome moanes, Euang. Do-
produceth teares from a contrite heart, giueth eloquence to the minical.
speech, promiseth euerlasting rewards to them that labor, increaseth Idem ad Re-
spirituall riches, quaileth babling and vanitie, and inflameth a desire gulam 4. D.
of Christ and our heauenly countrey. The Scripture is a table, Benedict.
furnished with heauenly iunkets, which giueth to the wearie, rest; to
the sicke, health; to the fallen recouerie; to them that stand in the faith Berno Augi-
fortitude, by which they may take the wings of an Eagle, and flie and ensis epistola
not faint: there are all muniments of our saluation. Could *Cal-* ad Eberhan-
uine, or *Peter Martyr,* or any of our learned Diuines at this dum Præsulé.
day, say more? or more plainly to inuite and prouoke the dull De S. Marci
appetite of weake and soule-sicke Christians, to take medi- Euangelio.
cines for their maladies, before their diseases grow desperate? and yet heare more not of this last hundred yeares, which
is the farthest allowance our aduersaries will vouchsafe vs,
for our religion. The holy Scripture is called a Testament for Radolph. Ar-
three causes, because it *is as it were the Charter which testifieth* denf. Domini-
the couenant betweene God and man: because it also *testifieth vnto* ca 12. post
vs the diuine will which we are bound to obserue: & because *it is a* Trinit.
testament of that inheritance which God hath promised vs. Then is
it not fit deare Christians, that you should peruse your char- * Coccius l. 6
ters? know how to frame your obedience? seeke after the art. 30. ex Ro-
crowne of immortalitie and eternall life? dolph. Flaui-
22. The * Author from whom I haue gathered these hath Cantuari.
many choise sentences to this purpose, all for the people a Idone Carno-
gainst the Romane robbers. He is not our friend, he is our tenfi, Giberto
sworne enemy, deuoted to the Romane sinagog, in defence & alij.

whereof

whereof he hath written great volumes. And therefore if any Romane Catholike hath care of his owne foule, he may tafte the fweetneffe of thefe ancient fentences, from the hand of a knowne and affured friend. Which if he fhall not difgorge, but digeft with patience, and thereby learne what belongeth vnto his peace, he will certainly find reft for his tyred foule, fo long mif-led in the mifts of ignorance, darkneffe of fuperftition, and almoft a very hell of infidelitie and idolatry. And if he will not hearken to any of thefe, or to them all, yet let him heare one, whom he is bound to obey aboue all, and that is a Pope, accounted a learned Pope, and a ftout Pope too, and therefore fpeaketh with knowledge and courage.

Innocent, 3. Dominica 5.poft.Epiph. in Euang.
Quoties nobis graues tentationes emergunt, recurrramus ad teftimonia Scripturarum: As often as great temptations do affaile vs, let vs recurre vnto the teftimonies of the Scriptures. The counfell is very good: happie is he that followeth it.

23 He is defperate that runneth wilfully vpon his owne death; he is mad that refufeth all medicine, that may reftore his wits or recouer his health. Be not fo defperate, be not fo
Abac. 2.4.
mad: you muft liue by your owne faith, and you muft exa-
1.Cor.11.28. 2.Cor.13.5.
mine your owne felues, before you receiue the Sacrament, yea and whether you be in the faith or not. Your Paftors may preach vnto you, but you muft take heed you be not deceiued. Learne to diftinguifh wholefome food from poyfon; it will be too late to examine it when you are poyfoned with it. If you be already, yet is there a remedie. *Non eft Pharmacum*
Wifd.16.12.
neque malagma: There is neither herbe nor medicine, *but thy word O Lord, which cureth all things. For thou haft the power of life and death, thou bringeft to the graue, and reduceft backe againe.* O Lord fuffer them not to die in their ignorance, to whom thou haft offred the knowledge of thy truth. It is (by thy mercifull prouidence) come neare vnto them, let them receiue it, imbrace it, and loue it to the comfort of their confciences, and the fauing of their poore foules.

24 Let no man thinke he may fay, that his trade or calling will not admit fuch diligent fearch, neither their bufineffe permit them to fpend fuch time as in this cafe is required. He

muft

muſt rather remember, that he who giueth vs time and lendeth vs life, may iuſtly challenge time for this. He may ſhorten his meales, abridge his ſleepe, detract from his pleaſures,
to do this dutie, and neuer loſe any thing in his eſtate; nay, it
hath a promiſe of Gods bleſſing, *To meditate in the Law of* Pſal. 1. 2.
God day and night. Let Saint *Hierom* rowſe and raiſe ſuch ſlug-
gards from their ſecuritie, vnto whoſe graue taxation and
cenſure I will leaue them. *Inertiæ ſe & otio & ſomno dantes,* Hieron. in
putant peccatum eſſe ſi Scripturas legerint, & eò qui in lege Dei Tit. 1.
meditantur, &c. Such as giue themſelues to idleneſſe, ſloth &
ſleepe, thinke that they ſinne when they reade the Scriptures,
and hold them but as bablers, and vnprofitable that do meditate therein day and night.

25 Be not rebels againſt the light, be not ignorant of the Iob. 14.
wayes of God; but returne out of your owne wayes to him,
by his wayes. You cannot hate the light if you know it; becauſe you know not the light, therefore you loue darkneſſe Iohn 1.
more then light: or at leaſt like children borne in a darke
dungeon and there brought vp, play and ſport themſelues
without deſire of light. So your deceiued ſoules hauing bene
borne and bred in the darkneſſe of Romane ſuperſtition, delight your ſelues therein, and haue no deſire to ſee the light
of truth. In which caſe S. *Gregorie* meeteth with proud men
that diſdaine to follow what they know, and S. *Auguſtine,*
the ignorant that will not know what belongeth vnto their
peace; and both of them deliuer the iuſt iudgement of God
vpon both the proud and the ignorant. Saint *Gregorie* thus:
Quia ſuperbi nolunt facere quod cognoſcunt, &c. Becauſe the Moral. l. 16.
proud will not do what they know, they are puniſhed with this paine, c. 2.
that they ſhall not know the euill they commit. For *becauſe they
firſt became rebels, afterward they are blinded that they cannot ſee
that they might know.* This is a iuſt iudgement vpon the learned of the Court of Rome, who will not reſt vpon the light
of Scriptures, and therefore are blinded with the ſpirit of error. And therefore they walke in *darkneſſe as if they were in the* cap. 29.
*light, for they are as pleaſant in their dungeon preſent, as if they en-
ioyed the libertie and light of their countrey, and are as iocond in the
night*

* Peccati.
Soliloqui c.
33.
vident.

night of *error, as if they were cōpaſſed with light of the truth, Saint *Auguſtine* thus. *Neſciunt aliquid de lumine æſtimare, quorum eſt in tenebris habitatio:* They know not how to value light, whoſe dwelling is in darkneſſe. They ſee darkneſſe, and darkneſſe they loue, and darkeneſſe they approue, and ſo proceed from darkeneſſe to darkneſſe, and know not where they fall. They fall with open eyes, and deſcend aliue into hell. Firſt, into the hell of a cruſted, ſeared and obſtinate conſcience, then into the hell of euerlaſting perdition and damnation, prepared for ſuch as either loue not God becauſe they know him not, or wil not know him whom they ſeeme to loue. God be mercifull vnto them, and forgiue them, that they may at the laſt know and loue God according to his word.

CHAP. III.

What true Antiquitie is, with the bounds and limits thereof;
when it began, when it ended.

F pretended *Antiquity* being admired and admitted, be ſo dangerous and damnable to the Catholike Chriſtian Church, and to each member thereof, that by it may be ſo ſoone and ſhreudly deceiued; it is high time that men ſhould be made to know, what true and vndoubted *Antiquitie* is, what bounds and limits it hath, where it beginneth, where it endeth, ſo as they may repoſe their truſt and confidence in it. For that ſeemeth ancient enough to ſome, that was done in their fathers dayes, a generation or two before them. But this is not *Antiquitie.* We muſt aſcend like a Pſalme of degrees, not with the *feet of our bodies,* but with the affections of our hearts, as Saint *Auguſtine* ſpeaketh. We muſt paſſe by the middle region, by diſcretion and triall of ſpirits, and in all humility from the foote of *Iacobs* ladder, clime vp to the top *which reacheth to heauen.* What *is Trent* Councell to *Chalcedon, Conſtance* to *Conſtantinople, Baſil* to *Epheſus?* the ſecond to the firſt Councell of *Neece?* What are all latter Conuenticles to thoſe foure generall, not Popiſh

Præfac. in.
Pſal. 123.

Gen. 28. 12.

pifh and factious, but indeed Imperiall and impartiall Councels? and yet there are euidences more ancient then thefe.

2 A forry & filly tenant, that was neuer out of a hel of beggery and mifery, and therefore knoweth no better hauen of reft and felicity, will brag of his fathers Copies or leafes, as if they were Euidences of fuch Antiquity, that could be found no where but in the Tower. So many pretend old Councels, and old Fathers, and old ftories; but for the greateft, and groffeft part of their religion, they haue but a few partiall affemblies, or late borne baftards, in their late fathers dayes. Is it not ridiculous to heare a prodigall princocke vanting of his gentility, becaufe his father was an vpftart of a few yeares ftanding? when an other can auouch *Codrus* or *Iaphet* for his progenitor.

3 Will you aske a Romane writer, a man of great note, a virulent wit and a peftilent pen, to tell you who be old fathers whom you may truft? He will cofin you; for he faith, *Hæc eft fententia Diui Thomæ, quam præter omnes eius difcipulos* Suarez in 3. *frequentius fequuntur antiqui Doctores & fancti Patres. This is* part. Thomæ, *the opinion of S. Thomas (Aquinas) which befides all his difciples,* difput. 54. *the ancient Doctors and holy Fathers do moft commonly follow.* fect. 4. Would not a ftranger to the Iefuiticall bafted and brauing language, expect *Iuftine Martyr, Irenæus,* or *Cyprian* before the great *Nicene Councell*; great *Athanafius, Hofius*, that were at that Councell, or at leaft *Bafil, Nazianzen*, and *Chryfoftome* amongft the Græcians, or *Ambrofe, Ierome, Auguftin,* & *Gregory of the Latine Church,* or Saint *Thomas* the Apoftle aboue and before them all? Yes verily. But here is nothing leffe: *Parturiunt montes, the hils trauell,* & bring forth a moufe; great crie, little wooll, much ftirring, and nothing to do. If thefe be not they, who are thefe *antiqui Doctores, & fancti Patres,* Quo ftabant thofe *old Doctors and fainted Fathers?* Forfooth *Bonauenture,* pueri cum to-*Richard, Albertus, Carthufianus, Alenfis, Antonius, Turre-* tus decolorif-*cremata, Waldenfis.* Are thefe your *ancient Doctors?* your fet Flaccus & *great holy Fathers?* Thefe children were cockered and pam- hærerct nigro pered, when *Auguftine* and *Ambrofe, Hierome, Chryfoftome* and Fuligo Maro-
ni.
            other

Iuuenal.Satyr. other ancient Doctors lay dusty and worm-eaten, and almost
7.   forgotte. We may answer *Suarez*, as *Acasius* answered *Eleusi-*
Concil.   *us; Quomodo Patres hos nominas, ò Eleusi, cum illorum non recipias*
Chalced.   *Patres? How can you call these Fathers,(father Suarez) when you*
                   receiue not their fathers? though *Acasius* his cause were euil, yet
                   his question was reasonable.

    4 These are but yong boyes in comparison of old men,
imberbes iuuenes, beardlesse youthes, conferred with that *vene-*
randa canicies, those *venerable gray haires*, which are for their
authoritie to be reuerenced. *All the Iesuits will shortly be cal-*
led Fathers of the Church, because in their pride they willbe en-
led Fathers aboue and beyond all their Orders, and then they will
Mun.ciuit.   *haue Fathers more then a good many.* But one of *Suarez* brother
sanctæ fund. Iesuits hath giuen better aduice from an ancient Father in-
1.ex.Ambros. deed: who saith, that out of the mouth of two or three witnes-
Epistola. 66. ses euery word shall stand. *Sed illis testibus qui ante hodiernum*
diem aut nudius tertius, non fuerunt inimici ne irati nocere cupiät, ne
læsi vlcisci se velint. Such witnesses who start not vp yesterday,
nor the day before, and were not our enemies, lest being
angry they seeke to hurt vs, or being offended, they seeke
to reuenge themselues vpon vs. This is a good caution.

    5 Therefore if the blacke guard be thus brought against
vs, we appeale to the great Guard, from them to the Pentioners, from them to the Nobles, from them to the King himselfe. Why should any man be barred of his best refuge? Will
you produce the Schoolemen? we appeale to their Masters.
Will you appeale to their Masters? we prouoke to their fathers. Wil you alledge their fathers? why may we not preferre
their *Grand-fathers*, their great grand-fathers, and so to the
Prophets, Apostles, and Christ our Sauiour himselfe? This is
plaine and euident dealing, from the bottome to the top,
from the kitchin to the hall; from the feete to the head of
the Church. As for *Suarez* old Doctors, and *sainsted Fathers,*
the oldest of them reacheth not 500 yeares past. These are but the
yong dayes of the corrupted Church : these sprang since Sathan was loosed, and Antichrist began to reigne and rage in
the Church. We dare not admit any thing for truth vpon
                                   their

their credit. They are domeſticall and partiall witneſſes, as farre ſhort of *Antiquity*, as they are of their forefathers *Integrity*: who as ſoone almoſt as they ſprouted out, they were deuided into diuers factions: that *Ariſtotle* did not ſo much oppoſe *Plato* his old maiſter, or any one ſect of Philoſophers another, as the *Thomiſts* and *Scotiſts* did both diſpute and write in their vehement contradictions; as if all diuinitie and religion were brought into a ſcholaſticall quarrell, to be entertained with wits, tongues, and pennes; yea almoſt, if not altogether, to plaine fiſts, buffets, and drie blowes: and all againſt their beſt maiſters and oldeſt fathers.

6 Wherefore we muſt not hold *Antiquity* to be that which is *Old*, or is no older then theſe young Doctors; but that which is *oldeſt*, that is firſt and primitiue, without any mixture, or deriuations, or mingling, or medling with following ages, and after times. Water is beſt tried in the fountaine, before it hath paſſed by the many varieties of diuers ſoiles. Truth muſt be ſearched in the Originall, before it hath bene ſtrained through the multitude of mens wits. *God onely is true, all men are liers and deceitfull.* The *Comforter, that is, the Spirit of truth*, who hath reuealed himſelf in his word, he hath taught the truth, and manifeſted it vnto all whom he hath ordained to eternall life. $\quad$ Rom. 3. 4. / Iohn 16. 13.

7 I knew not whom better to appeale vnto among late writers, then a prime Ieſuite, our aduerſary, an oppoſite to the Goſpell, a friend of Antichriſt; yet in this caſe as the diuell confeſſed Chriſt to be the Sonne of God, ſo he ſubſcribeth to that true and certaine antiquitie which we would haue: and proueth it by Saint *Paul. Paulus ait, illam eſſe veram & omni acceptione dignam doctrinam, qua Antiquitate præcellit, & in vniuerſum recepta eſt, vt quicquid alienum ab illa prædicatum fuerit, ſuſpectum eſſe intelligamus.* Saint *Paul* ſaith, that, that is the true doctrine, and without all exception, which is moſt ancient, and vniuerſally receiued, ſo that whatſoeuer is preached diuers from it, we may iuſtly ſuſpect it: *Hanc regulam tradit Apoſtolus, This rule the Apoſtle giueth to beleeuers.* There turne downe your leafe. For this we accept not as your $\quad$ Salmeron in Epiſt.B. Pauli. l. 1. part. 1. diſp. 9. can. 12. / Galat. 3. / Rom. 16. 17.

D $\qquad$ grant,

grant, but as Gods allowance, and therefore our due. For nothing can be auouched older, nothing so commonly receiued, as the Scriptures.

8 Traditions are questionable, both in their beginning & acceptation. If we rest and rely on men, what is truer then that of the *Poet*, which daily experience maketh manifest, *Quot homines, tot sententiæ, How many men, so many minds,* euery man his owne fashion? I will not say that euery man is wedded to his owne will, but euery man hath his owne conceipt, euery man aboundeth in his owne sence, and it often falleth out, that *suum cuique pulchrum*: A crow as blacke as she is, thinkes her owne bird fairest, and euery man easily fauoureth his owne deuice; an Ape and an Asse of all brute creatures most admire and dote vpon their owne young. This may be obserued among the best writers, that haue liued since the Apostles times, euen in the best ages.

9 They that conceipted more gods then one, imagined (and not without cause) that they had more affections and distractions then one, or once:

> *Mulciber in Troiam, pro Troia stabat Apollo,*
> *Æqua Venus Teucris, Pallas iniqua fuit.*
> Vulcan against Troy, for Troy Apollo stood,
> Venus well pleased, Pallas another mood.

This is most certaine with men, and would be without question as sure among the gods, if there were as many gods as men. But our God is one, *Euen one God and Father of all, who is aboue all, and with vs all, and in vs all.* Our Sauiour Christ was God and man; when he was man, yet he remained God: to shew that there was but one will in God, though two in himselfe, he protesteth that *he came not to do his owne will, but his Fathers will that sent him.* So that mans will can haue no mixture with Gods will, except his will be conformed to the will of God, *Who doth all things according to the pleasure of his will.* And therefore S. *Paul* when he should deliuer the doctrine of the Sacrament to the *Corinthians,* the institution whereof belongeth to God, saith, *Quod accepi à Domino, hoc tradidi vobis, What I receiued of the Lord, that haue I deliuered to you.* He
neither

1.Cor.8.6.

Iohn 5.30.

Ephes.1.5.

1.Cor.11.23.

neither deriueth his doctrine from himselfe, nor hangeth it
vpon the authority of men, but vpon the Lord Iesus Christ,
that was God and man.

10 Wherefore if you will aptly define true *Antiquity*, take
Saint *Hilary* his counsell, *Antiqua sunt quæ modum non habent,* In Psal. 138.
quæ indefiniti temporis significant vetustatem: Antiquitie hath no
bounds, no limits, it signifieth the age of indefinite time. In this
case it is no sophisme, *Petere principia, to go backe where we be-*
gan. We must lay our hand vpon the first knot of *Ariadnes*
threed, or else we may labor in the Labyrinth, as the *Sodomites*
groped for *Lots house,* and could not find it.   Gen. 19. 11.

11 Therefore all was not to be counted old, that went
not long before *Luthers* time, (as the simple imagine) when
ignorance had some few hundred yeares couered the face of
the Romane Church, as the darknesse did Egypt, when the Exod. 10. 22.
Israelites in *Goshen* saw well enough Wherein many, as with
candles in a house, saw the light of truth, though the Sunne
was intercepted with a cloud, or in eclips or interposition of
the earth, in that night of darknesse. Those times had their
limits, they were not indefinite, and therefore are not worthie the name of *Antiquity.* Which indefinite time though
in it selfe it passeth by all things created, and resteth onely in
that infinite Maiesty, beyond whom there is no time, with- Deus anti-
out whom there is no *being,* from whom there lieth no ap- quus dierum.
peale; yet by way of comparison, or in the tender of humane
capacity, we may yeeld vnto time, and giue a beginning vnto
that *Antiquity,* for which we search, and wherein we may rest,
as in the hauen where we would be.   Psal. 107.

12 This *Antiquity* is found primarily and principally in the
first reuelation of Gods will, which though it passed from
hand to hand, vntill the giuing of the Law in writing: yet
was it euer preserued by the voice of God, and ministery of
Angels, in the race of the faithfull: few in number, weake in
strength, despised of the world, persecuted by the wicked. If
you aske why God gaue them no Law in writing, as afterward he did? we know not what they had. Some are of opinion that diuers things were written before the floud, and
                        D 2   engrauen

engrauen in ſtone, and it may be there were writings which
were afterward loſt in their captiuity in Egypt. But theſe
things need not any curious diſquiſition. An ancient writer
in our aduerſaries computation, hath giuen a reaſonable ſentence for our inſtruction, and that times want of Scriptures.

Io. Catacuze- *Nos omnes indigemus Scripturarum auxilio, propter infirmitatem*
nus Apoc.4. *noſtram. Iuſtus verò Noe & Abraham, & qui illorum tempore*
floruerunt, pura mente prediti -- Scriptura non indigebant, ſed hæc
„ *in ipſorum cordibus inſcripta & adumbratafuit.* We, euen all of
„ vs, do want the helpe of Scriptures, by reaſon of our infirmi-
„ tie. But iuſt *Noah* and *Abraham* and others that flouriſhed in
„ their times, endued with pure vnderſtanding, wanted not
„ Scripture, but that was written and decifered in their hearts.

Hebr.1.1. But we haue a better teſtimony to giue vs ſatisfaction in this
caſe. *At ſundry times, and in diuers manners, God ſpake in old time*
to our fathers, by his Prophets; in theſe laſt daies he hath ſpoken to
vs by his Sonne. How God taught them, what is that to vs? If
we haue a rule, we muſt be directed by it: if none, we muſt do

Euſeb.hiſt.lib. as we may. Reade but *Euſebius*, how he deliuereth Chriſt and
1.cap.6. Chriſtianity from the ſuſpition of noueltie, and giueth the
Fathers before *Abraham* the title of Chriſtians, becauſe they
did exerciſe Chriſtian vertues, and caried themſelues in all
Gods ſeruice as Chriſtians do. So ſay we; we worſhip God
as the Apoſtles did, we hold their faith, and obey Gods direction as they haue deliuered; we are younger in time, but
we are equall in the profeſſion of the ſame faith.

13 Againe, this *Antiquity* which thus lay ſecretly ſealed
vp in one little familie, and a few ſcattered dependants, was
by the giuing of the Law, opened and reuealed in more maieſtie to a people, though from the ſame roote, yet growne
into more branches, and to a greater number, and more emi-

Ioſuah 1.7. nency in the eyes of the world. It was commended vnto *Io-*
ſuah the Captaine of the people, and vnto the Prieſts and Le-
uits, that he might gouerne, they might teach, all might worſhip God, & worke righteouſnes according to the direction

Deut.18.15. thereof. And to preuent defection herefrom, God promiſed
Ierem.7.25. Prophets, like vnto *Moſes, whō they ſhould heare,* which accordingly

dingly he performed, *Rising vp early and sending them.*

14 These Prophets in their times, changed nothing, but renewed the ruines of this ancient building, & restored true *Antiquity* to its old and worthy reputation. And therefore neuer altered any thing the Law had commanded, but for all matters of doctrine or conuersation, they prouoked to the Law, as is cleare both by the story of the Kings and Chronicles, and by the Psalmes and other Prophecies, which vndoubtedly were learned and receiued from God, and deliuered vnto the Church for the direction thereof in his will and wayes. And therefore, the King and Prophet *Dauid* who had vse thereof in his gouernment, besides the guidance of his priuate life and cariage, commendeth this as a great mercy and token of the loue of God, that he had giuen his *word vnto Iacob, his statutes and ordinances vnto Israel.* And the Pro- Psal.147.19. phet *Isaiah* sendeth all thither, as vnto the very rocke and foundation of true *Antiquitie, Ad legem & testimonium, To* Esay 8.20. *the Law and testimony, they that speake not according to that word, the mornings light is not in them.*

15 When the Prophets deliuered immediate reuelations, which concerned promises of blessings, or denunciation of iudgements to come, then they came with *Hæc dicit Dominus:Thus saith the Lord*; or *Os Domini locutum est: The mouth of the Lord hath spoken it.* But in matter of Gods seruice, and true godlinesse, all was onely to bring them to serue one God according to his Law, to reduce them from, either grosse Idolatry, which they committed like other nations, or from outward ceremonies, to the inward marrow and pith of the Law, and from their works *Ex opere operato,* that is, from presuming of Gods fauour for the worke wrought without sanctifying of the heart, (as if God were bound to shew mercie for their sacrifices, when they liued in their sinnes and wrought all iniquity) vnto a sincere and hearty conuersion, which is the perfection of true repentance. So religiously stood the Prophets to the *Antiquitie of the Law,* that they must go *ad legem & testimoniū,* to the Law and the Prophets, if euer they would be partakers of the mornings light, as is said.

16 The

16 The next fucceffion of this true *Antiquity*, was in the time of *the Meffiah*, when our Sauior appeared in the flefh. He was by his aduerfaries vrged with the *Tradition of the Elders*, their cuftomes and obferuations were euer preffed vpon him. But as he proued his own authority, fo alfo his doctrine, both of beleefe, and manners, as grounded vpon no other *Antiquitie*, but the *Law, the Prophets*, and *the Pfalmes. What is written in your Law?* and the like phrafes were *euermore* our Sauiour Chrifts defences. *He came not to breake the Law*, but to fulfill it. He giueth it a more fpirituall vnderftanding then the later old times had giuen, condemning not onely the outward act, but the firft motion and finfull thought. In what was amiffe, though very anciently permitted by *Mofes* himfelfe *for the hardneffe of the peoples hearts*, he tendered his reformation with the *oldeft Antiquity, Non fuit fic ab initio: It was not fo from the beginning.*

17 Vpon which faire and folid ground I may be bold to lay this fure foundation for all mine intended building, that the *True and vndoubted Antiquity began with the entrance of the law of nature*: continued in the Law and Prophets, was ended and confummate in the Gofpels and hiftories of the Euangelifts, the Epiftles and writings of the Apoftles. The very fimpathy (as I may fay) & concurrence, or facred method of the old and new Teftament, do glue a certaine maieftie & certainty vnto both, as when the Gofpels anfwer the Law, the Acts, the hiftories: the Epiftles, thofe books of mixt argument; the Reuelation, the Prophefies of the old Teftament. And as the old is determined and ended by the Prophets, fo is the new Teftament finifhed with the Reuelatiõ. In al likelihood to fignifie, that as the old Teftament was compleate when the Prophets ceaffed, fo the Scriptures of the new Teftament were full and abfolute when Saint *Iohn* had done writing. *Malachie* the laft of the Prophets, *Iohn* the laft of the Apoftles, in time and writing. Thefe are the true and certaine bounders of facred, vnimpeached, and that reuerend, refpected, and renowmed *Antiquity*, which all thofe whom we call the ancient Fathers of the Church, admired

and

Luke 24.25.

Mat. 5.17.

Mat. 19.8.

and admitted. Hereunto in all controuersies, they veiled their bonnets, and strooke their top-sailes, as in the chamber of Gods presence, and to the kings royall ships; as vnto the chaire of Gods estate, and the Admirall of that great Emperours Nauie in the turbulent sea of the troublesome and contradictorious world. Beyond these nothing hath bene reuealed with like maiestie vnto the sonnes of men. Since these, there hath bene no other word or *Gospell*, whereunto our consciences may be tyed, as vnto the sure anchor of secure safetie. Neither can it be euer proued, that any of the oldest ancient Fathers, prouoked or appealed to any other *Antiquitie.*

18 Vpon this foundation, *Tertullian* builded, when he wrote, that (except he were deceiued) *Antiquior omnibus est veritas, The truth is ancienter then all men, or all other things.* And so *Antiquity doth profit him if it be grounded vpon diuine learning, that was a treasure to be preferred, before all after wisedome.* Of which, and of which onely, we may say as the same ancient writer, *Against truth no man can prescribe, no length of time, no patronage of persons, no priuiledge of nations:* whose words would be farther pressed, for they are very significant, and remarkable. For custome it hath its beginning, *for the most part, from some ignorance* of Gods holy will reuealed in the Scriptures, or else *by simplicity: And by succession it is strengthened with vse, and so it is defended against truth.* But *our Lord Iesus Christ called himselfe Truth, not Custome. If Christ be alwaies, and before all, then truth is ancient and euerlasting. Let them therefore looke to it, which hold that for new which in it selfe is old: For heresies are not conuinced by their noueltie, but by the truth. Whatsoeuer sauoureth against the truth it is heresie, be it neuer so ancient a custome.* Thus and more *Tertullian.* Here is no other *foundation layd then Iesus Christ*, no custome pretended, but the truth iustified, not any writings but the diuine Scriptures offered, against heresies, the deadliest and most dangerous enemies of Christ, and his Church.

19 Shall this then stand for a Rule ? *Id esse verum quodcunque primum, Id esse adulterum quodcunque posterius. That is*

Apol. cont. gentes, c. vlt.

Idem de velandis Virginibus.

Sempiterna & antiqua res.

Tertul. aduersus Praxeam.

truth

truth which is first, that is adulterous which cometh after. This is all we defire, we aske no more. But then we muft vnderftand withall, this *First,*to be no fecondary, much leffe latter age, or time, but that which hath no antecedent, and is of it felfe primarie: and fo is not onely *Antiquum ancient, in the positiue,* but *Antiquissimum,*moft ancient in the fuperlatiue degree: otherwife there will be no ftay, no reft, no repofe for a confcience to be fatisfied with *Antiquitie.*

20 For as *Antiquitie* is vfually taken, and fo commonly abufed, it is nothing but a very glofe and outfacing with after times, when corruption began to grow in the Church, and euery particular Father of thefe Ancients, who fucceeded the Apoftles, and whofe writings are extant, and open to the world, had not only their little blemifhes but their great fpots and ftaines, fuch as they who now pretend themfelues to be their greateft friends, and vndertake to defend them with all their power, cannot hide them with all their skill, nor excufe them with all their wit. And therefore thefe by no meanes are to be taken for that eminent, predominant and binding *Antiquitie,* which may ftand without controllment, and be admitted without iuft exception. *Qui errauerit in vno, reus eft omnium,* It is not onely true of the Law, whereof *Saint Iames* fpeaketh, but of all mankind. He that erreth in one thing, may be guilty, & fo erre in many things. This priuiledge refteth with God alone, and with the penmen of the *holy Ghoft* in the facred Scriptures: *Deus folus verax, God only is is true,* and as true it is, that *All men are lyers.* No mortall man that fucceeded the Apoftles, was euer priuiledged againft this generall corruption of the fonnes of *Adam.* Which if any fhall gainefay, and pleade probabilities or poffibilities, of thofe that immediatly fucceeded the Apoftles times: I wold anfwer as *Saint Hierome* in a like cafe, vnto the *Pelagians: Noli ponere in cœlum os tuum, vt per effe, & effe poffe, ftultorum auribus illudas. Set not thy mouth againft heauen, that by likelyhood and possibilities thou mayft delude the eares of the fimple:* neuer tell me any man can do that, which neuer man did. Inftance but in one and take all.

Iam. 2.10.

Rom.3.4.

Dial. aduer. Pelag.cap.2.

21 The

21 The same *Saint Hierome* in this case, vpon a iuft exception, hath offered a good rule, which the rather muft be refted
vpon and holden for good, becaufe the Romanifts produce
this teftimony to obfcure the truth. *Cur poft* 400 *annos, why*   Ad Pamach.
after 400 *yeares laboureft thou to teach vs that which we neuer*   & Oceanum
heard before? Why doeft thou bring forth that which Peter and   de error. Ori-
Paule neuer taught? the Chriftian world euen vntill this day hath genis.
bene without this doctrine; I will keepe that faith in mine old age, in
which I was borne, baptized, and brought vp. This *ancient* Father,
and light of Gods Church we admire for his learning, and
this his paffage with one confent we imbrace : and wifh from
our hearts nothing more, in thefe dayes of contradiction, but
that this his rule might hold for the triall of *Gods* truth, that
the *oldeft religion* which flourifhed before *Saint Hieromes* time,
which *Peter and Paul* taught, and which the primitiue Church
beleeued, might be receiued, admitted, accepted, and reuerenced in the whole world. In this cafe we accept the Iefuits
challenge: *Oftendant nobis Lutherani, & qui illis pofteriores funt*
alij hæretici, Let the Lutherans and after heretiques fhew vs,
that the Apoftles were their leaders, that their paftors came into the
Apoftolicall function by lawfull authority, that their doctrine was
approued in all ages from the Apoftles times, in any village or ham-
let, but by an open heretique. If we cannot fhew this, as well as
Iofiah could, when he found the Law, and reformed : or if we   2. King. 22. 9.
cannot proue our religion in all things older, and of more
certaine continuance then our aduerfaries, I will come vnto
them, and ferue the king of their Antichriftian Babylon during my life. This we are able, and dare proue, and neuer   Mun. ciuit.
breake our fhins with a leape neither, as that Iefuite feareth or   fanctæ fund. 3
rather drunkenly dreameth.

22 For it is not onely true which *Iefus Syrach* the wife man
faith, *An old friend is better then a new:* but alfo Iefus Chrift the   Eccl. 19. 13.
wifeft of all men, & the eternal wifedome *of his Father* prefer-
reth old wine before new, and faith *that the old is better,* as before   Luke 5. 39.
was faid. *We know there is wifedome in old yeares, and that re-*
uerence is due to gray haires. And, *Interrogate Patres veftros,* is a   Deut. 32.
fage counfell of the *holy Ghoft.* And it is good *to confider the*   Ier. Lam. 3
                                                        dayes

Pſal.77. 5.
Pſal.78. 1.
Pſal.44.1.
Iob 8 8.9. 10.
dayes of old, and the yeares of ancient times : and it pleaſed God to aduiſe vs, *to incline our eares to his mouth, when he declareth high ſentences of old, euen ſuch as our fathers told vs.* And *Iob prayeth vs to enquire of the former age, and to prepare our ſelues to ſearch our fathers.* The Romaine Fathers are but of *yeſterday, and know nothing:* theſe may diſſemble, like idle & ſlow bellies, but thoſe will *teach, and tell, and ſpeake with their hearts.* But in our honeſt ſimplicity whereby we humble our ſelues vnto our anceſtors and forefathers, we muſt vſe this prudence and prouidence, that we take not proffered new friends for approoued old Fathers, freſh men for ancient Doctors, children for parents, yongſters for Aldermen, euery Courtier for a graue and iudicious Counſeller : for ſo a man may be ſoone and ſoundly deceiued. For as honorable age is not that which

Wiſd. 4. 8.
hath bene of long time, *Neither that which is meaſured by the number of yeares;* ſo neither doth the honourable *Truth of God* ſtand vpon the ages and times, ſucceſſions and ſuffrages of ſinfull men, but on his Word, which is before all time, *the author and God of time and truth.*

23 In which caſe, we haue a preciſe caueat to take heed of ſuch vncertaine and vnapproued *Antiquitie. The Lord hath*
Zach. 1.4.
bene ſore diſpleaſed with your fathers,—Therefore turne vnto me, ſaith the Lord of Hoaſts. Be not as your fathers, vnto whom the former Prophets haue cried, ſaying, Thus ſaith the Lord of Hoaſts ; Turne you now from your euill wayes, and from your wicked works: but they would not heare nor hearken vnto me, ſaith the Lord of Hoaſts. Your fathers where are they? And do the Prophets liue for euer? But did not my words and my ſtatutes, which I commanded by my ſeruants the Prophets, take hold of your fathers?

This Prophet after the peoples captiuity, admoniſheth them, that as they returne to their countrey from their thraldome and bondage, ſo ſhould they returne to the truth, and that God who had chaſtiſed their fathers for their error from that truth, would alſo chaſtiſe them if they alſo erred. So
Ezech. 20, 18.
Ezechiel, and not long before, *Walke you not in the ordinances of your fathers, neither obſerue their manners, neither defile your ſelues with Idols.* What cautels are theſe, not to reſt vpon later
Antiquitie,

Antiquitie, built vpon some, not many yeares past;but vpon Gods booke, the spring that riseth out of Gods owne sacred breast?

24 And therefore the Prophets, as they call the people from their fathers wayes and workes, so do they not leaue them like sheepe without a shepheard, to wander in the wildernesse without direction: or like a ship on the Ocean sea, without a compasse, and the load-starre that should guide them in the darknesse of the night; but leadeth them to the *great Shepheard of their soules,* & to the hauen of health where they should be, for their best repose and security. *Turne vnto* Malach.3.7. *me, and I will turne vnto you, saith the Lord of hoasts.* And *I am the Lord your God, walke in my statutes, and keepe my Commandements, and do them.* This is that *terminus à quo,* and *terminus ad quem,* from whence we haue our being, in whom we enioy our well being, whither, and to whom we must returne, for our euerlasting being. There is the fountaine of truth; from thence flow all the riuers of truth, therein rests the whole Ocean of truth. It began with the Patriarkes, it continued vnder the Law, taught by the Prophets, it is consummate in the Gospell, which was written by the Euangelists and Apostles, all inspired by the holy Ghost.

25 This is our *Nihil supra,* and our *Nihil vltra,* nothing aboue it, nothing below it, nothing before it, nothing after it, nothing any way beyond it, for age or truth. This came from heauen, is protected by heauen, and shall bring vs to heauen. There we find Gods loue in electing vs, Gods power in creating vs, Gods mercy in calling vs, Christs merits in redeeming vs, Christs righteousnesse in iustifying vs, Christs grace in sauing vs, the holy Ghosts wisedome inspiring vs, his knowledge teaching vs, his sanctification working vs, and conforming vs to the will of God; *By mortifying the deeds of* Rom. 8.13. *the flesh, and renewing the spirits of our mindes,* vnto obedience, Ephes. 4.23. in faith, peace, and holinesse, *without which we shall neuer see the* Heb.12.14. *Lord.*

26 Here we find the great *mysterie of godlinesse, God mani-* 1.Tim.3.16. *fested in the flesh, iustified in the spirit, seene of Angels, preached vn-*

to the *Gentiles, beleeued on in the world, and receiued vp into glory.*
Here is taught that vnspeakable mysterie of the blessed Trinitie, *The Father, the Word, and the Spirit, and these three are one.*
Our *God, Lord, Comforter: Loue, Grace, and Counseller: the beget-*
ter, the begotten, and the Renewer. The very light of the very light,
and the very Illumination. The spring, the floud, and the watering;
of whom all, through whom all things: of whom, through whom, and
in whom are all things. The liuing life, the life from the liuing , the
quickener of such as liue. One of himselfe, one of one, one of two. A
being of himselfe, a being of an other, a being from both. The Father
is truth , the Sonne is truth, and the holy Ghost is truth. In one
word, here we find that *which is able to make vs wise vnto salua-*
tion through faith which is in Christ Iesus. And that *all Scripture*
is giuen by inspiration from God, and is profitable for doctrine , for
reproofe, for correction, for instruction in righteousnesse, that the man
of God may be perfect, throughly furnished to all good works. Therefore what need we more? where may we find better ? what is
more certaine? what more powerful to pierce the hard buck-
ler of mans obstinate heart? what more learned to teach the
grosse capacity of mans vnderstanding in spirituall things?
what more effectuall to informe the conscience of man that
it may be conformed to the will of God? finally, what of more
Antiquity, to command all following ages vnto the obedience of certaine truth?

    27 To conclude, what can we aske for the strengthening
of our faith, but here we may haue it ? where may we seeke
that *precious pearle for which a wise man would sell all that he hath*
to buy it, but onely here, where onely it may be found ? At
what gate may we knocke to find the certaine entrance into
euerlasting life and glory, but at this doore which is opened
by him which hath *the Key of Dauid, which openeth and no man*
shutteth, shutteth and no man openeth? This is the gate of the Lord,
let vs enter into it : let vs passe through it, repose and repast
our selues in it. *Better be a doore-keeper in the house of God, then*
to dwell in the tents of vngodlinesse. Better to rest in the plaine
and simple vnderstanding of this vnquestioned & vndoubted
verity of holy Scriptures, then to dwell in the profound
science

1.Ioh.5.
Aug. in solilo.
cap.30. si sit
Aug.

2.Tim.3.15.

Mat.13.44.

Apocal.3.7.

Psal.84.10.

science (falsely so called) of Schoole Diuines, yea or in the *1.Tim.6.20.*
multitude of Fathers, neuer so many, neuer so learned who, as
hath bene said, and must still be thought , were all subiect to
that censure of the *holy Ghost : All men are lyers.* *Rom.3.4.*

28 I must therefore conclude and determine, that the
most certaine beginning , the most vndoubted continuance,
and the most firme and finall conclusion of the *oldest Antiqui-*
tie, against which there is no exception, is that which began
with the Fathers of the old world, was registred by *Moses* in
his sacred histories and Law, continued by the Prophets before Christ, and is concluded by the Euangelists and Apostles
in the new Testament. Of which , as our Sauiour vpon the
crosse in the worke of our redemption said, *Consummatum est,*
It is finished: So we may say and say truly, and seale it vp with *Iohn 19.30.*
the seale of God, (*He knoweth who are his* , and he knoweth
what is his,) for our comfort and instruction, *Consummatum* *2.Tim.2.19.*
est, It is finished. And therefore it is questionlesse not without
diuine prouidence, that in the last booke of the whole Bible,
last written of all the Scriptures , containing prophecies of
the last times, euen to the last end of the world , and in the
last Chapter, yea and last words of that last Chapter, there is
a seale, with the inscription of a fearefull and dangerous curse
to them, that shall *Adde to, or take from any thing contained in the* *Reuel.22.*
booke: yea (as I am perswaded)or in any other booke of holy
Scripture, whereof this booke standeth as the last period and
conclusion ; after which there remaineth nothing but the expectation of him, who is the chiefe, the principall, and I may
say the onely subiect and matter of all Scriptures, that is, Iesus Christ himselfe and his members, who saith, *Surely I*
come quickly, Amen, Euen so come Lord Iesus, & againe shutteth
vp all with *Amen.*

29 If the Romanists wil prouoke vs to following ages &
succeeding Bishops , this is not onely to step , but to leape
from *Antiquitie, which is true Antiquitie indeed, vnto Noueltie, in* *Mun ciuit.*
the comparison, from elder to yonger both times and persons, *sanctæ.*
that may breake not onely shinnes, but the necke too. For as
Adam of all Fathers was onely in Paradise , and saw the tree
of

Gen.3.

of life in the midst of the garden, which none of his posterity euer saw in the flesh, though many of them were saued by lesse meanes then *Adam* had; so the Euangelists and Apostles, who enioyed the presence & sight of our Sauiour Christ, that tree of life, saw and heard, and published to the vse of the Church, that which their successors neuer saw, though they learned Christ sufficiently for their saluation, and were excellent lights in the Church, and were Martyrs and Confessors, that loued not their liues to the death, for the testimonie of the Lord Iesu. Yet were they children in respect of those Fathers, and did euer submit themselues vnto their writings, as vnto the grounds of their faith. And required no more credit to themselues, then they deserued by their neare imitation of those their Ancestors: to whose authority they referred the censure of all their doctrine, as vnto that *Lydius lapis, that touchstone*, whereby all coyne is tried to be good or counterfeit. So much esteeme gaue they vnto this oldest *Antiquitie;* so little did they euer arrogate vnto themselues or new deuices.

30 First aske the Fathers what they say of themselues, and others like themselues, for their owne defects: then what they write of the Scriptures for their omni-sufficiency, and that will easily decide this question of true *Antiquitie*, what it

De incar. Dominic. sacrament. cap.3.

is, and where it was determined. *Nolo nobis credatur, Scriptura recitetur,* saith Saint *Ambrose, Non ego dico, sed audio; non effingo, sed lego. I will not desire you to beleeue me, let the Scripture be alledged. I say it not, but I heare it; I make it not on my fingers ends, but I reade it.* This Father asketh no credit to himselfe, but giueth all to the Scriptures, and therefore that he may proue

Lib.1.cap.7.

semper idem, the same man still, he saith to *Gratianus, Facessat nostra sententia, Paulum interrogemus: Beleeue not what I say, but let vs aske Saint Paule.* And Saint *Hierome, Sine Scripturarum*

Hieron. in Tit.cap.1.

authoritate garrulitas non haberet fidem; Without the authoritie of the Scriptures, prating should neuer get credit: as if all were but pratling that was spoken without that booke, or were not consonant and agreeable thereunto.

31 It is a faire offer that Saint *Augustine* makes to *Petilian* the

the hereticke: *Sunt certi libri Dominici, Certaine books of God,* De veritate
vnto which we both yeeld consent , there let vs seeke the Church, Ecclef.cap.3.
there let vs discusse our cause. I will not haue the holy Church made cont. lit.
manifest by humane doctrines, but by diuine Oracles. Can he offer Petil.
his aduersarie fairer? Can he speak more peremptorily for the
diuine Scriptures against the Doctrines of men? Yet he doth
say more in that booke, *Ne Catholicis quidē Episcopis consentien-* Cap.10.
dū est, We may not consent no not to Catholicke BB. if in any thing
they *be deceiued, or erre against the canonicall Scriptures.* And
what an humble acknowledgement doth he make of his
owne weaknesse, euen openly before his auditors, with reference of soueraignty to the Scriptures? *Quod dicimus fratres,* Auguft.in
hoc si non vobis tanquam certum exposuero , ne succenseatis: homo Pfal.85.
enim sum; & quantum conceditur de Scripturis sanctis, tantum
audeo dicere, nihil ex me. Brethren, if what we speake we deliuer it not to you for certaine , be not offended : for I am a
man, and as much as is granted out of the holy Scriptures,
so much I dare affirme , but nothing of my selfe. And elsewhere, *Let our Papers be cashiered from among vs , and let Gods* In Pfal,57.
booke haue place with vs, let Chrift speake , let the truth be heard.
Nay this Father is not afraid, *to set aside* one, or a few men and
their opinions, in comparison of the volume of Gods booke,
but 318 Fathers at once, and these gathered in a solemne
Councell, to determine a great & chiefe Article of Chriftian
faith, when it was called into queftion, by ftrong and violent
aduersaries; where he reasoneth with *Maximinian, Neither* Lib.3.c.14.
will I offer the Nicene Councell against thee, neither shalt thou al-
ledge the Councell of Ariminum against me, as preiudiciall in this
controuersie, but let vs trie by the authoritie of the Scriptures, and
let matter with matter, cause with cause, reason with reason
contend.

32 Infinite for number, eminent for authority, euident for
perspicuity, and excellently cordiall for a weake conscience,
are the sentences of the Fathers to this purpose difperfed
through all their works. And therefore we aske leaue in
this behalfe of the Romanifts, if they will not giue it, we will
take it, and haue good reason so to do, to say of all the Fathers,

Iuel againſt
Hardiog.

thers, as one ſaid of another without offence giuen or taken:
Da veniam Cypriane: *Pardon me Cyprian*; No holding with
Cyprian, though a learned Father and a Martyr, if *Cyprian*
hold any thing againſt the Scriptures. Or as *Auguſtine* ſaid
of as reuerend a Father as euer the Church ſaw in his time or

Aug. Epiſtola
19.

ſince: *Non puto frater te velle libros tuos legi, tanquam Apoſtolorum*
& Prophetarum, de quorum ſcriptis, quòd omni errore careant du-
,, *bitare nefas eſt: I thinke not brother that you would haue your books*
,, *read as thoſe of the Apoſtles and Prophets, of whoſe writings ſo*
,, *much as to doubt is ſacriledge.* This they beleeued both of themſelues and others, and of the holy volume of the ſacred Bible,
& therfore they haue ſpoken, yea and haue written it, as their
conſtant iudgement vnto poſterity.

33 And thus much (as afterward ſhall more largely appeare) do we attribute to Councels, to Fathers, to all inferior
Antiquitie, with this onely, Salua in omnibus, ſauing in all things
the authoritie of the Canonicall Scriptures. But in no caſe can

Rabbi She-
lomo.
Deut. 17, 11.

we be ſo frantickly mad, as a Rabbin, who becauſe it was written, *Thou ſhalt not decline from the ſentence they ſhall ſhew thee,*
ſaith, that a man may not depart from it though they ſay, *The*
right hand is the left, and the left the right; This may be a rule

Gloſſ diſt. 9.
Noli. meis.

for Rabbins, it can be no warrant for Chriſtians. Yet in the
B. of *Romes* diuinity, there is as much in effect, *Tenenda eſt ſen-*
tentia Patrum hodie vſque ad vnum iota, *The Fathers ſentence is*
now to be holden to the vtmoſt pricke. Yea both more and worſe

Rubrica in c.
In Canonicis
diſt. 19.

then this: *Inter canonicas Scripturas Decretales Epiſtolæ cõnume-*
rantur: *The Decretall Epiſtles are to be numbred among the cano-*
nicall Scriptures. How farre is this from blaſphemie; and yet
fathered moſt falſly vpon Saint *Auguſtine*: whoſe words im-
port no ſuch thing. Neither may we ſafely admit that ſuperlatiue reſpect to the beſt Father that euer wrote ſince the

Diſt. 15. c. vlt.
Diſt. 9. Noli
meis.

Apoſtles dayes, which *Gelaſius* giueth vnto *Leo* for one of
his Epiſtles, and the Gloſſe ſeemeth to attribute vnto all. He
that admits it not *vſque ad vnum iota*, vnto the leaſt letter or
pricke, *or diſputes of it, or receiueth it not in all things, Anathema*

Ieremy. 17. 5

ſit, let him be accurſed. Nay rather *Curſed is he that truſteth in*
man, and maketh fleſh his arme, and withdraweth his heart from
the Lord,   34 All

34 All this we hold to be exorbitant, and beyond all mediocrity, like that of the Councell of *Basil*: *Non solùm Ecclesiæ decreta & sententiæ authenticæ sunt*, *Not onely the decrees and sentence of the Church are authenticall*, vnto which *we must stand without contradiction*, *but also all the deeds and Customes*, *must be holden as the sacred Scriptures*; *for there is the like reason for the Customes of the Church that is for the Scriptures, and the like affection of pietie is due vnto them both.* Ex epistolis synodal. Concil. Basiliens.

35 We rather approue the modestie of the Fathers themselues, who (as before is said) deferred soueraigne respect vnto diuine Scriptures, and acknowledged themselues men subiect to error. *I know* (saith *Hierome*) *how to esteeme the Apostles, and how to respect other writers* : *those I know euer say true, but these sometimes do erre like men.* And Saint *Augustine* againe, *Ego solus eis,* &c. *I haue learned to yeeld that honor & reuerence to those onely writers, who are counted Canonicall, that I dare not thinke or beleeue they euer erred* : *or if I finde any thing in them that seemeth contrary vnto truth, I cannot thinke, but that either it is false written, or that the interpreter attained not vnto the meaning of that which is said*; *or that my selfe cannot reach vnto the true meaning of it. But others be they of neuer so great holinesse, neuer so great learning* (and holinesse with learning will go far in perswation,) *yet can I not thinke they speake truth because it is their opinion, but because by other authors, and canonicall reasons, and probabilities, which are not abhorrent from truth, they do perswade me.* Not to burthen my reader with ouer frequent allegations, if he wil take the paines to reade the ninth distinction in *Gratian*, he shall finde much to this purpose, out of other Fathers. Epistola 62. cap. 2.

Epistola 8. inter Epistolas Hieron.

36 Neither haue some of the Romanists best friends & fauorites bene far from this minde as touching the Fathers: not onely for their commenting vpon the Scriptures, but also for other writings, wherein they are found to haue erred from the truth. *Vix reperias quenquam qui non in aliquo errarit:* *You can hardly finde* (*of the Fathers*) *any one, who hath not erred in somewhat,* saith *Canus,* a B. and no meane souldier in the Roman Legion. And *Lyra* no contemptible author among them, Canus loc. com. l. 11. c. 7

E   will

will not haue his nofe fo holden to the grindleftone by a Father, as that he may not plucke it away when he feeleth it

In Mat.1. fmart. *Non enim fic ab eis teftimonia proferuntur, vt aliter fentire non liceat: For their teftimony is not fo without exception, that a man may not thinke otherwife.* And *Caietan* a learned Cardinall (a

Præfat. in lib. fault not incident to very many of that fraternity) faith mo-
5.Mofis. deftly, *Nullus deteftetur nouum facræ Scripturæ fenfum, ex hoc*
　　　　　,, *quod diffonat cum prifcis Patribus &c. Let no man deteft a new*
　　　　　,, *fence giuen of the holy Scripture, becaufe it foundeth not with the*
　　　　　,, *ancient Fathers.* He faw that fome were fo tyed to the regard of this vncertaine *Antiquitie*, as that nothing fmelled wel but what fauoured of a Faher; nothing tafted well, but what was receiued from a Fathers cooking; nothing founded well but what was fet to a Fathers tune. Howbeit in thefe there is fome meane and modefty, but in the others there is neither manners, nor mediocritie.

　　37　In which cafe we fay, and fay full truly, the eftate of the Church in her teachers, may be compared with the image of
Daniel.2.32. *Nebuchadnezar* which he faw in his dreame: *The head was of gold*, the breaft and armes of filuer, the belly and thighes of braffe, the legges of iron, and the feet partly iron, and partly clay. Chrift in his Apoftles and Euangelifts was the head of gold, the learned Fathers of the primitiue Church were that breaft and armes of filuer, the firft Orders of laboring and preaching Monks the belly and thighes of braffe, the fchoolemen and Cafuits the legs of iron, the moderne Iefuits & Priefts the feet part of iron & part of clay: to fignifie, that
Pfal.19.10. *all written in Scriptures was pure as gold, yea purer then gold, yea*
Pfal.12.6. *then much fine gold, fuch as hath bene tried feuen times in the fire.* The Fathers were filuer trumpets that aftonifhed the heretickes of the primitiue times with the found of the Gofpel,
Iofua.6.23. and ouerthrew the wals of vnbeleeuing Ierico; that gathered the elect into the Sanctuary of God. The beft and firft Monks that followed thefe times of the Fathers were more fubiect to corruption and ruft, and yet ferued as the meaner veffels and inftruments of the Temple. The fchoolemen and Cafuits, and I may ad the Popes Canonifts to them, were not

　　　　　　　　　　　　　　　　　　　　　　　　　onely

onely iron vp to their very faces and foreheads, but ruftie iron, cankred at the very heart: a very iron cage of vncleane birds, that (as *Harpies* in hell) fnatch from the people the *fincere milke of the word, that was able to faue their foules,* and in- I.Pet.2.2. clofed them in the iron grates of intricate and infenfible di-ftinctions, which they vnderftood not that heard them, nor thefelues that taught them. And finally, not as at the loofing of Satan, when as yet he had not wrought his ful worke in *the children of difobedience,* but as in the fit of madneffe, and rage Ephef.2.2. of *Antichrift* and the diuell, this mixture of iron and clay, Ie-fuites and Priefts, are broken not onely out of the earth, but out of the bottomleffe pit, like thofe locufts *with iron haber-* Reuel.9.10. *gions, and ftings in their tailes,* whofe affertions are impudent, their meditations earthly, their Religion fuperftitious, their zeale obftinacie, their hypocrifie deepe, their conuerfation wicked, their promifes deceitfull, their conditions crooked, their crueltie more then brutifh, their flatterie more then doggifh, their defignes dreadfull, their proiects pernicious, their practifes hellifh and diuellifh, (a ftrange medley,) as lightening to the eye, thunder to the eare, fire to the feeling, poyfon to the heart, and finally the very mixture of coales, fulphur, and fait-peter, that is, plaine gunpowder to the fmel, nay to all the fenfes. By them kings are murdered, Nobles maffacred, Eftates ruined, Churches profaned, the whole Chriftian world turmoyled, as if heauen and earth fhould be Qui cœlum turned into heapes, to be caft into a chaos, and hell of horror terris mifcent, and defolation with themfelues. The onely difference wher- & qui mare in thefe Iefuites & Priefts are vnlike vnto thefe feet of earth cœlo. and iron, is, that they cleaue too well together, who were to be wifhed, without breath of Chriftian charity, that they might hang together as well as they hold together, except they would become more faithfull Chriftians, honefter men, & better fubiects. Who how much foeuer they pretend *An-tiquitie,* yet are they in truth not *vindices veritatis,* protectors of truth, but *Veteratores,* crafty Foxes & falfe deceiuers, who pretend *Antiquitie,* but do nothing elfe but *antiquare Anti-quitatem,* not onely derogate from truth, by glofing vpon it,

but

but vtterlie abrogate truth, by their purging, or rather accu-
sing and condemning Index.

38 I haue digressed I confesse, as from the comely countenance of Christs beautifull spouse, *whose garments are all
glorious within,* vnto the filthy feet that neuer walked in the
way of peace. Yet haue I bene drawne by the due consideration of times and ages, wherein corruption crept into the
Church;& from those glorious and blessed beginnings, vnto
these dismall and desperate times, the last and worst dayes,
whereunto the world hath declined.

39 In which meditation we haue iust cause to bethinke
our selues, where we would rest for the safety of our soules:
whether in this clay, wherein a great part of this world stic-
keth vntill the muddie waters go ouer their soules; or in the
iron, wherewith another part of the sonnes of men do fight
against Gods truth; or with the brasen age, so subiect to ero-
sion and consumption; or in the siluer mines, mixed and blended with some drosse of imperfection; or in that golden
crowne, as pearles and precious stones, to shine gloriouslie
on that golden head. This is a mettall that admitteth no rust,
no canker, no corruption. It wil bring vs to the golden world
againe, to the Apostles faith and doctrine, to their patience
and constancie, to their manners and conuersation. In it we
may see our Sauiour in the flesh, and behold him crucified
before our eyes. There we may heare the gracious preaching of Christ the Sonne of God, and him publishing the Gospell in our streets. There our *hands may handle the word of life.*
There is no defect, no error, all sincerity, all verity: and therefore without all doubt or danger, without all deniall or contradiction: there, and there onely is that faithfull constant, vntainted, and most certainly true *Antiquitie,* which
we seeke for, may trust to, and must when all is said and done,
relie and rest vpon.

40 If therefore any ignorant or wilfull Romanist, shall
aske that ouertroden and outworne question, which is so
triuial in euery mans mouth, as if it were the very essence
of his tongue: *Where was your religion before Luthers name:* we

may

Gal.3.1.

1.Iohn.1.1.

may eafily and as truly anfwer, *It was in the Scriptures, where yours neuer came.* It wanted not a being from the beginning, but it wanted a reuiuing or renewing, after negleEt or contempt. It was as *Mofes* Law hid in a wall. It was a treafure for a time buried vnder ground: the time of reuelation being come, it pleafed God to make that manifeft which for a feafon was fecret, & this is the doEtrine which we now preach. By which oldeft breath, from the mouth of the Ancient of daies, now Antichrift is reuealed, and fhall ere long be deftroyed. Let the prefent Romanifts proue their religion, or any part thereof, from *Saint Paules* Epiftle to the Romans, and we will be all fuch Romanifts with them. We will not onely heare it with patience, but yeeld vnto it with all dutifull obedience, and vnfained loue.

2.King. 22.8.
2.Chr. 34.14.
Math.13.44.

2.Theff.2.8.

CHAP. IIII.

That this only Antiquitie præcedent, being firft and therefore oldeft, is a true and certaine note of the true Chriftian, Catholike and Apoftolicke Church and religion, without any exception or limitation.

Here hath bene long, and yet is a folemne and ferious controuerfie, what are the notes of the true Church. *Cardinall Bellarmine* tels vs, that fome will haue feauen, as *Luther*: fome two, as the reformed Churches; That *Auguftine* would haue fixe; *Hierome* would haue two; *Vincentius* would haue three; *Driedo* and *Petrus à Soto* would haue other three; *Hofius* would haue foure. *Sanders* would haue other fixe; *Michael Medina* would haue ten, and addeth the eleuenth; *Cunerus* would haue twelue. Himfelfe, contemning and reieEting vs and ours, as no bodies and no things, and forfaking the Fathers, and theirs, as wanting and defeEtiue; cafhiering and cafting his owne fellowes and theirs behind him, as infufficient and fhort: left fhort fhooting might lofe his game, bringeth forth his fif-

De notis Ecclefiæ, cap.2.

Cap.3.

E 3   teene

2.Sam.9.10.   teene sonnes, like the sonnes of *Ziba* the seruant of *Mephi-*
19.17.   *boseth*, that betraied his maister, and belied him shamefully,
and set in for all, but gat halfe his inheritance. As *Cardinall*
Bellarmine that aduentureth for a Popedome, but hath gotten
a Cardinals hat; or perhaps he would build the Romane
Church to the imitation of *Salomons* house in the forrest of

1.King. 7.2.3.   *Lebanon*, that had his pillars fifteene in a row: Or peraduenture he dreamed of the prayers called the *fifteene Oes*, in the
Office of the virgine *Marie* ; or some mysterie of iniquitie
there is in it: For he will haue iust fifteene ; which he extorts
by a retort, like an alchymist out of foure, as those fifteene pillars were in foure rowes : yet notwithstanding he dares not
giue his word for them all, that they wil proue the Church in
veritie, but onely in credibilitie, that is, plaine incertaintie.
Socolouius ouerstrips *Cardinall Bellarmine*, and will haue a iust
score, though *Salmeron* is contented onely with foure as
the vndoubted notes of the Church, and excludeth some of
Bellarmines notes by name, as *Honestie of life, and miracles*, and
may full wel, for they haue abandoned honestie, and their
miracles are counterfeit; others by necessary consequence:
For if there be but foure, then *Bellarmine* hath eleuen more
then needs, and *Socolouius* sixteene.

    2 Another Iesuite in a fresh assault runs vpon vs with his

In B. Pauli E-   thousand markes, *Whether is our Church Catholicke or yours,*
pist.lib.1.part.   *ô you Protestants, Lutherans and Caluinists ? Nostra profectò mille*
3.disp.3.4.   *indicijs, vestra nullis ; nostra de vitâ sanctè instituendâ multa, ve-*
Muri.ciuit.   *stra inani fide contenta, nihil aut parùm docet: nostra vitæ sanctimo-*
Sanctæ,fund.8   *niam magnoperè prædicat, & ad illam suos seriò adhortatur: vestra*
contumeliosè exagitat, & ab illà dehortatur : nostra per sedecim sæ-
cula vitæ sanctitate illustres plurimos numerat, vestra primo hoc suo
sæculo, nondùm primum, nondùm numeri initium habet. Ours
“ certainly (quoth he) hath a thousand notes, yours not one;
“ ours hath much for the leading of our liues holily; yours
“ contented with idle faith, teacheth little or nothing thereof.
“ Ours mightily commendeth sanctitie of life, and seriouslie
“ exhorteth thereunto; yours railes vpon it, and dehorts from
“ it. Ours in sixteene ages can number many famous for vp-
rightnesse

vprightneſſe of life: but yours in this her owne age hath not ,,
yet the firſt, no not the beginning of number. Where he na- ,,
meth a few other, but neuer a word true, as our conſciences
beare vs witnes,& as it is knowne to all that know the truth;
(but as a ſcolds tongue, ſo a Ieſuites pen is no ſlander.) In
which caſe he dallieth as a boy was wont in a ſchoole, of
whom we euer knew what money was in his purſe iuſt, by
his wagers: but if he had none at all, his common wager was
a hundred, or a thouſand pounds. One hath wagered his
three notes, ſome foure, others ſixe, one ten, another eleuen,
another twelue; *Bellarmine* fifteene, *Socolouius* his twentie:
this fellow belike guilty of the emptineſſe of his owne purſe,
wageth a thouſand, as much to ſay, he hath not one, no not
one of a thouſand. But I meane not to diſcourſe of the number, whether they ſhould be moe or fewer, whether older
or yonger, whether better or worſe, whether certaine, credible, probable or laudable; but reſting vpon that old axiome, What needeth a man go about the buſh, when he may ,,
eaſily ſtep ouer? or beate the buſh, when he ſeeth the Hare ,,
on foote?   ,,

3 I will with patience and good leaue of all, ſaue a labour
and without vilifying (yet cenſuring) thoſe notes of the Roman Synagogue, or magnifying of our own Church, or medling with moe of the Fathers notes, *content my ſelfe with one,*
whereby as my owne vnderſtanding is conuinced, and my
conſcience ſatisfied; ſo would I offer it to all Romane
Catholiques, for their ſufficient euiction; to all Chriſtian
Catholiques for their abundant ſatisfaction; that is, *The true,*
and oldeſt Antiquitie. For this is certaine and vnfallible, it doth
agree, *omni, ſoli, & ſemper*, vnto the Church: It is proper to
all true Churches onely, and euer vnto the true Church. It is
not an accident ſeparable, that may be preſent or abſent
without the deſtruction of the ſubiect: but it is an eſſentiall
propertie, yea very naturall and reall, which can be no more
ſeparated from the Church, then the ſoule can from the body, without the diſſolution and death thereof. And therefore theſe propoſitions, *That is the true Church,* or that is the

true religion, quæ est antiquissima, which is the oldest, is as true as to say, *Homo est animal risibile,* A man onely is capable of laughter.

Vbi supra.
disp. 4.

4 This *Cardinall Bellarmine* hath set vp for a second prop of his tottering & declining Synagogue; but both foolishly and falsly. Foolishly, because he hath inuerted the order of nature and ciuilitie: For in nature the Church was, before it was Catholike or common; it had a being, before it was vniuersall, which being was in the first man, before it was qualified by that title, or had a Catholike existence: and it is ciuility to set the first begotten in the first place. Therefore *Antiquitie* should haue bene the first, as it is principall, and (I say) the onelie necessarie note of the true Church and religion. So *Salmeron* placeth it for his first, and commends it for the chiefest note of the Church, as it well deserueth. Yet *Socolouius* not so ciuill or so propicious, maketh it the fourteenth of his twentie notes, & that not without great commendation, which I could right well approue. *Quartumdecimum sit ciuitatis Dei insigne, Ecclesiam catholicam* ἀεχα ζειν *semper, hoc autem est, antiquitatem & vetustatem sequi, vt id maximè laudet quod vetustissimum & antiquissimum, id peculiariter sequatur, quod cum maiorum instituto ac doctrinâ coniunctum est; recipiat nihil nisi illud* εὐαγγελικῶς καὶ πατρικῶς *simul; vt post Mag. Basilium Damascenus loquitur, dicatur: vt contrà hæreticorû fuit semper* νεοειζειν, *hoc autem est, nouitati in omnibus adhærere.* The

Vt supra.

" foureteenth badge of that citie of God is, it must be euer *An-*
" *cient,* that is, it must follow *Antiquitie,* and old age; that it
" please most which is oldest, and most ancient: that it follow
" that which is ioyned with our ancestors institution and doc-
" trine, that it receiue nothing except it be both euangelically
" and fatherly deliuered: as after great *Basil* speaketh *Dama-*
" *scen.* As contrariwise the heretickes do euer looke yongly,
" that is, in all things they cleaue vnto noueltie. All this is ve-
rie true, I would he and his would duly obserue it. Howbeit this matters not, set it where you will, it will beare out it selfe with sufficient authoritie.

5 Howbeit let vs looke to that which is worse. *Cardinall Bellarmine*

Bellarmine and all his brethren, yea and his Romane Father too, haue falſly and ſurreptitiouſly vſurped this title, which belongeth to others, not at all vnto them : *Antiquitie* denieth them her ſuppoit.

For the Romaniſts vſe *two paralogiſmes* or ſophiſtications, or in plaine Engliſh, falſhoods & coſening tricks in their diſputation of *Antiquitie*; whereby ſimple wits are circumuented, contentious humors tickled, & the truth of God quite outfaced. The one is, they call that *Antiquitie* which is not: the other, they challenge *Antiquitie* for their owne, which they haue not; and ſo aſſume all as granted which is moſt in queſtion. For when we ſeeke for *Antiquitie* (as before is premoniſhed)we muſt not inſiſt vpon the poſitiue, This is old, therfore true; for ſo an hundred hereſies may claime the priuiledge of many yeares, and yet neuer the better: No more in the comparatiue, This is elder, therefore truer : for ſo many errors were crept into the Church of God, before ſome truths were plainly and diſtinctly reuealed. But, this *is oldeſt*, therefore trueſt; this holdeth water and leaketh not, this wil abide the touchſtone without changing colour : this it that golden head, or that foundation whereon nothing can be built, but gold, precious ſtones, or ſiluer at the worſt, that will abide the fiery triall : hay, ſtraw, ſtubble, cannot endure the flame of Gods Spirit which appeared in fierie tongues, to ſtay by it, or continue in it, but is conſumed of it.   1. Cor. 3. 12.   Act. 2. 3.

6 *Cardinall Bellarmine* ſeemeth to lay this foundation for his Romane head & popiſh Synagogue: *Sine dubio vera Eccleſia antiquior eſt quàm falſa, quemadmodùm Deus antè fuit quàm fuit diabolus.* It is without all doubt, that the true Church is before the falſe, as there was a God, before there was a diuel.   De notis Ecleſiæ, cap. 5.

> *Dij Damaſippe tibi donent tonſorem :——*
> *Verum ob conſilium.*
> *His Saints graunt the Cardinall a cunning barber,*
> *For mouing his counſell in ſo ſafe a harbor.*

A wiſe conceipt, whereby he ſheweth himſelfe onely to be no *Manichæan* hereticke, that conceipted *duo principia, bonum & *

& malum, two beginnings, good and euill; giuing them e-quall time, without antecedence or consequence, but what is this to our purpose? as if the question were betweene God and the diuell, or the Church of celestiall Angels, and the dungeon of infernall spirits, or not rather and indeed of the Church of men among themselues in the visible state thereof. His rule must be this, *Quo antiquius eo melius*, By how much the elder, by so much the better. But this rule is like many rules in Law, which will admit moe exceptions and limitations, then it containeth words; or it must be fortified with *cæteris paribus*, or *in eodem genere*, due paritie and in the same kind, or els it will neuer hold.

Decius de reg.iuris.

7 For though God were before the diuell, yet was the diuell before men; though *Adam* was before *Caine*, yet was *Caine* not onelie before *Abel*, whom he murthered, but also before *Seth*, that continued the righteous seede, and from whom the true Church was propagated in the flesh, vntil the coming of the *Messias*.

Was not *Nahor Abrahams* ancient? yet was he an idolater, *Abraham* the Father of the faithful. Was not *Ismael* elder then *Isaac*? yet was *Ismael* base and sonne of a bond woman, *Isaac* of the free woman, and heire of the promise. Was not *Esau Iacobs* eldest brother? yet God would haue the elder serue the yonger. *Iebuse* was before *Ierusalem*, and *Ierusalem* had degenerated to a cage of vncleane birds, and the Temple was made a den of theeues before our Sauiour taught in it, or preached the Gospell. And therefore *Cardinal Bellarmines* bare *Antiquity* though he fetch it from the diuell that old dragon, hath not that vigor & force to stand in the gap against any falshood, which is rather fauoured and fostered, then confuted and condemned by his *Antiquitie*.

8 We must go (as is said) *ad Antiquum dierum*, to the ancient of dayes, from that *Alpha* that is *Omega*, which was first, and shall be last; euen from the Father, his Law and Prophets in the old Testament, to the Sonne, and his Apostles in the new Testament, to that holy Spirit of them both; which both inspired the truth that was euer, and doth preserue

ſerue and keepe it in the true Church of God for euer. Therefore we muſt not be deceiued by appearance : for *Quædam
videntur & non ſunt,* Some things appeare to be, that are not;
there is great ods betweene *bonum apparens & bonum verum* :
a ſeeming good and a true and vndoubted good. All is not
gold that gliſtereth : for although the good ſeed be ſowne
by the husbandman before the cockle by the enuious, yet the
weed often ouertoppeth the corne, and ſeemeth by ſtature
and growth the ancienter, though it be yonger in time, and
worſe in proofe. So hath experience the miſtris of fooles,
if you will, (though they be wiſe that take heed by her warning) and time the mother of truth, made it manifeſt, in
Chriſtian Churches.

 9 In *Ieruſalem* was the ſeed of the Goſpell ſowne by the Luke 3.38.
Sonne of man, who was the Sonne of God : and the Apoſtles
by his charge when they had receiued the promiſe of the Father (which promiſe was the holy Ghoſt) were to teſtifie of
him in *Ieruſalem,* after in all *Iurie* and *Galilee,* and then vnto
the ends of the world. Then was Rome a yonger ſiſter, nay
yet vnadopted into Chriſts family at all. *Epheſus* in *Aſia, Corinth* in *Greece,* with many other Cities in both, yea whole
countries and nations receiued the faith before *Rome,* as *Pon-
tus, Galatia, Cappadocia, Aſia, Bithynia,* or at the leſt with them: 1.Pet.1.1.
yea when ſhe perſecuted the truth and her litle flocke vnto
bonds, impriſonment and cruell death : and therefore were Acts 2.9.
they her ancients in time, and for the time, her betters in
grace.

 10 Will you ſay that thoſe Churches had their candle-
ſtickes remoued to *Rome?* That they loſt their birthright and
ſhe got it? That *Peter* in probabilitie, *Paul* in certaintie preached there, eſtabliſhed there the faith, & both ſealed it with
their blood : in ſo much that *their faith was made famous* Rom 1.8.
throughout all the world? And what of all this? If we can proue
Rome and her children to be *pares culpâ,* in the ſame fault with
them, will it not be as eaſie to proue that they may be *pares
pœna,* vnder the ſame iudgement and puniſhment with them
alſo? If God hath done this to *Ieruſalem* and her idols, why Eſa.10.10.
                   not

not to *Rome* and her images? And is not this a righteous thing
with God, that they which with-held the truth of God in
vnrighteousnesse, should commit sinne with greedinesse?
and that they which will forsake the truth, should beleeue
lies? and being led by hypocrisie should, be mis-led by the
spirit of error, deceiuing and being deceiued? Let not *Rome*
therefore boast what she hath bene, let vs rather consider
what she is.

> *Nam genus & proauos & quæ non fecimus ipsi,*
> *Uix ea nostra voco.*
> " 		*Lineall descent, and what we not atchieued*
> " 	*Is scarce cald ours, or to our selues deriued.*

They that will be *Abrahams* children must haue *Abra-*
hams faith, or else they shall neuer enioy *Abrahams* promises.

> *Mallem Thersites similem me gignat Achilli,*
> *Quàm me Thersiti similem progignat Achilles.*
> *I'de rather be Achilles borne from Thirsit's breed*
> *Then Thirsite sprong from stout Achilles seed.*

11 Blessed was *Iosia*, the good grand-child and sonne of
wicked *Manasses* and *Amon*; and cursed might they be who
descended from the loynes of gracious *Hezekiah*: many good
fathers haue had wicked sonnes, and many good sonnes haue
had as wicked fathers. Many haue sowne in the spirit, and
reaped in the flesh: begun well, ended ill: bene Apostles,
become Apostates: created and ascended Angels, degenerated and descended diuels. We haue seene, saith Saint *Au-*
gustine, Men walke in the midst of fire like starres, that haue falne
to the ground and become dong of the earth: we haue seene others as
dust among the stones, and yet aduanced to the firmament as
starres. This is the Lords doing, and it is maruellous in our
eyes; God setteth vp one and casteth downe another. Those
Cities, those people, those nations, those kingdomes, Monarchies, Churches haue risen and fallen, haue enioyed their
prime, and felt their periods. And yet God hath euer preserued a sanctified seed vnto himselfe, neither tying his mercies
to persons or places, but in euery nation he that feareth God,
and

Rom.1.18.

2.Thess. 2,11.

Gal.3 3.

Aug.1

Psal.118.23.

and worketh righteousnes,shall be accepted of him.*Non sunt* Acts 10.35.
filij Sanctorum qui tenent loca Sanctorum, sed qui sequuntur opera Hieron.
eorum, They are not the sonnes of Saints that succeed them ,,
in their places,but that follow them in their workes.Where- ,,
fore although this note of *Antiquitie* be a true marke, and
a certaine, of the Church, yet it is no euidence at all for the
Synagogue of *Rome*, which is neither the oldest Church
her selfe; neither hath kept the old faith, which was first
planted by the Apostle Saint *Paul*,and *Peter*, if you wil; neither hath any interest from the vndoubted monuments of
the true Church.In which case if we will seriously seeke,and
carefully trie which is the true Church, which is the true religion,it must not be by a generall challenge, without particular euidence; but by a diligent search and suruey of all
the ancient monuments of the Church, in each particular
doctrine and controuersie that haue risen since the first founders and foundation thereof.

12 An intruder may enter by force,may creep in by fraud,
may hold by violence,may presume vpon a potēt party,may
boast of an ancient title, and may defend himselfe for a time,
by forged cauillation; but all this cannot proue *bonæ fidei pos-
sessorem*,a true and vndoubted heire, a rightfull and lawfull
possessor. How shall this title be tried? what euidence shall
beare it? The oldest, say we, and the Romanists pretend the
same. Let them stand to it,we aske no other triall; but the
greatest,the farthest,the oldest *Antiquity*.Herein we wil rest,
and by this we will be tried,not onely for the whole in common,but for euery inclosure or peece of ground,wherein we
claime the right of inheritance.

13 We will grant that which our aduersaries so much
desire, and hold for their greatest aduantage. They receiued interest and inuestiture into the Church with all the liberties, priuiledges and immunities thereunto belonging.
They did shine as a starre in the firmament and midst of hea-
uen.They had the euerlasting Gospell preached by such An- Reu.14.6.
gels and messengers as God sent vnto them. All this is liberally granted:but we iustly lay to their charge,that they haue
broken

broken the conditions of their old Charters; they haue forfeited their intereſt; they denie their ſeruices, they will haue
what they liſt, and do what they pleaſe againſt the Lords wil
and pleaſure: and yet claime their eſtate to be as certaine as
in their firſt enfranchiſment. This againe they denie:
This againe and againe we affirme. By what or whom ſhall
we be tried? With one conſent al our party is agreed to ſtand
to no other trial,but this one,the oldeſt Charter,the ancienteſt euidence, which our aduerſaries boaſt was in their own
keeping. If this they refuſe or alter, they pretend *Antiquitie*
in ſhew, but deny it in very truth.They raile vpon **vs** as if we
denied all *Antiquitie* , and we proteſt before God and all the
world, that we will be tried by none other. By this we find
the Church, by this we offer and vndertake to defend the religion we profeſſe, or elſe to yeeld our poſſeſſion, and giue
them the day.

  14. Put this caſe in a ciuil action. There are lands left in
common to Tenants by one Lord *Paramount* , to be holden
of him to them and their heires in *Capite:* but as it often fareth,*communia quæ ſunt negliguntur* , things in common are
worſt husbanded, this Land lies waſte, ſome is abandoned,
ſome by others neglected , by little and little it growes to a
wildernesſe; that which was faire and fruitfull is barren and
ouergrowne with buſhes and bryers , vnwholſome weeds,
and rotten trees.The greateſt free-holders grow careleſſe of
this decay; the multitudes are carried with the ſway and
corruptions of the time,and do as others do,are content with
the homely , perhaps vnwholſome food which the vnma-
nured earth bringeth forth of it owne accord. At length in
ſucceeding ages,ſome few,either by learning the husbandry
of other countries,or by their triall of concluſions, and their
owne experience,find meanes to bring this Land into tilth,
would roote out or cut downe what is vnwholſome , or vn-
handſome , and by labour and induſtrie finde that it would
produce excellent fruite , if it were well husbanded. Yea
ſome good husbands increaſe in wealth , reioyce in their labours, and deſire to make all their neighbours partakers of
                                                their

their skill and knowledge. This perceiued by the idle, that take more pleaſure in their lazie eaſe, then in diligent labour, ſeeke to diſturbe thoſe induſtrious men of their inheritance, exclaime againſt their deuices and manner of husbandrie, offer violence to their perſons, wold deueſt them of their right, as innouators and brochers of new inuentions. It cometh to ſuite of Law, how will theſe pretenders be tried ? By the cuſtomes and manners of our fathers and grandfathers who haue liued a few ages before, ſaith the one partie. Nay, but by our oldeſt euidences which we receiued at the firſt from our capitall Lord, which your ſelues haue kept (as you pretend,) diuers hundred of yeares, ſaith the other partie. The ſlow-backs and lazie bones will none of this, whatſoeuer they pretend: theſe writings, ſay they, are but parchment and inke, they are but dead letters, crooked rules, dumb iudges, we wil not ſtand to theſe, except you will let vs interpret them as we liſt, blot out, raſe, enterline, put in what we wil our ſelues; we plead poſſeſſion, be it good or ill, right or wrong, we wil hold that we haue, and be tried by none but our ſelues and our friends.

15 This is a long circumſtance, you will ſay, and a tedious parable. But it is the very caſe in queſtion, a *Nathans* vnderſtanding will eaſily apply it, and ſay to the Romane Catholiques, You are the men. O that they had but a *Dauids* heart to confeſſe it, and crie *Miſerere mei Deus, Haue mercie vpon me O God, and renew a right ſpirit within me.*

16 Our Lord Ieſus Chriſt, Lord *Paramount* of his Church, hath beſtowed a goodly inheritance vpon his Apoſtles and diſciples, & to their ſucceſſors & inheritours of the ſame precious faith; hath deliuered writings containing his whole wil & pleaſure: what ſeruices are due, what rents to be payd, how the Land ſhould be vſed, that when this great Lord ſhould come, he might find all as himſelfe appointed. This Land, this Church, this Goſpel of the Son of God, is by ſome abandoned, by ſome trampled vnder foote, as an vnholy thing, Heb.10.29. euen as ſwine do pearles, or dogs holy things. Time by neg- Mat.7.6. lect, ignorance, ſloth, careleſneſſe of ſome, wilfulneſſe and

deſpe-

desperate madnes of others, maketh this Church a *cage of vncleane birds, a denne of errant theeues.* Briers & thorns theearths curse, are suffered to grow in it; errors and heresies in faith, corruption and dissolutenes of maners are furthered and fostered therein; true faith and honest life are exiled and banished therefrom. Long peace bringeth ease, ease pleasure, pleasure contentment, contentment neglect, neglect securitie, securitie a very Lethargie, or rather a Catalepsie, which is *stupor vigilans*, *a sleep of forgetfulnesse, or a waking stupidity,* vpon the heads, senses, and hearts of men, that though they see, yet they perceiue not.

Ierem.7.11.

17 This was not so generall, but some were either vtterly free, or at least not so desperatly possest with these incurable diseases, but groaned vnder a burden, and were grieued to see so great disorder, but were not ofpower to helpe it. At length some better aduised, either finding the truth abroad in other Churches among some few, brought it home to this Church which it had forsaken, and made it more publique: or by reading of the oldest euidences, which were the Scriptures and word of God, they sought to reduce all vnto the first beauty & integrity. The Priests and Leaders make head, they cry out against innouations, though it be for the better; they will confesse no faults, though their owne hearts conuince and condemne them: all is heresie, or schisme, or error at the least, that sauoureth not their fancies, or answereth not their credits, or at least profits. And therefore they persecute with fire and sword, massacre men, ouerthrow families, depopulate Cities, ruine nations, confound, shall I say, heauen and earth, or rather earth and hell together, to preserue their some few yeares continued superstitions & idolatries, for which they vniustly prescribe. They are offered the old writings, the very Testamēt which their Lord left sealed with his owne most precious blood, which issued from his crucified blessed body, safely reserued in the Register of the sacred Scriptures; the very first, and therefore the very best muniments betweene the Lord Iesus and his Church; by these the title of truth shall be tried, or the suite ceassed. This

by

by no meanes will be accepted. The Scriptures are infinitely Infra cap. 6. difgraced, with obfcuritie, with infufficiencie, with defect of authority, and what not? At a word, this beft, this onely, the moft true and al-fufficient euidence will not be admitted.

18 Now let any indifferent man iudge, yea and for me determine, whether is the likelier to haue the better caufe? efpecially if we duely confider that the Romanifts in fhew ftand all for *Antiquitie*, and fill their followers eares with nothing more then with clamorous outcries, that we refufe all *Antiquitie*, that our religion is meere noueltie, rather fuddenly ftart vp, then iudicioufly propofed; difclofed, laid open within thefe hundred yeares. Whereas in truth we are very well contented to be tried, yea iuftified or condemned by this oldeft, moft vndoubted, moft impartiall *Antiquitie*, not onely as a iudge among many, but as the only both witnes & iudge in all our differences. Let them but ftand to this *Anti-* Supra cap. 3. *quitie*, we defire no more.

19 Otherwife if they bring fathers for grand-fathers, grand fathers for great grandfathers; *Lamech* that defcended from curfed *Cain*, for *Adam* the father of all, we cannot endure it, we cannot heare it, for fo we may eafily be deceiued. Religion and truth (as we may fay) gaue the flip to *Cain* and his pofteritie, and defcended by the pofteritie of *Seth*, a Gen. 4. 19. yonger brother, but a better man.

20 *Symon Magus* was nearer the Apoftles in time and Act. 8. 13. place, then many Saints of God that kept the faith, and gaue their liues for the teftimony of Gods truth. If therefore we reft by the way, and not afcend vnto the very top of the hill, we may as well ftay vpon *Cain* the elder as *Seth* the yonger, vpon *Symon Magus*, as vpon *Iuftin Martyr*, or *Ireneus*, or any other that followed the Apoftles age. The Law that God gaue to *Adam* in Paradife, *They fhall not be two, but one flefh*, was Gen 2. 24. good, and by our bleffed *Sauiour* applied for a rule of refor- Mat. 19. 5. mation in a matter of great confequence But what *Cain*, or *Seth* taught, what is that to vs? Let it be to vs fufficient, that we haue *Adam* in Paradife before he had finned, nay God in heauen that neuer finned, as our firft founder; his certaine

F

Law,

Law, his vndoubted Prophets, Chrift our Sauiour himfelfe, and his Apoftles and Euangelifts infpired by the holy Ghoft, for the authors, builders, finifhers, and Preachers of our faith.

21 If we paffe by all intermediate *Antiquitie* , be it as an-cient as *Simon Magus*, as old as *Cain*, yet is not that the *Antiquitie* which we grant to haue bene, and define to be, the cer-taine and true marke of the Church, & euidence of the truth. But let vs reft vpon this, and fo conclude vpon all hands, that this *Antiquitie (and none other)is the true and certaine note of the true Chriftian Catholique Church and Religion, without excepti-on or limitation.*

Supra cap.3. 22 What this *Antiquitie* is , hath bene before deliuered, viz. that is the firft truth which was deliuered to *Adam*, or the Patriarchall Prophets; was their Rule of faith ; the Law which was firft giuen to Mofes, continued, and bound vntill the comming of Chrift. The Gofpels , Epiftles , and other books which were firft written by the Euangelifts and Apo-ftles, ftand ftill vnto all Catholique Chriftians , as the onely certaine doctrine , by which we muft be inftructed in faith and informed in manners , while we liue, and whereby we muft be iudged and faued in the laft day. For this *Antiquitie* the *Ancienteft Fathers* pleaded in their generations; vnto this with them we fubmit our felues, and our whole religion, and euery Article thereof at this day.

23 It is a moft melodious harmony, in the eare of euerie one that hath it open vnto truth, to heare all the Fathers that may be reputed Fathers indeed , as worthy of that reuerend name, how they all confent , and giue this glory to the do-ctrine of Scriptures , to be the onely and moft certaine *Anti-quitie* whereon to build faith, and to eftablifh the foundation of the Church. Of whom diuers are before alledged; yet to make vp the melody with the more pleafing concord , be-tweene thofe Ancients and our prefent Church and profef-fors of the fame truth, heare how they anfwer each other, as *Saint Auguftine* and *Saint Ambrofe* in their *Te Deum lau-damus.*

24 *Chry-*

24 *Chryſoſtome* with his golden mouth, when any thing is offred him that hath not the authoritie of this *Antiquitie*, ſingeth thus: *Hanc arborem non Paulus plantauit, non Apollos rigauit, non Deus auxit. Sed plantauit rationum intempeſtiua ſcrutatio, rigauit ſuperbia ſtolida, auxit ambitioſa cupiditas. This tree Paul neuer planted, Apollos neuer watered, God neuer increaſed:* „ *but the vntimely ſearch of reaſon planted it, fooliſh pride watered it,* „ *and ambitious luſt gaue it increaſe.* What remaineth, but that „ ſuch a plant ſhould be plucked vp by the roots? not onely blowne downe by the breath of Gods Spirit, but burnt vp too, with the fire and *brightneſſe of Chriſts appearing?* And he giueth the reaſon a little before of the heretiques errour, to be the ignorance of this doctrine of *Antiquitie*: as our Sauiour did of the *Sadduces. Sic animus Anomæorum cultu Scripturæ ſacræ priuatus, & carens doctrina ſancta & Chriſtianæ munere ſponte & ſuopte motu ferocem iſtam & horrendam prompſit hæreſim*: Thus the minde of the *Anomæans* depriued of the furniture of *holy Scriptures, and wanting the gift of holy and Chriſtian doctrine, of his owne accord and proper motion, brought forth this cruell and horrible hæreſie.* The ſame we may iuſtly ſay of the Romaniſts, and the moſt part of their articles. Did *Saint Paul* plant it? Did *Apollos* water it? did God ſend the increaſe? Their ſouls are depriued of the light of holy Scripture, therfore they run into all exceſſe of error. Heare how ſweetly we anſwer in the ſame tune.

25 *What I reade in the word of God, that I beleeue: what I do not reade, that I do not beleeue.* The very ſame thing in a diuers phraſe of ſpeech. Againe, *Saint Auguſtine authoritate Scripturarum contentus ſimplicitati dedere potius ſtudeo, quàm tumori; Contented with the authoritie of the Scriptures, I ſtudy rather to ſubmit my ſelfe to ſimplicitie, then to pride.* And doth not that gracious profeſſor D *Whitaker* ſing the ſame ſong, *Quæ non reperiuntur in Scripturis nõ refert quà diù in Eccleſiis durauerint. Nam quicquid eſt Scripturæ doctrina poſterius, et ſi ſtatim ab Apoſtolorũ temporibus doceri cœptum eſt, tamen nouum eſſe affirmamus, & contra quicquid Scripturæ docent, illud antiquiſſimum eſſe dicimus. Whatſoeuer is not found in the Scriptures, it mattereth not how* „

Marginal notes:
Chryſoſt.hõ.3 de incomprehenſibili Dei natura aduerſus Anomœos.

Mat.22.29. Ibid.

D.Bilſon Biſhop of Wincheſter, of Redemption pag 41. Contra Fœlic

De notis Eccleſ.c.3.p.247

,, *long it hath continued in the Church: for what is later then the do-*
,, *ctrine of the Scriptures , although it began presently vpon the A-*
,, *postles times, yet we auouch it to be new: & on the other side, what*
,, *is taught in the Scriptures, that we hold to be most ancient.* Leo a
Bishop of Rome, and one of the learnedst of that ranke, as-

Epistola. 81.　keth these questions in this very case: *Hoccine à Prophetis ;*
hoc ab Euangelistis ; hoc ab Apostolis didicisti ? Learned you
this of the *Prophets, of the Euangelists, of the Apostles ?* as who
should say, If these be not your founders, you not onely
stumble but founder, and shall neuer attaine vnto the truth.
Learned, yea thrice learned Doctor *Rainolds*, hath the true
descant to this faire plain-song, in other words, but to the

D. Rainolds　same sence, *Consequens est quidcunque Christianum vllum scire*
Thes.1.p. 64.　*deceat ad vitam æternâ obtinendam, id totum ex vberrimis Scrip-*
turarum fontibus hauriendum tradi: This followeth (out of certaine
forelayed premises) whatsoeuer it becometh any *Christian* man to
know, for the obtaining of eternal life, al that is deliuered to be drawn
out of the plentifull fountaines of the Scriptures. But perhaps our
Aduersaries wil hearkē better to their Saint *Thomas Aquinas*,
who tuneth the very same note. *Quicquid ille, i. Christus de su-*
is factis & dictis nos legere voluit , hoc scribendum illis tanquam
suis manibus imperauit. Whatsoeuer (*Christ*)would haue vs reade
of his workes or words, that he commanded to (his *Disciples*) as it
were his owne hands. Do not all these make one pleasant con-
cent & harmony, following to an haire that gracious coun-

Philip.2.2.　sell of the blessed Apostle Saint *Paul* ? Fulfill *my ioy that you*
be like minded , hauing the same loue , being of one accord, and one

1.Cor.3.　*iudgement.* For no man can *lay any other foundation then this,*
which is Christ, as he is reuealed in the Scriptures. And who-

Gal.1.8.　soeuer preacheth any other doctrine, be he an *Angell of God*
he is accursed. This *Antiquitie of faith and truth,* is that *Rocke*

Mat.7.24.　of which our Sauiour speaketh: *Whosoeuer heareth these my*
words and doth the same , I will liken him to a wise man that built
his house vpon a Rocke. He hath a good foundation and a good
building, the ground-worke is Christs word , the building
is the doing of the same. We neede seeke no further to be
saued.

26 *Such*

26 *Such as the man is, such is his strength,* & such as the strēgth, Iudic.8.21.
such is the man. Faith that is grounded vpon this foun-
dation, declareth the man in whom it is, to be in the certaine
and vndoubted way of saluation. A man that is established
on this Rocke, is sure that *the gates of hell shall neuer preuaile* Mat.16.18.
against it or him.

27 This hath bene euer the strength of the Church, and
the very Foundation of all the Religion of the true God. It
was *Moses* credit that he brought a Law vnto the people, Exod.20.
written with the finger of God : that he made the Tabernacle according to the patterne *that was shewed him in the mount:*
that he did all things as the *Lord commanded him.* In the day
of distresse *Fugiendum ad montes,* saith *Saint Hierom, we must* In Nahum.
fly to the hils. Ad montes Scripturarum, Mosen, &c. To the hils ca.3.
of the Scriptures, Moses, &c. This was then a sure foundation
to prouoke to the Scriptures, for the triall of doctrine. When
Religion decayed was to be reformed or restored by the
good Kings of *Iuda, Iehosaphat sent Priests and Leuites, haben-*
tes librum legis Domini, hauing the booke of the law of the Lord.
Hezekiah operatus est rectum & verum coram Domino iuxta le-
gem: He did that which was right and true before Lord; according
to the Law. Iosiah, when *Helchiah* had found and brought him
the Law, first caused it to be read vnto the people, then
made a couenant with God, then tooke an oath of his sub- 2.Chr.31. 21.
iects, *Vt facerent quæ scripta sunt in volumine illo quod legerat,* 35.
That they should do those things which were written in that booke
which was read. This was the rule whereby these holy Kings,
so much commended by the Spirit of God, reedified the ruines of Gods Church, by their elders defaced.

28 For although the Apostle call the Church the *Pillar* 1.Tim.3.15.
and ground of truth; yet it is but as a nurse, not a mother; as a
pillar to support it, as a ground to set it in, not as the foundation to build it on, much lesse as a mistris to ouer-rule it. The
hils are good foundations to build vpon, not onely for beautie to the shew, but for strength against flouds & inundatiōs.
Yet the hils haue their foundations, *God touched the foundati-* Psal.18.7.
ons of the hils. So the Church is a good foundation, yet she
　　　　　　　　　　　　　　　　　　　hath

hath her foundation alſo. A pillar ſupporteth a houſe, but yet the houſe is better then the pillar; it furthereth the wel-being, it maketh not the being of truth. A pillar alſo is as well for memorie, ſhew, or inſcription, as for ſtrength, de-

Plutarcb.in
Lucullo.

fence, & ſupportation; as in Ilium the apparition of *Minerua* in a ſweate was written vpon a pillar for perpetuall memorie. As thoſe pillars erected and ingrauen with the learning of thoſe times before the flood, left and ſeene afterward by the poſteritie. *Herculus* ſet vp pillars with *Nihil vltra*. *Abſalom*

2.Sam. 18.17.

reared vp a pillar for his memorie. Theſe pillars were not better then their inſcriptions, or thoſe whoſe monuments they were. So is the Church a pillar whereon the holy Scriptures are as it were ingrauen; as a pillar it preſerueth them, and it ſheweth them to all the world; yet is it not better then they, nor to be preferred before them. So is the Church *the ground of truth alſo*, the ground not onely to ſet it on, but alſo to ſow it in, that it may bring forth fruite; not to ouerwhelme it, and ſtifle it, that it can bring forth no fruite. The field is the Church, the ſeed is the word: of this ſeed that is thus ſowen, ſome falleth vpon good ground, ſome vpon bad; but all the ſeed is commended and committed to the ground, and ſo may be truly called, *The ground of truth*, that is, the ground for truth to be ſowen in. For in the Church or by the Church, is the truth ſowne and reaped, and by none or no where elſe. Thus is it *The pillar and ground of truth*.

Pſal.87.1.
Eſay 2.2.

28 She is likened to mount Sion, and is built in *montibus*, on the hils. *A mountaine prepared on the top of the mountaines.* Theſe mountains *Saint Hierome* calleth *Montes Scripturarum*, the mountaines of Scriptures on which the Church is built.

Eſay.28.16.

Iſaiah the Prophet ſpeaketh *of a foundation of foundations. Fundauit fundamentum fundatū*, or as *Tremellius, Fundationem fundatiſſimam the deepeſt and profoundeſt foundation*, and therefore the ſoundeſt and moſt certaine of all others. This is our *Oldeſt*, firſt, and chiefeſt *Antiquitie*, which we aske and will ſtand vnto without all exception. Behold how directly the

Eph.2.19.

Apoſtle followeth the Prophet, *Citizens of the Saints, and of the houſhold of God, are built vpon the foundations of the Apoſtles*

and

and Prophets, Iefus Chrift *himfelfe being the chiefe corner ftone. In whom all the building coupled together groweth vnto an holy temple in the Lord. In whom ye are alfo built together, to be the habitation of God by the Spirit.* Where it is euident that the Church is built vpon the Apoftles and Prophets, that is, their writings; they vpon Iefus Chrift, which is his doctrine: for he is onely that *fundatio fundatiffima, that profoundeft foundation,* whereon the Church is built, fupported by the Apoftles and Prophets as pillars, who are immediaty founded vpon Chrift himfelfe.

30 *Cardinall Bellarmine* conuinced in his confcience by this place of *Saint Paul,* is not onely driuen to confeffe, but promifeth to defend againft all gainftanders, that, *Verbum* C. Bellarm. *Dei miniftratum per Apoftolos & Prophetas effe primum funda-* de verbo Dei *mentum noftræ fidei: That the word of God miniftred by the A-* lib.3.cap.10. *poftles and Prophets, is the firft (and therefore the chiefeft) foundation of our faith.* And therefore *we beleeue whatfoeuer we do beleeue, becaufe God hath reuealed it by his Apoftles & Prophets.* But we adde, *That befide this firft foundation, there is required a fecond foundation,* that is, *The teftimony of the Church.* We will grant this alfo as well as you; Giue the word of God, deliuered by the Apoftles and Prophets, its due and deferued preheminence and foueraignty in determining articles and queftions of faith, and we will admit willingly the Churches teftimonie both for the Scriptures, and of them, and will receiue whatfoeuer fhe commendeth vnto vs, if it be grounded vpon the firft foundation. And this Church we fay is ours, and not yours, euen by the witneffe of that firft foundation, which can neuer be ouerthrowne.

31 If we haue not this Church, fhew it vs elfewhere, and we will come to it; If ours be it, why are you fo flacke to come to vs? You call your Church the *Catholique Romane Church*; we fubmit not our felues vnto it, neither dare we. But put *Apoftolique* for *Romane,* and proue your felues of that Church, we come vnto you, embrace you, loue and reuerence you, and will defire to liue and die with you.

32 The fumme of all is this: giue vs *Antiquitie* of doctrine, and veritie, we aske no more, neither do we acknowledge any other *Antiquitie*, but onely this, for the triall of all controuerfies, and affoyling all doubts. For it is both firft in time, and chiefeft in preheminence. So will I confeffe it, not onely to be a note of the Church, and religion to reft in, and rely vpon, but alfo the onely note thereof, without all exception or limitation, as hath bene faid. Difpoffeffe vs of this one foundation, we yeeld in all you lay to our charge. If you cannot, giue vs leaue to hold our title, vntill you euict vs, and we will poffeffe our foules in patience, and expect that Ancient of dayes, who will come and will not tarrie, and giue end to all our controuerfies.

D. Whittak. de notis Ecclefiæ. ca. 3. pag. 251.

33 Though this veritie hath bene fufficiently proued, by that which hath bene faid, yet our aduerfaries confeffion in this cafe, may yeeld much fatiffaction to fuch as ouer deepely dote vpon their owne writers. *Panormitane* their great *Canonift* faith, *Vbicunq; funt boni Chriftiani, ibi eft Romana Ecclefia*: Wherefoeuer good Chriftians be, there is the Church of Rome, he meaneth certainly the true Church. And further, that *Apud vnum folum fidelem, licet fœminam, poffit confiftere recta fides*: with one onely beleeuer though a woman, true faith may be refident. He maketh the profeffion of true faith, (which cometh by hearing of the word within the Church) to be the true note of the Church, though but in one. Which he exemplifieth in the bleffed Virgine *Marie*, during the time of Chrifts death and his manifeft refurrection. And againe, that the Church is cleared, not only to be, but to haue wel-being, *Si remanet vera fides in vno folo*, If true faith remaine onely in one. True faith is ftill the note. Whom another writer of theirs foloweth & faith, that Chrift from the time of his death to his refurrection dwelled only in the bleffed Virgin, by *true beleefe*, that fhe had, and all the Apoftles were departed from him by misbeleefe; & concludeth, that in that time, it might be efpecially faid to her, *Our Lord is with thee*, that is, by true faith and beleefe. True beleefe poffeffeth Chrift, misbeleefe eiecteth Chrift, True faith and beleefe ioyneth

An old Englifh booke tranflated (as it feemeth) out of Bonauenture de vitâ Chrifti, with fome additions, part. 1. die Lunæ, c. 3. ante finem

neth

neth the members to the head, and each member to another.

34 And yet another, *Semper manent aliqui, in quibus ser-* _{Fortalitium}
uatur veritas fidei, & iustificatio bonæ conscientiæ : Some euer re- ^{fidei lib.5.}
maine in whom is reserued the truth of faith, and testimony ,,
of a good conscience. And *Ioannes de Turrecremata* a famous ,,
schooleman, and a great Cardinall alledgeth two Fathers, to ,,
this purpose with good assent thereunto. *Ecclesia non in parie-* Summa de
tibus consistit, sed in dogmatum veritate, vbi vera fides est, ibi est cap.3.
*Ecclesia.*The Church standeth not in walls, but in the truth of ,,
doctrine, where true faith is, there is the Church. So *Hierome.* ,,
And *Chrysostome* very neere in the same words, altogether in
the same sence: *Vbi fides ibi Ecclesia, ibi sacerdos, ibi baptismus,*
ibi Christianus ; vbi non est, ibi Ecclesia non est. Where faith is, ,,
there is the Church, there a priest, there baptisme, there a ,,
Christian ; whereas faith is not, there is not the true Church. ,,

35 But what shall I stand on these, or the ancient Fathers, Mat.18.20.
who all concurre in the same opinion? Where two or three
are gathered together in my name, I will be in the midst *of* Iohn 10.3.16.
them, My sheepe heare my voice. Hereby shall ye be knowne to be ^{13.35.}
my disciples if you loue one another, if ye keepe my word. These ^{Iohn 14.23.}
words of our Sauiour make this position stronger then any
Father. But perhaps the Romane Catholique will beleeue a
Iesuite better then Iesus.

36 *Bellarmine* himselfe, the last and worst of the Romane
crew, and a Cardinall too, that knoweth the mind of the head
and body of that Synagogue, confesseth as much, and that by
way of conclusion out of *Ioannes Driedo, Ex quo sequitur, quod*
si sola vna prouincia retineret veram fidem, adhuc verè & propriè
diceretur Ecclesia catholica, dummodò clarè ostenderetur eam esse
veram, & eandem cum illa, quæ fuit aliquo tempore, vel diuersis in
toto mundo, &c. Whereof it followeth, that if onely one pro- ,,
uince should hold the true faith, it should be still verily and ,,
properly called the Catholique Church, prouided that it be ,,
clearely shewed, that to be one & the same with that which ,,
hath bene sometime, or diuers times in the whole world. ,,
We subscribe to this, we will aske no more. Not onely one
                                                prouince.

prouince, but all our Kings Maiesties dominions, with all those kingdomes or prouinces which professe the Gospell and reformed religion, haue the true faith, and therefore yet may be called, and that truly and propely the Catholique Church, with the Cardinals prouiso and all. For we vndertake and haue clearely proued to all the world, that the Apostolicall Church, for a good time, in diuers places of the world, and we may say, in the whole world, held that faith, truth, doctrine and religion, which at this day by the mercifull blessing of almightie God we maintaine, and which we are ready to iustifie with expence of our blood. This if we haue not done, or cannot do, we yeeld.

37 If our Romane aduersaries agree with vs thus farre, then my conclusion is demonstratiue, by our enemies owne witnesse : That the truth of doctrine and faith *contained in the Scriptures, is the proper and certaine note of the Church, truly conuertible therewith, yea and with it onely.* Where the true faith of Christ is professed, as it is reuealed in the holy Scriptures, there, yea that is the vndoubted true Church; where the true Church is, there the true faith is certainly and onely professed: For *Extra Ecclesiam nulla fides, nulla salus,* Out of the Churh there is no faith, no saluation. Vnto this punctually accordeth

Lactantius, Inst. diuin. lib. 4. cap. vlt.

Lactantius an ancient and learned writer of the Church, *Sola Catholica Ecclesia est, quæ verè Dei cultum retinet, hic autem est fons veritatis, hoc domicilium fidei, hoc templum Dei. quod si quis non intrauerit, vel à quo si quis exierit, à spe vitæ & salutis æternæ alienus est.* That onely is the Catholique Church which retaineth the true worship of God, for here is the fountaine of truth, this is the houshold of faith, this is the Temple of God, into which if any man shall not enter, or out of which if any shall depart, he is a stranger from the hope of life and eternall saluation. All this is very true, and our very case, against the Church of Rome at this day. If we can proue we haue the true worship of God, as hath bene done abundantly, then haue we the Scriptures, which are the fountaine of truth; then are we Gods houshold, Gods temple, out of which we dare not depart to the Church of Rome, without dreadful

dan-

danger of eternall condemnation. For this is the onely true, conuertible and effentiall marke of the Church and of true Religion. Take all the other markes in their full number, weight and meafure, yet are they but accidents, which may induce vnto probabilitie, but can neuer conuince as by demonftration: as Cardinall *Bellarmine* hath before confeffed. For example take a view of all his notes, and they will all proue plaine notts, for not one of them without veritie confonant to the Scriptures, is worthy to be taken vp for a note of the Church, nor can more make the true definition thereof, then the painted proportion and lineaments of a man vpon a wall, may perfwade vs to beleeue it a liuing creature.

38 Firft it is to be obferued, that whatfoeuer the Fathers write of the Catholique Church, the Papifts wreft to the Church of Rome onely, and whatfoeuer they apply to the Church and BB. of Rome then in their dayes they prefume to attribute to them now : then which nothing can be more abfurd. For neuer was that Church by all the Fathers deemed the Catholique Church ; neither do they deferue that now, who are murtherers, which their anceftors deferued who were Martyrs, or at leaft, learned and good men.

39 But let vs more exactly confider the name Catholique, which is *Bellarmines* firft note, or the fignification of the name, which is, *common* or *vniuerfall*. Neither is it fo ancient as the name Chriftian, except *Pharifæi erant Catholici*, Pharifies were Catholiques, as *Genebrad* makes them: or as the diuell whofe peregrination or perambulation was the whole earth. Neither hath it authoritie of Scripture as this hath, though it afterwards was iuftlie receiued and admitted into the Creed. Wherein what fhould hinder but that *Catholica Ecclefia* the Catholique Church, may be taken for the *inuifible Church*, and *Communio Sanctorum* the Communion of Saints, for the vifible ? And therefore the Church was without it, and fo may be, and yet haue the thing without which it cannot be. And as for the fignification, Arianifme was

Catholica. 1.
"
"
Chronolog. lib. 2.
Iob. 1. 7.
1 Pet. 5. 8.

once

once more common then orthodoxall faith. And Turcifme with the branches thereof at this day, is more vniuerfall then the Romane Synagogue, or all that profeſſe the Chriſtian religion. The Church of *Sardis had a name to liue, and was dead*, a name of life, and a ſtate of death : a dreame of a feaſt, and rife an hungred: a badge of glorie, a liuerie of ſhame: a fame to be rich and ful, and wanting nothing, and in truth is poore **Reuel. 3.**   naked, wreched, miſerable, like the Church of Laodicea. And therefore take this name, or the ſignification thereof, there may be as Catholique an error as a truth, and therefore the name of Catholique is nothing without truth.

Eſt nomen ſine re proiectà vilius algâ,
A name without the deed
Is worſe then any weed.

40 But beſides if you wil apply it to the Church of Rome, you abuſe the word, yea and the nature of the word too. For it can no more be Catholique and Romane then it can be publique and priuate, common and proper, vniuerſall & particular, then which what can be more abſurd? Not much vnlike a wife that would be fine at her feaſt, and hauing her beſt affection ſet moſt vpon one of her gueſts ſaid, Neighbours, *I drinke to all in ſpeciall, and to you Miſtris in generall.* Was not this a wifedomely Goſſip? *Non ita pugnant inter ſe* **Satyre.**   *Romanum & Catholicum nomen, vt pro Hircacerno, aut Chimera*
" *Romani-Catholici derideantur, conueniunt optimè.* The Romane
" and the Catholique name are not ſo oppoſite betwixt them-
" ſelues, as that the *Romane Catholiques* ſhould be derided like
" a monſter that is part a goat, and part a Hart, or ſome *Chime-*
" *ra* ; they agree paſſing well. They agree like *Ienkins* and *Ger-*
" *mans* lips. It is a very Centaure, compounded of diuerſities, if not contradictions. Howbeit we muſt not except againſt it, by whomſoeuer it be attributed, and howſoeuer applied. Yet what was Rome but a ſpeciall Church, when Saint *Paul* wrote his Epiſtle, as *Corinth, Galatia, Epheſus,* and others then were? That was after *Chriſt* promiſed *Peter,* and *Peter* had poſſeſſion, as our aduerſaries pretend. But where was the Catholique Church when Rome was no Church, and then

then not written to more then all the beleeuers difperfed, to whom they were indeed written. This is meere dalliance, a bable for a foole, yet the Papifts will not leaue it for the Tower of London.

41 *Antiquitie* without verity, is but *vetuftas erroris*, Antiquitas.1. the *Antiquitie* of error. The Turks haue florifhed and increafed a thoufand yeares, or very neare as long as the *Pope* hath bene knowne by the name of *vniuerfall Bifhop*, and as long as the Romanifts may well auouch their religion to be continued in the world. The Gentils were before them, and infidelitie is much ancienter then Chriftianitie. Seuer then *Antiquity* from Scripture veritie, and it can be no true or certaine note of Chrifts Church & religion. Of this is, or fhall be fpoken more or leffe, almoft in euery Chapter of this booke. For the prefent it is fufficient, that we profeffe for *Antiquitie*, and ftand with it more precifely and truly then the Romanifts do or poffibly can do, howfoeuer they boaft of that they haue forfaken, and therefore haue not.

42 *Continuance* the third note, whether you refpect the Duratio diu-experience of times paft, or hope of time to come, it can be turna 3. not fo much as a probable note, much leffe a certaine. If you will confine it to time paft, that is the fame with *Antiquitie*, which is nothing without verity. If to the time to come, that is onely knowne to God, vncertaine to vs, further then God hath promifed and affured, that *Babylon* fhall fall, and the Reuel.17. 16. *whore that fitteth on the feuen hils*, fhal haue her period. If both, we conteft and ftand againft them, both in our owne experience for all ages paft, and in our confident hope vnto the end of the world. For the time paft we will fay with that learned and religious Diuine, *Nos nifi poffumus probare noftram* D. Whitakers. *doctrinam femper fuiffe in mundo Chriftiano, docuiffe eam Chriftum, docuiffe Apoftolos, & Ecclefiam etiam quæ Apoftolorum tempore fuit, eandem tenuiffe; & Papiftarum dogmata è contrà noua effe, hærefeos nec crimen, nec pœnam deprecamur:* If we cannot ,, proue our doctrine euer to haue bene in the Chriftian world, ,, that Chrift taught it, that the Apoftles preached it, and that ,, the Church which was in the Apoftles time held it; and that ,,
the

„ the Papiſts poſitions, on the contrarie ſide, are new, we will
„ neither refuſe the name nor puniſhment, due to hereſie. For
the time to come we haue this aſſurance, that *though heauen*
and earth paſſe away, yet ſhall not one iote of Gods word faile, till all
be fulfilled. Their continuance without verity, is no note of
the Church; if with truth, it belongeth to vs & not to them.
For we haue and ſhall againe proue that they haue bene miſ-
led through hypocriſie, and haue erred from the truth, and
beleeued lyes.

Mat.5.18.

43 *Amplitude* or *multitude*, is further from being a true
note of the Church then any other. *Follow not a multitude*
to do euill, is a diuine precept: a multitude then many draw
vnto euill, therefore can it not make a certaine argument for
good; Neither agree in a controuerſie to follow many a-
gainſt truth, which is Gods redoubled commandement.
Aliquando in ſolo Abel Eccleſia erat, & expugnatus eſt a malo &
perdito Cain. Aliquando in ſolo Enoch Eccleſia erat, & tranſlatus
eſt ab iniquis. Aliquando in ſola domo Noe Eccleſia erat: & pertu-
lit omnes qui in diluuio perierunt, & ſola arca natauit in fluctibus,
& euaſit in ſiccum. Aliquando in ſolo Abraham, &c. The Church
„ was ſometimes in *Abel* alone, and he was ſlaine by wicked
„ and loſt *Cain.* Sometimes the Church was in *Enoch* alone,
„ and he was tranſlated from the vngodly. Sometimes the
„ Church was onely in the houſe of *Noah*, and God ſuffered
„ all to periſh in the floud, where onely the arke floated vpon
„ the waters and eſcaped to drie land. Sometimes it was one-
„ ly in *Abraham* &c. Saint *Auguſtine* hath a diſcourſe not much
vnlike this: out of which, or in imitation whereof, this *Lum-*
nius ſeemeth to haue written. If the Church were but in *A-*
bel onely, (as here is ſaid) where was the Church when *Abel*
was ſlaine? well I wot there was not then a multitude, or
afterward if it were only in *Enoch* and he tranſlated, he could
not leaue a multitude behind him ; ſo of the reſt named,
though they were not ſo alone, but that they had ſome with
them, yet were they farre from a multitude, and ſo continued vntill *Iacob* and his familie went into the land of Egypt.
And therefore if we ſet *Noah* & his houſe in the Arke againſt
                                                          the

Amplitudo
ſeu multitu-
do.4.
Exod.23.2.

Ioannes Fre-
deri.Lumnius
in Theſauro
Chriſtiani ho-
minis, de
Chriſto & e-
ius Eccleſia.
lib.2.cap.1.

Aug.in Pſal.
118.con.29.
in fine.

the drowned world: *Lot* against his fiue cities, the *Israelites* a-
gainst Egypt, yea against the face of the whole earth: *Micha-* 1.King.22.6.
iah against the foure hundred false Prophets, and *Eliah* with
those secret 7000 *that had neuer bowed their knees to Baal* , a- 1.King.18.20
gainst all Israel that cómited shamefull idolatrie: nay *Christ* &
his Apostles against not onely the proud Priests, the learned
Scribes, & the seeming-holy Pharises, but against all the multitude of the Iewes , yea and the Gentiles also, *who gathered* Psal.2.1.
themselues together against God and his Sonne Christ , whose Act 4.25.
flocke is a little flocke, and whereinto though many be cal- Luke 12.31.
led, yet few be chosen; we shall find that the multitude was Mat.22.14.
euer the worst, truth had the least partie. The aspect of an ordinary map will easily confute this argument ; where a man
may see with this his eye, that *Europe* is not the twétieth part
of the world, that are Turks and Infidels, and a great part of
Europe subiect to the same infidelity. And it is proued before
that not only two or three gathered together in Christs name
haue the promise of his presence, as the head with his members, but that the Church may be in very few, yea in one, and
that a woman. Therfore multitude without verity, is but like
a great beast with many heads, it holdeth no proportion, nor
forme to make a Church.

44 *Succession* is the fift, but this is worse, as if the Cardi- Successio E-
nall were resolued to fall *à malo in peius* , from naught to piscoporum 5
worse. Is it probable? is it possible? Did God euer tie his mercies or promises to places, or a succession of persons, as
though no sinne were able to make a diuorce , if the spouse
do play the harlot ? Many a good father hath a wicked sonne
in naturall propagation. Manie a good King and Priest haue
had as wicked followers in ciuill succession. It is often to be
remembred, that *Non sunt filij Sanctorum qui tenent loca Sancto-* Hierom.
rum , sed qui sequuntur opera eorum. They are not the sonnes ,,
of the Saints , that sit in their seates, but that imitate their ,,
maners, as before is remembred. God can *raise out of stones chil-* Mat.3.9.
dren vnto Abraham , and God can cast out *the children of the* Luke 19.40.
kingdome into vtter darknesse. Who had greater promises then
Dauid for his seed , euen concerning the temporall kingdome?

do me? yet had it no further obligation, than, *If thy feed shall walke in my wayes, and obserue my statutes.* What promise of the priesthood to *Aaron?* how was it sealed to *Phineas?* how afterward continued to others? yet not without due conditions, which *Cardinall Bellarmine* himselfe confesseth are to be vnderstood, though they be not expressed in the promises of God. The kingdome was alienated to a stranger, the high Priesthood was bought and sold for mony, and inuaded by the most wicked traitors vnto the Law and vnto the people of God, and that before the coming of the *Messiah.* Who gaue end both to that kingdome and Priesthood, and erected a priestly kingdome and royall Priesthood ouer all kindreds, nations, tongues & people of the earth. As great promises were made to *Salomons* Temple, to the Citie *Ierusalem*, to the High-priest in the chaire of *Moses*: and yet al these failed, or at least fowly fainted, for a time, vntill the coming of our Sauiour: and after were destroyed, and that worthily for their grosse sinnes, and manifold backslidings from their God, and his Law.

margin: Psal.89.30.

margin: Machab.

45 But suppose this note were somewhat of it selfe, if it were true, yet can the Romanists neuer shadow themselues vnder this arbor, whereof the leaues haue so often fallen, and the flowers faded, that there remained nothing to be seene but the rotten stickes, euill fauouredly crossing one another, to their open shame in the view of the whole world. That whereof *Liuie* complained, *Tantos errores tempora implicare, &c.* That times inwrapped so many errours, so that they knew not who were *Consuls*, nor what was done each yeare, *&c.* the same may be said of the newer Romans, they know not who were Popes in the first ages, nor what was done in their Popedomes, in such varietie and vncertaintie of Authors.

margin: Liui. lib.2. ab vrbe condita.

46 For first, there is no certainty who succeeded *Peter;* some wil haue *Linus*, some *Clemens*, some *Cletus*, after *Linus*, some *Clemens* before both, the most after them both; some *Anacletus* for *Cletus.* But none can tell certainly who was the man in truth and indeed. The best historians of them all cannot tell in order who was the second, third, fourth and fifth

margin: Irenæus.
Eusebius.
Epiphanius.
Ruffinus.
Hierome.
Sabellicus.

fifth Pope. Yet of late a Iesuite, excellent in laying foundati- | Muri ciuit.
ons with precious ſtones, ſaith that *ea fuit Clementis modeſtia,* | ſanct ſund. 5
vt dum in viuis Linus & Cletus eſſent, nollet tenere Cathedram.
Ita ex Petri deſignatione Clemens, ex Clementis modeſtiâ Linus
& Cletus primi poſt Petrum Romani Epiſcopi eſſe debuerunt. Such „
was *Clements* modeſty, that *Linus* and *Cletus* liuing, he would „
not hold that Chaire ; ſo that by *Peters* deſignment, *Clement*, „
by *Clements* modeſty *Linus* & *Cletus* ought to be the firſt Ro- „
mane Biſhops ſucceeding *Peter.* Put out mine eye with ſuch „
a modeſt Pope in theſe our dayes or the laſt thouſand yeares.
This diſtinction is *point deuiſe*, yet note that *Peter* appointed his ſucceſſor, without a Colledge of Cardinals, or conclaue to houſe them.

47 But what do they ſpeake of ſucceſſion at all, the certaintie whereof ſtandeth chiefly in the Biſhops certaine election? the forme whereof hath bene often altered, and without all queſtion, from that which Chriſt and *Saint Peter*
appointed (if they appointed any) to be their vicars or ſucceſſors. They will all haue it, that Chriſt appointed *Peter* ;
and *Peter* his followers two or three. It continued ſo in *Sal-* | In ſecund. fig-
merons iudgement vnto *Alexander* and *Sixtus*, who were the | no certo Ec-
ſixt and ſeuenth BB. of that ſea, as in the verſe. | cleſig.

Sextus Alexander Siſto commendat ouile.
When Alexander the ſixt his life did end,
His flocke to Siſtus then he did commend.

48 If this election was according to Chriſts inſtitution,
why was it poſted ouer to the Cleargie and people? then to
the Emperour with them, and ſometime to him alone ; now
to the Cardinals, the neweſt forme? If the firſt was good, why
was it altered ? if this laſt be onely good, as is now defended,
then the former Popes had no true and formall election ; and
ſo could they neuer haue any true and certaine ſucceſſion.
The very leaſt inconuenience they incurre, is, that they haue
changed *Antiquitie* for *Noueltie*, and Chriſts inſtitution for
their owne inuention. Volumes haue bene written of
often ſchiſmes, long for time, furious for malice, tempeſtuous for troubles ; and of their Popes, infamous for man-
G   ners,

ners, hereticall for opinions, difanulling of acts, condemning one another, nay poyfoning, murthering, maffacring,
detefting, defaming, yea excommunicating, fentencing,
condemning and executing their dead carcaffes and very
bones. Once a woman, often wicked men, fometimes children both in age and knowledge; fchifmatiques, heretiques,
idolaters, inceftuous, blafphemous, coniurers, forcerers, monfters and incarnate diuels, haue vfurped that feate whereunto they would tie this fucceffion. God will haue no fuch de-
Hofius. puties, or vicegerents: Saint *Peter* will neuer acknowledge
any fuch fucceffors. *Cardinall Hofius* his plea fhall neuer
hold out before that vncorrupt Iudge in the day of Chrift: *Iu-*
,, *das ne an Petrus: Whether Iudas or Peter held that fea and chaire*
,, *of Rome*, it mattereth not. He hath fufficient holineffe from
Muri ciuit. the feate. Which a new vpftart Iefuite fhames not to fecond.
fanct.fund. 5. *Fac aliquem Pontificum manifefta hærefi maculatum effe, animum*
ille fuum, non Petri Cathedram, feipfum non facerdotale officium
,, *maculauit, qui fequutus non hæretico expontifici, fed catholico ponti-*
,, *fici succeffit, quid vitij in fucceffione eft?* Grant that fome Pope be
,, defiled with manifeft herefie, he hath berayed his own foule,
,, not *Peters* Chaire; himfelfe, not his Prieftly office. He that
,, followes fucceds not an hereticall-no-pope, but a Catholique B. what fault is in the fucceffion? If it be in the Chaire
or office, and not in the perfon, then if there be *Peters* owne
Chaire ftill, there is no fucceffion; if there be a new Chaire,
then is it not *Peters*. A wife matter that the Iudge of the
world, and that in diuine and heauenly things, in the deter-
ming of all caufes, the decifion of all controuerfies, muft reft
vpon the wit, the vertue, the holineffe, the vnderftanding,
the knowledge of a ioynd ftoole or a wainfcot Chaire. If it
Act.3.6. be of gold or filuer, I am fure it was none of *Peters*, for *filuer*
and gold he had none in his purfe, much leffe in his chaire. Succeffion without truth therefore is nothing. If you fay that
Tertullian, and other Fathers attributed much vnto this fucceffion, it is true: but it was in thofe times when they had not
yet departed from the truth, and in many places where the
fucceffion then continued as well as at Rome. But now the
cafe is altered, they haue abandoned the truth, and the truth
hath.

hath forſaken them.

49 *Conſpiracie in doctrine*, is *Cardinall Bellarmines* ſixt note. Conſpiratio If he had left out doctrine, and had reſted vpon conſpiracie, in Doctrinâ.6 I would allow him this note aboue al others, as moſt properly belonging to the Romane Church. But take conſpiracy in what ſence you will , they haue it, we yeeld it them, viz. conſpiracy both theoricke and practicke , in doctrine and action, in ſchooles and in the tents. For greater conſpirators againſt Kings and States there neuer liued on the face of the earth , whereof all Chriſtendome can ſufficiently teſtifie. The Maſſacre in France, the vnholy League, the murther of two kings : in the low Countreys the Prince of *Orange*; in England the whole life of that famous, and neuer to be forgotten Queene *Elizabeth*, with daggers, dags, poyſon, inſurrection, & what not ? Our glorious and gracious King *Iames*, by aſſailing his perſon alone, him with his children, his ſonne beſide him, as is by forreine writers ſuſpected , and may by good probabilitie be proued.

50 The Powder-treaſon, which may very iuſtly be conuinced to haue paſſed the heads and wits of all the Ieſuites in Chriſtendome; witneſſe *H. Garnets* plea of the ſecreſie of confeſſion, & *Martin del Rio*, that hath put the caſe *eiſdem terminis* , in the very termes that moſt pregnantly expreſſe the very fact as it ſhould haue bene executed, if God in his wonderfull mercie had not preuented it. *Confitetur maleficus ſe vel* Diſquiſitionū *alium, poſuiſſe pulueres, vel quid aliud ſub tali limine , & niſi tol-* magicarum. *lantur, domum comburendam, Principem interiturum, quotquot* l.6.Sect.11 *vrbem ingredientur egredienturq̃, in magnam perniciem aut periculum venturos.* A wicked villaine confeſſeth, that himſelfe ” or ſome other, hath put powders , or ſome ſuch like matter ” vnder ſome certaine entrie, and except they be taken thence, ” the houſe may be burnt, the Prince may be ſlaine, as many as ” go into, or out of the Citie, may fall into deſtruction or dan- ” ger. The queſtion vpon this caſe thus put by the Ieſuite is, *Whether a ghoſtly Father may diſcouer this, to preuent this miſchiefe ?* He concludeth againſt almoſt all the ancient ſchools and Doctors for ſecreſie, as *H. Garnet* pleaded. This was writ-

G 2　　　　　　ten

ten fiue yeares before this powder-plot was difcouered, by a
Iefuite and a ftranger. By which it is manifeft, that it was a
thing long proiected, confulted and determined, as well as
by *Winters* trauelling into *Spaine*,and conferring with the Iefuites there. Theretore *Confpiracie* is indeed,and we confeffe
it a fingular and proper note of the Romane Catholicke
Church. Howbeit I erre from Cardinall *Bellarmines* mind, he
meaneth not confpiracy in fact,but in *doctrine*.

51   If I would take aduantage againe of the doubtful-
nes of the word, I may iuftly allow them alfo this as a true
marke of their Church, proper to them,againft all that euer

Io.Mariana.   writ before them,or befides them. For *Ioannes Mariana*,and
other writers of theirs following him, maintaine the *doctrine*
of confpiracy, for murthering Kings, and fubuerting States. So
that we may iuftly fay, and proue it, that that Church, and
that onely,teacheth and preacheth *confpiracy in doctrine*.

52   But you will fay, that neither was this the *Cardinals*
meaning. *Conspiracy in doctrine, is confent and agreement in the*
fame opinions. Then this is not any certaine note of the true
Church; and if it were, yet agreeth it not with the Church

Pfal.2.2.   of *Rome. Conuenerunt in vnum: They gather themfelues in one a-*
gainft God and againft his Chrift. This was prophefied, and it
was by experience found true. The Scribes and Pharifees con-
fpired with the Elders in mifinterpreting the Law, in obferuing traditions, and all they with the Priefts,to put our Sauiour *Chrift* to death, and to perfecute his Apoftles. Confent without veritie is a meere confpiracy; as *Herod* and *Pi-*
late were made friends,when they were both the enemies of
Chrift; and *Ephraim* and *Manaffes* to deuoure *Iuda*.

53   But fuppofe it were a probable marke, as Cardinall
Bellarmine would haue it, yet is the Church of *Rome* neuer
the nearer. For either he meaneth their confent and agreement with the ancient Fathers, or their neare friendfhip and
concurrence of opinions amongft themfelues. That they vtterly diffent from the ancient Fathers, or reiect or debafe, or
abufe them as they pleafe,and as they ferue or ferue not their
turnes, fhall in the 8.Chapter be proued. For themfelues,
                                                              their

their *Thomists* and *Scotists*, their *Nominals* and *Reals*, their *Dominicks* and *Franciscans*, their *Iesuites* and *Seculars*, do sufficiently demonſtrate their infinite differences, and that in many matters of doctrine.

54 That may be a Catholique doctrine in one place and not in another, at one time or in one age of the Church, which may not be at another; and the Scriptures themſelues are to be taken *secundùm præsentis Ecclesiæ praxin*, according to the practiſe of the preſent Church. Nay, at one time, that may be a Catholique doctrine in one place, which is heretical in another. A man may ſafely profeſſe, that the Croſſe ſhould not be worſhipped with diuine worſhip in *France*, but in *Italy* he may not. In *Spaine* one may be burnt for it, as Frier *Ægedius* in *Seuill.* Is not this a goodly and cloſe agreement in doctrine? How vehemently writeth *Ambroſe Catherinus* the Biſhop of *Compſa* againſt *Thomas de Vio Caietanus*, a Cardinall of the Romane ſea? We need no other witneſſe then Cardinall *Bellarmine* himſelfe, who in moſt controuerſies ſetteth downe the diſtracted and torne opinions of his owne friends. At one word, I would aske no better euidence to condemne al the writers of the Romane Synagogue, then that of Doctor *Kellison*, where he ſaith, *that one onely opinion in a matter of faith, obſtinately defended againſt the Churches authoritie, is ſufficient to diſmember a Chriſtian from the myſticall body* ” *of Chriſts holy Church, in that it depriueth him of infuſed faith,* ” *which is the glue, yea the ſinew, that vniteth the members and the* ” *body together.* Take writing, liuing, prouing, auouching and ” dying in an opinion, for obſtinately defending, and you ſhal hardly find any Popiſh writer, who doth not in ſome materiall point or other differ from the common hold and current of other Doctors and writers, who write in the defence of the Romane Synagogue.

55 Therefore that which they write of our diſagreement mattereth the leſſe. For as it is very falſe that we are deuided and diſtracted in opinions, as they pretend; ſo they which will waſh a cup cleane, muſt haue a cleane hand; and that hypocrite that *will ſpie a mote in his brothers eye,* muſt *firſt plucke* Matth.7.5.

Marginal notes:

Azor.inſtit. mor.l.2.c.13.

Cuſan. de authoritate Eccleſ. & Concil.

Suruey l.2. c.4.pag.102.

Matth.7.5.

*out the beame which is in his owne eye.*They fight like Centaurs;
or if they agree in any thing,it is but as *Sampsons* foxes, they
hang by the tailes to set the world on fire.We differ as brethren may,sometimes do, as *Paul* and *Barnabas*,yea *Paul* and
Peter, *Augustine* and *Hierom*, *Irenæus* and *Victor*,and many o-
ther Saints of God haue done , and yet *keepe the vnitie of the
Spirit in the bond of peace.*

Act.15.39.
Galat.2.14.

7.Vnio mem-
brorū inter se
& cum capite.
,,

56   *Vnio membrorum inter se, & cum capite,* The vnion or
hanging together of the members among themselues or
with their head, that is,the vnion and neare coniunction the
Papists haue one with another , and they all with the Pope.
Egregiam verò laudem. A goodly catch. All the Turks agree
together with themselues and with their head , the little
Turks with the great Turke ,as the pettie Papists with their
proud Pope;therefore that is the true Church. Much of that
which hath bene said in the former note,may be applied vnto
this : which sufficiently discouereth the distractions euen *ad
pugnos*,to very fists. Hereunto might all the histories be applied , when the Emperours fought against the Popes, the
Popes against the Emperours, the Popes one with another,
and the Cardinals against their great Maister.

Sleid. com-
ment.l.6.

57   Where was the vnion of members when *Charles* the
fifth,by the Duke of *Bourbon* and other Catholicke souldiers
sacked *Rome*, besieged the Pope in his Saint *Angelo*, tooke
him prisoner , made his conditions at his pleasure ? What
vnion of members when Cardinals haue called Councels a-
gainst Popes? What vnion when Popes were deposed by
Councels ? Cardinals persecuted and slaine by Popes ? &c.
when they pretended to be all of one profession , all of
one religion,yet a greater confusion,more effusion of bloud,
more hatefull and desperate malice,more cruell and dreadful
disasters were neuer in the citie of *Ierusalem* among the sedi-
tious , then hath bene stirred and continued, supported and
maintained in the Synagogue of *Rome.*

58   And therefore neuer tell vs what Saint *Cyprian*, Saint
Augustine, and other Fathers told of their dayes, or former
times, when the Church was persecuted, or newly breathed
from

from perſecution.The caſe is now altered.We may ſay of the beſt Biſhop now , if we compare him with the worſt that were in their dayes, *Quantum mutatus ab illis?* What a change now,from thoſe then ? *Rome* gates may admit with ſhame e- nough, the diſgracefull inſcription of a notorious diſſolute heires houſe that deſcended from noble anceſtors : *O domus antiqua,quàm diſpari domino dominaris?* O ancient citie , how vnlike are thy preſent glorious Biſhops to their gracious pre- deceſſors? Then the faith of Chriſt flouriſhed in that citie, the beleeuers riches were then in their hearts, not in their purſes; their Biſhops were Martyrs, they made none as now they do. The other Churches were ioyned to it, and it vnto them,not as head and members, but all as gracious members of that glorious head *Chriſt Ieſus*, knit together in the vnitie of faith, and girdle of peace and loue which is the bond of Coloſſ.3.14 perfection.

59 Proue your preſent Church to be ſuch as thoſe Fa- thers found and left it, we will ioyne with you in the ſame v- nitie of faith, and profeſſion of the Goſpell: but if you be de- generated from them, and are turned *Babylon*, giue vs leaue to come forth, as *Lot* out of *Sodome*; we will not be partakers of your ſinnes, leſt we alſo partake of your plagues. Turne vnto Chriſt,and we will meete you; we will not be diſſolued from Chriſt,to be ioyned with you.

60 *Sanctitas doctrinæ, Holineſſe of doctrine.* Cardinall *Bellar-* 8.Sanctitas *mines* dalliance is to be noted in this note aboue all others. doctrinæ. For he ſaith nothing with any proofe at all, but againſt Infi- dels,Philoſophers,Iewes,Turks, and heretikes. That which he ſpeaketh of his owne partie,is onely preſumed , the con- trary may be moſt euidently prooued : and that which he di- recteth to vs in generall or particular, either is not euill as he imagineth, or is moſt maliciouſly laid to our charge without iuſt proofe, as hath bin by diuers ſufficiently anſwered : yet Iuel. this is euer their moſt iniurious complaint againſt our do- Fulk,&c. ctrine,euen to this day, as in this, fitter to be applied to the Pope then to *Luther. Noſtri mali à malâ ſuâ voluntate, non Ec-* Muri ciu.ſact. *cleſie Catholicæ conceſſione; veſtri non tantùm ſuo vitio, ſed etiam* fund.8.

G 4   *Lu-*

,, *Lutheri indulgentia tales sunt* : Ours are euill from a peruerse
,, will, not by permission of the Catholike Church; yours are
,, such, not onely by their owne viciousnesse, but by *Luthers*
,, indulgence; he might better say, the Popes pardons. And a li-

Ibid. tle before he saith, *Arbor doctrina est, fructus vita; sancta doctrina, sanctæ vitæ, mala malæ certè origo est. Qui apud nos mali sunt,
non doctrinæ Catholicæ, sed prauo voluntatis impulsu tales sunt, qui
boni ita instituti sunt Qui apud vos mali, aut minùs boni sunt, Lu-*
,, *thero Magistro sic viuere didicerunt.* Doctrine is the tree, the
,, fruite is life; the originall of a holy life is a holy doctrine; of
,, a wicked doctrine a wicked life. Who with vs are euill, are
,, such not from the Catholicke doctrine, but a peruerse insti-
,, gation of their will; who are good, are so instructed. Who
,, with you are euill, or lesse good, haue learned so to liue from
,, their Maister *Luther.* A most wicked and damnable slander,
and certainly against their owne conscience.

61 *Luther* perhaps saith as he alledgeth, (*in Præfa.Gal.*2.)
that he doth *nescire legem, ignorare opera,* not know the Law,
and is ignorant of works. But they know that he meaneth in
the act of iustification, wherein neither the Law nor our
works haue any part, and not otherwise for life and conuersation. It would aske a great labour (though the matters be
apparent, yet are they such a multitude) to set downe all the
blasphemies, absurdities, superstitious and villanous opinions, more then *Hercules* was put vnto in the purging of *Au-*

Bellar. *gæus* stable. Beside, as diuine worship to the Crosse, which
Cardinall *Bellarmine* himselfe confesseth cannot be defended
but with distinctions which themselues vnderstand not. A-
doration of images, against the direct law of God, in the old
and new Testament. Murthering of Christ euery day in the
Masse, and crucifying of him afresh. Making prayers by numbers, and vaine babling, to be meritorious, *ex opere operato,*
so it be done, it mattereth not how. Murthering of Kings and
Princes, against the law of God and man, detestable and damnable in heauen and earth. That simple fornication is no sin,
or at most a *peccadilio,* a litle sin; nay adultery, which is more,
and that in a Clerk, is *inter minora crimina,* among small faults,
           and

and, as hath bene thought, if not taught by some of yours, in greater sinnes then this, euen in infidelitie.

Extra.de Iudicijs.cap.At si clerici.§.de adulterijs.

62 When *a Spanish Captaine* came to confession, and had opened the truth in many grosse and damnable sins, his ghostly father asked whether he had disburdened his conscience in all? He answered, in all sins of the larger size, in breaking the commandements of the holy Church, and in whoredome and bloudshed, &c. but one little pettie *peccadilio* remained, not worth the speaking of. His ghostly father would needs haue that out too: with much ado he answered, *Io no credo in Dios*, I beleeue not in God. I haue no better author then a souldier: but it may well be true, considering their miserable ignorance for want of teaching. In their learning, the stewes is *malum necessarium*, at the worst a necessary euill. Dispensations with incestuous mariages, and an hundred like to these, if not worse. And to speake shortly of all their religion, it is sacrilegious, in robbing God of his glory, and giuing it to creatures, in pride and pompe of the Pope and Prelates, in policie and cousenage of all the world, in crueltie and tyrannie against the best members of Christs Church, in vaine shewes and shadowes to please the senses of such as are children, yea babes in vnderstanding, and may be deluded with any thing vnder pretence of holinesse.

63 I could wish that the holinesse both of doctrine and manners might determine our quarels: our strife would soon be at an end, if *we would walke before the Lord in holinesse and righteousnesse all the dayes of our liues.* In meane time til it please God to worke this excellent worke, which our sinnes do yet hinder, we can manifest and iustifie to all the world, in the sight of God and men, that it belongeth vnto vs, which you wrongfully vsurpe vnto your selues, out of Saint *Augustine*, *Nihil in (nostris) Christianis Ecclesiis turpe & flagitiosum spectandum imitandumq́, proponitur, vbi veri Dei aut præcepta insinuantur, aut miracula narrantur, aut dona laudantur, aut beneficia postulantur.* You cannot verifie this of your Churches, we can of ours. In our Christian Churches there is no filthy, no flagitious thing set forth to be seene or imitated, where either the

Bellar.nota 8. ex August.de ciuit.Dei.l.2. cap.28.

,, the commandements of the true God are infinuated , or his
,, miracles reported , or his bleffings praifed , or his benefites
,, prayed for. Where is any of your idolatry ? your cenfing of
images, and facrificing for quicke and for dead? your feftiuals
and Legends, with fuch like trafh ? Looke vpon all the Litur-
gies of the reformed Churches, and fee what is in them, but
confeffion of finnes, begging of pardon, praying to God and
praifing his Name, magnifying Gods works and his mercy
that is aboue all his workes; reading of diuine Scriptures,
preaching the Gofpell, the very fubftance of that which Saint
Auguftine fpeaketh of. Heare our preaching , and obferue

1.Tim.1.5.   whether the fubftance of all be not *Loue out of a pure heart,*
and of a good confcience, and faith vnfained. And therefore we
conclude, as Cardinall *Bellarmine* out of him , *Perfuadebatur*
veritas noua confuetudine, fed non contraria rationi : We haue
,, taught and perfwaded the truth , which is new to your cu-
,, ftome, but not contrary to reafon. We teach the truth before
God, and lie not.

9. Efficacia   64   *Efficacie of doctrine.* What, is the *Cardinall* out of his
doctrinæ.   wits? Firft he impudently beggeth this, that all who haue bin
conuerted in times paft , haue bin conuerted by the Popes
and Church of *Rome*, and men of their now new religion.
The Apoftles and their fucceffors for diuers of the firft ages
we claime as ours. What haue they fince done, but peruerted and corrupted all religion ? Onely fire and fword, murthers and maffacres in Chriftendome; moft barbarous, fauage
P.Martyrs de-   and vnheard of cruelties in the Weft Indies, inforced rather
cads.   then perfwaded any to their fuperftitiö: which will be abundantly iuftified, & is lamented by fome of their owne writers.
    65   If they fend vs after their Iefuites to *Iapan, China,*
Cataia, the *Moluccan Iflands,*

              vltra Garamantas & Indos,

we will not beleeue them, they may equiuocate and lie, to
the aduantage of their Order. But if they will try with vs in
Europe, let them but confider how their greateft boaft is,
that all was theirs before *Luthers* time, as truly as all the
Mat.4.   world was the diuels to beftow vpon Chrift. It muft necef-
                                      farily

farily follow,that all that are turned from them,which is now
in the Weſt Church, almoſt as great a part as theirs,haue bin
brought vnto vs by the *efficacie* of our doctrine : which euidently hath had more power to draw from them, then they
had retentiue force to withhold from vs . The nations that
were conuerted from you, ſtand to vs : the Romane Church
loſeth ground euery day, bleſſed be the Name of God. And
did not our lenitie toward you concurre with your crueltie
toward vs,you would ſhortly euen by the power and efficacie of the word preached , be confounded and brought to
nothing. It would throw downe your ſtrong holds, and de-
moliſh your *Babyloniſh* tower to the ground.This is no note
of the preſent Romiſh Church, *They are fooliſh Paſtors, of no* Zach.11.15.
value.

　　66　*Holineſſe of life of the Authors and firſt Fathers of our re-* 10.Sanctitas
ligion. Here againe is a miſerable and baſe begging of the vitæ.
matter in queſtion. It is very true that *holineſſe of life* in them
that are the preachers of pietie , auaileth much to perſwade,
though as wicked a Prophet as *Balaam* may tell and foretell
a truth.Yet we grant that the fathers and founders of all true
religion vnder God were holy and good men, (though Cardinall *Bellarmine* doubteth of *Salomon* a pen-man of diuine Bellar.
Scripture) as the Patriarchs, the Prophets, the Apoſtles and
their ſchollers. But we ſay, they are none of yours,but ours,
and we proue it.*If you be my ſheepe,you will heare my voice,*ſaith Ioh.10.3.
our Sauiour. If you will be Chriſts diſciples, the Patriarchs,
Prophets and Apoſtles ſucceſſors, you muſt hold their doctrine,you muſt imitate their manners: you came from them,
we confeſſe, but you are not, neither euer were of them: for 1.Ioh.2.19.
if you had,you would haue abidden with them.

　　67　Your heads haue bin brainleſſe and brainſicke Popes,
lecherous and laſciuious Cardinals , Canoniſts ignorant of
Gods truth, Schoolmen that defiled the truth of God with
philoſophicall and ſubtill diſtinctions ; you haue nothing to
do with the doctrine contained in good Fathers bookes,and
expreſſed in their liues. But if I ſhould,or had leiſure to diſcouer that in this ſhort diſcourſe,which is extant in *Platina,*
　　　　　　　　　　　　　　　　　　　　　　　　　　in

in Benno, in Guicciardine, yea in all your owne hiſtories of the liues of your Popes and Cardinals, it would cleare this note from the Church of Rome eaſily.

68 But *Cardinall Bellarmine* ſoone giueth this the ſlip, and would faine compare the common people of their Church with ours, from the teachers to the hearers. Of their owne he ſaith, *Sunt equidem in Ecclesiâ Catholicâ plurimi mali, ſed ex hæreticis nullus bonus:* There are truly in the Catholike Church verie many that are naught; which is very true; but amongſt the heretiques (as he calleth vs) not one good; which is very falſe. To proue this he alledgeth a few inuectiue ſpeeches of ſome of our Preachers againſt the ſinnes and ſinners of their owne times. The ſame from him with ſome more large am-
Muri ciuit.   plification and impudency hath a yonger Ieſuite, in his rub-
ſanct. fund. 8.   biſh amongſt his pretēded precious ſtones, that their Church hath *innumerabiles bonos & multos illuſtres Sanctos,* innumera-ble good & many famous Saints; ours *malos ſine numero, nullum Sanctum habet,* wicked ones without number, but not one Saint.

69 Verily we cannot excuſe our ſelues, we muſt ingenu-ouſly confeſſe, that we are not as we ſhould be, our conuer-ſation anſwereth not our religion, as it ought, and as we moſt heartily deſire. *Many profeſſe they know God, but by works de-*
Tit.1.16.   *nie him, and are abhominable and diſobedient, and to euery good worke reprobate.* So were ſome of Gods people in the wilder-neſſe, ſuch were ſome in the Apoſtles times, and ſuch haue bene, are, and will be to the end of the world. Whereſoeuer the Church enioyeth peace, there ſinne wil abound; becauſe all are not choſen that are called, many liue with vs, that are not of vs.

70 It is no wonder to ſee ſome make Chriſtian libertie a
1.Pet.2.1.   cloake of their maliciouſneſſe. But what of this? are our people worſe then theirs? Reade the Preachers in the time of moſt barbarous darkneſſe, when the world was ſo blind they could hardly ſee ſinne to be ſin, were it neuer ſo groſſe and palpable. If our Preachers haue diſcouered a line full of

ours,

ours, they a leafe full of theirs: ours in a word, or a ſhort paſſage; they in whole treatiſes, ſermons bookes, yet extant to
the eye and view of all the liuing. In this caſe you cannot
blame vs, but you ſhame your ſelues. As for Pagans, Iewes,
Turks, and other heretiques, what haue we to do with them,
that are not of the Church?

71 *The glory of miracles.* Is this a note of the Church now,
which many of the ancient Fathers counted none in their
times? *Signes are not for beleeuers, but for vnbeleeuers.* If the Romaniſts aske now for ſignes to proue the Goſpell reuealed
and confirmed by miracles and wonders abundantly in the
prime of the Church, they ſhew themſelues infidels, and not
Chriſtians. The time was when they were markes, as the Author of the imperfect work ſaith, but in his time (and he was
ancient) it was not onely no marke, but a ſigne of the contrarie. And *Chryſoſtome* is of the ſame minde vpon *Iohn*, and accounteth it a temptation to aske a ſigne, & thoſe but block-
heads in compariſon, that were led by them: for *Qui craſſiori
erant ingenio ſignis trahebantur; acutiori verò Prophetis & doctrinâ:* They that were of groſſe capacity were drawne by miracles; thoſe of ſharper iudgement, by the Prophets and doctrine: and a little after, he maketh it a plaine ſigne of infidelity to aske ſignes: *Si fidelis es, vt oportet, ſi Chriſtum diligis vt
diligendus eſt, non indiges ſignis, ſigna enim incredulis dantur:* If
thou be faithfull as thou ſhouldſt, if thou loue Chriſt as he is
to be beloued, thou needeſt no ſigne, for ſignes are giuen to
vnbeleeuers. And *Auguſtine* ſaith, *Poſſem quidem dicere neceſſaria fuiſſe (miracula) priuſquam crederet mundus, ad hoc vt
crederet mundus. Quiſquis adhuc prodigia, vt credat, inquirit,
magnum eſt ipſe prodigium, qui mundo credente, non credit.* I
may well affirme, that miracles were neceſſarie before the
world beleeued, to the end the world might beleeue.
Who ſo requireth wonders that he may beleeue, himſelfe
is a monſter, who whiles the world beleeueth, beleeueth
not.

72 Of the ſame minde is *Theophylact* and other Fathers: If
an *Angell from heauen ſhould bring vs another Goſpell, then that*
which

Gloria mira-
culorum. 11.
1. Cor. 14.

In Mathæum
hom. 49.

Homil. 23.

”
”
”
”
”
De ciuit. Dei
li. 22. c 8.
”
”
”
”
”

Theophil,

which we haue receiued out of the holy Scriptures ; we would not aske him a signe, but we would not beleeue him if he wrought mira-

2.Pet.1.19. *cles.* For we haue a sure Word, not onely of the Prophets, which the Iewes had, but of the Apostles also, *To which we shall do well to giue heed, as vnto a light shining in a darke place,* (euen in the midst of Popery) *vntill the day dawne, and the day-*

Staplet. im-
pudenter ob- *starre appeare in our hearts.* What need *Luther,* or *Caluin,* or
ijcit in prom- any other to worke miracles for this doctrine, that hath bene
tuario mor. confirmed by so many signes, done by our Sauiour and his
Dom.24.post Apostles? If we came with a Law that was neuer written be-
Pent. num.4. fore, as *Moses* did, and to deliuer a captiued people out of a tyrants hands, to conuey them into the wildernes, and there leade them fortie yeares, and then bring them into a promised Land, possessed by others : miracles were necessarie to approue our calling, and perswade the people, as they were

Heb.7.12. vnto *Moses.* Or if we were to translate the Law and Priest-hood, which God himselfe hath established, and to abrogate all the ceremonies which had diuine *authoritie,* as Christ did, then also were miracles as necessarie for Christ as for *Moses.* Or if we were to withdraw the Gentiles from their so long continued idolatrie, miracles might be of as good vse as they were to the Apostles. But now there is no such thing. We alter nothing of that God hath prescribed ; we stand to that doctrine that is an vndoubted truth, we do but reduce to the considerations of the old euidence, out of which we pleade our cause, and by which we desire to be tried, and so wil stand or fall to our Lord *Paramount,* who hath deliuered it, as his owne Word, and Scepter of his kingdome.

73 We derogate indeed from the doctrines and traditions of men, from rites and ceremonies, wherwith the Spouse of Christ hath bene disfigured, and defiled. We haue remoued images out of Churches, disauowed absurd and monstrous opinions, against nature, against reason, against Scripture. Doth this require miracles? Proue any article of our Religion not taught in the booke of God, either by direct letter, or such necessary and ineuitable deduction, that will make a demonstration, you shall neede to aske no miracle to

make

make good your confutation, we our selues will condemne
our owne opinion. Howbeit this presumption (without all
proofe) that theirs is the oldest Church, ours is the new; that
all the Fathers are theirs, and we haue none but *Luther*, and
Caluin, and a few *Nouellants*, makes our aduersaries so blind,
that they cannot see truth; so giddie that they *cannot discerne
the things of God.*

74 Moreouer it is easily proued, that miracles haue bene
wrought by infidels and heretiques, (whatsoeuer *Cardinall
Bellarmine* idlely conceiteth to the contrarie) and by those
that haue bene called gods, euen very diuels. *The god of this
world hath blinded many eyes that they beleeue lyes, because they
will not obey the truth.* And as it hath bene foretold that signes
and wonders should be wrought in the time of *Anti-christ*,
whereby the very elect might be peruerted, if it were possible; plaine & euident enough to delude and condemne those
that were seduced by them. For the miracles of the primitiue
Church, we admire & reuerence them, & giue God the glory.
Those were ours, not yours, for we haue their doctrine, & not
you. But for your *Legends & festiuals, & fained stories* of Monks
and Friers, and such like, the Church of Christ hath learned by
sufficient experience not to trust them. *Surius*, and *Lipomanus*,
and *Antoninus*, are too yong to cozen vs with their fables ;
though some of them with sin and shame enough haue presumed to steale into the Romane new reformed *Breuiarie*.

75 That which is obiected by *Cardinall Bellarmine* to *Luther* & *Caluine*, of their counterfeiting of miracles, is refuted
by two ineuitable arguments. The one, that they both, with
all our teachers, hold miracles vnnecessarie, and therefore
need counterfeit none. And the other, that there is not one
that testifieth any such thing of them, but runnagats, apostates, and their mortall & damnable enemies, a sufficient exception in Law against their testimonies. That of *Caluine*,
changing the name, the place, and a few immateriall circumstances, is registred to haue bene done by the Dominick Friers, to deceiue the *Franciscans* about the pure conception of
the virgine *Marie*, before *Caluine* was borne, by *Bernardinus*
                                                                de

Marginal notes:
Aug de ciuit. Dei.lib. 10. c. 16. & l.21.c.6
2.Cor.4.4.
2.Thes.2.11.
Bolsac.
Prateolus.

In ferm.de ex-
cell.glor.virg.
Mariæ, de có-
cep.lect.5.&6

de Busto, where he hath the same counterfeit tricke, *totidem verbis,* in the same words, with the wiues railing, & scolding, and all, *Sicq̃, gloriosa Virgo puritatem & integritatem suam, hoc insigni miraculo cum maxima aduersariorum confusione demonstra-uit:* and so the glorious Virgin, by this notable miracle, made manifest her puritie and integritie, to the great confusion of our aduersaries. This was done, not by *Caluin,* but by *Dominicke* Friers; not for his profession, but theirs. The miracle was in the discouery rather then in the fact: it shameth the Papists, but not vs, sauing that we are ashamed on their behalfe, when we see them so shamelesse, as to impute that to others,

Gen.39.20.

which they do themselues. So was *Ioseph* made the delinquent, when the queane his mistris was onely in the fault.

76 As for the Papists miracles in our time, either they are pretended to be done *apud Antipodas,* in the furthest part of the world, (and trauellers may lie by authoritie) or they are supposed to be miracles when they are none, as most of *Philip Nereus* his miracles. He was sent for, or came to one desperatly sicke, prayed for him, and he recouered; so haue I done, I thanke God, to an hundred, and yet no miracle neither. Or they are onely *teste seipso,* vpon their owne word, which we are not bound to beleeue, except we had more proofe of their honestie. Or they cosen some credulous scholer, such as *Iustus Lipsius* was of late, better learned in humanitie, then deeply studied in Diuinitie, (and the greatest Clerks be not euer the wisest men:) or such as *Gregory* or *Beda* were, who being honest, and withall credulous and trusting others, swallowed many a gudgeon, as in effect *Melchior*

Loc. commū.
l.11.c.6.p.337

Canus a learned Bishop on your part censureth.

77 Yea, Sir *Thomas Moore* (yours so sound at heart, that he lost his head for his great Maister, against his best Maister *Christ*) doth not onely note, that Saint *Augustine* was deceiued by ouer much credulitie in this case, but also gathereth good obseruations, and giueth good aduertisements against the like impostures, in an Epistle written to *Ruthelus,* set before *Lucians* Dialogues: *Hunc sanè fructū afferet iste dialogus, vt neque*

neque magicis habeamus præstigijs fidem, & superstitione careamus,
quæ passim sub religionis specie obrepit: tum vitam vt agamus mi-
nùs anxiam, minùs videlicet expauescentes tristia quæpiam, & su-
perstitiosa mendacia: quæ plerumq; tanta cum fide & authoritate
narrantur (vt beatissimo etiam Pat. Augustino viro grauiss. hostiq;
mendaciorum acerrimo, nescio quisnam veterator persuaserit, vt
fabulam illam de duobus Spurinis, altero in vitam redeunte, altero
decedente, tanquam rem suo ipsius tempore gestam pro verâ narra-
ret, quam Lucianus in hoc Dialogo mutatis tantùm nominibus, tot
annis antequam Augustinus nasceretur, irrisit. This profit hath „
that Dialogue, that we neither credit magicall impostures, „
nor giue way to superstitions, that so far spread themselues „
vnder the shape of religion; but may liue lesse anxious, to „
wit, lesse fearing dolefull and superstitious lies, which for the „
most part are related with such credit and authoritie (that I „
know not by what cosener, that blessed Father *Augustine*, an „
austere and bitter enemy against lies, could be inticed to be- „
leeue that fable of the two men, the ones reuiuing, and the „
others dying, and to report that for a truth, as a thing done „
in his owne time, which *Lucian* in his Dialogues, the name „
onely changed, so many yeares before derided. Which sen- „
tence though it be since libd out of Saint *Augustines* name
in a new impression, yet notwithstanding it hath left a deepe
impression both of Sir *Thomas Moores* iudgement, and of
the Papists dangerous imposture, in falsifying their fathers
and friends writings, who might leade them into the way of
truth.

78 Finally, many pretended miracles are either such as
any Iugler can do, with their *deceptio visus*, blearing the eyes
of their beholders; or such as are done by the power of Satan, and such as Antichrist is prophecied he should do at his
coming.

79 These Doctor *Stapleton* calleth *potiùs miranda quàm* Prompt.mor. Dom.24.pest Pentecost.n.4 Aug.lib.83. quæst.
miracula, rather maruels then miracles: and farther proueth
out of Saint *Augustine*, whose words he alledgeth at large,
that *vera miracula non solùm Antichristus ipse eiusq; proximi*
præcursores, sed quilibet hæretici, non secùs quam magi, Deo per-

H *mittente*

,, *mittente operari poterunt :* not onely Antichrift himfelfe, and
,, his immediate forerunners, but euery hereticke, no other-
,, wife then magicians (God giuing permiffion) may worke
,, true miracles : As our Priefts and Iefuites in *England,* where
they need, and accordingly make, miracles of al forts, to perfwade thofe abfurdities, wherewith they fafcinate and be-
witch fimple and ignorant foules. What miracles do they
that we heare of?They caft out diuels forfooth;but that may
be by the confent or confort with diuels, as witches and coniurers do. This,you will fay,was falfly obie&ed to our Saui-

Matth.12.24. our: fo it may be to thefe. No,here is great oddes. Our Sauiour Chrift did caft diuels by his word and commandement
out of men that were knowne of all the countrey to be pof-

Sir Geo.Pec- feffed : thefe perfwade men and women that they be poffef-
hams houfe. fed, and make them beleeue that they are difpoffeffed, and
D.Harfnet. do it with holy water, abufing of Scripture, croffes and ex-
orcifme,which is in plaine Englifh coniuration. Chrift did it
openly in faire day light,before multitudes, & fome of them
his enemies : the Priefts do it clofely in chambers, and by
night, without any witneffe but domefticals. Chrift fometimes in his abfence from the partie; the Priefts are prefent
with all their trinkets. Chrift did many other miracles befides, as curing ficke, cleanfing leapers, halt, blind, lame,
none came amiffe vnto him; he raifed the dead in the bed,in
the coffin, in the graue : thefe cannot cure a halting dog, or
a lame horfe; they can do nothing,but that onely about diuels, and therefore are certainly impoftors,if they boaft of
this for a miracle.

79　I conclude with one of their owne, not Poets, but
Preachers,who certainly faw that this was no mark to know
the Church by, though he were in their Church as bright as

Stella in Lucā a ftarre: *Vt mundus Apoftolis adhiberet fidem, miracula opera-*
9.v.2. p.252. *bantur,&c. That the world might giue credit to the Apoftles,*
they wrought miracles, which now to do were fuperfluous, becaufe
now we beleeue thofe things which Chrift preached: and if any fuch
miracles fhould be now done, they would rather weaken the faith.
Like as if a man had his caufe fufficiently proued in iudgement,yet
　　　　　　　　　　　　　　　　　　　　　　　　　　　he

he would proue it againe,and make his cause doubtfull, as if it wan-
ted proofe. So in this case if now we should proue our faith by mira-
cles,it were as much as to call it into question, and so might depriue
it of her dignitie, and that were dangerous. This is left by the
Spanish *Index Expurgatorius* vncorrected , therefore no
fault.

80   *Lumen Propheticum,* the light of prophecie. Is this a
proper note of your Church?Nothing lesse. For neither was
the gift of prophesie either promised before Chrifts coming,
or performed to the Church as a perpetuall gift , more then
the gifts of healing,tongues,and such like: nor Prophets giuen for perpetuall vse more then Euangelifts and Apoftles.
There were in the primitiue Church,we grant, but we deny
that to be your Church. But our question now is that which
was not then.At that time as the prophesies continued,there
was but one Chriftian Church difperfed into diuers nations,
but faft bound vp in one vnitie of faith , that all men might
fee and know the Church of Chrift by their confent in one
truth according to the Scriptures , and fo might be knowne
without prophecying,and therefore this was not a neceffary
note then; for there were diuers Churches planted by the A-
poftles that had no Prophets , and yet were true Churches;
as alfo the Church of the Iewes was without Prophets from
Malachi to Chrift, about three hundred yeares, and yet was
the onely true Church of God.

81   But the question prefent is,where is the true Church
now?You fay with you,you will proue it by the *light of pro-*
phesie. Shew vs your Prophets,who are they ? what foretell
they? that we may heare and beleeue them . You haue none
that you dare auouch,except the wench that cofened *Ludo-*
uicus de Granada, and prophefied of the Spanifh *Armada* in
1588. Then why fhould this be counted your badge , when
it is not fo much as pinned to your fleeue? Cardinall *Bellar-*
mine faith,we haue no Prophets : we confeffe that none profeffe themfelues to be fuch; neither haue they any fuch ; and
therefore we are both deliuered from the labour of proofe
for this point.Only this I adde,that although God be onely

H 2   able

12.Lumen
Propheticum.

able of himselfe to foretell contingents, and things to come,
yet haue diuels, and Gentiles, and hereticks, at sundrie times
prophesied by the permission of God. Neither did *Balaam*
foretell onely what should be truly performed in Christ, or
the time of Christianitie, but also concerning the Israelites
and the Moabites; and yet he proued not himselfe the true
Church wherin he liued. The *Sybils* among the heathen prophecied not onely of Christ, as *Cardinall Bellarmine* pretendeth, but of many other things which fell out among the
heathen themselues, as by historie appeareth. And God pro-
uideth by his Law, that if a Prophet shall foretell a thing to
come, & it come to passe, yet the Lord may send it to tempt
or trie, whether men will stand to the truth of God. Such
prophecies and Prophets there may be sufficient to deceiue,
and that by Gods permission, and yet they neither in nor of
the truth and true Church. Therefore *nota quòd hæc nota ni-*
hil valet, note that this note is worth nothing. Which experience in all ages, and in all places hath confirmed, and is
manifest by many idolatrous people in both the Indies at
this day.

Confessio ad-
uersariorū. 13.   82 *Confessio aduersariorum*, Confession of aduersaries. A
man would not thinke, that a Cardinall Iesuite, so ancient a
graue Doctor should be so boyish, so childish, so babish, as
to please himselfe with such bables. He is certainly as mad,
as *Thrasilaus*, that thought al the ships with their lading, that
came within the Pireum at Athens, were his, & would require
accounts of the Factors and Mariners as if all had bene his
owne. What else doth *Bellarmine*? *Plinius Secundus* and o-
ther infidels commended the Christians in the primitiue
Church: *Iosephus* and other *Iewes* admired Christ as a good
man, & the *Messiah*. *Mahomet* and his Turkes acknowledge,
that Christians may be saued, and that Christ was a great Prophet. *Totilas* an *Arian* king had *Saint Benedict* in great honour and admiration; therefore the moderne Church is
the true Church. *Bellarmine* like mad *Thrasilaus* challengeth all these commendations as belonging to himselfe.
Our question is of the present Church of Rome? Prouo
                                                        Rome

Rome to be as these commended Christians were, and we will ioyne with it, as with an excellent member of Christs Catholike Church, as then it was.

83 All that professe Christ, and are called by the name of Christians, may claime these praises as well as the Romanes, and therefore this note belongeth not to them now, howsoeuer the ancient Church deserued these and greater commendations. But as the case standeth, the Papists are detested euen of Iewes and Turks for their most grosse and heathenish idolatrie. The Turkes hate those Christians most that worship images, and those are the Romanists. A Iew being asked why he would not embrace the Christian religion, it being so pregnantly proued by the conference of the old and new Testament; answered, that there were three impediments which did withhold him. The first was, that Christians worshipped images, and maintained it, against the expresse commandement of almightie God; *We should not fall downe before them nor worship them.* The second, that *Christians* professedly did eate that God whom they did worship. The third, that *Christians* were mercilesse to the poore. If Cardinall *Bellarmine* wil haue a Iewes testimony, let him take this, and apply it where it best deserueth, he will haue little cause to boast of Turkes or Iewes. If other infidels were neare them, they would detest them, or at least enuie them, that they are greater idolaters then themselues. As an Indian asking, whither the Spaniards went when they died? It was answered to heauen; Then will I neuer come there, quoth he, where Spaniards are. So good are Romane Catholiques in infidels eyes.

84 Those whom Cardinall *Bellarmine* calleth heretiques, *Luther*, *Caluine*, haue written reuerendly of some things in the Popish Church: so the Church of Rome hath the commendation of her aduersaries. This he holdeth a testimonie *omni exceptione maius*, beyond and aboue all exception, *vel inimicis iudicibus*, euen enemies being iudges. If this be an argument of so great force, why doth Cardinall *Bellarmine* vse so often *domestica testimonia*, homely and from home brought

H 3   arguments,

arguments, which be of no force? *Cocleus, Prateolus, Bol-*
facke, and such like runnagates and apoflates, *qui femper funt*
,, *perfequutores fui ordinis*, who are euer perfecutors of that re-
,, ligion from whence they are fallen, are his authors, for himfelfe againft vs, which he and his fellowes fet before decei-

Occidit mi-
feres crambe
repetita ma-
giftros.

ued foules, not onely like *Crambe bis cocta,* but *millies recocta,*
not onely like coleworts twife fodden, but a thoufand times
boyled to mafh, anfwered and anfwered againe, and difpro-
ued moft pregnantly. But that hellifh malice can be fatisfied
with nothing. In this, if any of ours be contented to approue
that in your Synagogue, which anfwereth the feruice of the
temple in Ierufalem, and to picke no more quarrels then may
iuftly be conuinced againft your Church, it is our modefty
and charitie.

85 If your hearts be fo big, and your ftomacks fo great,
that you will commend nothing in vs, or that ours is, we are
fatisfied, contented and paid with this : He is commended

Rom.14.4.
Marke 5.7.

whom the Lord commendeth, and *Euery man ftandeth to his*
owne maifter. If we fay the diuels confeffion, *that Chrift is the*
Sonne of the liuing God, was true without exception, yet we
thereby place him not among the Angels, but hold him a diuell ftill. If you fay we are heretiques, and wine bibbers, glut-
tons, finners, and worfe if worfe may be, as your tongues and
pens are now no flander; fo can you not depriue vs of Gods
grace in this life, nor his glorie in the life to come. Praife
your felues, we enuie it not; difpraife vs, we refpect it not. But

Act.24.14.
Ib.v.1.

know that *by the way which you call herefie we ferue the God of*
our Fathers, beleeuing all things that are written in the Law and
the Prophets, and in the writings of the Apoftles and Euan-

lib.v.5.

gelifts. Though *Ananias the high Prieft, and the Elders, and Ter-*
tullus the oratour, that is the Pope, his Cardinals and fworne
vaffals, and hyred oratours, fay we are *peftilent fellowes, mo-*
uers of fedition among Chriftians, through all the world, and chiefe
maintainers of fects, and polluters of the temple, we are neuer the
worfe, no more then Saint *Paul* was againft whom they were
fpoken. And what derogateth this from vs? Nay, it addes
great comfort to our foules, and affureth Gods bleffing vnto

vs,

vs, as a feale of gracious profeſſion. *Bleſſed are you when men* Mat. 5.11.
reuile you, and ſpeake all euill againſt you, for my Names ſake, for
great is your reward in heauen.

86 We will fet your flanders as a garland on our owne
heads, and account them as our comfort, our ioy and our
crowne. What if you curfe vs? may not we bleſſe you? What
if you raile on vs? may not we fpeake kindly to you? What
if you perfecute vs? may not we pray for you? Giue vs this
as we deferue it, we beg it not as your due. It ſhall ſtand as
a true note that we *are the children of our heauenly Father, who*
is good euen to his enemies : when your railing tongues and Render to
malicious hearts, and virulent fpirits, ſhall proue you the our neigh-
brats of your owne fires, *Belzebub, Lucifer, Sathan the accu-* bour ſeuen
fer of the brethren: much good do it your harts with this note, fold &c. Pſal.
it is yours not ours.   79.12 13.

87 *The vnhappy, or diſmall, or deſperate ends of the oppoſites.* Infœlix exi-
Here Cardinall *Bellarmine* feeketh to fetch his Church from tus oppug-
aboue the Moone, & beyond the Sunne, that neuer reached nantium. 14.
to the clouds : or if it did, yet no farther then to that Princes kingdome that rules in the aire. *Pharaoh* in Egypt perfe- Epheſ. 2.2.
cuted the Iſraelites, the then onely true Church of God, and
he was drowned for his labour. What is this to the Syna- 2. Macha. 9.
gogue of Rome? *Antiochus* breathed out threatnings againſt
the Iewes, and was eaten with wormes. *Pilate* vniuſtly and Mat. 27.18.23
againſt his owne confcience condemned our Sauiour Chriſt
to pleafe the Iewes, and killed himſelfe. The three *Herods,*
Aſcalonita, the Tetrarch, and *Agrippa,* kild the infants, put *Iohn*
Baptiſt to death, and mocked Chriſt, ſlue *Iames* with the
fword, impriſoned *Peter;* and all came to miferable and
ſtrange ends, by the iuſt iudgement of God. *Emperours* perfecuted the Primitiue Church the firſt three hundred yeares,
and died fearefull and vntimely deaths. Old heretiques haue
likewife bene plagued with the immediate hand of God.
What is this to the Romanes, that are not fuch a Church as
that which was then perfecuted? What is it to vs that are
not fuch tyrants or heretiques as thofe were? Befides, many
a good King hath died an vnimely death in warrre; and many

a wicked tyrant hath died quietly in his bed. To build vpon such euents, is but a weake foundation to erect the faith of a Church vpon. But as a man in danger of drowning, layeth hand on any thing he toucheth, though it be but a thorne that runneth into his hand: so Cardinall *Bellarmine* in his desperate cause, when he seeth the ship in the sea of *Rome* splitted and ready to sinke, he raketh any thing, though he sting his conscience, which fasteneth his hand vpon that which cannot helpe, but is sure to hurt his cause.

88 If we looke into the state of the later Romane Church, since it was corrupt and rotten at the heart, we shall find matter enough to proue both many Popes and Cardinals, Emperours and Kings in your religion, wicked and damnable, by the disastrous ends of such as haue persecuted our Church. How many Popes haue had either vnhappie reignes, or fearful ends? The Emperour *Charles* that through heartbreake turned foole, and was shut vp in a Monastery. King *Philip* the second of *Spaine* is storied to be consumed with *Sylla* his consumption of lice, or that Egyptian plague, which made the sorcerers cōfesse, *Digitus Dei est hic*, the hand of God was on him. Queene *Marie* had no great happinesse in her life, nor ioy in her mariage, lesse in her sorowful death, least in the losse of *Calice*, one of the greatest crosses that euer happened the English red Crosse.

Plutarch. in Sylla. Historie of Spaine.

89 We admire the hand of God in these euents, but we make them no mark of our Church. We insult not ouer your fals, but commiserate your blindnesse, that cannot see the hand of God against you in your Spanish *Armado*, whereagainst, God vsed the wind and sea for his weapons of destruction: Nor the peaceable end of that noblest Queene that euer liued, after so many conspiracies; and the miserable deaths of all her enemies that rose against her: Nor the preseruation of his Church against al that the Pope or his maister the diuel can do.

15. Fœlicitas temporalis.

90 *Temporall felicitie.* If euer Cardinall *Bellarmine* slept, or dreamed, or doted, (and God wots, though perhaps he be too busie to sleepe profoundly, yet he dreameth and doteth often)

often) then hath he shewed his carelesse hart and feared conscience, in making *temporall prosperitie a note of the true Church:* Of his it may be, of Chrifts it is not, neither euer was, neither find we any promise that it shall be, as long as it is in this world. Our Sauiour Chrift saith, *My kingdome is not of this world:* himfelfe neuer enioyed in his owne perfon, neuer promifed his followers, any earthly preferments. *I fend you forth as sheepe in the midst of wolues:* what *temporall felicitie* haue fheepe in fuch company? Not to runne ouer hiftories that would aske a volume: from the bloud of *Abel* to the bloud of *Zacharias* the fonne of *Barachias,* what fuch *temporall felicitie* had the Church? From *Noah* to *Abraham,* from *Abraham* to *Moses,* from *Moses* to the *Kings,* from the *Kings* to the King of Kings the Lord *Iefus:* from *Chrift* to *Conftantine,* from *Conftantine* all the ancient Fathers times; from thence vntill this day, could euer the true Church of God fhew the colours of profperitie to draw her fouldiers to their Captaines quarter? When it was confined vnto one family, that one family often oppreffed by famine, oppofed by aduerfaries, in bondage in Egypt, wandring in the wildernefle, girded in with enemies, had pricks in their eyes and thornes in their fides, perfecution of Prophets, murdering of Saints, erecting of idols in the very temple of God, long captiuities, fubiection to infidels in temporall gouernment, prouoked to idolatry with hazard of their liues, depriued of Prophets diuers hundred yeares; reduced to Chrift, and a few Apoftles and Difciples, the head crucified, the members difmayed, the fhepheard fmitten, the fheepe fcattered, beleeuers hated, defpifed, murthered without pitie or mercy. Saint *Paul* to the *Hebrewes* fheweth the ftate of Gods Church vnto his time.

   91   The multitude of Martyrs and Confeffors in the primitiue Church vnder flourifhing Emperours, rich Proconfuls, pompous Prefidents, vnder the *Goths* and *Vandals,* vnder *Arian* heretiques, vnder proud Prelats and tyrannous Popes, can fufficiently confute this note of Cardinall *Bellarmine,* that it neuer belonged to the true Church. Our Sauiour more then once admonifheth his Apoftles, neuer to expect

any

Ioh.18.36.

Mat.10.16.

Mat.23.35.

any such matter; and therefore shewed his calling to be with a powerfull (ἐνεργία πνεύματος) working of the Spirit, that had such followers; and neuer promised them any temporall good, but the contrary: proposing no preheminence, but

Matth. 10. foretelleth subiection; no honour, but contempt; no pleasure, but paine; no laughing, but mourning; no peace, but a sword; all quite contrary to Cardinall *Bellarmine*, nay in opposite contradiction to his learning. If he had but spent a little meditation vpon the 73. Psalme, or had read the 21. of *Iob*, or had but cast his eye to the 12.of *Ieremie*, and withall considered the perplexitie of those beloued men of God in this very question, he would haue paused, and gone into the temple of God, and made better enquiry before he would haue blotted his paper with so vaine a conceit, nay so dangerous, so vntrue, against all experience by sacred or profane stories.

92 Where will this note of your owne Church appeare in the dismall dayes of your imagined Antichrist ? Your selues say, he shall flourish with riches, power, victories, building of *Ierusalem* and temple, no man or earthly force shall

2.Thess.2.8. withstand him, Chrifts coming must onely abolish him : you and yours must be driuen into wildernesse to holes and caues of the earth, must be slaine and turned out of the world. If *temporal felicitie* shall proue the Church, you must lose it, Antichrist must haue it. If he alledge Cardinall *Bellarmine* in that case, what can be answered, but that it was onely one Doctors opinion ? Or would Cardinall *Bellarmine* take the aduantage, and proue his owne proposition true, by turning to his Antichrists prosperitie, and *enioying the pleasures of sinne for the season*, take that for the true Church which most aboundeth with worldly glory, and so by sauing his life lose his soule ? Certainly he must either eate this word (and *temporall felicitie* is a sweet morsell) or else he must be deuoured with the apostasie of the time. Cardinall *Bellarmines* proofe for this note, is onely this, that the victories of the old Testament were famous, of *Abraham, Moses, Iosuah, Gideon, Samuel, Dauid, Hezechiah, Iosiah*, the *Machabees*. Therefore

fore Cardinall *Bellarmines* Church is the true Church. I say not therefore:but becaufe that Church was the true Church, therfore God fhewed his mightie power in the protection & defence thereof,and fent them Sauiours whē they conuerted and turned vnto him : otherwife when his Church finned, he raifed enemies againft them,who ouerthrew them, fpoyled them,tooke their citie,burned their Temple,caried them away captiues,and liued Lords ouer them many yeares.

93   Then belike they were not the true Church when they were in fuch preffure : but they were when they had *temporall felicitie.* But Cardinall *Bellarmine* knoweth well enough,that this is farre from being any certaine note, or fo much as probable, feeing it may fo eafily *adeffe & abeffe fine fubiecti interitu.* The Church may haue it or want it,without preiudice or benefit.If the Church haue it,fhe muft be thankfull; if fhe haue it not, fhe muft be patient : neither hindreth the wicked, neither hurteth Gods children . Let profperitie come to the wicked like the comfortable Sunne , yet it either hardneth them like clay in their malice, or melteth them like the fat of lambes to their confumption. Let aduerfitie befall the righteous, it will either foften them to repentance if they liue,or paffe them vnto glory if they die.Both are like fire to gold or ftubble . *Ignis accedens ad aurum fordem tollit,* accedens ad frænum in cinerem vertit:* Fire applied to gold doth feparate the droffe, applied to ftubble conuerts it to afhes. The gold remaines folid and precious; the afhes by the blaft of Gods iudgement are fcattered from the face of the earth.

94   If the Cardinall fhall obiect Gods promife of earthly bleffings which he hath propofed to his children : or that of our Sauiour to them that *firft feeke the kingdome of God and the righteoufneffe thereof, cætera adijicientur,* other things fhall be caft vpon you; or the like : we anfwer, that the promife of temporal profperitie hath its manifold limitations,and muft be reftrained to a competencie,not enlarged to fuperfluitie: mediocritie of food and raiment, not mountaines of wealth and honour.Saint *Peter* had this promife as well performed, when he faid , *Siluer and gold haue I none,* as euer any Pope

Lumnius ex Auguft. in Pfal.128.

Deut.28.vnto 14. Matth.6.33.

Act.3.6.

that

that hath vſurped his pretended Chaire. The Preacher hath
anſwered the Cardinall ſufficiently in this caſe, that by theſe
outward things no man can *know who is worthy of loue or ha-*
tred. Weale and wo, proſperitie and aduerſitie, health and
ſickneſſe, yea life and death, can make no certaine difference
betweene the good and bad, Gods election and reproba-
tion. In theſe things he ſheweth his mercie, in making *his*
Sunne to ſhine, and his raine to fall vpon the good and bad, the
righteous and vnrighteous. The wicked may liue to fill vp the
meaſure of their iniquitie, the godly may be taken away from
the euill to come; and who is ſufficient to iudge of theſe
things ?

95 Thus hauing eaſily not onely runne ouer, but alſo o-
uerrunne, and ouerturned theſe fifteene notes of Cardinall
Bellarmines Church, which if they were certaine notes of a
true Church, yet they belong not to the Church of Rome:
it remaineth that nothing being oppoſite to this our note of
the *Antiquitie* of that verity which God hath reuealed in the
Scriptures, it muſt needs be granted that this muſt ſtand as
the onely foundation of Chriſtian religion, the ground-
worke of our faith and beleefe, the onely reciprocall and
conuertible note of the true Church. So that of this, and of
this onely we may truly ſay, *Where verity of doctrine gathered*
out of the Scriptures, which is the moſt ancient truth, and ſo is
faithfully preached and rightly beleeued, there and no where elſe is
the true Church. And againe, that you may ſee how the definition agreeth with the thing deſcribed, and maketh it a
certaine note, that admitteth no exception or contradiction,
note this, *That is the true Church where the veritie of doctrine*
gathered out of the Scriptures of God, which is moſt ancient, is
faithfully preached and rightly beleeued. Againſt this neither
the altars of Rome, nor the gates of hell, ſhall neuer be able
to preuaile, *Rumpantur & ilia Codro,* though the Pope and his
Cardinals burſt their hearts to withſtand it.

96 This cannot be verified or iuſtified by any one of *Bel-*
larmines notes, no not of them all, though twiſted in a rope
together. Let them be remembred once more, & that ſhortly.
                              For

For what can the name Catholique more priuiledge the Ro- Catholique.
manifts from Apoftafie, then the name of Ifrael did the Iewes
from their idolatry? All were not Ifrael that were fo called;
there is an Ifraelite according to the flefh, & an Ifrael which
is of God: there is a circumcifion of the flefh, and of the fpi- Rom.2.28.29
rit; an outward in fhew, an inward in proofe. So fay we of
the Romanifts ; they haue bene fometime a good Church,
they afterward bare the face of a Church, but they are finally
declined and fallen from the Church. This if they deny, we
can proue it. Let them adde the truth of doctrine to Catholique, and we wil profeffe our felues to be of the true Catholique Church : otherwife the bare name, which is but the
fhell, we leaue vnto them ; truth of doctrine, which is
the kernell, we referue to our felues. So is Antiquitie Antiquitie.
without veritie, nothing but a blaft of vanitie. Truth of a
dayes birth, muft be preferred before it. That which is now
oldeft to vs, was once new, when it was firft made manifeft,
and new *Ierufalem* fhall furpaffe the old. As Chrifts new
commandement was not preiudiced becaufe it was new, fo
neither muft a renewed truth be condemned when it appeareth. *Veritie* may be fomewhat graced by the grauitie of *Antiquitie,* as a beautifull bride by her comely handmaid: but
nuda veritas, naked truth, and that alone, without all colour
or ornaments, is more acceptable to her fpoufe, moft comfortable to them that attend the bridegroome. *Ueritas temporis filia,* New dayes may produce old truth.

For continuance in neuer fo great length. The diuell may Duratio diu-
claime it better then the Pope, and his lies are more ancient turna,
then the Popes equiuocations : and in this he is furer, that he
hath continued in his owne perfon with all his Angels ; the
Pope by fucceffion and change in himfelfe and his members:
yet the one may continue in his malice in this world, or in
hell fire, as long as the other. Many falfe opinions in doctrine, and errors in life haue continued long in the world,
which maketh them neither commendable to God, nor acceptable to his Saints. But *Verbum Domini manet in æternum,* Efai.40.8.
the word of the Lord endureth for euer; and this is the word
                                                   which

which we preach: whatſoeuer is againſt or beſide this, the longer it hath continued, the worſe it is.

Amplitude or multitude.

What is multitude without the truth of Gods booke? It is but a confuſed army without a Captaine, a very beaſt with many heads, a helliſh diuell with many legions, that will crie *Hoſanna* to the Son of *Dauid*, and, Crucifie him, Crucifie him, in ſixe dayes; yea confeſſe that he is the Sonne of God, and yet aske what they haue to do with him.

Matth.21.9.
Matth.27.23.
Matth.8.29.

Succeſſion of Biſhops.

Is Succeſſion of Biſhops any thing without truth gathered from the Scriptures? By no meanes. For ſo curſed *Chams* progeny might as well deduce their pedigree from *Noah* as *Sem*; the Prieſts of the Iewes from *Aaron*, and the people from their father *Abraham*. And thus they would haue preſcribed againſt our Sauiour, and ſo they did; but with as much validitie as the Romaniſts againſt vs.

Conſpiracie in doctrine.

Will they ſtand vpon Conſpiracie without truth of doctrine? This is like *Ephraim* and *Manaſſes* againſt *Iuda*, *Herod* and *Pilate* againſt Chriſt. Their contradictions both paſt among Schoolmen, and preſent in ſundry points, are infinite; if they agree, it is but as *Simeon* and *Leui*, brothers in euill. Many heretickes haue better agreed each with other, then themſelues; and the moſt of their doctrine is but conſpiracie againſt Chriſt in matter of faith, or againſt Princes in matter of obedience.

Vnion of members.

Shal Vnion of members iuſtifie the Romane Church without Gods truth? Both Iewes and Gentiles fretted and gathered themſelues together againſt the Lord and againſt his Chriſt. This may well be ioyned with the former. Such as *the man is, ſuch is his ſtrength*. Such as their vnitie is in the members, ſuch is their conſpiracie in doctrine: wicked men, falſe doctrine.

Iudg.8.21.

Sanctitie of doctrine.

Holineſſe euen in precepts as well as life, wil make a great and a good ſhew where it is, and muſt be holden worthy of all eſtimation. This is very true, but yet not without truth in the myſteries of Chriſtianitie. Not to ſpeake of many Philoſophers morall precepts conducing to vertuous holineſſe: The Scribes and Phariſes ſate in *Moſes* chaire, and bade men

do

do that which was holy and good; yet were they our Sauiour Chrifts moſt implacable enemies; and their righteouſnes was ſuch, that if ours exceed not theirs, we *ſhall neuer enter into the kingdome of God.* But to ſay as we ſhould, *Sanctitie and truth of doctrine* is all one, which either *Bellarmine* muſt diſtinguiſh, or elſe he concludeth for vs, that the truth of doctrine which is oldeſt, is a note of the Church.

The *Efficacie of Doctrine* may ſeeme exceeding prepotent in this caſe; but this is nothing without the *truth of doctrine.* For both heathen Orators haue bene powerful to perſwade, and Antichriſts doctrine ſhal leade men powerfully through hypocriſie to beleeue lies, when Chriſts doctrine may harden many children of vnbeleefe, and become the power of God vnto their condemnation. Some may be pricked at their hearts, when others may grind their teeth at the ſame Sermon. Some may ſay, God is in them of a truth; others may ſay, the Preachers are full of new wine. At a word, we haue perſwaded more from their falſhoods, then euer they induced to Gods truth. *Efficacie of doctrine.*

What is more acceptable vnto God from his faithfull ſeruants, then holineſſe of life, without which *no man ſhall euer ſee God?* This may moue much, if it be ioyned with Gods truth: it is otherwiſe but hypocriſie and blind deuotion. If they take holineſſe for auſteritie of life, many Turks and Infidels, and idolaters haue gone before them. If they meane an honeſt, Chriſtian, and charitable cariage in the courſe of godlineſſe, we dare compare with them, and may be iuſtly ſaid and proued to go farre before them. *Holineſſe of life. Heb.12.14.*

The working of miracles may breed admiration, yea aſtoniſhment, and from the ſimple may wreſt a beleefe; but many ſhall caſt out diuels and worke miracles, to whom Chriſt ſhall ſay, *Depart from me, I know you not.* And *Iannes* and *Iambres* may reſiſt *Moſes*, and yet be but iugglers or ſorcerers, far from true worſhippers of God. The Romaniſts haue none now but counterfeit; we haue had many wrought by the mightie power of God, in the often and wonderfull deliuerance of his Church and Saints from the tyrannie of the *The glorie of miracles. Matth.7.22.*

Ro-

Romane Antichriſt.

Light of pro-
pheſie.
Glorious and bright hath bene the light of propheſie in Gods Church; yet an old Prophet hath deceiued a yong Prophet, when he left the charge of God, and heaikned vnto him. Their Prophets propheſie lies in the name of the Lord, we are commanded to auoid them.

Confeſſion of
Aduerſaries.
Let not onely your aduerſaries approoue you in ſome things, but your friends alſo applaud you in all things; and either in charitie the one, or in flattery the other, ſpeake better then you deſerue. How doth this acquit you from the errors you hold and maintaine againſt the truth of Gods Scriptures?

The vnhappie
end of ſome
oppoſites.
If you ſpeake of the old Romane Church and the then perſecuting tyrants, you ſay ſomewhat that may moue: but Infidels made the ſame obiection to Chriſtians. But if you ſpeake of later times, I would you durſt compare. Suppoſe that ſome of your oppoſites haue had vncouth ends, they were puniſhed for their ſinnes, it iuſtifieth not your diſobedience. A *Ioſiah* may die in the field, as well as an *Ahab*; the one puniſhed with temporall, the other with eternall death: and *Ionathan, Dauids* ſworne friend, may die with *Saul, Dauids* forſworne enemy. But turne your eyes to your Popes, obſerue Gods iudgements vpon them, we need no worſe examples to ſtop your foule mouthes.

Fœlicitas
temporalis.
If all the twiſts of Cardinall *Bellarmines* fifteene fold cable rope be diſſolued into this, I may iuſtly ſay, or at leaſt hope, that this will neuer preſerue the Romane ſhip from the reuenging hand of God. *Diues* had more aduantage againſt *Lazarus*, the perſecuting Emperours againſt the perſecuted Biſhops and Chriſtians, then the Cardinals Church hath againſt vs. And therefore I conclude, that the truth of God reuealed in the Scriptures, will ſtand alone without all theſe; but all theſe can neuer hold out without that truth.

CHAP.

CHAP. V.

All aforesaid notwithstanding, we will not so confine Antiquitie in triall of veritie to that one euidence which is the Scriptures onely, but for all mens more abundant satisfaction, we will enlarge the bounds of Antiquitie to ancient Councels, Fathers, and Histories, which are the largest borders of probable Antiquitie.

T is ill putting a sword into a mad mans hand, or to yeeld any so much as seeming aduantage vnto a boysterous & vntractable aduersarie. If we hold our owne, as soone may a dwarfe wrest *Hercules* club out of his hand or fist, as our Romanists recouer the truth out of our possession. For *veritas*, truth, is not only *magna* great, as *Diana* of the *Ephesians* was vnworthily styled and proclaimed, but *& praualet*, it preuaileth too: which is the end of all our expectations, and the summe and rest of all our desires. Now the chiefe hand that holds it, the strongest locke that secures it, the best munition that defends it, is the written word and Scriptures of God: and that is ours by *Bellarmines* inuincible argument, *Inimicis iudicibus*, our enemies being iudges, as hereafter shall more euidently appeare. It may Infra.cap.6. be perhaps imputed vnto me as an vndiscreete aduenture, that may giue aduantage to the Papists, to yeeld any thing besides Scriptures, for the triall of our Religion, which we haue receiued from the pen-men of Gods holy Spirit: yet notwithstanding, for our aduersaries more full satisfaction, I will be contented to enlarge the bounds of *Antiquitie*, and yeeld them *ex superabundanti*, of our curtesie, & aboue that we need, or they make good vse of, besides the Scriptures (with reseruation of their supereminent and superexcellent authoritie) the *Councels*, the *Fathers*, and the *Histories of the Church*, for the due & true triall of *Christian veritie*, not as theirs, but as indifferent witnesses for both.

2 For although that one *Antiquitie* of the Scriptures, be

euery way in it selfe sufficient to decide & determine al matters in Religion, to demonstrate the Church, to assure vs of
the truth, and to guide vs vnto euerlasting life; as one saith,
Si quæritur quæ sit Dei voluntas, habes Dei præcepta quæ per
Mosen Dei voluntate sunt vulgata; habes Dei filium, qui Patris
voluntatem sciens, quæ erant abscondita, reserauit, & quæ obum-
brabantur in lucem transfudit. If it be demanded what is the
" will of God, thou hast the commandemēts of God, which by
" *Moses* according to Gods appointmēt were published. Thou
" hast the Sonne of God, who knowing the will of his Father,
" hath vnlocked what before was hid, and hath brought to
" light what before was shadowed. And then what need we
" more to know then the will of God, reuealed in the old and
new Testament? And what need we do more then the will of
God so reuealed? Yet as those that professe themselues Maisters of defence, will not for their credite refuse to trie their
skill at any weapon, so we are content to satisfie our aduersaries thus farre, that if they will take vp any of those weapons, we will either by *fine* force-take them out of their
hands; or themselues for feare, and with shame shall like
cowards cast them downe, and like obstinate and malicious
men runne to fire and sword, darts and mortall things, the
most potent weapons that euer they vsed, for the support
of the walls of their tottering Babel, or the defence of
that whore that sitteth on the seuen hils; or we will be
contented to yeeld them the day, and be seruants to their
Maister.

3 I know not what other euidence they can so much as
pretend except *Traditions*, which *Socolouius* will, shall *eandem*
vim penitus habere ad fidem Christianam faciendā quam Scriptu-
ra, haue the same force with the Scriptures to beget a
Christian faith. But how vaine those *traditions* are, which he
valueth at so high a price, the following discourse shall a-
bundantly proue, and so, as they shall haue little cause to
vaunt of them, or trust to them. Yet he, aboue and beyond all
others (not *ex professo*, but by the way perhaps or in a flourish
or bragge,) addeth more by foure vnto these fiue, which I
find.

Fortunatus in
orat. Domi-
nicam.

Prou. 26. 18.

Campion
hath thē not.
Socolouius
partit. Eccles.
pag. 758.

Infra cap. 10.

Idem ibid. p.
156. and 757.

find not in any other so much as intimated, much lesse vrged as *Reuelation*, which himselfe counteth perillous, & so do we Popes decrees, schoolmen, both Diuines & Canonists, which we haue cause to like worse or as ill, and finally the Rabbins whom neither approue, but the histories are left out. Howbeit indeed we vtterly except against these latter, as either vaine or partiall, or such as neither partie may well credit. The rest which I haue before named, are such as our aduersaries seeme to vrge against vs with great vehemencie, and we refuse not vpon equall conditions. Now we will trie who hath title to them, who haue them, who make most account of them, who least abuse them, best employ them, with such like occurrents and circumstances, as the cause shall require.

4 The Romanists neither do nor can denie, but that we haue the Scriptures, for they cal vs for this cause *Scripturarij,* Prateolus.alij, *Scripturemen.* But they take such exceptions against our possession, that by their good wils they would haue them do vs on benefite at all. For first they say we haue got them surreptitiously, & haue cosened the Romane Church of them. Secondly, that when we stole them we left the best behind; we got the shels, they the kernels; we the barke, they the body, we the roote, they the sap, we the letter they the Spirit, we the sentence, they the sence, we the *bare Scriptures,* they D. Kellison the meaning and vnderstanding of them; this in effect saith his suruey. D. *Kellison.* And another somwhat fresher then he saith: *Ecclesia* l.1,c.2. *fcripturā,hæreditario iure possidet. The Church possesseth the Scriptures by right of inheritance, not onely the shell of the dead letter, but the kernell of the liuely meaning.* All this we grant if he meane the true Church; but taking Catholike as proper and peculiar to the Church of Rome he saith most falsly. *They which glorie of holy writ out of this Church, they boast of the shell without the kernell, and brag of their robberie.* So confident are these Romanists that the Scriptures are no bodies but theirs and their heires by fee tayle.

5 Vpon the former they ground (though we neuer granted it, and they shamefully begge it) that we haue no

title to the Scriptures forſooth, but what we haue from the Romane Church; that they are by right theirs, and none but theirs; they had the credite of the keeping of them. Yet our Doctor grāteth this vnto vs as a courteſie, that we know the Scriptures to be Scripture, yet by no meanes Idem. but only by the Romane Church. *Let vs ſuppoſe*, quoth he, *that they beleeue that the old and new Teſtament are holy Scripture becauſe the Romane Church ſaith ſo.* Neuer ſuppoſe it, for my part I neuer thought it. No? ſaith the Doctor, *Catholiques* (by which he meanes *Catholique Romanes*, (as after in the ſame ſection) *haue had the Scriptures in their keeping time out of minde, as all hiſtories, all Councels, all ancient Tradition will witnes for vs. And ſo at leaſt by præſcription, Catholiques are the true and lawfull poſſeſſors of the Scriptures, yea hiſtories and the ancient bookes of the Fathers, &c.* Where you ſee they haue *All Hiſtories*, yea and *Hiſtories* too. And withall obſerue that he hath theſe fiue parts of *Antiquitie*, which I ſpake of, *Scriptures* firſt, *Councels, Fathers, Hiſtories,* and *Traditions.* Againe he ſaith, *Luther and Caluin and all found the Bible in the Catholique Romane Church,* they tooke it without the true owners leaue; therefore they are theeues, and no lawfull poſſeſſors: and therefore haue no right to vſe it, eſpecially *againſt the true owners;* wherein there ſeemeth great reaſon, *Leſt,* ſaith he, *they cut our throats with our owne weapons.* Is not this a faire ſpoake?

6 What if we ſhould tel the Doctor, that we had the Scriptures from the ſame hand that they had receiued them? The old teſtament from the Iewes in the naturall tongue wherein it was written, the new Teſtament from the Greeke Church in the tongue then moſt common in the world, wherein it was alſo indited? If the Iewes kept the Scriptures for their betters (ſo the Romaniſts repute themſelues,) why might not the Papiſts keepe them for vs, and yet we their betters? Or is not the gate as open for vs, to leade vs vnto the Scriptures, as for the Romanes? Or will they haue the Iewes of their Catholique Romane Church? Or will they haue the Greeke and Romane Church all one, who haue liued and do liue in diuiſion vnto this day? The *Grecians* waſhed their altars,

tars, after a Romane Prieſt had ſaid his Maſſe. The Romanes take the Greeke Church to haue bene a very long time ſchiſmaticall, and for ſome hundred yeares hereticall: yet had they the Scriptures in their naturall language, more true and vncorrupt then the Romanes (by their more then a good many tranſlations) had. And therefore we may iuſtly ſay, that as it hath pleaſed God the *Philiſtins* ſhould keepe the Arke of God for a time, without violation, though it was their [1.Sam.5.&6.] ſcourge and plague: ſo it pleaſed him in his prouidence to make the Iewes and Grecians his keepers of the treaſure of holy Scriptures, without corruption, to their ſhame and confuſion, from whom both you and we haue receiued them. If otherwiſe we haue receiued them from you, it was at the laſt and worſt hand, corrupted by your tranſlations, and therefore we are not beholding to you, ſo much as we both vnto them: and it fareth with you from vs, as with them from vs or you, for you are well curried and cudgelled with them by all our writers, as well as they by either of vs.

7 Were it not a fine diſpute of the Iewes and Grecians, to tell the Romanes that they are theeues, *and no lawfull poſ-ſeſſors, and therefore haue no right to vſe* (*the Scriptures*) *eſpeci-ally againſt the true owners?* Chriſtians may not vſe the Law and the Prophets againſt the Iewes, to proue that Ieſus Chriſt is the true *Meſſias* : nor the Weſt Church againſt the Eaſt, to proue that the holy *Ghoſt* proceedeth from the Father and the Sonne. For they had no right to vſe them *againſt the true ow-ners.* Or will they pretend that thoſe were neuer the true owners? They may as well deny that God was the author of them. For they all were written in their tongues, and moſt for their ſakes principally, and accordingly ſent vnto them.

8 Did any of the ancient Fathers reaſon thus with the moſt damnable heretiques that euer were? that they neuer knew Scriptures to be Scriptures, but by the Church? that they vſurped them frō the true owners? that they might not vſe them without their leaue? Nothing leſſe. But when the heretickes alledged Scriptures, the Fathers anſwered by Scriptures, as our Sauiour Chriſt did the diuell, for whom

the Scriptures were neuer written, and to whom they were neuer committed, but are common to all Gods children. According to a right good obseruation of *Iustus Orgelican*, a Saint, as Cardinall *Bellarmine* intitleth him, and an ancient writer, on the *Canticles*, vpon these words : *Sicut turris Dauid collum tuum, mille clipei pendent* : Thy necke is like the tower of *Dauid*, a thousand bucklers hang thereon. *Potest hæc turris Scriptura canonica conuenienter intelligi, quæ per Spiritum sanctum velut turris excelsa extructa est. In hac sanctà Scripturà omnis armatura fortium reperitur, ex qua, vel contra diabolum, vel contra ministros eius fortiter depugnatur. Nam & ipse Dominus, cum in deserto à diabolo tentaretur, ex hac turri arma produxit, cum eum ex prolatis ex Scriptura sacra testimonijs vsque quaque deuicit.* This tower may conueniently be vnderstood the Canonicall Scriptures, which by the holy Ghost is built much like a stately castle, in which is found the whole armory of the valiant, from whence both the diuell or his ministers are couragiously resisted. For euen the Lord himselfe, when he was tempted of the diuell in the desert, brought weapons from this tower, with which testimonies vrged out of the holy Scripture, he foiled him at euery assault.

9   But suppose the Scriptures had bene so yours, as that you could not onely prescribe against all the world, but also hold them so close, that no man had them in his hands but you ; yet could you neither say that they were not written for the common good of all, no more then you can say, that Christs death was not sufficient for all: neither that they were to be kept so close, but that your owne friends should see them and haue them. What if one of yours should lose them, and another should find them? and in perusing of them, should also find, that he stood entituled by them to an inheritance as well as he that lost them? What should hinder, but that the finder might make his best benefit, and pleade them for his owne right, as well as the other that lost them? yea and iustly complaine, that he hath bene too long and vniustly kept from them? *A man that hath writings, whereby another mans title may be cleared, the Iudge may command him to bring them*

Chap. 4. v. 4.

Iust. Orgel in Cant.

Mich. Salon. in 2. 2. q. 70. art. 1. cont. 3. conclus. 1.

them forth. If he hath no commandement, yet charitie will bind him, if he know it, to produce them. This may not be, left *they cut our throats with our owne weapons,* fay you Maifter Doctor. If you fpeake for your owne fafety and fecuritie, you fay wel, for they will cut your throats indeed. But if you fpeake of iuft and right, you fpeake exceeding ignorantly, by your leaue, and vncharitably, by another Doctors opinion of your owne.

10 It is not fafe for a theefe to fuffer a true man to take away his weapon; but if a true man find a theeues weapon, or can wreft it out of his hand, it is lawfull and iuft for a true man to vfe it in his owne defence, to faue his purfe and life; much more his foule. *Hercules* tooke from the Lion his skin, and *Thefeus* from *Periphetes the robber* his club; fhewing that this club which he had gotten out of another mans hand, was inuincible in his owne. This was their honour; this is our glorie, when we glory in thefe fpoiles of our enemies, and beate them with thofe weapons which they account their owne. *Bellarmine* makes it an inuincible reafon that is drawne from his enemies owne confeffion, and in truth it is fo in law : *Illud quod quis pro fe inducit, etiam contra ipfum induftum non decet reprobare, vt inftrumenta, & qua fimilia funt :* The euidence ,, that a man offereth for himfelfe, he may not reiect, if it be ,, brought againft himfelfe, as inftruments and fuch like. I am ,, verily perfwaded they would vtterly difclaime this in all, as they do in part, for their witneffe, fo we might be debarred with them.

11 Doctor *Kellifon* holds it an iniurious vfurpation and a groffe abfurditie, to ouerthrow enemies with their owne weapons: quite contrary is very true. It is prouerbially faid, that when two ride on a horfe, one muft ride behind; fo when two fellowes croffe and contradict one another, one muft prooue a foole or a knaue, except they will counterpoife themfelues, and be both alike. Was it not *Dauids* great glory, that he cut off *Goliahs* head with his owne fword? and was not that fword laid vp for a monument of that victorie? What differs our cafe? Antichrift of *Rome* claimeth the Scrip-

Plutarch. in Thefeo.

Dift.19.c.Si Rom.in gloff. Vbi plura.

1.Sam.17.51. 1.Sam.21.9.

I 4   tures

tures for his owne fword, will haue it clofe to his owne fide, and tied at his girdle; what if a valiant *Dauid*, a nobodie in the giants eyes, fhould take this fword of the Scriptures from him, and cut off his head? were it not a token of more valour? were it not worth the laying vp to *Dauids* vfe for euer? To this fence was that prouerbe vfed, *Suo fibi iugulo gladio*, I ouer-came him with his owne weapon, I confuted him with his owne argument, I got my poffeffion by his owne euidence. All this by way of fuppofition. For we will neuer grant, that the Scriptures are more theirs, or fo much theirs as ours, or that we had them otherwife from them, but as from *Communes cuftodes*, common treafurers after Iewes and Grecians.

12 Yet let vs make the fame fuppofition againe, that the Scriptures are theirs, and theirs onely. Why then do they fo debafe and vilifie them? why do they refufe al triall by them? why do they call them, bare Scriptures, contemptuoufly, dead letters blafphemoufly? or if they forfake them and caft them from them, why may not we take them vp, and make our iuft benefit of them? They are like a dog in a manger, neither can eate themfelues, nor fuffer thofe that could. They wil challenge the keeping of the *key of the kingdome of heauen*, *but they wil neither enter in themfelues, nor fuffer thofe that would.* This is certainly a dogged and fpitefull nature. They wil nei-ther acknowledge the foueraigntie of the Scriptures, nor fuffer others to take benefit by them: they denie their autho-ritie, and will boaft of their poffeffion. In this there is neither rithme nor reafon, no glory but fhame. For all this claime of Doctor *Kellifon*, the Chapter following fhall fufficiently proue, how they vfe this pupill, whom they thus pretend to be committed to their charge. How bafely they reiect it, and make this Scepter of Chrifts kingdome, this glorious Kings fonne, this birth of the morning, this rule of righteoufneffe, a very fcullian in their bafeft feruices, a very darkneffe of the land of *Egypt*, a crooked rule, by which nothing can be di-rected. Howfoeuer they pretéd their tutorage ouer it: which notwithftanding it recouereth its ftrength, and remaineth it felfe to be at the leaft the firft and chiefeft part of *Antiqui-tie*,

Mat. 23, 13.

tie, if they will not allow it to be the onely. In this cafe we fay of their fo much bragd of poffeffion, as Saint *Hierome* Præfat.in Io-writes of the Iewes. *Illi habent libros, nos librorum Dominum:* nam. *illi tenent Prophetas, nos intelligentiam Prophetarum; illos occidit litera, nos viuificat Spiritus; apud illos Barrabas latro dimittitur, nobis Chriftus Dei filius foluitur.* You Romanifts, as the Iewes, haue the bookes, but we haue the Lord of thefe bookes; you hold the Prophets, we the meaning of the Prophets: the letter kils you, the Spirit quickeneth vs; you let loofe *Barrabas* the thiefe, that is, your traditions, we fet at libertie Chrift the Sonne of God.

13 Doctor *Kellifons* other cauill is, that though we *fo willingly alledge Scriptures, yet we decide all by the bare letter of the Scripture.* This he amplifieth prettily with a fimilitude of D.Kellifon. a fowle and beautileffe maid (not like fuch as waite on chaft l.1.c.2. Iefuits & modeft Priefts in their chambers here in England, howfoeuer they fhift with their deuoted hofteffes in other countries,) and fuch like conceipts, in effect thus much. That we deceiue the *people with bare Scriptures*, without the fap and fence, the pith and marrow of them; as if we went but to the huskes, or fed on bare bones, and that therefore the people fhould take heede of vs, and not *beleeue their Minifters when they proue what they preach by Scriptures.* (No? not when they proue by Scriptures? (the words proofe goes farre;) becaufe forfooth heretickes do fo. Becaufe *Tertullian refufeth flatly to difpute with Heretickes by bare Scriptures, and therefore no maruell if we refufe to decide controuerfies with them by bare Scriptures. For bare Scriptures is of a waxie nature.* Thus farre and much more, but all to the fame purpofe, hath Doctor *Keilifon* made a bare tale. Will any man beleeue him in a cafe fo apparently falfe? fo oppofite to his owne and fellowes confciences of vs, if they fhould be well examined, of that they dayly heare, and reade of vs and ours? Or need I now anfwer him that which hath bene anfwered by B. *Iewell* B. *Bilfon*, by D. *Rainolds*, D. *Whitakers* in this very cafe? What importunitie is this? What art of railing & falfe accufations is here? As if our Sauiour Chrift may not proue by

the

Mat.4.
the Scriptures becaufe the diuell alledged them, or Chrift muft not be beleeued though he proue by Scriptures, becaufe the diuell prefumed fo to do. *Non debet ouis pellem fuam deponere, quòd lupi aliquando fe ea contegant,* The fheepe muft not part with his skin, becaufe wolues fometimes couer themfelues therewith. The Scribes and Pharifes, and Sadduces had more modeftie then thefe men. When our Sauiour had once folidly côfuted them by the Scriptures, they were afterward filent, *and no man durft aske him any more queftions.* The diuell himfelfe departed, after three wounds receiued; our aduerfaries ftand defperatlie to it, though they receiue a thoufand.

Aug. de fer. Domini in mont.l.2.

14 *Campion* complaines that they hauing the letter we will haue the figure: D. *Kellifon*, that they haue the fence and meaning, we, as he pleafeth to ftyle it, the *bare Scripture.* Which of thefe is the truer? *A nobis verba funt* (faith *Campion*) the words are for vs. What are thefe words, but the bare letter? We defire the meaning by conference with other Scriptures, by the antecedents and confequents of the text; as Saint *Auguftine* would haue vs: neither will we deny the harmonie of the Fathers concurring with fuch expofition. Haue you not giuen vs a fword to cut your owne throats? Or if you will claime both fwords, as your Pope doth, you are verie cowards; Will you affaile with both, and haue vs defend with neither, when both are in our hands, as well and fafer then in yours? If we vrge the words, you crie for the meaning: if we vrge the meaning, you crie for the words. What ftrange prefumption is this, that you will haue it as you lift? we muft haue it as you will allow it? You will haue, *hoc eft corpus menm,* taken according to the letter, we otherwife, in figure. We would haue thofe words *There is but one God, and one mediator betwixt God and man,* to be taken according to the letter: you, not without a ftrange diftinction, abhorrent from the Scripturer. We muft defcend vnto you; you will not yeeld an inch vnto vs; are you not partiall in your owne conceipts? We know and will ingenuoufly confeffe, that there are many places of the Scriptures plaine, and

1.Tim.2.5.

Iames.2.4.
Saint Francis.

to

to be taken according to the letter , and all other fences will
be abfurd. There are other places , that if they be taken according to the letter,they will kill, as our Sauiour fpeaketh, Iohn 6.
and as Saint *Auguſtine* obferueth vpon his fpeech , *Except* De doct.
you eate my fleſh and drinke my blood. Flagitium aut facinus vide- Chriſt.lib.
tur iubere, vtilitatem & beneficium vetare, figurata loquutio eſt. 3.c.16.
He feemeth to command a wicked thing or an hainous
crime, to forbid that which is profitable and beneficiall,this „
is a figuratiue fpeech. If ill be commanded or good forbid- „
den, there is a figure. And he exemplifieth it by thofe words „
of our Sauiour.

15 But if you will preffe vs with the fence onely , why
take you the letter? If you be reproued for the letter,why do
you vfurpe it your felues ? Let vs be bound to the fame law,
and we will aske no more libertie then your felues do take.
Though in this your contradiction you do both together little leffe,then grant vs both, while one faith we haue the letter; the other,that we haue the fence. Howbeit what need
we thus difpute ? a flat negatiue were fufficient in this behalfe. If a man may fpeake it in ciuilitie, you flatly and falfely
bely vs ; we ſtand not on the bare letter of Scripture , more
then you. We profeffe with Saint *Ierome*,that the Gofpell
doth confiſt,*Non in verbis Scripturarum,ſed in ſenſu,*not in the Com. in Gal.
words of the Scriptures,but in the fence;not in the barke but 1.
in the fap, *not in the leaues of the words , but in the roote of the*
meaning. Non in legendo , ſed in intelligendo, not in the rea- Contra Lu-
ding,but in the vnderſtanding of them , as the fame Father cifer.
fpeaketh.

16 This haue all our writers profeffed; this do we ſtand
to in the fight of God and man ; this we defend in the face of
our enemies. What need D. *Kellifon* or father *Campion* bleare
the eyes of their filly profelytes (whom they make feuen
fold the children of hell worfe then themfelues) with this
ſlanderous imputatió,as if we had nothing but *bare Scripture*
without any true fence or meaning thereof? If this proteſtation yeeld not fatiffaction to their imperfwafible iealoufie &
implacable malice,we wil giue it in D.*Kellifons* own words,
and

and wiſh from our hearts,he would ſtand to his own doome, and that might be the iſſue and end of all ſtrife,He ſaith thus.

D.Kelliſon.
l.1.c.2. *If they giue vs the letter of Scripture with the true meaning, which is the formall cauſe and life of the word, we will reuerence it as the word of God, and preferre it before all the decrees of the Pope and Church.* I would it were in our power to giue you this; or the grace of God were in you, to receiue it. As you can in no reaſon yeeld vs leſſe, ſo we in our conſcience would aske you no more, but that the letter of Scripture *with the true meaning might be preferred before all Popes and Church.* This had bene a ſufficient *ſuperſedeas* to your Councell of *Trent,* and would ſoone ſtop your mouthes euery day. But this is againſt the whole current & ſwinge of your Synagogue, as will in the next *Chapter* moſt manifeſtly appeare; and therefore we are like to receiue anſwer as in many other caſes,that this *is but one Doctors opinion.*To conclude,we are agreed that the Scriptures ſhould be the firſt and chiefeſt *Antiquity* of the Church and true Religion, though our aduerſaries allow it

Socolouius.
partit. Eccleſ.
pag.756. not the onely.*Locus ſecundus ordine, fide verò primus, eſt Scriptura ſacra.* The holy Scripture is ſecond in order, but firſt in credit.

Conncels. 17 The ſecond euidence of *Antiquitie* is the Councels; which I place next vnto the Scriptures & before the Fathers, becauſe many witneſſes are to be preferred before one,eſpecially many vnited before any or many diſperſed; and our Countriman *Campion* in his *Thraſonicall* challenge ſo placeth them, and ſo do others; but this greatly mattereth not.

18 Theſe alſo our aduerſaries claime as theirs,and none of ours, by any title. Theſe made *Campion* a cocke of a hen, ſet a combe on his head, and ſpurres on his heeles, and made him ſtep into the cocke pit, with a *reſolute and preſent minde,*

D.Kelliſon.
l.4.c.2. and would proue vs all crauens and runnawayes. Theſe D. *Kelliſon* ſaith we *contemne; Caluin, Beza and others deſpiſe all the Councels;* and he refers vs to his firſt booke,fourth and fift Chapters,for their words, where I finde not a word againſt

Mur. ciuit.
ſanct. fund.6. Councels, but that which is, ſeemeth againſt Fathers. Another, *Quid adeò Catholicos homines recreat atq̃, tranquillat,quid adeò*

adeò terret & exanimat exitiales hæreseos apros, vineæ Catholicæ
vastatores,atque saluberrima summáque Conciliorum authoritas?
What is that doth so recreate Catholicke men and con-,,
tent them? what is it doth so terrifie & exanimate the deadly ,,
hereticall bores, destroyers of the Catholike vineyard, so ,,
much as the most wholsome, and eminent authoritie of the ,,
Councels? saith this boasting Iesuite. If they apply this or a-,,
ny of this vnto vs, they egregiously wrong vs, and shame
themselues.For besides that we all giue much reuerence vnto the ancient approued Councels, & receiue what by them
was concluded against the most infamous heretickes in their
times,as all our writers do affirme;so some of our aduersaries
are contented to acknowledge the same. First, our friends;
Concilium quid aliud est quàm flos & tanquam epitome Ecclesiæ?
saith D. *Whitakers.* What is a Councell,but the verie flower D.Whitakers
& abridgement of the Church?And a little after,*The name of*
Councels is large, their faith singular, authoritie great. And the
former Iesuite confesseth of *Luther: Lutherus magnoperè com-*
mendat & euehit laudibus Concilia. Luther greatly commends ,,
and with prayses extols Councels. Though because *Luther* ,,
will not be conie-catched by them, the Iesuite saith he doth
depraue them. The truth is,he doth sift and examine them:
and good reason, when they haue bene in *Romane fin-*
gers.

18 We do not indeed equall the first and best,to the foure
Euangelists,as you would seeme to make Saint *Gregorie* do,
but we hold their conclusions against those heretickes, who
by the Scriptures were first learnedly confuted, & then iustly condemned by them. And Saint *Gregorie* giueth the same Dist.15.cap.
reason of his so high conceipt of them. Our indifferent and Sicut artie.21.
religious estimation of them is deliuered in the published ar- Art.21.
ticles of our professed religion. We are further contented
to stand bound vnto them, as far as our aduersaries practise
affoordeth vs example.We dare not, as is said, hold that the
foure first Councels were as authenticall as the foure Euangelists, and that the Councell of Trent (one of the most partiall that euer was) is to be receiued like the ancient, and so
make

Ratione.4.

make it as good as the Goſpels , as *Campion* doth. Otherwiſe we ſhew & manifeſt our reſpect vnto them in the higheſt commendations we can. Yea maiſter Doctor *Whitakers* in the reuerence of them taxeth the ſentence of *Gregorie Nazianzen*, as ouer hard and harſh againſt Councels. *Neque*

D.Whitakers

ego Conciliorum dignitatem verbis conabor extenuare : & Nazianzenū miror de Concilys tam iniquè iudicaſſe & acerbè ſcripſiſſe, quandoquidem nullius vnquam Synodi felicem exitum vidiſſet : Neither will I go about to extenuate the dignitie of Councels;and I wonder why *Nazianzen* did ſo vniuſtly iudge,and ſo bitterly write of Councels , that he had determined with himſelfe , *and vtterly reſolued euer to auoid the meetings of Biſhops,*for that he neuer ſaw an happy end of them.

     20 This might haue bene ſufficient to them that ſaw theſe proteſtations ſo long in print before they wrote , to conceiue of vs,that we abandoned not the authoritie of ancient Councels , as our aduerſaries in euery new booke lay vnto our charge. Yet *Bellarmine*,a meere ſtranger to vs and our countrie , a man ſufficiently obliged and deuoted to the Church and her great maiſter of *Rome*,is more propitious to our credite then our owne countrimen (that we may find it true by experience,a mans greateſt *enemies are thoſe of his own*

Bellar.de Cō-
cil lib.1.cap.
5.in fine.

houſhold:)for he ingenuouſly confeſſeth,that we accept a third part of thoſe which himſelfe and his receiue , and thoſe the firſt ſixe and vndoubted beſt. By that time I haue well examined the matter, it may haply approue that they receiue not,eſteeme not,approue not, ſo many as we.

Cap.6.

     21 For the reſt,beſides theſe 18 by the Cardinal named,ſome are generall,and yet reprobated.Therfore generall Councels may erre, elſe why are they reprobated? Some in part admitted,in part reiected,like two in bed,one takē,the other

Luke 17. 34.

forſaken;two at the mill, the one choſen,the other forlorne. One alone by it ſelfe is neither manifeſtly bild nor manifeſtly caſhiered, like one alone in a bed,that can take no warmth. Hereby it euidently appeareth,ŷ the Romaniſts admit ſome, exclude others: they yeeld their reaſons,and hold them ſufficient for their iuſtification.We offer our ſelues bound to the

ſame

fame law,we wil meate with the fame meafure.They are curfed if they haue diuers weights in their bag,one to buy with, Prou. 6.
another to fell with; yet fo they vfe vs.We are contented to
do as we are,or rather would be done vnto; and therein we
wrong them not.Let this be fufficient for the indifferent reader, that we admit the Councels next after the Scriptures, as
a moft beautifull handmaid that lookes on the hands of her Pfalm. 123.2.
Miftris;but not as the Ladie,that hath power ouer the whole
houfe; giuing not onely primacie of order,but fupremacy of
authoritie vnto the booke of God. We preferue that due re-
fpeƈ that belongeth vnto the graue and gracious affemblies
of learned men. Our aduerfaries do no more, nay not fo
much.We offer, we intend, we will performe no leffe , and
therefore in this we ftand on equall termes with them : yea
better termes then they.But I doubt our aduerfaries will appeare to flinch from this they pretend. Except perhaps they
produce new conuenticles in ftead of old Councels, as the
moft of them do,euen to the very Trent,or vnder a thoufand
yeares,as *Schoppius* in the cafe of Pardons:*Ecclefiam Indulgen-* De Indul-
tias approbaffe,That the Church hath approoued and granted par- gentijs. c.12.
dons, fo many generall Councels do witneffe , and begins with
Clarimontanum,a cleare name,but an obfcure affembly,1096,
and fo downe to a Lateran or two, and fuch like of fmall refpeƈt,God knowes.

   22   The Fathers writings alfo we receiue, as excellent e- Fathers.
uidences of Gods truth. They are as *Dauids* Worthies:they
haue bene valiant in fighting Gods battels : they are of the
thirtie,but attaine not the firft.Thofe *Campion* was fure were
all his, euen as fure as *Gregorie* the thirteenth. But if *Campion*
had not bene as fure *Gregories* , it had bene better for him
by his head and quarters. Thefe not onely *Campion* but all
our Romanifts claime,from the cedar in Lebanon,to the hyf-
fope that groweth on the wall,from the firft to the laft,from
the greateft to the fmalleft;from the beft to the worft : from
the fteward of the houfe to the fcullion in the kitchin,that is,
from the firft and primitiue Fathers, to the moft barbarous
of the Schoolemen , as truly as all was the diuels to beftow
                       vpon

vpon Chrift. But what hath darkneffe to do with light? why fhould error prefume vpon the protection of truth? The Fathers were famous and excellent in their generations, their memory is bleffed, their writings refpected, their learning admired, their authoritie efteemed as much and more then themfelues defired, or perhaps fometime more then the credit of humane teftimony may admit. And yet thefe whom we loue fo well, whom we reuerence fo much, muft be none of ours : the Romanifts claime all, they will not allow vs one.

22 The Apologie of the Romifh and Rhemifh Seminaries will needs haue them all, and onely theirs, and wil allow them

Cap.5.   to no body elfe. *All the foules of our Chriftian Fathers, all the Saints in heauen, all their actions, works, writings, liues and deaths profeffe for vs.* And not much before, when he had foundly fcoft at vs, for auowing Gods meere word, faith of himfelfe and fellowes: *We truft the learned Fathers of all ages,* and therefore *fweare all that take degree (according to the ordinance of the*

Seff.4.   *Councell of Trent) that they fhall during their life in all their preaching, teaching, difputing, writing and otherwife expound the holy Scriptures as neare as they can, fecundùm vnanimem confenfum Patrum,* according to the vniforme confent of Fathers. And yet more like a *Thrafo* or *Signior Bragadochio, If any thing be objected againft vs, we fay to it roundly, and thus fuch and fuch a Doctor expounds it, thus the Fathers interpret it.* Thus *Rabfheca*

2.King.18. may fpeake to the people that fit on the wall, and perhaps fome malcontents may beleeue him and murmure. But *Hilchia* and *Shebna,* the learned will neuer beleeue him. *Trie ere you truft, and beleeue as you find,* are good rules. All is not Sun that fhineth; the faireft fhewes haue not euer the beft proofe.

Infra.Cap.8. They haue well faid, but they neuer yet did it, as fhall afterward appeare.

23 But as for vs, we are fo far from thinking any good of Fathers (or elfe Friers be liers,) that *we reuile and mif-call the ancient Fathers: that we contemne Church, Councels, Fathers, and chiefe Paftors :* that we *vfe vnreuerent and reuiling fpeeches againft the Fathers:* that we *are defcended of paricides and reuilers*

of

of ancient Fathers. What can be spoken more bitterly, more spitefully? what can be written more impudently, more shamelesly? what can be vttered more slanderously, more villanously? and all in *lie*, with *lie* and all : which I thinke he receiued from Doctor *Heskins*, who layeth this to the particular charge of Bishop *Iuel*, *that he did not onely abuse, but did mocke and scorne the learned and holy Fathers, contemne their learned Commentaries with scoffes, reprehended their graue authoritie, played and dallied with them, &c.* How often hath this damnable slander bene most fairly and euidently answered? How haue all our writers, not onely gainsaid it by word, but manifested the falshood of it by proofe and practise in all their books, so ful farced with the true allegations of the most ancient Fathers? Let the godly and learned Bishops Chalenge (to trie by the Fathers of 600 yeares after Christ) confute you. Let his bookes extant, not onely in Englifh, but also in Latine, so full of Fathers sentences, stop your mouthes. Yet one comes but yesterday, and saith, *Adsunt ante oculos fideliss. Cathol. veritatis testes, veterum Patrum volumina, recentiorum Doctorum libri, aliquorum Conciliorum tomi, Synodi Tridentinæ decreta, ab his abundè licet discere quid doceant Catholici. Sed hi tam luculenti testes prætereuntur, non inspiciuntur, non audiuntur, &c.* There are before your eyes very faithful witnesses of the ,, Catholique veritie, the volumes of the ancient Fathers, the ,, books of moderne Doctors, the tomes of the ancient Coun- ,, cels, the decrees of the *Tidentine* Councell : of these may be ,, abundantly learned what the Catholiques teach. But these ,, so manifest witnesses are passed ouer, are not lookt on, not ,, heard, &c. This sentence of a stranger is somewhat more ,, milde, but equally false, as shal appeare. But obserue how the Councell, or rather conuenticle, or rather conspiracie of *Trent*, is ranged with Fathers and ancient Councels, which sufficiently maketh their malice, or at least partialitie against the truth, manifest.

24 Let Doctor *Rainolds* margines of his *Theses*, and other writings, and allegations in his readings, satisfie you. Let *Peter Martyr* and all the writers of our part, with their learned

works,

Margin notes: Epist.to B.Iuel · B.Iuel. · Muri ciuit. sanct Fund.1.

works, full ſtuffed with Fathers, content you, or at leaſt ſtay your rage. Let the profeſſions and proteſtations of all our writers conuince and condemne you. For we ſay, that we reuerence the Fathers, as much and more then you : we reſt in their authoritie as much and more then you : we giue them all their due commendations, as much and more then you : we haue them, we reade them, as well as you, perhaps better : we preſerue them ſafe and ſound in their firſt integritie , and ſo would leaue them to our poſteritie , ſo do not you : we haue them, we vſe them, we ſtudie them, we alledge them, we beate and bombaſt you with them ; yet are you ſo blind you cannot ſee it, ſo dull you cannot perceiue it, ſo ſenſleſſe you cannot feele it ; or ſo obſtinate and obdurate againſt

Plutarch.

truth, that you will not confeſſe it , like *Lacedæmonian* boyes.

Ratione 5.

25 How impudently doth *Campion* charge, that *Tobie Mathew,* and now the moſt reuerend and moſt worthy Archbiſhop of *Yorke,* with a ſpeech, as if no man could reade the Fathers, and be of that opinion which he profeſſed. This that eloquent and learned Doctor (in a publique and famous Latine Sermon in *Oxford,* yet to be ſeene , and I am ſorie it is not publiſhed as it is worthy) doth vtterly diſclaime and denie : yet for more abundant ſatisfaction, heare his obteſtation and proteſtation, in his owne words : *Teſtor beatum illud & ſempiternum numen Deum Patrem creatorem cœli & terræ; teſtor vnigenitum Dei Filium Ieſum Chriſtum Seruatorem noſtrum, ſcelerum & mendaciorum vindicem, Iudicem viuorum & mortuorum; teſtor Spiritum qui olim ferebatur ſuper aquas, Spiritum Paracletum, Spiritum ſanctum, Spiritum veritatis, præpotentem & immortalem Deum, trinum & vnum, quantum mens mea reſpicere poteſt præteriti temporis ſpacium, inde vſque cogitando ac recordando repetens, nunquam hoc mihi, aut huiuſmodi, vel ſcripto vel dicto, vel ſerio vel ioco, vel vigilanti, vel ſomnianti excidere.* I ,, call to witneſſe that bleſſed and eternall power, God the Fa- ,, ther, Creator of heauen and earth: I call to witneſſe the onely ,, begotten Sonne of God *Ieſus Chriſt* our Sauiour, the auen- ,, ger of wickedneſſe and lies, Iudge of quicke and dead: I call

to witneſſe the Spirit that moued vpon the waters, the Spirit „
of comfort, the holy Spirit of diuine truth, prepotent and „
immortall God, a trinitie in vnitie, as far as my thoughts can „
recollect the time paſt, and from thence repeating, can me- „
ditate and remember, that neither this nor any ſuch ſpeech „
fell from me, either by writing or word, in earneſt or ieſt, „
waking or dreaming. Whereby he then gaue abundant ſatiſ- „
faction to the preſent and moſt frequent auditorie; and may
ſtop the mouth of malice it ſelfe, were it not opened by a lying, and impudent, and maleuolent Ieſuiticall ſpirit. Yet
comes Doctor *Kelliſon,* who perhaps heard him (in all pro- Suruey.lib.1.
babilitie heard of him and of his proteſtation, after ſo many c.4.
yeares) and brings it in againe, as if it were without queſtion
true, and granted without any contradiction. Whereof what
better confutation can there be, then an oppoſition of their
reputations and credits, to ſay as his Grace in that Sermon
did, alluding to the plea betweene *Varrus* and *M. Æmilius
Scaurus: Ille ait, ego nego, vtri creditis?* He ſaith it, I denie it,
whom will you credit? A malcontent, a fugitiue, an enemy,
a Papiſt, a traitor ſaid it: a contented, conſtant friend, a Proteſtant, a learned and loyall ſubiect denies it, a Biſhop, an
Archbiſhop, yet reſolutely renounceth it, and is ready to depoſe the contrary euen to this day. What would they do if
he were dead, when they deale thus with him being aliue,
and able to anſwer the proudeſt Archbiſhop in *Europe* if he
dare oppoſe him? as *Beza* liued to anſwer the ſlanders of his
ſuppoſed death. If any vrge this farther, I will ſay no more
but as one ſaid merily, *Domine Audax,* you are too ſaucie:
Accipe ſtultum, & ſede aſſe, Take a ſtoole, ſit downe and pleaſe
your ſelfe.

26 His *Grace* had read the Fathers (as his owne hand in
al his books, and ready turning of them ſufficiently teſtifies,)
his fit and frequent applying them in all his Sermons, can yet
iuſtifie him; and as him, ſo all that profeſſe any learning, eſpecially in matter of controuerſie. And thus much in dutie be
ſaid for my moſt reuerend Maiſter, whoſe reading, diligence
in ſtudie, frequent preaching, I know, and perhaps may pub-

liſh, if I ouerliue him, when I cannot flatter him, though I would, as I will not now though I could.

27 We make no idols of the Fathers; we take them not to be Fathers of our faith, but followers of the truth; not deuoid of all error, yet great lights of Gods Church; faire, yet not without blemiſh; true, yet not without eſcapes; faithfull, yet not without fault; fruitfull, yet not without wants; profitable, yet not without ſome loſſe; ſafe, yet not without ſome danger. Excellēt are they and full of good matter, yet but excellēt men, not Gods, no nor Angels. As *Iohn Baptiſt* was not y *Lambe of God that taketh away the ſins of the world,* but pointeth at him with his finger, and ſheweth him vnto the world, profeſſing himſelfe his inferiour, not worthy *to ſtoope downe and vnlooſe the latchet of his ſhoo.* So the Fathers they are not *Gods,* they point at *God,* their writings are not Canonicall Scripture, they direct vs to the Scripture, and acknowledge themſelues vnworthy ſearchers of them, for *who is fit for theſe things?* Let this therefore be no more laid vnto our charge, that we contemne, deſpiſe, reiect the Fathers: for as much as we hold our ſelues, and that iuſtly, as farre intereſſed in them as you, keepe them ſafer then you, vſe them better then you, yeeld them as much authoritie as you ſhould giue them, as themſelues do require, as pietie will ſuffer, which commandeth ſoueraigne ſubmiſſion to Gods Scepter, that is, his word, wherein is reuealed and taught all certaine truth concerning Gods ſeruice and our ſaluation.

28 And this we will not aſſume onely (as you do in moſt things) but prooue it alſo, which afterwards ſhall more euidently appeare; where what account your partie maketh of them, ſhall be, I hope, ſufficiently prooued. This was thought reaſonable to an heathen Philoſopher, *Vnumquemque Deum ſic coli oportere quemadmodum ipſe præſcripſit:* God muſt be worſhipped as himſelfe preſcribeth: the rules whereof muſt be receiued from God, not from man; from the writings of God, not from the writings of men. Thus are we contented to vſe Fathers as an euidence approued in the third place.

29 Hiſto-

Ioh.1.8.

Mat.3.11.

2.Cor.2.16.

Cap.8.

Socrat. apud
Auguſt. de Ci
uit. Dei.

29 Hiſtories are the laſt which we can allow, or our ad- Hiſtories.
uerſaries can aske, as a *Commune principium* common to vs Plutarch.
both. In which we are priuiledged as they, and they as we.
They are witneſſes of former times and ages, and the occurrents of them. We alledge and vrge them, and can iuſtifie
our ſelues, and condemne our aduerſaries by them. The more
ancient they are, the more authoritie we giue them. The
later are more partiall, and therefore of leſſe credite. While
the Church ſtood in her intregritie, men were not ſo drawne
vnto parts, as after they were. It could not be ſaid then, ſome
were Papiſts, and ſome were Imperials, (by which diſtinction many hiſtories are by our aduerſaries drawne into ſuſpition) but either before the Church medled with Emperors,
but to ſend them humble Apologies; or the ciuill State with
it, except to perſecute it; or after the common-wealth was
ioyned with the Church, the ciuil with the Eccleſiaſticall,
the Emperors with the Biſhops; when there was ſuch an harmonie of mindes, that each wrote the truth of other, and
both of themſelues, as neare as humane frailtie commonly
doth: yet not ſo without exception, but that there may be
found errors in Chronologie, and the diſtinction of times, in
relation of matters receiued by report on the credite of o-
thers, with ſuch like iuſt exceptions which our aduerſaries
will allow vnto themſelues, and therefore cannot denie vnto vs.

30 Howbeit this may ſerue for our iuſtification in this
behalfe. We will admit all *Campions* Catalogue, which he
onely nameth and challengeth as his owne (an eaſie claime,
and as true as if we ſhould ſet downe a catalogue of Popes
names, and ſay they were all ours,) and will except againſt
none of them, whom ſome of their partie hath not excepted againſt. We will alledge and auouch nothing for our
ſelues and againſt them, but it ſhall be out of ſuch hiſtories
or reports, as themſelues admit for their owne, or that cannot (by our aduerſaries concluſions) be ſaid to be ours, or in
the leaſt matter partiall for our ſakes. We wil not name a *Bol-
ſec*, nor a *Prateolus*, nor ſuch like, as they do none other; that

is, we will not produce an enemie, no not any they account their aduersarie , to teftifie of the hereticall doctrines, and damnable liues of their Popes, or his Cleargy, or the multitude that adored the beaft. *Hoc de apoftatarum fictis rumoribus nafcitur.Neq, poffunt laudare nos qui recedunt, aut expectare debemus,vt placeamus illis qui nobis difplicentes & contra Ecclefia rebelles,folicitandis de Ecclefia fratribus violenter infiftunt. Quare & de Cornelio,& de nobis, quæcunque iactantur, nec audias facile,*

99 *nec credas frater chariffime.*This fpringeth from the falfe rumor
99 of Apoftates: neither can they praife vs who depart from vs,
99 neither can we hope to pleafe them, who difpleafing vs, and
99 being rebels againft the Church, do violently infift to intice
99 brethren from the Church. Wherefore whatfoeuer is caft a-
99 broad,either of *Cornelius*, or of vs, deare brother, do not ea-
99 fily heare it, muft leffe beleeue it. This *S. Cyprian* requefteth on the behalfe of his friend & himfelfe,& that of a friend: we will aske but the fame rule for our felues,or againft our moft deadly and defperate enemies. For though *Melancthon*, *Pantaleon*,*Functius*, *Sleiden* , and the *Centurifts*, yea and our Maifter *Foxe*,are all excellent hiftorians:haue & deferue their due cõmendations with vs; yet we are content not to beleeue the againft our aduerfaries, except they produce fuch munimēts and records as may fufficiently ftrengthen their authoritie. Let vs haue the fame meafure,they fhal find vs foone fatisfied.

31 They deale not fo with vs: but like lazy & foggy hounds, if one yelp before,all come barkng after;game or no game,it matters not, they follow by the eare like curres , not by the fent,like good dogs. So if one of your partie,be he neuer fo wicked, yea & knowne vpon good reafon fo to be, yea condemned by your felues for a lewd cõpanion; yet if he do but open before, you all follow after , not vfing that fagacity is required either in Iudges or witneffes,but drudge doggedly after,without care or confcience;as if all that is againft any of vs were as true as the Gofpell, whofoeuer writes it, whofoeuer fpeakes it. As it was faid of a drunken fot , *Tam naribus quàm oculis videt* ; He fees as well with his nofe , as with his eyes;fo of thefe:They fmell better with their eares,then with

their

Cyprian.e-
pift.52.

their nofe.But this argues their groffe ignorance, or profane fecuritie, or careleffe profaneneffe,or notorious partialitie.

32 If we fpeake of your Popes liues,do you thinke we will call D. *Barnes*, Maifter *Bale*, or the *Centurifts* to witneffe ? By no meanes. But as diuers of our men haue written compleat hiftories of former times,to whom vpon good caufe,we giue deferued credit , and to whom your felues are beholden ; fo we receiue them as witneffes of truth : but we will admit nothing they fay, as a difdaine vnto your partie , except we fmell the fent of verity from former and more vnfufpe-cted authors, or fuch pregnant teftimonies or records,as are without exception.

33 Thus if you will admit hiftories as you are bound, we will concurre with you, & ftand to them as farre and further then you will or dare do. As in the proper Chapter of hifto-ries fhall by the grace of God moft euidently appeare. This *Infra.*c 9. in the meane time,I hope, will giue abundant fatisfaction to euerie indifferent reader , that this falfe imputation where-with our aduerfaries fo impudently afperfe vs ftill , (though our frequent proteftations be againft it ,) that we refufe and renounce all *Antiquitie faue onely the Scriptures*, and of them we haue but the fhadow,without the fubftance, the bodie without the foule ; but as for Councels, Fathers, and Hiftories,we difclaime them , and cut them off at one ftroke, is vtterly vntrue. Thus doth *Socolouius* moft impudently flan-der vs , when he faith. *Quanquam Lutherana & Augustana fecta,Ebionis, Arij,Macedonij, Apolinaris hæresin non sit sequuta, ea tamen habet doctrinæ principia, ea fundamenta, quibus stantibus non modo Arij , & Macedonij hæresin renasci & germinare necesse sit, sed omnes alias quæcunque aliquando orbem vexarunt Christi-anum : qualia sunt , nihil recipiendum esse præter ea quæ claré & expresse in sacris reperiuntur Scripturis: Priuatum sensum cu-iusque in Scripturæ interpretatione sequendum esse: veterum Con-ciliorum atque Synodorum paruam vel nullam habendam ratio-nem. S. Patres nullo precipué S. Sancti dono illustratos fuisse; li-bertatem de fide decernendi pænes omnes æqualem permanere: Ma-gistratus spirituales in fide atque moribus,nullam coercendi vim ha-*

K 4 *bere:*

bere:omnes paſſim ſacerdotes, Doctores, Paſtores eſſe; aliaq̃ cius ge-
,, *neris.* Though the *Lutheran* and *Auguſtane* ſect, follow not
,, the hereſie of *Ebion, Arius, Macedonius, Apolinaris*; yet hath
,, it the ſame principles and grounds of doctrine, which ſtan-
,, ding, it is not onely neceſſarie that the hereſie of *Arius* and
,, *Macedonius* ſhould bloſſome and reuiue, but all others what-
,, ſoeuer in times paſt haue vexed the Chriſtian world: of which
,, ſort are theſe, Nothing is to be receiued, ſaue what is cleare-
,, ly and expreſly found in the holy Scripture. The priuate ſence
,, of each part of Scripture is to be followed in the interpreta-
,, tion thereof. Little or no account is to be had of the ancient
,, Councels or Synods. The holy Fathers were inſpired by no
,, ſpeciall gift of the holy Ghoſt. The libertie or priuiledge of
,, diſcerning faith is vnto all alike. The ſpirituall Magiſtrates
,, to haue no power of coertion in faith or manners. In each
,, place all are as Prieſts, Doctors, Paſtors, or of the like kind.

    34 Euerie word of this is a moſt falſe ly; we denie it euery
word, and proteſt againſt it; and all this booke, and manie
before, ſhall and haue conuinced them to be moſt iniurious
imputations, anſwered many hundred times before this was
written. But that this may be ſeene the better not to be mine
offer, take that which was offered in the triall of one of the
greateſt and groſſeſts points of the Romiſh Idolatrie, and interpretation of that place which they chiefly vrge, before
D. *Kelliſon* wrote, or many others, who yet continue vntrue
ſlanders againſt the profeſſors of the reformed religion. *Nul-*
lam in hoc iudicio antiquitatem refugio, nullum Concilium, nullum
Patrem, nullum omninò ſincere vetuſtatis monumentum repudio. I
,, flie or ſhunne in this triall no *Antiquitie,* I reiect no Councel,
,, nor Father, no not any monument at all of ſincere *Antiqui-*
,, *tie.* This we all profeſſe as one man. Enter the liſts of your
owne practicall conditions, with any of thoſe weapons; we
giue you the challenge & will dare you at your owne dunghill; the very gates of *Rome,* the Caſtle Saint *Angelo:*
your *Lateran* and *Saint Peters* Church : your very *Achelda-*
ma and field of blood, that was bought with the thirty peeces
of ſiluer for which Chriſt was ſold, and is now at *Rome,* or
                                   pre-

D. Whitakers
in Campi.
Rat, 2.

pretended to be: I maruell by what miracle. And therefore deceiue no more your nouices with this brag : I will proue you refufe, contemne, yea condemne all thofe witneffes your felues, or elfe my felfe will yeeld vnto your *Inquifition,* which is worfe then Purgatorie, perhaps as hurtfull as hell, yet honoured with Saints, to your euerlafting fhame, and Gods euerlafting glorie.

CHAP. VI.

Whether Proteftants or Papifts (as the Chriftian world is now deuided or ftiled) do admit or reiect the firft and chiefeft Antiquitie, which is the Scriptures.

He ancient Philofophers differed men from beafts, and therefore preferred men before beafts, becaufe they haue the vfe of reafon. Saint *Auguftine* (if the booke be his) almoft equalleth men with Angels, becaufe they haue reafon as well as they; the principall emploiment whereof is in action, to diftinguifh betweene good and euill, in opinions betweene truth and error. To do an action without reafon, is to do it like a beaft, which may do good or euill by chance or nature, or by the ouer-ruling power of Gods prouidence, who difpofeth all creatures in his feruice for his own glorie. This *Tullie* cals *officium medium,* *quod cur factum fit ratio probabilis reddi poteft,* that for which a probable reafon may be giuen. To beleeue any thing without reafon, is to beleeue more like a beaft then a man, who is bound to beleeue nothing without reafon. And therefore though many things to be beleeued, exceed all difcourfe and reach of reafon, yet do we beleeue nothing that concerneth the greateft myfteries of our religion, and by it of our faluation, but we haue good reafon to beleeue it. *Quæcunque dicit diuina Scriptura, ea credere oportet quod funt, quomodo verò funt, ipfi foli cognitum eft:* Whatfoeuer the diuine „ writ affirmeth, ought to be beleeued that they are fo; but by „

In Soliloquijs cap.7.& 8.

Offic.l.1.

Epipha.hærel.70.

what

,, what meanes they are fo, it is knowne to God onely. That a Virgin did beare a fonne: that the God of glorie was crucified: that fo many wondrous works were done, and miracles wrought by our Sauiour *Chriſt*, and his Prophets, and Apoſtles, are all aboue and beyond reaſon; yet haue we great reaſon to beleeue them, becauſe they are regiſtred in the volume of Gods written booke, the authoritie whereof is a Chriſtians ſufficient reaſon for all opinions and aſſurances of faith. For which cauſe Saint *Peter* willeth *euery man to be readie to giue a reaſon of the hope that is in him*; not that the articles of the faith be made ſubiect to reaſon, but that all the world may ſee that we haue reaſon to beleeue as we do. *Fides noſtra ſuper ratione quidē eſt, non tamen temerariè & irrationabiliter adſumitur. Ea enim quæ ratio edocet, fides intelligit; & vbi ratio defecerit, fides percurrit : non enim vtcunque audita credimus, ſed ea quæ ratio non improbat: verùm quod conſequi ad plenum non po-*,, *teſt, fideli prudentia confitemur.* Our faith indeed is aboue rea-,, fon, yet is not held raſhly or againſt reaſon. For what reaſon ,, teacheth, faith conceiues; and where reaſon failes, faith goes ,, on: for we beleeue them not howſoeuer we may heare ſay, ,, but as they are not contradicted by reaſon : but what cannot ,, be ſearched to the full, we acknowledge with a faithfull ,, prudencie.

2 When *Plato*, ſurnamed *Diuine*, (becauſe of all Philoſophers he drew neareſt by drift of reaſon to the contemplation of the Godhead and diuine nature) had read the firſt Chapter of *Geneſis*, becauſe it ſauored and fauoured his owne opinion of the creation of the world, againſt *Ariſtotles* opinion of the *non-creation* thereof, who deemed that *mundus* was *æternus*, the world was eternall; ſaid more like a reaſonable Philoſopher as he was, then a conſcionable Diuine which he was not; *That Moſes wrote the truth, but he wanted reaſon to proue it.* Chriſtians that beleeue it, haue reaſon ſo to do, becauſe *Moſes* in the Law, the Prophes in their times, our Sauiour in the Goſpell, haue affirmed it. Thus we do not reſt the truth of God vpon mans reaſon: *Nos vniuſcuiuſque quæſtionis inuentionem non ex proprijs rationibus dicere poſſumus, ſed ex*

Scriptu-

Eſai.7.14.
Matth.1.21.
Acts.

1.Pet.3.15.

Iunilius de partibus diuinæ legis.l.2. c.vlt.30.

Epiphan.hæreſ.65.

*Scripturarum consequentia:*We cannot demonstrate the inuen-,,
tion of euery quettion from our owne reasons, but by the ,,
consequence of the Scriptures. Therefore when any thing ,,
in Scripture is aboue and beyond reason, we imitate *Pytha-*
goras schollers, whose Maifters *ipse dixit* was to them a sufficient reason. So say we that are Chriftians, in matters of faith
& religion, this is our reason, *God* hath spoken it in the Scriptures. And none but this may secure a conscience of the
truth of God, as the beft, or indeed the only euidence thereof. Of which holy booke, men may more iuftly say that which
Seneca faid of *Sextius* booke, which he affected and admired,
*Viuit, viget, liber eft, supra hominem eft:*Gods booke is a liuing
booke, a booke of life, flourifhing, a booke indeed moft free
from error, aboue the deuice of man to inuent it, aboue the
reach of man to vnderftand it, aboue the reason of man to
comprehend it. It hath aftonifhed the moft prophane, it hath
conuinced the moft peruerse, it hath taught the moft learned, it hath inftructed the moft ignorant, it hath made a secret found in filence, it hath giuen light in darkneffe and in
the fhadow of death; although the Gofpell was to the *Iewes*
a ftumbling blocke, to the *Grecians* foolifhneffe, yet to as 1.Cor.1.23.24
many of them as fhould be faued, it was (and remaineth e-
uer) the power of God and wifedome of God. And there-
fore what Saint *Peter* wrote of the old Teftament, may much 2.Pet.1.19.
more be fpoken of the whole, both old and new, We haue ,,
a fure word of the Prophets and Apoftles, to which we ,,
fhall do well to giue heed, as vnto a light that fhineth in a ,,
darke place, vntill the day dawne, and the day-ftarre arife in ,,
our hearts. This word being agreed vpon on all hands, to be ,,
the certaine word of God, doubted of by neither part; we a-
uouch and proteft to be the onely true and perfecteft rule of
truth, as before is fufficiently proued. Yet becaufe the Reader Chap.5.
fhall find this oppofed by the aduerfary in this Chapter, I wil
ftrengthen it with more reasons, that obferuing the reuerence which is due, and we beare vnto the Scriptures, our
aduerfaries contempt and difcountenance of them may the
better appeare.

3   It

3 It was the credit of *Moses*, and of the Law he brought vnto the people (not that he had receiued it from *Ioseph*, or *Iacob*, or *Isaac*, or *Abraham*, or *Noah*, or from *Melchizedech*, or *Adam* himselfe by tradition, but (as the heathen said, *à*

Exod. 20. *Ioue principium*) that it was written with the finger of God,
Exod.sæpe. that he made the Tabernacle and Altar, not like *Iacobs* at *Bethel*, or *Abrahams* in mount *Moriah* , but according to the patterne which God shewed him in the mount *Horeb*: who did all things as the Lord commanded him, which is exceeding often repeated . The Prophets afterwards held themselues to that rule , and neuer stretched beyond this teth,

Zachar. 1. with *Dicit Dominus, os Domini locutum est*, or *ad legem & testi-*
Esai. *monium* . Thus saith the Lord , the mouth of the Lord hath
Esai. „ spoken it : to the law and to the testimonie; they that speake
 „ not according to this word , they shall neuer haue the mornings light. These are the bounds God hath set at the foote of the hill; all must come neare, that they may heare, but not

Exod. 19.24. go ouer the railes lest they die, and be thrust through with a
Heb. 12.20. dart . All must come to the Scriptures, that they may heare and learne ; no man may beyond them search into Gods secrets, lest he be oppressed with his glorie. And therfore howsoeuer a man may write with good reason *De Ecclesiasticâ Hierarchiâ*, of the gouernment of the Church , I know not

Dionys. de how he should write *de Cœlesti*, of the gouernment of hea-
cœl.Hierarc. uen.The heauen of heauēs is the Lords, the earth hath he gi-
Psal. uen to the children of men.Therefore we must giue vnto men (as vnto *Cæsar*) that belongeth to them, to God that belongeth to him.Saint *Paul* heard words in heauen that were not to be vttered out of heauen ; so hath God reuealed whatsoeuer is for the wel being and well doing of the Church militant vpon the earth , but not what the Angels and Saints do or shall do in heauen farther then praise the Lord. Saint *Hi-*

Hil.de Trinit. *larie* teacheth a better lesson then to meddle with the secrets
l.3. of heauen, when he saith, *Bene habet vt ijs tantùm quæ scripta sunt contentus sis*: It is well with thee if thou canst be content

Amb.Hexam. with that is written. And Saint *Ambrose* as well:*Ego, quid fa-*
l.3.c.3. *cere potuerit Deus, nunc prætermitto; id quod fecerit, quod apertè Scriptu-*

Scripturarū authoritate non didici,prætereo. I now ouerſlip what ,,
God might haue done ; what he hath done, that manifeſtly ,,
I haue not learned by the authoritie of Scriptures, I let paſſe. ,,

4   It is vaine curioſitie to enquire what we ſhould do
there, it is worke enough to ſtudie how we may come thither; and therefore though Saint *Ierome* (as before is noted)
ſaith,*fugiendum ad montes*,we muſt flie to the mountaines,yet
he reſtraineth with limits, *Ad montes Scripturarum* , to the
mountaines of the Scriptures : and leſt we ſhould therein be
deceiued,and take falſe Scriptures for true , he yet giueth a
ſtricter limitation,*Ibi inuenient montes Moſen,Ieſu Naue,mõ-
tes Prophetas, montes noui Teſtamenti Apoſtolos & Euangeliſtas,*
There they ſhall find the mountaines *Moſes,Ioſua,*the mountaines the Prophets , the mountaines of the new Teſtament, the Apoſtles and Euangeliſts. And when one is come
vnto theſe mountaines , and is exerciſed in the reading of
ſuch mountaines, if he cannot finde ſuch a one as may teach
him, *(for the harueſt is great,but the labourers are few)*yet ſhall
his endeuour be approued , becauſe he fled into the mountaines;and the ſloth of his Maiſters ſhall be reproued & con-
demned.The good Kings did like the good Prophets; when
Religion was neglected or decayed, they reſtored it by this
rule onely. *Iehoſaphat* ſent *Prieſts and Leuites, habentes librum
legis Domini* , hauing the booke of the Law of God. *Heze-
kias* did that which was right and true before the Lord,*iuxta
legem,*according to the Law. *Ioſias* made a couenant with
God , tooke an oath of his ſubiects,that they ſhould do that
which was written,*in volumine illo quod legerat,*in that volume
which was read , that was the booke of the Law , that was
found by *Hilchias* in the wall. The deformed Church was
thus beautified, the decayed Church thus reedified,the corruptions of the Elders were reſtored, reformed.

5   *Chriſt* our *Sauiour* by the Scriptures confounded the
diuell,and vſed no other weapon againſt him that brought
the Scriptures, and was as well skild in them, as the greateſt
hereticks that euer wrote. Yet as *Hierome* ſaith,*Falſas e Scripturis Diaboli ſagittas, veris Scripturarum frangit clypeis;* Chriſt

brake

Margin notes:

In Naum.
Cap.3.8.

Mat.9 37.

1 Kings
2 King.18.3.

2 King.23.

Tho.Aquin.
Ca.taur.in
Mat 4.

,, brake the falſe arrowes of the diuell drawn out of the Scrip-
,, tures, with the true bucklers of the Scriptures. So ſay we, If
Chriſt be our Captaine, let vs follow him, in his manner of
fight againſt the greateſt enemie that euer oppoſed his kingdome. You are preaſſed with Scriptures, anſwer with Scriptures. If you aſſaile vs by Scripture, we will aske no other
defence, but that two edged ſword of the Spirit, which is the
word of God, either to proteċt our ſelues, or confute our
aduerſaries. Out of the Scriptures Chriſt taught his Apoſtles, confirmed the multitude, confuted the Scribes, blan-
ked the Sadduces, and confounded the diuels. What is written in your Law? What readeſt thou? Know you not what
is written? What ſaith your Law? Is it not written in your
Law? Therefore you erre, becauſe you know not the Scriptures. Chriſts preaching, his praċtiſe, his words, his workes,
his life, his death, hath confirmed the written word to be
the rule of truth. His Apoſtles following him as their maiſter, in their Sermons, in their conferences, in their Councels,
in their writings, ſilenced their aduerſaries, inſtruċted their
diſciples, cōforted the Churches, confronted the Iewes, conuerted the Gentiles, onely by the power and euidence of the
Scriptures, as by the Aċts of the Apoſtles, and the old Eccleſiaſticall hiſtories, it is cleare and manifeſt.

Eph.ſ.6.17.

Luke.24.
Mat.21.42.
Luke 10.17.
Mat.22.29.
Iohn 10.34.

6 From the Apoſtles to deſcend vnto after times, in the
chiefe prime of the Church; though *Laċtantius, Tertullian, Ar-
nobius*, and *Auguſtine*, when they wrote againſt the Gentiles,
dealt moſt by reaſon, by the workes of God, and their owne
writers, as *Varro* and others, yet they vſed alſo the collation
of Scriptures, of the old and new Teſtament, as the ſtrongeſt
arguments to conuince truth againſt them. But when *Irenæus, Epiphanius, Auguſtine* wrote bookes, or rather volumes
againſt the Iewes and heretickes, did they confute them
by the authoritie of the Church? or Councels, or Fathers,
or Traditions not written? or by any things elſe but onely
by the Scriptures?

7 I cannot finde, and I am perſwaded it can neuer be di-
reċtly proued, that any of the ancient Catholique and approued

ued Councels, euer vſurped theſe words of the Apoſtles, *Videtur Spiritui S. & nobis.* It ſeemeth good to the holy Ghoſt &
to vs, (though *Bellarmine* be of opinion they may:) but e- A&. 15.28.
uer ſubmitted themſelues vnto the Scriptures in all their determinations and concluſions. Yet the *Rhemiſts* would faine Rhem.Teſt.
finde one, by the teſtimonie of Saint *Cyprian* in an African in A&s.15.
Councell; wherein the Biſhop ſeemes (as they take it) to vſe Cyprian. E-
the ſame words. For neither are the words the ſame with piſt.54.nu.5.
thoſe in the Apoſtles Councell, neither do the words depend lib.4.epiſt. 2.
vpon their owne ſence, but on antecedent proofes ; neither
ſeemeth it to haue bin a Councel of Biſhops ſolemnly aſſembled, but rather counſell communicated one to another. The
Apoſtles words are, *It ſeemeth good to the holy Ghoſt and to vs.*
But in Saint *Cyprian,* It hath pleaſed vs by the ſuggeſtion of the
holy Ghoſt. The Apoſtles had not onely the holy Ghoſt breathed vnto them by our Sauiour, but receiued him in the vi
ſible ſigne of clouen tongues. And therefore they knew the
mind of the holy Ghoſt by immediate ſuggeſtion, and might
well ſay, It ſeemeth good to the holy Ghoſt and to vs. But
theſe African Fathers, after they had alledged many Scriptures, and vrged many reaſons out of them, by this immediate ſuggeſtion of the holy Ghoſt within thoſe Scriptures,
and by thoſe reaſons before giuen, do conclude: For theſe
are the certaine ſuggeſtions of the holy Ghoſt. Which may
be further probably conceiued by the very poſition of the
words. The Apoſtles put the holy Ghoſt firſt, themſelues after, to ſignifie they had the immediate ſuggeſtion; the other
put themſelues in order before this ſuggeſtiõ, the holy Ghoſt
after, to note they had the mind of the holy Ghoſt in his reuealed word, & neither by viſiõs or ſights: wherby they were
more perſwaded of the mind of the holyGhoſt. So the words
haue not dependance of the Fathers themſelues, but on thoſe
allegations and reaſons before ſuggeſted and produced. And
finally, this ſeemeth not to be an aſſembled Councell, but a
conference, either by letters, or communicating one with another, and ſending for ſubſcription or conſent; which appeareth by the beginning of the Epiſtle, where they mention
not

not a Synod or Councell, but rather *participato inuicem confi-lio*, hauing conference or taking counfell one with another: which may as wel be in abfence as in prefence, as well at fundry times as at once, as well by fome, and fome often, as by an affembly altogether. For there is as much difference betweene *Concilium*, that is, a Synod or affembly, and *confilium* which is an aduice, as there is betweene *decipere* and *defipere*, that is, to play the knaue, or the foole; or with nearer refemblance if it may be, a Maifter *incipiens* and *infipiens*, the firft may begin well, the other may begin, continue, and end an Affe.

8   I maruell the *Rhemifts* were fo ill aduifed to alledge this to proue it a rule, that all Councels may vfe the Apoftles phrafe, feeing they haue none but this, that I can find by mine owne fearch, or enquiry of others as yet, and this farre vnlike that: neither is this a Councell in their owne account; and if one, yet a priuate one, that can giue no rule nor good example to generall Councels, by their owne learning; yea and that one fo priuate, yet prefuming to fet their names before *Cornelius* the great Patriarch and Pope of Rome, being themfelues but meane Bifhops, and to call him Brother, that *in ftylo nouo*, in the new ftyle is the Papifts *Pater Patrum*, the Father of Fathers: and fo to preuent thofe heretical doctrines that afterwards inuaded that Sea, when they concluded, before the Pope heard of it, (what a facriledge is this in the Romane Synagogue?) and to teach that all muft receiue the cup of the Lord: which ancient cuftome is now abolifhed by good *Cornelius* his wicked fucceffors. Certainly if the Rhemifts had a better or another, they would neuer haue brought forth this.

9   But let this paffe, both it (if it were a Councell) and all other ancient and approued Councels, ftrengthened and concluded their pofitions, their determinations, not *authoritate fuà*, by their owne authoritie, neither prefumed of the immediate fuggeftion of the holy Ghoft, but by the authoritie of the Scriptures, whereby *Arius*, *Macedonius*, *Neftorius* and *Eutyches* were learnedly confuted, and iuftly condemned in
                                                                          the

the foure first generall Councels.

10   There is a memorable and remarkable storie to this purpose, in that most famous and first generall Councell of Nice, whereof *Constantine* the Great (a graue and Bishop-like Emperour) like an Angell of heauen (as *Eusebius* repor- De vita Con-teth) was the chiefe. When he saw controuersies rather multi- stan. l. 3.pag. plied, then made fewer, rather kindled, then quenched, made 169. this exhortation vnto all the Bishops assembled : *Euangelici & Apostolici, nec non antiquorum Prophetarum oracula, plane* Theod.l.1.c.7 *nos instruunt sensu numinis. Proinde hostili deposita discordia su-* σαφῶς. *mamus ex dictis diuini Spiritus explicationes quæstionum.* The Euangelicall and Apostolicall bookes, together with the ora- „ cles of the ancient Prophets, do plainly (and we may well „ say fully) instruct vs in the knowledge of the Deitie; and „ therefore laying aside all hostile contentions, let vs take from „ the sayings of the holy Ghost, the explications of our que- „ stions. Which the reuerend Bishops did so respect and ob-serue, that when they had resolued against Priests mariages, or retaining their wiues, one *Paphnutius homo Dei*, a man of Ruffin.l.1.c.4. God, commended for chastitie, a Confessor that had one eye Socrat. l. 1.c. boared out for the testimonie of Chrifts truth, was haught 11. in the ham, and was condemned to the mines, withstood the whole Councell with one sentence of Scripture (*honorabile coniugium inter omnes*, mariage is honorable amongst all men) and to this one man, that with one eye saw more then the whole Councell, bringing but one place of Scripture, they all yeelded, and gaue due reuerence to the written word of God, as vnto the surest author and stay of truth. Here was not truth preiudiced with number of voices, nor the Scriptures ouer-swayed by the pretended authoritie of the Church, nor the Popes pleasure attended, what it might please his Holinesse to conclude.   In Concil.

11   Euer in old time, and in the first and best Councels, the Chalced. Act. bookes of the Gospels were laid in the midst before the Fa- 1. p. 740. thers & Bishops, as in the Councell of Chalcedon; so was it in Act. 2. p. 288. the Councell of Constantinople. So in the Councell held by & 5. pag.308. *Theodorus* Archbishop of Canterbury, wherof mētionis made edit. P. Crab.

L   hist.

Nota in Cô. *Hiſt. Angl.* l. 4. *cap.* 17. So they did, ſaith *Binius* in his notes
1.Nic p. 314. vpon the firſt Councell of Nice. And ſo they did in the firſt E-
In Annot.
Tom.1.p.918 pheſin Councell, ſaith the ſame *Binius.* And *Baronius, In medio*
Tom 5.ad *Patrum conſeſſu ſedem cum Euangelio collocarunt , cuius intuitu*
annum 431. *omnes admonerentur, Chriſtum omnium inſpectorem & Iudicem*
num.50. *adeſſe, ſynodiq, præſidem agere.* In the midſt of the Fathers they
Binius Tom.
1.p 918 vide placed a deske with the Goſpell, by beholding whereof they
Baro.in annal. might all be admoniſhed that Chriſt was the ouerſeer of all,
ad annum and a preſent Iudge and Preſident of their Synod. That which
325.nu. 60. the Chalcedon Councell did in practiſe , was not to the ſhew
of the eye, or for ſome ſolemne ceremonie ; but they obſerued it indeed , and made their concluſions and reſolutions accordingly, *Sicut olim Prophetæ vaticinati ſunt, & ipſe Chriſtus
nos inſtruxit.* As the Prophets foretimes foretold vs , as Chriſt
himſelf hath taught vs. *Et Concilium Syrmienſe: Sicut Scriptura*
„ *ſanctæ dicunt:* As the Scriptures of God deliuer and teach , *Se-*
„ *cundùm Propheticas Euangelicaſq, voces,* According to the voice
„ of the Propheticall and Euangelicall writings; nothing in the
Eccleſiaſticall faith but the Scriptures. Whoſoeuer pretendeth
Hiſto. tripart. it, the rule is good, & without exception. Yea the very Creeds
l.5.c.34. that follow that of the Apoſtles, haue this for their authority,
euen concerning the common grounds of Chriſtianity, according to the Scriptures.

    12 Which wreſted out the confeſſion from *Panormitan* the
great Canoniſt (I am ſure no Proteſtant Iſraelite , but rather
Panormitan. a *Goliah* among the Romiſh Philiſtims) to ſay , *Plus creden-*
dum eſt vni priuato fideli quàm toti Concilio & Papæ, ſi meliorem
„ *habeat authoritatem & rationem.* A man may better beleeue
„ one priuate Chriſtian, then a Pope with a whole Councell, if
„ he alledge better authoritie and reaſon. This we aske of our
aduerſaries, but they will not yeeld it. This we haue taken
from the practiſe of all ages, and perſons in the Scripture and
ſince, and this we will by the grace of God hold, againſt the
Synagogue of Rome, and citie of Satan. And good cauſe why.
Pſal.19.7.8. For it conuerteth ſoules , giueth wiſdome to the ſimple, light
„ to the blind, reioyceth the heart, endureth for euer, is righte-
„ ous altogether. More precious then gold, ſweeter then the ho-
                                      nie

nie and the honie combe. This neither deceiueth,nor can be ,,
deceiued. It is not giuen by any priuate motion; we are ſure 2.Pet. 1.20.
that thoſe holy men wrote as they were inſpired of the holy
Ghoſt. Theſe were written for our learning, that through pa- Rom. 15. 4.
tience and comfort of the Scriptures we might haue hope.
Theſe were inſpired from God,and are able to make the man 2.Tim.3.16.
of God perfect and abſolute vnto euery good worke. Theſe Ioh.20.31.
were written that we might beleeue, and beleeuing haue e-
ternall life.Without which we cannot beleeue.For faith com- Rom.10.17.
meth by hearing, and hearing by the word of God preached.

13 Seeing therefore holy Kings and Prophets,our Sauiour
Chriſt and his Apoſtles, Councels and Fathers in the time of
the Law, and in the dayes of the Goſpell, againſt Iewes and
Gentiles, errors and hereſies, men and diuels, haue vſed the
Scriptures,as all-ſufficient,for defence of truth,reproofe of ſin,
exhortation to vertue, for ſauing of ſoules, and glorifying
God, who is bleſſed for euer : why ſhould this ſo ſoueraigne
a medicine, ſo direct a rule, ſo cleare a light, ſo pure a fountaine,ſo glorious and fixed a load-ſtar,ſo certaine a guide,that
vnum neceſſarium, be reiected, contemned, nay vilified, with Luke 10.42.
opprobrious, ſacrilegious and blaſphemous words, writings,
deeds? If we of our Church do this, eiect vs, excommunicate
vs, pronounce with ſound of trumpet againſt vs *Anathema
maranatha*,confiſcate our goods, ſeiſe on our lands,burne our
bodies, ſet on vs the markes of reprobates, while we liue,
and lay on vs the puniſhment thereof when we are dead.
But if the Romaine pretended Catholicks, do all this, yea and
much more, to the diſcountenancing, diſgracing, and tram-
pling vnder foote of the Teſtament ſealed with Chriſts
blood, this precious word of life, that is able to ſaue our
ſoules; good readers at leaſt ſuſpect them, and ſuſpend your
iudgement, vntill you haue made farther ſearch into this euidence. And the Lord Ieſus open your eyes, that ye may ſee
your manifold errors, and eſchue them, and ſoften your frozen hearts, that ye may diſcerne the truth of God, and
obey it.

14 Howbeit attend a little, and heare what eftimation is

Math.13.44. 45.
made of this precious pearle and treafure (for which a wife man would fell all that he hath to buy it,) by the profeffors and teachers, yea hearers and followers, of the Romane religion. And then determine with your felues, and iudge accordingly betweene vs and them. In which cafe fhall I tell you what I haue heard with mine eares? I confeffe, not of Maifters, but of Scholers, but fuch as in all probability fpake as they had learned. I alledged to one, for the generall vfe of mariage, among men of all callings, that of the Apoftle

Heb.13. 4.
Saint *Paul, Mariage is honourable among all men.* He anfwered, Did you neuer reade that S. *Paul* fpoke like a foole? fo (quoth he) did he then. I heard a Recufant Gentlewoman (who had afterwards a child by a Recufant Gentleman, he married, fhe fingle) that cald the word of God the word of a dog, the Scriptures fcraptures, the Bible a bable, and the *Pfalmes* the *fhames of Dauid.* Which out of queftion came from a greater wit, and as little grace. If you fay, this is but a poore argument to prooue the generall eftimation or contempt of the Scriptures, of all Catholickes Romaine, by fuch particulars, know that I crie but cuittance with *Bellarmine,* who telleth a tale of an Englifh woman, that hearing the fiue and twentieth of Ecclefiafticus read in the Church, in the vulgar tongue, flang out of doores and faid, (as his words are) *Hoccine eft verbum Dei? immo eft verbum diaboli.* Is this the word of God? it is the word of the diuell. Thus vpon the credit of an Englifh Gentleman that told it, and a curft queane that fpake it, he would prooue it inconuenient, if not vnlawfull, to reade the Scriptures in a knowne language, that might be vnderftood of the people. Let thefe teftimonies beare the credit they deferue, and prooue eithers intention as they may, I will vrge them no farther, but *iam fumus ergo pares.* You haue as good as you bring; and God knoweth I report the truth.

In Apol. ad Clau. de Sanit.
15 Haue the learned Sorbonifts and other Diumes of *Babylon* (that accurfed citie) any better opinion of the Scriptures of God? In which cafe fhall I ask *Beza?* he will tell you

that a Sorbonist said,*Melius habituram Ecclesiam Dei si Pau-*
lus nullam Epistolam scripsisset, It had bene better with the „
Church of God, if Saint *Paul* had written neuer an Epistle. „
Shall I aske *Sibrandus Lubbertus?* he will report of another
that said, that were it not for the authoritie of the Pope, he De Princip.
would giue no more credit to the Scriptures then to *Æsops* Christia. dog.
fables. These are fearfull blasphemies. Or shall I tell you what L.1.c.5.
Gregorie Valentia said of one that vrged him with Scripture? Hassenmull.
Nugator vrget contra me τὸ ῥητὸν, this trifler vrgeth against me c.9.
that same word; I cannot deny, but that he and other *Luthe-*
rans haue for themselues the letter, but we neither care for
the letter nor literall sence, but we require the Catholique
vnderstanding. And this you must vnderstand to be the
Popes interpretation, from whose determination it is vnlaw-
full to dissent. And againe to a certaine *Lutheran*: *Si vis esse* Idem c.6.
egregius Catholicus, ne occuperis esse Biblicus : If thou wilt be a „
noble Catholique, neuer desire to be a Bibler. For the De- „
crees of the Church be sufficient for a good Catholique vnto „
saluation: these may you trust, so may you not the Scriptures. „
The Church hath the Vicar of Christ for her head, which is „
the Bishop of *Rome,* whose faith cannot faile, who hath all „
laws in the closet of his breast, and cannot erre. What of *Ho-* Idem c.9.
sius?Non ipsum verbum nec verborum sensus, sed Ecclesiæ Romanæ „
mens tibi contemplanda est : Neither the word it selfe, nor the „
sence of the words, but the mind of the Church of *Rome* „
must thou thinke vpon. We must take all Scripture and vn- „
derstand it in that sence which the Bishop of *Rome* deliuereth „
it, who is Chrifts vicar; and whereas he is head of the Church, „
the pillar and foundation of truth, he cannot erre. And again: Idem c.6.
What need we reade the Bible, when we haue the whole- „
some commandements of the Church, which vnto Catho- „
liques is in stead of the Bible? There were Christians before „
the Bible was written; the dead letter can saue no man: let „.
vs heare the Church, and we shall be safe; for that is the li- „
uing tree, and the very Law of God, which neither erreth „
nor deceiueth. Or that of *Turrian* : *Non Pauli verba,* Not „
Pauls words, but the Churches interpretation is to be hol- „

„ den, for fhe is the liuely interpreter of *Pauls* words; the

Idem c. 9.   words of *Paul* are but a dead letter. Or another: The Bible

„ will fooner make an hereticall *Lutheran* then a Romane Ca-

Idem.cap.6. tholike. Or another:That the Pope and their General,are fet

Decalogus & aboue all law,and are our ten commandements and Law.Or

lex noftra.

Idem.cap.9. another: *Quid mihi profers facram Scripturam , quam quilibet*

„ *hæreticus profe citat?* What bringft thou me the holy Scrip-

„ tures,which euery hereticke citeth? This is a dumbe iudge,

„ it can giue no fentence; therefore not the Scripture, but the

„ Bifhop of *Rome* and the Romane Church is the iudge of con-

„ trouerfies,and we muft ftand to them,and not to that,if euer

„ we will haue an end of controuerfies. Or the Iefuites of *Co-*

Idem 16. *len*, that call the Scriptures *Sermonem abbreuiatum,* a curtall

„ word, and an imperfect doctrine, which doth not containe

„ all things neceffary to faith, good manners, and the ob-

„ taining of a bleffed life; that it is to be perfected by traditi-

„ ons. For out of the Scripture can be nothing taken that is

„ certaine and fure, but it is a leaden inftrument,which both

„ Catholickes and heretickes may apply to their purpofe both

Idem c.6. alike. Or as *Fabricius* the Iefuite : *Hæretici femper hæretica in*

„ *nos vrgent Biblia*: The hereickes euer vrge againft vs hereti-

„ call Bibles : but we haue the Bifhop of *Rome* , whom if we

„ follow, we can neuer erre, nor be deceiued. The Pope alfo

„ may interpret himfelfe , fo cannot the Bibles; and therefore

„ we may fafelier truft his decrees,then the others obfcurities.

Idem 16. Or as father *Iulius* : As the Prophets might fafely truft the

„ words of the Lord, fo may euery Catholicke fafely truft the

„ Decrees of the Church:for in them he doth heare the Bifhop

„ of *Rome* fpeake, to whom by name and fingularly the holy

„ Ghoft was giuen, and who is placed aboue all cafualtie of

„ error.

     16 Thefe barbarous and monftrous fpeeches againft the bleffed word of life,and fountaine of liuing waters, I could not beleeue,they are fo bafphemous, neither would, becaufe I haue receiued them from domefticall teftimony, they are our friends;the Romanes and Iefuites aduerfaries that write them. Yet can I not but truft them, and expofe them to the

be-

beleefe of others, becauſe they containe the very ſubſtance of the doctrine holden in the Popiſh Church. And though theſe words may paſſe away,or be denied,or qualified,or otherwiſe conſtrued, yet *litera ſcripta manet*, that which is in their bookes,they ſhall not deny, they cannot excuſe, they wil not refuſe for brats of their owne begetting,and botches of their owne breeding, in the vniuerſall corruption of their vaine and wicked imaginations. You ſhall heare no baſe nor beggerly authors, but the chiefe writers of the Romiſh Synagogue, the great Cardinals and Pentioners of that Court.

17 *Ecchius* cals the Scriptures,*Theologiam atramentariam*, an inke Diuinitie : *Pighius*, *Naſum cereum*, a noſe of waxe: *Melchior Canus*, *Iudicem mortuum*, a dead Iudge . Another, *Euangelium nigrum*, a blacke Goſpell. *Pennas anſerinas*, gooſe quils.*Regulam Leſbiam & plumbeā*,A *Leſbian* and leaden rule, a dead and dumbe letter,a killing letter, the matter of ſtrife. *Sphinges* riddles,*Sybillas leaues*,*Protagoras principles*. *A doubtful, obſcure,various,changeable, inſufficient ſhop of heretiks.**Dead ink*. **Scriptura eſt res inanimis*, The Scripture is a thing without ſoule, as other politique lawes.**The weake and falſe caſtle of holy Scriptures*. Theſe are but phraſes, or ſingle words,or ciaculations. Heare their graue ſentences : *Hæc eſt ſanè omnium intelligentium ſententia:* This is the opinion of all that vnderſtand ſoundly, who do place the authoritie and vnderſtanding of Scriptures in the approbation of the Church , and not on the contrary, who place the foundatiō of the Church in the authoritie of Scriptures. And afterward, *Dico nulla eſſe Chriſti præcepta, niſi quæ per Eccleſiam pro talibus accepta ſunt :* I ſay there are no commandements of Chriſt , which are not receiued for ſuch by the Church. Another, *Apoſtoli quædam conſcripſerunt, non vt ſcripta illa præeſſent fidei, & religioni noſtræ, ſed potiùs vt ſubeſſent:* The Apoſtles haue written certaine things,not that they ſhould be ouer our faith, but rather be vnder it.Is not this good reaſon ? And *Ecchius* againe: *Scriptura non eſt authentica ſine Eccleſiæ authoritate.* It is euident that the Church is more ancient then the Scriptures , and

Enchir.cap.4.
Hierar.l.3,c.3.

Lib.2.c.8.

*Lodou.Can.
Latar.in orat.
hab. in Conc.
Trident.
*Epiſc. Picto-
rienſis.
*Briſt.mot.48
Cuſan.ad Bo-
hem.epiſt.2.

Piggh.Hierar.
l.1.c.20.

Porcinum os
quocunque
cibo ieiunia
ſedat.

L 4   that

that the Scriptures haue no approbation without the authoritie of the Church . *Hofius* a Cardinall faith of the Pfalmes
of *Dauid*, which *Athanafius* fo highly commended, Saint *Auguftine* and many Fathers illuftrated in part or in all by their
Commentaries; yea Chrift our Sauiour and his Apoftles
haue alledged and commended them as commanding Scrip-

Aduer.Brent.
de legit.iudic.

tures, written by a king and a Prophet, *Quid ni fcriberet? Scri-
bimus indocti, doctiq; poëmata paffim.* Why fhould not *Dauid*
write? Euery Poet and piper can write Poemes. And therefore feeing this bafe eftimation is made of the holy Scrip-

Controu. 3.
de Ecclefia.

tures, is it maruell if *Pigghius* thinke that man mad that will
be ouerruled by the Scriptures? *Si dixeris hæc referri oportere
ad iudicium Scripturarum, communis te fenfus ignarum effe com-
probas*: If thou faift that thefe matters are to be referred to
the iudgment of the Scriptures, thou doeft manifeft thy felfe
to be void of common fenfe. Or may we not think it ftrange
that *Canus* faith , *Peftem effe fi omnia referantur ad iudicium*

Lib.3.cap.1.

Scripturarum : It were a plague if all things fhould be referred to the iudgement of the Scriptures . Or may we not
wonder that another dares fay and pretend , that *quidam ex
veteribus*, a certaine ancient Father belike there was, *qui ver-*

Socolou.de
veræ & falfæ
Ecclef.difcri-
mine.l.2.c.2.

*bum Dei , facramq; Scripturam pulcherimæ imagini fimilem
effe dixerit, qua vnum quidem & verum afpectum habeat, foli ip-
fius artifici Spiritui fancto & Ecclefiæ Dei cognitum, ita affecta
eft vt ex quacunque parte quis conftiterit, eum afpicere videatur,*
„ who faid the word of God and the holy Scriptures were
„ like a beautiful image, which indeed had but one true afpect,
„ knowne onely to the artificer, the holy Ghoft, & the Church,
„ notwithftanding fo affected, that on what part foeuer a man
„ ftands, it may feem to behold him. Where the good man ob-

Idem Partit.
Ecclef.p.758.
Trad.l.6.ar-
tic.30.

ferueth not how he plucketh out his owne eye to blemifh
ours; for he hath *The word of God, and Scriptures*, but the word
of God is as wel Traditions as Scriptures; and then what certaintie at all will he leaue, when both Tradition and Scriptures may deceiue with their glancing eyes? Yet in this he
faith true, that the Scripture glanceth on euery man, for fo it
doth, and maketh many a confcience blufh . *Coccius* layeth

to

to *Swenkfeldius* charge, that he saith *de Euangelio scripto : Doctrina Euangelij est humanum Euangelium, Scriptura est incerta, & flexibilis doctrina, quæ patitur se in varios sensus trahi:* Of the 🙶 written Gospell, The doctrine of the Gospell is a humane 🙶 Gospell, the Scripture is an vncertaine and flexible doctrine, 🙶 which permits it selfe to be wrested into diuers sences. How can he see this mote in his brothers eye, & not see the beames Mat·7· 3· in his owne and fellowes eies?

18　Let Saint *Chrysostome* aske these great Doctors this short question: I will leaue them to answer, at their leasure. Chysost.ad *Quid igitur accedis si Scripturis fidem non habes? Si Christo non* Popu·Anti-*credis? nunquam talem Christianum dixerim, sed potiùs & gen-* och.Hom.50. *tilibus peiorem.* What do you coming, if you giue no credit 🙶 to the Scriptures? If you beleeue not Christ? I will neuer 🙶 hold such a one to be a Christian, but rather worse then an 🙶 infidel. In meane while let him answer himselfe, *Frustra iactat* 🙶 *se Spiritum Sanctum habere, qui non loquitur ex Euangelio.* In vaine doth he boast to haue the holy Ghost, that speaketh 🙶 not out of the Gospell. But *Pigghius* knowing his fellowes 🙶 mindes, and feeling their distresse, not without cause complaines, (after a tedious, odious, loathsome and sacrilegious comparison of the certaintie of the Churches traditions against the word of God) *Si huius doctrinæ memores fuissemus,* Lib.3 c.1. *hæreticos scilicet non esse informandos aut conuincendos ex Scripturis, meliori sanè loco essent res nostræ : sed dum ostentandi ingenij, & eruditionis gratia cum Luthero in certamen descenditur Scripturarum, excitatum est quod nunc (proh dolor) videmus incendium.* If we had bene mindfull of this doctrine, that heretickes were 🙶 not to be taught or conuinced by Scriptures, certainely our 🙶 cause had bene much better; But whiles for ostentation of 🙶 wit and learning, we fell to the disputing by Scripture with 🙶 *Luther*, we see (wo worth vs) what a fire it hath kindled. Full 🙶 well did *Pigghius* perceiue that the Romish religion would neuer stand if it were tried by the touchstone of the written word of God. And this do they all most euidently confesse, while with one consent and voice they flie the triall of the Scripture.

19 For

19 For this caufe they equall and preferre any thing almoſt before them , they take vpon them to difpence with them; they will giue them no authoritie for that maieſtie they haue in themſelues , the Prophets and Apoſtles that wrote them, that fauing Son of God that confirmed & ſealed them with his blood: but from the authoritie of that Synagogue or rather Court, which(as hath bene proued)hath euer deteſted and abhorred them. *Papa poteſt diſpenſare contra ius diuinum.* The Pope can difpence (not onely with, but) againſt Gods Law. *Papa poteſt diſpenſare contra Apoſtolum,* The Pope may difpence (not onely with, but) againſt the Apoſtle. *Papa diſpenſat contra nouum Teſtamentum,* The Pope doth difpence, not onely with , but againſt the new Teſtament. *Papa poteſt diſpenſare de omnibus præceptis veteris & noui Teſtamenti,* The Pope can difpence with all the precepts of the old and new Teſtament. *Quæ hæc ſententiarum portenta,* What ſtrange? what monſtrous ſpeeches are theſe? And yet if worſe may be heare worſe. *Summa rei eſt, nullum verum argumentum è Scriptura, quæ vel maximè perſpicua videatur, erui poſſe, quod fidem Catholicam generet niſi accedat authoritas & interpretatio Eccleſiæ Catholica.* The ſumme of the matter is this, that no true
” argument can be drawne out of the Scripture be it neuer fo
” plaine, which may beget the Catholicke faith, except the au-
” thoritie and interpretation of the Catholicke Church do
” concurre. This he endeuoureth to iuſtifie by the example of *Eſau* and *Iacob: Iſaac non potuit eos diſtinguere , ſed Rebecca potuit. Iſaac* knew not one from the other, but *Rebecca* did. As who fhould fay, the Church knoweth the Scriptures, better then God that made them. For if ſubtill *Rebecca* muſt be the Church, then blind *Iſaac* muſt ſtand for God ; for he was her husband, as Chriſt was the Churches. Yet his ſpeech may ſtand good, though his proofe be naught. For if he take the Catholique faith for the preſent Romane faith, it is very true, that no pregnant place of Scripture cleareth it; but if he take it for the truth of God, euerie Chapter, euerie ſentence proueth it. But this mattereth little , for elſewhere thus he faith, abuſing a place of *Turtullian* which he wrote to a

good

lb.q.1.quicunque in gloſſ.
Diſtinct.34. lect.82. prejbit.
Panor extra. de diuortijs. cap.Fin.fum.
Angel.dict. Papa.

Socolouius partit. Eccleſ. p.767.

good purpoſe: *Nihil proficiet congreſſio Scripturarum, niſi pla-* Socol. de ve-
nc vt ſtomachi quis ineat verſionem & cerebri : The triall of the
Scripture profits nothing, except it be to bring a man in- Socol. de ve-
to the turning of his ſtomacke and braine; which is true, ræ & falſæ
as theſe old heretickes, and theſe new Catholiques abuſe Ecclef. diſ-
them. crim.l.1.c.1.

20 Our aduerſaries crie out againſt vs, that we do *delum-* Campion.
bare,diſioynt,mangle, or maſſacre the Scriptures, becauſe
with all *Antiquity* we ſeuer the certaine from the vncertaine,
the pure from the vnpure, the word of God,from the word
of man.And yet we leaue an honorable reſpect euen to thoſe
we eſteeme leaſt, for their grauitie and antiquitie, and giue
them the next place vnto the Scriptures, and perhaps ſeate
them ſomewhat too neare them. But all this will not ſerue
our turnes.They are not aſhamed to ſay, we blot out the A- Muri ciuit.
poſtolicall writing. The Romaniſts pretend and vndertake ſanct.fund.2.
the patronage of all the Scriptures,as *Demoſthenes* Tutors fund.3.
did him and his fifteene talents; in the moſt ſolemne and ſe- Plutarch in
rious manner. Yet ſee how they ſcorne them, deride,ſcoffe, Demoſthen.
blaſpleme them. They leſſen their authoritie,denie their ſufficiencie,make voide what they liſt,retaine what they pleaſe,
corrupt it by falſe tranſlatiō, miſ-interpret it by curſed gloſ-
ſes, diſpence with it and againſt it,as with the lawes of ſinfull men. Good ſubiects dare not,would not if they durſt,ſo
diſgrace the lawes of a mortall King,as theſe vaſſals and veſſels of wrath dare preſume to deface, and diſcountenance
the word of the King of Kings.

21 *Bellarmine* will not haue the Pope *Anti chriſt*, becauſe C.Bellar.de
he is Chriſts Vicar, and ſo profeſſeth himſelfe:but *Anti chriſt* Roman.Pon-
effert ſe ſuper omne quod dicitur Deus,lifteth himſelfe aboue all tifice.l. 3.c.1.
that is called God,& therfore the Pope being but Gods Vi-
car,maketh himſelfe vnder God,& therefore cannot be *Anti-*
chriſt:this is his reaſon. But obſerue the propheſie,and apply
it. Neuer was there garment ſo fitted to a bodie, as this is
ſhaped to the Popes iuſt feature, and that two wayes; firſt
the Apoſtle doth not ſay,*quod eſt Deus*,which is God,but *quod*
dicitur Deus, which is called God.All Magiſtrates,eſpecially
of

of high eſtates, as Princes,Kings,and Emperors, and Angels
too, are called Gods: the Biſhop of Rome lifteth himſelfe a-
boue all theſe, as farre aboue the Emperour as the Sunne is

De Maior. & aboue the Moone ; and commandeth Angels, to carrie and
obedientia,c. recarrie ſoules at his pleaſure. God is God in earth and in
Solitæ. heauen ; but the Pope is aboue God in earth, though God
Staple.inprȩ- be aboue him in heauen,or elſe God is not in earth at all,but
fat. doſt. in heauen onely. For the Pope is ſaid to be *ſupremum in terris*
princ. ad *numen*, the ſupreme god-head in the earth. And peraduen-
Greg.13. ture would be taken for God in heauen, or for his Sonne *Ie-*
Margar. de *ſus Chriſt*; as *Margarinus* words may well intimate:*Te vnum*
la Bigne in
fine epiſtolæ *reſpicio Pontificem,qui ſcias & poſſis compati infirmitatibus meis,*
ad Greg.13. *tentatus per omnia pro ſimilitudine* : *Itaque adeo cum ſiducia ad*
in tom.pri- *thronum gratiæ tuæ, vt miſericordiam conſequar & inueniam apud*
mo Bibliot.
ſanſto. Patrũ. *te gratiam in auxilio opportuno.* I looke towards thee alone
Heb.4.15.16. *as the Biſhop* which knoweſt and canſt feele my infirmities,
„ and art in all things tempted in like ſort.Therefore I flie with
„ confidence vnto the throne of thy grace, that I may obtaine
„ mercie, and find grace with thee in time of need. This to
Gregorie the thirteenth, ſcarſe a Saint, much leſſe a God.
Therfore he ſetteth himſelfe without queſtion aboue all that
is called God,in heauen and in earth, and yet is not a God.
And if there were no other, yet this were a very probable,if
not a demonſtratiue reaſon, to proue him *Anti-chriſt*:for he
ſetteth himſelfe aboue all that are called Gods, and yet in
truth are no Gods.But this is nothing,the Pope exalteth himſelfe aboue the onely very true God,& his Son Ieſus Chriſt,
whom he hath made heire of all things ; and by whom he
Hebr.1. made the world. For what elſe doth he when he taketh his
Scepter out of his hand? will giue his Lawes no farther allowance then may ſtand with his liking? that diſſolueth
what God bindeth?that tieth what God looſeth? By which
he doth not only ſay in his heart,there is no God,like a foole,
but alſo doth manifeſt vnto the world, that he holdeth none
other to be God,but himſelfe alone,like a mad diuell.For he
that giueth authoritie to a law, is aboue the law maker, as
Iuſtinian was aboue *Paulus, Vlpian, Pomponius, Trebatius,* and
others

others. He may deny this in word, but he doth this in deed, *quid verba audiam cum facta videam?*

22 Let him neuer smeare it ouer with faire words, when his ouert deeds do make his sacrilegious presumption and madnesse to be so knowne to all men, that we may iustly say, as one did vpon like occasion : *He that knowes not this, is vn-* Aug. *learned; he that will not acknowledge it, is peruerse, he that dissembles it, is an hypocrite; he that denieth it, is impudent, he that defends it, is desperate and damnable.*

23 They do confesse in word and writing, that all the Canons of the Scriptures, yea and more then God would haue in the Canon, are the word of God; and yet are no farther allowed then they are authorized by man. Aske *Salmeron*,and he will vouchsafe you a good discourse,why God would haue his word of the old and new Testament committed to writing. And he giueth approoued reasons, as well in respect of $\begin{smallmatrix}\text{Tom. 1. Pro-}\\\text{legom.25.}\end{smallmatrix}$ the Gentiles, of Apostate heretickes, and also of the faithfull. And answers, why God gouerned his Church without Scriptures before *Moses* (though that be vncertaine,) and a while in the Apostles time before they were written . For first, the Church was but in few, and they taught in great measure by Gods Spirit. The Apostles liued to whom all questions and doubts might be referred. And in substance concludeth, that the Church could neuer haue consisted in truth and peace, without the will of God had bene written in Scriptures. Yet like a good Cow, that had giuen a good meale of milke, he kicks downe all this with his heele; and telleth vs plainly with diuers reasons, *That the Euangelists are not sufficient wit-* Tom. 1. Pro-*nesses for that they wrote. First,they were not present at euery thing* legom. 32. *Chrift did, Marke and Luke at very few. Mathew and Iohn not* ,, *at all. Secondly, they bring no witnesses for that they did not see.* ,, *Thirdly,they note not all the times. Fourthly,not all places. Fifthly,* ,, *Rurfus neque vt teftes confcripferunt , quandoquidem nec iurati,* Quis vnquam *nec rogati , nec de mandato Iudicis teftificantur .* Againe, they ab hiftorico iuratores exewrote not as witnesses, for that they were neither sworne,nor git? &c. required , nor testified by the commandement of the Iudge. Seneca. de morte Clau-Sixtly, *Dicendum itaqne Euangeliftas fcripfiffe tanquam hifto-* dij Cæfaris. *riographos*

riographos, quorum non est omnibus quæ enarrant, dum gerantur,
,, *interfuisse.* We muſt therefore hold the Euangeliſts to haue
,, written like hiſtoriographers, of whom it is not required they
,, ſhould be preſent at all was done, and recorded by them. *Non*
negamus Apoſtolos oculis vidiſſe, & manibus contrectaſſe: ſed hæc
nobis modo fidem non faciunt indubiam, niſi quatenus ab Eccleſia
illa viſio Apoſtolorum & contrectatio comprobata eſt. Quamobrem
Euangeliſtæ nunc nobis fidem non faciunt, ſatis eſt eos fidem am-
,, *plam ipſi Eccleſiæ ab initio feciſſe, &c.* We denie not the Apoſtles
,, to haue ſeene with their eyes, and to haue handled with their
,, hands; but theſe make no vndoubted credit vnto vs now, but
,, ſo farre forth as that viſion and handling of the Apoſtles is
,, approoued by the Church. Wherefore now the Euangeliſts
,, giue vs no certaintie; it is ſufficient that they made abundant
,, faith from the beginning, vnto the Church. He ſaith elſewhere, *Si autem Eccleſiæ ſecluſo teſtimonio, Euangeliſtæ conſide-*
rentur, quantum ad humani iuris viam attinet, fidem plenam, imò
ſemiplenam non faciunt, quia neque vt notarij, neque vt teſtes ro-
,, *gati, vt suprà dictum eſt teſtificãtur.* For if the Euangeliſts ſhould
,, be conſidered, the Churches teſtimonie being ſecluded, as
,, farre as belongeth to the courſe of humane law, they beget
,, not a faith either perfect, or halfe perfect, becauſe they wit-
,, neſſe, (as before is ſaid) neither as notaries, nor as produced
,, witneſſes. *Credere ergo ſanctam Eccleſiam, omnium articulorum*
eſt præcipuus & maximus, quo credito, omnia fide accipiuntur quæ
credenda ſunt; illo verò non credito, nihil perfectè ad ſalutem credi-
tur. Imò immedicabilis efficitur homo, quia peccat in Spiritum ſan-
ctam, Eccleſiam regentem & illuſtrantem, quod quidem peccatum
,, *non remittitur ei, neque in hoc ſeculo, neque in futuro.* Therefore
,, to beleeue the holy Church, of all articles is the chiefe and the
,, greateſt; which beleeued, all things are receiued which ought
,, to be beleeued; but this not beleeued, nothing is perfectly be-
,, leeued to ſaluation; yea that man is made vncurable, becauſe
,, he ſinneth againſt the holy Ghoſt, gouerning and enlighte-
,, ning the Church, which ſinne certainly is not remitted to him,

Salmer. Tom.
1. Prolegom,
8. pag. 4. neither in this world nor the world to come. And in farther
diſcourſe he ſaith, *(Scripturæ) canonicæ propterea dicuntur, quod*

in

in ſacrorum librorum canonem ab Eccleſia receptæ & repoſitæ ſunt,
& quia rectè credendi, & benè viuendi nobis ſunt regula : denique
quoniam omnes alias doctrinas, leges, ſcripturas, ſiue ſunt Eccleſi-
aſticæ ſiuè apocryphæ, ſiue humanæ, regere & moderari debent. Nam
quatenus illis conſentiunt eatenus admittuntur, repudiantur verò
& reprobantur, quatenus vel in minimo contradicunt. Scripturam
verò diuinam facit authoritate ſua Spiritus ſanctus, canonicam ve-
rò facit iudicium Eccleſiæ Catholicæ, illam eſſe à Deo declarans. Fur- ”
thermore the Scriptures are ſaid to be canonicall, becauſe they ”
are receiued and placed in the Canon of the holy bookes, and ”
becauſe they are our rule of beleeuing rightly, and liuing well: ”
Finally, becauſe they ought to gouerne and moderate all o- ”
ther doctrines, lawes, ſcriptures, whether Eccleſiaſticall, or ”
Apocyphall, or humane. For in as much as they agree vnto ”
thoſe, in ſo much are they admitted; but reiected and refuſed ”
in as much, as in the leaſt thing they diſagree from them. The ”
holy Ghoſt by his authoritie makes the Scripture diuine, but ”
the iudgement of the Catholicke Church makes it Canoni- ”
call, declaring it to be from God. There was neuer Canoni- ”
call Scripture therefore, before the Councell of Trent; for
there was neuer any generall and œcumenicall Councell,
which is the Church repreſentatiue, that euer made any Con-
ſtitution, for placing of the Scriptures in the Canon before it.

24　*Soto Maior,* a greater ſot, concurreth with theſe. And Soto Maior
Doctor *Stapleton, Per comparationem dilucide oſtendit ex voce* in Cant. c. 2.
ſeu teſtimonio, iudicio & authoritate Eccleſiæ Catholicæ conſtare In antidotis
nobis que ſint Scripturæ, ſacræ, diuinæ & Canonicæ; quanquam ip- Euang. Ioan.
ſa Eccleſia ſacras, diuinas ac canonicas non faciat, ſed tantum vt ipſi c. 13.
libri, ſacri, diuini & canonici, pro talibus habeantur, & cognoſcan-
tur, certo certius, quemadmodum in illa mulierum duarum concer-
tatione: He manifeſtly ſhewes by compariſon, from the voice ”
or teſtimonie, iudgement and authoritie of the Catholicke ”
Church, it is appointed to vs which are the holy, diuine, and ”
Canonicall Scriptures; although the Church it ſelfe make not ”
the Scriptures holy, diuine, and Canonicall (*this is contrary to* ”
Salmeron,) but onely that thoſe holy, diuine and Canonicall ”
　　　　　　　　　　　　　　　　　　　　　　bookes

,, bookes fhould be fo accounted, and more certainly knowne
,, to be fo then certainty it felfe,like as in that contention of the
,, two women.

1. Kings.   25 Aske a * Pope and he will tell you, *Si vetus nouumq́;*
* Nicol.Papa *Teſtamentum ſunt recipienda,non quod codici Canonum ex toto ha-*
diſt. 19. *beantur annexa,ſed quod de his recipiendis ſanĉti Papæ Innocentij*
prolata eſſe videtur ſententia; reſtat nimirum quod Decretales Ro-
manorum Pontificum Epiſtolæ ſunt recipiendæ; If the old and new
,, Teſtament be to be receiued, not becauſe they are accounted
,, wholly to be annexed to the book of Canons, but becauſe the
,, determination of holy Pope *Innocent* ſeemeth to be giuen for
,, their receipt,it remaineth verily that the Decretals of the Ro-
,, miſh Biſhops are to be receiued. Wherein are included many
blaſphemies, but two principall; the one that the authority of
the Scriptures depends on the ſentence of a Pope,a mortal and
miſerable, a ſinfull, and a ſhamefull,or rather ſhameleſſe man.
The other, that the Decretall Epiſtles, ſome fooliſh,ſome partiall, ſome erronious, ſome hereticall, ſome dangerous, ſome
ſuperſtitious, ſome blaſphemous,ſome idolatrous,are made of
equall authoritie with the Scriptures of God. O moſt damnable impietie,and wicked Idolatrie! What good Chriſtian can
endure it? What honeſt heart will not deteſt and abhorre it?
Yet are the Romaniſts ſo paſt all ſhame, that with brazen af-
ces and iron foreheads, and whoriſh hearts, they abbet, approoue,and publiſh the ſame with one conſent as before; and
Turrecrema. yet more may be alledged. *Ioan.de Turrecremata,* a Cardinall
as others aboue named,ſaith: *Quod illis libris (id eſt,Scripturis)*
ſit credendum firmitèr, non conſtat, niſi per authoritatem Eccleſiæ;
,, *vnde Auguſt. Euangelio non crederem:* That we ſhould ſtedfaſt-
,, ly beleeue the Scriptures,appeareth not but by the authoritie
,, of the Church, as S. *Auguſtine* writeth : *I would not beleeue the*
*Goſpell, but that I am mooued by the authoritie of the Church.*As
much to ſay, if the ſonne had not made me know his father, I
had not bene acquainted with him, therefore the ſonne is his
fathers better.

26 The Samaritans reaſoned much better then ſo. They
were firſt told of the Meſſias by the woman, and vpon her
word

word they beleeued, and came to Chriſt: but when they
heard him, they beleeued, not becauſe of her words, but becauſe they had ſeene him and heard him themſelues. It is
often obiected out of *Auguſtine, Euangelio non crederem, niſi* In Ioh.4 tract.
Ecleſiæ me commoueret authoritas: I would not beleeue the 35.in fine.
Goſpell, but that I am moued by the authoritie of the
Church. True it is, his firſt motiue was the Church, but his
certaine perſwaſion came from the Scriptures, as by this example: *Primò per fœminam, poſtea per præſentiam, ſic agitur hodie:* Firſt by the woman, then by his preſence, ſo fareth it now
with *thoſe that are out of the Church, and are not yet Chriſtians.
Chriſt is taught by Chriſtian friends, as it were by the woman, that
is, by the Churches inſtruction. They come to Chriſt, and beleeue by
this fame, and many more, and with more confidence beleeue in him
that he is the Sauiour of the world,*after they had heard himſelf;
where we ſee Saint *Auguſtines* meaning. The Church leadeth
men to the Scriptures, as a ſeruant vnto the maiſter: but the
maiſters will muſt be knowne at his owne mouth. *Philip*
brought *Nathanael* to *Chriſt*, therefore *Nathanael* muſt reue- Ioh.1.45.
rence *Philip* aboue *Chriſt*. *Naaman* had not knowne nor 2.King.5.3.
heard of the Prophet *Elizeus*, if his maide had not told him,
or them that informed him; therefore ſhe is their better, and
they her Lords. The reaſons are all one: both abſurd, and a-
gainſt common ſenſe. Yet another Cardinall now liuing, Viuit, imò in
flouriſhing, and a part of the ſacred Conclaue, followeth Senatū venit.
his fellowes for company, and ventures his ſoule with them,
and ſaith, *Sanè credere hiſtorias Teſtamenti veteris, vel Euange-* Bellar. de Ec-
lia Marci & Luca, eſſe Canonica ſcripta, imò illas eſſe diuinas cl.mil.l.3.c.14
Scripturas, non eſt omninò neceſſarium ad ſalutem: Verily to be- ”
leeue the hiſtories of the old Teſtament, or the Goſpels of ”
Marke and *Luke* to be Canonicall writings, yea that they be ”
diuine Scriptures, it is not at all neceſſary vnto ſaluation. ”
This is the learning of this preſent age.

27 The Lord threatned his people for their ſinnes, thus:
Behold you deſpiſers, and wonder, and vaniſh away, for the Lord Habac.1.5.
will worke a worke in your dayes, a worke which you ſhall not be- Act.13.41.
leeue, though a man tell it you. If euer there were a wonderfull
M   plague

plague of excæcation, blindneſſe and hardneſſe of heart; this
is it which an honeſt man could neuer beleeue, though it
were told him, it is ſo incredible, but that it is ſo vſuall; the
wicked cannot conceiue, becauſe they are hardened in their

Marius Victo- ſinne. *An Scripturas quas legimus vanas epinaris? ſi vt nomine*
rin de genera- *ita & re Chriſtianus eſt quiſpiam, neceſſe habet venerari Scriptu-*
tione diuina. *ras:* What? (ſaith an ancient writer) doeſt thou thinke the
" Scriptures we reade are vaine? If any, as in name, ſo in deed,
" be a Chriſtian, it is neceſſarily required he ſhould reuerence
" the Scriptures. But may we take *Bellarmine* at his word? is it
his conſtant opinion? will he not? hath he not retracted it?
No: this was no ſodaine motion, he had ſaid as much and
more before, and therefore this is *ſecunda cogitatio,* his reſolued opinion, which to vnderſtand the better, heare what he

De verbo Dei ſaid: *In Scripturis plurima ſunt, quæ ex ſe, non pertinent ad ſidem,*
non ſcripto.l.4 *i. quæ non ideo ſcripta ſunt, quia neceſſariò credenda erant, ſed ne-*
c. 12. *ceſſariò creduntur quia ſcripta ſunt, vt patet de omnibus hiſtorijs*
Teſtamenti veteris, de multis etiam hiſtorijs Euangelij & Actuum
Apoſtolorum, de ſalutationibus in Epiſtolis, alijſq, id genus rebus:
" There are many things in the Scriptures, which of themſelues
" do not appertaine vnto faith, that is, which were not there-
" fore written becauſe they were neceſſary to be beleeued,
" but they are neceſſarily beleeued becauſe they are written,
" as is euident by all the hiſtories of the old Teſtament, and
" many alſo of the hiſtories of the Goſpell, the Acts of the A-
" poſtles, the ſalutations in the Epiſtles, and other things of
" that kind. This is *verbum abbreuiatum* indeed, leſſe then an e-
pitome of the Scriptures. If this be not delumbation of the
Scriptures, I know not what is. Firſt, he makes God do much
in vaine, yea to take his owne name in vaine: *Fruſtra fit per*
plura, quod fieri poteſt per pauciora: It is vaine to go about, when
one may go the nearer way, or to make more coſt thē needs.
If it were not neceſſary to be beleeued, why was it written?
What conſūption of Gods creatures, pen, ink & paper? What
exhauſting of labor? What waſte of time, if leſſe would haue
ſerued? What is the end for wᶜʰ the Scriptures were written,
but to teach vs faith and obedience? May we thinke God ſo
tedious

tedious in the Scriptures, which indeed are the moſt cōpen-
dious bookes, to containe ſo much matter, that euer were
written, as that he would vſe ſo many words to ſo litle purpoſe, being not needfull or neceſſary to be beleeued? It was
better ſaid by ancient writers, *Dicere verbum aliquod in Scrip-* Orat. 1.
turis redundare, eſt graue nefas; quod ſi nihil redundat, nihil eſt ina-
ne, nihil ſuperuacaneum: To ſay (ſaith *Gregory Niſſen*) any word
in the Scripture is more thē needs, is a grieuous offence. For
if nothing redound, nothing is in vaine, nothing is ſuperflu-
ous. And Saint *Hilary* ſaith, *Dei ſermo & vera ſapientiæ doctri-* Lib. 12. de
na, quæ loquitur, & perfecta & abſoluta ſunt : Whatſoeuer the Trinit.
word of God and the doctrine of true wiſedome ſpeaketh, ”
is perfect and abſolute. We may ſee the difference betweene ”
reuerend antiquitie and preſumptuous noueltie; they ſpake
of the Scriptures as Gods bookes, our aduerſaries as ill as of
any prophane authors, if not worſe. Some qualification
might be giuen to the Cardinals words if they had bin vttered alone, yet conſidering that which followeth in him, and
is before ſet downe by me, it cannot be, but that his direct
meaning is to derogate from the abſolute perfection of the
Scripture, as if in ſome things it were ſuperfluous, in others
defectiue. From ſuch damnable conceits, good Lord deliuer vs.

28 But is it not ſtrange, that all our aduerſaries with one
voice hold, *that the Scriptures containe not all things neceſſary to*
faith and manners, or to ſaluation? and yet *Bellarmine* is of opinion, that welnigh three parts of the Bible was more then
needed to be beleeued. I could wiſh that this Cardinall had
conſulted with his ancient and better : Saint *Chryſoſtome*
would haue taught him a more wholeſome leſſon : *Nihil in* In Gen. hō. 28.
Scripturâ ſacrâ inuenire licet quod abſque ratione aliquâ ſit ſcrip-
tum, quod non & latentem in ſe habeat vtilitatem: A man can find ”
nothing in the holy Scripture that is written without ſome ”
cauſe, or that which hath not in it ſome hidden profit. *Bel-* ”
larmine ſlipt a *gaudie*, when he ouerskipt this authoritie,
which is as oppoſite to this of his, as light is to darkneſſe,
truth to error. A good [vnpartiall Biſhop of the primitiue
　　　　　　　M 2　　　　　　　Church,

Church,to a nouellant,flattering,glauering,afpiring, ambitious Cardinall of Antichrifts traine and family. How will
Rom.15.4. he anfwer Saint *Paul*,that faith, *Whatfoeuer things were written aforetime,were written for our learning, that we through patience and comfort of the Scriptures might haue hope.* This the Apoftle fpake of the old Teftament, much more of the new, fay the Rhemifts. Set this againft *Bellarmines* words , and what are they but a flat contradiction ? *They were not written therefore, becaufe they were neceffarily to be beleeued,* (faith *Bellarmine.*) *All that was written (euen all hiftories and all) were written for our learning, that we might haue hope,* faith *S. Paul.* Can Cardinall *Bellarmine* be true to *S. Peters* keyes,that will be fo falfe to *S.Pauls* fword?

29 As lafciuious talke founds to a modeft and chaft eare, or loathfome meate fauours to a found palate, fo do thefe wicked, ghaftly,and hellifh deprauations of Gods word and holy Scriptures vnto an honeft hearted Chriftian. But fuppofe,as the truth is,that the Scriptures of God be their moft implacable enemy, and that they ftand in the way againft Antichrift, aboue all other armour, munition, weapons offenfiue and defenfiue ; yet they cannot deny but that they are the word of that God whom they profeffe to ferue, and of his Sonne Iefus Chrift,whom they call their Sauiour, and of the holy Ghoft whom they acknowledge their fanctifier. Me thinkes that for Gods fake who is the God of truth, and for his Sonne Iefus Chrifts fake , who is the way, the truth, and the life; and for the holy Ghofts fake, that infpireth and leadeth into all truth, they fhould beare more reuerence vnto them,then fo to deiect,vilifie,debafe,and fcorne the word and Scriptures of God with fuch fcurrilous and fcullianly termes, as I haue not heard or read giuen vnto the moft contemptible bookes that haue bene written, fhall I fay by ancient Chriftians? nay I dare fay by any ancient Philofophers, Orators,or licentious Poets.

30 Is it not fufficient to fay, *Scriptura non fufficiunt,* The Scriptures are not fufficient to the doctrine of faluation? or that they haue bene approoued by the Catholicke Church
of

of *Rome*? or that the Pope, or his Church, or both, fhould haue the greateft,and if you will, the onely fwinge and fway in the interpreting of them?(which notwithftading are falfe, and cannot without impudencie be affirmed, moft certainly can neuer be proued,) but they muft call it an inkie, a blacke Gofpell, a mute and dumbe Iudge, and fuch like groffe titles aud teatmes as before are out of themfelues difcouered, and giue it no authoritie in refpect of the Author principall, which is God; or fecondarie, which were Prophets and A-poftles; nor from the maieftie and holineffe of the word it felfe: but all as fhall be allowed by their fupreme God in earth, the Bifhop of Rome, a principall partie in the contro-uerfies now depending? It were lothfome to run ouer what hath bene before faid in this Chapter,of our Aduerfaries info-lencie,& vnmannerlineffe, impudency & gracelefnes againft the Scriptures. A good and deuout Chriftian will be forie to heare or reade them once, will take no pleafure to repeate them often. Let euerie gracious heart deteft and abhorre fuch proud, peremptorie, wicked and pernicious blafphe-mies; and learne to giue vnto the word of truth and life that due refpect which it worthily deferueth. And let all decei-ued Papifts confider how they may in any matter truft them with any inferiour Antiquity,that dare thus abufe the books of Gods owne librarie.

31 He that is not *faithfull in little, who will truft him with* Luke 16.10. *much ?*but he that is not faithfull in much, who will truft him with any thing? They that are fo fawcie with Gods, will they not be bold with mens writings? Trie them as far you as wil, but truft them not; *No man that doth a miracle in my name,* Mark.9.39. *(*faith our Sauiour*)can lightly fpeake euill of me.*Verily if *Bellar-mine* and his fellowes could worke miracles in Chrifts name, as they pretend they do, they could neuer fpeake fo wicked-ly of his word.

32 But herein they demonftratiuely manifeft themfelues, *not to be of God,becaufe they heare not Gods word;* For *they that* Ioh.8.47. *are of God heare Gods word,* and reuerence and loue it; will 1 Ioh.4.6. neither fpeake nor heare euill of it, becaufe they reuerence

and

and loue and honor God the author of it. Howbeit, as that Sorbonist said, it had bene better *if Saint Paul had neuer written any Epiſtle* ; ſo am I verily perſwaded by that I reade, and is before deliuered, that there is no obſtinate, reſolued, learned Papiſt, but would thinke it a faire day, and would warme himſelfe heartily at that fire wherein all the diuine Scriptures in the world ſhould be burned. Such is their ardent and furious zeale towards them. Witneſſe their often burning of Bibles in vulgar tongues, vnder pretence of corrupt tranſlations; their traducing of the Originall of the old and new Teſtament, in compariſon of their corruptions which they would obtrude vpon the Church of God; their railing on it vnder colour of the letter and bare Scripture; their preferring their Church, yea their Pope before it; and finally *are ſo iealous of, and thinke ſo dangerous ſome parts of Scripture, as*

The Epiſtles of Saint Paul. *Saint Paules Epiſtles*; that as a worthy and learned knight heard *by credible report (though he ſaw it not) ſome* Ieſuites of late in Italy in *ſolemne Sermons, &c.* cōmend *S. Peter for a worthy ſpirit, and haue cenſured Paul as a hot headed perſon, tranſported with pangs of zeale* : with worſe then this. By all which they ſhew their venimous tooth and cankered heart againſt the Scriptures, which they could wiſh in one fire, as the Tyrant wiſhed his Nobles heads all on one neck, that he might

Irenæus. cut them all off at one ſtroke. *Ex Scripturis conuicti in accuſationem vertuntur Scripturarum* : *Being conuinced by the Scriptures they turne to accuſe the Scriptures* : as the dog byteth the ſtone, which is throwne at him, though he hurt his teeth, and not the ſtone.

33 But ſuppoſe we grant them all this, that they are the onely and ſole poſſeſſors of the Scriptures; they may raile on them as they liſt, they may authoriſe them at their pleaſure, or caſt them off, when they will; the Church may interpret them ; the Pope may expound them; his ſenſe muſt be the true ſenſe, neuer to be altered or gainſaid. Will all this, if it were granted, ſatisfie them? May an honeſt Chriſtian Catholicke reſt vpon this ; That the truth is determined by the Popes and Churches expoſition, whereunto we muſt ſtand

and

and truſt? No, ſaith Cardinall *Cuſanus*, it mattereth not
how Pope, or Councell, or Father, or any haue interpreted
or expounded them, they *muſt be taken according to the cur-* Epiſtola ſe-
rent practiſe of the Church. The preſent time, muſt giue the true cunda ad Bo-
tune of the Scriptures, as much to ſay, as the preſent age muſt emos.
controll if need be, all the ancient expoſitions and interpretations of the Scriptures, whether by Fathers, or Church,
or Pope, or whomſoeuer; and the greateſt *Antiquitie* muſt
ſtrike ſaile and fall vnder the Lee of the freſheſt Noueltie, to
be braued and boarded at their owne pleaſure.

34 Is not this ſtrange learning? In another epiſtle to the Epiſtola 3.
ſame people he ſaith, *That a man muſt change his minde as the
Church changes hers, and ſhe may vary by the power of the keyes,
as ſhe will, in diuers caſes. Vti quondam vita coniugalis virginali,
poſthæc virginalis prælata coniugali exiſtit.* As in times paſt the ,,
maried eſtate was preferred before virginitie, but now vir- ,,
ginitie is preferred before Mariage. And ſo that which by ,,
their learning was more meritorious in times paſt, is now
leſſe; that which was then leſſe, is now more. Thus may they
preferre a yong deuice before an old, and yet claime *Antiquitie* againſt all the world: in ſo much that God himſelfe is
ſubiect to mutabilitie if the Church alter: *Sicut quondam
Coniugium præferebatur Caſtitati per Eccleſiam, ita apud Deum
remunerantem; & poſtea mutato iudicio Eccleſiæ, mutatum eſt &
Dei iudicium.* As mariage was ſometime preferred before ,,
Chaſtitie by the Church, ſo was it with God the rewarder of ,,
it: afterward when the iudgement of the Church was alte- ,,
red, ſo was Gods iudgement alſo. What is this but to call ,,
good euill, and euill good, ſweet ſoure, and ſoure ſweet, Iſa.5.20.
which God abhorreth in men? How ſinfull then is it aboue
meaſure to make God acceſſarie to ſo great an iniquity?

35 *If God iuſtifieth, who ſhall condemne?* If God in the beginning thought Mariage good and rewarded it, as is confeſſed,
can it be made euill by the Church, and condemned or puniſhed, as is pretended? This is to make that vncleane which
God hath ſanctified: nay more, they will make God himſelfe
to account that profane, which he hath hallowed: and ſo

do binde God to the mutabilitie of the Church., which for
waxing & waining, and variablenesse & changing, is likened
to the Moone. As good a rest to leane vpon, as the brokē reed
of Egypt, which when a man trusteth vnto, it pierceth the
hand, nay the heart and conscience, which is thereby led out
of the way, & wounded, as the man that between *Hierusalem*
and *Iericho*, feil among theeues. This one would not onely
say, but might iustly sweare, especially if the Church be taken as it is now contracted into the person of the Pope, who
is made by the Iesuites all in all; and yet may be such a one as
Pope *Leo* the tenth, who in comparison of many was tollerable, and yet could call the *Gospell, the fable of Christ, Quid
mihi narras istam de Christo fabulā* ? What telle st thou me this
fable of Christ? He might haue lent it his eare, though he likt
it not in his heart, for he held his riches and honour, his title
and triple crowne vnder pretence of it. The farther consideration whereof must be deferred, till I shall speake of the
crackt and rotten props of the Romane Synagogue. Meane
while let the courteous Reader but seriously and with an
honest heart consider, what reuerence and respect we beare
to the holy Scriptures of God, as the purest fountaines of
liuing waters; and make them not onely our chiefe, but our
onely *Antiquitie*, whereby we would gladly trie our cause,
and proue our selues the true Church; and how basely and
blasphemously our aduersaries speake of it, write of it, abuse
it, refuse it for any euidence at all, but when, and where, and
how themselues list, and account it as a very fable. But I will
conclude in one of the Popes white sonnes words, but better
applied then he doth: *Nihil contra Petri ædificium arena casula:
What are sandie grounds to Christs foundation ? the threshold of
hell against the gates of heauen ? the Synagogogue of Antichrist,
against the fold of Christ ; or heresie against the Church of God ?*
or all Traditions against Scripture, on which we are contented onely to rely and rest.

36 Doctor *Kellison* draweth all our positions that we hold
against the Churches vnlimited and transcendent authorities
or the Popes soueraigne & omnipotent infallibility in allowing

Marginal notes:
2. King. 18. 21
Balæus.
Muri sanct.
ciuit. fund. 4.

ing and interpreting the Scriptures at their owne pleasure, and their best aduantage; vnto the open way to Atheisme and infidelitie: yea he will haue almost all things we teath to tend vnto vtter apostacie, and irrecouerable damnation, euen this triall of truth by the Scriptures, being to vs a very *Rhadamanthus*. But we call heauen and earth to witnesse this day against him and them all; and iustifie, that the Papists not onely open a gap, or prepare a way, but haue opened the very gates of hell, and proclaimed Infidelitie and Atheisme to the whole world, while they thus disgrace & make voide the singular preheminence and predominant power of Gods written word, which is the ground, foundation, rule, and touch-stone of all truth.

37   The Physitions haue their *Galen* and *Hippocrates*, the Lawyers their *Iustinian*, the Philosophers their *Aristotle*, the Mathematicians their *Euclide*, euery facultie hath an author to rest vpon; whom to reiect or refuse is a shame, and deserues a hissing out of the schooles. Onely Diuinitie hath no *Commune principium*, no Author to rest and relie vpon; the holy Scriptures are cashired from the schooles of Diuinitie. They daily brag and braue vs with challenge of disputations, as diuers haue done; though we neuer did, neither do, neither will, refuse them, yet may iustly say, *Contra principia negantem, non est disputandum*: Against him that denieth the principles of Art, there is no disputing. They would haue vs run to them into other nations to trie our valour, as one *Pompedius Silo* said to *Caius Marius*: If thou be *Caius Marius* that Plutarch in noble Captaine, leaue thy campe and come out to battell. To C. Mario. whom *Marius* answered, If thou be a noble Captaine, come plucke me out by the eares to the battell. So we to our aduersaries, Let them fight with these weapons, and plucke vs out of Gods vineyard by the eares, if they dare.

CHAP.

CHAP. VII.

◆Whether Proteſtants or Papiſts admit or reiect the ſecond
Antiquitie, which is the Councels.

Rom Scriptures we deſcend to Councels, as
from mount *Nebo*, and the top of *Piſga*,
where we might beſt ſee the land of promiſe
with *Moſes*, vnto the valley of *Iordan*: a
fruitfull countrey we confeſſe, but nothing
ſo pleaſant, or ſo comfortable, as where we
might ſee more plainly the good promiſes and bleſſings of
God; as from mount *Sion* where God dwelleth in perfect
beautie, to the citie *Ieruſalem*, where the faithfull inhabite; as
from *Sanctum ſanctorum* and the Arke of Gods ſtrength, to the
Tabernacle of the congregation, where the people aſſemble:
as from the immediat ſcepter of the immortall God ſitting in
his Maieſtie, to the aſſemblies of mortall men gathered together in his holy Name. No queſtion but *Zerubbabels* temple
was very faire, but farre from the glorie of that was built by
Salomon: that though the people ſhouted with a great ſhout,
and reioyced, yet many of the Prieſts and Leuites and the
chiefe of the Fathers, ancient men, when they remembred the
glorie of the one, and ſaw the foundations of the other, they
could not refraine to declare the ſorrowes of their hears, with
the teares of their eyes: *They wept with a lowd voice*: not ſo
much miſdeeming of Gods prouidence in the latter, that
was meaner, as admiring Gods Maieſtie in the former, and
lamenting the ruines of that which was moſt excellent.

    2 So gracious is the name of Councels, ſo venerable is the
aſſemblies of Fathers. Some of them are for time ancient, for
truth receiued, for care of Gods Church renowned: yet if we
compare them with the honour of the Scriptures, which are
the vndeniable and inuincible power of God *vnto ſaluation*
to all that beleeue: The knowne power of God and wiſdome of God,
which ingrafted in vs doth ſaue our ſoules: though men may
with good cauſe reioyce, that God hath prouided ſuch gra-

cious

Deut. 34. 1.

Ezra 3. 11. 12.

Rom. 1. 16.
Iam. 1. 21.

cious meanes, to preferue truth in his Church, and to tranf-
mit it vnto pofteritie; yet the Priefts and Leuites, and chiefe
of the Fathers, ancient men, haue good caufe to lament with
teares, and to bemoane with griefe of heart, that the Scriptures of God, the word of truth, the Gofpell of Chrift,fhould
be all on ruinous heapes, as of leaft, or no reputation at all,
in the triall of faith, and reformation of manners; and Councels not onely compared, but rather then faile, preferred before Scriptures of God; as if God fhould be filent,when men
giue the fentence.

3 We hold the ancient Councels in eminent authoritie,
but they are not like the wifedome of God, who built his
word as he formed the world in the creation, when he did all
things, *Numero, pondere & menfura*, in number, weight and Wifd.11.17.
meafure, and eftablifhed it for euer, and faw that all he had
made was good. There were no fuperfluities, no difproportion, no defeéts, no blemifh in the Scriptures, as is prooued.
In the Councels it hath not bene fo, by our aduerfaries owne
confeffion, as will afterwards appeare. There was not an iron 1.King. 6.7.
toole vfed, no noife heard, in the building of the firft temple,
which was fo beautifull. But at the fecond, the oppofition of Nehe.4.17.
importable and implacable enemies, made them woike on
the wals of the citie, with working inftruments in one hand,
and their weapons in the other. So when it pleafed God to
haue his Scriptures written, there defcended the immediate
influence of Gods Spirit into the hearts of the pen-men,who
though difperfed into diuers parts of the world,yet all agreed
whē their writings were conferred. It was not fo with Councels, they had need of the countenance & proteétion of Emperors, and weapons of warre, and the guard of fouldiers.
Though many were gathered into one place, yet they came
not all with one mind, they handled not matters after one
manner, there were high words, long difputations,vehement
contradiétions, change of fentence, from worft to better
fometimes, and not feldome,from better to worfe. Therefore
call them the Church, or what you will, you may perhaps account them in *armatura fortium*, but they are not that perfeét
Panoplia

Panoplia that armeth at all points,and defendeth at all aſſayes.

4 I could find in my heart to affoord that vnto the Councels in compariſon of the Scriptures,that I would vnto the bleſſed *Virgine Mary* in reſpeſt of her Sonne. And our aduerſaries ſlander vs in both alike. Becauſe that we miſlike, that the honour due vnto the onely begotten Sonne of God, the onely Sauiour of the faithfull, ſhould be attributed to a creature, though ſhe be the mother of God, we are accuſed to ſpeake euill and diſdainfully of her, and preferre euery woman that hath more children, before her. When God knoweth, as the truth is, there is no title of honour giuen vnto her, by the holy Scriptures, or any ſolide or primarie antiquitie, but we will yeeld it with all reſpeſt and reuerence: onely we dare not place her in her Sonnes throne, and giue her the worſhip due vnto him. She hath doubtleſſe, as *Bathſheba*,a ſeate on the

1. King. 2. 19. Kings right hand, and muſt haue her due reſpeſt,as the Kings mother; but we giue her not ſo much, much leſſe triple honor in reſpeſt, in the preſence of her Sonne; That ſhe ſit, and he ſtand,ſhe with a crowne and he none;ſhe with three crownes In diuers vpon one head,in the forme of a Popes triple crowne;he with pictures. one ſingle or perhaps a crowne of thornes. We like a meane, we miſlike exceſſe; we would giue all due, but preſume not to rob God of his owne glorie. This very account we make of Councels. We like and allow them: we giue them a reuerend ſeate by the throne of the holy Scriptures, euen at the right hand, but as a ſubieſt, not as a ſoueraigne; as a wife, if you will, but not as a husband; to moderate the affaires of the houſhold committed to her charge, but not to checke and o-uerrule the Lords gouernment.

.5 Examine all our writers and their writings,and ſee whether they do not ſpeake of Councels in this manner, and as the ancient Fathers did in their times.Search our Apologies,Confeſſions, Anſwers,Replies,or what you will, that ours is; you ſhall find much more reſpeſt giuen vnto them by vs then by our aduerſaries. In matters indifferent we giue them power to determine, for comlineſſe and order, and the preſeruation of peace in the whole bodie. For interpretations of Scripture, we we will not derogate from them, but wil either accept of thē, or anſwer them with due reſpect. For matters of fact we will beleeue them, for their times, as diligent ſearchers after the truth. For behauiour and manners, we admit their counſels, as the ſeruants of Gods, our ancients, our fathers. For the matters of faith and religion, we likewiſe confeſſe, that principall articles of Chriſtian beleefe, haue bin determined and concluded by them, which we receiue as ſolid and certaine truth, and pronounce *Anathema* with them, againſt all that ſpeake againſt them. But we may not ſo bind our ſelues to euery thing they ſhall impoſe vpon vs, as if euery word were a law, becauſe they conclude it, but becauſe they conuince it, out of the fountaine and foundation of truth, that is, the word of God. They may not preſume vpon immediate inſpiration, that were Anabaptiſticall; but muſt reſt and rely vpon the demonſtration of Gods reuealed word.

6 Neither will we truſt them as we do the Apoſtles, when they ſaid, *Videtur Spiritui ſancto & nobis*: It ſeemeth good to the holy Ghoſt and to vs; except they can ſhew vs the mind of the holy Ghoſt, as it is written in the Scriptures. For themſelues hold now, that *Authoritas generalis Concilij non eſt immediatè à Deo, ſed à Papa*: The authoritie of a generall Councell is not immediatly from God, but frō the Pope. And therefore now the Councell muſt ſay, *Videtur Papæ & nobis*, It ſeemeth good to the Pope and vs. For the Pope cometh betweene the holy Ghoſt and them, as ſinne may come betweene Gods mercy and our helpe: and ſo be an hinderance, not a furtherance of our ſaluation. And if we conſider Councels without theſe limitations and bounds, we ſhall eaſily find they haue bene but men, many of them ignorant and vnlearned, many partiall and preiudicate, many louers of men more then louers of God, eſpecially in the latter and declining times of the Church.

7 Beſides, ſeldome haue Councels bene concluded with generall and vniforme conſent, as that of the Apoſtles; but for the moſt part the greateſt number of voices paſſeth and concludeth. Neither hath it bin vnuſuall, that *maior pars* did

vincere

Act. 15. 28.

Supra cap. 6.
Sil. Prierias,
verbo Papæ.
§. 1.

*vincere meliorem,*the greater part ſwayed and caried it againſt
the better.Neither are we ignorant that the whole aſſembly
doth not take notice of euery matter, further then their *placet* or *diſplacet,*their voice for,or againſt : but there are a few
Committees or Delegates choſen to diſpute of the matter,
and theſe may be perhaps a few hungry Friers , as in the
Councell of *Trent,* that diſputed more for their bellies that
were their gods, then for the God of heauen and earth. It is
hard to bring the belly by perſwaſions vnto reaſon,that hath
no eares. Of which Councell we may well ſay, as Saint *Auguſtine* of the Donatiſts, *Superfluis & moratorijs proſequutioni-
bus geſta cumularunt, nihil aliud magis viribus agentes niſi vt ni-*
,, *hil ageretur :* They heapt vp all they did with trifling and
,, delaying proſecutions , ſeeking nothing elſe with all their
,, power, then that nothing might be done . And experience
hath taught,that one good man, reputed one of the moſt ignorant and leaſt reſpect,hath found and euinced that,where-
in the greateſt clearks haue bene grauelled, and gaue ouer
the bucklers.

     8   This may be exemplified by a very remarkable ſtory,
regiſtred in the preambles to that firſt and famous Councell
of *Nice*; where a great diſputation was held betweene the
moſt learned Biſhops and certaine heathen Philoſophers, in
matter of religion and defence of Chriſtian truth . The Phi-
loſphers were ſo pregnant in wit , ſo ſubtill in diſtinctions,
ſo learned, ſo wiſe,ſo eloquent, that they not onely held the
Biſhops hard to it,but ſeemed to ouercome them.One of the
vnlearnedſt,or to giue it in his owne words,*(Quidā ſimpliſſi-
mus naturà vir, & nihil aliud ſciens, niſi Chriſtum Ieſum & hunc
crucifixum,*A ſimple man by nature, who knew nothing but
Chriſt Ieſus,and him crucified, intreated to encounter thoſe
boaſting challengers , with confidence to ouercome them.
All preſent were as fearfull to commit the triall vnto him , as
Saul and his army doubted to ſend *Dauid* againſt *Goliah.* But
the ſimple mans reſolute importunitie, firſt ouercame his
friends to aduenture him , and then ouerthrew the Philoſophers,and conuerted them, as *Dauid* ſlue the vncircumciſed
                                                    Phi-

Marginal notes:

Plutarch.in
M.Catone.
De geſtis cum
emerito.

P.Crab.inprę-
amb.Concilij.
p.235.

1.Sam. 17.33.

Philiftim, and faued Ifrael. The like befell in the very Councell it felfe, when one *Paphnutius*, by alledging Scripture,
brought all the Bifhops to his mind, as before hath bene ob- Supra cap.6.
ferued. And if not the fame, yet the very like is recorded by
Socrates and *Sozomen*, who report it to be done by a fimple
lay-man: *Quidam ex Confefforibus Laicis, fimplicem habens fen-* Hift.tripart.
fum, One of the lay Confeffors, hauing a fimple meaning. l.2.c.3.
And *fenex fimplex & innocens ac probatiſſimus Confefforum*, An
old fimple innocent man, moft approoued of the Confeffors,
&c. Which manifeftly euinceth, of what authoritie the
Scriptures were at that time, and in that famous Councell.

9 In which cafe we know it fareth with the God of truth,
as it doth with the Lord of hoafts; he can ouercome in the
day of battel, as well by few as by many; fo can he maintaine
his truth as well by a handful as by a heape; by two or three Math.18.20.
gathered together in his Name, as by a multitude affembled
at a mans cōmandement. And although (as the prouerbe is)
Plus vident oculi quàm oculus, More eyes fee more then one;
yet fometimes one that ftands by, may fee, or at leaft perceiue
more then many that are actors. Our Sauiour promifeth not
fo much to many at once, as to one alone, that fhall ftand a-
gainft neuer fo many in defence of truth : *Be not carefull what* Math.10.19.
to anfwer, it fhall be giuen you euen in that houre what you fhall
fpeake. A great promife, performed to many in the dayes both
of the firft and latter perfecutions; when many a fimple man
was able by the Scriptures to conuince a great many that
thought themfelues both wife and learned. Whereby it is
euident, that God tieth not himfelfe to numbers of voices;
but as the wind bloweth where it lufteth, fo the Spirit of
God infpireth where he pleafeth. Moreouer, it is not vn- Ioh.3.8.
knowne, what preiudice fome of the Fathers had of Councels, as *Gregorie Nazianzene* that neuer expected or had feene
a good end of them. What wrong fome Fathers had by
them, as *Athanafius*, who was turmoiled and toffed, &c. How
the former were reformed by the latter, the fathers by their
fonnes, as Saint *Auguftine* obferued ; and all this in the firft Auguft.
and

and pureſt times of the Church. By all which it appeareth, that neither the Fathers, who liued ſo neare them, both in time and place, gaue them ſuch vncontrollable authoritie, as if all were Goſpell they ſpake, or that the Councels had euer that good reſpect as was wiſhed and expected; and therefore they muſt needs come ſhort of that ſoueraigne and ſuper-eminent authoritie, which we may giue by good right vnto the Scriptures of God.

10 But if we ſhall ſpeake of the later ages of the Church, we can by no meanes yeeld that their Councels were either lawfully ſummoned, or indifferently managed, or happily concluded; whereof afterward there will be occaſion to ſpeake more at large: vntill then, all courteous and iudicious Readers may plainly ſee, and, I hope, will as ingenuouſly con-feſſe, that notwithſtanding we are traduced by our aduerſa-ries to ſet light by Councels, to deſpiſe and reiect them, yet we haue a due eſtimation of them, as much as may ſtand with the ſafetie of truth, and the honour of Gods word, written in the Scriptures. Which is more then our aduerſaries will performe, whatſoeuer they promiſe and pretend to their o-uer-credulous diſciples. For when they ſpeake of Councels in generall, they would make the world beleeue, that we for-ſake and renounce them all, that they receiue and admit eue-ry one. There was a well conceited friend, that would euer boaſt his neighbours with his owne liberalitie, in diſtribu-tion of his apples, in compariſon of another that was very kind indeed; and would ſay, he is miſerable, he giues his ap-ples but by diſhfuls or ſtroakes, but I am bountifull, that giue mine by quarters. Whether would you take for the franker man? He that gaue by quarters, you would thinke. But it was not ſo: he talked of quarters, as if they had bene ſacks full; but they were but quarters of one apple cut into foure parts. Euen ſo it fareth with the Court of *Rome*. They will be tried by the Councels, and they will tell you of ſo many in *Peter Crabs* Edition, ſo many and ſo good of *Surius* his ſetting forth, yea more and better done by *Dominicus Nicolinus* in fiue volumes, by *Binius* beſt of all, ſo fairely
printed,

printed, fo diligently perufed, fo carefully correéted, according to old Copies, in fiue greater *Volumes.* You would
think the Church of Rome offred vs quarters, that is, whole
fackfulls of Councels, but come to receiue them, they proue
but quarters in a leffe volume. They admit but eighteene
without exception, a very few to fo many pretended; and
the beft of thofe not only drawne violently to their purpofe,
but fufpended or hanged (in plaine Englifh) at their pleafure,
yea embowelled and quartered too, except they can make
them to ferue their purpofes. The former was a merrie, but
this is a dangerous equiuocation.

11 And not to defraud your expeétations longer in this
behalfe: firft vnderftand our aduerfaries dealing with the
body of the Councels. They exclude all prouinciall and Nationall Councels, not out of their books, but put them out
of credit, when they make againft them, or not for them; fo
do not we. And though they feeme to allow as many as are **Greg.de Val.**
confirmed by Popes, they receiue not all the generall; no
more do we. They refufe many better Councels and accept
worfe; fo will not we. They except againft fome particulars
in the beft; we not fo much, nor fo often as they, but euer
vpon better caufe then they yet euer haue done, or I feare
will do. They will admit or reieét what they lift, in the fame
Councell; we defire to be equally obliged, to all, or to none.
For that Councell that erreth in one, may erre in more, and
fo in all; and that that bindeth in one, bindeth in all, or not at
all. I remembred before, that when *Bellarmine* diftingui- **Supra cap.5.**
fheth of generall Councels, fome are approued, fome reproued or reprobated, fome partly confirmed, partly reieéted;
one neither manifeftly allowed, nor manifeftly difallowed.
To omit the others for a while: confider how a generall
Councell is by *Bellarmine* defined. *Generalia dicuntur ea qui-* **Concil. E-**
bus intereffe poffunt & debent Epifcopi totius orbis, nifi legitimè **phefinum ad**
impediantur, & in quibus nemo reétè præfidet nifi Romanus Ponti- **tuendam vir-**
fex aut alius eius nomine. Thofe are called generall Councels, **ginis dignita-**
at which all the Bifhops of the whole world may be, and **gatum.**
fhould be, except they be lawfully hindred; and in which „

N   no

„ no man may rightly be Preſident but the Biſhop of Rome, or
„ ſome other in his name. The firſt part of this definition is impoſſible, the other is vnreaſonable. Whereupon I may iuſtly
inferre, that ſince the Apoſtles time there was neuer generall Councell in the Church; & that there neuer can be generall Councel with any indifferency. For the firſt, neuer could,
neuer ought, much leſſe euer did, all the Biſhops of the whole
world gather together into one Councell. When were euer
the *Abiſens*, or the *Æthiopians*, or the *Indians*, either ſummoned that they might come; or ſtayed for, till they could come;
or were cenſured for not coming; or talked of, as members miſſed in that body? I trow neuer. Therefore there
was neuer generall Councell whereunto the whole Church
muſt ſtand obliged. And it is impoſſible that euer there
ſhould be.

12 For *Biſhops* are to be preſuppoſed ancient men before
they are choſen, and ſo are for the moſt part; (except the Romane boy Biſhops, and boy Cardinals, and boy Popes too, if
you will.) It will aske diuers years to ſend & receiue anſwers
from ſome, wherin may be ſo many changes vnknowne and
vnheard of, by the deaths of men, that no certaintie can be of
their aſſembling.

13 For the Popes precedencie it neither was in the firſt
generall Councels, nor required, neither ought it to be euer
or at all, as hereafter ſhall appeare. Beſides, we deny that in a-
ny of the firſt & chiefe Councels the Pope was Preſident, &
therfore by the Cardinals definition they were no Councels.
But we will ſuppoſe them to be generall, which *Bellarmine* &
others that write of Councels call ſo. Of ſome of thoſe generall Councels, ſome are approued, ſome not. If they be generall they may not be reiected, for they haue the confluence
of Biſhops & the Pope Preſident, elſe are they not generall.
Dico Concilium illud non poſſe errare quod abſolutè eſt generale &
„ *Eccleſiam vniuerſam perfectè repreſentat* : I ſay that the Coun-
„ cell cannot erre which is abſolutely generall, and perfectly
„ repreſenteth the whole Church. Being ſo generall, and the
body & head cleauing together, why ſhould they be reprobated?

Bell. de Con-
cil. aut. l. 2. c. 1.

bated? Why fhould they not be approoued? Either they were
not generall; or being generall, by your owne learning they
could not erre,and then no reafon to reprooue them.Or finally, being generall, they did erre, and therefore were iuftly reiected. The fame may be faid of the part which is faid of the
whole. If they were generall, why are they not approoued, as
well in all as in part? If they be not generall,why do you giue
them that title? And why refufe you them in part, and not in
all? I know not what to fay to the poft-alone, that is neither
manifeftly reiected,nor manifeftly accepted.It may not be admitted becaufe *Antonius* faith,it was *Conciliabulum illegitimum*,   Anton.
an vnlawfull Conuenticle,and becaufe it rather increafed then
diminifhed the fchifme. If it be without doubt reprooued,
then without doubt *Alexander* the fixt fhould not haue called
himfelfe the fixt, but the fift. A perillous matter. What is the
fumme of all this? Verily thofe Councels that make for them
in all,thofe are all theirs; thofe which haue any thing for the,
thofe are in fo much theirs; thofe which haue ought againft
them,are in fo much none of theirs.They haue a great facilitie
in fauing themfelues harmeleffe.

14 *Bellarmine* confeffeth, *Concilium legitimum poffe errare*   Bell.de Cocil.
in his qua non legitime agit, & de facto erraffe, quando ab Apofto- l.2 cap.7.
*lica fede reprobatur.*A lawfull Councell may erre in that it doth   Infra p.139.
vnlawfully, and fo hath erred when it hath bene reprooued „
by the Apoftolicall Sea. As much to fay, it may do vnlawful- „
ly, and then when it doth fo,it erreth;and fo when it may erre,
it erreth, and feeing it erreth it may erre.Againe,*Concilia in iu-*   Bell. de Con-
dicys particularibus,nec non in praceptis morum, qua non toti Ec-
clefia, fed vni tantum 'aut alteri populo proponitur,errare poteft.
Councels in their particular iudgements, as alfo in precepts of „
manners, which are not propofed to the whole Church , but „
for one onely people or another, may erre. They may erre in „
particulars: but the whole doctrine of faith and manners confifteth of particulars , and they all make the generall. If they
erre in all particulars but one, they erre not in the generall,
much leffe if in any, leaft of all but in one. Yet it is Romane
learning, that if the fhip leake at the leaft hole, it will finke at

laſt, as well as if there wanted a whole planke. And a man may be as well damned for one particular hereſie as for many. How then will ſuch a Councell eſcape, that erreth in particulars? They may alſo erre in manners; but men may be damned, as well for corruption in life, as error in faith. If *good manners maketh man, then ill manners marreth man.* But theſe muſt not concerne the whole Church, but one or ſome people. But as he that conuerteth one ſoule, ſhail haue his reward, ſo he that ſubuerteth one ſoule, much more a Church or people, ſhall incurre a iuſt condemnation. And wo is him that offendeth one little one.

Mat.18.6.

15 Againe, Councels may erre in words. But among men words expreſſe the meaning of the heart; we muſt anſwer for euery idle, much more erronious word, and not ruling the tongue may make ones religion vaine. *By thy words thou ſhalt be iuſtified, and by thy words thou ſhalt be condemned.* Sometimes Councells may define matters, not as certaine, but as probable. But faith and manners muſt be built vpon certainties, and not probabilities. Againe Councels may erre in *quæſtionibus de facto & in paruis,* in queſtions of fact, and matters of ſmall moment. *But he is curſed that iuſtifieth the wicked, and condemneth the innocent, and he that is not faithfull in a little who will truſt him in much?* Adde vnto all this, what Cardinall *Turrecremata* ſaith, *Eſt de neceſſitate ſalutis:* It is of the neceſſitie of ſaluation, to hold that the Councell hath ,, not his immediate dependance, or authoritie from God, but ,, from the Pope. God deliuer vs from thoſe Councels, where God is not Preſident, or where the Popes authoritie ouerruleth.

Mat.12.36.
Iame.1.19.

Bell.de Rom.
Pont.l.4.c.11.

De Ecclef. l.
3.cap.30.

Staplet. doct.
princip. lib.8.
c.14.15.&
lib.11.c.6.

16 Doctor *Stapleton* confeſſeth, that though generall Councels cannot erre in their concluſions, yet they may erre in applying Scriptures to their concluſions. If they may or dare abuſe Scriptures, they need not feare a greater ſlip. Biſhop *Canus* doth alſo confeſſe, that *Concilium generale etiam congregatum Romani Pontificis authoritate errare in fide poteſt.* A ,, generall Councell, yea gathered by the Biſhop of Romes au- ,, thoritie, may erre in matters of faith. And with Cardinall
Bellarmine

Canus.l.4.c.5.
loc.com.

Bellarmine, that the Fathers in a Councell may erre in small Lib.5.c.5. matters; and that it may be holden without herefie, that the Church in some law and custome may erre: and that often _Maior pars vincit meliorem_, The greater part preuaileth a-Ibid. gainst the better; because _Sapientes pauciſſimi ſunt, cum ſtulto-_ ,, _rum infinitus ſit numerus_: Wise men are very rare, but fooles ,, without number. Such are the most part of the Popes Councell. All which this Bishop illuſtrateth by many examples. Put all this together, or the ſubſtance of it into one ſentence, and then tell me, you that ſay Councels cannot erre, whether euer there were Councels that might not erre? or whether themſelues do not confeſſe that a Councell may erre? and what in effect we ſay, which our adverſaries do not approue, though they moſt cenſoriouſly reproue vs for that themſelues neither can nor do deny.

17 Finally, to make vp this conſideration of Councels in general, let a Pope giue his definitiue ſentence, and conclude all: _They tell me_ (ſaith _Paſcalis_) _that this ſtatute is not found in_ Paſcalis? _the Councels; as though Councels can prefixe any law to the Church_ ,, _of Rome, whereas all Councels from the Church of Rome receiue_ ,, _being and ſtrength; and in their Canons the authoritie of the Biſhop_ ,, _of Rome is euidently excepted._ In this the Pope makes himſelfe ,, not a Chancellor, but a canceller of Councels, tearing them, and making them void at his pleaſure. Who will ſtriue with ſuch a mightie man? who will go to law with ſuch a Iudge? An old Councell cannot bind a new Pope. They tell of making the Scriptures a noſe of waxe; what do they with the Councels. but make them ſhip-mens hoſt? Like him that dexterouſly diſtinguiſheth vpon the 18. Chapter of Saint _Marks_ Goſpell, that hath but 16. in all. _Sic ego euado, ſic tu euades:_ Thus I can ſhift, and thus thou maiſt illude and eſcape. This will ſerue my turne, and this thine. If you allow but 18, why do you trouble the world with ſo many? If you put forth ſo many in ſhew, why approue you ſo few in deed? _Tenet hoc, non illud: tenet in hoc, non in illo:_ This holds, if it make for you: this holds not, if it make for vs. Or thus much is ours, none at all yours. Is not this fine, and faire worke? playing the

N 3 Gipſies,

Gipſies, *faſt and looſe.*

18   Now concerning Councels in particular; which can
you name more ſacred then the firſt *Nicene?* yet how many
doubts and ſcruples about this Councell? Who called this

Conc.Nice.1.   Councell? the Emperour, or the Biſhop of *Rome?* All the E-
Euſeb.   piſtles and Prefaces to the Councel conuince it was the Emperour, and *Euſebius* with others concurre therein. The Romaniſts will haue the Pope to ſummon this Councell, and
not the Emperour, without all authoritie or probable rea-

Ad an.Dō.325   ſon. *Baronius* doth confeſſe, that the Councell of *Nice* was
pag.240,241. *indu*ℏ*um à Conſtantino, perſuaſum à Sylueſtro, facilè perſuaſum.*
In vnum locum coëgit, per literas acciuit, neque mandatum dun-
taxat erat ad hanc rem datum, edictum promulgatum fuit, &c.
,, commanded by *Conſtantine,* perſwaded by *Sylueſter,* and ea-
,, ſily intreated. He gathered them into one place, ſummoned
,, them by his letters; neither was his commandement giuen
,, onely to this purpoſe, but alſo decreed and publiſhed,&c.

19   Who was Preſident of this Councell? *Hoſius* Biſhop
of *Corduba* in *Spaine,* or the Biſhop of *Rome* by his Legates?
Hoſius was takē ſo to be, and ſtandeth yet firſt in the ſubſcription. How many Canons were there of this Councell? All

Concil. Car-   the copies that could be found within leſſe then foureſcore
thag.6.   yeares after that Councell in Eaſt and Weſt, vpon the
moſt diligent ſearch of the 217 Fathers, whereof Saint *Au-*
guſtine was one, were brought and conferred; and that vpon
Zozimus Biſhop of *Rome* his producing of a forged copie to
proue his vſurped title; and there could be found but twentie Canons, and no more. *Baronius* alſo acknowledgeth directly but twentie Canons, though *Ruffinus* nameth two and
twentie, yet he hath indeed but twentie in ſubſtance, but di-
uideth otherwiſe then the ordinary account, and concludeth

Annal. ad an.   thus: *In quibus omnibus editionibus,* 20 *tantummodò Canones e-*
Dom.325.   *numerantur,* in all which Editions there are onely twentie
pag.279.   Canons numbred. And farther: *Sed & Theodoretus viginti Ca-*
nones tantùm in magna Synodo ſtatutos affirmat, totidemq̃, recep-
tos eſſe, in archiuis Alexandrinæ, Antiochenæ, & Conſtantinopoli-
tanæ Eccleſiæ, cum illi magnà diligentià perquiſiti ſunt, ab Epiſcopis
Afri-

Africanis, dictæ Synodi ſextæ Carthaginenſis, acta, & epiſtolæ eà de cauſâ tunc ſcripta certiſſimam fidem faciunt.Theodoret auoucheth „ but onely twentie Canons, and that no more were receiued „ in the libraries of the *Alexandriā, Antiochian,*and *Conſtantino-* „ *politan* Church, whē they were ſearched with great diligence „ by the *African* Biſhops of that ſixt Councell of *Carthage,* the „ Acts and Epiſtles then writtē for the ſame cauſe, giue certain „ faith or teſtimony thereof. His after coniectures are idle, „ not liked of himſelfe,confuted by many, conuinced by their owne improbabilitie.

20 *Zozimus* his ſucceſſors, *Boniface* and *Celeſtine,* who ſtood vpon the ſame title of their prerogatiue, yet could not with their honeſties (a rare vertue in moderne Popes) or would not for ſtarke ſhame, vrge that pretence any farther or longer.Yet *Gratian* will haue 70 Canons, and that by the teſtimony of a counterfet *Athanaſius.* And if any aske,how this number is decreaſed? we muſt ſay (though it be a ſtarke lie) that certaine *Chapters* of the *Nicene Councell were out of cuſtome in the Romiſh Church,* craftily leauing ſome vnderhand ſuſpitiō,that they might be found in the Greek Church, though after moſt diligent ſearch they could not be found there. If this ſhift will not ſerue, *Gratian* will haue another: How they were loſt, it is doubtfull, moſt thinke they are inſerted into the Councell of *Antioch.* Is not this cunning iuggling? *Bellarmine* being not ſo impudent as *Gratian,* is contented to renounce *Athanaſius* teſtimony, that there were more then twentie Canons, and ſaith: *Hoc argumentum ridetur à Magdiburgenſibus, & verè non eſt ſolidum*: This argument is derided by the *Magdiburgenſes,* and in very deed it is not found.

Diſtinct.18.
c.70.

Bell. de Rom. Pont.l. 2.c.25.

21 Yet he laboureth by far-fetched arguments to proue there were more Canons then twentie, to ſaue *Zozimus* credit, if it were poſſible. Firſt he excuſeth him, that he tooke the *Sardican* Canons for the *Nicene,* and ſo nameth the one Councell for the other,which was an eſcape indeed,but worthy no blame forſooth. What? no blame, for an vnerring Pope that cannot lie,in ſome caſes if he would? Yes, he is

either

either blame-worthy, or no body. Or he thinketh that in the Councel of *Nice* , this was decreed implicitly and obfcurely, that appeales lie to the Bifhop of *Rome* : or perhaps the *African* Councell was corrupted concerning thefe Canons : or that fome marginall note crept into the text; or it may be probable, that the three Canons which *Zozimus* vrged, were not plainly in the Councell of *Nice,* but they were called the Canons of the *Nicene* Councell, becaufe the Councel of *Nice* and *Sardica,* were taken for one and the fame; and that the Canons of both thofe Councels were ioyned together in a *Romane* library : the ignorance whereof troubled the *African* Fathers. All *Baronius* idle coniectures of the corruption of the fixth Canon, are by thefe reafons confuted. None of the twentie Canons was vrged by *Zozimus* : none of them were excepted againft by the *Carthaginian* Fathers. Falfe would neuer haue bin tendred, if they had a true : and the Pope would rather haue complained of the corruption of that Canon, then forged others, if neceffitie had not bene without

Baron. ad an. 325.pag.279.

law. And the fame Cardinall confeffeth, that the Canon of Appeales was none of the twentie : *Qui inter* 20 *illos nequaquam numeratus habetur* , which was not numbred amongft thofe twentie Canons. What fhifts are thefe of a graue Cardinall ? He is onely honeft in this, that he refufeth the authoritie of *Athanafius* counterfeit teftimony to *Marke* Bifhop of *Rome.*

Panop. l.4. c.89.

22 *Lindan* will needs haue 70 Canons of this Councell, the fame Epiftle of *Athanafius* to *Marke* , (fo will hungry dogs eate dirtie puddings,) though *Marke* was dead before that Epiftle was forged. Or if this will not ferue his turne, he will find the 70 Canons out of fundry Authors, like the fcattered planks of a wracked fhip, or the chips of *Noahs* Arke; and for ought I know, may be feeking them yet in *Purgatorie,* for on earth they were neuer found to that day. Yet fince forfooth there are found in *Alexandria* 80 Canons, that is, ten more then they would haue, or fought for, or fo much as

Baron. epit. pag.239.

thought of, (or elfe a Iefuite lies, and that is no miracle) and that in the Arabian tongue, and tranflated into Latine by a Iefuite.

Iefuire. Againe, though *Bellarmine* would haue *Zozimus* miftake chalke for cheefe, and a fearne-bracke for a fox, the Nicene for the Sardican Councell ; yet *Lindan* will not haue that by any meanes; *Nec D.Zozimum pro Sardicenfi, Nicenum allegaſſe, S.Zozimus* alledged not the *Nicene* Councell for the „ *Sardican.* And *Baronius* taketh his part, and will haue *Zozimus* „ take his allegation out of the Councell of Nice: *Quem (Canonem) Theodoretus digito ſignat*, which Canon *Theodoret* pointeth at with his finger. All this about the number of the Nicene Canons. But one *Contius* a Lawyer of their owne re- Annot.in diſt. folueth all doubts, and faith peremptorily, *That their baſtardie* 16.cap.70. *is prooued euen by this, that no man, no not Gratian himſelfe durſt alledge them.* As who fhould fay, if any would be fo audacious and graceleſſe, it would be he. Thefe miferable fhifts and contradictions confidered, let any modeft Chriftian iudge, whether it be likely, thefe doubtfull, vncertaine, obfcure coniectures, fhould be of more force in this end of the world, to proue that there are 70. or 80. Canons truly tendred by Pope or Papifts, in their owne cafe; or rather beleeue the 217. Bifhops of the Carthaginian Councell, whereof Saint *Auguſtine* was one, that had made diligent enquirie by the learned and famous Bifhops of the Eaft, *Alexandria, Antioch, Conſtantinople,* that is, the Greeke Church within 80 yeares after and leſſe, (befide *Cæcilianus* copie at Carthage, who was prefent at the Councell, and brought it with him) nor in any other copie Greeke or Latine.

23 All which notwithftanding there comes a frefh fellow, and he defperatly grounds vpon the 39 Canon in *Arabico,* that all is the Popes, and that his authoritie ftretcheth ouer all ftates and perfons, not onely Ecclefiafticall, but Ciuill, as if his rule were as leuell, as any vndoubted Canon of that Councell. *Ille qui tenet ſedem Romæ, caput eſt & princeps omnium Pa-* Coccius tom. *triarcharum, quandoquidem ipſe eſt primus, ſicut Petrus cui data* 1.l.7.art. 4. *eſt poteſtas in omnes principes Chriſtianos,& omnes populos eorum, vt qui ſit vicarius (hriſti Domini noſtri ſuper cunctos populos, & vniuerſam Eccleſiam Chriſtianam, & quicunque contradixerit à Synodo excommunicatur.* He that holds the chaire of Rome, is
head,

,, head, and Prince ouer all Patriarches, for as much as he is firſt,
,, as *Peter* was, to whom all power was giuen ouer all Chriſtian
,, Princes and all their people, as who is the vicar of Chriſt our
,, Lord ouer all people, and the vniuerſall Chriſtian Church: and
,, whoſoeuer contradicts this is excommunicated by the Councell. But if there be but twentie Canons, then this is none, and
therefore needeth no other anſwer.

    24 Now for the interpretation of the ſixt Canon of
this Councell, there is almoſt as great variety. We alledge
this Canon to proue, that the Biſhop of Rome for his iuriſdiction is confined, as an Archbiſhop or a Patriarke, at moſt to
his Prouince and countries adioyning, as *Alexandria* and *Antioch* are to theirs. And that he hath no more iuriſdiction ouer
them, then they ouer him. Which we ſay is plaine in the text
in all editions, and all tranſlations. This our aduerſaries are
ſo farre from granting, as that they would not onely haue it
not abet this truth, but would wreſt it, and wreath it, quite

Can. 6. contrary. The words as *Bellarmine* hath them are: *Mos anti-
quus perduret in Egypto, vel Libya & Pentapoli, vt Alexandrinus
Epiſcopus horum omnium habeat poteſtatem, quoniam quidem &*
,, *Epiſcopo Romano parilis mos eſt.* Let the ancient cuſtome conti-
,, new in Egypt, or Libya and Pentapolis, that the Biſhop of A-
,, lexandria hath power ouer all theſe, becauſe the Biſhop of
,, Rome hath the like cuſtome. The ſence whereof we take to
be, that Alexandria ſhould exerciſe iuriſdiction ouer thoſe
Churches neare vnto it, as Rome did thoſe near vnto her: *Bellarmine* keepeth a foule coile about this Canon. Firſt he telleth how Pope *Nicolas* would haue it, or there wants ſomewhat in the Canon before: *Eccleſia Romana ſemper habuit pri-*
,, *matum,* the Church of Rome euer had primacie. But this is
added without ſufficient authoritie; contrary to all approued
copies.

    25 Then he propoſeth foure expoſitions. One of *Ruffinus,*
Hiſt. Eccleſ. l. 10.c.6. the oldeſt and trueſt; *That the Biſhop of Alexandria ſhould haue
the charge of Egypt, as the Biſhop of Rome had the charge of the
Churches adioyning.* Thus we take it, and therefore haue *Antiquitie* for vs. The ſecond is of *Theodorus Balſamon* and of *Nilus,*

lus, *That the Bishop of Alexandria should haue the same charge*
of all Egypt, as the Bishop of Rome had of the West. *Bellarmine*
likes them better for their liberalitie, that they giue more
then *Ruffinus* giues; yet he will not haue his Maifter tyed
vp in so fhort a tether, *Aut Cæsar, aut nullus*, either all or none.
We could thinke well of this as the times then were, when
the Church was confined into a narrower roome then fince it
hath bene, when the charge is too big for him, were he as big
againe. It is too heauie for *Atlas* that was fained to carrie
heauen on his fhoulders. The third is of *Caranza* the epitomi-
zer of the Councels, who telleth (though *Bellarmine* omitteth
it) *That he was shewed an old edition by a Cardinall, where in stead*
of Romano Episcopo, was Metropolitano Episcopo, in ftead of Romane was Metropolitane. This alfo maketh for vs with great
aduantage, written by a Papift, fhewed by a Cardinall, both
our aduerfaries, and therefore good witneffes for vs, out of an
old copie, which fauours of *Antiquitie*, but all thefe are all one,
or none at all with *Bellarmine*. He hath a crotchet in his owne
head, and will reach a note aboue *Ela*, but he will fetch it; and
therefore he bringeth a fourth expofition, and I beleeue you
will thinke a very ftrange one. *Becaufe the Romane Bishop was*
fo accuftomed, which is not in the text by *Bellarmine* himfelfe
alledged : that is, becaufe the Bifhop of Rome before any definitions of Councels, did vfe to *permit vnto the Bishop of Alex-*
andria the gouernment of Libya and Pentapolis: Siue confueuit per
Alexandrinum Episcopum illas prouincias gubernare; Or that the ,,
Bifhop of Rome accuftomed to gouerne thofe prouinces by ,,
the Bifhop of Alexandria. The laft and the worft. Curfed be ,,
the gloffe that corrupteth the text ; neither hath he the letter
of the text, nor any probable reafon, fo much as to conceipt
it, and yet he concludeth there is no other probable expofition
but this; it is true, to ferue his turne.

26　*Turrian* maketh this Canon plaine for the Bifhop of **Dogmat:**
Rome, *Habemus huius iudicij primi ad Pontificem pertinentis au-* **Charact.lib.**
thores grauissimos, fanctissimos, ac plurimos Niceni Concilij Patres **3. fol. 123.**
318. *Vigeat (inquit) & firma sit prisca confuetudo, quæ eft in E-*
gypto, Libya & Pentapoli, ita vt Episcopus Alexandriæ horum
omnium

omnium poteſtatem habeat,quandoquidem Epiſcopus Romanus hoc
conſueuit, & ſimiliter vt per Antiochiam & alias prouincias præ-
*,, rogatiua ſeruetur Eccleſiis.*We haue moſt graue,moſt holy,and
,, thoſe many Fathers of the Nicene Councell, euen three hun-
,, dred and eighteene,for this principall iudgement appertaining
,, to the Pope.*Let* the ancient cuſtome flouriſh and ſtand firme,
,, which is in *Egypt, Libya,* and *Pentapolis,* ſo that the Biſhop of
,, *Alexandria* may haue the power of all theſe, foraſmuch as the
,, Biſhop of Rome accuſtomed ſo, and in like manner through
,, *Antioch,* and the reſt of the prouinces,the prerogatiue may be
,, preſerued to the Churches. Thus he firſt corrupteth the text,
then he gloſeth thus: *In confirmanda iuriſdictione Alexandrini*
Patriarchæ & Antiocheni,Nicæna ſynodus iudicium & autohrita-
tem Epiſcopi Romani ſecuta eſt. Perindè eſt enim hoc quaſi diceve-
tur, quia Epiſcopus Romanus iam olim à principio ſolitus eſt conce-
dere Epiſcopo Alexandrino iuriſdictionē Egypti Libycæ & Penta-
polis. Nicæna quoque Synodus eius authoritatem & normam ſe-
quuta, poteſtatem iſtam & aliquam iuriſdictionem, quam Epiſco-
pus Alexandrinus iam olim ab Epiſcopo Romano, accepit,vt idem
,, *teneat,concedit.* In confirming the iuriſdiction of the *Alexan-*
,, *drine* and *Antiochian* Patriarchie, the Nicene Councell follo-
,, wed the iudgement and authoritie of the Romane Biſhop.
,, Which is as if they ſhould haue ſaid thus: becauſe the Biſhop
,, of Rome hath bene accuſtomed, in times paſt, from the be-
,, ginning, to grant vnto the Biſhop of *Alexandria* iuriſdiction
,, ouer the *Egyptian, Libyan,*and *Pentapolitan* Churches, the Ni-
,, cene Councell following his authoritie and rule, granteth
,, that he may retaine the ſame power and iuriſdiction, becauſe
,, in times paſt the Biſhop of *Alexandria* receiued it from the
,, Biſhop of Rome. Where he hath much babblement to the
ſame purpoſe, as idle as this; from whom it ſeemeth Cardinall *Bellarmine* hath much of his : yet *Turrian* ſeemeth much
more audaciouſly impudent.Let any man of iudgment lay this
building to the Councels rule, and they ſhall eaſily diſcerne
the crookedneſſe, yea the wickedneſſe of it.

27 *Andradius* the Champion for the Councell of Trent
miſliketh one ſhift, becauſe it is againſt all the old copies, and
foiſteth

foisteth in another worse , that by custome *his iudgement is* Lib.2.
vnderstood. The glosse vpon the Decrees would haue it thus.
According to the old custome , let due honor be reserued to euery Dist.65.c.m
prouince; to the Bishop of Alexandria, who is like the Patriarch of antiq.in glo
Rome. Parilis mos, like custome, that is, in something, becaufe both
may depose Bishops, else say, Romano, id est, Constantinopolitano, to
the Bishop of Rome, that is, to the Bishop of Constantinople. „
For this is subiect to the Pope , as the rest. The last that I haue
seene is the most impudent of all other, and faith plainly:
Niceni primi & antiquissimi verba sunt. Ecclesia Romana sem-
per habuit primatum. The Church of Rome had euer the primacie; and as confidently alledgeth the 36 Canon beside, as
the sixt wrongfully.

28 *Gregorius de Valentia* hath yet another hole to creepe out Anali. fidei
at: That *Ruffinus* copie agreed not in this Canon with the co- Catho.l.7.
pie sent by the three Patriarkes to the Fathers of the Coun- c.11.
cell of *Africke,* for by that copie they are safe enough. *Ther-* „
fore this Canon doth not deny .the authoritie of Primacie to the „
Bishop of Rome, which he hath otherwise as the successor of Peter „
ouer all Churches. But he verily signifieth that he hath also a „
certaine speciall authoritie of a Metropolitan ouer the Churches „
that lye neare the diocesse of Rome. Which authoritie the Councell „
of Nice would haue reserued to euery Archbishop Metropoli- „
tane in his owne prouince. Yet there is a fetch more in the „
corruption of the Chalcedon Councel, where the words are
set downe positiuely and conclusiuely, that should be ambi-
guously and doubtfully. Which the compilator vpon the Compilator.
Epistle of *Iulius* more then infinuateth. *Hoc statutum solum*
reducibile est ad quintum & sextum caput Niceni Concilij, verùm
apertè non inuenitur. This Decree may only be reduced to the „
fift & sixt Chapters of the Nicene Councell, but in very deed „
ouertly is not there found. What is in all this said that a „
conscionable Christian may rest vpon? Onely all men that
haue eyes to see , may see , and all that haue eares to heare
may heare the wicked and gracelesse attempts of the Papists,
who seeke either to contradict flatly , or to falsifie cunning-
ly, or to vndermine deceiptfully, all true euidences of *Anti-*
quitie;

quitie; and will either rifle forged writings, as that of *Atha-thanaſius*; or corrupt wilfully, as the Chalcedon Councell; or gloſe ſhamefully, as *Gratian* and many others; or dig down old walls, perhaps vndermine very priuie places, to outface good Chriſtians with their forged deuices ; and fetch 50 yea 60 Canons, for a need, of the firſt *Oecumenicall* and beſt Councell; after many ages , and that after ſuch ſearch , as *Torrenſis* would make the world beleeue. I might adde vnto all that hath bene ſaid, that there are diuers things diſperſed in the 4. 5. 8. 11. 14. 17. 20. Canons of this Councell, which are not obſerued of the Church of Rome , neither of long time haue bene; which, if the obligation of Councels autho-ritie were ſo ſtrong as is pretended , might not be omit-ted.

   28 I haue ſtood the longer about this Councell, be-cauſe it is worthily reputed the firſt in the peace of the Church, and the beſt for the excellent doctrine concluded therein againſt the moſt clamorons heretikes (but Papiſts) that euer were. That it may appeare there is not ſo much ſo-liditie , and certaintie of truth in Councels , neuer ſo great, neuer ſo old, as in the Scriptures. That our aduerſaries are as irreſolute in theſe as in other writings : that if they make this ſhamefull ado to ſupport the triple crowne by ſuch deuices, they haue no cauſe to traduce vs vnto their miſerable decei-ued Proſelytes, as if we onely did except againſt generall Councels , and that they onely were the preſeruers and ob-ſeruers of them.

   29 *Bellar.* alledgeth the ſecond generall Councell which was the firſt of Côſtantinople, for the Popes ſupremacie, out of the Epiſtle of the Councell written to *Damaſus* (as he pre-tédeth) as it is in *Theodoret*. Where he would haue the Coun-cell ſay : *Se conueniſſe apud vrbem Conſtantinopolim ex mandato literarum Pontificis per Imperatorem ad ſe miſſarum, & ibidem fa-tentur Romanā Eccleſiam caput eſſe, ſe autem membra:* That they
,, aſſembled at the citie of Conſtantinople by the commande-
,, ment of the letters of the Pope, ſent vnto them by the Em-
,, peror. And there they confeſſe, that the Church of Rome is
                                                   the

Concilium Côſtantinop.

De Rom.Pô-tif.lib.2.c.13. Hiſt.lib.5.c.9.

the head, they the members. But this was from the Councell, „
not from *Boniface* himfelfe; neither was this *Concilium fecun-*
dum, but after the Bifhops colle&ed the yeare following. Is
it poffible that *Bellarmine* could be miftaken in a matter fo e-
uidently contrarie? He hath not one materiall word true.
For this Epiftle was not written to *Damafus* alone, but to
him with all the reft affembled with him, of whom diuers
are named with the fame title of honor with him in euery
refpe&. *Dominis reuerendiffimis & pijffimis fratribus & collegis*
Damafo, Ambrofio, Brettoni &c. & cæteris fanctis Epifcopis.
To our moft reuerend Lords and moft holy brethren and „
collegues *Damafus, Ambrofe, Bretto &c.* and the reft of the ho- „
ly Bifhops. This is no more to *Damafus* then to any of the „
other Bifhops. But that he hath the firft place, not aboue, but
common with the reft; not one fillable of other preference.
Againe, *Tanquam veftra membra nos quoque his literis fumma* In another
pietate Imperatoris accerfiuiftis: You inuited vs alfo as your reading.
members by the letters of the moft religious Emperor. From Nos illuc tan-
hence *Bellarmine* gathereth that which was neuer fcattered, quam mem-
that the Church of Rome was the head, they the members, bra propria
and *that the Emperor was the Popes Carrier*. There is neither literis Deo ad
Rome nor Church, nor head in this fentence; but they call Principis ad-
themfelues their members, as fellowes and brethren in the uocaftis.
fame feruice.

30 And whereas *Bellarmine* would haue *the Emperor the*
Popes porter to carrie his letters, it is very plaine that the Bifhop of *Rome* with his collegues, had procured the Emperors
letters to them, to procure the Bifhops at Conftantinople
to ioyne with thefe that were affembled at Rome. Cardinall Lib. Recog.
Bellarmine retra&eth his conceipt, about this Councell and de quatuor
Damafus his letter in many words, and might haue feene this, Concilijs &
but that it is an old faying a and a true, that none fee worfe, Ecclef. pag. 46
then they that wil not fee. He loues a frog, and takes her for
Diana. But if it had pleafed his *Carnalitie*, to haue obferued
how the Bifhop of Rome is called, not *Father*, but *brother*,
not *mafter*, but *fellow*, themfelues not *fubiects* to a head, but
members of a body, he would neuer in a cloud of witneffes,
haue

haue dared to auouch so many,so grosse,so manifest vntruths.

Ecclesia anti- He would not turne his eye to that which they speake of
quis. & plane the gouernmēt of each prouince within it selfe,as was ordai-
Apostolica in by the Councell of *Nice*; which giueth sufficient light to find
Syria. Ibid. the meaning of the sixt Canon we before spake of. So doth
the second Canon of this Councell of Constantinople.
Where is their admiration of Councels,that thus abuse their
authoritie to support their pride and supremacie?

De Christo.l.   31 It is the common opinion of the Schoolemen; and
5.c.9.& 10. *Bellarmine* and all Romanists defend it at this day , that our
Sauiour Christ *did merit by his suffering,as well for himselfe as for
others.* This is direct not onely against the Scriptures , but
Concil.Ephes also against the third Councell generall , which was the first
primum.   at *Ephesus. Qui dicit quod(Christus) pro se obtulisset semetipsum
oblationem, & non potius pro nobis solis, (non enim eguit oblatione,
,, qui peccatum omnino nesciuit) anathema sit.* He that saith Christ
,, offered himselfe an oblation for himselfe,and not for vs one-
,, ly ;(for he needs no oblation that knew no sinne) let him be
,, accursed. The reason standeth necessarily thus. If Christ merited as well for himselfe as for vs ; then he offered himselfe,
as well for himselfe as for vs. But he offered not himselfe
for himselfe. For the greatest merits of Christ were his passion,and that oblation once offered for our sinnes;and therfore if Christ offered 'not for himselfe, he merited not for
himselfe;and so *Bellarmine* crosseth this Councell and is therfore accursed of it.

Concil. Chal-   32 The Councell of Chalcedon is the fourth. Is this free
ced. prim. from the Romanists cauillation? It is cleare that the Fathers
act.16.   of that Councell equalled the Bishop of Constantinople to
the Bishop of Rome , and ordained that they should vse
the same priuiledges, and yeeld Rome the primacie , not
as by Christs designement,or by succession from Saint *Peter*,
but because it was the chiefe Citie , and then reigned ouer
the world. This is an euidence vnauoidable, vndeniable.
How do they answer it? The words are pregnant and plaine,
they cannot denie them for shame.They canno t *effingere com-*
Index. expur. *modum sensum* , pretend any interpretation of them , to fit
in Bertramo.   their

their purpofe, as in fome cafes they craftily deale with the
Fathers.What then will they do? Thus *Bellarmine* illudes it,
*Leo epift.*35 *ad Anatolium,* 54 *ad* *Martianum,* 55 *ad Pulche-* De Conciliis
rium, agnofcit Chalcedonenfem Synodum legitimam fuiffe, & ta- l.2.c.7.
men non dubitat ei attribuere ambitionem & inconfultam temeri-
tatem: *Leo* in three Epiftles acknowledgeth the *(Chalcedon* ,,
Councell to be lawfull, and yet he makes no fcruple to taxe ,,
it with *ambition* and *inconfiderate rafhneffe.* What? a lawfull ,,
Councell, a generall Councell, one of the firft foure, equalled
by Saint *Gregorie,* and from his authoritie by learned Catholickes, to one of the Gofpels and yet fubiect to *ambition* and
inconfiderate rafhneffe? Me thinks this is a ftrange imputation.
If it would not be thought to be halfe and more herefie, I
would rather cenfure the Pope for this *ambition* and *incon-*
fiderate rafhneffe, then thofe 650 *Deo amantiffimorum Epifcopo-*
rum, Bifhops moft beloued of God. For he fpake for himfelfe, ,,
his owne honour, his owne benefit, perhaps his owne belly, Venter non
and therefore could heare the worfe what that venerable Cato.
Councell determined; they not for themfelues, but Gods
Church, and the peace thereof.

33   This the Pope may fay peraduenture, becaufe he is
not fubiect to controlment. But what will or dare a Cardi- Hoc cap. p.1.
nall fay of fuch a reuerend Councell? Cardinall *Bellarmine* de Concil.
will anfwer as before: *Refpondeo, Concilium legitimum poffe er-* l.2.c.7.
rare in his quæ non legitimè agit, & de facto erraffe, quando ab A-
poftolicâ fede reprobatur: I anfwer (faith the Cardinall) that a ,,
lawfull Councell may erre in thofe things which it doth vn- ,,
lawfully; and in fact hath erred, when it was reprobated by ,,
the Apoftolicall Sea. Which anfwer is halfe foolifh, halfe ,,
mad. It erres in that wherein it erreth, and is vnlawfull
wherein it is vnlawfull; or it is vnlawfull in that wherein it
erreth. Wherein he directly concludeth, that this Councell
erred. The mad part is, *in fact it hath erred, when it is reproued*
by the Apoftolicall fea. It hath erred in the preterperfect tenfe,
if the Pope reproues it in the prefent tenfe. As much to fay,
though it was once lawfull, yet if the Pope afterwards reproue it, then it is vnlawfull. Alas poore Councell! I fee the

                    O   Ca-

Catholike Romane god in earth, is not like our God in heauen; nor the Councels in earth, like the euerlaſting counſell

Ioh. 13. of the God of heauen. *Whom our God once loueth, vnto the end*
he loueth them; but their *Lord god the Pope can like and diſlike,*
approue and reproue, loue once, and yet hate euer after : their
Councels though conſtant in themſelues, yet to be repealed
or reproued by their great Maiſter. If Popes be ſo fickle, truſt
them that liſt, I will not. If Councels may be ſo eaſily con-
trolled, reſt on them that dare, I dare not.

    34   Yea but the Cardinall preſumeth not thus to anſwer

Epiſt. ad Mi- of himſelfe, he hath two Popes more to helpe him. Pope *Ni-*
chaelem Imp. *colas* **1.** had a tooth againſt this Councell; and *Gelaſius* in part
allowes it not, becauſe *Alia per incompetentem præſumptionem*
„ *prolata, vel potiùs ventilata ſunt:* Some things were by incom-
„ petent preſumption vttered, or rather ventilated. Is not this
fine ſtuffe ? that Popes ſhould vſe Councels like their cooks
or their ſcullians: if they dreſſe his meate to the Popes liking,
he eates it, deuoures it; if they dreſſe it, though cleanly and
wholeſomly, yet if it be not to his tooth, he loathes it : and
either will not eate it at all, or caſts it vp againe. And therefore *Bellarmine*, the Popes ſewer, is bold to take the meate,
and caſt it in the cooks face, that it neuer came to his maiſters
ſight, for feare of troubling his queazie ſtomacke, and tels
vs plainly, like a diſſolute gentleman : *Reſpondeo, Decretum*
illud illegitimum fuiſſe , quod reclamantibus ijs qui Concilio præſi-
„ *debant, factum ſit:* I anſwer at a word, that Decree was vnlaw-
„ full, becauſe it was made when the Preſidents of the Councel
„ diſclaimed it. This is plaine dealing indeed, but ſeldome vſed
by the Cardinall. But in this, his and his fellowes madneſſe
is made manifeſt vnto all men ; that what maketh for them,
they can be contented to entertaine it ; that which is not for
their profit, lightly to regard it : that which makes againſt
them, vtterly to diſcard, and caſt it to the middin or dunghil.
Would they vſe the foure Goſpels as the foure firſt, and (I
ſay ſtill) beſt Councels are vſed? If for ſhame they might, they
would, euen as plainly : which they do in ſome ſort, though
with ſome more ſhew of wit in couering more cloſely their
trechery.

trechery. Wil they vfe later Councels better,that abufe thofe fo wickedly?Or how may we thinke they regard any, feeing they refpeét thefe fo litle?Or how can *Bellarmine* and his pue-fellowes hold, that *Councels confirmed by the Pope,cannot erre?* as he endeuoureth to proue in a whole booke by poore ar-guments,God wot; and yet confeffeth plainly,that they do erre.

35　The firft that fubfcribed in the fift generall **Councel,** was *Eutyches, Epifcopus Conftantinopolios noua Romæ* , the Bi- An.Dom.553. fhop of *Conftantinople* which is new *Rome*:the next, *Apolinæus* Iuftiniani pri-*Epifcopus Alexandriæ,* Bifhop of *Alexandria.* The Bifhop of mi,27. *Rome* fubfcribeth not at all, neither feemeth he to haue bene there,either by himfelfe or his Legats.Thofe are mentioned in euery feffion or collation, and none from *Rome.* For this fift Councel(which Saint *Gregory* honoreth as the firft foure) Diftinét.15. although I find nothing by our aduerfaries contradiéted in Sicut. it, yet *Bellarmine* putteth a doubt which it is. *Many thinke it* De Concil.l.1 *not that which was celebrated vnder Agapetus and Menno, and* cap.6. *which is in the fecond Tome of Councels, vnder the name of the fift Councell,for that was particular, and went before the fift Councel.* The other that he held to be the true fift Councel,the fecond of *Conftantinople,* he faith, *That the great Bifhop was not there by himfelfe,nor his Legats.* Here is a double doubt, referued perhaps for fome aduantage. If a man fhould take the for-mer, and alledge it for the fift generall Councell , that is de-nied to be it, and therefore will be eafily put off. If the other fhould be vrged, the Pope was not there by himfelfe, nor his Legats;therefore that is nothing. Yea but the Pope did con-firme it by his libell or letters: *Nicephorus* is witneffe. What account *Nicephorus* is made of by the Papifts,wil afterwards Infra cap.9. appeare,when we fpeake of Hiftories. Why fhould we truft him,whom themfelues difcredit? But the truth is, the Pope was not there by himfelfe,nor any other, nor confirmed it, as if it could not ftand without him. But the Fathers thought they might lawfully, and did in faét, both confult and con-clude without the Pope. But *Bellarmine* is loath it fhould be fo,and therefore will not confeffe it though it were fo.

36   *Iuſtinian* in his Epiſtle to this fift Councell, hath, *Sem-*
per ſtudium fuit orthodoxis & pijs Imperatoribus, Patribus noſtris,
pro tempore exortas hæreſes per congregationem religioſiſſimorum
Epiſcoporum amputare, & rectâ fide ſyncerè prædicatâ, in pace ſan-
,, *ctam Dei Ecclesiam cuſtodire.* The orthodoxall and religious
,, Emperours, our progenitors, euer had this care, to lop off
,, the new ſprong hereſies, by a religious congregating of Bi-
,, ſhops; and by faith ſincerely preached, to preſerue the holy
,, Church of God in peace. After this he remembreth the former foure generall Councels : of *Nice* againſt *Arius*, that it
was *congregata*, gathered by *Conſtantine*, who was in the
Councel, and had holpen the Fathers. Of the ſecond, which
was at *Conſtantinople* againſt *Macedonius*, that *Theodoſius, Con-*
gregatis in regiâ vrbe 150 *ſanctis Patribus, cum & ipſe particeps*
fuiſſet Cócilij, damnatis prædictis hæreticis, vnà cũ impijs eorũ dog-
,, *matibus, fecit rectã prædicare fidem: Theodoſius* calling together
,, 150 Fathers in the regall Citie, when himſelfe was a part of
,, the Councel, condemning the ſaid hereticks together with
,, their impious opiniós, cauſed them to preach the right faith.
Of the third, which was at *Epheſus* againſt *Neſtorius*, it is ſaid:
Theodoſius Iunior piæ recordationis, congregauit Priorem Epheſi-
nam Synodum, cui præſidebant Celeſtinus & Cyrillus ſancti Pa-
tres, & directis Iudicibus qui deberent Concilio intereſſe, compulit
& ipſum Neſtorium ibi peruenire, & iudicium propter eum proce-
,, *dere : Theodoſius* the Yonger, of religious memory, gathered
,, the firſt *Epheſine* Councell, ouer which was ſet *Celeſtinus* and
,, *Cyrillus,* holy Fathers. And the Iudges directing who ought
,, to be preſent in the Councel, compelled euen *Neſtorius* him-
,, ſelfe to be preſent, and iudgement to proceed againſt him.
Of the fourth, at *Chalcedon* againſt *Eutyches: Piæ recordationis*
Martianus congregauit Chalcedone ſanctos Patres, & magnâ con-
tentione inter Epiſcopos factâ, non ſolùm per ſuos Iudices, ſed etiam
per ſeipſum in Concilium peruenit, & ad concordiam omnes per-
,, *duxit : Martianus* of pious memory, gathered the holy Fa-
,, thers at *Chalcedon ;* and a great contention ariſing amongſt
,, the Biſhops, not alone by his Iudges, but by himſelfe com-
,, ming to the Councell, he bringeth them to an agreement.
                                                                                    More

More afterwards of the care of *Leo* the Emperour to write
to all Bifhops, *Ad omnes vbique Sacerdotes fcripfit, vt vnufquif-
que propriam fententiam manifeſtaret de eodem ſanꝶo Concilio.*
He wrote vnto the Priefts of euery place, that euery man ”
fhould make knowne his owne opinion of that holy Coun- ”
cell; at laſt faith, *Nos fequentes ſanꝶos Patres, & volentes re-* ”'
ꝶam fidem ſine quadam maculà in Dei Ecclefiis prædicari, &c.
We following our holy Fathers, and willing the true faith ”
without pollution to be preached in the Churches of God, ”
&c. with like fentences of religious Emperours.

37 Whereby it is cleare, how much, not onely by their
fauour and counfell, but alfo by their authoritie they encou-
raged good Bifhops, and called Councels to the rooting out
of herefies, and eſtablifhing of the truth of the Gofpell. Indeed *Vigilius* Bifhop of Rome refufed the other Bifhops in a
Councell, becaufe there were few Wefterne Bifhops, as if
that would preiudice a Councell called by the Emperours
authoritie. But it was anfwered, there were but few in o-
ther Councels, and that it mattered not much whether
there were or not. So little then did the Bifhops of the Eaſt
refpeꝶ the Bifhop of Rome, or his fellowes of the Weſt.

38 If I fhould enter into an exaꝶ difcourfe of the Romaniſts dealing with the fixt Councell, efpecially to acquit *Honorius* late Bifhop of Rome, from the taint of the *Monothelits*
herefie, it would aske more then an Herculean labour. It was
called vnder *Conſtantine* the fourth, *Pogonotus*, in the yeare
678, againſt the *Monothelites*, and confifted of 171 Bifhops,
who were gathered together againe with others, to the number in all of 227. Bifhops, and fate in *Trullo* the Emperours
pallace. This is fometimes a good Councell, fometimes a bad,
fometimes the fift, fometimes the fixt, fometime neither, but
Quini-fextum, the fift-fixt Councell, like an Androgenus or
an Hermophrodite, neither male nor female, but both, or either, or neither, or what they liſt themfelues, to their beſt aduantage.

39 *Surius* thinketh it pittie to cafhire it quite, for a few ill
Canons that make againſt the Romane fynagogue, becaufe
O 3   he

*De Canoni-
bus fextæ fy-
nodi admon.*

he finds other that feeme to ferue his turne. *Turrian* a Iefuite will haue it true and good, forfooth it furthers his pur-

In Diatrib, l.
5.cap.1.

pofes. But *Albertus Pighius* a Canon will none of it, but both
it and the next are adulterous and baftard; thefe are both Romane Catholickes: whether will you beleeue? *Pighius* is confident aboue meafure. *Albertus Pighius vir doctus & pius* (faith
Melchior Canus) *Pighius* a learned & a godly man, doth fhew
by many arguments, that the acts which are carried about vnder the name of this Councell containe many errors. Yea he
calleth it *ter execrandum Concilium*, a thrice accurfed Councell. And, *Quod ad Concilium Constantinopolitanum (quintum &
fextum, refpondet enim vtri(que) non fuit legitimum.* As for the
Councels (fift and fixt, for he anfwers to them both) it was
not lawfull. And afterward faith, it was neither called nor
confirmed by the Bifhop of Rome, neither was it vniuerfall,
becaufe many of the Wefterne and Eafterne Patriarkes and
Bifhops were wanting.

40 But this *contentious pertinacy of Pighius must be reproued*
(faith Canus) who to man out an opinion, that he hath once broa-
ched, aduentures to weaken by vaine coniectures, Councels which
haue bene receiued by the Churches Decree. How far may the ftu-
die of contention and peruerfe obstinacie preuaile, when heate boiles
vp? And may not another Papift be as peruerfe and dogged as
Pighius is prefumed to be? The Councell *Quini-fextum Bel-*
larmine calleth profane, as *Pighius* his fixt thrice-accurfed.

Lib.5.c.6. lo-
co com.
Summa Con
cil.pag.328.
Tom. 1. difp.
54.fect.1.

Canus confuteth their Canons in many words. But *Caranza* in
his Epitome will haue them, and giueth them full authoritie;
fo doth *Suarez* the Iefuite, who alledgeth one of them with
great approbation of all. And *Gratian* alledgeth them in great
good earneft. Euen as they ferue their turnes fo they approue or reiects thofe Canons. See *the battell of the frogs and
mice.*

41 Though Bifhop *Canus* faith, *Abiat nunc Gratianus qui*
„ *Trullianos Canones fexta Synodo tribuit.* Farewell to *Gratian,*
„ that would charge the fixt Councel with the *Trullian* Canons.

Tom. 2.qu.
35.fect.2.

Yet *Suarez* the Iefuite when he had cited the 79 Canon for
the pure deliuerie of the bleffed Virgine *Mary*, faith, *Qua de-*
finitio

finttio magnam habet autohritatem, quoniam illi Canones praterquā
quod plus quàm à 220 Patribus editi funt, in feptima Synodo, Ca-
none primo approbati videntur. Which definition hath great au- „
thoritie, becaufe thofe Canons befide that they were fet „
forth by more then 220 Fathers, they feeme to be approued „
in the firft Canon of the feuenth Councell. And this he pro- „
ueth by *Surius,* who hath alfo obferued, that the faid Councell,
and that of *Florence,* and *Adrian,* and *Michael,* Bifhops of
Rome, vfed the *authoritie of thefe Canons, which Innocentius* re-
citeth alfo out of the Decrees of *Gratian,* as they were cited
by him. Which befell *Thomas* of *Aquine,* and other learned
men fometimes, that trufting *Gratians* diligence, alledge the
chapters of the Decrees, with lying Authors and titles.

42 Is not *Gratian* a perillous fellow, that deceiueth Popes,
Councels, Saints and all? And yet he is the beft founder and
Patron of the Popes law. Maifter *Harding* our countreyman
was taken in the fame fnare; for he citeth this Councell in
Trullo to be a very ancient one, to proue S. *Iames* his Maffe Replie, art. 5.
to be worth the acceptation. And *Gregorius Holoander* one of
Cardinall *Bellarmines* catholicke Authors, was caught in the
fame fpringe, *Sancta fexta Synodus grauiffima fententia Apoftu-*
licos Canones agnouit: The fixt holy Councel by their graue fen- „
tence acknowledged the Canons of the Apoftles. So was Car- „
dinall *Turrecremata* fet by the heeles. For he vpon *Gratians*
word faith, *Ex quibus fatis apertè apparet,* By them it appeareth
clearely. Vfing the authoritie of them as clafficall.

43 *Suarez* notwithftanding to faue all whole, and his caufe Vbi fupra.
and friends harmleffe, faith, *Quamuis quorundam Græcorum*
temeritate aliqui eorum deprauati effe dicantur, hic tamen (de quo
agimus) nunquam in dubium reuocatus eft. Although fome of „
thefe Canons be faid to be corrupted by certaine of the „
Greeks temeritie: yet this (of which we fpeake) was neuer „
called into queftion. Where he leaueth in fufpence and fufpi- „
tion, all faue that which feemeth to ferue his owne turne. Yet
Bellarmine fearing that they may make more againft him then De Rom.
for him, will rather cafhier a few friends, then admit for their Pont.l.2.c.18.
fakes many enemies, and faith plainly, *Nullus roboris funt ifti*

,, *Canones*, theſe Canons are of no force. *For they are not the Ca-*
,, *nons of the true, lawfull, and generall Councell; but of another cer-*
,, *taine conuenticle, which entituled her ſelfe falſely by the name of*
,, *the ſixt. Councell. Whence it followeth, that this ſixt falſe Synod,*
,, *either was not generall, or was not lawfull: For generall, and law-*
full it cannot be, where the authoritie of the firſt Sea is wan-
ting.

44 So many and ſo intricate queſtions growing about
this Councell and the Canons thereof, will its greateſt aduerſaries refuſe it *in toto* in all? No, that will they not, by any
meanes. *Honorius the Pope, heretickes honour ſaued,* they will do
reaſon to ſerue their turnes. Firſt, *Bellarmine* of the ſame
Councell and Canons ſaith, *Hos ergo Canones dicimus partim*
,, *reprobatos.* That theſe Canons are partly reproued, *Becauſe the*
,, *Pope was not there by himſelfe nor his Legates, while theſe Canons*
,, *were caſting:* and partly approued, *becauſe although thoſe Canons*
,, *haue no force of themſelues, yet ſome of them were afterwards ap-*
,, *proued by the Pope, or other lawfull Councels.* He neither knowes
nor cares whether, but *ad bonum ordinis,* to do him ſeruice: as
the 82 Canon of painting images was receiued by *Adrian* the
Pope, and the ſeuenth Synod.

45 But in my mind he giueth a better reaſon in another
place, maruellous plauſible in the Pope and his merchants
eares, and that is *ab vtili,* from profit: which more preuaileth
at Rome then the words of a Prophet. Becauſe *ille Canon 82*
,, *de picturis vtilis erat eo tempore,* That Canon the 82 of Images,
,, was profitable at that time to the queſtion *then handled.* So I
dare ſweare he will ſay of more of them, if they fit his foote
as well. And *Bellarmines* brother *Melchior Canus,* as hard
a friend as he is to that *Trullian* Councell, and the Canons of
it, yet he can take the 19, and diſcharge it valiantly againſt
Caietan, as the *Midianites* that ſlue one another.

46 Varietie they ſay breeds delight, but certainely this
diuerſitie breeds confuſion. How can a man reſt vpon Councels thus traduced, mangled, maimed, abuſed, aboue all meaſure or meane? Theſe are the firſt ſixe, which *Bellarmine* of
his bountie affoords vs, as accepted & reuerenced by vs. We
enter-

De Concil. l. 1. c. 7.

De Concil. l. 2 c. 8.

Lib. 7. c. 3.

entertaine them with loue, we yeeld them their due honour,
we will not aske fo much as *Bellarmine* muft allow: That we
may vfe the lawes, themfelues impofe : that we may vfe the
Councels as they do; though we may not with our credits,
we will not for our honefties. Let them thus abufe them,
that defpifed credite, and renounced honefty. I will conclude all I will haue faid of thefe fixe Councels with *Bellar-*
mines laft fhift, and that they are almoft all corrupted by
the Grecians that enuied and emulated the Romanes honour.

47 *Dico fine dubio*, without all doubt, I fay, *That the name* Bell. de Rom.
of Honorius was inferted among the names of thofe who were dam- Pont.l 4 c.11.
ned in the fixt Councell, by thofe that enuied the Romane Church;
and fo whatfoeuer was there faid of Honorius. Secondly, it was al-
moft an ordinarie cuftome amongft the Grecians to corrupt bookes.
The fixt Councell found many corruptions made by heretickes in
the fift. And Gregorie faith, that Conftantinopolitans corrupted
the Councell of Chalcedon, and fufpects the fame to be done in the
Ephefine; *and addes, that the Romane copies are truer then the*
Grecians, and giueth a ftrong reafon. *Quoniam Romani ficut*
non acumina, ita nec impofituras habent : Becaufe the Romanes
as they haue blockheads , fo they haue litle wit ; and little
wit, little craft. *Cicero* had a better conceipt of his owne
countrie and countrimen, when he faith, *Sed meum iudicium*
femper fuit, omnia noftros vel inueniffe per fe fapientius quàm Gra-
cos, aut accepta ab illis feciffe meliora, &c. My iudgement euer Tufc.lib.1.
was, that the Romanes were more wife for inuention then
the Grecians , or made things better which they receiued
from them ; and I am fure the Grecians declined when the
Romanes florifhed, as a fubdued people are debafed vnder
their coquerors. *If the Grecians haue corrupted the third, fourth,*
and feuenth Councels, what maruaile is it if they corrupt the fixt ?
In what cafe are men, if the firft and chiefe Councels be thus
corrupted, nay be fo diuerfly handled, may be thruft out, and
brought in, in part, or in all, when thefe Doctors lift ? How
can we truft them? How can we repofe confidence in them?
And this of the firft fixe Councels.

48 To

48 To deſcend vnto the reſt in this manner were a bur-
denſome labour vnto me, and a tedious taske for the reader,
and perhaps needleſſe for either. Yet I will beſtow a few
lines in ſome, and thoſe not many. The reſt I will leaue to
be cenſured by thoſe,I haue,or ſhall mentiõ. A good Mathe-
matician may meaſure *Hercules* by his foote.

Bell.de Rom.
Põtif.l.2.c.15.

49 *Sardicenſe Concilium conſtat vniuerſale eſſe probatum*: It is
euident that the Sardian Councel was vniuerſally approued;
more vniuerſall then the great Councell of *Nice*,ſaith Cardinall *Bellarmine*. For there were 376 Biſhops; which were
more then were in the *Nicene* Councell by 48: as well approued, for it is taken to be the ſame with the *Nicene*. *Non mi-*
,, *nor eſt authoritas Sardicenſis,quàm Nicenæ Synodi*, The *Sardican*
,, Councel is of no leſſe Authoritie then the *Nicene*,becauſe the
,, moſt part of the Fathers that were at the one were alſo at the
,, other. And no new thing appertaining vnto faith is added to
the one, that was not in the other. *Gregorius de Valentia* will

Anal.fid.ca-
tho.l.7.c.11.
Epit.pag.281.

alſo haue it a generall Councell , by the teſtimony of graue
authors. And *Baronius* will haue it a generall Councell in all
points. Why then is not this numbred among the generall
Councels that are approued by *Bellarmine?*Becauſe they haue
no other ſhift to excuſe *Zozimus* the Biſhop of *Rome* his forgerie of the *Nicene* Councell, to the African Fathers. Why
doth he put ſo generall,and ſo approued a Councell amongſt
his demie-reprobates ? Forſooth becauſe there is a coale at
one end will burne his fingers , to ſaue himſelfe harmleſſe
he will hold it at the other end, to put out the fire. A
craftier companion there neuer liued. Haue not *Romanes*
their wittes about them now as well as euer the *Grecians*
had?

Canon 36.

50 We alledge the Councell of *Elibertine* againſt making of Images,and placing them in the Church , *Placuit pi-*
,, *ctaras in Eccleſia eſſe non debere,ne quod colitur & adoratur,jn pa-*
,, *rietibus depingatur*: It ſeemeth good vnto vs, that pictures
,, ſhould not be in the Church, leſt that which is worſhipped
,, and adored ſhould be painted on walls. It it ſport to ſee

De Imagini-
bus l.2.cap.9.

how *Bellarmine* ſweates and tewes , to anſwer this with the
vtmoſt

vtmoſt bent and extent of his *Romane* wit. But I leaue thoſe anſwers. This to our purpoſe. When we produce this very ancient peece of euidence,*Bellarmine* diſgraceth the whole authoritie of the Councell. It was but a Councell of 19 Biſhops,but a prouinciall Councell, and not confirmed, and it ſeemeth to haue erred in other Decrees.When *Sixtus Senenſis* ſhould anſwer this Canon, which he nor all the Papiſts in Chriſtendome can do,with any ſo much as probabilitie, for their life,he prefaceth and diſgraceth it:*Prouinciale Concilium Elib. à decem & octo duntaxat Epiſcopis , in Hiſpania peractum.* A prouinciall Councell of 18 Biſhops only holden in Spaine. ,, *Bellarmine* as the truth is,ſaith 19,but *Sixtus* thought belike to curtall them by one, that another may come after and ſay 17. So by little and little to make them no body. But both, and indeed others of their ranke , take this exception, that they were ſo few. *Bellarmine* might haue remembred what he had ſaid before , where he gaue a better note then he doth now take notice of, or put in practiſe himſelfe: *Omne Concilium non eſt tanto melius quanto maius,&c.* Euery ,, Councell is not by ſo much the better , by how much the ,, greater: for *the Councell of Ariminum* (which was an here- ,, ticall Councell) *had* 600 *Biſhops, the firſt of Conſtantinople but* 150.

51 *Suarez* keepeth a ſell coyle about this Councell, Diſp.54.ſect.1 in the matter of Images. *Difficilius explicatur decretum Concilij Elibertini,&c.*The decree of the *Elibertine* Councel is more difficultly explaned.*That becauſe it was but prouinciall,and but of a few Biſhops, Canus doubteth not to grant that it erred; but others anſwer,that that Councell did onely forbid the proper images of God, and others ſay,that it forbad images to be adored, and painted after the manner of the Gentiles. Sed hæc ſine fundamento dicuntur* : But all this is ſaid without ground, for the words of that Canon, in the firſt *Tome of Councels and in Gratian,are,* Diſtinct.4. that what is worſhipped in Churches,ſhould not be painted on wals. c.Placuit. *Out of which words it may not obſcurely be gathered , that images there,are not ſimply forbidden, but that they ſhould not be painted vpon wals , which law at that time might be profitable. For that*
Counſell

Councell was about the time of the Nicene Councell, when as yet Idolatrie floriſhed. Wherehence it might eaſily fall out, that images of Saints painted on wals, might by the inſidels be irreuerently handled. So anſwereth *Allen, dial. 5. c. 16. Sanders lib. 2. cap. 4. Ayala lib. de trad. 3. p. c. de Antiq. imag. who giueth another reaſon of that Decree, to wit, becauſe images painted on walls might be eaſily defaced. But becauſe this inconuenience by diligence may be auoided, and that old neceſſitie is now ceaſſed, therefore that Decree is abrogated by vſe, and in the ſeuenth Synod ſuch images are admitted to be painted on walls.* Thus dally they with the ancient reuerend Councels, when they ſpeake againſt them.

 52 But will they vſe them ſo when they make for them? No I warrant you. For *Melchior Canus* alledgeth it, and that rightly, for the Epiſtle to the *Hebrewes* without all exception. And *Bellarmine* himſelfe (as little account as he makes of it in our caſe) doth not onely alledge it, but vrge it, for his faſting vpon Saturdayes. And good reaſon: for the caſe is altered, quoth *Ployden. Perſpicuum eſt ex Concilio Elibertino*, it is cleare by the Councell of *Elibertine.* Now this Councell is a cleeare witneſſe, in this caſe and againſt mariage of Prieſts, Biſhops, Deacons and Subdeacons. The three and thirtieth Canon is authentique without derogation or impeachment, either of Canon or Councell. And *Noͨturna peruigilia ſublata ſunt omninò Elibertini Concilij Sanͨtione*, ſaith *Sixtus Senenſis.* Night watches are taken vtterly away by the Decree of the *Elibertine* Councell. Beſides, *Gratian* hath at leaſt ten of this Councels Canons diſperſed in the Decrees which ſtand for good law. And *Ino* whom *Bellarmine* placeth in the liſt of his Romane writers, and *Gratians* good Maiſter, finding it not ſo good for his great Maiſter of *Romes* profit, hath left it quite out.

 53 Thus they cheate the whole world vpon all aduantages, as if they were bound by obligation, and ſolemne vow *to do nothing for the truth, but againſt the truth. Quis vos faſcinauit?* Who hath ſo bewitched you? I could adde vnto theſe the Councel of *Alexandria,* ſo commended by *Ruffinus,*
           that

Lib. 2. c. 9.

Bellar. de o-per. bon. in particulari, lib. 2. cap. 18.

Bibl. Sanͨt. l. 6. annot. 152.

Gal. 3. 1.

that beareth the praife, which the former Councell iuftly deferued; *Few they were in nūber, but for integritie of faith and man-* Hift.lib.2.c.28 *ners, many.* Yet this Councell is now no Councell, no not fo much as vouchfafed a roome among the Councels, or by *Bellarmine* among good, or indifferent, or naught, or any at all.

54 *Pererius* (fpeaking of the interpretation of *Caietan* In Gen. c. 19. and *Thoftatus*, of *Pluit Dominus à Domino*, The Lord rained §.35. from the Lord) faith of the *Syrmian* Councell, *Verùm ante omnes Patrum authoritates:* But before all authorities of Fa- ,, thers, the *Syrmian* Councell feemeth to make certaine this ex- ,, pofition. And afterward: *Neither may we doubt of the credit of* ,, *this Councell,* as well for the determination of other Councels approuing theirs, as Saint *Hilarie* his authoritie, who acknowledgeth this Councell for *Catholicum & fincerum,* both Catholicke and fincere. How could a man conceiue of this Councell, but that it was abfolute and without exception? Yet *Pererius* himfelfe in the next *Paragraph* but one, doth fomewhat derogate from it: *Sciat Lector Concilium iftud poftea fuiffe probatum, non quoad omnia:* And yet the Reader muft ,, take notice, that this Councell was afterwards approued, but ,, not in all things. It is preferred before all the authorities of ,, Fathers, the credit of it muft not be doubted of, it is Catholicke and fincere, and yet it is not approued in all. And *Bellarmine* turnes it to the order of *Hermophroditi,* and faith, it was a generall Councell, yet in part approued, in part not.

55 Such are the Councels of *Frankford*, of *Conftance*, and *Bafil,* though called by themfelues, confirmed by their Popes. *Frankford confirmatum fuit quoad illam partem,* Confirmed in one part, and reprobated in another, becaufe it is againft the idolatrous worfhip of images, allowed by the fecond of *Nice. Bafil* alfo is currant, *quantum ad primas Seffiones,* as farre as the firft Seffions go: but bafe coine, *quantum ad vltimas Seffiones,* as farre as the laft Seffions reach. I had thought, that *pofteriores cogitationes* be *falubriores,* the laft the beft. The worft of thefe is that of *Bafil,* which is approued in nothing, but

but about the diſpoſitions of certaine Benefices , which was
yeelded vnto for peace and quietneſſe ſake . Aske *Gregorius*
Greg.Valent. *de Valentia* , which Councels were approued by the Pope
and he will tell you, that all are good that are in the Tomes
of the Councels,&c.ſauing the Councell of *Baſil.*

56 Yet aske of him againe in particular of the Councell
Greg. Valent. of *Conſtance*, and you ſhall heare what he ſaith : *Reſpondetur,*
analyſ.cathol. *Decreta illius quidem Seſſionis Concilij Conſtantienſis non habere*
l.8.c.7.   *certam authoritatem.Nam ea tantùm Martinus quintus probauit*
quæ eſſent circa fidem determinata conciliariter, hoc eſt, adhibita
priùs diſputatione & ſententiarum collatione, rectè atque ſedatè,
,, *ſicut fieri in Concilijs aſſolet, inſtituta*: It is anſwered, the De-
,, crees of that Seſſion of the Councell of *Conſtance*, haue no
,, certaine authoritie . For thoſe onely which *Martin* the fift
,, did approue were good, which were determined concerning
Conciliaritèr. the faith *in good earneſt*, that is, were concluded after diſputa-
,, tion permitted, and collation of ſentences rightly and quiet-
,, ly, as was wont to be vſed in Councels . *Illa verò Seſſio*
quinta Concilij Conſtantienſis' edita fuit , importunitate tantùm
quorundam ſchiſmaticorum,non niſi admodum tumultuariè, vt ex
actis Concilij conſtat, & benè à Caietano, & ab alijs animaduer-
,, *ſum eſt*: But that fift Seſſion of the Councell of *Conſtance* was
,, decreed onely vpon the importunitie of certaine ſchiſmatiks,
,, and that very tumultuouſly, as it is euident by the acts of the
,, Councel, and hath bene by *Caietan* and others wel obſerued.
Porrò Concilium Baſilienſe nunquam fuit confirmatum : etſi ante
apertum ſanè ſchiſma fuerit habitum pro legitimo, quoad inchoati-
onem quidem, & proſequutionem eius Concilij attinebat, vt rectè
,, *quoque notauit Caietanus*: Moreouer, the Councell of *Baſil*
,, was neuer confirmed, although verily before the opē ſchiſme
,, it was holden for lawfull, concerning the beginning indeed,
,, and proſecution of that Councel, as *Caietan* alſo hath rightly
,, noted. Here is the beginning approued, and the end diſanul-
led; the end embraced, and the beginning reiected, iuſt as it
pleaſeth them. And as they can apt it to their purpoſes, ſo hath
it force, or no validitie.

57 I will note but one more, and that is that of *Africke*
or

or *Carthage*, whereof Saint *Auguftine* was an honourable
member, among 217 Bifhops more then were at the firft
Councell of *Conftantinople*, or the firft of *Ephefus*, two of the
firft foure generall Councels, and therefore of much reuerence. This Councell, efpecially for the laft Canons fake,
which feemeth to make for the Romanifts in numbring the
bookes of the Scripture, as if thofe which we iuftly hold *A-*
pocryphall, were of the fame authoritie with the Canonicall
Scriptures, Cardinall *Bellarmine* and the reft of his brethren
hold in great account. And therefore it is oppofed to the *Lao-*
dicene Councell, long before it in time, and fo (*if Antiquitie*
haue predominancie) the better: *Concilium Carthaginenfe eft ma-* De Concil.
ioris authoritatis quàm Laodicenfe, tum quia pofterius, tum quia l.1.c.8.
nationale fuit, & præterea confirmatum à Leone quarto : The ,,
Councell of *Carthage* is of more authoritie then the *Laodi-* ,,
cene Councell, both becaufe it was the latter, and alfo becaufe ,,
it was Nationall, and befides was afterwards confirmed by ,,
Leo the fourth . Three reafons to giue this Councell prefe- ,,
rence befòre the *Laodicene*, one becaufe it was later, therefore Antiquitie hath not preference in Councels; another,
becaufe it was *Nationall*, the other but *Prouinciall*: a third,
becaufe this was confirmed by Pope *Leo* the fourth, the other
was not.

58   Thefe men that fo much pretend *Antiquitie*, now
preferre *Noueltie*, the latter before the former. And it was
alfo confirmed by the fixt generall Councel, and Pope *Adri-*
an, as appeareth in the Decrees. And this in the Cardinals o- Dift.16. c.
pinion, makes a *Nationall* or a *Prouinciall* Councel to be in the Quoniam.&
nature of a generall : *Aliquando reperitur Concilium vnius na-* cap.Sextam.
tionis aut regionis dici vniuerfale, ficut in Concilio Africano: Ioh.Turreci.
Sometimes a Councell is found in one Nation or Prouince, l.3.c.3.
to be called vniuerfall, as the Councell of *Africke*. Howfoeuer ,,
the poore Councell of *Laodicene* may fhift, I know not, yet
you heare it hath the approbation of another general Councell and Pope. But the Councell of *Carthage* is without queftion authentiqne in the Romanifts opinion, who haue not a
like euidence for the authorifing of *Apocryphall* Scriptures
                                                              in

Can.   in all their learning. This Carthaginian Councell we alledge
for the abridging of Appeales *ad tranſmarinas partes*, beyond
the ſeas, and againſt the pompous titles of the ſea of Rome:
Non appelletur princeps ſacerdotum , aut ſummus ſacerdos , Let
him not be called prince of prieſts or higheſt prieſt:or as *Gra-*
tian addes vnto theſe words , *Vniuerſalis autem nec etiam Ro-*
manus Pontifex appelletur: But as for vniuerſall, the Biſhop of
Rome ſhall not be ſo called. What will Cardinall *Bellarmine*
ſay to the authoritie of this Councell, now it ſo plainly and
DeSum.Pont. pregnantly maketh for vs? *Quidam locus in Concilio Carthagi-*
l.2.c.25.   *nenſi vel corruptus eſt,vel è margine irrepſit in textum:* There is a
,, place in this *Carthaginian* Councell corrupted, or crept out
,, of the margine into the text. Or if that will not ſerue them,
that which graced it in reſpe& of the *Laodicean* Councell, It
was a nationall,therefore to be preferred,Now it is a Natio-
De Concil.l.2. nall with a *But.Concilium Carthaginenſe nationale fuit, nec fere-*
c.8.   *bat leges vniuerſæ Eccleſiæ, ſed tantùm Epiſcopis Africæ , itaque*
neque prohibuit, neque prohibere potuit,ne Rom. Pontif. diceretur
,, *princeps ſacerdotum:* The Councell of *Carthage* was *Nationall,*
,, and made no lawes for the vniuerſall Church , but onely for
,, the Biſhops of *Africa*; therefore neither did it forbid , nei-
,, ther could it forbid,that the Biſhop of *Rome* ſhould be called
,, the Prince of Prieſts.

          59 What will Biſhop *Lindan* ſay to this malepart cenſure
Panopl.l.3.c.4 of the *African* Fathers ? *Quod Concilij Africani tertij cui diuus*
Auguſtinus interfuit,decretum, in 8 *Synodo in Tullo congrega-*
ta , quia fuit approbatum, atque in Rom.Pont. Eccleſiæ͜q, Apo-
ſtolicæ authoritate roboratum, in dubium vocari nequit à pio Ca-
,, *tholico,Eccleſiæ͜q, Chriſti filio:* Which decree of *African* Coun-
,, cell,wherein Saint *Auguſtine* was preſent, was confirmed in
,, the eighth Councell in *Trullo* , and afterward ſtrengthened
,, with the conſent of the Biſhop of *Rome:* and the authoritie
,, of the Apoſtolicke Church, cannot be called into queſtion
,, by any pious Catholicke,and the ſonne of Chriſts Church.
How is Cardinall *Bellarmine* then either a pious Catholicke,
or a ſon of Chriſts Church,who extenuateth that which is ſo
ſtrongly barocadoed by ſuch inuincible fortifications,as his
                                                      owne

owne fellowes, his deare mother the Church, his vnerring father the Pope? yea himſelfe alſo in ſome caſes? Yet like an vngracious ſonne of his mother the Court of Rome, and his great father the Pope, he can ſay,that theſe African Fathers De Rom. were deceiued *by ignorance.* A ſawcie and fooliſh part of a Pont.l.2.c.25. Frier (he was no Cardinall when he wrote this,) ſo malepartly to confront and taxe ſo ancient, ſo graue, ſo learned Biſhops, ſuch Saints gathered together in ſo great a number, their Decrees confirmed by the Pope himſelfe, another Councell, the whole repreſentatiue Church; and therein to contradiƈt himſelfe, who approueth the ſame Councell in other caſes. Let him looke to it,whether it can ſtand with religious integrity, or ciuill honeſtie; with learned conſtruƈtion, or reaſonable perſwaſion, to commend and diſclaime, to aduance and caſt downe, to magnifie and vilifie, to build and deſtroy,vpon all aduantages.

60 Or if they will vſe this large and vnbounded licence, why may not we vſe our lawfull and reaſonable libertie,in taking iuſt exceptions vnto ſome Councels, when good occaſion is offered? I will conclude theſe conſiderations of Councels in particular, with a reaſonable motion of the Ieſuite himſelf vnto *Caluin;*I wil aske no more but that he returne & reflect it vpon himſelfe. *Caluinus contra inuocationem Sancto-* De Saƈt. bea- *rum, Caluin* againſt the inuocation of Saints, *bringeth as a* titu.l.1.c.10. *chiefe argument, a teſtimonie from the third Councell of Carthage, but in the ſame Councell, Chapter 47. the bookes of Machabeis are approued,either therefore let Caluin receiue the bookes of Machabeis as Canonicall and diuine, or let him not terrifie vs with the authoritie of this Councell, from the inuocation of Saints. Neque enim dicendum eſt eos Patres in vno ſapere,in altero delira-* There is re.For we may not ſay the Fathers did wiſely in one thing,and much doubt doted in another. May not we ſay the ſame to the Ieſuite and of the 47 Ca- his fellowes, not onely of this Councell, but alſo in their beſt all of the o- and moſt approued Councels, but eſpecially of thoſe that are ther. partly receiued, partly reieƈted. Either let Cardinall *Bellarmine* renounce in the Biſhop of *Rome,* the name of vniuerſall Biſhop,*and chiefe Prieſt, and Prince of Prieſts* : Let him diſplace

P   place

place images out of Churches; giue no more iuriſdiction to
the Biſhop of Rome, then other Archbiſhops, Metropolitans, and Patriarks haue in their Churches. Let Conſtantinople be equall in authoritie and iuriſdiction with the Romane
Church : and hold that Councels are aboue the Pope, that no
appeales may be out of *Africa*, to any beyond the ſea, &c. or
neuer let him deterre vs with the authoritie of Councels. *For
no man will ſay, that the Fathers gathered in Councels were wiſe in
one thing, and doted in another*. I neuer read of any on our
part, that haue thus vſed any Councell, or ſpoken that of any,
which Cardinall *Bellarmine* hath ſaid of many. And therefore
certainly he and his Synagogue yeeld farre leſſe reuerence to
Councels of any ſort, then our Church doth, whereby they
iuſtly depriue themſelues of the ſecond euidence of *Antiquity*,
which is the Councels.

61 Wherefore our Sauiours counſell may ſtand for our
Mat. 22. 21. direction, *Giue vnto Cæſar that which is Cæſars : giue vnto God
that which belongeth vnto God*: That vnto Councels that belongeth vnto Councels, that vnto Scriptures which belongeth
De Baptiſ. cō
tra.Donatiſt.l.
2.c.3. vnto Scriptures. Which Saint *Auguſtine* expreſſeth moſt ſigni-
ficantly in more words : *Quis neſciat ſanctam Scripturam, &c.*
,, Who knoweth not the Scripture *Canonicall both of the old and
,, new Teſtament, is contained within its certaine bounds, and that it
,, is ſo farre to be preferred before the following Biſhops letters, that
of it no man may doubt, no man may diſpute, whether it be true
or right, whatſoeuer is knowne to be written therein? But as for
Biſhops letters which haue bene, or are written after the Canon
once confirmed ; and peraduenture by the more wiſe ſentence, of
ſome more skilfull in the ſame point, and by the more graue authoritie of other Biſhops, and the wiſedome of the more learned, and by
Councels may be reprehended, if they haue erred in any thing from
the truth. Yea the Councels themſelues which are held in diuers
regions or prouinces, do yeeld, without any circumſtance to the authoritie of more full Councels, which conſiſt of the whole Chriſtian
world. Yea and thoſe plenary Councels often haue bene amended the
former by the latter, when by any experience of things, that was
opened which was ſhut, and that was knowne which before was ſe-*
cret,

eret, and without any fwelling of facrilegious pride, without any ftiffe necke of arrogancie, without any contradiction of cankred enuie, with holy humilitie, with Catholicke peace, with Chriftian charitie.

62 Happie were the ftate of the Chriftian world if this might be faithfully obferued : and thus farre we fubfcribe moft willingly. Let Gods booke the holy Scriptures keepe its due refpeƈt and predominate ouer all, as it beft deferueth; then let one Father be examined, yea and correƈted, if need be, by more; the Fathers by *Prouinciall* Councels, thofe by *Nationall*, thofe by *Generall*, the former by the latter, if they will, by learning and wifedome be reformed, without partialitie, with *à faluo iure*, a fauing the right *of the blessed Bible*, the holy, canonicall, vndoubted, Scriptures of God.

63 If this method of Saint *Augustine* cannot be admitted and obferued by the Romanifts, I will fay with the fame Father, in the fame cafe, in the words before going. *Certè nobis obycere foletis Cypriani literas, Cypriani fententiam, Cypriani Concilium. Cur authoritatem Cypriani pro veftro fchifmate affumetis, & eius exemplum pro Ecclefia pace refpuitis?*—*You Donatifticall Romanifts, you vfe to obieƈt the decrees of Fathers, the Canons of Councels*, the authoritie of ancient both times and perfons; but why do you alledge their miftaken, or mifapplied authorities to fupport your errors and idolatries, and yet refufe the Councels and Fathers when they make for the truth of the Gofpell, and peace of the Church? This your partialitie makes your obftinate madneffe manifeft to all that are not diftraƈted by the fame frenzie. This fhameth your Champion with his more then *Goliathian* brag of Councels, *Concilia generalia mea funt, primum, vltimum, media, his pugnabo:* Generall Councels are mine, the firft, the laft, and all betweene, with thefe I will fight. When God knowes, and a great part of the Chriftian world fees, and I hope the ingenious and religious Reader by this time perceiueth, that the Romanifts haue deuefted themfelues of Scriptures and Councels. They will none of them, they care little for thefe: and therefore we enter as in our owne right vnto the quiet and peaceable poffeffion of

Campion. Rat. 4.

P 2   them

them both, being abandoned of the pretended poſſeſſioners; but indeed tyrannicall intruders vpon this precious inheritance of God and his Church.

64 And therfore concluding,that our aduerſaries haue neither the firſt, nor the beſt Councels, we can affoord thē a few of the worſt and the laſt Conuenticles. Neither yet indeed care they for any at all , but onely to make ſhew , and deceiue the world. Their very Councell of *Trent* is not receiued, nor euer was in this land , and therefore cannot blind vs. Nay, I cannot ſee how any old Conncell can oblige many nations, that are not now ſubiected to their Canons,in as much as they were not receiued in ſome places, nor heard of in others many yeares after.For,*Decreta Concilij generalis,quæ per decennium in aliquâ prouinciâ nonſunt recepta, amittunt vim ſuam,& deſinunt obligare*: The Decrees of a generall Councell, which in ten yeares is not receiued in a Prouince, doth loſe its force ,, and bindeth no longer. Doth he not make a Councel a ſtrong foundation of truth , when it may be ouerthrowne for ten yeares diſcontinuance ? We vſe not Councels ſo.If we did,we might well be aſhamed, and ſo might the Romaniſts, if they were not paſt ſhame.

Leonardus Leſſius de Iuſtitiâ & iure. lib.2.c.22.dubit.13.

C H A P. V I I I.
Whether Proteſtants or Papiſts admit or reiect the third euidence of Antiquitie, the Fathers.

Cannot ſufficiently maruell, that ſo long experience, and ſo euident proofe,of our ingenuous acceptation,and daily vſe of the ancient Fathers, cannot moue our aduerſaries conſciences, ſo much as to confeſſe, that we haue a reuerend and due regard of them , as of a good and profitable euidence of *Antiquitie.* For as before is obſerued,Biſhop *Iuell* of famous memory,a precious iewell indeed, when he was employed to fight the battels of God in the Church militant, (now ſet in the glorious Diadem of our bleſſed Sauiour in his Church triumphant) made an open,

Supra. c. 5. B. Iuell.

reſolute,

refolute, and iuſt Challenge, to all the rabble of the Romiſh Catholickes,offering the triall of our cauſe to all the *Antiqui-tie* which next fucceeded the Apoſtles of our Sauiour Chriſt, in the firſt 600 yeares, and that in 27 articles, that are in que-ſtion betweene vs and them: He performed his Challenge, obtained victory ouer his aduerſaries,and yet triumpheth glo-rioufly. His workes remaining without farther anſwer in the whole(although fnarled at,and railed on in ſome parts)aboue halfe an hundred yeares;and I am perſwaded will ſo ſtand ſtill to the worlds end.

2 Reade all or any of the writers in the reformed Churches. Their bookes do not onely teſtifie, but proclaime the ſame,to any eye that doth not winke, to any eare that is not ſtopped, to any heart that is not either frozen in the dregs of darke ſu-perſtition, or inflamed with the furie of Romiſh malice and idolatrie. Doctor *Reinolds* hath bene complained on by a ma- D.Reinolds, leuolent aduerſarie,as I haue heard(and it may be true)for ha-uing his margine larger then his text: That he hath more alle-gations then lines, and ſo his learning is not his owne , but other mens ; for he ſaith little or nothing but he hath an au-thor for it. Is not this a ſhrewd fault? Much like a Lady that without cauſe found fault with her bread, and ſending for her Baker, rated at him for that the bread was naught, but could not tell wherein the fault lay.The Baker being required to tell the fault himſelfe,confeſſed there was a fault,to pleaſe his La-dy,andhe thought it to be, ẙ there was too much floure in the bread; the Ladie (like a good houſewife) was well ſatisfied, and bad the Baker amend it,& put in leſſe.Thus it fareth with the minions of Babylon, they find a fault , and the fault is, there is too much floure of Scriptures , Councels , Fathers , Hiſtories, and all kind of learning , and this is turned to our reproofe.

3 To inſiſt vpon particulars were infinite , let this ſuffice the indifferent Reader, that we profeſſe our reuerence to the Fathers in our preachings, in our writings , in word , in pra-ctiſe, in conferences, in diſputations, in Cities,in Vniuerſities, among our ſelues, againſt our aduerſaries.This we haue done,

do yet, and will do; neither fhall the ftrongeft fonne of the
Romane *Haraphath* be euer able to wreft them out of our
hands.

    4 All this and much more notwithftanding, our aduer-
faries are not afhamed yet to fay, *Explodunt Patres aduerfarij,*
Our aduerfaries hiffe out the Fathers, as *Campion.* Or, *The Pro-*
teftants fcorne the Fathers, as Doctor *Hill.* Or, *They make no more*
account of the Fathers, then of Adam Bell, and Beuis of
Hampton; Or, *Fathers, Councels, Antiquitie, Church, common con-*
fent, all thefe the new *Apoftles haue reiected :* as D. *Kellifon.* Or,
Nullius fæculi politiam & formam Ecclefiafticam admittunt, omni-
um fæculorum ritus & ceremonias damnant: contra vniuerfos Pa-
,, *tres & Scriptores Ecclefiafticos excipiunt, &c.* They admit the po-
,, licie or forme Ecclefiafticall of no age, they damne the rites
,, and ceremonies of all times, they except againft all the Fathers and Ecclefiafticall writers; as Doctor *Stapleton.* Or as
yet they crie out againft vs as well abroad, as at home, euen
yet after all our proteftations and practife: *We abandon Fa-*
thers, as a frefh Iefuite raileth. Or as Doctor *Kellifon* againe,
Whiles our Reformers refufe the authoritie and doctrine of the Fa-
thers, they cut themfelues from the Church of Chrift. Let him
vndergo this cenfure that is conuinced to be guiltie of thefe
accufations. *He that hiffeth or explodeth the Fathers, that fcornes*
them, that makes no more account of them then of Adam Bell and
Beuis of Hampton, that reiects them, excepts againft them
all, (or againft any one vnworthily) *and refufeth their doctrine*
and authoritie (wherein they all confent, or the moft of them,
which are our aduerfaries owne limitations) let them be cut
off from the Church; yea if they dare venture the doome,
as we dare, woe worth them that do all things which
they lay to our charge; but indeed themfelues do them,
not we.

    5 To iuftifie our felues in the fight of all men, let the in-
different reader perufe Saint *Auguftine,* not in a few fentences, but whole bookes, *de Prædeftinatione & gratia, de Na-*
tura & gratia, de Gratia Chrifti, de Prædeftinatione Sanctorum, de
Bono perfeuerantia, de Prædeftinatione Dei, de Gratia & libero ar-
bitrio:

Marginal notes:
Campion.
Rat. 5.

Suruey. l. 1. c. 3

Prompt. Ca-
thol. Domi-
nica. 7. poft.
Pentecoft.
Muri ciuit.
fanct. Fund. 7.
Suruey. l. 1. c. 4

bitrio: Of Predeſtination and grace, of Nature and grace, of „
the Grace of Chriſt, of Predeſtination of the Saints, of the „
Good gift of perſeuerance, of Gods predeſtination, of Grace „
and freewill, and other points of Chriſtian religion, againſt „
the Donatiſts, and the Pelagians, wherein he is wholly ours, „
none of theirs. In theſe moſt abundantly, in all other points
moſt ſufficiently, he maketh for vs, and we frequently
alledge him. Aske *Melancthon* of Saint *Auguſtine.* *Huius* Melanc.præ-
ætatis errores, vt emendarentur, ſaltem aliqua ex parte, Auguſti- fac.in Sanct.
num Deus excitauit, hic mediocriter expurgauit ; nec dubito ſi tom. opruem
iudex eſſet controuerſiarum huius ætatis, habituros nos eum ὁμο-ϕρ- Lutheri.
ϕov, certe de remiſſione gratuita, de iuſtitia fidei, de vſu Sacramento-
rum, adiaphoris expreſſe nobiſcum ſentit. God raiſed vp *Auguſtine,* „
that the errors of that age, at the leaſt in ſome part, ſhould be „
amended, he hath indifferently purged them; neither doubt I, „
ſhould he be iudge of the controuerſies of this age , but we „
ſhould haue him of the ſame mind with vs. Truly his iudge- „
ment is expreſly with ours, concerning free remiſſion, iuſti- „
fication by faith, the vſe of the Sacraments, and things in- „
different. Where he hath much more of the ſame Father, to „
the like effect. And commendeth other ancient writers,
who from his light ſaw the truth, and publiſhed it in many
things.

6 Saint *Hierome* aboue any Father moſt skilfull in the
tongues, diligent in his ſtudies, induſtrious in his ſearch,
vntired with labour at home, vnwearied with trauell a-
broad, reſiding moſt in the Eaſt, where the moſt monuments
of *Antiquitie* , for plentie and authoritie, were then to be
found; diſcerned and diſtinguiſhed betweene Canonicall
Scriptures and Apocryphall. Not as reſting vpon the Canon of the Iewes, but as all learned Chriſtians had done before him, and then did, together with him, as might be now,
and after ſhall be plainly proued.

7 *Ambroſe* for iuſtification by faith onely : *Epiphanius* not
onely againſt Images, but againſt diuers other hereſies now
defended by the Romaniſts, *Gregorie* againſt the Supremacie both of all others, and his owne Sea. *Iuſtinus Martyr,* for

Apolog.

the plaine and simple administration of the Lords Supper, without Massing or sacrificing, eleuation or adoring, carnalitie or transubstantiation. *Theodoret* for Christs spirituall presence in the Sacrament, without such tricks and quaint deuices and distinctions, as the Romish * *Mophti* hath conceipted. *Chrysostome*, for reading Scriptures in knowne languages, and the common vse thereof among the Laytie both in hearing it at the Church, and reading it at home in priuate houses.

The Tuikes Pope.

8 Not to presse infinite particulars; we auouch and auerre, that many of the ancient Fathers were eminent in some things aboue the rest, (as in these mentioned:) all of them in most things we professe, yea in all things fundamentall in the reformed religion, most pregnant. And therefore we deny not their *Antiquitie*, we refuse not their authoritie; we reuerence their age, we reiect not their workes, we counterfeit nothing in their names, we neither cast them into *ignis purgatorius*, to consume or obscure them, nor castrate them, by an Index expurgatorius to maime or marre them, we neither burne them with fire, nor brand them with infamy. All which our aduersaries haue done, and worse, with sinne and shame to them and theirs for euer.

9 In which case it fareth with the Romanists, in their malicious slanders against vs, as it did with their ancestors the persecutors of the true Christians in the Primitiue Church. The heathen obiected to the beleeuers worse idolatrie & filthinesse to be done by them in secret, then their Priests did openly and in the sight of the Sunne. Themselues they could not iustifie that were indeed guiltie, and therefore impeached others of greater crimes falsly; that their grosse Idolatrie might seeme, if not in all tollerable, yet in part excusable in the comparison. So deale the Romanists with the faithfull professors of Christs truth at this day. To shade their owne shame, they would impose that on vs which we neuer imagined in thought, but themselues haue openly practised in deed, in the view of the whole world. And yet glorie vnder pretence of *Antiquitie,* as if they onely entertained

Euseb.l.4.c.7.

tained,and we cafhiered the Fathers; when in very deed and truth, themfelues abufe them moft intollerably, reiect them moft contemptuoufly, raile on them moft contumelioufly, and entertaine them onely as mercenary fouldiers, for prefent neceffitie, not to aduance them to dignitie, or preferue them in honour. Or as counters, that ftand fometimes for a thoufand pounds,fometimes for a farthing. Or like Players, that are brought on the ftage, fometimes like Kings, with great admiration,¦ fometimes like fooles or clownes,with as great derifion.They are angry with vs,as if we did not admit them, or any of them, without all exception: they will take libertie themfelues to vfe, or rather abufe them, at their owne indifcretion, and no man may fay, blacke is their eye.

10 It is true, that diuers of our writers haue branded fome,that haue bene brought vnder the name of Fathers,to be children for yeares, and baftards for generation, in comparifon of the Fathers that were ancient indeed, and of vndoubted birth. Then outcries were made, that when they could not anfwer the authoritie,they would difcountenance the author. Now *Bellarmine, Baronius,Poſſeuine*, and *Sixtus Senenſis* are afcended to our opinion, and acknowledge their minoritie and illegitimation as well as we.

11 It is as true, that exception hath bene taken againſt diuers corruptions of editions,tranſlations,and fome forgeries. This hath bene alfo taxed as an iniurious imputation, wrongfully and without caufe pretended, but impoffible to be proued. Some of our friends haue feemed to appeale from Fathers,or to except againſt them, as *Bellarmine* noteth. De Miſſa.l.1. You fhall heare what our aduerfaries do on that behalf, how c.15. they take the fame exceptions themfelues, and iuftifie vs in that they haue formerly condemned vs: and yet feeke ſtill to outface vs and the truth, as if they were the very *quinteſfence* of *Antiquitie*, and we the very *feces* or *excrements* of debafed noueltie; *cuius contrarium verum eſt* : but you ſhall find the contrary, and in time *Wiſedome ſhall be iuſtified of her chil-* Mat.11.19. *dren*, and iuftifie them too. And God will reueale that vnto
the

the moſt ignorant, that now is manifeſt onely to the learned. That not we, but the Romaniſts, do that moſt palpably, with which they challenge our Church moſt impudently and in-iuriouſly, as the gentle Reader, euen with ſhort attention, ſhall moſt eaſily diſcerne and perceiue. Wherein they haue vſed moſt egregious impoſtures, and ſuch as they which know them not, will hardly beleeue them. Thoſe which ſhall know and vnderſtand, will deteſt and abhorre them, if they haue any zeale of Gods glorie, any remorſe or ſence of a good conſcience, any compaſſion of the Churches afflictions, any deſire of the ignorants conuerſions, any regard of the Fathers credits, any care or deſire of their owne ſaluation. My hearts deſire onely is, that all partialitie and fore-priſing laid aſide, the very truth of God may appeare on this behalf, and that each partie, according to the euidence thereof, may be iuſtified or reformed.

12   The worſt that we ſay of the Fathers in generall, or in particular, or that we would any other ſhould ſay, is, that moſt of the Fathers had their errors, their blemiſhes, their ſpots. They were not without their ſlips, their faults. Some of them erred in many things of leſſe moment, ſome in mat-ters of greater conſequence. I need not deſcend vnto ſingu-lar perſons or opinions, they are noted by thoſe painfull and induſtrious Chroniclers, in the 4. Chap. of almoſt euery Cen-turie. Some by *Luther, Melancthon, Peter Martyr, Caluin, Iuel,* and other writers of the Chriſtian Catholicke Church. The moſt are confeſſed by the late and ˌmoderne Romane Courtiers. *Iuſtine Martyr, Irenæus, Papias, Tertullian, Victo-rinus, Lactantius, Apolionarius, Seuerus, Nepos;* moſt of the Fa-thers were of mind, that becauſe the world was created in ſixe dayes, therefore it ſhould end in ſixe thouſand yeares: *I-renæus, Hilary, Lactantius, Hierome, Iuſtinus Martyr;* and how many beſides, were Millianaries? A fearfull opinion. How er-red that holy Martyr Saint *Cyprian in rebaptization? Auguſtine* in damning Chriſtians children vnbaptized, to hell fire? not to a conceited *Limbus,* with their *pœna damni* onely, but to the damneds hell, with *pœna ſenſus.* In giuing the Euchar[st
to

Reade Ca-nus l.3.c.3. of the Fathers errors, which both he with vs, and we with him, ac-count holy, Auguſt.

to children as foone as baptized? How *Tertullian* and *Origen*, Bellar.de Pur-
by our aduerfaries condemned for heretickes in many parti- gat.l.2.c 8.
culars? How *Hierom* in fecond mariages? How *Benedict*,that
*commanded the Eucharift to be giuen to a woman that was *quære.
dead? I am loth to rip vp this old fore, which hath bene, and
well may remaine couered vnder the veile of reuerence and
charitie; vndeniable by any, confeffed by our aduerfaries in
the generall often : and humbly acknowledged by themfelues, that they may eafily, and haue certainly erred often.
That either they might fay of themfelues, while they liued,
with Saint *Hierom*, *Errauimus iuuenes, emendemur fenes* : We Hierome.
erred when we were yong; as we grow elder,fo let vs waxe
wifer. Or of their writings after their departure, with Saint
Auguftine : *Neminem velim fic amplecti omnia mea, vt me fequa-* De bono per-
tur nifi in ijs quibus me non errare perfpexerit : I would haue no feueran.c.21.
man fo to embrace all my writings,that he fhould follow me
in any thing,but wherein he perceiueth I erre not. Or better
if better may be: *Homo fum, & quantum conceditur de Scriptu-* Aug.in Pfa.85
ris fanctis, tantum audeo dicere, nihil ex me : This I fay to you
brethren,but if I expound not as certaine,be not angry; I am
a man, and as much as is granted vnto me out of the holy
Scriptures,fo much I dare fay, nothing of my felfe. Thus modeftly do the Fathers fpeake of themfelues; thus do we reuerently refpect them ; I would our aduerfaries could but
affoord them thus mnch.

13   Of them all we may fay with Saint *Hierom*,without
impeachment of their credit, aduantage to our captious aduerfaries,or derogation of our duties towards them: *Scio me* Epift.61.c.2
aliter habere Apoftolos , aliter habere reliquos tractatores ; illos
femper vera dicere,iftos in quibufdam vt homines aberrare:I know ,,
how to efteeme the Apoftles , and how other writers ; that ,,
they euer fpeake the truth, but thefe in fome things as men ,,
do erre. God knoweth that this is true ; and we will write, ,,
we will fpeake, we will thinke no worfe of them. That as it ,,
pleafed God to lay open in his word the manifold imperfections of the beft Patriarchs,Prophets and Apoftles,to fhew
that all had finned,*and were deftitute of the glorie of God:conclu-* Rom.3.23.
                                                    ding

Rom.11.32. ding *all vnder sinne, that he might haue mercie on all :* so it hath pleased the same God, that knoweth all men to be lyers, to suffer the Fathers of the Church to erre , that we may know they were but men, and that we are onely bound to the truth of God, which he hath gracioully reuealed in his word. As for the Fathers, they may all conclude with Saint *Augustines* pe-

Aug.in Psa.85 riod: *Ergo fratres siue illud, siue illud sit, hic me scrutatorem verbi Dei, non temerarium affirmatorem teneatis:* Therefore brethren, howsoeuer it be, take me here to be a searcher of the word of God, not a rash affirmer. A graue and gracious speech.

14 Thus much are our aduersaries bold to say of them when they please, which is ingenuitie , yea vertue in them. But (in their Censure) this very same, or lesse then they say, is impudencie and vice in vs. What would they say of vs? what

Abb.Vsperge. tragedies would they make, if we should say, *Resistendum est*
pag.412. *quibuscunque in faciem, siue Paulus, siue Petrus sit, qui ad verita-*
tem non ambulat Euangelij: We may resist any man in the face, be it *Paul,* be it *Peter,* if he walke not after the truth of the Gospell? Yet thus said *Pius* the second without controlment. And no doubt he alludeth to *Pauls* reproofe of *Peter. Lyra,* whom *Bellarmine* claimeth for one of his classicall authors of the Romane Church, is bold to say of the Priests, of whom

Deut.17.12. God said , *He that will not heare , or stand to the sentence of the Priest, he shall die :* yet saith, *Si Sacerdotes quicquam dicunt fal-sum, quodȝ à lege Dei est alienum, non sunt audiendi:* If the Priests shall say any thing that is false , or auerse from the Law of God, they are not to be heard. And therefore he addeth his owne practise, and groundeth it on Saint *Augustines* autho-

In Matth.1. ritie: *Non debet aliquis moueri, &c. No man may thinke much if I depart in this from the opinion of Hierom. For the sayings of the Saints are not of so great authoritie, but that it is lawfull to hold contrary vnto them, in those things which are not determined by the Scriptures*; as *Augustine* saith in his Epistle to *Vincentius, of the writings of the holy Doctors:This kind of writing is to be distin-guished from the Canonicall Scriptures , for testimonies are not brought out of them, as if a man might not thinke otherwise .* A sound practise vpon a good rule.

15 Not

15 Not onely the current, but the torrent of our aduersaries tread the fame path, whether we do it or not; as *Torrenfis*, *A man may lawfully diffent from the Fathers, fo he do it with mo-* Confeff. Au-
deftie. But who fhall iudge of this modeftie? If one of ours guft.l.1.cap.
fhould fay fo, our modeftie with them, and in their conftru- 11.tit.1.
ction, would feeme plaine impudencie. *Stapleton* our bitter
countreyman, and virulent aduerfarie, confeffeth of the Fathers, that fometime, and in fome cafes, *Hallucinantur inter-* Princip.Doct.
dum & male colligunt, They are deceiued fometimes and ga- l.7.c.6.
ther amiffe. *Melchior Canus* a Bifhop of their owne, is bold
with the Fathers, with fome by name, with fome if they be
but two or three, with fome if they be more, if they be not all;
and faith plainly, that neither one or two, nor halfe, no nor the
moft part, make a certaine proofe in matters of faith. As to
reiect one or two were impudency, *fo to admit them and hold* Lib.7.c.3.
them for certaine, were more imprudencie; neither may any man be
led by this error: That if Ambrofe or Hierome hath done or fpoken
any thing againft the cuftome or doctrine of this time, it is lawfull
for him to do the fame; with much more in that Chapter to this
purpofe.

16 But what if they fpeake againft the truth of Scriptures,
which is more then cuftome and the doctrine of the time?
Cardinall Caietan as learned as any of his ranke, is bold in this
behalfe; and faith, that God hath not tied the expofition of
the Scriptures, *vnto the fences of the Fathers, but that a new fence* In præfac.
agreeable to the text, though it go againft the ftreame of the Fa- Com.in lib.
thers. may be good. This *Melchior Canus* reputeth a rafh and Mofis.
hard fpeech, yet *Andradius* defendeth it, neither doth *Canus* Canus lib.1.c.
himfelfe vtterly condemne it. And to fay truth, faith he, *to fol-* 3.
low our Anceftors in all things, and to fet our feete in their fteps, as Defenf. Trid.
children do in fport, it is nothing elfe but to condemne our owne Conc.l.2.
wits, and to depriue our felues of our owne iudgment and ftability to
fearch out the truth. I like well the fpeech of *Ambrofius Amfber-* Præfac.in A
tus, concerning Saint *Hierome* and Saint *Auguftine,* which I pocal.
could wifh were obferued *in cenfuring all the Fathers,* that
were Fathers indeed. Firft, he commendeth them both highly,
then he prefumes not to preferre either in comparifon, left he
fhould

fhould feeme to detract from one to giue to the other, yet concludeth, that *no man fhould reprehend him, fi quem ex his mihi placuerit, fecutus fuero* , If he pleafe himfelfe in choofing whom he would follow. Here is great wifedome, modeftie and difcretion : which I defire to find in all that profeffe learning on either partie. For certainly the learnedeft now are in many things beholding to the Fathers that liued in ancient times. He would not be fo tyed to the Fathers, but that he might depart from them when they flide from the truth. And indeed why may not a poore wife man, by long experience, and much reading, and diligent obferuation, deliuer a Citie by his wifedome, when all the graue Senators haue either not feene the danger, or ouerflipt the opportunitie ? Or why may not Saint *Auguftine* be vfed by a later learned man, as he vfed Saint *Cyprian*, vpon iuft occafion? who confidered of his writings by the Canonicall; and what he found agreeable to the holy Scriptures authoritie, he receiued it with his due commendation ; what was otherwife, he would refufe it by his leaue.

Cont. Crefco. Gram. lib. 2. c. 32.

17   It cannot be denied, but that few of the Fathers had farther skill in other tongues then in their owne : the Greeke Fathers haue little fhewne that they vnderftood the Latine tongue at all; the Latine Fathers make it euident, that they had no great skill in the Greeke tongue; very few (though fome) had in-fight in the Hebrew tongue at all. If a writer or Preacher in thefe dayes haue good knowledge in all thefe learned tongues, be able of himfelfe to vnderftand the old and new Teftament in the prime language wherein they were written, hath the helpe of all the Fathers writings before him, queftions ventilated by which Scriptures were debated in exacteft manner ; what reafon is there, but that fuch a learned man now, may amend that which was amiffe in former times ? What hinders but that time with thefe adiuments and helpes may produce a hidden truth, and fucceeding age may find that treafure, which (though knowne to heauen yet hid in earth,) may reforme the Church to her firft integritie?

18 Vnto

18 Vnto thefe I may adde *Bellarmine* a *Cardinall* as well as *Caietan*, and of his mind, which he very modeftly vttereth, *Quis neget multos veterum Patrum habuiſſe excellentèr donum interpretandi, & fuiſſe ſpirituales? Et tamen conſtat quoſdam ex præcipuis eorum non leutèr in quibuſdam lapſos.* Who can denie „ but that many of the ancient Fathers had the gift of interpre- „ ting excellently, and were ſpirituall? Yet it is euident that „ ſome of the chiefe of them, fell in ſome things not of ſmall „ moment. *Doctor non proponit ſententiam ſuam vt neceſſariò ſe- quendam, ſed ſolùm quatenus ratio ſuadet* : Which verily is true and ingeniouſly written; A Doctor propofeth his ſentence, not that it muſt neceſſarily be followed, but as farre as reaſon perſwadeth. But if we ſpeake but ſuch a word as their Catho- licke Cardinals, and other their fellowes haue done, *Medea* of *Rome* would bring the Moone from heauen; and the whore of *Babylon* if ſhee could not with her curſes moue God, with her blaſphemies ſhee would riue and turne vp hel againſt vs. *Quis veterum Patrum* (ſaith *Marianus Victorius*) *eſt qui idem teſtimo- niũ diuersè interdũ non interpretetur, & qui modò vnius opinionis fuit, alterius poſtea factus non ſit?* Which of the ancient Fathers „ is there, which doth not interpret the ſame teſtimonie in di- „ uers manners? and which was of one opinion now, and was „ not afterwards of another? A great imputation, yet no harme, a friend, a fellow, a follower, that is, a Papiſt writes it: and thē it is well enough. For ſome of our writers to haue ſaid but as much, or ſcarſe ſo much as theſe, in this matter and man- ner, in them is an inexpiable tranſgreſſion, a contempt, a de- baſing of all *Antiquitie.*

19 *Non propterea damnandi ſunt Patres quod aliquando erra- rint, quia Deus fabris in domo ſua operantibus indulget, etiamſi non ſemper aurum vel gemmas, ſed interdum quoque fœnum & ſtipu- las ſuperſtruant.* The Fathers are not therefore to be con- demned, becauſe they ſometime erred; for that God doth pardon workemen in his houſe, although they do not euer build with gold and precious ſtones, but ſometime hay and ſtubble. And againe, *Palàm eſt Patres omnes, quantum- libet inſignes vitæ innocentia atque eruditione, ſubinde verbo, ſcrip- tóve*

De verb. Dei lib. 3. c. 10. ad arg. nonum.

Bellar.ib.

Non leuitèr.]

Cœlo dedu- cere lunam. Flectere ſi nequeam ſu- ſeros, Ache- ronta moue- bo. Victorius.

Villauin. de rat. ſtud. The- ol. l. 4. c. 6. obſ. 2.

Idem ib.

tóve offendere; It is euident that all the Fathers, although eminent for innocencie of life and learning, yet did sometime slip in word or writing; which he doth illustrate by many examples in that obseruation. Thus farre our aduersaries and we concurre, that the Fathers may and do sometimes erre, and therefore are not in all things to be followed; beyond this I protest that I neuer read any Author, I neuer heard any Preacher write or speake in derogation of the Fathers, on our part.

Dialogo 1.   20 I am not ignorant how vehemently *Feuerdentius* fretteth, as if he were in a fit of a burning ague, and taxeth *Melancthon*, and *Caluin* and others for despising and vilifying of the Fathers. For *Melancthon*, he alledgeth an impression of his workes in 1544, which I could not attaine vnto. That which I haue seene hath no such thing. What his censure is of Saint *Augustine*, and some other Fathers is deliuered before.

Eod. cap. A booke called *Scutum fidei*, which he also produceth, I haue not seene, neither know I the Author. But for *Caluin*, his words of him are, that he calleth *Augustine Theologastrum, blaterantem nugas, quòd* τον λογον, *Latine reddiderit verbum*, a pettie Diuine, pratling trifles, becaufe he misinterpreted a Greeke word. The railer either neuer read the place vpon S. *Iohn*, or elfe speaketh againft his owne confcience a manifest vntruth. For vpó the firft of *Iohn Caluin* faith, in the difcuffing of another word : *Rectè ergo Augustinus*, Saint *Augustine* faid well. And afterwards againe, *Excusatione digni funt veteres Ecclesiæ scriptores*. The ancient writers of the Church are worthy excufe. The words that found towards *Feuerdentius* flander

Caluin in Ioan.c.1. are: *Miror quid Latinos mouerit, vt* τον λογον *transferrent, verbum. Sic enim vertendum potius effet* τὸ ρ῀῀ημα. *Verùm vt demus aliquid probabile secutos esse, negari tamen non potest quin sermo longè melius conueniat. Vndè apparet quam barbaram tyrannidem exercuerunt Theologastri, qui Erasmum adeò turbulentè vexa-*
,, *runt ob mutatam in melius vocem.* I wonder what moued the
,, Latines, that they fhould tranflate the Greeke word with fo
,, vnapt a Latine word. For they fhould haue fo tranflated ano-
,, ther Greeke word, more properly. But to grant they had fome
                                             probability,

probabilitie, yet it cannot be denied that another word is „
farre more apt; wherehence it appeareth what barbarous „
tyrannie thofe pettie Diuines vfed, who fo turbulently vexed „
Erafmus, for turning a word by a better then was vfed „
before.

21   *Caluin* hath not an euill word of Saint *Auguſtine*;
but of the *Bardi* and barbarous bellie-burſt Diuines, that
vexed *Erafmus*, which Saint *Auguſtine* neuer did. Another Feuerdentius
place from *Caluin* he hath out of his *Inſtitutions*. *Simulque* Ibid.
eius(id eſt Auguſtini)acuta,erudita & pia commentaria dicit falſa,
profana,inepta,abſurda,pluſquam anilia deliramenta, effiɗa fabu-
larum inſomnia,allegorias pueriles & frigidas, hominem in omni
doɗrina varium & in conſtantem, quem de crepida vetula amoue-
ant deſideria. And he calleth his (that is, *Auguſtines*) acute, „
learned and religious Commentaries, falſe, profane, fooliſh, „
abſurd, worſe then old wiues tales, fained dreams of fables, „
frozen and childiſh allegories, a man in all learning wauering „
and inconſtant, one that would turne vp an old womans ſto- „
macke. In the place thus quoted there is not one of theſe „
ſcurrilous words of Saint *Auguſtine*, no not one. He is once
named, twiſe alledged againſt Poperie, and in the margent Calui n. Inſti-
of one Edition which I haue ſeene, there are theſe words: tut.lib.3. c.20.
reſponſio clariſſima authoritate Scripturæ & Auguſtini teſtimonio § 20.
firmata. An excellent anſwer confirmed by the authority of „
the Scripture, and *Auguſtines* teſtimonie. What a lamenta- „
ble caſe is this, that fo without all care or conſcience any
ſhould fo wilfully lye, and ſlander? *Caluin* indeed faith
ſomewhat of Saint *Hierome* vpon the 19 of Mathew, but not Hierome in
without cauſe. I hope *Feuerdentius*, nor any of his fellowes Mat.19.
dare defend all that S. *Hierome* ſpeaketh of mariage, which is
the matter wherein *Caluine* iuſtly taxeth him. That of *Beza*
againſt Saint *Hierome* is as idle, for it reſteth rather vpon *E-*
raſmus report, then vpon *Bezaes* cenſure: and if ſuch was *Hie-*
roms mind, he erred.

22   It is made a great matter, that *Luther* in the confidence
of the truth which he profeſſed, and which he knew to be
grounded vpon the Scriptures, once ſaid : *Dei verbum ſupra*
                              Q   *omnia*

*omnia,diuina maieſtas mecum facit , vt nihil curem, ſi mille ᴄAu-
guſtini, mille Cypriani, mille Eccleſiæ Hieronimianæ contra me ſta-
rent.Deus errare & fallere non poteſt, ᴄAuguſtinus,& Cyprianus,
ſicut omnes electi,errare potuerunt & errarunt.* Gods word is a-
" boue all, the diuine Maieſtie is on my ſide, ſo that I need not
" care though a thouſand *Auguſtines*, a thouſand *Cyprians*,a
" thouſand *Hieronima* Churches ſhould oppoſe me. God can
" neither erre nor be deceiued. *Auguſtine* and *Cyprian*, as all
" other the elect, both could and haue erred , and did erre.
There is much modeſtie in theſe paſſages; but heare a Papiſt,
and compare their ſpeeches without reference to God or
his word, which *Luther* doth: *Ego vt ingenuè fateor, plus vno
ſummo Pontifici crederem, in his quæ fidei myſteria tangunt, quam
mille Auguſtinis ,Hieronimis,Gregorys,ne dicam Richardis,Scotis,
Gulielmis.Credo enim & ſcio quod ſummus Pōtifex in his quæ fidei
ſunt errare non poteſt , quoniam Eccleſiæ authoritas determinandi,
quæ ad fidem ſpectant, in Pontifice reſidet.Et ita Pontificis error v-
niuerſalis error Eccleſiæ eſſet;vniuerſalis autem Eccleſia errare non
poteſt. Nec mihi dicas de Concilio, credo enim quod plus atteſtetur
Spiritum ſanctum regere Eccleſiam,ſi iudicium pænes Pontificem ſit,
quàm ſi pænes Concilium ſit. Humanæ quippè ſapientiæ opus videri
poteſt quod Conciliū Patrum non erret.At videri non poteſt niſi Dei
opus eſſet, ſicut reuera eſt, quod vnus homo qui ſuaptè natura facilè*
" *errare poteſt,nunquam erret in fide,&c.*I,as I ingenuouſly con-
" feſſe, would more credit one Pope,in matters that concerne
" the myſteries of faith, then a thouſand *Auguſtines, Hieromes*
" *Gregories*,not to ſpeake of *Richards,Scotoes*,or *Williams*. For
" I beleeue and know,that the chiefe Biſhop in matters of faith
" cannot erre , becauſe the authoritie of the Church in deter-
" mination of things belonging to faith, is reſident in that
" Biſhop. And ſo the error of the Biſhop ſhould become the
" error of the vniuerſall Church. But the vniuerſall Church
" cannot erre. Speake not to me of a Councell, for I am con-
" fident that it is certaine the holy Ghoſt doth better gouerne
" the Church, if the iudgement be referred to the Pope then if
" it be referred to a Councell. It may ſeeme to be the worke of
" a humane wiſedome, that a Councell of Fathers doth not
                                                            erre.

*Cornelius
Muſſus in
Rom.cap.*

erre. But it cannot otherwise be ſuppoſed thẽ the worke „
of God (as it is indeed) that one man who naturally is „
apt to erre, ſhould not erre in faith &c. Obſerue this paſſage „
well.

23 See the difference. *Luther* preferreth God the Father,
and his diuine Maieſtie before all; which is religiouſly ſpoken. But here the Pope in his power is ſet before all, with
ſuch monſtrous amplifications as are incredible, and vnpoſſible, and ſauour of the higheſt blaſphemies. Now would it
be conſidered, how farre in peremptotie tearmes, and in continued practiſe, the Romane Catholique writers go beyond
this, firſt in generall of them all, then in particular of ſome:
whereby it will appeare, what account they make of this e-
uidence of *Antiquitie*, when it ſtandeth in their way.

24 *Sylueſter* ſaith, *Ecclesiæ conſuetudini magis ſtandum eſt, quàm* Summa de
authoritati Auguſtini & aliorum Doctorum: A man muſt rather Bapt.4.num.5
reſt vpon the cuſtome of the Church, then vpon the authori- „
tie of *Auguſtine* and other Doctors. Cuſtome, one of the vn- „
certaineſt things of the world, which may be pictured blind,
and vpon a wheele, as the heathens did Fortune; which hath
moſt damnified the Church, both in her temporall ſtate, & in
her ſpiriturall ſeruice of God, is preferred before the Fathers.
We dare not ſay ſo much; if we ſhould, thoſe that loue vs not,
would and might iuſtly condemne vs. Let the thing in queſtion be what it will: yet Cuſtome ſhould neuer preuaile
againſt authoritie, except it haue better reaſon and authoritie to ſupport it. Yet ſo are our aduerſaries wedded to blind
and vnconſtant Cuſtome, that they not onely preferre
it before the Fathers, but equall it with the very diuine
Scriptures of God, *Non ſolùm Ecclesiæ decreta, & ſententiæ au-*
thenticæ ſunt. &c. Not onely the Decrees & ſentences of the „
Church are authenticall, whereunto without contradiction „
we muſt ſtand, but alſo her very practiſe and Cuſtomes are as „
the holy Scriptures. For the holy Scriptures & the Cuſtomes „
of the Church haue equall right, and the ſame affection of „
pietie is due to both. How many Cuſtomes were there in „
the time of the Fathers which are not now? How many now

that were not heard of in thofe dayes?

Lib.7.c.3.   25 *Melchior Canus* auoucheth, that the holy Fathers, after the writers of the Scriptures, were inferiour and humane. That fometime they fainted, and fometimes brought
forth a monfter, beyond the order and courfe of nature. If
a Proteftant had fpoken or written fo monftroufly of the Fathers, he fhould haue bene houted and fhouted at, like a
De Rom. monfter indeed. But *Bellarmine* flily faith of the Pope, *Si*
Pont.l.2.c.27. *ipfe vt pater ab omnibus honoratur, non habet ipfe vllos in Ecclefia*
» *patres, fed omnes filios*:If he be honored of all men as a Father,
» then he hath no Fathers, but all are his childrenn. The Popes
head hath all the Fathers wit, his braines are their braines, he
Doct. Prin.l. one for all; is not this a compendious courfe? But *Stapleton*
7.c.10.l.10.
c.11. fteps to it more defperatly, and Magiftrally concludeth, that
neither Councels, nor *Fathers*, *nor any thing but the Pope is*
iudge of all Controuerfies: proue this and take all for me. But
who are thefe to *Iames Gretzer*, the moft vehement and virulent fpirit that euer fet pen to paper? He goes to it (without feare or wit) with downe right blowes, and knockes all
the Fathers in the head, as one man at one ftroke, in *Bertrams*
perfon, whofe cafe wold be difcuffed more at large. By whofe
vfage we may fee and perceiue how our aduerfaries efteeme
of *Antiquitie*.

26 This *Bertram* liued in the dayes of *Carolus Caluus* (as
our aduerfaries grant,) this was about the yeare of Chrift
870. He wrote a booke of the *Eucharift*, wherein he confuteth and confoundeth the doctrine of the reall prefence, for
Tranfubftantiation was not then hatcht, nor heard of. This
booke could not be fuppreft, and that is the Roma-
Index Belgi- nifts griefe; but he is fo trimd in their *Index expurgatorius*,
cus. that they deuife many trickes to fhuffle ouer his authoritie,
with denying, glofing, fophifticating, a *quid pro quo*, an *inui-*
fibiliter, for a *vifibiliter*, with fuch like difhoneft fhifts, as the
bafeft Mountbanke and fhame of Phifitions, the vildeft pet-
tiefogger and ftaine of Lawyers, the wranglingft fophifter
and blemifh of Logitians, would be afhamed, and blufh, to
make, or offer. This is laid to their charge, by the learned on
                                                            our

our part. Some are fo nice, as to hold their peace, for feare the more it be ftirred, the more it will fauour ill in the fenfe of any confcionable Chriftian. Some fay very litle, becaufe they will not fay nothing. But *Iames Gretzer* like a mad man, paffing through thicke or thinne, faith what they all thinke, and that is this : *Dum prohibetur, negamus prohiberi Patrem*; Lib.2.c.10. When *Bertram* is forbidden, we denie that a Father is for-,, bidden. For he is faid to be a Father, who feedeth and nou-,, rifheth the Church with wholefome doctrine, &c. For this ,, is not an vfuall matter, to damne errors and errants, if by ,, hurting they become new. We haue an example of this in ,, Pope *Gelafius*, who by a publifhed law fhooke *Tertullian* and ,, *Origen*, and others, thought exceeding ancient, out of the ,, hands and vfe of Chriftians. For this right euer is, and hath ,, bene, and fhall be in the Church, that fhe catefully remoue ,, fuch things as may be hurtfull to the flocke ; and if fhe may ,, prefcribe a whole booke, it may be lawfull for her to cafhiere ,, a part of a booke, whether much or litle, either by cutting it ,, out, or wiping it off, or blotting it, or fimply leauing it out, ,, and that for the Readers benefit. Thus he.   ,,

27 And what can more difcouer their groffe impuden-cie, in offering all manner of violence and defperate deftru-ction to all Antiquitie ? The practife whereof, in an Edition of *Ambrofe, Iunius* difcouers, as an eye-witneffe in *Lyons*, be-Innius in Præ-ing fhewed it by the Examiner of *Frelonius* print: where two fat. Indicis Friers, againft the full confent of all ancient Copies, blotted Expurg.Belg. out, and put in, at their pleafure, to the great loffe of the Printer, the fhaming of themfelues (but that they are paft fhame) and to the cofening of all that fhould buy and truft that corrupted Edition. Which makes me rather beleeue that which *Helias Haffen Mullerus* reporteth alfo of his owne Triüph.Papal. knowledge, as both an eare and an eye-witneffe : In a Li-brary at *Lampfperg*, *I faw* (faith he) *Chryfoftomes and Hieroms workes, in whofe bookes thofe things that fauoured a little of Po-pery, either were couered with papers, or rafed forth, or blotted with inke. And when I asked father Lutzius what that meant ? he anfwered, becaufe that reading did not feeme Catholicke, and*

that

that yong fchollers might eafily be offended at them.

28 If this be not the ready way to the vtter ouerthrow of all *Antiquitie*, let any Chriftian that hath a heart iudge. *Facilis defcenfus Auerni*: It is an eafie matter to runne headlong to hell; and no way directer then this. Or at the leaft may we not iuftly fay that to you, which M. *Harding* layeth vniuftly to our charge? *The ancient Fathers are but men,if they pleafe you not : but if you find any colour of aduantage but in the new Schoole-men, ye make much of it ; fo that your owne opinion is the rule to efteeme them or defpife them.* Or doth not *Gretzer* giue the fame aduantage againft all the Fathers, as againft that one? Or do not the Romanifts by their *Index Expurgatorius*, and their *Index librorum prohibitorum*, verifie and iuftifie in the fight of all men,*that their owne opinion is the rule to efteem them, or defpife them?*

29 To conuince our aduerfaries yet more clearly(though it need not) [in this their abufage of the ancient Fathers, we will defcend vnto particulars, and obferue how they take old for yong, and yong for old, few before many,fome with opprobrie, and open, not onely contradiction, with more fawcineffe, but with bafe and contemptible termes (as they do the Scriptures) which in vs were plaine blafphemy; certainly in them it is extreme impudencie.

30 Aske *Bellarmine* the meafure of *Antiquitie*, and he will giue you a rule : *Qui ante annos fexcentos fcripfit, videat an recte recens appelletur:*He that wrote aboue fix hundred yeares ago take heed how you call him a frefh man.Stand vpon this rule. Let *Bellarmine* alledge a miracle for the fecret of his Maffe, *Vfus eft antiquiffimus*, though not fixe hundred yeares fince; and if the cuftome began after that,it were moft ancient. Ancient if you will, but not moft ancient. But let vs alledge *Oecumenius*,an author approued by *Bellarmine* himfelf, and often alledged by him and others, as an ancient Father of the Church,for the ftate of Antichrift ; either he will adde to his text,*tantum*, and that is fhame enough ; or elfe he will leffen his authoritie, as if he were a new writer, though he wrote not long after *Bellarmines antiquiffimus vfus,* his moft
ancient

Refpon. ad Apol.apud Iuel.p.22.

Apolog. p.1.

De Miffa.l.2. cap.12.in fine.

ancient vſe; with much more impudencie in himſelfe, and
not without a note of baſe contempt to the Father. *Sed neque* Apolog.
tanti faciendus eſt, cum ſit author recens. I wiſſe you need not ,,
make ſo much eſteeme of him, ſeeing he is ſo new. Some are ,,
ſo ſtale, that they may ſtinke, like *Bellarmines* miracles; ſome
are ſo new, that they may be too ſweete for his quezie ſtomacke. This *tantum & tanti*, ſhewes *Bellarmine* to be partiall:
tantus, quantus. Will not this ſerue to ſtop *Bellarmines* mouth
for euer, when he alledgeth *Oecumenius?* yea or *Theophylactus?*
yea or *Bernard?* or *Anſelmus?* or *Hugo de Victore?* or any other
that hath written ſince, or about their time? You need not
make ſuch an account of theſe, they are too freſh, too new,
too yong to reſt vpon.

    31   Theſe and their yongers will ſerue to proue *Peters*
primacie, and ſuch like Pontificiall and profitable queſtions,
as make for the pompe and benefit of the Romane Biſhop,
or the facing out of falſhoods in matters of religion. But if Bellar.de Ro-
they ſpeake for vs, they are too yong, and great reaſon, for Pont.l.2.c.25.
the caſe is altered. Suppoſe theſe are too yong for their palate, wil they vſe the old better? By no means. They vſe them Fers aliquid?
as the Court of *Rome* do their ſuiters. If they bring nought, Fero quod ſa-
they are kept out; if they bring ought, they are let in. So the as Philip ſaid,
Fathers, if they make for them, they receiue them with all Ξίνος ἴλθεε
friendly titles & applauſe; if nothing, they care not for them: ὅςτε ὀνήσει.
if againſt them, they are worſe then no bodies; nay they eſ- Veniat qui
cape not without contumely and reproach. pes.

    32   Shall I begin with a Greeke or a Latin? *Origen* and Ipſe licet ve-
Tertullian, both of great antiquitie? There are almoſt none nias Muſis
more frequently vrged in many caſes then theſe, by *Bellar-* com.Hom.
mine, and other writers on their partie. *Origenes viſus eſt in* attuleris, ibis
Gehenna ignis cum Ario & Neſtorio: quinta Synodus, c. 1. dicit A- Hom.foras.
nathema Origeni, ſicut Ario, Neſtorio, & cæteris hæreticis: Origen Bellar.de Scri-
was ſeene in hell fire with *Arius* and *Neſtorius*; and the fifth ptorib.Ecclef.
Councell accurſeth *Origen* as *Arius*, *Neſtorius*, and other he- Idē de verbo
retickes. He is beſide ſet in the moſt Catalogues of Hereticks, Dei.lib.1.c.9.
as a principall. Yet when he will bring him to anſwer Saint Prateolus de
Ierome, and all antiquitie, about thoſe *Apocryphall* peeces hæreſ.
Q 4   which

which are bungled and clouted to the Prophet *Daniel*, he commends his authoritie; and good reason, for he speakes for him. And to make vp a muster of Fathers, *Parsons* in his three Conuersions hath this *Origen* and *Tertullian* also, as famous writers, and Catholicke Doctors, within the first three hundred yeares. And *Gilbert Genebrard* plainly defendeth him.

Three Conuersions, part 2.c.2.§.12.
So do all Popish writers.
M.Cooke.

De Rom. Pon l.2.c.5.
De Monachis l.2.c.34.

33   *Tertullian* is with *Bellarmine* when he pleaseth him, *grauissimus author*, a most graue author, a famous writer, and Catholicke Doctor. By *Parsons* and them as ordinarily cited as any other Father that hath written, (as hath in part bene said) none more : yet if *Tertullian* offend him, he is an here-

De Ro. Pont. l.4 c.8.

ticke; and if he answer him, he will tell you: *Respondeo, non esse omnino fidem adhibendam Tertulliano in hac parte:* I answer, that
" no credit at all is to be giuen to *Tertullian* in this case. In an
" other case he may perhaps be beleeued, but not in this. If

Canus loc.c6.
l.11.c.2,

Melchior Canus answer him, he will say, that *Irenæus & Tertullianus conuincuntur erroris*, *Tertullian* and *Ireneus* (his anci-
" ent) are conuinced of errors : therefore disenabled to be sufficient witnesses for a controuersie. But these two were both tainted with heresie, neither is it denied by vs, and therefore we refuse them as well as they. This is true : but this is the difference; we make no account of them in matter of controuersie to conclude by them : our aduersaries not onely make vse of them for illustration, but vrge them also as oc-

De rat. stud.
Theo. l.4,c.6.
obs.1.2.

casion requireth for probation. *Villa Vincentius* doth not only taxe these, but with them, *Irenæus, Victorius, Papias, Methodius, Cyprian, Hilary, Epiphanius, Ambrose, Hierome, Augustine*: all of reuerend Antiquitie, to erre in some particulars, as all the Fathers else, neuer so much obserued for innocencie of life or learning.

34   I need not set forth all the Fathers with those praises they right well deserue; neither to paint them with those colours wherein our aduersaries do adore them; nor to yeeld them those ornaments of reuerence, which we do and can well affoord them: onely let me deliuer how rigid censurers our aduersaries and theirs are, when they speake not to their

purpose,

purpofe, or fing not to their tune. Will you haue an expedite
anfwer vnto Saint *Auguftine*, who is fometimes *hæreticorum* Muri ciuit.
terror, Catholicorum defenfor, magnus Auguftinus, Africæ decus: fanctæ.fund.
The terror of heretickes, the defender of Catholickes, great ²
Auguftine, the ornament of Africa? *Si rurfus obycias Augufti-* De Sacram.
num refpondeo (faith *Bellarmine*) *Auguftinum non expendiffe hunc* Euch.li.c.11.
locum diligenter. If you againe obiect *Auguftine*, I anfwer that „
Auguftine did not confider of this place diligently. Which is „
cleare by this, that he fhortly fhifted himfelfe of this difficul-
tie, faith the Cardinall. Againe, *Adde Auguftinum ex fola igno-* De Rô. Pont.
rantia linguæ Hebræa effe deceptum: Adde this, that *Auguftine* by lib.1.cap.10.
meere and onely ignorance of the Hebrew tongue was decei-
ued. *Stapleton* of *Auguftine*; it was *lapfus humanus*, a humane Doct. princ.l.
flip, caufed by the diuerfitie of the Greeke and Latine tongue, 6.c.3.
which either he was ignorant of, or marked not. Will you
haue Maifter *Hardings* anfwer to the fame Father, and ano- Contra Apo-
ther more ancient then he with him; *If in a fecret point of lear-* log. p.92.
ning, Saint Auguftine or Saint Cyprian teach fingularly, we follow
them not. Will you haue *Albertus Pighius* anfwer this learned De peccato
Father? *Non multum me mouet Auguftini fententia*. I am not orig.
much moued *with Auguftines* opinion. *Mihi non placet Augu-* „
ftini ea de re definitio & fententia. In that point *Auguftines* defi- „
nition and fentence pleafeth me not. Will you fee this bold „
fellow more defperatly fet on him? *Quòd Auguftini fententia,* Contro. 1.
&c. That *Auguftines* opinion is not onely vncertaine, but falfe; „
thus me feemeth I can proue; and his conclufion is, *That the* „
fentence of Auguftine is not onely vncertaine, but certainly falfe; I „
haue fufficiently demonftrated faith he. He is fo angrie, that he „
neuer Saints him, though he name him often in this place.
Was there euer liue dog, that fo barked at a dead Lyon? If
Pighius alone were thus fawcie, it fhould be our fatisfaction,
that the fact, or words of one fhould not be imputed to all; or
that fome of his owne fellowes had reproued him for his ma-
lepertneffe. But Maifter *Harding* and Cardinall *Bellarmine* follow him in the fame fteps. S. *Auguftine* is to them as he pleafeth them, and then what reuerence hath he for his *Antiquitie?*
God forbid we fhould fo abufe S. *Auguftine.*

35   Saint

35 Saint *Hierome*, a learned man, and an ancient Father.

In Proph.Ioel Yet *Nicholaus Lyra* firſt is bold with him, *Sauing his reuerence,*
c.1.ver.1. *he will not be of his opinion in that caſe.* *Non probatur ſententia*
Lib.2.cap.11. *Hieronimi à Gelaſio,* ſaith *Melchior Canus: Hieroms* opinion is
not approued by *Gelaſius* in ſetting downe the Canon of the
Scriptures. Cardinall *Bellarmine* is bold with him; in one caſe
De Rom.Pōt. he ſaith plainly, *errauit,* he erred. Againe, I admit (ſaith he)
l. 4. *Hierome was of this opinion,* as who ſhould ſay, what if he be?
or let him be, it maketh the caſe neuer the better, he is made
but as a chip in a keale pot, as a Gentleman ſaid of a certaine
ceremonie, it neither did good nor harme : the Cardinall is
De verbo Dei not perſwaded by him. Yet againe, when *Caluins* obiection
l.1.c.10. out of *Hierome* is to be anſwered; *Sacerdotes qui Euchariſtiam*
conficiunt, & ſanguinem Domini populo diſtribuunt : when the
Prieſt prepareth the Euchariſt, and diſtributeth the bloud of
the Lord to the people. The Cardinall anſwereth nothing but
De Sacram. thus; *Nihil noui audimus,* we heare no newes; would this ſa-
Euch.l.4.c.26. tisfie a Catholicke Romane, if one of vs ſhould make ſuch an
De Clericis.l. anſwer? In another caſe, *Eſt hoc loco obſeruandum,&c.* In this
1.c.15. place it is to be obſerued, *that Saint Hierome ſeemed not to be*
ſo very conſtant in his opinion ; *In ſo much that it is very probable*
De R6. Pont. *that he was not very certaine.* Yet worſe in another caſe, *Quæ*
l.1.c.8. *ſententia falſa eſt & refellenda* : Which ſentence is falſe, and in
his place to be refuted; *ſatis pro imperio.* The Cardinall might
haue ſpared ſo plaine a ſpeech, to one as good as himſelfe. For
Saint *Hierome* was a Cardinall, as well as he, or elſe painters
and Papiſts lye. And though this Saint *Hierome* giue a great
Epiſtola 7. ad teſtimonie of Saint *Hilarie,* and perhaps too great, *That in Hi-*
Læt. *lary libris pietas fidei non vacillat* : In *Hilaries* bookes the pietie
Annal. Eccleſ. of faith wauereth not; yet Cardinall *Baronius,* better ſighted
Tom.4.ad an. then Saint *Hierome,* can find ſome holes in his coate, and tell
369. vs, *Nec ipſe Hilarius næuis caruit,* Neither *Hilarie* himſelfe wanteth his blemiſhes; and to conclude, *Melchior Canus* is yet
bolder with Saint *Hierome* ; *Quod Hieron. tradit ex veteri Hi-*
″ *ſtoria, pace tanti viri dixerim, in re ſine dubio fallitur* : That which
″ Saint *Hierome deliuereth* out of the old Hiſtorie, by the leaue
″ of ſo great a man, without doubt in this he is deceiued.

36 That

36 That librarie of learning and fchoole of vertues, Doctor *Reinolds*, faid in a matter wherein he had good caufe of
exception, onely, *Da veniam Cypriane*, Pardon me *Cyprian*.
Wherein he rather imitated Saint *Auguftine*, then enforced a-
deuifed conceipt of his owne: And for this is fo canuafed and D. Harding.
courfed like a princocks boy, as if he had fpoken blafphemie
againft all the Fathers. How much bolder is Cardinall *Bellar-*
mine with Saint *Cyprian*, who anfwereth his authorities thus, De verbo Dei
Refpondeo, Cyprianum hæc fcripfiffe, cum errorem fuum tueri vel- l.4.c.11.
let, & ideo non mirum (i more errantium, tunc ratiocinaretur. I an- „
fwer, that *Cyprian* wrote this, when he would defend his er- „
ror, and therefore no maruell if he then reafoned as erronious „
men do. Yet for all this to giue a plaifter to Saint *Hieroms* „
broken head, in another cafe *Canus* is content to preferre this
one *Hieromes* opinion before *Eufebius, Nicephorus, Hippolytus*, Lib.11.c.3.
Ambrofe, Epiphanius, and Hillarie: He is here a Captaine to
command a multitude, he was before, *gregarius miles*, a common fouldier, fcarfe worthy of a pay.

37 Saint *Chryfoftome* that excellent Preacher, who obtained his furname of golden mouth for his precious eloquence,
is ancient, and worthie all credit, yet heare how he is ferued:
In the expofition of a place of Saint *Iohns* Gofpell, *Tollet* thus Tollet.in Io.7
taxeth him, *Enthimius*, and other *Fathers, Chryfoftomus, Enthi-* fi quis fitit.v.
mius & alij antiqui Patres, de fiti doctrinæ hæc exponunt verba, fed 37.
rectius & commodiùs interpretabitur de doctrina, & de quouis
bono gratiæ, &c. Chryfoftome, Enthimius, and other ancient Fa- „
thers, do expound thefe words of the thirft of doctrine; but „
they may more rightly and commodioufly be expounded of „
doctrine it felfe, and of euery good gift of grace. Adde as ma- „
ny as you will to *Chryfoftome*, they muft all veile bonnet to a
frefh Iefuite Cardinall. Yet againe, *Chryfoftome, Enthimius &* Idem ibid.
Theophylactus, conueniunt in vno; fed expofitio hæc violenta eft & Annot.23.
incongrua: Thefe agree in one, but this expofition is violent and „
incongruent. Another expofition though it be true, yet it is Idem in 4.Io.
confufed and wants a commentarie; *Neither is Clemens Alex-* an.23.
andrinus to be followed. *Canifius* alfo is bold with Saint *Chry-* De Maria
foftome and others. *Chryfoftomus, Amphilochius, Theophylactus*, virg.l.4.c27.

in

in the interpretation of thefe words, The fword *fhall pierce thy foule*, *impegerunt*, ftumbled. And to fay the truth, it is a

De Sacra.Bap. good horfe that neuer ftumbled. And *Bellarmine* faith, that
l.1.c. 5.   *Chryfoftomi fententia quam fequitur Theophylactus defendi non poteft*, The fentence of *Chryfoftome* which *Theophylact* followeth cannot be defended. And in another cafe, he hath Saint
De Purgat.l. *Leo* with them, and difcards them alltogether. And that is re
1.c.4.   markable that a Pope cannot paffe the Cardinals cenfure, if he ftand in his way; but this he doth as a Iefuite, who will ouertop to the Pope, not as a Cardinall that muft be his vaf
De Concil.   fall. In another place he miflikes his opinion, and ioynes *Ire*
auhtor.l.2.c. *næus* and *Cyprian* with him, becaufe they thought not well of
8.   things ftrangled, forbidden Act. 15. *Contra fidem omnium codicū Græcorum & Latinorum*, Againft the truth of all books both Greeke and Latine.

De R.ō. Pont.   38 *Theodoret* when he pleafeth Cardinall *Bellarmine*, he is
l.4.c.1.   *etiam inter Græcos Patres eruditiſſimus*, euen among the Greeke Fathers moft learned : yet *De errore damnatus eft*, He was con
De Euchar.   demned of error. *Gregor. de Valen.* faith, *Theodoretus damnandus*, he is to be condemned, and was indeed condemned in the
Lib.11.c. 6.   fift Councell, quoth *Melchior Canus*. And indeed the Coun
5. Synodo.   cels fentence is very terrible, *Si quis defendit impia fcripta Theo*
Act.4.cap.13. *doreti*, &c. *anathema*, If any man defend the wicked writings of *Theodoret*, which are fet forth againft right faith, let him be accurfed. Yet *Bellarmine* to iuftifie his title of *Eruditiſſimus*,
De Imag.fan- giueth him and *Origen* (two fometime damned heretikes, in
ctorum.l.2. c. the Romanifts iudgments, and by the firft Councell) the buck
5.   lers, againft, or before the confent of all other Fathers, in the diftinction of *Image* and *Idole*. But when *Bellarmine* meeteth with him in the companie of both their betters, he fares with the reft for all his *Eruditiſſimus*. *Ambrofe, Hierome, Auguftine, Gregorie*, the foure Cardinall Doctors of the Latine Church, in number like the foure great Councels, in number and pi
Bellar.de Pur- ctures, with a Man, a Lyon, an Oxe, and an Eagle, fo ordinagatorio,l.1.c.4 rily painted as they do the foure *Euangelifts* : yet cannot priuiledge *Theodoret* and *Oecumenius* with their companies, but they are all reiected; and *Bellarmines* owne opinion grounded

vpon

vpon a few light coniectures, is preferred before them all. *Sexta est sententia, quam omnibus anteferimus* : The sixt opinion we preferre before all. When, for ought I see, it is one of the worst of all, as he that goes through the wood, and chooseth the crookedst sticke. *Vt mihi videtur* (saith *Maldonatus:*) In Mat.16.2 As it seemeth to me, *quamuis Chrysostomo & Theophylacto secus videatur*: though it seeme otherwise to *Chrysostome* and *Theophylact*, one Iesuite to two ancient Fathers, yea to tenne if that will serue the turne; and that with a *teste meipso*, he preferreth himselfe, which is great arrogancie.

39 Against the full streame of all the Fathers, I verily beleeue without any exception, the *Franciscan Friers*, and the Iesuiticall Fathers Societie, with their new found Sodalitie, and the Pope accessorie, and the Councel of *Trent* more then wincking at it, hold; that the blessed virgine *Marie* was with out all actuall or originall sinne. *Sancti omnes qui in eius rei mentionem incidere, vna asseuerant*, All the *Saints* that euer fell into the mention of that matter haue together affirmed it, that she was not without sinne. He numbreth them for feare of failing, *Ambrose, Augustine, Chrysostome, Emissenus , Remigius, Maximus, Beda, Anselmus, Bernard, Erard, Anton. Paduanus , Bernardinus , Thomas, Vincentius, Antoninus, Damascen, Hugo de Victore*; you may adde *Fulgentius*. In the same chap. *Canus* sheweth by two other examples , how Saint *Augustine* alone is preferred first before *Basil, Eusebius, Chrysostome, Damascen, Ambrose, Gregorie, Hierome, Beda, Raban, Strabo*. And then againe , before *Hierome, Gregorie Nazianzen, Gregorie Magnus , Chrysostome , Cyrill , Euaristus* Pope , and *Origen*. Where is their oath enioyned by the Councell of *Trent* , to all that should take degree in diuinitie, to follow *vnanimem consensum patrum*, the vniforme consent of the Fathers? when thus they cannot onely preferre one to many, but none to all the Fathers? And make them all ciphers in *Algurisme* (as they say) when they please, and dispence with their oath without a Popes Bull.

40 *Epiphanius* his Epistle *ad Ioannem Hierosolymitanum*, is alledged by vs against Images, and so by consequent against

Canus. l.7.c.1
xvij. Fathers
and children
cashiered at
once.
De fide ad
Pet. Diacon.
c.26.

Epiphanius.

the

the Romane Idolatrie, which, to fay truth , giueth it a great
blow. Of this Epiſtle, firſt obſerue, that it is in Popiſh editions, printed in Popiſh Vniuerſities, hath this grace added
vnto it, that where the workes of *Epiphanius* are ſet downe in

Printed at Pa-
ris, 1564. Catologue thus: *Eiuſdem Epiphanij Epiſtola ad Ioannem Con-
ſtantinopolitanū Epiſcopum, varia eruditione ſalubríque admoni-*
,, *tione plena. D. Hieronymo presbytero interprete.* An Epiſtle of
,, the ſame *Epiphanius* to *Iohn* Biſhop of Conſtantinople, full of
,, diuerſitie of learning, and of wholeſome admonition, Saint
,, *Hierome* presbiter interpreter. What the myſtery here ſhould
be, that *Iohn* is is called Biſhop of Conſtantinople, and the
ſuperſcription of the Epiſtle it ſelfe ſhould be called *Iohn* Biſhop of *Hieruſalem*; or whether it be a miſtakïng of the Printer, or other miſpreſſion, I know not. But the booke printed
at Paris, ſet forth by a Doctor of *Sorbon*, dedicated by an E-
piſtle to all the children of the Catholique Romane Church;
this very Epiſtle of the Father confeſſed to be full of all diuerſitie of learning, and wholſome admonition, interpreted
by Saint *Hierome*, and therefore queſtionleſſe approued by
him ; hath a note of aduantage in the margent (euen in the
place which we vrge,) ſeeming to make for Pilgrimage; *pere-
grinationis Antiquitas*, the *Antiquitie* of Peregrination, alled-

De Clericis,
l.1.c.1. ged by *Bellarmine*, euen in the very midſt & marrow of thoſe
words which are againſt Images , is notwithſtanding ſo
ſtrangely vexed, and tormented with the ſhifting anſwers of
thoſe *Romaniſts*, that an honeſt man would wonder how it
were poſſible, men ſhould ſo run to perdition, againſt their
owne conſcience. Doctor *Harding* was not come to the
quinteſſence of theſe deſperate wits that now outface the
world with vtmoſt impudencie. But as granting the authoritie, his anſwer is; *If he be of the opinion you make him, yet
is he but one man ? Or, What, if this place maketh not againſt
the vſe of Images ? Or, It was not againſt all Images.* Poore
ſhifts.

He liued a-
bout the
yeare 1350.
Dialog. 2. 41 *Cope* in his Dialogues ſetteth the authoritie of *Symen
Mataphraſtes* againſt this ſo ancient Father : as if a ſcullian
ſhould controll his Lord and Maiſter. And for further
                                          helpe,

helpe, in part out of *Thomas Waldenſis*; not ſo ſalt as bitter Tom.3.tit.19 cap.157.
an enemie to the truth, denieth the Epiſtle, reproueth the
tranſlation (though tranſlated by *Hierome,*) and when nothing will ſerue, he flies in the Fathers face, and ſaith he was
an hereticke of the *Authropomorphits* ſect, and therefore tare
the Image of Chriſt. A thing of all other moſt vnlikely, for
that ſect would haue Images: or that he was a Iew; or it was
not Chriſt Image: or of any Saint, but it was the image of
Hercules or *Iupiter*. *Conuitiare audacter aliquid adhærebit:* Slander hardly, ſomewhat will ſticke on. This is the tricke of a
right ſcold indeed. *Baronius* ſaith, It is *confictum aditamen-* Epit.anal. p. 416.
tum male aſſuetum ab aliquo Iconclaſta, A counterfeit patch,
clouted on by ſome Image breaker; or ſaith he, *vt detur eſſe* „
Epiphanij, to grant it is *Epiphanius*; for indeed it cannot be
denied, yet he hath another ſhift; that *Epiphanius* was angrie that the Image of ſome profane man painted vpon the
holy vaile, ſhould be hanged for the Image of Chriſt, or
ſome *Saint*, at the entrance. This is againſt all the circumſtances of the text; for who would imagine that a profane mans
picture was brought into the Church? Secondly the Father
doth not doubt of the picture in his memory, whether of
Chriſt, a *Saint*, or a profane man: but whether Chriſt, or a
Saint, he well remembreth not whoſe, & therefore it was not
the picture of any profane man, but either Chriſt, or a *Saint*.
Becauſe this double dealing will not ſerue. *Sixtus Senenſis*, Bib.ſanct. l.5, annot.247.
goes to it with a threefold cord out of *Damaſcene*. *Dama-*
ſcenus occurrit Epiphanio tribus reſponſionibus, Damaſcene occurs „
Epiphanius with three anſwers; firſt, *Either this skipt or crept* „
out of the margent into the text; or it was not the old Father E- „
piphanius, but ſome other of that name, or finally one ſwallow makes „
no Sommer. But of all theſe fancies and follies, ſhifts aud ſub- De Imag. Sanctorum, l.2.c.9.
tilties, *Bellarmine* thinks the beſt anſwer to be that which is
commoneſt, *verba illa eſſe ſuppoſititia,* that the words are foiſted
in. Let *Bellarmine* himſelfe be iudge of theſe anſwers, and
turne the perſons.

42 *Hermannus* anſwereth a place of *Baſil de Spiritu Sancto;*
Iſta omnia non eſſe Baſilij, ſed inſerta eſſe in libro Baſilij, ab aliquo
Nebulone

,, *Nebulone*: All thefe were not *Bafils*, but added to him by fome
varlet. Whereunto *B. Harmine* anfwereth , *Quæ fanè expedi-*
tiſſima reſponſio eſt. Sic enim facile eſt omnia ſoluere argumenta.
,, This verily is an expedite anfwer, for thus it is eafie to af-
,, foile all arguments. I vndertake not to difpute on what
grounds *Eraſmus* was moued to reiect part of this booke,
whom *Hermannus* followeth , but he that readeth Maifter
Cookes Cenfure vpon that booke, he fhall finde more then
the ftyle, & more then probable arguments to difenable that
part which *Eraſmus* reiecteth. But marke all the anfwers before made vnto *Epiphanius* : *That he was but one man; that one*
ſwallow makes no Sommer, that the Father was an hereticke, that
wrote againft herefies: *and a Iew : That this part is a counterfeit*
patch, That the words were foiſted. And may you not fay to the
beft of them, as *Bellarmine* to *Hermannus, Hæc ſanè? &c. This*
verily is an expedite anfwer. Thus Doctor *Harding,* Cope, *Wal-*
denſis , Baronius, Sixtus Senenſis , Damaſcene and *Bellarmine,*
may eafily aſſoile all arguments. What *Antiquitie* will ftand be-
forethe face of fuch flipftrings, more diuerfe in their anfwers, and as quicke as a Camelion in changing colours ?

43 Infinite are the examples that may be produced, of a-
bufing the ancient Fathers in this kind; fometime they prefer
fome before others, as Saint *Auguſtine* is preferred before
Cyprian and *Gregorie,* and before *Clemens Alexandrinus,* Saint
Hierome, & alijs multis, and many others, *quia eius ſententia eſt*
probabilior, becaufe his opinion is more probable. Sometime one before all other, againft *Bellarmines* proteftation.
Nos ſequimur Patres quando ſimul aliquid doceant , We follow
the Fathers when they teach all one thing.

44 *Auguſtine* and he onely, yet he both fo, and otherwife,
perhaps conceiting it fomewhat to make for the proofe of
the *Trinitie* of perfons in the Deitie, deuided the tenne
Commandements into three and feauen againft all *Antiqui-*
tie of Stories, and Iewes and Fathers, both before him and
with him, and fince, that euer deuided them into foure and
fixe. All their Catechifmes and Offices with the Schoolemen hold the former deuifion, which Saint *Auguſtine* alone
of

Bell. de verb.
Dei n5 Scrip-
to. l. 4. c. 7.

Bell. de Rom.
Pont. l. 1. c. 16.

De Rom.
Pont. l. 1. c. 26.

of any they can name. He for one caufe to build a certaine
truth, though vpon a weake foundation; but thefe vpon a
wicked purpofe, to hide the fecond commandement from
the eyes of the people, left it fhould difcouer their groffe i-
dolatrie. Though they know that the conference of the text,
the 20. of *Exod.* with the fift of *Deut.* and Saint *Paul* making
the commandement of luft but one, (which Saint *Augustine* doth alfo) do euidently ftop the mouthes of all contradiction. Befides that, Saint *Augustine* himfelfe doth not vfe this di-
uifion abfolutely, but indifferently; fometime fo, fometime otherwife: but they moft conftantly abufe it, as if it might not be otherwife. Which their Seminaries of *Doway*, in their *annotations* vpon the 20. of *Exodus*, endeuour to defend, a-
gainft their oath, and all *Antiquity*; and fo do they moft mife-
rably, onely vpon Saint *Augustines* authoritie, one againft all other, befides the circumftances of the text making againft them. *Iofephus*, of credit for *Antiquity*, hath them deuided into foure and fixe, which queftionleffe was as the Iewes tooke it, at and vntill his time. *Aben Ezra* hath the fame diuifion. The author of the imperfect worke attributed to *Chryfoftome*, and the Comment vpon the *Ephefians* afcribed to *Ambrofe*, ancient authors by *Bellarmines* confeffion. *Ori-
gen* before them deuideth as we, and faith, that they which make but three in the firft Table, cannot make vp the number of ten commandements. *Athanafius* as we; *Gregorius Nazian.* in *Carmin.* Saint *Hierome* deuides the firft two as we, and calleth that of images the fecond, that of honouring parents the fifth. *Ionas Arialenfis* alfo hath our diuifion, and parteth that of worfhipping images from the firft of hauing one God, about eight hundred yeares fince. *Polydore Virgil* conuinced in his confcience of this veritie, numbreth them in the order that we do. But this by the *Belgian Index expurgato-
rius* is blotted out, as an eye-fore to the Romanifts, being fo oppofite to their idolatrie. All which confidered, let our aduerfaries be iudges whether they or we fticke clofeft to *An-
tiquity*, or do come neareft *ad vnanimem confenfum Patrum*,
to the vniforme confent of Fathers.

Enar. in Pf. 57.
Ad Ianuar. ep.
119. quæft. in
Exod. 71.
Contra ad Bo-
nifac. contra
2. epift. l. 3. c. 4.
written after
the former
works, and fo
his after cogi-
tation. Autor.
quæft. vet. &
nou. Teftam.
c. 7. which is
S. Auguftines
ancient by
Bellarmines
confeffion: for
he was more
ancient then
S. Ambrofe
who côuerted
S. Auguftine.
de fcript. Eccl.
in Amb. &
Auguft.
Iofeph. Antiq.
l. 3. c. 6.
Homil. 49.
Vbi fupra.
In Exod. c. 20.
hom. 8. in
Synopfi.
Pag. 467.
De inuétione.

R   45   In

45　In another cafe of difcerning betweene *Canonicall* and *Apocryphall* Scriptures (wherein Saint *Auguftines* authoritie may admit an anfwer, by a neceffary diftinction, that he taketh not the word *Canonicall* fo exactly for a rule, but for holy bookes fit to be read; and excepteth againft fome of thofe bookes, as not fufficient to euince an article of faith. They reft vpon Saint *Auguftine*, and a doubtfull Canon of the *Carthaginian* Councell, by the Romanifts in fome cafes refufed; and a few doubtfull and obfcure teftimonies, to which Doctor *Rainolds* hath taken iuft exception; againft all Conncels and Fathers that were before him without exception, that euer I read, or by fearching could find. I need not name them, they are all that euer wrote of that fubiect, of the Iewes, the Greeke Fathers, or the Latins. Where is their *vnanimus confenfus?* where is their anfwering roundly with the Fathers, and other euidences of antiquitie?

Lyra.
Bretto.
Caietan.
Driedo.
Lib.2.epift. 1.

46　Some whom they challenge for their owne, haue confeffed with vs, before and fince the Councel of *Trent*, that thofe, or the moft, or at leaft fome of thofe bookes are *Apocryphall*. They are like thofe of whom Saint *Cyprian* fpeaketh, *Scimus quofdam quod femel imbiberunt, nolle deponere, nec facile* ,, *mutare*: We know fome that will neuer difgorge what they ,, haue once fwallowed, nor eafily change if they be once fetled, though perhaps vpon their dregs. I will dilate no more examples, I will but relate them, and leaue them to the Chriftian readers cenfure, to iudge how our aduerfaries vfe this excellent euidence of *Antiquity*, when they lift.

De verbo Dei
l.1.t20.

De verbo Dei
l.1.c. 2.

De verbo Dei
l.2.c.2.

47　*Origen, Tertullian, Irenæus, Clemens Alexandrinus, Athanafius, Caffianus, Eufebius, Ruffinus, Hierome*, are all reiected by *Bellarmine*, for their cenfure of the booke of *Hermes*. In another cafe he fetteth downe two opinions, and alledgeth for either opinion (which indeed are diuers) the authoritie of many Fathers, but concludeth with *Nobis igitur dicendum videtur*, when all is done, fay they what they wil, *Thus it feemeth good to vs to fay*. Yet in another cafe, *Driedo* who in fome things is by his fellowes reiected, yet is his meere coniecture preferred before all *Antiquity*. In another cafe, *Bafil,*

Theodo-

Theodoret, Sedulius, Haymo, Primasius, Peter Lombard, D. Thomas, & alij quidam ex Latinis, and other Latin writers, and some of his own best friends, Greeks, Latins, old, new, some, and more, ordinary men, and Saints, are all neglected and set aside, and *Bellarmine* concludeth all himselfe, with *Vera igitur sententia est*; as who should say, Be it as it may be, *this is the truth which I say.*

48 If Cardinall *Bellarmine* taxe *Luther* of impudencie, because he preferreth his owne interpretation before the *Rabbins, Theodoret, Hierome, and the 70 interpreters,* and, as saith *Ezechiel,* (which is vntrue, for the word, *Luther* taketh as *Bellarmine* himselfe and all the others do) of an impudent face; may we not say, that *Robert himselfe* is *robustus facie,* of an impudent face, that will thus outface so many? In another case, *Tertullian, Ambrose, Chrysostome, Oecumenius, Epiphanius, Theophylact, Theodoret, Sedulius, Anselme, Haymo, Thomas,* and *Caietan,* old men that were like to be indifferent, the yonger frie, that if they be partiall, it is on our aduersaries part, yet all haue one entertainment. These twelue are cashiered, as vnable to interpret a Scripture. And the resolution resteth vpon *Ephrem, Petrus Cluniacensis, Dionysius, Hugo* and *Gagnio.* A companie of doubted, base, late, vpstart companions, set to outbeard and outface them. When *Rehoboams* yong play-fellowes counsell shall be preferred before the wise, graue, and ancient Sages of *Salomon,* boyes before men, children before fathers, yong before old, schollers before Doctors, yea vizards before faces: is it not strange that men should be so impudently shamelesse, as thus to pretend *Antiquity,* and yet preferre noueltie and euery *nouellant* before it? I am sure this is not to interpret *secundùm vnanimum consensum Patrū,* the vniforme consent of Fathers. Let all the ancient Fathers writings be searched and ransacked, if you will, and you shal euer find them our equall witnesses for truth, especially in those things, when many agree, and each is constant in himselfe, as in those particulars before remembred, and in the expressing of God by any image; thirteene by name, besides *a* lij, others, added to make it vp.

Bellar.de Ro. Pont.l.3.c.17.

a Bellar.de Im. Sanctor.l.2.c.8.

R 2 49 Take

49   Take a few examples for the interpretation of Scrip-

Ierem.1.10.

tures: God faith to the Prophet *Ieremy, Conſtituam te ſuper regna,&c. I will ſet thee ouer kingdomes, that thou mayſt plucke*

Extra. de ma- ior.& obed.C. Solitæ.

and roote them out, that thou mayſt build and plant. This *Innocentius* the third applieth in effect to the depoſing of Kings, and diſpoſing of kingdomes; it ſtandeth yet in the text of the Canon law, in a Decretall Epiſtle, equalled to the *Canonicall Scriptures.* But what one Father euer ſo tooke it? much leſſe hath it the generall conſent of all the Fathers. It is pitie *Innocentius* had not taken the *Trent* oath. In the ſame Epiſtle is

Pſal.136.8.9.

alledged, *Deus fecit duo magna luminaria,* God made two great lights, the greater to rule the day, the leſſer to rule the night. What Councell euer defined? what Doctor euer dreamed, that this ſhould meane 2 powers in the Church, the *ſpirituall ſublimitie* and *ciuill dignitie?* That the Pope ſhould gouerne the day, that is, ſpirituall things; the Emperour ſhould gouerne the night, that is, temporall things? till the ſame *Innocentius* ſo applied it? Which is done in ſo good earneſt, that

Gloſſ.ib.

the Gloſſe calculateth how farre the Sunne is greater then the Moone, by iuſt Geometricall proportion, that no man, may doubt how farre the Pope is aboue the Emperour. *Terra eſt ſepties maior Luna, Sol octies maior terra:* The earth is ſeuen times as big as the Moone, the Sun is eight times as big as the earth; therefore the Pope is fortie ſeuen times as big as the Emperour. He ſhould haue ſaid, fiftie ſixe times, for that is ſeuen times eight; and it is maruell he would loſe in his account, when he ſpake for the Pope. But this vnskilfull ac-

Falſa latinitas non vitiat te- ſcriptum.

count ſhall no more preiudice the Popes ſupremacie, then the Popes falſe Latin ſhall abate his Decretall.

50   Howbeit leſt this ſhould not be ſufficient, *Laurentius* maketh a better account, and more authenticall, by *Ptolomies authoritie: Manifeſtum eſt quod magnitudo Solis continet magnitudinem terræ centies, quadrageſies ſepties & duas medietates eius:* It is manifeſt that the bigneſſe of the Sunne containeth the greatneſſe of the earth one hundred fortie ſeuen times, and two medieties thereof; and therefore *palam eſt,&c.* It is manifeſt that the Sun is bigger then the Moone by 7744 times

and

and one medietie. Wherein there are two things remarkable:
The one is the myfterie of this number, feauen and feauen,
foure and foure, the feauen heads of the beaft which are feauen hils, and the feauen fpirits which inflict feauen plagues
vpon the earth; the foure, is the foure Orders of Friers, that
fupport the foure corners of the Popes Canopie; and carrie
like foure whirlwinds the Popes doctrine, to the foure places
of diftreffed foules, *Limbus Patrum, Limbus puerorum, Purgatorie,*and *Hell*: The medietie is the Iefuites, which make the
myfterie of this number to feeme the truer; as the bottle of
hay giueth credit to the tale of *Garagantuas* buttons. The o-
ther is the exact calculation of this proportion; they will
not giue the Emperour one inch in meafuring with the
Pope.

51 Where hath fuch or fuch a Doctor; fuch or fuch a Father; nay where hath any fober man, fuch or fuch phantafti-
call, or rather braine-ficke, and plaine franticke imaginati-
ons?Yet nothing of all this in text or gloffe is reformed by any *Solitæ benig-*
new edition that I haue feene, nor by the Spanifh *Index*, *nitatis.*
which notwithftanding hath fet their *deleantur* to diuers
Chapters in the fame title. In the fame Epiftle there is a place
of Saint *Peter*,*Subditi eftote omni humanæ creaturæ*, Be ye fub- *1.Pet.2. 13.*
iect to euery humane creature for Gods fake. *Apoftolus fcripfit*
fubditis fuis; The Apoftle wrote to his owne fubiects, to pro- „
uoke them to obedience. For if *Peter* had meant this of a „
Prieft, then euery feruant fhould be a Priefts maifter, becaufe „
he faith,to euery humane creature.That which followeth *Regi* „
tanquam præcellenti, To the king as to the moft excellent, we „
denie not but that the Emperour is moft excellent, in tempo- „
rall things, (though this be now denied) but the Pope in fpi- „
rituall things. Although it be not fimply faid,*Subditi eftote, fed* „
additum fuit,propter Deum; be you fubiect, but there is added „
for Gods fake;as if God were *terminus diminuens*, & did dero- „
gate from kingly *authoritie*: neither is it fimply written to the „
King moft excelling,but not without caufe is added *tanquam*,
not moft excellent, but as it were more excellent. Certainly
this was not Saint *Hilaries optimus lector*, his beft Reader, *Qui*

dictorum intelligentiam expectet ex dictis, potius quàm imponat.
Who expect not the fence out of the words, but rather bring their
owne fence to the words. Neque cogat id : Neither let him conftraine that to be in the words, which his owne prefumption
conceited before he read them.

52 This was a Pope indeed, or rather a puppie or a poppy,
to bring one afleepe in careleffe ignorance; yet reputed
one of the learnedeft of thofe times. But who euer of the ancient Fathers thus interpreted this place? a thing fo infenfible,
prepofterous, prefumptuous, intollerable, impious and blafphemous, as if a man had ftudied and laboured of purpofe to
proue himfelfe out of his wits.

53 *Chrift* himfelfe faith, All power is giuen me in heauen
and in earth. *Ergo, Chrift* hath giuen to his Vicar *foueraigne*
temporall power, faith *Sixtus Quartus.* And fortifieth it with
another text prophefied of Chrift himfelfe; *His dominion fhall*
be from fea to fea, and from the floud to the ends of the world. Hath
Sixtus any Doctor, any Father for this? *Boniface the eight* moft
grofly abufeth thefe texts, *Vnus Paftor, vnum ouile,* One Shepheard, one fheepfold; *Ecce gladij duo,* Behold two fwords, &,
Pone gladium tuum in vaginam, Put vp thy fword into the
fheath: and concludeth by them thus; Verily he that fhall denie the temporall fword to be in *Peters* power, he ill hearkens
to the word of the Lord, that biddeth him put vp his fword
into his fcabberd. Which concludeth *à baculo ad angulum;* I
may fay, from heauen to hell. Will you fay, this was in thofe
dayes? or thefe were Popes not fworne according to the order in Trent Councell, and therefore whatfoeuer they haue
faid is good, though it be neuer fo abfurd? I know not what
elfe may any way be anfwered; certainly there is little credit
in it. *Stapleton* lately hath vpon this authority of *Boniface* prefumed vpon the fame interpretation. Which *Bellarmine* dareth
not well do, but more fearefully and with more modeftie, and
notes it but by the way, that it may be vnderftood of a fecondary Paftor. So it may indeed, to ferue their turnes, but not in
truth. What dare not thefe men do when they deale with
men, if they be not afhamed to deale thus with the euer bleffed

fed Sonne of God, and his holy word, the fcepter of his fpirituall kingdome? What Fathers or Father euer tooke any of
thefe Scriptures as thefe *Romanifts* haue done?

54 That place, *Super hanc petram*, Vpon this rocke will I
build my Church, is by ª *Auguftine*, ᵇ *Gregorie Nazianzen*, a De verbo
ᶜ *Cyril*, ᵈ *Chryfoftome*, ᵉ *Ambrofe*, or who was the author of ┌Domini, Ser.
thofe Commentaries vpon Saint *Pauls* Epiftles in his name, │13.
ᶠ *Hilarie*, yea and many others, haue taken the Rocke, either ┤b In Teftimo.
for *Peters* confeffion, or for Chrift whom *Peter* confeffed. ├ex v. Teftam.
Whereunto I find not a better anfwer then that of *Stapleton* ├cont. I.
before mentioned to Saint *Auguftine*. It was an humane flip, ├c De Trinit.
caufed by the diuerfitie of the Greeke and Latine tongue, ├l. 4.
which he was either ignorant of, or marked not. But what ├d In Math.
will he fay to *Cyril* and *Chryfoftome*, that vnderftood the ├hom.55.
Greeke tongue as well as he? Againe, that all the *Apoftles* re- ├e In Eph.2.
ceiued the *Keyes* with *Peter*, and that all were the foundation, ├f De Trinit. l.
we haue ᵍ *Auguftine*, ʰ *Ambrofe*, ⁱ *Origen*, ᵏ *Hilarie*, ˡ *Ierome*; ├2.c.6.
and thefe will not ferue vs, were they more, were they ├g In Ioan.
better. ├Tract. 118.
├h In Pfal.38.
55 If we fhould meafure all this by *Parfons* rule, our ad- ├i In Math.
uerfaries do vs and the religion we profeffe exceeding wrong. ├Tract.1.
For faith he, Whenfoeuer any doctrine is found in any of the ├k De Trinit.
ancient Fathers, which is not contradicted, nor noted by any ├l.6.
of the reft, as fingular; that doctrine is to be prefumed to be no ├l Aduerf. Io-
particular opinion of his, but rather the generall of all the ├uin l. 1.
Church in his dayes; for that otherwife it would moft cer- ├3. Conuer.
tainly haue bene noted and impugned by others; whereby it ,, ├part. 1. c.5.
followeth, that one Doctors opinion or faying, in matters of ,, └& 24.
controuerfie, not contradicted or noted by others, may fome- ,,
times giue a fufficient teftimonie of the whole Churches fen- ,,
tence & doctrine in thofe dayes, which is a point very greatly ,,
to be confidered. Thus he. And it is not altogether improba- ,,
bly fpoken. If this may be true in one, and is fo greatly to be
confidered in any, what fhall we fay to fo many, yea fometimes all, and yet not at all obferued, much leffe duly confidered? This line entangleth vs, but guideth them. It is true, into
a Labyrinth, but not out.

R 4　　　　　　56 If

56 If one of our Church ſhould write; that Saint *Bernard*
by the euils which he ſaw in his time , ſuſpected *Antichriſt* to
be nigh , as *Cyprian* , *Hierome* and *Gregory* did: and yet both
theirs and Saint *Bernards* ſuſpition was falſe , no man contradicted them in their times , no man then wrote againſt them;
therefore this was the opinion of their times. Why now reiected? Infinite might be the examples in this kind,but this may
ſatisfie any indifferent Reader,to know them as a leaper by his
muffler.

57 *Neque mihi probatur quod dicit Cyrillus* , Neither do I
approue that which *Cyrillus* ſaith, (ſaith *Tollet the* Cardinall:)
boldly ſaid , but well enough if he be a Romane Catholicke.
Herein *Bellarmine* deſerueth commendation aboue any other
of his partie, that he ſtandeth as indifferent to the Fathers that
were long ago , as to his owne friends and fellowes , if they
ſtand in his way. And like a right Midianite, if he do but
thinke he hitteth an Iſraelite , he will not ſticke to ſheath his
ſword in his fellowes bowels, as Doctor *Reinolds* well obſer-

ueth. Through *Caluins* ſides he killeth *Andreas Maſius*, *Arias
Montanus* , *Genebrard*, *Poſſeuine*, the Spaniſh Inquiſitors, Ieſuites,men pious, learned in his owne iudgement, the Popes
Cenſors,the flower of Rome, the Pope himſelfe, and the Generall of his owne order, euen all his owne fathers, brethren,
fellow ſouldiers , fighting vnder the ſame ſtanderd of Antichriſt; and yet leaueth *Caluin*,but a light ſcarre:and againe, he
doth the like, to diuerſe in the ſame Chapter ; who all ſtreng-
then *Caluins* opinion,who in *Caluin* by the Cardinall are confuted, and confoded.

58 May I not ſay at the leaſt of theſe Romaniſts,as S.*Hie-*

rome in his time of ſuch? *Iſti tantam ſibi aſſumunt authoritatem,
vt ſiue dextra doceant, ſiue ſiniſtra, id eſt, ſiue bona, ſiue mala, nolint*
 ,, *diſcipulos ratione diſcutere, ſed ſe prædeceſſores ſequi.* Theſe aſſume
 ,, ſo much authoritie to themſelues , that whether they teach
 ,, truth or falſhood, good or euill, they will not haue their ſchol-
 ,, lers diſcuſſe with reaſon, but follow them as their foregoers,
like the *Pythagoreans*. This is not to perſwade , but to command the faith of men; this is not to intreate, but to compell;
not

not to leade, but to driue men, to hold what they lift, without fearching for the truth, like their *cœca obedientia*, their
blind and mufled obedience; or their implicite or intricate
faith, which leads them into darkneffe, and leaues them in
the fhadow of death: but can neuer guide them into the way
of peace and light of truth.

59   Or may we not vfe *Bellarmines* annotations out of De facram.
Ioannes à Louanio, againft himfelfe and his fellowes? *Patribus* Eucharift.
in rebus grauioribus nihil credunt, In matters of greateft mo- l.4.c.26.
ment they giue no credite to the Fathers. Certainly they do
not, but when they lift, and as they pleafe to ferue their own
turnes, and no farther. For as before was noted out of *Sta-*
pleton, whatfoeuer can be faid or done, nothing ftandeth for
certaine truth with them but the Popes determination, who
is fole iudge of all Controuerfies. Which *Ioannes de Turre-*
cremata, a Cardinall & a principall pillar of the Romane Synagogue, deliuereth in plaine words, without all hypocrifie
or diffimulation. Which were it true, a quicke end would be
to all controuerfies. *Facilè eft intelligere ad Romani Pon-* In Sum.deEc-
tificis authoritatem fpeƐtare, tanquam ad generalem totius orbis clef.l.2.c.107.
principalem Magiftrum ac doƐtorem, determinare ea quæ fidei funt,
& per confequens edere fymbolum fidei, facræ Scripturæ interpreta-
ri fenfum, & doƐtorū fingulorum diƐta ad fidem fpeƐtantia, approba-
re vel reprobare. It is an eafie matter to vnderftand, that it ap- ,,
pertaineth to the authoritie of the Bifhop of Rome, as vnto ,,
the generall and principall Mafter, and Doctor, of the whole ,,
world, to determine matters of faith, and by confequence to ,,
fet forth a Creed, to interpret the fence of holy Scriptures, ,,
and to approue or difproue the fayings of all Doctors which ,,
appertaine vnto faith. Here is the merry fong, Pleafe one ,,
and pleafe all. Let all the Romane Catholiques in Chriftendome, or *vltra* Garamantas & Indos, proue this one propofition, which with tooth and naile is labored to this day, and
for my part I will be theirs in *toto*, as they are the Popes in
Affe. And this may faue labour to all difputes, giue a *Super-*
fedeas to all Schooles, preuent the trouble of calling Councels, fettle the confciences of all Chriftians: *Ipfe dixit*, will be
the

the conclufion to all arguments , be the premifes what they will, or may be.

60 If this they cannot proue,(as God and his Sonne *Chrift* ruling by his word, they neuer fhall) then we may moft certainly conclude, that though in fhew they pretend themfelues the onely treafurers of the Scriptures, the onely keepers of the Councels, the onely preferuers of the Fathers;yet when they are brought to the iffue, they neither care for the Scriptures, nor reft on Councels, nor refpect Fathers, but as the old Romanes their flaues to ferue their turnes, or the Turke his vaffals to fill ditches. What they can ingenioufly, fairely, faithfully, and confcionably anfwer vnto this, I proteft I know not. If they fay, they alledge moft of the Fathers in fundry controuerfies, we deny it not. But we aske, with what finceritie do they alledge them ? and what confidence they repofe in them, when they make againft them? This is manifeft by that which hath bene faid : whatfoeuer Friar *Valentia* faith to the contrarie, in his vaine boaft and maledi&ion. *Non fectariorum more pauculas quafdam fententias obfcuriores hinc indè in monumentis Patrum venantur, fed locos ipfos* ,, *perlegunt & cum iudicio conferunt:* They hunt not out, after ,, the manner of fectaries, a few obfcure fentences here and ,, there in the monuments of the Fathers, but they reade the ,, places themfelues,and conferre them with iudgement. Thus faid he of the conftant doctrine of the Romifh Church. If I had him by the nofe, as S. *Dunftan* had the diuell with a paire of tongues, I would not let him go, till he had recalled this lye. For he knoweth it as well to be vntrue, as the diuell knoweth that he is a lyer, and the father thereof.

Greg.de Valentia.l.6.c.12

61 If they fay, that we, or fome of ours haue refufed fometimes, or giuen fome harfh tearmes to fome of the Fathers, we grant it. I haue neither read nor heard it. But if they refufe, yet they do but as our aduerfaries do, and vpon better ground then they do it. If they vfe any vnreuerend fpeech of any approued Father, we defend them not ; we wifh they had not; and we are right fure not worfe then our aduerfaries themfelues haue done, nor fo ill by much, as I verily beleeue.

62 I omit the Romanifts fuppreffing of fome Fathers, reiecting of fome, corrupting of the beft, correcting of the moft without caufe, preferring of the worft. All which are as euident as noone day. *Gretzer* directly maintaines they may do it, and therefore all may put vp their pipes, when they talke of the Fathers. We will conclude our purpofe and promife with Saint *Hierome*, (whom to follow is credite in this cafe, for he fpeaketh wifely and learnedly, as if he would not be deceiued, and could iudge of that he read:) *Meum pro-* Ad Minriū. *pofitum eft Antiquos legere, probare fingula, retinere quæ bona funt, & à fide Ecclefiæ non recedere:* My purpofe is to reade the An-" cients, to proue euery thing, to hold that which is good," and neuer to depart from the faith of the Church. Cauill not" that you are the Church, we appeale to that Church whereof Saint *Hierome* was, from that which is pretended now to be, from new, to the old Romane, preferuing the credite and prerogatiue of *Antiquitie.* So we may reade and reuerence *Antiquitie* of the old writers, and admire both their learning and diligence: but we muft take heed of their errors, as in *Origen* & *Eufebius*, yea & in many, if not in all others. Gold is found in the earth, and Pearles in the fand, and the mudde of *Pactolus* may be richer then the waters of the riuer. So haue the Fathers excellent learning, yet fometime ouerfwayed with the current of the time. We will take their wheate in the eare, though couered with chaffe; it is our difcretion to feuer it before we vfe it for our food. Gods holy Spirit onely difpenfeth out of the garners of the Scriptures, that which is pure without mixture, and that fay we, is fufficient to faue our foules. Vnder thefe premifed conditions, which our aduerfaries cannot with their credite deny vs, becaufe they no otherwife vfe or admit the Fathers themfelues, we wil fay with one of our mortalleft enemies; we wil C. Hofius cõ-renounce the vfe of light; & wil fuffer our felues to be depri- feff.L.2.c.32.
ued of any thing that is moft deare to mortall men, fo we p.520.
may walke in the fteps of our firft forefathers, (in the faith) which we wil defend with our liues, it being grounded vpon the fure foundation of Gods booke.

CHAP.

CHAP. IX.

Whether Proteſtants or Papiſts admit or reiect the
fourth euidence of Antiquitie; Hiſtories.

Cicero de o-
ratore, l. 2.

Ncient Hiſtories bring much truth to light, and are worthily called the witneſſe of times, and light of truth, the life of memory, and miſtreſſe of life, and the meſſenger of *Antiquitie*. By them we conuerſe (as it were) with our anceſtors, and may behold the order of former ages, and obſerue the Goſpell propagated to diuerſe nations: how God hath protected his Church from tyrants and hereticks; how he hath ouerthrowne his enemies: ſometimes by miracle, ſometimes by meanes, for his owne glorie, for his Churches good. Vnto theſe, both we and our aduerſaries ſometime appeale, rather as vnto probable, then neceſſarie and vndoubted witneſſes.

Loc.Com.l.
11.c.4.

2 So ſaith *Melchior Canus*, *Præter authores ſacros nullus Hiſtoricus certus eſſe poteſt*; *Beſide diuine Authors, there can be no Hiſtorian certaine, that is, Fit to make certaine faith in Diuinitie, but ſuch as are graue and worthy credit, miniſter a probable argument to a Diuine.*—But if all ſuch agree in one, then their authoritie may ſtand for vndoubted: with much more in the ſame Chapter; where he hath ſome good rules in this matter of Hiſtorie.

Rat. 7.

3 Whereof our countriman *Campion* ſaith, *Priſtinam Eccleſiæ faciem hiſtoria priſca detegit, huc prouoco. The ancient Hiſtorie doth diſcouer the old face of the Church. I challenge you at this weapon, or abide you in this field. And what do they deliuer? the prai-*

Ergo their
Church had
changes.

ſes of our prædeceſſors, our proceedings, our * *changes, our enemies.* But firſt trie and theu truſt. Firſt ſeeke, and you ſhall find the cleane contrarie: For they are either ours, or we are not Chriſts: not that Hiſtories make vs Chriſtians, but that they demonſtrate vs to hold the true ancient and Chriſtian faith, taught by our Sauiour and his Apoſtles, and continued vnto

vs

vs till this day And that the Religion which our aduerſaries call Catholicke, is a falſe and counterfeit noueltie, without any true face or countenance of Antiquitie.

4   Although *Bellarmine*,according with *Canus* by way of obiection,ſaith, *Hiſtorici* (*Diuinis exceptis*) *non rarò mentiun-* tur, *& certè non firmam & infallibilem fidem faciunt* : Hiſtories (excepting the Diuine) do not ſeldome lye, and verily they make not certaine and infallible proofe ; yet the Hiſtories and Chronicles of the firſt ages do clearly deliuer the integritie of faith and the innocencie of manners in the Primitiue Church : as that about thirtie Biſhops of the ſea of *Rome* were all Martyrs, loued not their liues vnto the death, and ſealed their holy profeſſion and doctrine with their bloud. The other ſucceeding Biſhops, for about 300 yeares after, by litle and litle declined, till the number of the name, and myſtery of the Beaſt began to be written in capitall letters in the forehead of the Romiſh harlot; and the ſeruants of Antichriſt ſo inuaded the Church, that all that do but runne by the hiſtories of the Church may reade it, and but lap as the dogs by Nilus, may taſte and feele, that when Deuotion had brought forth riches, the mother was deuoured of the daughter, and then wealth wanted not iſſue; for it begat pride, pride begat ambition, ambition ſchiſme, ſchiſme hereſie, hereſie corruption both of faith and manners.

5   So that if we will obſerue the paſſages which the Chronicles deliuer of the Romane Church, with her proceedings and changes, you ſhall find that by theſe ſteps and degrees all the hiſtories do deſcend,as it were linked one in another, through the ſucceeding generations, ſhall I ſay? or degenerations of that Synagogue ? In the firſt period was *Truth, Patience and Martyrdome* : in the ſecond was *Learning, Reſolution and eaſe* : in the third was *Riches, Honour and Securitie*: in the fourth was *Power,Oppreſſion and Diſhoneſtie* : and from thence to this day, plaine *Impudencie, Tyrannie and Apoſtaſie.*

6   To particularize theſe gradations and decrements, would aske me more moneths to reade, then I haue dayes to write.

margin: Bellar.de Con cil.lib.2.cap.9

write. For all histories do fully discouer these things. In which behalfe shall I commend my Reader vnto the *Centuaries, Carion, Bale*, or *Barnes*, that write of the liues and acts of the Romane Bishops? or to our M. *Foxe* his Acts & Monuments? This though iustifiable enough in it selfe, and might saue labour of further search, in as much as they write not their owne, but what they receiued from more ancient authors; yet to our aduersaries it would be a scorne, and reiected as a *Domesticall* and insufficient testimony, where againft they would peremptorily except, though this be their owne perpetuall vse.

7 When they will raile against *Luther*, or *Caluin*, or *Beza*, or any professor of the reformed Religion, none so frequent, with *Prateolus* and the Iesuites, as *Fredericus Staphylus, Cocleus*, or *Bolsac*, or such like railers, and for the most part Apostataes, who desperatly detest the truth, from which they were fallen, and are the cruellest persecutors of that Religion they once professed, and haue forsaken.

<aside>Omnis Apostata & persequutor sui ordinis.</aside>

8 But we will be bound to *Canus* his rules, or *Campiont* Catalogue, as farre as the Romane Court in their practise vse to do, yea and farther: otherwise they shall not do vs that wrong, as to bind vs vnto that law which they themselues will not endure. We will go with them *pari passu, in equall steps:* we will *not be drawne, non passibus aequis, with vnequall conditions.*

9 Let the Authors be, *Eusebius, Damasus, Hierome, Ruffinus, Orosius, Socrates, Sozomene, Theodoret, Cassiodorus, Gregorius Turonensis, Vsuardus, Regino, Marianus, Sigibertus, Zonoras, Cedrenus, Nicephorus*; why not *Platina, Sabellicus, Abbas Vspergensis, Ioan. Parisiensis, Guicciardin?* why not *Beda?* why not *Martinus Polonus*, and such other, whom they will not grant to be ours, and before *Luther* was heard of, were euer acknowledged by themselues to be their owne, till they made the Romanists winch and gad, as vnable to endure the imputations they iustly layed vpon the Antichristian Pope, and his Locustian Cleargie.

10 Concerning all which, this shall be our rule: We will

not

not except against the former, but will either shew sufficient reason out of our owne obseruations, or out of our aduersaries owne confeffions, who moft bafely reiect the moft
and the beft,as after fhall appeare. Neither will we adde any
other vnto them, but fuch as were euer reputed Romane
Catholiques for their religion, and for their faction plaine
Papifts.

11 As for later Legends,which are now as graue ftories,
as *Antoninus, Lippomanus,Onuphrius, Surius, Sedulius,* and men
of the like temper in their faces as *Nabuchadnezzars* image
was in his feet,which neither had good mettall,nor yet hung
together: of whom we may fay, as *Tully* of *Herodotus,* whom
he cals *Patrem Hiftoriæ, The Father of Hiftories* ; and yet taxes
him with this, that he had *Fabulas innumerabiles,Innumerable
fables,* as *Theopompus* had. We care not for them,we will not
admit them,we plainly reiect them. For they wrote *vt Poëta,
non vt teftes,* as Poets, not as witneffes : and forgat that
they had diuers rules; they wrote for pleafure, not for
truth.

12 By the moft ancient and moft approued Hiftorians,
we affirme and iuftifie, that the Bifhops of *Rome* continued
long as vaffals and fubiects to the Romane Emperours; yea
when they were Chriftians,they were at their election and
at their commandement.Which is cleare, as well by the ftories, as by their mutuall Epiftles that paffed betweene them:
wherein the Bifhops euer gaue titles of honour and fuperioritie to the Emperours, and humbled themfelues by fubmif-
fiue petitions and requefts . For this I may referre the iudicious Reader to the firft Tome of the Councels, and the beginning of the fecond, to *Eufebius, Theodoret,* yea and *Gregorie the Great,* who all concurre in this paffage, without any
iuft exception to my knowledge.

13 By the fame Antiquitie and Authoritie it is pregnant, that the Emperours called the Councels, fummoned
the Bifhops with words of Soueraigntie, prefcribed them
limits of time, place,and matters to be handled . If the Bifhops of *Rome* did any thing, it was by petition and humble
　　　　　　　　　　　　　　　　　　　　　　　　fuppli-

De Legibus,1.

supplication before, dutifull thanks and gratulation after; without all pretence of the present power now claimed and defended by the Romane Catholickes, as if no Councell may be summoned, but onely by the bellowing of the Popes bull. Which challenge is meere new, and flatly Antichristian.

14   Reade *Eusebius in vita Constantini,* and *Theodoret* of the calling of the *Nicene* Councell, and the Emperours Christian behauiour in exhorting the Bishops, composing differences, allaying contentions, perswading of peace, and managing euen the matters of faith and religion, in offering *Codicem diuinum,* the *booke of God,* by his Imperiall maiestie. A thing now so abhorrent from the Romane eares in these later dayes, that though they know it as well as we, yet will they not belecue it, or at least confesse it, to saue their soules.

15   If we suruay all the first sixe generall Councels, we shall easily find the Emperours by their Edicts calling them, the Bishops of *Rome* intreating, the Legats subscribing, after *Hosius* Bishop of *Corduba* in *Spaine,* in the first and best Councell of *Nice,* not at all, or not by name, *Bellarmine* confesseth, *neque per se, neque per Legatos, neither by himselfe, nor by his Legats,* in the first Councell of *Constantinople,* congregated as the Fathers confesse in their Epistle to the Emperour, *ex mandato tuæ pietatis, at the commandement of your pietie.* The first of *Ephesus, Sanctum & vniuersale Concilium ex Edicto pie-* ,, *tatis studiosissimorum Imperatorum Ephesi coactum : The holy* ,, *and vniuersall Councell assembled at Ephesus by the Edict of the* ,, *pietie of most religious Emperours.* And againe, *Cum ex pio edicto* ,, *coacti essemus, When by that pious Edict we were assembled,* say the Bishops there.

16   The greatest generall Councell of Chalcedon was summoned by *Martianus* the Emperour. *Leo* the Bishop of Romes submissiue letters to him, his imperiall acts extant, in the same Councell. Adde vnto this the fift and sixt Councels which were both at Constantinople, the one called by *Mauritius,* the other by *Constantine* the fourth. In the later, most

of

Episcop.318.

De Concil.l.1
c.19.

Episcop.150.
Episcop.200.

Episcop.650.

of the actions begin with *Præſidente piiſſimo in Chriſto dilecto* Concil. Con-
magno Imperatore: The pious and great Emperour beloued of ſtantinop.6.
Chriſt, being Preſident. And againe, *Secundùm Imperialem ſan-
ctionem Synodus congregata: The Synod gathered according to the
Imperiall Decree.* The Councell of Nice, diuerſe Councels at
Toledo, the third, ſeauenth, eight, tenth, twelfth; In France,
in Germany, in Italy, in Rome it ſelfe, by Kings and Emperours in theſe times, as in the ſeuerall Councels it is cleare: alſo by the letters, actions, and other paſſages, which any man
of meane reading may ſee and obſerue, our aduerſaries themſelues cannot without ſhamefull impudency denie.

17   Many other ancient monuments there are regiſtred in
the beſt Hiſtories, and the appertenances of the Councels
themſelues, which all enforce the calling of Councels, and
ordering of them by Chriſtian Emperours. Not that they
preſumed to determine in matters of faith, as *Vzza laid his* 2.Sam.6.6.
hand to the Arke, and as Vzziah that would play the Prieſt : but 2.Chron.26.
they commanded the Biſhops to aſſemble, preſcribed them 16.
orders and bounds, made lawes and conſtitutions to obſerue
the religion which in the Scriptures was taught, and as by the
learned it was preſcribed. Chriſtian Kings would haue this
power now; it is not permitted them, it is vſurped by another,
that neuer made claime to it in the firſt, and moſt vncorrupted
ages.

18   I could exemplifie this paſſage with ſundry other particulars, but this being the maine foundation of the Romiſh
Synagogue, the very thing whereon the gates of Saint *Peters*
Church, and the Port-cullis of the caſtle *Angelo* hangeth, that
is, the Popes ſupremacy, and ſole power to call and authoriſe
Councels, I ſhall content my ſelfe with this which hath bene
ſaid, ſaue that it would not be forgotten, what Edicts the ancient Chriſtian Emperours made for the publication and eſta-
bliſhment of the greateſt myſteries of faith, and ordering of
the Clergie, both for their religious and ciuill behauiour. As
De ſumma Trinitate & fide Catholica, Of the glorious Trinitie Cod. tit.1.3.3
and Catholicke faith, of holy Churches and their priuiledges, of 4.5.6.
Biſhops and the other Clergie, &c. of Epiſcopall audience ; of Here-
S   *tickes,*

ticks, of Apostataes. By which it is demonstratiuely proued, that the Emperours did order Church gouernment, in the best times of the Church, as *Dauid, Iehosaphat, Hezekiah, Iosias,* Kings of *Iudah* did in their kingdomes; then which, what soundeth more harsh or absurd to a Catholicke Romane at this day? Yet all this by Histories and other old monuments of *Antiquitie,* we directly proue.

19 We may adde vnto these the Histories of Popes liues, who are as deeply branded with infamie, by ancient writers after their death, as their consciences were seared with iniquitie in their life. In so much as if we should compare the liues of some Popes with the most wicked Kings and Emperours that euer liued, as *Plutarch* doth the Romanes with the Græcians, that had bene for the most part famous for their vertues; we should find the Popes peerelesse, not onely in respect of the worst Christians, but the most detestable and damnable heathens. *Tarquinius, Dyonisius, Nero, Heliogabalus, Iulian the Apostata,* may be in many respects, put into the Romane Calendar for Saints, before and in comparison of the Romane Popes, *Anastasius, Iohn the twelfth or thirteenth, Iohn the three and twentieth, Hildebrand that was Gregorie the seauenth, Boniface the eight, Benedict the ninth, and Syluester the second, Alexander the sixt,* and diuers others. What blasphemies, villanies, adulteries, incests, heresies, apostasies, tyrannies, murthers, poysonings, treasons, and all manner of outrages against God and man do all Histories, all Chronicles, publish vnto the world, as vpon a stage, not onely to be lightly heard, but euen seene and felt by all hearers and spectators? some of whose godlesse and gracelesse misdemeanors may

Infrà. cap. 15. haply in this following Discourse be in part touched, if not fully discouered.

20 That which concerneth our present question of this euidence of *Antiquitie,* which is the Histories, I will propose two or three examples, wherein in this case the Romanists either miserably, absurdly, and doggedly snarle at all *Antiquitie,* or vtterly reiect and denie it; the most expedite course they can deuise to ouerthrow that, which in truth would ouerthrow

throw them. There is firft the ftorie of Pope *Ioane*,the female
Pope, and the whore of Babylon, not onely in figure, or fpiri-
tually, but in very deed really and carnally. Which is witneffed by more then a double grand Iury of fufficient witneffes,
older and later, Greeks and Latines,domefticall and forreine,
Diuines, Lawyers and Phyfitions, Philofophers,Poets and o-
ther humanitians; Priefts, Bifhops,in their account Saints,and
Cardinals, Friars, Monks, and Canons, yea and whole Vniuerfities, not one of them an enemy, nay not fo much as one
of them, not a friend to the Romane Catholicke Court and
religion.*To whom* may be added a teftimonie of good authoritie, out of an ancient Hiftorie without name indeed, yet of
vntainted credit for ought I know. *Fuit & alius Pfeudopapa*
cuius nomen & anni ignorantur, nam mulier erat,vt fatentur Ro-
mani,& elegantis formæ,magnæ fcientiæ, & in hypocrifi,magnæ vi-
tæ. Hæc fub virili habitu latuit quoufque in Papam eligitur, &
hæc in Papatu conoepit, & cum effet grauida Dæmon in Confiftorio
publice coram omnibus, prodit factum, clamans ad Papam hunc
verfum. Papa pater patrum, Papiffæ pandito partum, Et tibi tunc
edam, de corpore quando recedam. Chronica compendiofa ab initio
mundi. There was another baftard Pope, whofe name and
yeares are not knowne.But a woman fhe was as the Romanes
confeffe, of elegant beautie, great fcience, and in hypocrifie
of good conuerfation. She long lay hid vnder the apparell of
a man, vntill fhe was chofen Pope, and when fhe was with
child, the diuell openly in the Confiftorie before all bewray-
eth the fact,and cryeth to the Pope: *O Fathers Father, difclofe*
the fhee Popes little heart. Then will I tell truly when from thee Ile
depart. And take vnto them all the teftimony of three as famous Vniuerfities as any in *Chriftendome, Paris, Oxford, and*
Prage, Ioannes fucceffor Leonis 4, circa ann. Domini 854, & fe-
dit annis duobus & menfibus quinque: fœmina fuit, & in Papatu
impregnata. Iohn the fucceffor of Leo the fourth, who fate two
yeares and fiue moneths,was a woman,and in her Popedome was begotten with child. *Epiftola Parifienfis, Oxonienfis, Pragenfifq, V-*
*niuerfitatis,Romanis omnibus.*All before *Luthers* time,or at leaft
Luthers aduerfaries,and fuch as either wrote againft him,or in

Marianus
Scotus Sanct.
Martinus Po-
lonus.
Sigibert,Vo-
lateran.
Bergomenfis.
Sabellicus.
Tritemius.
Luitprandus,
Nauclerus.
Stella.
Chalcocõdila.
Barlaam.
Krantius.
Lucidus.
Rodeginus.
Fafcic. tem-
porum.
Bapt. Mantu-
anus.
Io. Pa n t.on.
Textor.
Platina.
Fulgofus.
Io. de Parifijs.
Petrarch.
Gotf. Viterb.
Boccace.
Rad.Ceftrenf.
Laziardus.
Alphonf. à
Cartagena.
Theodoricus
de Niem.
Schedel.
Gaffarus.
Charanza.
Barth.Caffan.
Carolus Mo-
lineus.
Flores tem-
porum.
Io.de Turre-
cremata con-
ftare dicit.

defence of the Popifh faction, whofe euidence is fo pregnant, fo apparent, ioyned with the ancient caruing at Rome, where her monument lay, till by *Pius* the fift it was demolifhed and caft into Tiber; and an ancient painting in Sienna, till it was defaced very lately by *Baronius* meanes and fuite; and in a pi-

De tempori-
bus mundi, æ-
tate 6. vel li-
ber Chroni
corum cum
figuris & ima
ginibus &c.

cture with a child in her armes in two impreffions, one anno 1494, the other anno 1497, both before *Luther* preached aboue twenty yeares, is to be feene vnto this day. Vpon fuch a cloud of witneffes, euen from their owne friends, in vn-fufpected times, before reformation of religion was either in-tended or pretended by *Luther*, can any be thought fo impu-dently paft fhame, as to deny it?

21 Yea we may call heauen and earth (perhaps hell, where fuch are, & wicked fpirits with whó they are)men, & Angels, and God himfelfe as witneffes againft them. Yet one *Onu-phrius* a Friar, *ergo* a lyar (according to the old prouerbe) hath broken the ice, to hard, frozen, brazen, iron impudency, that hath either fought to fhift off all authoritie, or to caft off all authors, as corrupt, or partiall, or with fome vniuft exception or other, with finne and fhame enough, to make voide this ftorie: fome others haue followed him in his fteps, haue ouer-taken and gone before him in his folly, madneffe, and out-facing impudencie : whofe vaine exceptions I will not dif-cuffe, onely that one I cannot omit : where fhe is termed *Io-*

Harding.

annes Anglicus Maguntiacus , as if it were vnmeafurable ab-furd to call her *Anglicus Maguntiacus* : as if it fhould fignifie an Englifh woman, borne at *Ments*, which indeed were ab-furd. But why cannot *Anglicus be* her furname, *Ments* the Ci-tie of her birth (as many haue anfwered,) and aboue other Maifter *Alexander Cooke* in his Englifh Dialogue, as well as the affigned Bifhop of *Bofonenfis*, is named *Iofephus Angles Va-lentinus: Iofeph Englifh* of *Valentia?* which fufficiently anfwe-reth M. *Hardings* friuolous quarrell . But I would aske this plaine queftion of our Romanifts, whether hiftories may ftand for times rule of *Antiquitie* to perfwade a truth?They will an-fwer as before out of *Canus*, that euery one or a few do not, efpecially if there be contradiction in others. But if all with

one

one confent, that were neareft thefe times, concutre in one, and no man till many hundred yeares after fome of them, and fometime after all, for aduantage, and to a purpofe excepteth againft the ftories, then is it certainely true as farre as humane authoritie can giue it certaintie. Yet becaufe this ftorie doth preiudice the vaunt of their perpetuall fucceffion; doth make vncertaine their pretended onely fufficient ordination; giues a fhreud fhake to their counterfeit rocke, which God knoweth hath wandered like a floting Iland this many hundred yeares, and with beating againft other fhores, hath fomed out her owne fhame; fiue or fixe and thirtie authors, conftantly, in diuerfe countries, in many ages, in Catholique Vniuerfities, Citizens of Rome, and officers in the Popes owne Court, fecular and religious, muft be all corrupted, falfified, denied, difcredited, fhaken off, branded with infamy, and all without fappe or fence, truth, or honeftie, learning or credit, onely to faue that frothie Sea from this filthy queane. And all this begun and fet on foot by that one confciencelcffe *Onuphrius*, whom Cardinall *Bellarmine* himfelfe reiecteth, as a contradictor of all *Anti-* De Rom. *quitie*, and auouching that, for which he hath no authoritie. I Pont.l.2.c.6. maruaile how they laugh not one at another, when they fee how they gull the fimple world, as the Arufpices did among Arufpex Athe Gentiles. The beft reafon they haue to weaken this ftorie, is, that *Anaftafius Bibliothecarius*, who liued about thofe times, maketh no mention thereof: but one of their own fellowes can moft wickedly fay, *Quàm impotens eft argumen-* Sonnius de *tum negatiuum fumptum ab authoritate Scripturarum?* How falfe verbo Dei is a negatiue argument drawne from the Scriptures? Then cap.14 15. how impotent, and impudent, is a negatiue argument, from a balductum hiftorian, an Abbot at moft of the Sea of Rome, that may be iuftly fufpected partiall, to faue his Maifters credit, whofe vaffall he liued and died? But fee how *Bellarmine* can helpe himfelfe in the like, if he haue but two authors, and thofe his friends, and liuing, the eldeft 500 yeares after Saint *Gregorie*, they muft be fufficient againft all filence. *For a thing may be true, though omitted by many: but to thinke that to*

*be falſe, which ſo many graue men and moſt worthy credit haue af-
firmed, may not be admitted.* But the caſe is altered, here they
ſpeake for themſelues, there they ſpeake againſt vs.

22 There was another Pope, *Sylueſter* the ſecond, that did
infeofe Antichriſt in the Roman Sea by Liuerie and Seiſin,
yea tradition and poſſeſſion of his owne perſon, into the
hands and power of Sathan, to the vſe of Antichriſt and his
ſucceſſors, till Chriſt ſhall aboliſh him by the brightneſſe of
his coming. This Pope obtained the Archbiſhoprickc firſt
of Rhemes, then of Rauenna, laſtly of Rome, *malis artibus*
by wicked meanes, by Symony, by the helpe of the diuell, to
whom he gaue himſelfe both body and ſoule, on condition
to liue till he ſaid Maſſe in Ieruſalem. The diuell accepted
the condition. *Sylueſter* entred poſſeſſion. The condition
expired, he reſigned his breath, and the diuell had his prey.

Polonus.
Platina.
Bembus.
Naucler.
Pet. Præmon-
ſtratenſis.
Tilmanus.
Anton.
Lyranus in 2.
Machab.
cap. 14. qui
allegat Guli-
erm. in Chrō.
Bellarmine.
Baronius.
Papyr. Maſſ.

All this *in full effect* is reported by a whole Thraue, or a com-
plete Iurie of twelue men, all Catholique Romaniſts of
vnſuſpected faith', when they ſerue our aduerſaries turnes.
It hath bene painted in a Chappell of holy roods called Ieru-
ruſalem, in Rome, as a Seminarie Prieſt acknowledged to
my ſelfe, and ſaid he had ſeene it himſelfe, or had very cre-
dibly heard it, I Remember not well whether. This paſſed
current ſome hundreths of yeares for a truth, without contradiction, now it is newly called into queſtion, and with
tooth and naile diſcredited and diſcarded, and *Sylueſters* reputation ſalued and patched vp, by wits ſet on malice, as
if the worſt were that he was a learned and skilfull Mathe-
matician, and in the ignorant world, onely reputed a
Magitian, or a Coniurer, that otherwiſe he was a learned and honeſt man. And let an *Onuphrius* of fiſtie
yeares old, or a *Bellarmine* vnder fortie, or a *Baronius* vnder thirtie out-beard and out-face all former *Antiquitie.*

23 The ſame may be ſaid of *Gregorie* the ſeuenth, of *Marcellinus,* of *Liberius,* and moſt of the moſt wicked Popes :
Iuab. de Va-
lentia, &c. who by great *Antiquitie* of Hiſtorie are diſcouered
to be rather monſters then men, rather Vicars of hell
then

then Vicars of Chriſt; and yet by our new Maiſters are iuſtified , commended , and they want little of Canonizing (ſome of them) for their Churches Saints.

24 That Pope *Iohn*, who in his life was moſt deſperatly wicked, in his death moſt damnably marked, a very incarnate diuell, if euer there were any: yet the moſt that *Bellarmine* ſaith of him is, that he was *Paparum ferè deterrimus*, al- *Bellarmine.* moſt the worſt of the Popes. If he ſay no more, he was bad inough, if he wanted but little of the worſt; but worſe then he none could be but the diuell himſelfe. Thus much for a taſte of our aduerſaries reiecting Hiſtories in the ſtories of the Popes.

25 If I ſhould ranſacke *Antiquitie*, from the villanies and diuelliſh tyrannies of the Popes, to the corruption of manners , in the citie and Court of that Sea, the conſpiracies of Cardinals, the preſumption of Prelates , the ignorance of Prieſts, the hypocriſie of Monks and Fryers , the helliſh confuſion of that infernall Hierarchie and Court; great volumes would not ſerue to contract that which is diſperſed in the bookes , of the Popes Secretaries, Chamberlaines, Bibliothecaries, friends , fellowes , followers , fauorites , men of their faſhion and faction. We haue their bookes, we made them not , our aduerſaries acknowledge them their owne and not ours, they abuſe them againſt vs, we vſe them aginſt their owne pewfellowes; Saint *Bernard*, *Gulielmus de Amore*, and who not? with many other learned men in their Treatiſes, their Sermons, their diſcourſes, yea as before is ſaid in the remembrance of Pope *Ioane* , Preachers , and painters and Poets in all tongues haue filled bookes, if not libraries, with the report of theſe things.

26 Yet now theſe ages are made moſt innocent , our times moſt corrupt; their Priſts then, as learned forſooth, as our Miniſters now are ignorant. All ſowre is ſweet , and Eſay 5. 20. ſweet is ſowre; error truth, and truth error; euill good, and good euill; if theſe new actuaries may be beleeued in this laſt age of the world , when they write grieuous Eſay 10. 1. thing. But wo vnto them that *iuſtifie the wicked for re-* & 5. 23. *wards*

S 4　　　　　*wards*

wards, and that take away the righteouſneſſe of the righteous from him.

27 Of theſe dayes, if euer it might be ſaid as the Prophet ſpake to the people of Iuda and Ieruſalem, ſo to Rome

Eſay 1.5.

and her Romaniſts: *They reuolted more and more, the whole head was ſicke, and the whole heart heauy. From the ſole of the foote, euen vnto the head, there was no ſoundneſſe* (in the Romane Synagogue,) *but wounds and bruiſes, and putrifying ſores, which were not cloſed, neither bound vp, nor mollified with ointment: Except there had bene a remnant left, they had bene as Sodome, and like vnto Gomorrha.* Such was the lamentable eſtate of theſe ignorant and ſecure times, by the report of all them that then wrote or ſpake; yet all this now not onely excuſed, but iuſtified, yea magnified in compariſon of the cleare Sunne-ſhine of the Goſpell of peace. Beleeue Hiſtories, you ſhall finde all this to be true; refuſe them, you ſhew that you deſpiſe an eminent euidence of *Antiquitie.*

28 Thus much being ſhortly ſaid of Hiſtories, it is a matter conſiderable, what theſe good men ſay of Hiſtoriographers, that haue left their painefull monuments to poſteritie. *Firſt, Melchior Canus* with one blaſt blowes away

Canus l.11.c.6

the credit of all Greeke Hiſtorians. *Græcorum (Hiſtoricorum) fides maiore ex parte fracta & debilitata eſt:* The credite of the Greeke Hiſtorie writers is for the moſt part crackt, and weakened. And afterward of *Diodorus,* of whom he ſaith, That he trifleth much in his Hiſtorie, and attributeth to him, as to all the Grecians, a very facilitie and facultie of lying, with this reaſon : *Quid enim leuius eſt in mentiendo quàm Græciæ regio vana, & ad omnem impulſum mobilis ?* For what is lighter in lying, then the vaine *Countrie of Greece, inconſtant vpon euery occaſion?* But I will proceede vnto particulars, and take all or the moſt part in *Campions* Catalogue, who are not onely receiued by him, but commended by other Catholique Romanes, yea and vſed ſometimes, abuſed often, as they make or ſeeme to make for their purpoſe.

29 *Euſe-*

29 *Eusebius* is the firſt; he is condemned à *Gelasio, à Ni-* E   Euſebius.
cena Synodo secunda, quòd Arianæ hæresis aſſertor; *of Gelasius,* of Canus l.11.c.6
the ſecond Counncell of Nice, becauſe he was an abettor of the Arian diſtinct.10.cap
hereſie. And againe: *Ne illa quidem quæ Euſebius ibi refert vera* Canus ibid. Sancta Rom.
ſunt omnia, quin reperias aliqua quæ verè reprehendas: Neither
is that verily which *Euſebius* reporteth, all true, but that you
may find ſome things worthy to be reprehended. Another
faith plainly, *Reijcitur Euſebius & cæteri: Euſebius is reiected* Sixt.Senenſis
and others, who in the ſupputation of the kings of the Medes and Bibl.ſanct. l.8.
Perſians, and in accounting their names and times, followed fabu-
lous Herodotus. Yet heare Cardinall *Baronius: Euſebius ended* Epit.pag.238.
his Chronicle in the twentieth yeare of the Emperour Conſtantine.
That is come to vs too, but mangled and corrupted. Hierome tur-
ning it into Latin, augmenting it vnto the time of Valentinian.This
is maimed and corrupted alſo. What credit is to be giuen to
him, that is condemned by a Pope and a Councell for a fa-
uourer of the Arians hereſie? that is *deceiued by a fabler in ſup-*
putation of times, perſons, names and numbers? that is mangled
and corrupted *in the originall and in the tranſlation?* Yea with
Bellarmine, he is in one place, *Grauiſſimus author, A moſt graue* De verbo Dei
author; in another place, *Erat hæreticis addictus,* He was too l.1.c.20.
*much addicted to hæreticks.*He giues him a plaiſter, and breakes lib.1.cap.26.
his head. And yet faith more, *Reſpondeo, locum Euſebij ſine du-*
bio eſſe corruptum: I anſwer, that the place of *Euſebius* is without doubt corrupted. What? of, and on? In this they play all
Ambidexters, as they do with all *Antiquitie*; and therefore
deſerue to be caſt ouer the barre.

30 The ſecond is *Damaſus,* a Biſhop of *Rome,* a frequent
author in the reformed Breuiarie, whom *Bellarmine* to proue De verbo Dei
Saint *Marks* Goſpell to be written in Latin, (a manifeſt vn- l.2.c.7.
truth) and for many other things throughout his works, maketh a claſſicall author, and faith, that he maketh that manifeſt, this cleare and almoſt out of queſtion.By whom he confuteth *Platina* and *Polydore Virgil,* and vpon his credit, giues
them the downeright lie. Would any reaſonable man thinke
that ſo great a man ſhould euer vndergo a rigid or hard cen- De Miſſa.lib.
ſure? you ſhall find he is not ſpared. For beſide *Binius,* *Baro-* 2.cap.15.
nius

mus and *Poſſeuine,* do ſentence his Pontificall to be none of *Damaſus* his doing; *Bellarmin* himſelf, who vſeth his authority as often as any man, & that in many things, as before is noted, yet with ſome paſſage of contempt reiects him. After he had caſt out *Faſciculum temporum,* and *Paſſionale* (and that perhaps worthily, though they haue now and then ſerued his friends turnes in ſome profitable affaires) with a *Meritò contemnimus,*

De Ro.Pont. lib.2.cap.5. *We worthily contemne them;* he addeth, *Nec multum me mouet Pontificalis Damaſi,* Yet am I not much moued with the authoritie of *Damaſus Pontificall,* or *Sophronius,* and *Simeon Metaphraſtes,* or what they ſay in the *life of Linus, that he died before Peter.* For *Sophronius* and *Metaphraſtes are but of the freſher ſort.* And *the booke that is attributed to Damaſus, is of vneertaine credit in this matter.* In this *matter?* but *he vſeth him in many other matters,* with euery blaſt he turnes as the weather-cocke.

Editio Concil. Veneta.tom.1 p.617.& 684. Tom.2.p.463 31   Another ſaith, that he doth *pugnare cum probatis & receptis omnibus hiſtorijs : He fights againſt all (euen all) approned and receiued hiſtories.* If this be true, what a ſhame is it, that Leſſons and ſtories ſhould be read in the Church vnder his name, that is not author of the booke? Or why ſhould the Breuiarie giue credit and countenance to that which hath no authoritie of it ſelfe?

De Sacramen. Euchar.l.2.c.1 *Bellarmine* hath a reaſon to proue the vaine ſtorie in the counterfeit Epiſtle to the brethren in *Achaia,* concerning Saint *Andrewes* martyrdome: Becauſe it hath bene read in the Church ſeruice. Why hath not this giuen the ſame reputation to *Damaſus?* Or why may not it make Friar *Surius* in time a claſſicall Author, whoſe geſts, or rather indeed ieſts, are ſo ſolemnly infarced into that now Romane reformed Breuiarie? Certainly the neweſt Legends ere long will outface the oldeſt ſtories of the Church, becauſe they are purpoſely prouided to ſtand in ſtead, vpon any aduantageable occaſion, though not now, yet perhaps hereafter. So prouident are they to deceiue their poſteritie. So either *Campions Damaſus* is no body, or *Campions* betters be deceiued.

32   Saint *Hierome* is next, one of the moſt laborious Fathers

thers of the Church. How he is vſed, is partly deliuered in
the former Chapter, among the Fathers. But in matter of ſto- Baron.epit.
rie, he hath his wipe too. His *tranſlation* and continuation of Pag.293.
Euſebius his Chronicle, is mangled and corrupted; therefore Bellar.de ver-
without credit. *Lyra* an old friend of the Romane Church, ſcript.l.2.c.10.
was miſ-led by him, who then will truſt him? Two Cardinals
crackt Saint *Hieromes* credit; how can we reſt on him that is Canus l.11.c.7
thus diſgraced? Yea when *Ioſephus* the Iew hath not leſſe credit in his ſtory then he.

33 *Ruffinus* is next, his opinion is approued by Cardinall De Concilijs
Bellarmine in one caſe, he is reiected in another : *Falſa expo-* l.2.c.8.
ſitio eſt, His expoſition is falſe. And *Melchior Canus* ſaith, *Quod* De Ro.Pont.
Ruffinus aſſerit, ex Patrum traditione eos libros à Canone reijcien- Canus.
dos (pace Lectoris dictum ſit) Patrum traditiones ignorauit : That
which Ruffinus ſaith, that by the traditiō of the Fathers thoſe books
were reiected out of the Canon (be it ſpoken by the Readers leaue)
himſelfe was ignorant of the Fathers traditions. A fickle anſwer
to ſo ancient an authoritie. In a caſe ſo true, that without all
exception, excuſe, or tergiuerſation, all the Fathers that mentioned the canon of the Scripture before *Ruffinus*, did exclude
all theſe *Apocryphals* ; yet this Catholicke anſwer ſerues, *He*
was ignorant of the Fathers traditions. But if he had not ſaid ſo,
he had ſhewed himſelfe ignorant of the Fathers traditions
indeed.

34 *Socrates* and *Sozomene* follow, whom I ioyne, becauſe I find them together in their reproofe. It is a wonder
that either *Campion* would name theſe, or *Canus* number Canus.
them ſuperlatiuely among *nobiliſſimos hiſtoricos*, ſeeing Cardinall *Baronius* ſaith of their ſtory of *Paphnatius* in the *Nicene*
Councell, *Falſum eſſe oportet, This muſt be falſe.* And for failing, in the margent is noted, *Falſi ſunt Socrates & Sozome-* Epitom.238.
nus: Socrates and *Sozomen* are falſe fellowes. And yet in the
ſame booke he alledgeth *Socrates* for the Biſhop of Romes
authoritie, without derogation to his credit. And good cauſe
why, for he makes for him.

35 *Cope* cals the ſame ſtory of *Paphnutius* into queſtion Dialog.n
(for in truth it drawes bloud from the Catholicke cauſe) becauſe

caufe *the whole matter depends vpon Socrates and Sozomen, of whom, one was a Nouatian, the other commends with great praifes Theodore Mopfueftenfis, who was condemned by the fifth Coun-*

De Imag.l.2. c.12.

cell. Cardinall *Bellarmine* can alledge them often when they make for him; but when they touch his freehold, and impeach the holy Fathers Crowne and dignitie, he accufeth and refufeth them at his pleafure, & that in very vile termes:

De Concil. authorit.l.2.c.8.

Non debet illis authoribus credi, Thefe fellowes are not to be beleeued. He taxeth *Socrates* with many lies, and that he was a *No-*

De cultu Sáct. l.3.c.20.
De Pœnitent. l.3.c.14.
De Cœlibat. c.6.

natian hereticke. And as for *Sozomen, Et non ignoramus Sozomenum in hiftoria multa mentitum,* We are not ignorant that *Sozomene in his hiftory hath lyed in many things.* And *Valentia, Non ignoramus Sozomenum multa alioqui mentitum effe: We are not ignorant that Sozomen lyed otherwife in many things.* What could be faid worfe of the impudenteft lyers that euer deferued the whetftone? Their credit is left paft all recouery. *So-*

Locorum.lib. 11.c.6.

crates hiftory pleafeth me not, faith *Canus*: he is a patron of *Origen, excufeth Neftorius, biteth Cyril.*

36   *Theodoret* hath the next place: he hath bene reafonably well bombafted among the Fathers, neither fcapeth he

Canus l.11.c.6

fcotfree among the Hiftorians; one for all: *Theodoretus fuit hoc nomine damnandus, Theodoret* was to be damned *euen vnder this title, who in truth was condemned in the fifth generall Councell.* Howfoeuer the matter be, *this patronizing of erronious fellows, weakens the authoritie and credit of his hiftory,* quoth *Canus.*

37   Now comes *Marianus Scotus*, fometime called *Sanctus*, a man ancient for yeares, vnfufpected for partialitie, no witneffe domefticall, our aduerfaries challenge him as their owne, he is in *Bellarmines* Catalogue of Catholicke authors:

Annal.tom.1. ad annum 34.

and *Baronius* hath entituled him a noble *Chronologer*: yet *Marianus* fares no better then his fellowes, nor worfe then his betters. In the ftorie of Pope *Ioane*, he is corrupted, as they would haue it appeare, by fome new found written copies in *Flanders*. A flim flam tale, deuifed to alleuiate his authoritie in that ftorie. But they go a nearer way to worke. Cardi-

De Ro. Pont. L.2.c.5.

nall *Bellarmine* faith peremptorily, *Marianum Scotum contemnimus, We contemne Marianus Scotus:* as who fhould fay,
he

he were not worth the naming, a Saint, a base fellow. What if a Proteſtant had anſwered thus?

38 Is *Sigebertus* any body? No: for either *aliquis impudens* Barnarſius, *Nebulo interpolauit ſcrepta eius, Some impudent Knaue hath corrupted his workes*; or there be diuerſe editions or manuſcripts, that will helpe out at a dead lift; or if no other honeſt ſhift will ſerue them, then cut him downe with *Sigebertus in hoc eſt fide indignus, In this matter Sigebert is worne out of credit*, as Cardinall *Bellarmine* will haue it, who may do what he will, De R6. Pont, for he is ouer his worke: Or, *O ſcelus, ô impoſtura, ô fraus, O wickedneſſe, O impoſture, O coſenage*, as Cardinall *Baronius*. Why? was he not one of their owne? Thus like filthy birds they betray their owne neſts. lib.4.cap.13. Analium. Tom.9 ann. 774.

39 *Zonoras* a Monke alledged and approued by Cardi- De R6.Pont nall *Bellarmine* againſt all *Antiquitie*, in the caſe of *Honorius*, l. 4.c.11. as if he were the onely Paragon, whoſe teſtimonie went beyond all. Yet in another caſe of the diſpute betweene *Sylueſter* De Concilijs and the Iewes, cauſed by *Helena* the mother of *Conſtantine*, he l.1.c.20. is reiected by the ſame Cardinall.

40 *Nicephorus* ſhall follow: and what of him? *Semper mihi audacior eſt viſus, He euer ſeemed to me ſomewhat too ſaw-* Maldonatus *cie or malapert* ſaith *Maldonatus*. As he erred with the Græ- præfat. in cians in his Diuinitie, ſo was it no maruell *that there are not a* Lucam. *few errors in matter of Hiſtory*, as is *euident by the Annales of* Bellarm. de Cardinall *Baronius*. A few more there are in *Campion*, in *Ca- ſcriptoribus nus* and others, accounted *inter nobiliſſimos Scriptores, the moſt* Eccleſi. in *noble writers of Hiſtorie*. But partly, I may ſay of the moſt part Niceph. of them as of theſe; partly if they thus deale with the beſt, what care they for the worſt? partly theſe are enough for examples in this kind; partly I haue not read ſo many pregnant exceptions againſt ſome others as againſt theſe, though I dare ſay they are very few that beare not their marke for ſome defect or other.

41 An example or two more. *Iulius Africanus* is forſaken Bellarm. de in that worke which is taken for his. He calleth the ſtorie of ſcript. Eccleſ. *Suſanna* a fable, therein he erred, *following the error of moſt lear-* Canus l. 11.c *ned men*. And therefore it was pittie that for one fault, he 7. ſhould

fhould be caft of by *Gelafius*, feeing his fault was common with fo many that were learned. Yet he is in this refufed, becaufe it maketh againft the Grand-maifters opinion, yea though he erre with the learned and with the moft of the learned.

De R6.Pont.
lib.2.cap.27.
Canus lib. 11.
cap.7.
42   *Epiphanius* a Greeke, a moft ancient and approued Author, faith Cardinall *Bellarmine*, *Nihil prorfus mouere nos debet : He fhould not moue vs at all*, faith *Canus. Firft*, becaufe in the difpofition of matters and times, *he neuer vfeth to follow any graue Authors, and againe he is deceiued vnto he remembrance of thofe things. Anaftafius Bibliothecarius* is fometimes a great man; not onely his word, but his very filence in the caufe of Pope *Ioane*, is more then a probable argument againft the great number and fhew of other writers that mention the ftorie. Yet *Caranza* doth fet him on the pillorie for *forgerie, for corrupting Damafus his Pontificall. Turrian* alledgeth a De fexta Synod.
De Concil.l.
1.cap.7. certaine *Hiftorian*, one *Theophanes*, but Cardinall *Bellarmine* likes not his opinion. Infinite more are there, fome of their owne, fome of more ancience times, whom either they difcredite and caft off in groffe, or except againft in fome particulars, or prohibite not to be read; or refine, or rather defile, if not in their purgatory fire, yet in their partiall fingers. And as they deale with other Authors, they make them fay what they lift, or vfe them as they pleafe.

43   We deale not thus with our aduerfaries. We take old Authors at their hands. We leaue them as we find them. We chaftife them not. We commit them not to the houfe of correction, nor burne them in their eares like rogues. We banifh them not out of the Church. We giue them their due and deferued refpect, and wifh with heartie defire, that they may be heard with indifferencie. For they teftifie not fo much the honour and vertues of the Popifh Church (as *Campion* pretendeth) as the incroachments of Popes vpon not onely their brethren and followers, but their Lords and Maifters. The Simonies and fchifmes, briberies, and braueries, the lawleffe luxurie and vnbridled tyrannie of the Sea of Rome . Not onely the violent and vniuft excommunications, but the murders

ders and maſſacres committed on the bodies of Saints: if they haue but touched the triple Crowne with their leaſt finger. Whence haue we the impious liues, the deſperate deaths, the craftie deſignes, the cruell executions, the palpable ignorance, the groſſe idolatry, the declining of religion and pietie, the increaſe of ſuperſtition and apoſtaſie of the Romane Synagogue, but onely in ſuch as they haue claimed for their owne Stories? written by Popes, by Cardinals, by Biſhops, by Abbots, by Monkes, by Friars, before *Luther* was heard of in the world; ſo that we may iuſtly ſay, *Ex ore tuo te indicabo, ſerue nequam*: Chriſt will iudge thee out of thine owne mont, thou wicked ſeruant.

44   Theſe foure euidences, *Scriptures, Councels, Fathers,* and *Hiſtories,* being the onely either certaine, or probable monuments of truth and *Antiquitie,* either by our chiefeſt aduerſaries challenged, or by vs granted; the firſt accounted by vs ſufficient of it ſelfe: It and all the reſt ſo qualified or rather quelled, chaſtiſed, corrupted, debaſed, and caſt off by them: with what countenance not brazened; or with what conſcience not ſeared, can they either obiect nouelty vnto vs, or vſurpe *Antiquitie* to themſelues? All or any of theſe we are well contented to admit, ſome vnder better termes and conditions, euery one vnder the ſame themſelues do.

45   What then remaineth, but that we reioyce and thanke God, for that he hath not left vs without the certaine teſtimonie of the moſt true and leaſt doubtfull *Antiquitie,* both of ages, and perſons, that do iuſtifie the veritie of our faith and religion, ſo accuſed of noueltie by our aduerſaries? as if all we haue, or profeſſe, began with *Luther,* or *Huſſe,* or *Wickliffe* at the fartheſt: theirs from the Apoſtles, as they pretend, at the leaſt. But he that hath an eye to ſee, or an heart to vnderſtand, may diſcerne euidently, and know perfectly, that we may ſay to the Popes teeth:

Hæc nouitas non eſt nouitas, ſed vera vetuſtas,
Relligio, & pietas, Patrum, inſtaurata reſurgit,
Quam tua corrupit leuitas & nota tuorum, Segnities.

This

This Neweneſſe is not new, this is true age;
Our faith and workes we haue from Fathers ſage.
But thine owne lightneſſe, and notorious ſloth
Of thy bad brood, hath now corrupted both.

46   From all theſe foure precedent Chapters, I therefore conclude: that the Church which hath not euery one of theſe, though it miſſe but one, yet hath not all *Antiquitie*: and that Church which depraueth or refuſeth all theſe, hath no *Antiquitie*. Now let the Chriſtian readers free their hearts from the captiuitie of Antichriſtian ſlauery, wherein they ſtand bound to beleeue what they are taught by that ſtep-mother, that ſeeketh the ſubuerſion of their ſoules eſtate: and iudge by that which hath bene ſaid, whether Proteſtants or Papiſts admit or reiect *Antiquitie*. If we admit it, do vs right, and ſlander vs not. If they reiect it, do them no wrong, but beleeue them not. So ſhall we retaine ſafely, you recouer your owne ſecurely, without partialitie, to vs, or them.

C H A P.   X.

In place of Canonicall Scriptures *, the Romaniſts obtrude Apocryphals, Traditions, which they call vnwritten verities, but indeed are vncertaine vanities, and vnfit to be vrged or vſed in queſtions of faith or manners.*

E haue ſufficiently if not abundantly ſhewed, how Romane Catholickes not onely irreuerently extenuate, but alſo blaſphemouſly reuile and raile vpon the Captaines of the hoſt of the liuing God: how they deſpiſe Gods ſcepter, and trample the word of his Teſta-

ment, ſealed with his precious bloud, vnder their feete, accounting it as vaine a thing to ſaue a Chriſtian ſoule, as *a horſe*

to ſaue a man; which is fearefull to conſider. Yet leſt they may ſeeme damnable, paſt all ſhame, they pretend that they haue the word of God, though not all written in the Canonicall Scriptures, yet either written Apocryphals, and vnwritten verities, which they hold to be as good, if not better then the
written

written word of God in the Canon of the Bible. So that this is our difference.

2 We would haue all queftions of faith and mannners debated, all doubts refolued, all herefies confuted, all truths confirmed, onely by the written and vndoubted word of God which is common to vs both. Our aduerfaries will none of this, as before is fhewed. The fuppofed defect wherof they would feeme to fupply with Apocryphall writings, againft all *Antiquitie* : The Religious light whereof they would extinguifh with an vnknowne tongue, againft all reuerend authoritie: The certaine truth whereof, they would fophifticate by obtruding a barbarous and falfe tranflation, againft the authentique credite of the Hebrew and Greeke Originals : The certaintie whereof they would make voide, by doubtfull, obfcure, yea oppofite vnwritten Traditions, which they call vnwritten verities, but are indeede meare vanities, if not groffe villanies, as fhall appeare.

3 When *Alexander* the Great was dead, and as fome thought, poyfoned, his Monarchie was prefently diftracted into foure pettie Kingdomes in comparifon of the entire. Thefe *reguli* warring one againft the other, came to fpeedy and finall defolation, and became a prey vnto the Romanes, who erected a great part of their Monarchy by their ruine. Thus thefe our Romanifts after they haue fhifted, ftrangled, poyfoned, and murthered the precious word of God, written by the diuine infpiration of the holy Ghoft, and the vndeceiuing penne of the holy Prophets and Apoftles, in the facred Scriptures: one part vfurpe the Apocryphals as their refuge; others ignorance of true Scripture for their skonfe, others falfe interpretations, for their fuccour; and others Traditions for their chiefe Citie of repofe and Caftle of defence. But all thofe fhifts will not ferue them, they will rather make paffage and way to the victorie and conqueft referued for truth.

Diodor.
Plutarch.

4 To handle all thefe, is not my purpofe, becaufe their abufe of Scriptures hath it paffage and due confideration

Suprà cap. 6.

T   al-

already and their Apocryphals with them. I will onely ſtand vpon Traditions, wherewith our aduerſaries do not onely ſhoulder out, but trample vnder foote, the diuine and vndoubted Scriptures. Theſe are by Doctor *Kelliſon* thus defined. *Tradition is nothing elſe but an opinion, or cuſtome of the Church, not written in holy Scriptures, but yet deliuered by the hands of the Church, from time to time, from Chriſtians to Chriſtians, euen vnto the laſt age,* If he had ſtayd at the firſt words, *Tradition is nothing, as an Idoll is nothing,* he had ſaid well. This may ſerue all ſorts of Traditions of the Romane Church. Of which notwithſtanding *Melchior Canus* is bold to pronounce, that *Plus habent virium quam Scripturæ aduerſus Hæreticos: Traditions haue more force againſt heretickes, then the Scriptures.* Wherein I beleeue him, if he meane the reformed Churches, by heretickes; for the Scriptures are certainly for vs, their Traditions we acknowledge to be againſt vs. And it is as true, as that the Biſhop of Romes Decretals do better faſten the triple Crowne vpon the Popes head, then all the Scriptures of the old and new Teſtament. But they may more truly ſay and plainly, that more hereſies haue bene and yet are ſupported and maintained by Traditions then by the written word, which is the fire that conſumeth the chaffe of mens deuices, and the onely *Malleus hæreticorum,* the onely hammer, that either bruiſeth the hearts of men and ſofteneth them to repentance, or breaketh them in peeces, and beateth them to death through obſtinacie in misbeleeſe. If he meane heretickes indeed, it is vtterly falſe. For I dare boldly ſay, and all *Antiquitie will abet the ſame,* that all the heretickes of ancient time, with all their hereſies, haue bene confuted by the Councels and Fathers of the Primitiuetimes onely by the Scriptures.

5 As for vs, by that which they call hereſie, I may ſay often and iuſtifie it truly, *We ſerue the God of our Fathers, obſeruing all that is written in the Law and the Prophets, and haue hope towards God, that the reſurrection of the dead, which they themſelues alſo looke for, ſhall be both of iuſt and vniuſt.* Let them remoue vs from this hold, by theſe meanes, and we will confeſſe

Marginal notes:

Suruey.lib.8. c.3.

1.Cor.8.4.

Loc.com.l.3. c.3.

Ierem.23.29.

Act.24.14.

feffe our felues heretickes indeed, and increate to be reformed by them. They refufe this condition to trie with vs.
They cannot conuince vs of any errror by the Scriptures,
and therefore they flie vnto their vncertaine Traditions Of
which another of their locufts faith: *Si Paulus ille Tarfenfis.* F.Nicol.Hei-
If that fame Paul of Tarfus, that elecl inftrument of diuine Philo- brō de gene-
fophie, fhould condemne any Traditions of the Catholique Church, ralibus notis
yea of the Popifh, (for of this onely do we Orthodoxes depend) or Etiamnum
the Decrees, which for the common vtilitie, the edification of the Papifticæ.
faithfull and peace, are indulged as our aduerfaries ficlen : I would
confidently profcribe him, abandon him, pronounce Anathema,
with direfull execrations againft this Saule , (and would fepe-
rate him) *both from Chrift and from his Church.*

6 I neuer yet heard, or read, fo zealous a paffage either
fpoken or written, by any Papift, for, and in defence of the
knowne Scriptures, as this is for Traditions and Decrees.By
which we may eafily perceiue, what account is made of this
Dalila among the Romifh Philiftims. By helpe whereof they Iudg.16.19.21
would pollthe haire, & then put out the eyes of *Sampfon*, the
Champion of God. That which Saint *Paul* applieth to the
corrupters of the Gofpell , that this heart-burnt *Abaddonift,*
applyeth vnto the refufers of Traditions and Decrees. Yet
another Romanift, not a locuft of the wildernéffe, on which
Saint *Iohn* Baptift fed, but a depopulating locuft, that afcended out of the pit to confume Gods fruite, faith worfe in my
conceipt then all thefe, in fetting to fale this ware. *Quin imo* Socolouius.
in hoc Traditio fuperat Scripturam , quòd tempore prior fit , quòd Partit.Ecclef.
clarior, quòd latiùs pateat, nec corrumpi, nec interire, nec in varios pag.758.
fenfus ita facile torqueri poffit. This Tradition ouertoppeth ,,
the Scripture, becaufe it is older for time, clearer, larger; ,,
can neither be corrupted, nor perifh, or be drawne into di- ,,
uerfe fences, fo eafily as Scriptures may.   ,,

7 Cardinall *Bellarmine* hath a long difpute of this matter
of Traditions, and will haue fome Diuine, fuch as Chrift
taught and are not written in the Gofpels; fome Apoftolicall, preached by the Apoftles, but not written in their E-
piftles, Acts or Prophecies ; the third Ecclefiafticall, fince
Decreed

decreed by Councels, or determined by Popes, and receiued of that Church which they call, and onely accompt, Ca-
Bell.de verb. tholique: or to take *Bellarmine* in his owne words, *Not theſe*
De1.l.4.c.2. *which are decreed, but vſurped, and taken vp, as certaine ancient*
cuſtomes, begun, either by the Prelates or people, which by little
and litle, by the ſilent conſent of men haue obtained the force of a
Law. The diuine and Apoſtolicall haue the ſame authoritie
with the written Scriptures of the new Teſtament. Which
though they haue nothing but truth, yet containe they not
all truth in the Romaniſts conceipt, and therefore (as is ſaid)
their defeƈt muſt be ſupplied with theſe Traditions. The Eccleſiaſticall are of the ſame accompt with the written Canons, and regiſtred Decrees of the Councels and Popes:
which are ſometimes reckened to be equall with the foure
Campion. Euangeliſts, and Canonicall Scriptures; euen Trent, with the
rat.4. beſt former, and the laſt with the firſt Decretals; and ſo by
conſequent all theſe Eccleſiaſticall Traditions are as good as
the Apoſtolicall or Diuine, & ſo as the written word of God.

8   Our difference with the Romaniſts ſtands not in this,
whether the diuine and Apoſtolicall Traditions be equall
with the Scriptures; we will confeſſe it. For we doubt not,
but that the Apoſtles preached nothing but the ſubſtance
thereof is written: and let our aduerſaries direƈtly and de-
monſtratiuely proue, that Chriſt or his Apoſtles taught any of
thoſe things which they obtrude vpon the Church, (though
not written,) we will receiue them as the word of God. But
this they ſhall be neuer able to do: and therefore we deferre
the triall of all truth to the certaine and vndoubted written
word, that is, the Canonicall Scriptures of God. In which
caſe we may be bold to ſay, euen with the Conuenticle of
Seſſio.4. Trent it ſelfe, that we *receiue and reuerence* with equall *pious*
affeƈtion, all that Chriſt or his Apoſtles taught by word of
mouth, whether they concerne faith or manners, euen as well as
the Scriptures themſelues. For certainly they ſpake nothing
contrarie to that which is written. But there are many Traditions fathered vpon the Apoſtles and Chriſt himſelf, which
were neuer ſpoken of, or thoght of by the͂: & which are quite

kam

kam, and cleane contrary to the Scriptures. We will not be gulled with thefe vnder any pretence: proue them Chrifts, we accept them with all humilitie; if you cannot proue them, we reiect them with all feueritie. Of the Iewifh expofitions and Traditions, this hath *Solo-Maior: Cuiufmodi expo-* ^{In Cant.cap.4.} *fitiones feu Traditiones fuo idiomate appellare folent, Hebr ai, Caba-* ^{pag.935.} *la, Græce autem Deuterofes dicuntur, eafq; expofitiones feu Traditiones maximè venerantur, & quafi numen quoddam adorant Iudæi.* Such expofitions and Traditions the Hebrewes in their owne tongue call *Cabala*; but in Greeke *Deuterofes*; and thefe expofitions and Traditions the Iewes exceedingly reuerence and adore as a certaine diuine Godhead. The Papifts, with as good reafon, and no better, make Gods word of their vaine and idle Traditions, and worfhip and adore them as the very Scriptures of God.

9 I hold it but a fory confequent to fay, *Chrift did many* ^{Iohn 10.} *things which are not written* , therefore there is not fufficient written for our faith and faluation; for *fo much is written that we might beleeue, and in beleeuing haue euerlafting life.* Or that thefe were the things which Chrift did, or the Apoftles preached, which are now offered vnto the Church for fuch. We denie peremptorily that any of thefe Traditions , which are pretended, and concerne beleefe or manners, are either Chrifts or his Apoftles, if they be not in the Scriptures. For fome of them are erronious, fome blafphemous, fome wicked, fome idolatrous, fome contradicted, fome vtterly abandoned, fome old, now antiquated, fome were lately obtruded; none of thefe fo proued as may conuince the vnderftanding conftantly to beleeue them . And therefore one of the Romane Captaines faith ingenioufly, that, *Quj omnes Tradi-* ^{Lindan.Pano.} *tiones paris authoritatis putarit, infignis temeritatis, ne dicam ve-* ^{l.4.pag.478.} *fania, condemnandus eft; quædam enim funt nullius fidei: He that thinkes all Traditions to be of like authority, is to be condemned, not only of notable rafhneffe, that I fay not of madneffe; for fome of them are of no credit.* Let his fellow *Herburne* cenfure him for his fpeech, who would curfe Saint *Paul* if he faid fo much. For ^{Supra § 5.} certainly they haue all the like credit in the Romane fyna-

T 3　　　　　gogue

gogue for ought I know. But for their conuenience or near-
neſſe vnto the ſimilitude of truth, there may be difference,
ſome nearer, ſome farther off. The proofes in this caſe of ſuch
moment, muſt be demonſtratiue, and *luce clariores*, as cleare
as the Sunne. We cannot take one Father for one, and another for another tradition; eſpecially if they erre neuer ſo litle from the written word. But they muſt be deduced *à pri-
mordijs Eccleſiæ*, from the very beginning of the Church, continually teſtified by ſucceſſion of writers, Fathers and hiſtories, before we may iuſtly affoord them the reputation of
probabilitie: and on that condition, being not repugnant to
the Scriptures, we will accept them.

    10 We cannot ſuffer our ſelues to be made ſo very ſots,
Petrus à Soto. as to hold with *Petrus Soto* quite againſt *Lindan: Infallibilis eſt
regula & Catholica, quæcunque tenet, credit, & ſeruat Eccleſia
Romana, & in Scripturis non habetur, illa ab Apoſtolis eſſe tradita.*
*This is an infallible and Catholicke rule, that whatſoeuer is held,
beleeued and obſerued of the Romane Church, and is not in the
Scriptures, that is deliuered by the Apoſtles.* Vnder this veile
may infinite abſurdities lye couered, and any thing be thruſt
vpon the Church of God for diuine and Apoſtolicke traditions. And indeed it hath brought as many falſe doctrines
into the Church in truth, as *Pandoras* boxe diſperſed plagues
into the world in fiction. Yet if they will needs giue ſo much
credit to the Church, that we muſt receiue and accept, whe-
Hoſius. ther *ſcriptum* or *non ſcriptum*, written or not written traditions, *and meete them with both armes, and follow them with great
deuotion*: yet let vs receiue them from that Church that is
qualified as the Cardinall would haue it: *Vna, ſancta, Catholica, Apoſtolica,* the onely one Church of Chriſt, *the holy, vniuerſall, Apoſtolicke Church.* But this is not the Church of *Rome*,
which is neither one, but deuided; not holy, but wicked; not
vniuerſall, but priuate; not Apoſtolicke, but moderne, and
of yeſterday in compariſon of the Apoſtles times. She is the
mother of fornications. And therefore our Nouellants at this
day, either aſſume that which is not granted, and they can neuer proue, or implicate a contradiction, which they can neuer.

uer reconcile, to make their priuate the vniuerfall Church.
And therefore call it, *Ecclefia Catholica Romana, The Catholick*
Romane Church : that is, the vniuerfall priuate Church, as is
before remembred. The one, true, *holy, Catholicke and Apofto-* Supra cap. 4.
licke Church, neuer knew nor heard of many of thofe traditions which are now equalled, yea I fay preferred, before the
Scriptures of God. And therefore we cannot receiue them
from that holy Mother, who receiueth nothing but from the
hand of her fpoufe, and his vndoubted *Vicar,* which is the holy *Ghoft* : as Cardinall *Hofius* is contented to fay; and that not Tom.2.c.32.
onely fuppofed or furmifed, but as reuealed in that booke
which is fealed with the bloud of the Lambe, euen the will
and teftament of God the Father, and his bleffed Sonne Iefus
Chrift.

11   With what face then could *Pighius*, when he had
not onely grunted like a hog, but roared like a bull againft
the Scriptures, renouncing them for fole or fufficient iudges
in matters of faith, fay vnto the Pope? or how could his Apo-
ftaticall Holineffe endure to heare this impudent and fearfull
blafphemie? *Huic tam fœcundæ malorum omnium radici fecurim* Pigb.in præfa,
imprimis admouere vifum eft : I haue thought good principally to
lay the axe vnto this fertile roote of all euill, that is, triall by the
Scriptures. *To the plucking vp whereof by the rootes, I haue coun-*
ted it aboue all things neceffary, to demonftrate by moft cleare rea-
fons, that the Authority of Ecclefiafticall tradition is no leffe, that
I fay not more ample and powerfull, then the Scriptures? What a
plague do they account the Scriptures of God vnto themfelues? how do they feare them? how do they not onely e-
quall, but preferre traditions before them? and that not only
diuine or Apoftolicall, as Cardinal *Bellarmine* diftinguifheth,
but euen Ecclefiafticall alfo? for that is *Pighius* his word.
Whereby it is euident, that either he knew not the Cardinals diftin&ion, and fo flipt a gawdie, or elfe he voluntarily
puts in the very worft of all kinds, and preferres them to the
Scriptures. And left you may take this but as one Do&ors o-
pinion, let him take a Bifhop with him, who faith, that this
truth is moft certaine, whereby all the Lutherans herefies

Simanca de
Ecclef. §. 26. are plainly confuted. *Quòd Ecclefiæ Traditiones,&c.That Tra-*
ditions of the Church, in matters of faith and manners, although
they be not written, is no leſſe authority then the holy Scriptures.
And if this will not ſerue , he may take a Cardi-
nall to them both, who attributes as much to his *Tra-*
ditions as he doth: *Adeo non minùs graue flagitium viſum eſt Ec-*
cleſiaſticam conſuetudinem contemnere, quàm diuinam legem præ-
uaricari : It ſeemes no leſſe wickedneſſe to contemne Eccleſiaſticall
cuſtome, then to breake the law of God. It is not to be maruelled
then, that Cardinall *Hoſius* tels vs , that *Proprium ſemper hoc*
fuit hæreticorum axioma, nihil eſſe recipiendum præter Scripturas:
That this hath alwayes bene the proper axiome of hereticks, that
*nothing ſhould be receiued but the Scriptures.*For they haue found
a better thing for their purpoſe , and therefore leaue theſe
tanquam nullius in bonis occupanti, as no mans goods to the oc-
cupier, euen to thoſe that they call heretickes. Let me be one
of theſe hereticks that are ſo religiouſly affected to the written word, and will be ſaued by it. And let this be the counterfeit Catholicks generall rule, that what they cannot proue
by the certaine word of truth contained in the Scriptures,
they will defend by vncertaine, obſcure and baſe Traditions, yea many things quite contrary to diuine Scriptures.
The while, it is worthy obſeruation , how this monſtrous
Genef. brood ingenders a Mule from an Aſſe and a Mare.For *Bellar-*
De verbo Dei *mine* will proue that their Traditions be good, becauſe here-
lib. 4. cap 8. tickes will none of them. And Biſhop *Lindan* proues them
Panopl.lib. 2. as good, becauſe heretickes alledge them. Like *Sampſons*
foxes, though their heads be aſunder, their tailes meete together; their premiſes contrary, yet the ſame concluſion.

12   I cannot but hold it ſtrange, that after all theſe monſtrous ſpeeches of Traditions, one of their owne, that would
ſeeme to hold vp the walls of the holy Citie, vpon two foundations, that *Quis non horreat Catholicos, ſi de illis verè queſtus*
eſt Philippus, ſuas Traditiones longè accuratius ſeruari poſtulant
quàm Euangelion? ſed minimum hoc ſtolidiſſimi Philippici cerebri
phantaſma eſt. quod nec in animam, nec in os, nec in calamum vllum
33 *Catholicum venit:* Who would not but abhorre the Catholiks
if

if *Philips* complaint were true of them, that they require a ,,
great deale more obſeruation of their Traditions, then of the ,,
Goſpels; which neuer came into a Catholicke ſoule, nor ,,
mouth, nor pen . Reade but what is ſaid in the ſixt Chapter ,,
of contempt of Scriptures, and that immediatly before in this, Socolounis.
and it will make any holy Chriſtians heart abhorre Romane
Catholickes indeed. *Ex ore tuo te iudico*, nay, thou *iudgeſt thy
ſelfe* by thine owne mouth *thou wicked ſeruant*. Yet his after
ſentence is ſomewhat more modeſt then his fellowes; when
he ſaith, a Chriſtian may defend his faith two waies. Firſt, *Diuinæ legis authoritate, tum deinde Eccleſiæ Catholicæ Traditione*.
Firſt by the authoritie of the diuine Law, thē by the Tradition
of the Catholick Church. Here the Scriptures are firſt indeed,
but argued of defect, to be ſupplied by Traditions of the
Church, neither diuine, nor Apoſtolicall.

13 If the queſtion in this caſe were but of Ceremonies
and circumſtances, we would not ſtriue. For peace and vnitie, much would be yeelded vnto out of diſcretion: as
Saint *Paul* did, for a vow and ſhauing of his head, and a puri- Act.21.24.
fication; or as all the Apoſtles did for a time in things ſtran- Act.15.29.
gled and bloud. But our queſtions are of the matter and ſubſtance of Religion : to grant what they would haue we account preiudiciall to our ſaluation; the deniall whereof our
aduerſaries repute hereſie; and call vs heretickes, a grieuous
imputation, not to be borne. *Noli in ſuſpicione hæreſeos quen-* Hieron. ad
quam eſſe patientem , ne apud eos qui ignorant conſcientiam eius, Pammach.
*diſſimulatio conſcientiæ iudicetur, ſi taceat. Endure not any man
in the ſuſpicion of hereſie, to be patient, leſt among thoſe who
know not his conſcience, if he be ſilent, his diſſimulation be
taken for conſcience :* In which caſe no honeſt man may be
ſilent.

14 It is hereſie againſt the Romane Church not to beleeue Petrus à Soto.
rightly the *Oblation in the ſacrifice of the altar , Inuocation of
Saints, Merit of works, the Primacie of Biſhops of Rome*, moſt of
the *Sacraments* of their new religion, prayer for the dead, *Auricular confeſſion, neceſſitie of ſatisfaction*, to let paſſe diuers matters about the Sacraments: *As vnction of Criſme, conſecration of
water*

*water in Baptisme, the whole Sacrament of Confirmation, the ele-
ments, words and effects of the Sacrament of Order, Matrimonie*
Suruey lib. 8. cap. 3. §. 4. *and extreme Vnction.* Doctor *Kellison* confesseth also, that *The
Reall presence, the sacrifice of Masse, the fast of Lent, Images, holy
water, the signe of the crosse,* and such like, are Traditions. These
with diuerse others are capitall and deadly, defended by fire
and sword, and haue spilled the bloud of many a good Christian. We hold some of them superstitious, some blasphemous,
some both; all vnnecessary, vngodly, and derogatorious to the
truth of God, receiued in his word, the kingdome and merits
and mediation of the Sonne of God. There are many other of
great moment with them, that appeare vnto vs most vaine:
diuers that in the Primitiue Church were common, which
now are antiquated, forsaken and forgotten. Sundry of new
inuention which the ancient Fathers neuer heard of. Yet consider them how you will, and let them be what you will, this
is *Infallibilis regula, an infallible rule,* and Catholicke, that is ge-
Idem supra hoc cap. nerall, *That whatsoeuer the Church of Rome beleeueth, holdeth
and keepeth, and are not in the Scriptures, are deliuered by the A-
postles.* And again, *The obseruation of which, the beginning, author,*
Salmeron in Epist. Pauli, lib. 1. part. 3. disput. 8. *or origine, is not knowne or cannot be found, those are without
doubt Apostolicall Traditions:* but *extra sacras litteras,* they must
be out of the Scriptures, or no bargaine, no traditions.

15   Which rules holding *Infallible,* what Labyrinth may
the faith of Christians be led into, that no *Ariadnes* threed,
will bring it out? I purpose not to stand on the distinctions of
Traditions, how many sorts of them are mentioned by Authors, nor in the confutation of euery particular, or examination of their age or authoritie, which all are found in most
writers of controuersies on both parties, which is done e-
nough to my purpose out of *Bellarmine* alreadie. My only drift
is to lay open two notorious frauds in this question of Traditions, which our aduersaries haue vsually proposed and practised, to delude and misleade simple Christian people, and as
I verily beleeue, against their owne consciences.

16   First to colour the worst, they haue some which they
call Traditions and are not, for as they be plainly in the Scriptures,

tures, or by fuch neceſſary collection and deduction drawne
from thence, that they may iuſtly challenge their prerogatiue
from the Scriptures, as many of the Fathers, and namely *Epi-*
phanius taketh them, *Traditiones Patrum ex Prophetis, & lege,* Epiphan.
& Apoſtolis, & Euangeliſtis. The traditions of the Fathers out
of the Prophets, and the Law, the Apoſtles, and Euangeliſts:
ſo are they no traditions. Such may be certaine words, applied to matter in the Scriptures, as ὁμούσιον, or the *Trinitie,* or
the baptizing of children, and the like. And ſuch our aduerſaries pretend ſome of theirs to be, from which they ſince
are driuen. *Salmeron* ſeemeth to take Tradition in the
ſence with many of the Fathers. *Non omnia ſimul tradita ſunt,* In Epiſtolas
&c. Al things were not deliuered at once, *but Tradition increa-* B. Pauli. lib. 1.
ſed by little and little, the Prophets followed Moſes, and the Epi- part. 3. diſp. 8.
ſtles, the Goſpell. Whereof he ſeemeth to me to make a mad ››
collection. *Hinc colligi poteſt, Hence it may be gathered, that all* ››
things were not deliuered by the Apoſtles, but thoſe things which ››
for that time were neceſſary, and which were fit for the ſaluation of ››
the beleeuers; and he giues for this, as profound reaſons. For ››
otherwiſe, *we ſhould need neither Chriſt to be with vs, to the end* ››
of the world, nor the holy Ghoſt to inſpire vs, nor Paſtors and Do- ››
ctors to teach vs, yea we ſhould be worſe prouided for then the Sy- ››
nagogue, Neque bene eſſet conſultum ſimpliciter Eccleſiæ. Neither ››
plainly ſhould the Church haue bene well prouided for.

17 Vnder this colourable pretence they haue ſo peeced
their Traditions to the Scriptures, as they repaired *Theſeus* Plutarch.
ſhip, till it put the Philoſophers to their diſpute whether it
were the old ſhip, or a new. For ſo haue the Romaniſts confounded their traditions with the Scriptures, as that they know
not which is old, which is new, which in time they would
haue made like a Capuchins cloke that is neuer but one,
though it haue not one rag of the firſt left. Howbeit of theſe
Scripture Traditions, there is neither ſcruple nor queſtion betweene vs and them. Neither in deed can theſe by them be
called Traditions at all.

18 For they hold Traditions to be truths not contained in
the Scriptures, which cauſeth their diſtinction of the word of
God

God written, and not written. Whereby their egregious wickedneſſe doth moſt euidently appeare. For as long as ignorance blinded the eyes of men, and the veile of darkneſſe
was drawne ouer their hearts, all, or the moſt part of their Traditions, were they neuer ſo new, neuer ſo abſurd, were once a-
uouched from the Scriptures, as if they had bene moſt pregnantly proued by them. But when the ſophiſtications and abſurd conceits of the Romane Church were diſcried and diſcouered, and the true ſence of the Scriptures by diligent enquirie boulted out; then they had no other ſhift but impudently
to hold the concluſions, without their ancient premiſes, and
to diſpute like skilfull Lawyers, from *Titulo non ſcripto, lege
nulla, paragrapho nuſquam* or *nunquam*: Lawes vnmade,
words vnwritten, learning neuer heard of, neither any where
to be found.

The bee-hiue of the Romane Church

19 For example, take any of *Soto* or Doctor *Kelliſons* Traditions, or almoſt any other that are controuerted betweene
the Court of Rome and the Church of God, and obſerue
which of them hath not had the pretence of Scripture vpon
Scripture, text vpon text, and Apoſtle vpon Prophet to proue
them. Yet now they are only Traditions not written. Whereby it is notoriouſly euinced, that when they alledged Scripture
for theſe, and many other, either they did it out of groſſe
and palpable ignorance, ſpeaking that which they vnderſtood not, and that muſt be their beſt excuſe; or elſe out of
a deſperate hardneſſe of heart and wilfull malice, falſly alledging, and damnably abuſing the holy Scriptures of God,
for matters not at all contained in them, and that vpon their
knowledge.

20 The other is, that in ſtead of the onely written word of
God, of which there is no doubt or ſcruple, they ſubſtitute
and ſuborne, vncertaine, vnknowne, various, temporary and
tranſitory Traditions in their roome. Of which they can fetch
ſtore when they pleaſe, and from whence they liſt, and make
them outcountenance the gracious face of the bleſſed Sonne
of God, ſhining in the holy Scriptures of the Prophets and A-
poſtles.

21 *Poſſunt*

21 *Poſſunt eſſe nouæ Traditiones:* There may be new Tradi- In Rom.l.1.
tions, reſpecting both faith and manners, although they be neither
made nor deliuered by the Apoſtles, faith *Salmeron.* This Tradi- In Rom.l.1.
tion without all Apoſtolicall authoritie, *Eſt in primis adſa-* part.3.diſp.8.
*lutem neceſſaria,*faith he, is chiefly neceſſarie to ſaluation, and
more by *much, then the Scripture it ſelfe.* And this he indeuo- Adeo magis
reth to fortifie by many reaſons. As if we *could neither haue* quàm ipſa
the Scriptures canonized, nor a true tranſlation allowed, nor Scriptura.
a certaine interpretation approued, nor find the *iuſt num-*
ber of Sacraments; nor gouerne the Church, nor aſſoyle doubts,
*without Tradition.*Which is all vtterly falſe, except he meane
the Sacraments of the Roman Synagogue,which indeed can
neuer be found in Prophet or Apoſtle. Much more to
this effect hath the ſame Author in the ſame place, as abſurd as this, whereof let it not ſeeme tedious to reade a little more.

22   *Qui non credit Traditioni in Eccleſia recepta:* He that ,,
beleeueth not the Tradition receiued in the Church, but ſeeketh ,,
for Scripture, is like an euill debter, that will not pay his debt, ex- ,,
cept he ſee his obligation, whereas it is enough to produce ſufficient ,,
witneſſes. But if *ſometimes falſe and corrupt Traditions are* ,,
brought forth, we muſt not marueill thereat, becauſe heretiskes ,,
haue corrupted ſome Scriptures, yet notwithſtanding by Tradition ,,
we may know both falſe Scriptures and falſe Traditions. And yet ,,|
more : *Traditio eſt antiquior Scriptura,&c. Tradition is more* ,,
ancient then Scripture, yea by ſo much more ancient, as the prea- ,,
*ching of the Apoſtles in time preuented their writings.*Yet againe, ,,
The Scripture could not be Iudge of the emergent doubts which a-
roſe. And in ſhort concludeth, *Petenti ergo Scripturam,* oppo-
*nenda eſt Traditio quam commendat ipſa Scriptura:*To him therefore that requireth Scripture, oppoſe Tradition, *which the*
Scripture it ſelfe commends. I may inferre a better concluſion
vpon theſe words: Therfore the Romane Traditions are oppoſite to the Scriptures, by the Ieſuites confeſſion, though
this followeth not by demonſtration neither.

23   To expreſſe what hath bene ſaid more plainly, you
may obſerue of the firſt ſort of Traditions grounded vpon
the

the Scriptures, The myfterie of the Trinitie, which is the subfiftence of three perfons in one God. The confubftantialitie of the Sonne with the Father. The Baptizing of Infants, and fuch, as though the termes whereby the matter is expreffed, be not in fo many fyllables or words in the Scripture, yet the doctrine which vnder thofe words taught, are truly contained in them. So is it lawfull to deuife words to expreffe more plainely to our vnderftanding the true meaning of Gods word. But we muft not wreft Scriptures to

Hilari.

fhrowd falfhood vnder our words. *Non fermoni res, fed rei eft fermo fubiectus.* The matter may not be fubiected to the words, but the words muft be apted to the matter. So that neither are the doctrines contained in thofe words, holden by Tradition, but by Scriptures. Neither are the words whereby thofe doctrines are deliuered Apoftolicall, but by the ancient Fathers in approued Councels and their learned writings applyed vnto the Euangelicall and Apoftolicall Scriptures.

Partition.Ecclef.pag. 757.

24 *Socolouius* me thinkes giues not an ill obferuation in this kinde. *Sic filium Dei* ὁμοούσιον *Patri credimus. So we beleeue the Sonne of God to be confubftantiall with his Father, becaufe the Nicene Councell fo defined it, albeit this name be not found in the holy Scripture. So that the holy Ghoft is of the fame fubftance with the Father and the Sonne, and proceedeth from them both, be-*

Ex Scripturis ita fanxerunt.

caufe the Conftantinopolitan and Romane Synods at the fame time out of the Scriptures eftablifhed it. If our aduerfaries would bind 'themfelues to the imitation of thefe examples, we would heartily accept fuch Traditions, and ioyne with them.

25 Howbeit the Tradition which the Romanifts moft ftand vpon, and vrge vs with, is the authoritie of the Scriptures themfelues: which they hold cannot be knowne by the Scriptures, nor any other meanes, but onely by the Tradition of the Romane Paraclete, the Pope and his Church. This Doctor *Kellifon* prefumeth we muft confeffe; without which confeffion we can neuer know the Scriptures to be Scriptures, more, as one faith, then any other writings to be

the

the word of God. He faith farther, that there is no poſſibilitie to know them, but by the Romane Church : yea no re- Suruey.l.8,c.3
medy but we muſt fall into plaine Atheiſme, and flatly deny
that there are any Scriptures at all. For all which he giueth
doubty reaſons. We cannot beleeue the Scriptures without
the Romane Church, this is preſumed. We may not beleeue
them for the authoritie of the Romane Church. For we beleeue her not in other things, therefore we muſt not in this.
Though this be but a poore inference(for if ſhe hold nothing
true, the diuell is in her indeed,)yet as I ſaid already, ſo I ſay
againe: We beleeue it not for the Romane Church, but for
their Ancients the vndoubted and renowmed Churches of
the Iewes and Grecians, in whoſe tongue they were written, and from whom the Romanes themſelues receiued
them.

26 Neither do I ſee any reaſon why we ſhould be turned to the troubled riuers, when the cleare fountaines are
as open to vs as vnto them ; when our acceſſe is as eaſie, the
way as certaine, and all other meanes concurring to our iuſt
ſatisfaction, as vnto theirs. We will not confeſſe our ſelues
beholding to the Romane Church at all. The Iewes haue
theirs in Hebrue, the Grecians theirs in Greeke vnto this
day. Our learned men are as able, and ſhew themſelues
more wlling, to tranſlate them into Latine, and all other
tongues then they are; and therefore if their vulgar tranſlations, and what elſe they haue beſide, were not onely hid
in a wall, as the Law was when *Hilchia* found it in the dayes
of *Ioſiah* cut with a penknife, and burnt in the fire, as Ierem.22.
Iehoiachim did *Ieremies* booke, or buried in the graue with
the Romane ſuperſtitious *Numa*, we cold fetch it where they Plutarch in
ſcorne to ſeeke it, and bring it forth leſſe tainted then that Numa.
they onely offer vs. And therefore the Doctors reaſon in this
caſe is not worth a raiſin nor yet a currant.

27 He farther asketh, Will you alledge Tradition? and
without a fee anſwereth for vs. That ſo we ſhould giue contradiction to our owne poſitions. But who made him our
Atturney? we are old enough to anſwer the Srribes and Pha-

riſes

rifes our felues. His anfwer on our behalfe is falfe ; we deny not all Traditions that are fo called. For we accept them, if they be Apoftolicàll, and haue the confent of all perfons, in all ages, profeffing the fame faith. Bring vs any Traditions thus fortified, thus affured as the Scriptures are, we will meete them, receiue them, imbrace them and lay them next our hearts to obferue them. Wherefore though we can eafily confeffe this to be an excellent proofe, yet we hope to find as good, if not better.

28   The Doctor demandeth farther: May they pretend the authoritie of their owne new Church ? But firft, faith he, they muft proue their Church to be the true Church. That is not to do, if we had fpoken to men that had not loft their eares. I could wifh for their owne fakes, they could as well proue themfelues to be the chafte fpoufe of Chrift, as we haue done on our owne behalfe. For we know our felues to be the true Church of Chrift by the Scriptures, as a chafte matron is knowne by her husband. And we know the Scriptures by the Church, as the husband is knowne by his wife. His bleffings vpon her, his loue toward her, her faith and obedience towards him, are fufficient demonftrations to vs that we are his fpoufe; fufficient motiues to him, to continue our gracious and glorious husband. This can they neuer know, that vilifie his word, and oppofe themfelues vnto the law of Chrift, as the Courtly Church of *Rome* doth.

29   Yet the Doctor proceedeth to fight with his owne fhadow, and play with his owne imaginations. *They will alledge Scriptures,* faith he, *but thefe will not helpe them : for neither doth the whole teftifie of the whole, nor any part one of another; or if they do it, it fhould not. For euery part vnto a Philofopher or vnbeleeuer, is as much doubted of as the whole. So that the whole cannot teftifie for a part, nor any part for the whole.* We deale not with Philofophers or vnbeleeuers, or elfe they confeffe themfelues to be both. But Philofophers and vnbeleeuers do no more beleeue the Church, then they do the Scriptures; and then what hath the Doctor faid, that maketh not as much againft the knowledge of their Church to be
the

the true Church, as of the Scriptures to be the true Scriptures? But all that he hath said is palpably falfe. For the new Teftament approueth the old, and the old doth demonftrate the new. The new often alledgeth the old, and the old foretelleth that which is done in the new. Enough to conuince a very Infidell.

30 But more then this. The old Teftament was in the hands of the enemies of the Gofpell. The Gofpell was entertained of the Iews enemies. Thefe fortified both by ftrength of oppofition, and preferued both for their owne defence and fatisfaction. And many of thefe accorded each with other, induced, without ftanding vpon the authoritie of any outward Church, by the due conference of the Scriptures. Heretickes haue refufed both, when they haue made againft them: and the true beleeuers ftrengthened their caufe by them. Againe, heretickes alledged them when they could draw any fimilitude of truth from them; and the Chriftian Catholiks euidently conuinced all gainftanders out of them. And this we haue out of approued Ecclefiafticall hiftory, and monuments of the moft ancient Churches. This is a farre ftronger and more euident reafon, to proue the Scriptures to be Scriptures, then that they were (forfooth) preferued and approued by the Romane Church. What will they anfwer if we tell them, that the Scriptures were before the Romane Church was? and that neither all, nor fome, nor any part of them was more committed to her charge, then to any other Church to which they were written, as to them one, to the Corinthians two, and fo to others; but all for all, that all *through patience and comfort of them might haue hope.*		Rom.15.

31 The Doctor hath not yet done. *Shall they be tried by each mans priuate spirit?* faith he. *This may not be. For it is not probable, that one should discerne more then thousands: and if Councels and Fathers may erre, much more priuate men, to whom so large promises are not made.* I will not anfwer with *Panormitane,* that *one man bringing not onely Scriptures, but better reafon,* Panormitan. *is to be beleeued before the Pope and a generall Councel:* but I may well fay, that one *Elias* is to be preferred before all *Baals* 1.King.18.
				V					Priefts,

1.King.22.
2.King.6.
Gen.19.

Priefts; one *Michaiah* before foure hundred falfe Prophets; and that one *Elizeus* may fee, when a thoufand Aramites fhall be as blind as the Sodomites that could not find *Lots* houfe. The ftory is notorious of one *Paphnutius* in the Councell of *Nice*.

32   But I rather anfwer, that the Scriptures are fufficient to demonftrate their owne authoritie; not by their phrafe and ftyle onely (which the Doctor derides of all other arguments, for that, as he faith, *The profane man accounteth the ftyle bafe and barbarous,*) but by many reafons befide. Yet euen the very ftyle, fo folemne, fo graue, fo ftately; the matter fo full of iuftice, holineffe and fanctification: the hiftories fo true in the iudgement of all : the myfteries fo deepe, the maieftie fo great, as that vnto any indifferent iudgement, in all excellencies it is not onely in deed, but in fhew alfo the moft compleate and abfolute book in the world. Yet befide all this (as the Doctor faith well) the Antiquitie of the Scriptures before all other bookes : their preferuation fo many thoufand yeares, through fo many dangers, fo long captiuities, fuch potent and malicious enemies that fought to deftroy them: the conformitie and vniformitie of the bookes one with another, which were indited and tranflated, in diuers times, at fundry places, by feuerall perfons, without contradiction, or one dangerous pofition. All which if the Romane Church may auow, I fee not why any Chriftian Catholicke may not do the fame: and then all thefe are in equall ballance, and indifferent to vs as to them.

33   But we will come yet nearer them, and tell them that the Scriptures manifeft themfelues, as we difcerne hony by the tafte, the Sunne by his light, muske by the fmell, muficke by the eare, Phyficke by the working, our friend by his loue, our parents by their naturall affection. For they giue *light to the eyes, wifedome to the fimple*; they *are fweeter then the hony, more precious then the gold of Ophir : as the very day ftarre when it appeareth* in our hearts; more fragrant then the ointment, more foueraigne then any medicine made by the art of the Apothecary: by the very fent of it we follow the Lord.

Pfal.19.

Euthy-

Euthymius an ancient writer, alluding to the nineteenth Pſalme : *Scripturam nobis Deus legem tradidit, &c.* God hath Euthym.in giuē vs his Scripture for a law,by which we ſhould be taught diuine Pſal.19. prouidence and wiſedome. And he hath called it after diuers names: HIS LAW,*becauſe it ordereth and guideth our conuerſation of life.* TESTIMONIE,*becauſe it teſtifieth againſt ſinners.* IVSTIFICA-TION,*becauſe it teacheth that which is righteous. A* COMMAN-DEMENT,*becauſe it chargeth that which is to be done.* FEARE, *becauſe it is inexorable.* IVDGEMENT, *becauſe it pronounceth doome and ſentence.For the Law of the Lord is irreprehenſible,con-uerting ſoules. And what is in it that can be accuſed, ſeeing it is prouided for the conuerſion of ſoules? &c.* Haue we not all theſe marks in theſe Scriptures ? or do all theſe agree to any other writing in the world,but vnto our Scriptures ?

34 In them we haue the apparitions and viſions of God, the meſſages and ſongs of Angels , the expectation of the Patriarks, the ſure word of the Prophets, the ioyfull newes of reconciliation wrought by Ieſus Chriſt; the ſpirituall hymnes and Pſalmes diuinely compoſed to comfort our hearts.In them we haue the voice of our Father calling vnto vs in loue and iuſtice,promiſing his mercies, threatning his iudgements, doing his wonders, confounding his foes, de-fending his friends ; and in them we may find and feele the very fruition of heauen vpon earth. All the wiſe men of the world, all the Angels in heauen can neither amend them,nor make the like. By them Philoſophers moſt learned haue bin conuerted,Atheiſts reformed, heretickes confuted, and the very diuels of hell confounded. Theſe vndeniable euidences haue we of the Scriptures, from the Scriptures themſelues, without any externall adiument.Theſe with the former rea-ſons are vnto vs the ſauour of life vnto life, by which we be-leeue and embrace the Goſpell. If they be the ſauour of death vnto death to the Romanes , they may wilfully periſh in their ſinnes ; we will heartily praiſe God for our ſal-uation.

35 If Doctor *Kelliſon* and Cardinall *Bellarmine* ſhall yet Bellar. de ver-ſay, *Non aliunde nos habere Scripturam eſſe diuinam & qui ſunt* bo Dei,l.4.c.4

,, *libri facri, quàm ex Traditione non fcripta:* By no other meanes
,, do we know the Scripture to be diuine, and which be the
,, holy bookes, but onely from tradition not written. Let
them heare the Ancients fpeak, and let gray haires ftop their
mouthes, who demonftrate the Scriptures to be both diuine
and holy, by all thefe circumftances before noted, with ma-

Diuin.lectio.
lib.1.c.16.
An.Dom.530

Nicrietas.

Plus,

ny mo of like moment. *Intuemini fodales egregij,* (faith *Caffio-
dore*) *Behold my noble companions, how admirable and fweet the
order of words in the diuine Scriptures do runne, euer increafing
appetite, facietie without end, the glorious hunger of the bleffed,
where too much is not reproued, but rather ofte oportunitie is praifed, and that worthily: whereas the knowledge of wholefome things
is thence learned, and eternall life is performed to thofe that beleeue
and do thereafter. Where things paft are defcribed without falfhood, prefent things are fet out better then they appeare to be, things
to come are told as if they were paft. Truth ruleth euery where
in them, euery where diuine vertue fhineth in them, euery where are
layd open things beneficiall to mankind.* Shew me fuch a booke in
the world befide this.

    36 Whereunto I may adde the difcreete, wife and lear-
ned anfwer of another ancient and well approued Father; a-
gainft whom Cardinal *Bellarmine* taketh no exception among
Ecclefiafticall writers that liued about *ann.* 545, who propofeth our aduerfaries queftion euen in their owne words in
effect, and maketh anfwer for vs as directly as we would de-

Iuuil. African.
l.2.de partibus
diuinæ legis,
quæft.29.

fire. *Vnde probamus libros noftræ religionis diuina effe infpirations
confcriptos? Whence do we proue the books of our religion to be written by diuine infpiration?* He anfwereth himfelfe, *Ex multis,*
(not only by Tradition, as our aduerfaries deeme) but by many reafons: *Of which, the firft is the truth of the Scriptures felfe;
then the order of the matters, the confonancie of the commandements, the maner of fpeech, without bouts, and the puritie of the
words. To thefe may be added the qualitie of thofe that wrote and
preached it: that men did deliuer diuine things, vile men high matters, rude men profound fecrets, not without the fulneffe of Gods Spirit. The power of the preaching, which while it was preached (though
but of a few, and thofe defpifed) preuailed. There accurreth more-*

ouer

ouer to thefe the rectifying of contraries, as of the Sybils or Philofo-
phers, the ouerthrow of aduerfaries, the benefit of confequents, the
accomplifhment of thofe things which by collections and figures, and
exclufions of oppofites and prædictions, are foretold; and laftly, the
frequent miracles which were done vntill the Scripture it felfe was
receiued of the Gentiles. Whereof this is fufficient to the next mira-
cle, that it is knowne to be receiued of all men. Thefe are fuch demonftrations for the certainty of the Scriptures, that we need
not feeke the Vatican Library, nor the Popes Confiftorie for
a Tradition, they are fufficiently or rather abundantly warran-
ted of themfelues. To conclude, take yet an older then they
both, who though in fewer words, yet in equall fubftance deliuereth the fame : *Maieftatem Scripturarum fi non vetuftatem,* Tertul. in A-
diuinas probamus, fi negatur Antiquitas:We proue the Maieftie of pol. cap. 20.
the Scriptures, if not their Antiquitie.We proue them diuine, if you
*doubt of their age.*This haue the Ancients faid for vs, and therefore our aduerfaries in all they fay againft vs or them: *They*
haue fowed but wind, they cannot reape nothing but a whirle Ofee 8. 7.
wind.

　　37 Concerning the fecond fort of Traditions, fuch as cannot, neither I thinke will now be offered to be proued by
Scriptures, yet haue bene defended by many, I will not infift
vpon particulars, take thefe very few for a tafte: (for moft of
the reft are fubiect to the fame cenfure:) *The Primacy of Peter,*
the very foundation of the Popes fupremacy (for they muft
ftand or fall together) is taken by théfelues to be a Tradition
vnwritten, as before is faid; yet hath the Court of Rome not
onely fuperficially pretended, but vehemently vrged and preffed; that Saint *Peter* in the lift of the Apoftles is firft named :
that he asketh Chrift moft queftions, receiueth moft anfwers:
that he is not onely a *Petrus* of the Church, but that *Petra,* vp-
pon which the Church is builded. That of all the Apoftles he
had the fword, and handled it; that his faith fhould not faile;
that he conuerted fhould ftrengthen the brethren; that all
Chrifts lambes and fheepe were committed to him, as vnto
the vniuerfall Paftor of all foules : that he moued the election
of another in the place of *Iudas;* that he fpake firft in the

Councell of the Apoftles? All thefe Scriptures haue bene alledged for *Peters* primacy; yet now it is but a Tradition that
is not written; for indeed thofe Scriptures proue it not, they
know. Thefe are contradictorie members, Scriptures and
Traditions, as written and not written. So that in the language
of Popifh *Afhdod*, if it be Scripture, it is no-Tradition, if a Tradition, then no Scripture. The water of Iordan with feuentie
times feuen wafhings, can neuer cleanfe this leprofie. The
Balme of Gilead will neuer cure this defperate malady.

38 Let the other particular be the inuocation of Saints;
this alfo is a Tradition, yet defended by Scriptures, though mi-
ferably racked and detorted againft all fap and fence. Not
to name the places, I referre the Reader if he be a Scholler, to
their Authors: if he be none, to the credit of fuch whom they
may truft in the fearch. *Ecchius of the worfhipping of Saints* hath
aboue twentie places of Scriptures, befides reafons which he
feemeth to ground vpon Scriptures. Alfo without enumera-
tion of Authors names, I fay, all that write of the Inuocation,
Veneration, Adoration, Mediation, Interceffion, or any worfhip of Saints, they all haue and yet do alledge Scriptures,
thicke and threefold to proue their affertion; and that muft
needs be againft their confcience, for they hold al this by Tradition. And that which conuinceth moft their impofture, and
might reforme their confciences if they were not feared, is,
that they in manner all confeffe, when they haue alledged
Scripture, yet that this doctrine is not in the Scripture. Howbeit with fuch cautelous and euafiue fpeeches in moft of them,
that they dare not fpeake it fo plainly that it may admit no
fhift: but, that if need be they may change their tune and
turne tippet at their pleafure. As *Petrus à Soto: In Scripturis
non quidem docetur, fed infinuatur Sanctorum inuocatio: The
inuocation of Saints verily is not taught in the Scriptures, but infinuated.* And *Chemnifius* reporteth that the Iefuites write, *Non
apertè eam in Scripturis tradi, fed in myfterio: That it is not openly
deliuered in the Scriptures, but in a myfterie. Ecchius* faith, *Ex-
plicitè non eft præcepta Sanctorum inuocatio: The inuocation of
Saints is not plainly commanded:* and addeth reafons why it is
neither

Marginal notes:

Enchiridion
de Sanctorū
veneratione,
cap. 15.

Chemnif. Ex-
am. p.184.

Enchirid. cap.
15.

neither in the old nor new Teſtament. Biſhop *Canus* ſaith, *Sanctorum Martyrum auxilium precibus implorandum,&c.That* Loc.Com.l.3. *helpe is to be ſought by prayer to the holy Martyrs,* (and to them c.3. or to none, for they are the moſt certaine Saints, in the beſt Romane learning) *or that their memories ſhould be celebrated, &c. ſacræ litteræ nuſquam fortè tradiderunt* : The holy Scriptures peraduenture do no where deliuer. What a miſuſing is this of a matter of ſo high a nature,as concerneth the ſeruice of God, the gaine or loſſe of ſoules? It is *not taught*, forſooth, but inſinuated,not *openly*, but in a *myſterie*,not *plainly commanded*, but belike couertly inuolued; and if all theſe ſhifts of men will not ſerue, they will trie the diuels ſtratagem wherewith he deceiued *Eue*, and by her *Adam*, and in them all mankind:*Ne fortè moriemini, Leſt peraduenture you dye;peraduenture* (ſaith he) *it is no where written.*

39 Howbeit, to put it out of all peraduenture,Biſhop *Lindan* ſpeaketh plainly, and as the truth is. For in numbring vp Panoplia,l.3. many particulars not at all contained in the Scriptures (he c.5. hath *thoſe of Images, and inuocation of Saints*. If *Lindan* be not In 2. 2. Thoplaine enough, I am ſure that *Bannes* a Ieſuite is. *Orationes eſſe* mæ. q.1.art. *ad Sanctos faciendas neque expreſſe, neque impreſſe & inuolutè ſa* 10.concluſ. 2. *cræ litera docent* : The holy Scriptures teach, neither openly,,, nor ſecretly, or couertly, that prayers are to be made vnto ,, Saints. Yet you ſhall find another that will haue a ſalue ,, (ſuch as it is) to couer, though it cannot cure,this ſcarre:*That ſuch as this, and many other things of the ſame kind, the Catho* Canus. *licke Church holdeth as ſtrongly as if they were contained in the Scriptures.* This is like a *new peece ſet to an old garment,it makes* Mat.9.16. *the rent worſe*. For he more then inſinuateth, it is not in the Scriptures, & yet he holdeth it *as ſtrongly*,(which is ſtrangely) *as if it were Scripture*. The contrary I am ſure is directly proued by Scriptures, without all peraduenture, ambiguitie, or controuerſie, as in euery Common place booke our Diuines haue proued. And then may the wife ſo checke the husband, and Traditions ouertop Scriptures, that we muſt hold that ſtrongly for Traditions ſake, which the Scriptures as ſtrongly condemne for Gods glorie ſake ?

V 4   40 The

40   The Councell of Trent it felfe, which determineth all matters, without all modefty and fhamefacedneffe, though they decree Purgatory as *taught by the Church, by the holy Ghoft out of the holy Scripture,* (out of them indeed, for it neuer came there,) which notwithftanding is ordinarily called and accounted a Tradition by the Romanifts,yet in their mandate of praying to Saints they are contented to leaue out the Scriptures as the Scriptures leaue out it; and reft vpon *The vfe of the Catholicke and Apoftolicke Church, received from the firft times of Chriftian religion, the confent of holy Fathers, and Decrees of facred Councels.* This that they fay is much more then they can euer proue ; yet the Scriptures in this cafe they dare not enforce, whereby they fhew one fcruple of modefty, in a talent of impudency; a bafe allay.

41   This makes me the more to maruell at Cardinall *Bellarmine* and others, who haue written fince the Councell of Trent, and yet ftill feeke to defend that by the Scriptures, that is confeffed to be a Tradition,not contained in thē. In which cafe I could well commend the ingenious plaineffe of an ancient *Schooleman, æqualis Sancti Bernardi,* Saint *Bernards* equall, who for himfelfe faith modeftly: *Ego amplius iudicare non præfumo,&c. I prefume to iudge no farther,but onely this,that the Saints fee onely fo much, as it pleafeth him whom they behold; it is hard to iudge whether they heare the prayers of fuppliants, or not.* But this may not be abidden.For though he was *Vir egregius, non tamen allegabilis,*faith *Cunerus:*Though he was an excellent man, yet not to be alledged, a mad anfwer to fuch an authoritie. Yet *Hofmeifter* a later Diuine, hath made a *more modeft* almoft conclufion, with more certaine authoritie then his owne,which he taketh from S. *Auguftine,* if it be in Saint *Auguftine:Tutius & iucundius loquor ad meum Iefum: I fpeake more fafely and more fweetly to my Sauiour Iefus,then to any of the holy Saints of God. My Chrift owes me more then any of the Celeftiallfpirits.* But moft modeftly George *Caffander: Ego in meis precibus,&c. I in my prayers vfe not to inuocate the Saints, but I direct my prayers vnto God himfelfe,& that in the name of Chrift, for this I hold moft fafe.* But I trow their *Index expurgatorius* hath

Margin notes:
Seff. 25.

De Sanctorum beatitudine.l.1.c.19.

C. Bellar. de fcriptor. Ecclef. 1130.
Hugo de fancto Victore de facrament. part.16.c.11.
Locor. commun. de cultu diuorum.cap. 20.

Sanctorum fpirituum.

E Chemnifio. parte 3.exam. Trid.Concil.

hath whipt him for this, and hath let out this hereticall bloud
or that is worſe, cleane turned him out of their fellowſhip.
Such is the ſtrength of truth, that ſometimes in the dayes of
darkneſſe, it breaketh forth and giueth light vnto ſome more
vnpartiall hearts, who without preiudicate affections, ſearch
diligently for it till they find it; and when they haue found it,
dare make open profeſſion of it. I cannot forbeare to ioyne
Eraſmus his conceite, which I may adde vnto the former mo- Epiſtola ad
deſt paſſages, which though he ſeemeth to vtter merrily, yet he Sadolctum.
meant it verily, & ſo I take it: *Conſtat nullum eſſe locum in diui-*
nis voluminibus, qui permittit inuocari Sanctos, niſi fortè huc tor-
quere placet quod Diues in Euangelio opem imploret Abrahæ : It
is euident, that there is no place in the Diuine volumes, which ,,
(he ſaith not, teacheth, commandeth, or counſelleth) but that ,,
ſo much as *permitteth Saints to be inuocated, except* a man ,,
would wreſt that in the Goſpell, where *Diues* calleth vpon *A-* ,,
braham. A fit *Mœcenas* for ſuch learning, and Patron for ſuch
idolatrie. But *Eraſmus* is but *ſemi-Chriſtianus*, a moitie of a
Chriſtian with *Bellarmine*, and therefore this will be taken but
for a *Lucian* floute. Yet if it be a bourd, it is a true bourd, as
the Northerne prouerbe ſaith.

42 This paſſage might be amplified by the article of images, auricular confeſſion, and many others: but theſe are ſufficient to demonſtrate our aduerſaries fearefull abuſing of the
word, by alledging Scriptures euen againſt their owne conſciences, for ſuch things as themſelues call and hold to be Traditions, and confeſſe are not to be found in the Scriptures. What
is this but to draw the Scriptures to their owne ſence, not to
ſubiect their owne iudgement to the Scriptures? Which double dealing may ſufficiently detect our aduerſaries care and
conſcience, or rather, neither care nor conſcience, in ſeeking
and finding the way of truth. But that which is worſe, if worſe
may be, they are contented to reſt themſelues, and delude gracious Chriſtians with Traditions that haue no ground of probability in the Scriptures, or ſhew of authoritie, whereon a
deuout ſoule might relie and repoſe his faith, with hope to
hold faſt without fainting or falling. If they departed, but
from

from Mount Sion to mount Nebo neare vnto the land of
of Promife, it were fomewhat tollerable, though hope be
neuer fo good as fruition; or if they would trauell from
mount Nebo to Sion, we would ioyne with them, for this
were from the worft to the better. But to bring vs from the

Pfal.

hills from whence commeth our faluation, thefe foundations which can neuer be moued, to the marrifhes and boggs,
quicke fands, and blacke mud, or myerie clay of mens
Traditions, where no firme footing can be found, no
ground-worke can be laid, this is apparently from better to
worfe; that giueth no hope, but menaceth defperate, deadly,
and vnrecouerable damnation. Better haue Traditions with
fome probable fhew of Scriptures, then to bring them and
enforce them without all fauour or fap of authoritie. Yet is it
hard to iudge whether is the better.

43 For except they be either exprefly in the Scriptures, or
by neceffarie deduction without wrefting or writhing may
be concluded from them, they are without all credit for confirmation of faith, or perfwafion in matter of religion. Howbeit our aduerfaries haue for this an expedit way. For we need
not diue into the deep ocean of *Antiquitie*, nor delue into the
bowels of the earth for this bafe mettall, nor afcend vnto the
fecrets of long fince paffed times, if we will be ruled by the
Romane Court. For if they haue them, and the Pope allow
them, they are thereby approued without all queftion, as if
they were neuer fo old, and could be directly brought from
the Apoftles mouthes or pennes. And when they are thus
had and enioyed, yet they may be changed and altered, yea

Contra Bren-
tium.l.4.
En defpetto
di Dios.

difanulled and abrogated at the Popes owne pleafure.
In defpite of all heretickes (faith Cardinall *Hofius*, he might fay
as the ruffians in Spaine fometimes, In defpite of God) *the*
power hereof appertaineth to them alone who fit in Peters Chaire:
who for that they may euer háue at hand men fraught with wife-
dome and learning (fuch as often their Nephewes & fauorites
are) *whofe counfell they may vfe, to whom it is giuen to fee with*
many eyes, (as *Argus,* or *Efops* Miftris) *whether thefe Traditions*
either be for, or againft charitie, &c. & fo accordingly can caufe to
be

be omitted or intermitted,or changed into others (like Camelions) more cōmodious and profitable,he means for the Roman Church. In what cafe are Chriſtian ſoules vnder ſuch vnconſtancie?

44 See how fitly a wittie and ingenious Poet of our time hath likened the word of God to the Gnomon of a Sun Diall,theſe Traditions to a clocke,& the Pope to a wethercock. As himſelfe turneth with the wind, ſo he can ſet the clocke at his pleaſure : And it greeues him that the Dials Gnomon is ſo guided by the Sunne that it can not erre, neither will obſcure truth, do the weather-cocke what he can.

45 We are not ignorant of the frailtie of mans nature, how ſubieƈt it is to mutabilitie and change. And we as well know by long and great experience, (howſoeuer the Canoniſts, Schoolemen,and other the Popes creatures flatter) that the Biſhop of Rome is but a man, a fraile and ſinfull man, often times a moſt wicked and damnable man; yet all Chriſtianitie muſt hang vpon this one hinge,as heauen reſted vpon *Atlas* ſhoulders. No Scriptures, but of his allowing;no interpretation but of his deuiſing ; no Traditions but of his approuing; and therefore no faith ; no religion but of his making. Yet all this is not enough to ſupport the decaying walls of tottering Babylon, but we muſt haue alſo new ſtuffe added, euer prouided it be ſuch as is vſed in the Romane Church, admitted by the Popes authority, continued at his pleaſure, impoſed vpon his command, to be altered and changed for his aduantage.

46 The Scriptures of God, are counted but as a fit burthen for *Balaams* Aſſe: As if the Scriptures were falſe propheſies, as the Aſſes loade was a falſe Prophet. Like as our Romane Rhemiſts who fauour much of an Aſſe too˙, as if they were *Aſſians* borne, neare the riuer *Aſſus.* For they liken their tranſſubſtantiated hoſt to our bleſſed Sauiour,and the Prieſt that carieth him to an Aſſe. And this though it ſeeme abſurd, yet they will make it good in the handling : or as *Benedictus Pariſienſis*, that ſaith, *Balaams Aſſe ſignifieth the Church,and the Pope Balaam that ſitteth thereon*, and ſo may keepe together the feaſt of *Aſinarus*, where Saint *Francis* may be the Prieſt, na.

Nicol. Herbron in Monade, cap.1.
Scripturam quam Aſinus Balaam baiulare quivit. Annot. in Mat.21. with the bleſſed Sacrament, as it were Chriſt vpon an Aſſe. Concord. Bibliorum in verbo Aſi-

Prieft, that called his carkaffe his Affe ; like lettuce for fuch lips. Surely they are of the ancient ftocke of the *Bruti*, or *Cumani*, as *Iulius Cæfar* applied them. But Traditions need no Affe to carrie them, they haue life and actiuitie fufficient in themfelues. *Quid enim aliud funt Traditiones, quàm viuum quoddam, Euangelium?* For what are Traditions *(faith a Cardinall)* but a certaine liuing Gofpell? As much to fay, the Scriptures are fo old, they are decrepite they can not go nor helpe themfelues. But Traditions are nimble as tumblers, and can trauaile like luftie *Iuuentus*, or a landloper ouer the world. *They are the liuing Gofpell, the Scriptures are but dead letters.*

1.King.3.16. For thefe we ftriue as the two mothers before *Salomon*, both claime the liuing child. The harlots word is, Let it be neither thine nor mine, let it be deuided. The true mothers heart yearned. We thanke God our triall ftands before one wifer then *Salomon*, we doubt not but to hold our liuing child which is the Scriptures ; let them take their dead child who are the mother or damme therof, we wil not deuide the word of God into *Scriptum & non Scriptum*, written and not written. This is to kill the liuing word, the word of life. We are well contented to leaue them their owne vnto themfelues, for in their owne conceipts they cannot be bettered. For fome one of them may be as good as the whole Scripture, yea rather then faile, better.

47 The Strumpet Babylon taketh all the Scriptures infufficient to faluation. Not the one halfe, nay I may truly fay and fafely, not one iota of her doctrine, now by the reformed Churches reproued, hath any ground from the Scriptures Hofius ibid. of God at all. But one Tradition *is almoft enough to faue a foule* forfooth, and that is the figne of the Croffe, efpecially if it be skilfully made: *Beginning from the top of the crowne or the forehead* (at the leaft) *to the nauell, and then from the left fhoulder to the right,* and this is a Croffe in *folio* : as that ouer the lips when a man yaunes, is in *decimo fexto* : and prouided alfo it be done with three *fingers to fignifie the Trintie*, and then to a *rude countrie fellow who for the grofnes of his vnderftanding, is not able to attaine higher in other points, Vel hoc illi propè folum ad*
falutem

salutem sufficere queat: Euen this almoft alone may be fuffici- „
ent for his faluation. „

48 But this is not all. For as the admiffion of this ceremonious Tradition is fo fupereminently great, fo is the o-
miffion thereof as fuperlatiuely dangerous. And if we will
beleeue this Cardinall at euery word, the very *omiffion thereof* Ibid.
in contempt, is fo paffing and aboue meafure wicked, that *it is
finne againft the holy Ghoft.* I haue read of a Grammarian that
fwore, that the Pope, *ex plenitudine poteftatis,* by the fulneffe
of his power could not make a new Latin word. What a
ftrange vfurpation is this of a Cardinall, that can after all the
Doctors, Schoolemen and Popes, make a new finne againft
the holy Ghoft, which was neuer heard of in this world, nor
fhall euer be cenfured in the world to come?

49 The fumme of all is this; high and profound myfteries of Diuinitie are called into queftion, which concerne
the glorie of that dreadfull Maieftie whom we all pretend
to worfhip in truth and veritie. We appeale to the Scriptures, as vnto the written will of the Sonne of God, to trie
our claime to the mercies of God his Father, and the inheritance of life promifed to vs, purchafed by him. Herein we
are refufed, this euidence is defpifed, vilified, reiected. Our
aduerfaries call and crie for Traditions, left without writing,
either by our Sauiour or by his Apoftles, as they pretend, but
can neuer proue: or by the cuftomes of their Church, which
perhaps they may fhew, but we haue no reafon to allow.
Proue them to proceed from fuch diuine authoritie, we receiue them, accept them, reuerence them, and embrace them
with both our armes, and lay them to our hearts. Our aduerfaries will not admit any fuch condition.

50 Say what we can, if *Rome* get the maifter doome,
what the triple Crowne hath, that we muft hold (fauing the
gold and precious ftones thereof): what it refufeth, that we
muft deteft, with implicite faith and blind obedience, without asking queftion, or demanding reafon; as if we had heads
without braines, and carkaffes without hearts, meere blocks
without fenfe, and worfe then the horfe or mule that haue
no

no vnderftanding. But (deare Chriftian Reader) as we confift of bodies and foules, and haue the light of reafon and facultie of vnderftanding, whereby we are enabled to lay claime vnto the inheritance of light and life: fo we are refolued not to be remoued from the truth of God reuealed in his word, with any blaft of *Romes* falfe doctrine, who withhold

Rom.1.18.
Iude 13.

the truth of God in vnrighteoufneffe, and dayly fome out their owne fhame, to the great difhonour of Gods maieftie, and the vnfpeakable fcandall of his Saints.

51 Wherefore let the Romanifts pretend what omnipotencie they pleafe in their pompous Prelate, and infoift what Traditions they will into the title of the word of God, or tye the holy Ghoft to the Popes elbow or chaire ftoope, as his Parafites either vainly imagine, or elfe againft their owne confciences affirme; yet we know and haue proued, that after the publication of the Scriptures and deceaffe of the Apoftles, nothing may bind our abfolute obedience in the fubftance of our faith and religion, but onely they. And this we conclude, not out of our owne felfwils, but we build it vpon the ancient Fathers, and receiue from moft approued *Antiquitie*, which fhould bind them fafteft that pretend it moft, as our aduerfaries haue done, though now they leaue off to enquire of old yeares, or to be guided by gray haires, and onely betake themfelues to the moderne Tyrant, and the policie of his Court, as if the bleffed Spirit of God were at his commandement.

52 But if we aske our Fathers, Saint *Chryfoftome* wil tell vs, that *Qui propria loquuntur, falsò prætendunt Spiritũ fanctum,* ,, As long as they fpeake their owne, they falfly pretend the ,, holy Ghoft. Both Papifts and Anabaptifts (whom in this cafe I cannot feparate) are ftifled, and their breath ftopt, by the fame Father, who defendeth Gods caufe and ours againft

De fancto &
adorando
Spiritu.

them: *Si quid præter Euangelium fub titulo Spiritus obtrudatur, ne credamus: quia ficut Chriftus eft finis Legis, ita Spiritus Euangelij:* If any thing be thruft vpon vs befide the Gofpel, vnder the title of the holy Ghoft, let vs neuer beleeue it: for as Chrift was the end of the Law, fo was the holy Spirit of the Gofpell.

Gofpell. As who fhould fay, As nothing fhould be added
to the Law and Prophets (which is the old Teftament)after
Chrift came, who was the fulfilling of the Law and the Prophets: fo nothing, as neceffary to faluation, fhould be added
to the Euangelifts and Apoftles, that is, to the bookes of the
new Teftament, when the holy Ghoft had done writing by
them. Which we fhall eafily perceiue, if we well obferue the
bodie of both Teftaments with their fubftantiall parts. For
the old Teftament hath the Law of *Mofes*, the hiftories of
the Church, moralities for conuerfation, and prophefies,
chiefly of Chrift our Sauiours firft coming in humilitie, and
yet not without intermixture of each of thefe within o-
ther : So the new Teftament though in quantitie fhorter,
yet in qualitie both plainer and more eminent, hath the law
of Chrift in the foure Euangelifts, the hiftorie of the firft
Church in the Acts of the Apoftles, inftructiós both for faith
& manners in the Epiftles, and finally the prophefies of after-
times, vntill the fecond comming of the Lord Iefus in glorie; yet not without intertexture of euery in each, that
the harmonie of the Scriptures may be feene, and the
conftancie of the Spirit of God made knowne vnto all following generations. From thefe nothing may be taken; to
thefe nothing may be added, without deepe facriledge, and
high blafphemie, or both in either. Therefore to conclude,
all Traditions, efpecially if they neuer fo litle oppofe thefe
Scriptures, or vary from them with the leaft contrarietie,
howfoeuer they may be tendred, yet may they not be touched; and may be reiected with the fame facilitie they were
receiued or admitted.

CHAP.

CHAP. XI.

Inſtead of ancient Councels, the Romaniſts preſſe vs with late
partiall Conuenticles, which they call Generall and Oe-
cumenicall Councels, but are vnworthy
the Church of God.

Hat credit and reputation the firſt and moſt ancient Councels haue with our Aduerſaries the Popes vaſſals, is before in the ſeuenth Chapter euidently deliuered & made manifeſt. Now let vs behold, how, this notwithſtanding, they will haue Councels to bleare the worlds eyes, and appeale vnto them that are paſt, and call for more, marry vnder ſuch conditions as they will be ſure to take no hurt by them.

2 Such haue bene the later Councels of a few paſſed ages, congregated vpon faction, ouerruled by preiudicate affection, and concluded to the preiudice of the truth, onely for the ſupport of the kingdome of Antichriſt, and the honour of his tempeſtuous ſea. By any of which if he be benefited, then he bleſſeth them; if he be croſſed, he curſeth them. This hath borne and bred, maintaineth and defendeth yet

Bellàr.

that partiall diſtinction, of ſome Councels approued, ſome reproued, ſome in part accepted, ſome in part reiected; one not abſolutely to be receiued, nor peremptorily to be refuſed. Which is as much to ſay, as they will admit and condemne, as many and in as much as they liſt: which no honeſt man would aske, no wiſe man will yeeld vnto.

3 This myſterie of iniquitie, ſimple Chriſtians know not, and therefore are deceiued. For if an honeſt, ſimple, well meaning man ſhould heare all the great learned Catholickes

Ioh. de Turre-
crem. ſum. de
Eccleſ. l.3. c. 58
Hoſius contra
Berqium, lib. 2,

with one voice profeſſe and proteſt, that *Full generall Councels in matters of faith cannot erre*; or that, to call into queſtion, or ſo much as to ſay, *That the ſpirit of Councels may be tried, is a ſin againſt the holy Ghoſt* ; or he doth wrong to the iudgement

ment of a Councell, that shall reason or dispute against it after it Canif.Catech.
hath once determined: That all Nationall or Prouinciall Councels de præceptis
must stoope to the authoritie of an Vniuersall, without all stop or Ecclefiæ.
ambiguitie; he could not but admire their great authoritie. Io. Bunderius tit.17.art.1.
And in very truth if this were spoken of those oldest and best
Councels, we would conniue much for the innocencie of the
times, the grauitie of the Bishops, and the *Antiquity* of both.
But this is claimed for euery late Conuenticle, though neuer
so partiall. As if the last Chapter of Trent, were as good as the
first Councell of Nice; and *Pius* the fourth or fifth as good as
Peter and *Iames* in the Councell of the Apostles. Howbeit
God knowes the case is exceedingly altered. For vpon examination we haue found that the first and best Councels haue
not that credit with the Romanists which they pretend,
neither are the later such as they may iustly commend, or we
safely receiue without danger of miscariage, in chiefe articles
of our faith.

4 The first, as hath bene proued, were called by Emperours, maintained at their charge, protected by their armes,
concluded by their approbations, the time and place affigned
at their pleasure, whatsoeuer the Locusts or rather dogs of
Rome, snarle or barke to the contrary. These later must be
summoned onely by the Pope, appointed when he list, collected where he pleafe, onely he will be at no charge, as the
Emperours were: marrie the Emperours as his vaffals must
giue the commers protection. He alone must be Prefident, not
so much moderating with learning and difcretion, as ouer-
ruling with power and authoritie, commanding with pride
and infolencie, and concluding them with shame and infamie,
as wofull experience hath made euident to all the Christian
world. Whereas Saint *Augustine* in his time could say, that
sometimes old Councels were amended by the new, former
by later; we may iustly say, and proue it true, that since this
partialitie bare fway in the Church, the old haue bene corrupted, not corrected by the new; and the former by the
later, to the fubuerfion of faith, and ouerthrow of good
manners.

X　　　　　5 If

Concil. Lateran,
Trent,

5 If we fhould exemplifie this by particulars, but in the late Councell of Lateran vnder *Leo* the tenth, and the laſt of Trent, they would yeeld abundant matter to iuſtifie this aſſertion. In the former, befides all the abſurdities therein contained, this blaſphemie was there heard and vncontrolled, that the Pope had *Poteſtatem ſuper omnes poteſtates, tam in cœlo quàm in terra*: Power ouer all powers both in heauen and in earth. In the later, fo many groſſe errors determined, as if of fet purpofe they would not onely reforme nothing that all the world faw to be amiſſe, but fo maintained all the corruptions that fretted the confcience of many a Chriſtian, like a very Gangrene, that in many Countries and Vniuerſities, yea fome of them otherwife Catholicke, they are yet exploded and condemned. Cardinall *Hoſius* to fhew how in fome cafes the former Councels were amended by the later, doth beautifie it with this inſtance. *There is* (faith he) *a Canon Apoſtolicall, that a Presbyter which is a fornicator, ſhould be depoſed. This in the Councell of Gangren, as it is alledged by Gratian, is amended, and the paine mitigated.* Surely a very great commendation; to take away a feuere puniſhment, for fo groſſe a finne, that had a greater cenfure in the law of nature. But out of queſtion this mitigation was vpon good occaſion and difcretion approued. For if in thefe later ages all Prieſtly fornicators had bene depofed, there would fcarcely haue bene Curats to haue ferued at their altars, except *ſi non caſte, tamen cautè*, if not chaſtly yet charily had faued them harmleſſe.

Contra Brentium, l. 2.

6 If thefe be their reformatious, what then are their deformations? Obferue without preiudice the paſſages of moſt later Councels (not to fpeake of the African nor the Chalcedon) that haue bene fiue or fixe hundred yeares after Chriſt, and marke whether the primacy, or fupremacy of the Biſhop of Rome, or the honour of that turbulent Sea, the Popes benefit, vnder pretence of voyages againſt the Saracens or Turkes, the recouery of the holy land, and fepulcher of our Sauiour, with fuch like impoſtures, haue not bene chiefly ventilated in them; vnder what pretence foeuer they were called, they pretended an errand for one thing, but they intended another.

Furfur quære-
bam, fed pro
potu venie-
bam.

Againſt

Againſt all which,we haue iuſt caufe to except.

7 For the maine point of all controuerſies betweene the Romaniſts and vs, is, whether the Pope be Antichriſt? If it can be proued he is, then neceſſarily all his doctrines are but pretended without care of conſcience, though they were true; if they be ſtarke falſe, as the moſt are, then ſuch as the *man, ſuch is his ſtrength*,they are the liker to himſelfe.But theſe are they that are oppoſed by vs, theſe we deſire may be reformed, rectified, and one truth eſtabliſhed in the Church. What likelier meanes then to call a Councell of all the learned in Chriſtendome, to be ſelectedout of all kingdomes, to a conuenient number,that euery one may haue freedome of ſpeech and voice,no rule to guide them, but the word of God written, which is *Commune principium*, the onely vncontrouerted authoritie by all parties, and according to this rule to determine,that peace may be procured to the *Iſrael of God*? Gal.6.16.

8 The name of a Councell will be hearkened vnto perhaps (though the late Popes haue bene drawne vnto it like a Beare vnto a ſtake) and by much importunitie one may be granted. But who muſt ſummon it?onely vſurping Antichriſt,our capitall enemy, and of all truth and righteouſneſſe. Who muſt be Preſident ? The Pope onely,either in his perſon,or by his Legates. Who muſt haue voyces deciſiue? Onely Biſhops, or priuiledged Abbots, or Generals of the Locuſtian orders. What all? or the *maior* par? The *maior* part without doubt. Are all theſe learned? That mattereth not,they may be as very aſſes as the Pope, or may ſend their Proctors as very dolts as themſelues. Haue they all free voyces? No, they muſt be ſworne to the Pope,before they may breath in the Councell. Are they for number indifferent for all nations?By no meanes; there are more Biſhops in Italy, then in all Chriſtendome beſide. May theſe diſpute *de omni ente* , of all matters? No, they are herein tethered to the Popes pleaſure.May they reſolutely conclude; if the *maior* part , or all of them, agree? That were preſumption and beyond their commiſſion.May any man that wil,come to diſpute?Not without ſafe coduct.Will that protect him, if he diſpleaſe them? Nothing leſſe; faith is not to be Iohn Huſſ. Hierome of Prage.

X 2   kept

kept with Heretickes. Who are thefe Heretickes? All whom they will call fo. What if any thing remaine doubtfull? The Pope muft interpret it.What if it be plaine?The Pope may difpenfe with it.

9 Their great Maifter muft fend them the holy Ghoft from his Confiftory, or at leaft from his clofet, or elfe all conclufions are but confufions.If he be obftinate,or an hereticke, or what you will, faue that he fhould be, can the Councell correct him? That were ouer fawcie,for the members to queftion the head.May they proceed againft him *de facto?* He will deliuer himfelfe by his owne law. But for the good and peace

Bellarmine. of the Church may he fubmit himfelfe to the Councell? No, he cannot do that neither, though he would. To conclude, whatfoeuer the Councel would do without him,it is nothing; whatfoeuer he determineth without the Councell, it is good. This hath bene the ftate of many Councels paft,and is like to be of all to come, as long as the triple Crowne ftandeth fo faft on Antichrifts head. Therefore we iuftly difclaime fuch Councels; and the Romanifts do but delude and mocke Chriftians, when they offer them. More of this afterward in

Infra Chap.14 the Popes fole and abfolute power.Meane while,let the Chriftian indifferent reader meditate what thefe Romane teachers performe, whē they promife to proue their doctrine by Councels, when fuch partiall factions, I may truly fay,priuate and appropriate Chapters and Conuenticles fhall beare the name of Councels?

10 They are certainly but the Cumane Affe, a Lions skin couereth thē, their ftentorious braying fcareth fearefull creatures, but their eares will make their fottifhneffe knowne,and their dull pace will bewray them to any man of courage or confcience. If any man will thinke, that they attribute not fo much vnto thefe later Conuenticles,as vnto the former Councels, let them know that Cardinall *Bellarmine* alledgeth the Chapter of Trent as fauourly,yea for fome things, for which he hath no other authoritie, as if it were the firft Councell of Nice.

11 In that controuerfie about the Apocryphall Scripture,
Accedit

accedit postremò decretum Concilij Tridentini: For an vpshoote Bellar.de ver-
the *Decre of the Councell of Trent cometh in,—The authoritie of* bo Dei,lib.1.
which Councell is with Sixtus and all Catholickes * *greatest and* c.7.item.c.9.
most ancient, (he should say, *Maximè antiquanda,* Aboue all antiquissima.
to be abolished.) So doth *Sixtus Senensis* alledge it for the Bibl.Sanctæ.
authoritie of *Baruch.* So *Andradius* & all Papists. And aboue l.1.Baruch.
all, *Campion*; who when he hath by *Gregories* authoritie compared the former first Councels to the foure Euangelists,
promiseth(if his breath had not bene stopt) and vndertaketh
to demonstrate that Conuenticle of Trent to be *of the same* Ratione. 4.
authoritie and credit with those first, and therefore commends
it aboue the Moone: *What varietie of nations , what choice of
Bishops, out of the whole world? what brightnesse of kingdomes
and Commonweals? What marrow of Diuines? What holinesse?* Great crie &
What teares? What fasting? What Academicall flowers? What little wooll.
tongues?What subtiltie?(that is onely true) *What labour? What
infinite reading? What riches of vertue and studies? did fill that
maiesticall assembly?* To whom I may answer,Perhaps,and
most likely,neuer a one; or that which a Popish Gentleman
said to his Catholicke wife, of whom he made more then she
deserued, *How would I make of a good wife, that make so much of
thee?* How would *Campion* commend the first Councels,
that thus superlatiuely and hyperbolically emblasoneth the
last and worst , and percase the least, if not for number, I
am sure for reputation? Euery singular of our countreimans
sweet flowers,which he pretendeth to haue bene in that
Trident garland, I could oppose with more then twise as
many most filthy stincking weeds, more odious then *Assa
fœtida,*that would both blemish, and out-smell the Popes
Porphyrie and most priuie chaire. If the number of
the bawds and queanes , and such other necessarie imple-
ments of that personated Conuenticle,were compared with
the number of the Prelates, they would passe them by many
hundreds. There were indeed some secrets of that Councel,
but these are none.

12 As the number of Prelates of all nations are noted in
the end of that Councell, they were but 270 of all, the most

by their Proctors, more of Italy by 104, then of all other kingdomes: and for England, but one, and that was the Bishop of Saint *Asse. Similis simili gaudet*, Like will to like. And was not this a prettie Congregation, to compose all matters, yea euen of faith, and that for all Christendome? Especially if we consider, how all Cardinals, Archbishops, and Bishops are first sworne before they be admitted to be Prelates, that they will do nothing preiudiciall to the sea Apostolicke, as they call that pestilentiall chaire and seate of Antichrist. And to prouide for hereafter, lest any succeeding Councell should be hopefull for any good: *All* (according to the order *of this Conuenticle* and the Popes Bull or bable) *which shall be preferred to Cathedrall or superior Churches, or to other dignities, Canonries, or other whatsoeuer Ecclesiasticall Benefices,* and in effect all other Ecclesiasticall persons, regulars, or at least their gouernors, yea of Knights too, shall be bound, to promise, and sweare, that they will maintaine *the Orthodoxall faith* (they meane the Romane faith) and that they will remaine in the obedience of the Church of Rome.

Bulla Pij.4. super forma iuramenti professionis fidei.

13 The forme of which oath is worth the setting downe, as well to know how Antichrist seeketh to make all sure, by all seuere policie, as to let all good Christians see how little good was done in the late Councels, or what lesse hope is like to follow hereafter, if any thing be offered to be tried by a Councell. Which was indeed the cause why some Christian Princes, and learned men, refused to come to that Councell; & some afterward obseruing the exceeding partiall proceeding thereof, would neuer to this day yeeld their consent thereunto. But heare the oath: *I. N. Do faithfully beleeue and confesse all and singular things contained in that forme of faith which the holy Romane Church vseth, that is to say, I beleeue in one God, the Father almightie, maker of heauen and of earth, and of all things visible and inuisible; and in one Lord Iesus Christ the onely begotten Sonne of God, and *borne of his Father before all worlds: God of God, light of light, very God of very God, begotten not made, Consubstantiall with the Father, by whom all things were made*

*Natus.

made; who for vs men and our saluation came downe from heauen, „
and was incarnate by the holy Ghost of the virgine Marie, and was „
made man, and was crucified for vs vnder Pontius Pilate, suffered „
and was buried, and rose againe the third day according to the „
Scriptures, and ascended into heauen, sitteth at the right hand of „
his Father, and shall come againe with glorie to iudge both quicke „
and dead; of whose kingdome shall be no end: and in the holy Ghost „
the Lord and giuer of light, who proceedeth from the Father and „
the Sonne, who with the Father and the Sonne is worshipped and „
glorified, who spake by the Prophets; and one holy Catholique and „
Apostolicke Church. I confesse one Baptisme for remission of sins; „
I looke for the resurrection of the dead, and the life of the world to „
come. Amen.

14   Before I passe further in the particulars of this Oath,
note that this Romane Creed (though it be *Orthodoxall* and
good (*if natus may stand for genitus,* borne for begotten, or
γεννηθέντα for συλληφθέντα; which are the words in the Apostles Creed,) yet is it in many words diuerse from that of the
Apostles, not the same in some particulars with the Nicene
Creed, which it resembleth nearest. This, Master *Harding* a- Hard Apol.
gainst our English Apologie maketh a great matter. *In our* Part. 2.
fathers dayes before any change of Religion was thought vpon,
Christian people liued together in perfect vnitie. None was asha-
med of the common Apostles Creed; and much more to this effect, as if it were an argument of great leuitie, to professe
our faith in diuerse words. And yet you see the Romane
Church, and a Pope, may do it without blame.   Another
(becaufe some of our Church haue interpreted *descendit ad*
inferos, He descended into hell, to be the same, with, *he was bu-*
ried. with ancient *Ruffinus:* others for Christs agonies on the Ruffin. in
Crosse,) saith, that we leaue out an Article, or halfe an Article Symbol. apud
of the Creed; but in this Creed it is left out indeed. If it be Cyprianum.
the Nicene, then in that they agree and haue *Antiquitie;* if it
be the old *Westerne* Creed, of which *Ruffinus* speaketh, out of
which it was left in his dayes, it argueth they haue constancie: howsoeuer, they, nor any of theirs should so bitterly
taxe vs, when we generally haue the words, and but some

haue their priuate interpretation of them, and not accuſe
themſelues for doing that ouertly, which they pretend we
do couertly: which alſo, if they looke neuer ſo narrowly into all our Liturges,they ſhall neuer ſee.But they would faine
haue vs leaue out a peece of a queſtionable Article, to couer their moſt wicked idolatrie and ſacriledge in leauing out
a certaine vndoubtȩd Commandement of almightie God.
Now to procede in the Oath:

Traditions
before Scrip-
tures.

15 *I moſt conſtantly admit and embrace, all Apoſtolicall and
Eccleſiaſticall Traditions and ſuch like obſeruations and Conſtitutions of the Church. Item, the holy Scriptures I do admit ac-*
,, *cording to that ſence, which our holy mother the Church, (where-*
,, *unto belongeth the iudgement of the true ſence and interpretation*
,, *of holy Scriptures) hath holden and doth hold; neither will I euer*
,, *take or interpret them but according to the vniforme conſent of the*
,, *Fathers. I alſo profeſſe, that there be truly and properly ſeuen Sa-*
,, *craments of the new Law,inſtituted by Ieſus Chriſt our Lord, and*
,, *vnto the ſaluation of mankind, although they be not all neceſſarie*
,, *for euery ſingular man; that is to ſay,Baptiſme,Confirmation, the*
,, *Euchariſt,Penance,Extreme vnȼtion,Orders, and Matrimony;*
,, *and that they conferre grace. Moreouer,I do receiue and admit all*
,, *the receiued and approued rites of the Catholique Church, about*
,, *the ſolemne adminiſtration of the foreſaid Sacraments. All and*
,, *euery thing concerning originall ſinne, and of Iuſtification, which*
,, *were defined and publiſhed in the holy Councell of Trent, I embrace*
,, *and receiue. I withall profeſſe, that in the Maſſe there is offered*
,, *vnto God a true proper and propitiatorie Sacrifice, for the quicke*
,, *and dead: and that in the moſt holy Sacrament of the Euchariſt,*
,, *there is truly,really, and ſubſtantially the body and blood, together*
,, *with the ſoule and Diuinitie of our Lord Ieſus Chriſt: and that*
,, *there is made a ȼonuerſion of the whole ſubſtance of the bread into*
,, *the body, and the whole ſubſtance of wine, into the blood, which*
,, *conuerſion the Catholique Church calleth Tranſſubſtantiation.*
,, *I confeſſe alſo,that vnder our kind onely, all, and whole Chriſt,*
,, *and the true Sacrament is receiued.I conſtantly hold that there is a*
,, *Purgatorie, and that the ſoules there detained,by the prayers of the*
,, *faithfull are redȩemed. Likewiſe,the Saints which reigne together*
                                                            with

with Chri∫t, *are to be wor∫hipped and inuocated ; and that they offer* „
prayers to God for vs ; and that their Reliques are to be wor∫hipped. „
I do mo∫t firmly auouch, that the Images of Chri∫t, and of the euer „
Virgin mother of God, as al∫o of other Saints, are to be had and „
continued, and that due honour and wor∫hip is to be done to them. „
That the power of Indulgences was left by Chri∫t to his Church: Indulgentiæ
and I affirme their v∫e to be very wbole∫ome for Chri∫tian people. non innotue-
I acknowledge the holy Catholicke Romane Church to be the mo- ad Purgatoriū
ther and mi∫tre∫∫e of all Churches. And I promi∫e and ∫weare true ignem trepi-
obedience to the Bi∫hop of Rome , the ∫ucce∫∫or of ble∫∫ed Peter datum e∫t.
Prince of the Apo∫tles, and the Vicar of Ie∫us Chri∫t. Item, all other Fi∫ull.
things which haue bene deliuered, defined and declared in the holy „
Canons and generall Councels, and principally in this holy Coun- „ Principall.
cell of Trent, without doubting, I receiue and profe∫∫e: and together „
all things contrary, and what∫oeuer here∫ies condemned by the „
Church reiected or anathematized, I do al∫o damne, reiect and a- „
nathematize. This true Catholicke faith, without which no man „
can be ∫aued, which for the pre∫ent I voluntarily profe∫∫e, and truly „
hold, the ∫ame ∫ound and inuiolable vnto my la∫t breath of life, „
(God a∫∫i∫ting me) to hold and confe∫∫e , and to tho∫e which ∫hall be „
vnder me, and that ∫hall be committed vnto my charge, to be holden, „
taught and preached, as much as in me lyeth, I will be carefull. This „
I the ∫aid N. do promi∫e, vow and ∫weare, as God ∫hall helpe me, and „
the∫e holy Go∫pels.   „

16 This is the Oath that all mu∫t take, who are euer like
to haue voice in a generall Councell   What hope then can
there po∫∫ibly be, that euer any reformation may be effected
by a Councel ? The mo∫t and chiefe∫t things betweene Anti-
chri∫t and vs, are already in this Conuenticle concluded. Who
euer di∫puted again∫t them ? who euer contradicted them on
our part, till all was concluded at their owne plea∫ure, and to
their owne liking ? Our cau∫e had not an aduocate , not a
Proctor, not any ∫o much as a remembrancer. The witne∫∫es,
the Iudges delegate, the Iudges ordinary, the ∫upreme Iudge
in the∫e matters, were made, prouided, determined, re∫olued
again∫t vs. The ∫entence was giuen before the Councell a∫-
∫embled : onely a ∫hew of a Councell was made, like an *ignis*
fatuus,

fatuus, or a maske with drum and trumpet, as if great matters had bene in hand; but nothing altered, or at leaft nothing amended, nothing reformed : which was all the expeƈtation of the wife, and determination of the wicked before hand.

17 Such are the Councels which our Aduerfaries would haue. They confeſſe we receiue the firſt and beſt, they obtrude the later and worſt. We fubfcribe vnto the former; they falfifie, corrupt, and contemne them. We iuſtly refufe the later; they againſt all right and reafon vrge, magnifie and preſſe them. To conclude, fuppofe we would yet fubmit our felues to the determination of a Councel, and that al things ſhould be ended as our felues would haue it, faue onely the Soueraigntie of the Biſhop of *Rome* kept harmleſſe, and that we ſhould depart with contentment, and hope to enioy the truth with peace: the next newes we ſhould heare might be,

Extra, de ele-
ƈione & ele-
ƈi poteſtate.
cap. Significa-
ſti in fine.

Quaſi Romanæ Ecclesiæ legem Concilia vlla præfixerint, &c. As if any Councels can prefixe limits to the Romane Church; whereas all Councels by the authoritie of the Romane Church haue bene made, and received their ſtrength : and that in their Canons the Biſhop of Romes authoritie is euidently excepted, as before is remembred.

Silu. Prierias,
Panormitan.
Ioh. Andræas.

18 The Canoniſts vpon this text fpeake infinitely of Popes fupereminent and vnbounded authoritie, euen in Councels, and befide them, and aboue them. Therefore the Romaniſts do but mocke vs, and feeke to gull vs, when they offer vs thefe new Conuenticles for old Councels, whereby they know that they can onely choake truth, and make the credulous world beleeue that the Moone is made of a green cheefe, or that all the flocke of Chriſt is contained within the bounds of the Romane Church, as the Sunne is contained in the compaſſe of a cart wheele. Finally, yet once fuppofe that we would yeeld as much to all the Councels paſt, as hath bene or can be praƈifed or required; ſhall all their Canons ſtand vnuiolable? and may we reſt vpon either the old Councels, and new Conuenticles, and that with the Popes confent, without change or alteration? No, that may not be.

For

For if we fay, that the Papifts, *by the Church vnderftand Coun-* Defenf. Rob.
cels; *Gretzer* confeffeth, *Ita eft : fed præfentia, non præterita.* Bellar. l. 3. c. 10
Quia vt Pontifex qui viuere defiit, non eft controuerfiarum Iu-
dex, fed fuit: Ita Concilium quod olim celebratum eft, non eft præ-
fens controuerfiarum Iudex, fed fuit. Per Concilium igitur intelli-
gimus illud, quod præfens cum præfente, hoc eft, cum iam Cathe-
dram Petri tenente Pontifice controuerfiam dirimit, & fententiam
iudiciariam pronunciat : ita vt vox eius & fententia, ab omnibus
præfertim litigantibus, perſpicuè & euidenter audiri ac intelligi
queat. They vnderftand by the *Church the Councels. Marry the* ,,
prefent, not the paft. For as the *Pope after his death, is not the* ,,
Iudge of controuerfies, but was : fo a Councell that was celebrated ,,
in times paft, is not a prefent Iudge of controuerfies, but was. There- ,,
fore we vnderftand by a Councell, that which is prefent with the ,,
prefent, that is, with the Pope, Peters Tenant in poffeffion, who can ,,
end the controuerfie, and pronounce the finall doome. So that his ,,
voice and fentence may be perſpicuoufly and plainly heard and vn- ,,
derftood, eſpecially of thofe who are at ftrife. If this be the cafe ,,
of Chriftians in the Romane Church, why do they either
taxe vs for leffe regard vnto the ancient Councels? or fo
much brag to their difciples, that they haue all *Antiquitie?*
when perhaps in refpect of generall Councels, fome parts
of their Religion were neuer till the Councel of *Trent,* part
may be broached when they will, by this or the next Pope,
with or without any Councell at all. And fo all *Antiquitie*
is at one word, as at one blow, vtterly ouerblowne and deftroyed by this moft defperate Papifts one fentence.

CHAP.

CHAP. XII.

*For ancient Fathers, the Romanists offer vs new Fellowes with old
names. Some graue men indeed, but stript out of their owne comely
ornaments, and harrowed out of their wits, and so made incompetent Iudges, or witnesses for the truth. And for
abundant Cautell, they take their old Schoolmen, in defect of old Fathers indeed.*

He very name of Ancient Fathers hath bene
reuerend in the Church, and their authoritie
much, and that worthily efteemed. They
haue illuftrated the Scriptures by their learned Commentaries, inftructed the Church
by their zealous Sermons, Tractates and Homilies, confuted heretickes and their errors and herefies by
their wifedome and dexteritie in the word of truth; taught,
and difperfed the Chriftian faith in their elaborate writings
to all pofteritie. The fruites of their godly trauels are yet
fweet vnto the tafte of euery gracious man that readeth them
with difcretion, and doth fauour them with fobrietie. We
are to this day beholding to them. They hold vs faire light
to fearch the darkeft myfteries of the diuine Scriptures. They
prefent vnto vs the ftate of the Church in their times. They
leade vs the way themfelues haue walked to the kingdome
of heauen. Whofe bookes we reade with pleafure and profite; whofe vertues we endeuour to imitate in our life and
conuerfation; whofe children we defire to be called, and reioyce to haue them our Fathers.

    2   How they haue bene by our aduerfaries traduced in
Supra cap.8. their credits, and their workes corrupted, hath bene before
demonftrated. Now I would aduife a carefull Chriftian to
be cautelous, not to receiue all for Fathers who are offered
vnder that name; nor to truft euery thing that is alledged
out of a good and certaine Father, without due examination
and triall. For in the vnaduifed admittance of either of thefe,

                                                              a

a very honeſt heart may eaſily be deceiued. As *Sertorious* ſur- Plutarch in
priſed the *Gyriſonians*, whom when he had ouerthrowne and Sertorius.
ſlaine, he cauſed his men to put on the ſouldiers apparell, and
to take their weapons in their hands; which the Citizens ſeeing, and taking them for their owne friends, opened the gates
and loſt their Citie. So the Romaniſts murther the fathers by
their maledictions (as before is proued,) & then clothe themſelues with their apparell, to deceiue the ouer credulous and
weake Chriſtians. If a Bankrupt be brought in a faire Citizens
gowne, and with the name of an Alderman, it would be a
ſhrewd temptation to a plaine meaning man to giue him credit: Or if a Client ſhould bring into an open court, old euidences without date, that haue hand & ſeale, and are truly his
Anceſtors, ſo accepted and taken, and all this without doubt or
denyall; would not this dant and amate his aduerſarie, and
giue him good cauſe at leaſt to feare, if not quite to deſpaire of
his action? I trow it would.

3 Yet for all theſe faire ſhewes, a wiſe man will looke
eare he leape, and trie ere he truſt. He will be reſolued of the
perſon, before he take his word, or his bond either. And a
graue and ſage Counſellour will reade the euidences, and ſee
whether the thing in queſtion be conueyed by that deed, or if
it be, whether it may lawfully be ſo or not; or if it be ſo, & may
be ſo, yet he will ſpie for enterlinings, or prie for raſures, or cō-
pare it with Counterpaines, or ſearch the Rolles in the Chan-
cerie or monuments in the Tower, before he yeeld his Clients
cauſe. So muſt we do with our aduerſaries, when they produce Fathers. They may tell me this is ſuch a Father, and it
may not be the man; ſhall I take a knight (as they ſay) of the
Poſt, or a counterfeit cranke for a worthy Alderman in the
Citie of God? They may produce ancient euidences, that by
their ſtyle, and other probable circumſtances, may be proued
to be the old Fathers indeed. Muſt we take them at the firſt
ſight, and throw vp our cauſe before we make better tryall of
the deed? We muſt obſerue whether the caſe in queſtion be
there concluded. If it be, whether it may ſo lawfully be paſſed, as that no iuſt exception may be admitted againſt it; or if
there be no exception in reſpect of the maner of conueyance,

yet

yet look whether there be not enterlining, or rafures, or whether it agree with ancient copies in vnfufpeted Libraries. For
by any one of thefe, a good caufe may be ill ouerthrowne,
and an vnrecouerable loffe may fall vpon an innocent and
harmeleffe foule.

4 Our aduerfaries the Romanifts (howfoeuer *Bellarmine*
calleth them block-heads) as they are paffing wittie and
dexterous in all craftie deuices, and care not how they circumuent poore foules, deuout perhaps, but yet blinded
and amazed with fuperftition : fo they ceaffe not to put
them in daily practife, and are not afhamed in the noone
day of the Gofpell, to offer them to the world, as if all men
were as blind buzzards, as they make themfelues.

5 That excellent Father *Athanafius* was accufed before a
Iudge of incontinencie with her that was prefent, and laid the
fat moft impudently to the innocent Fathers charge. The

Ruffinus hi-
ftor.l.1. c.17.

Harlot not fparing her felfe withall, vrged the libell, as fhe
had bene inftructed; fuch circumftances were produced, as that
it poffeffed the Court with probabilitie at the leaft, that the
good Father was flandered with a matter of truth : vntill *Ti-*

Presbytero
fuo.

motheus the good Bifhops Chaplaine taking vpon him the
perfon of the accufed, asked (as if himfelfe had bene the man)
whether fhe knew him to haue bene in her houfe, and whether euer he had carnally knowne her : She not knowing the
Father, but imagining this to be the man, auouched her accufation as ftrongly to his face, as if he had bene *Athanafius*
indeed, whom fhe accufed. By which fhe was conuicted of
calumnie, the good Fathers aduerfaries confounded, and his
innocencie by Gods prouidence, and this Chriftian policie,
worthily cleared, though he not deliuered from his enemies
malice. It thus often fareth with the Romane ftrumpet, who
accufeth the holy Fathers, as acceffary to her fornications,
and that with fuch impudencie and importunity, that a right
iuft man may be eafily deluded, but a friend to the Fathers wil
detect her deceite, and faue their credit from her fhameleffe
accufation.

6 Before we enter the exemplification of thefe vngodly
                                                    ftratagems

ftratagems, in their particulars, it were good to confider a
few deceits in generall, well obferued by their owne friends.
Among (and I may well fay aboue)other,*Sixtus Senenfis* hath Bibli. Sancta
laboured well in this kind: and hath fet downe many meanes ad finem.l.4.
and occafions, why bookes are falfely intituled, fome honeft,
fome difhoneft,as he faith. Not to fpeake of thofe which he
calleth honeft, the difhoneft are principally two-fold; either
to play the knaues in the coufening the ignorant,or to broach
their owne errors vnder titles of credite: and this may and
hath bene attempted by the Authors themfelues. Howbeit
this alfo may be done by others, and that out of error, or deceit. Error by miftaking, through the identity or fimilitude
of names, or liknefle of ftyle, or nearenefle of the infcription,
or concurrence of matter, or fuch like. *Others for profit, gaine,
and filthie lucre, being Writers, Printers, Stationers, and Bookefel-
lers, will fometime to make the book more faleable, giue a good name
to a bad author, or at leaft a better to a worfe :* which *Sixtus* deliuereth & amplifieth in many words, but to this effect. Whereby fufficient warning is giuen, not to beleeue that all is gold
which gliftereth with the glorious fhew of an ancient Fathers
name, but to beware left a fnake be hid vnder greene graffe.
We receiue this cautele from our aduerfaries, both rules and
practife, and therefore haue iuft caufe to look about vs. Howbeit thefe are fuch common trickes, that they may impofe as
well vpon our aduerfaries as vs, and fo we may be all deceiued. But there are others which are fo appropriate to the
Church of Rome, that they onely inuent them, to circumuent
vs, and to outface a good caufe, with pretended countenance
of ancient Fathers, and that vnder thefe fhadowes.

7   There are fome ancient Fathers and Martyrs named in Auguft. de
old Hiftories, that notwithftanding wrote not at all,no more confenfu E-
then *Pythagoras* did his Contemplations, or *Socrates* his Pra- uangelift.l.r.
ctiks,but their difciples after them.Some of thefe haue books cap.
fathered in their names, fo the names are old, but the books Hieron.in Ca-
are new. There are others that indeed wrote, and their books tal.
are named by Saint *Hierome,* or *Eufebius,* or others, but loft Eufeb.
and perifhed. Thefe titles are fet to new books, vnder their Socrates.alij.
                                                      names

names, as if they were the fame that are remembred in older times. Thefe either haue bene written in times fomewhat elder, by heretickes, or fuch impoftors, and for aduantage are now admitted for clafficall authors in the Church of Rome: or they are inuentions of idle Monkes, that haue little elfe to do, and layed a while to ruft and canker in vaults, or old wals, and being found on the fudden (forfooth) of them that hid them, or a generation or two after, are produced for witneffes, as if they were elder then *Methufalem,* and were begotten long before their fathers were borne; and this were a miracle.

8 Of fome of thefe, and the moft of them that are pretended to be begotten fo foone, and yet borne fo late, we may iuftly fay as S. *Auguftine* doth of the counterfeit writings fathered vpon *Henoch and Noah, which are therefore fufpected both of Iewes and Chriftians for their ouer great Antiquitie, left vnder* **Aug.de ciuit.** *pretence thereof they may offer falfehood for truth. Nam proferun-* **Dci.l.18.c. 38.** *tur quædam quæ ipforum effe dicuntur:* **For there are certaine** *workes, which are faid to be theirs, of them, who out of their owne braines euery where beleeue what they lift. But the integritie of the Canon receiueth them not; not that the authoritie of thofe men is* **Plutarch in** *reiected, but becaufe the bookes are not beleeued to be theirs. Plu-* **Thef.** *tarch* was afraid of this in writing the life of *Thefeus* and *Romulus,* fearing the fables of Romes *Antiquitie, vnder the appearance of Hiftoricall narration:* and therefore craues pardon when he writeth of things fo old and ancient. For which caufe, we haue as iuft occafion to obferue carefully what we receiue, left vnder pretence of old, we accept new, to the preiudice of Gods truth, and aduantage of Antichrift: who hath made this not the leaft part of his diftempered morter, whereby he would daube vp the breaches of the battered walls of his Lateran and S. *Peters* Church. The moft of whom, though they haue bene of late in part difcouered by Cardinal *Bellarmine,* Cardinall *Baronius, Friar Sixtus,* and *Father Poffeuine,* and other Romane writers, & not long fince by that precious Englifh *Iewel* the worthy Bifhop of *Salifburie, and that librarie of learning Doctor Reynolds, and laftly moft exquifitely and iudicioufly by my*

late

late learned friend, Maister Robert Cooke, of Leeds, in an exact volume of these authors, with inuincible arguments proouing their baſtardy, ſo that now they can hardly deceiue a man of any reading and care to ſearch out the truth. Yet the dayes haue bene when ſcarſe any of them was auouched, but with a garland of Rhetorical flowers to adorne and preſent them to the acceptation of ignorant or careleſſe Chriſtians: I am verily perſwaded againſt their owne conſciences that ſet them forth, to deceiue the vnskilfull by theſe deuices.

9 Suppoſe we ſhould bring to you either the Canons of the Apoſtles, or their Conſtitutions, would you miſtruſt any thing that comes from thoſe elect inſtruments of Chriſts glory? eſpecially when Saint *Clement* is made the ſetter forth of them, and they are placed with his workes, and one wily Biſhop ſhall ſay, *They are certainly the Apoſtles?* another produce a Councell *that had them in great reuerence?* another vrge that they were *receiued of the Church euen preſently after the Apoſtles times?* their *authoritie approued by Anachtus Saint Peters ſcholer, &c.* and that *Damaſcene yeelds ſo much vnto them, that he ſeemed to number them with the Canonical books (of holy Scriptures)* of which ſome would haue none, ſome more, ſome fewer. So vncertaine are they, whether they be, or not; to whom to referre them, or what to do with them.

Canones Apoſtolorum, Conſtitut. Clement. Lindan.Chrō. prefixa Panopliæ. Bannes in Thomas Aquin.2.2.q.1. art.10.cont.6. Pigghius Hierar.l.2.c.10. Alphon.de caſtro. Bell.de Scrip. Eccleſiaſticis in Clemente.

10 *Gelaſius* a Pope and a Saint in the Romane Catalogue and Calendar, vtterly caſhires them. Which cannot be ſalued by Cardinal *Bellarmines* plaiſter which he laid on too faſt when he ſaid: *Canones Apoſtolorum, cum ſexta Synodo reijciuntur:* The Apoſtles Canons with the ſixt Councell are reiected. The like may be ſaid of the recognitions, *Conſtitutions, and other Apocryphals,* ſet forth in his name. Maſter *Harding* after he had floriſhed with great oſtentation, that the Doctors with one conſent, in all ages, in all parts of the world, from the Apoſtles time forward, both with example, and alſo teſtimony of writing, confirmed the ſame faith: muſtereth in great brauerie, as his champions in triumph, ſundry names without perſons:

Diſt.15.c.Romana. De verb. Dei, l.1.cap.20. Art.1.of priuate Maſſe.

Y   but

but take view of thefe Doctors as he aduanceth them: *Abdias*
Bifhop of Babylon , who was the Apoftles fcholer, and faw Chrift
our Sauiour in the flefh, and was prefent at the paffion and martyr-
dome of Saint Andrew. Would not all this almoft make a mans
lips water to heare what he faith that is thus qualified? yet
is hea ranke counterfeit, difcarded now by all the Romane
writers. His next Doctor, is a *Doctors Maifter: Saint Iames*
his Liturgie or Maffe; whom though that paire of Cardinals
will not vtterly difclaime , yet they confeffe it hath bene *fo*
enriched, (as *Bellarmine* faith) *hath fuch additions and briefe con-*
tractions, that it is not eafie to difcerne what part of it hath Saint
Iames for the author: but by many arguments it is moft euidently condemned. Saint *Martiall* is the next , *one of the 72*
difciples of Chrift, Bifhop of Bourdeaux in France, fent thither by
Saint Peter , not onely Sainted, but deified , that heard Chrift, and
faw Chrift, was a Confeffor, yea an Apoftle : yet when all this is
faid, that *Iames* and this *Martiall are falfe lads,* vnworthy
the naming among Chriftian authors. He hath alfo Saint
Clement with much honorable remembrance. Saint *Dionyfe*
with more , conuerted by Saint *Paul, mentioned in the Actes*
of the Apoftles , had *conference with Saint Peter, Paul, and Iohn*
the Euangelift, and much acquaintance with Timothy , yet when
all is done , thefe are but cofening Gibeonites , they belye
their names , their times, their countries; they are now de-
tected by their beft friends. Thefe Mafter *Harding* (as he
faith) giueth but for a tafte, as if he had much more of the
fame food to minifter to his hungrie friends ; but there is
mors in olla , death in the pot: thefe are not to be trufted , they
haue no credite.

11 The like may be faid of *Amphilochius, EphremDorothæus,*
and many more , who are now put into the volumes of their
Bibliotheca Sanctorum patrum, and haue bene alledged by
the Romane writers with great commendation. For they are
all wholly counterfeited , or horribly corrupted enery mothers fonne.

12 There are other *Fathers,* who were not onely Fathers
indeed, but that haue many, knowne, certaine, confeffed and
appro-

[marginal notes:]
Abdias.

Bellar. Baro-
nius alij.
Saint Iames.
his Liturgie.

Saint Martiall

Saint Clemēt.
Dionyf.

approued workes that admit no exception. Yet haue they intermixed in their volumes, many Pamphlets, Rhapsodies and Centons, that are some erronious, some hereticall, some friuolous; some ridiculous, some idolatrous, some blasphemous; that an honest Scholler would loath to reade them, be ashamed to alledge them, detest to defend them. Yet none more frequent in our Aduersaries margins of their bookes, then these. As there were very few writers after the Apostles & Euanglists, for the first 300 yeares which was before the Councell of Nice, so were there almost none of them that did write, but had some, nay many things foisted among their workes. *Iustinus Martyr* in Cardinall *Bellarmines* opinion, was the first after the *Apostles times*, whose writings reach vnto vs: who perhaps he accounteth in the *first hundreth yeare*, he was certainly not long after. The Cardinall numbreth his workes to be twelue. Of them there are but fiue in his iudgement truly fathered: seuen (the maior part) either are vpon good reason suspected to be none of his, or vtterly reiected as workes vnworthy of him. *Melito* was another. He had also a booke vnworthy so great a man, attributed vnto him. After them *Tertullian*, *Origen Cyprian*, the most famous, haue diuers things added to them. So had *Basil, Chrysostome* and others among the Grecians: *Ambrose, Hierome, Augustine, Gregorie*, and others among the Romanes. Few of any fame escaped this imposture, not to speake of the corruptions of their knowne workes since these dayes.

De Scriptor. Ecclesiasticis.

13 To prosecute each of these in their particulars, though it may seeme pertinent to this place, yet for feare of length partly, and because none but scholers are like to make search for them: I would referre them to the authors before named, especially to that of Maister *Cooke*; who hath most exactly searched into this argument. Which booke I could wish in euery yong Diuines hand, that purposeth to reade the Fathers, lest he take *quid pro quo*, one for another, a theefe for a true man; or if he purpose to studie controuersies, lest he be ensnared in a net wouen with Fathers names, without

Y 2   one

one threed of their spinning , and made a prey by Antichrist the child of perdition. There he may find an answer out of our aduersaries owne mouthes and pennes, to very neare two parts or more, very neare the one halfe of all that is brought for priuate Masse, Reall presence, Transsubstantiation, Inuocation and worship of Saints, Purgatorie, Pilgrimage, Popes supremacie, Pardons, Originall sinne, Iustification, Free will, Prayers in an vnknowne tongue, halfe Communion, Merit, seuen Sacraments, and whatsoeuer else they call Traditions. For the chiefe and most pregnant proofes the Romanists haue for these things, are all fished out of such puddles , as if they had so many ancient Fathers; when God knowes they are not the progeny of the Fathers, or the true children of the Church.

14 I may adde vnto all this, that the true Fathers, in their vndoubted and knowne workes, by new Editions and pretended Manuscripts are so corrupted and sophisticated with additions, subtractions, purgations, and almost euacuations, that it is as hard at first sight to know an ancient Doctor of the Church , as it is for a child to know his father neare the Popes Court. Where the Romanists talke of Doctors and Fathers, they are for the most part no other then hath bene said, they vse them no otherwise, as you shall proue.

15 It may possibly be, that out of a very Father indeed, so taken and approued, our aduersaries may sometimes find a sentence that wil make shew for them. Yet looke narrowly to it, and you shall find it some priuate opinion of his, confuted, or at least contradicted by other, or mistaken by himselfe, or misapplied, or misconstrued, or such a fault as cannot be excused, and if the father were liuing, would reforme it himselfe. Such are the souldiers which Antichrist brings against vs, such are the weapons with which our aduersaries assaile vs; which maketh vs the lesse to feare them, because we find them, but in shew bumbasted Gyants in very truth for pined dwarfs.

16 There was a tyrannicall King called in Hebrue *Abaddon,* and in Greeke *Apollyon,* that in a desperate cause, made

warre

warre with a peaceable Prince, euen the Prince of peace. He presseth into the field diuers choice men, valiant souldiers, furnished with their armour of proofe; yet because his claime is wrongfull, and his quarrell naught, they go no further then enforced, they fight with no courage, and are ready to turne their weapons against him that presseth them for his enemy: for he is not their liege Lord, nor they his subiects. The Tyrant flyeth, yet abating no malice, returneth againe with a rascall rout, and a forlorne hope, of out-lawes, vp-starts, boyes, and loose desperate companions, with shels for shields, with spits for swords, and will venture a new assault against the puissant armies of the great Prince. Wil not a wise Counseller rather thinke him out of his wits, then encourage him in his enterprise, or giue him comfort against the day of battell? This is the very case of Antichrist, who daily defieth the hoast of the liuing God. He hath pressed the Scriptures and oppressed them, when he long kept them in an vnknown tongue; enforced the Fathers by wresting them into his quarell, against their wils. They had good armour and weapons, but they would not vse them against the Prince of peace. By these this Tyrant could neuer come to his purpose; he flyeth the field; he returneth with his *Abdias* and his *Martial*, with scullions and kitchin boyes, perhaps with a few ancient and graue men among, but cut and maimed, because they refused his wicked designes. For this he searcheth vaults, plucketh downe old wals, ouerthroweth pillars, and perhaps spareth not to farme priuies, to find out such weapons as may serue for shew, but shall neuer stand in stead for proofe.

17 It fareth with them as with a man in danger of drowning, who catcheth at shadowes, which cannot helpe him, or thornes and briers, which rather hurt him. These are but shadowes, but thornes and briers, they are at most but an AEgyptian reed, which if you leane on, and trust vnto, it will breake, and the shiuers will runne into the hand, perhaps into the heart too; yet being driuen to this, they had no other shift, and therefore hold it as their best refuge.

18 When all these stratagemes are described, and their

euents difcouered, in thefe facrilegious abufes and violence
offered to *Antiquitie*, then they flie in ftead of Fathers to
children, to the Schoolemen of later yeares, whom they en-

Bellar.de Lai-
cis,l.3.c.6. title old Diuines, as *Thomas Aquinas ex Theologis antiquis*,
though they haue yonger fots, men drowned in the dregs of
Philofophie and humane reafon, fupported with Sophifmes,
and inextricable diftinctions, wherewith they quite marre
true Diuinitie, and amaze fimple and ignorant men, who are
neuer able to conceiue the truth in any euidence, but euer
labouring, and neuer profiting or proceeding in the way of
faluation, perifh in their errors and finnes. Of whom our Sauiour fpeaketh, *that many fhall ftriue to enter, and yet fhall neuer*.

Socol.de veræ
& falfæ Ecclef.
difcrimine,l.3.
c.11.in fine. Ere long we fhall haue *Socolouius* his catalogue or beadrole,
of *Sadolets, Pooles, Fifhers, Moores, Hofiufes, Lindans, Tappers,
Sottes, Canies, Medinaes, Oforiufes, Canifiufes*, and *Sanders*, lifted in the number of old Fathers, who haue exhaufted Scriptures, Fathers, Councels, and all *Antiquitie*, and haue all thefe
at their fingers ends.

19 Now courteous Reader, what authors bring we forth
that were neuer heard of before? what ftrangers haue we
brought into the Temple of God? what communion haue
we held with thefe fonnes of Belial? We are contented with
the Scriptures, which are confeffed to be truth on all hands:
we alledge no Councels, but the moft ancient; no Fathers,
but fuch as haue long bene approued in the Church of God;
or if any do for ceremonies or otherwife, they are more to
blame. Our authors are without fufpition, without exception. If they denie our tranflations, we appeale to the Originals, which they refufe. If they refufe our Editions, we are
contented with theirs, or fhew good caufe why we are not.
I canot conceiue why an honeft hearted Chriftian Catholike
fhould not herein reft fatisfied with vs, that in all things
deale fo apertly, and without intricate fubtilties, or outfacing
brauadoes, and offer fuch equall and iuft conditions in triall
of our caufe. Whereas they daily are yet feeking new fhifts
out of the old corners of Antichrifts or the diuell his maifters

Pfal.119. braines. *O Lord, let thy word be a lanterne vnto our feete, and a
light*

light vnto our steps; and for thy mercies sake by lawfull and honest meanes, let vs be led into thy truth, that we may walke
the way of euerlasting life.

20 Peraduenture some of our aduersaries will say, and
not altogether without reason, that some of our owne Captaines haue vsed such souldiers in the conflict of learning, as
well as they. It may be so, (we confesse) and better too, but
not worse, or so ill; wherein they may be worthily excused in
respect of them. For vntil the heresies of the Romane Church
were publikly and resolutely, not onely by preaching, but by
writing called into question , the Fathers writings were taken almost of euery man one from another, at second hand,
few saw them themselues in their owne likenesse. Neither
was it easie for them who contended about great mysteries
of faith, to make any diligent search in the discouering of
these impostures. In which kind notwithstanding , *Erasmus*
and some others following this businesse with sharpe sense,
layd open the counterfeits and forged Fathers, to more exact
view. Vntil then, some of ours took them as they found them
without scruple , and alledged them against *Rome,* as *Rome*
brought them against truth. Our difference was, that we examine the best and most certaine by the Scriptures; they vrged the worst, as binding proofes for their errors, whereby
they mis-led their disciples, and sought to outface their opposites. But now seeing the most of these haue bin examined
by the light , and are found ouer light to sway or ouerbeare
any controuersie of moment ; let them be discarded as they
deserue, on all hands, in point of controuersie. Which I wish
were and might be euer strictly obserued , not onely by our
aduersaries against vs, but by vs also against them, in all matters of faith : yea and among our selues also , betweene our
selues in matter of ceremonie ; for no man now can alledge
them without blushing after such discouerie.

CHAP. XIII.

When the ancient and approued hiftories will affoord no helpe to re-
paire the ruines of the Romane Synagogue, her builders
feeke reliefe from fables and Legends,the dreames
and deuices of Monafticall Locufts.

 Hat fupplies the Romanifts haue made for
Scriptures, Councels and *Fathers,* is fhortly,
but I hope fufficiently,deliuered . Rather
then they fhould not feeme to runne with
foure feet,like beafts,as they are,hauing dif-
countenanced all ancient hiftorians with

1.King.3.20. their hiftories,they haue againe prouided to put a dead child
into the liuing childs roome; and therefore haue coyned
old wiues tales, and lying Legends,which are the drowfie
dreames of Monks and Friers,the very fruites of idleneffe,va-
nitie,and ignorance of Gods truth, as is confeffed by one of
Canus loc.c8. their beft friends, *Ab hominibus otiofis fitta, à corruptis ingenijs*
l.11.c.6. *verfatæ:* Fained by idlers, and perufed by corrupt wits. And
left they fhould feeme to negleft in this purueyance either
Laitie or Clergie, they haue prouided for both.

2   For the Laitie, from whom all facred hiftories of the
Bible were immured and lockt vp in the darke dungeon of
an vnknowne tongue, they prepared the ftories of King *Ar-*
thur of *Brittaine* and his Knights of the Round Table; the
foure fonnes of *Amon; Valentine* and *Orfon,*with the like in
profe: *Beuis* of *Hampton, Adam Bel,*and fuch like in meeter.
Wherein many exploits and renowmed feats were defcribed to be done,after deuout hearing of Maffe, or orifons to
our Ladie,or fome other Saint, bleffing themfelues with the
figne of the Croffe: by thefe meanes to inftill the dregs of fuperftition and idolatry into ignorant hearts, with the delight
of a vaine ftorie, which was more then halfe Scripture,to
them that knew no better,nor other. I haue heard (but I cannot auouch my author, neither is it much materiall) that
                                                    fome

fome of the rude and vntaught borderers in the North (who would not beleeue that *Thou fhalt not fteale* was one of Gods commandements, but of King *Henries* new making) being reproued by a Gentleman for their barbarous ignorance in the points of Chriſtianity, anſwered, They would gladly learne if any would teach them: and if they could get but a gude buike, they would haue it read in their Chappell though they had no Chaplaine. The Gentleman in meriment lendeth them *Valentine* and *Orſon*, they thankfully accept it, get it read, and hearken it deuoutly. In the beginning when the mother was deſtitute of helpe, deliuered in a forreſt, a child ſurpriſed and nouriſhed by a Beare, with other lamentable accidents that befell the diſtreſſed mother and her innocent babe, with croſſings and bleſſings and lamentations, they fell a weeping, and ſtrake their breaſts in compaſſion, as if they had heard the ſtorie of *Ioſeph* making himſelfe knowne to his brethren, and tooke it for a very holy booke, if not for Scripture it ſelfe. But afterward hearing ſuch fighting and ſcratching, ſuch riuing and ſpoyling as followed in the tale, they returned with their booke, and asked in good ſadneſſe whether that were Gods buike or nay? for they found woe worke and fell fighting in it. Such was the diſmall darkneſſe of that forlorne people, and ſuch is it to this day, where they haue no better teaching. And what will not the *brutiſh and fooliſh man* beleeue, when he is vtterly ignorant of Gods truth, which the wiſeſt in the world forſaking, ſhall beleeue lyes? Gen. 45. 2.

2. Theſ. 2.

3 For their Clergie they had their golden Legends, Saints liues, Feſtiuals, Martyrologies, *Sermones diſcipuli*, and ſuch like wholeſome books, which were commended to Curats, with prefaces, with prologues, with concluſions, propoſing, promiſing, and warranting ſuch benefite by them, as they neuer auouched by the word of God; whereas they are ſo full fraught with lyes and fables, that the more learned Romaniſts are aſhamed of ſome of them. Doſtor *Harding* ſayes of the golden Legend, *Forſooth there is an old motheaten booke, wherein Saints liues are ſaid to be contained: Certaine it is that among ſome true ſtories there be many vaine fables written.* D. Harding.

But

But *Viues* that was no Proteſtant, ſaid more then Maiſter *Harding*; who ſaith onely that it mattereth *not who was the Author*, for whoſoeuer made it was *ferrei frontis & plumbei cordis,Of an iron face and a leaden heart,*which ſentence Biſhop *Canus* alſo alloweth. Howbeit that which was once gold is now but ſiluer,and that which is now motheaten and canker-fretten too, if you will, was freſh and faire, tranſlated into di-uers tongues, commended to *Curats,* read in Churches, hear-kened by the people in their owne tongue, when the Scrip-tures lay perhaps motheaten in a few libraries,and were ſcarſe to be found in one Prieſts ſtudie of an hundred:and were care-fully, but moſt wickedly kept from the people, as the ſecrets of *Numaes* & *Pythagoras* religion, in an vnknowne language, leſt they might ſee, and loue the true euidence of their euerla-ſting inheritance. To allure the readers the better to buy this Legend, the reaſon of the name was giuen in the end of the booke, with the vſe for the which it was written: *It is called Golden, that like as gold excelleth all other mettals, ſo this excelleth all other bookes.* And therefore is commended,&c. A further proofe for the eſtimation of that booke may be produced out of a wil of a predeceſſor of mine,in the Vicaridge of Hallifax, dated *anno Dom.* 1477; who giueth no booke in his will,but one, and that is (as I take it) this. *Item lego Ioanni Wilkinſon fi-lio Roberti Wilkinſon, vnum librum nominatum Legenda Sancto-rum, ſi ſit Preſbyter:* I bequeath to Iohn Wilkinſon my brother Ro-bert his ſonne,one booke called the Legend of Saints,if he be a Prieſt. By which we may ſee,what ſtore of books ſuch a man in thoſe dayes had; perhaps in all likelihood, he had not a better. For it is probable he would haue giuen him the beſt, or one of the beſt, hauing onely lay-men his executors, eſpecially it being giuen on this condition, that he were a Prieſt. For otherwiſe it had bene too good for him.

  4   There is a whelpe of this haire called, the Feſtiuall, drawne as it were out of the *Meditullio* the marrow of this Legend, and hath onely the quinteſſence of the fables and liues thereof. And it hath this prologue: *In mine owne ſimple vnderſtanding, I feele well, how it fareth, by other that be in the*

ſame

Canus loc.
commun.l.11
cap. 6.

Prologue to
the Feſtiuall

*same degree; and hauing charge of foules, and holden bounden to
teach their Parishens, of all the principall feastes, that come in the
yeare, (hewing what the holy Saints suffreden and deden for goddis
sake and for his loue, so that they shoulden haue the more denotion
in good Saints, and with better will come vnto the Chircke, to serue
God, and pray this holy Saints of their helpe. But for many excuse
them for defaut of bokies, and also by simplenesse of coming: therefore in helpe of such Clerkes this Treatise is drawne, out of Legenda aurea, that he that list to studie therein, he shall find readie in it
of all the principall feasts of the yeare, of each one a short sermon
needfull for him to teach, and for other to learne; and for this
Treatise speaketh of all the high feastes of the yeare, I will and pray
that it be called Festiuall, &c.* This wise booke was compiled
for the vse of Curats, in defect of better bookes: for supplie
of skill in stead of sermons; for publicke Seruice, as needfull
to be taught, as fruitfull to be learned; and all this of a brat
of that *Legenda aurea,* so debased by Maister *Harding,* so branded by others. The same may be said of *Vincentius Beluacen-
sis* and *Saint Anthony, quorum vterque non tam dedit operam vt
res veras certásque describeret, &c.* saith *Bishop Canus,* no friend   Canus loc.
of ours, *who both endeuoured not so much to set downe things true*   cōmun. l. 11.
and certaine, as to passe ouer nothing at all, that they found written   cap. 6.
in any shreads of paper. Yet one of these was a Saint, the other
a copious writer, both approued long, and allowed in the Romane Church.

5   Not a much vnlike iudgement giues Cardinall *Bellarmine* of *Simon Metaphrastes; whom Aloisius Liponanus* hath
translated, and put among his owne workes, and *Surius* hath
his part of him also in his liues of Saints. Thus saith the Cardi-   De scriptori-
nall: *Illud autem est obseruandum: This is to be obserued, that Hi-*   bus Ecclesiast
stories were written by Metaphrastes of the liues of Saints, to which ,,
he added much out of his owne wit, not as things were indeed done, ,,
but as they might haue bene done. For Metaphrastes addeth many ,,
conferences or Dialogues of Martyrs, and their persecutors, and ,,
some conuersions also of some of the Pagans standing by, in such ,,
number as seeme incredible. And moreouer many miracles, and ,,
those very great of the ouerthrowes of temples and idols by occasion ,,

of

,, *of the perfecutors, whereof there is no mention in the ancient wri-*
,, *ters. And you may obferue this alfo in him, that fome hiftories of*
,, *Saints are addedfince he wrote.* Yet this very fame Author is

In fefto Ni-
colai. 6. De-
cemb.
Blafij.Febr.3.
Alexij.Iulij.
17.
crept into the new reformed Romane Breuiarie as if he
were fome great and worthy author, and that very frequently.

 6 What fhall I tell you of *Damafus*, whofe name hath
long time giuen credit to *Anaftafius Bibliothecarius*, as if he
had written the liues of Popes, who liued *Anno Dom.* 367,
when the other was the author that liued *Anno* 850, and were
almoft 500 yeares betweene? And not onely *Ambrofe, Chryfoftome, Hierome, Auguftine, Athanafius*, and fuch like ancient
and approoued authors, in their moft fufpected workes, but
Gregories Dialogues, *Hincmarus, Bonauenture,* and fuch other
haue their equall authority for leffons in their feruice. Yea ma-
In Breui. Ró.
reformat.
ny vncertaine authors; *a Sermon of Saint Auguftine in manifcrip-
tis* : yea *Martyrologies,* and I wot not whom : *Platina,* and one
Barzo Clictoueus, Metaphraftes, and *Friar Surius* moft frequent, new vpftart fellowes of our owne dayes, or our late fathers, and yet now make vp part of their ordinarie feruice in
their Church; wherein they commit two defperate and dangerous euils.

 7 The one, that they fhut the word of the euerlafting
God, almoft quite out of that Seruice they pretend is done
for his glorie: and bring in the authoritie of finfull & fhameleffe men. The other, for that they giue authoritie to thefe
bookes in time to come, which are full of incredible tales
and damnable lyes, and caufe them to be receiued by the ignorant, for clafficall authors. The wrong they do to almightie God in the former is odious, the impofture they lay vp-
pon the Church in the other is moft dangerous.

 8 For the latter obferue what Cardinall *Bellarmine* doth
in a like cafe, and feare the confequent that may follow
Breuiar. in
fefto Andreæ.
thereof. The Cardinall brings a teftimony out of a booke
called, *The paffion of Saint Andrew the Apoftle*, written (as is
Bellar.de Eu-
char.l.2.c. 1.
pretended) *by his difciples that were prefent at it.* Of which
booke he faith. *Hunc librum legitimum effe fatis conftat, That*
this

this booke is of credit it appeareth plainely. His profound reasons are, becausc he knoweth none that haue called *the credit thereof into question*, *and that his words, Salue sancta crux, All haile holy crosse,are most famous in the Church; to let passe that in the Romane Breuiarie lately renewed and purged, the passion of Saint Andrew hath it place.* No man (it may be) denied it, becausc it was long ere it was found,and when it was found, so contemned that no man spake of it. And *Salue sancta crux* may be no elder then the storie, nor the storie then it, and both of new inuention: & as for the reformed Breuiarie,it is rather deformed,but only in a very few things,that could not stand with common sense. If thefe be reasons to proue this fables authoritie,what shall let, but that in halfe another generation, *Surius the lyer*, and whom you will befide shall be of as good authoritie as this? and to say truth, I thinke they be so. For befide that it smels of the Greeke herefie of the not proceeding of the holy Ghost: so it contraries the Cardinals owne opinion,that wil haue Saint *Andrew* faftened with nailes, as Chrift was.Whereas the Achaians fay he was bound with ropes, and that they were prefent and eye witneffes thereof. Neither is it improbable, but that the Cardinall had feene, or at the leaft he might haue feene Bifhop *Whites Diacofion Martyrion,*who long before the Cardinall euer wrote, had branded this ftorie, that it was *Apocryphall, absque controuerfia,* without all controuerfie. Neither is it vnlikely, but that the Bifhop finding it so fauourable vnto that caufe which he defended with all his heart, and to his vtmoft power, would haue falued and faued the credit thereof, if he had not great caufe to the contrarie; efpecially he would not haue faid with so ftrong affeueration, that it is *Apocryphall without controuerfie.*

> Bell.de Imag.
> l.2.cap.27.

9 Thefe are the fupplies of the ancient and receiued hiftories of the Church: so barbarous, so abfurd, so fenfleffe, so againft nature,reafon & poffibility,that they rather fauour the braines of mad men,then the wit and grauitie of any that had toucht with their lips the water of life, or the fire taken from the Altar of God. Howbeit, I muft confeffe that di-   Iohn.4.14. verfe   Efai.6.7.

uerfe of our late Romanifts haue ingenuoufly acknowledged,and boldly reproued,the abfurd and groffe tales of thefe
fomewhat elder times, or corrupted authors. And I thinke,
do wifh in their hearts, that their elders had bene wifer, and
more circumfpect then they were; as appeareth by Bifhop
Canus and others of his ranke. Yet I cannot but hold it
ftrange when I fee a continuance, or rather not onely a fmall
acceffe, but a great increafe of fuch fabulous writers, after
fuch|miflike as is fhewed by fome of their learnedeft wri-
ters; fuch hope of reformation thereof pretended by others,
that nothing is amended, but the worft that were, continued in their former reputation, others are added feuen times
worfe the children of perdition then the former were.

  10 For the old motheaten, leaden Legend and the foifty
and fenowed Feftiuall, are yet fecretly layd vp in corners,
read with folemne deuotion, kept clofe with great care,
fometimes in fearches loft, with great griefe vnto the owners,as if they were the beft bookes of their religion.Which
daily appeareth, when among other fuperftitious trafh,they
are taken from Recufants, and are as verily beleeued by the
ignorant Papifts, nay I may well thinke better, then the
bleffed booke of God himfelfe. As I haue heard of a fuperftitious ignorant woman, that when fhe heard the paffion of
Chrift read in her owne tongue, fhe wept bitterly,and ten-
derly compaffioned fo great outrage done to the Sonne of
God. After fome paufe and recollection of her fpirits, fhe
asked where this was done,& when: it was anfwered, many
thoufand miles hence at Ierufalem, and a great while ago,
about fifteene hundred yeares. Then (quoth fhe)if it was fo
farre off,and fo long ago,by the grace of God it might proue
a lye, and therein fhe comforted her felfe. This may be but
a tale,rather made by wit,then acted in deed; but certainly
as abfurd things as this haue bene faid, and done, both
by people and Priefts in the darkeneffe of ignorance and
the night of fuperftition and idolatrie. For they *knew not
the Scriptures,nor the power of God.*

  11 For the beft learning the moft people had in the very
letter

letter and ſtory of the Goſpel, was when they heard *per Chri-*
ſtum Ieſum Dominum noſtrum, they would put off their cappes
and make curteſie;. or if the Prieſt could end his words in *am*
and *um,* in *ant* and *vnt,* it was as good Latine as any in a pew-
ter candleſticke : *Some roſtum, ſum ſoddum, & ſum for Aliſon,*
&c.per ChriſtumDominū noſtrum. When the Prieſts were ſuch
aſſes to reade theſe Legends, no maruell if the people were
ſuch fooles to beleeue them. Neither may it ſeeme ſtrange,
ſeeing many of their learnedſt defend many as abſurd tales
as any in the Legend , and make the world beleeue, that
themſelues hold them for truth : or at leaſt they will conniue
and winke at all that ſerues their turne, and let it paſſe *pro bo-*
no Eccleſiæ, that is in plaine Engliſh , for the furtherance of
their cauſe. With which dumbe and deafe policy, which
is neither to ſee nor heare of any deformities in the Church,
they haue held the world ſo long bewitched with ſuch old
wiues tales, as if they were indeed true miracles , or reuelations from heauen.

12 Take this for one in an old booke new printed, as a
precious iewell pittie to be loſt or left out of hand. *Petrus*
Apoſtolus in PalatioDei eſt Ianitor conſtitutus: Peter the Apoſtleis
made porter of Gods Pallace, where ther are two gates, that is to ſay,
the gate of Iuſtice & of Mercy: by the gate of Iuſtice they enter who
are ſaued by the workes of righteouſneſſe; by the gate of mercy
they enter who are ſaued by the ſole mercy and grace of God
without workes — therefore is *Peter painted with two keyes,*
becauſe with one he openeth the gate of Iuſtice , to wit, vnto them
who can ſay with the Pſalmiſt, 118, *Open vnto me the gates of*
righteouſneſſe, that entring into them I may praiſe the Lord, &c.
But with the other he openeth the gate of Grace and mercy, to wit,
vnto them to whom is ſaid, Epheſ. 2, *For by grace you are iuſtified*
through faith, and not of your ſelues , it is the gift of God, not of
workes , leſt any man ſhould glorie. Now leſt this fiction
ſhould want credit, and that the peoples eyes may be as well
deceiued by the Romane legerdemaine , as their eares faſci-
nated with their charmes , theſe keyes were kept in Rome to
be ſeene, as is left by an ancient writer whom *Baronius* alledgeth

ledgeth, and not without commendation, for the Epiſtle of

De Scriptori-
bus Ecclef.
Theod, Studi-
tes.
Ieſus to *Abgarus*, and Cardinall *Bellarmine* intituleth him a Saint.*Theodorus Studites vir admirandus,& potens opere & ſer-mone: An admirable man, powerful in work & word* ſaith, *Proinde intelligo aſſeruari Romæ claues Petri, Apoſtolici ſenatus principis, honoris gratia, etiamſi claues nullas ſenſibiles dederit Dominus Petro, ſed ore tenus, in hoc, vt penes illum eſſet poteſtas ligandi & ſoluendi, eas autem argento confectas palàm adorandas proponunt.*
„ I vnderſtand that the keyes *of Peter the Prince* of the Apoſtli-
„ çall Senate, are kept at Rome for honours ſake. Although Chriſt gaue no ſenſible keyes to *Peter* : but by word of mouth, that he ſhould haue the power of binding and loo-ſing. But they offer them openly to be worſhipped; and in the margent, *Claues Petri venerabiles* : *Peters* keyes are vene-rable. See how long ago theſe impoſtures began in Rome ann. 820. Will the Romaniſts be ſo impudent as to defend this now? or are thoſe keyes loſt ? &c.

Loc.com.lib.
II.c.6.
13 Of ſuch tales Biſhop *Canus* tels two, one of Saint *Francis*, another of Saint *Dominicke*. How the former would take his lice againe, when they were bruſhed off; and would preach to birds and beaſts, and his brother wolfe, becauſe Chriſt bids his Apoſtles preach to all creatures; wherein if it were true, he ſhewed himſelfe ignorantly mad, and madly ignorant. The other compelled the diuell to hold a candle till he burnt his fingers and cried horribly, (and he might haue added, how Saint *Dunſtan* caught the diuel by the noſe with a paire of tongues;) and concludes, *Non poſſunt huiuſmodi ex-empla numero comprehendi* : *The number of ſuch examples can-not be comprehended* : *but in theſe few others may be conſidered,*
„ *whiſh haue obſcured the Hiſtories of moſt glorious Saints. But*
„ *they ſhould not ſo with falſe and counterfet fables haue blemi-*
„ *ſhed the true deeds of the Saints.* And to make vp the number, or rather meaſure of this iniquitie, take this for an vpſhoot: *Vpon the one ſide of Saint Peters Church* (at Rome) there lyeth a Church yard, that is called Gods field, and there be bu-ried poore pilgrims, and no other. And it is that land *which was bought with the 30 peeces that our Lord was ſold for. In an old*
Engliſh

*Englißh treatiſe of diuers matters concerning London, Cap.of the
whole pardon of Rome granted by diuers Popes , and the ſtations
that be there.* Saint *Brice* ſaw the diuell knocke his head a-
gainſt the wall:perhaps that the bloud ranne about his eares.
For ſuch ſpirits haue fleſh and bloud,and fingers, and noſes,
and corporall ſenſes , whatſoeuer the Scriptures ſay to the
contrary, that true ſpirits haue not.

14   They dealt with their Saints,as their Poets did with
their Champions and Worthies.They neuer thought they
commended them enough,except they killed fiftie or threeſcore men at a ſtroake; and it was nothing to cleaue a mans
head to his teeth , but bodie and all to his ſaddle *cropowne*:
yea ſometime ſaddle and horſe and all to the ground.As probable as that of foureteene thouſand killed in one battell, Plutarch.in
more then halfe were killed by *Romulus* owne hands , which Romulo,
the heathen Philoſopher derides.So did they with the Saints;
they cannot enough (as they thinke) commend them with
truths, and therefore deuiſe infinite lyes. Wherein they diſhonour God, abuſe his Saints, make their ſtories ridiculous,
and ſhame themſelues. And to be ſhort, they thought *it pietie to faine lyes for religions ſake.* Yet theſe things and ſuch o-
ther like , *will peraduenture pleaſe the readers better for their
ſtrangeneſſe and curioſitie, then offend or miſlike them for their falſhood.* As *Plutarch* ſpeaketh of the vanities of Mathema- Plutarch,
ticians.

15   As they dealt with their miracles , ſo did they with
their viſions. Euery Friers fancie was ſupported with reuelations, as frequent and as true as drunkards dreames , or the
Indians extaſies, after they haue carowſed *Tobacco*, and are Monardus.
inſpired with the diuel.This was common betweene the Dominicans and Franciſcans about the pure conception of the
bleſſed Virgin,(as Biſhop *Canus* obſerueth.) Contrary reue- Ibid.
lations were brought on both ſides, *which gaue* (as he ſaith*)
to the wicked no ſmall occaſion of laughter, to the godly of weeping.*

16   Thus farre wiſe men ſaw,and perhaps lamented; and
ſome wiſhed reformation therein , and were in hope to ſee
                                Z   it,

it, but their expectation was deceiued, for *Rome* neither can nor may reforme any thing. This author tels, that at his being at the Councell of *Trent,* he heard that *Aloysius Lippomanus the Bishop of Verona would salue this sore, by setting forth a storie in this kind, with constant grauitie.* This he neuer saw : neither euer should, if he had liued to this day : though Cardinall *Bellarmine* giues him a litle passage of commendations in this respect. For such a lumpe of paper (so slouingly blotted, and marred with as loud lies as euer any told before him) neuer burdened the world before. The onely difference is, that what was before disperfed in many, he hath scrapt and rakt together into one midden; neither hath he amended any thing that was amisse, nor left out any thing that makes for his partie and faction, be it neuer so absurd.

    17   This desire of reformation herein, if it take not the good effect in histories past and disperfed into many hands, yet it is strange that it hath not wrought some sparke of modestie in those that since haue written of old Saints or new: the powdered vp miracles and visions of elder times, or the fresh deuices of latest inuentions. In the former kind, *Laur. Surius* leapes ouer the bounds of all modestie, into the depth of all not onely improbabilitie, but impossibilitie. And yet his gests (which are worse then iests, as I said) are the most frequent authoritie in the Romane Breuiarie, newly deformed by his and such Friers tales. *Sedulius* in his Conformities of Saint *Francis,* though he came after him in time, yet hath he ouerstript him and gotten before him in detestable and abhominable lying , and may take the whetstone from him. The difference is, that *Surius* hath the more lyes, but *Sedulius* hath the greater, if greater may be.

    18   But these perhaps found their liues in bookes before them; and so like the silly men whom Bishop *Canus* bemoneth, beleeued all they found in print. Looke on the Epistles of the Iesuites from the East Indies , what miracles are daily wrought by the Crosse, by holy water, and such like trinkets. There are many such monstrous miracles, that none but mad men would beleeue them . I will not blot paper to

tell

(marginal note: De Euchar. l. 2 c. 1.)

tell their tales, of which we may well fay, as Biſhop *Canus* Loc.commū.
doth in his Spaniſh prouerbe, *De luengas vias,luengas menti-* l.11.c.6.
ras, Farre countries ſend loud lyes.

19 But thoſe which in this kind be moſt to be maruelled
at, are they which write in theſe laſt dayes, in ciuilleſt countries,and yet tell vs ſhameleſſe tales, as if they were done before the Floud, or brought from the *Antipodes*. I would remember but two of this kind, that is,*Iuſtus Lipſius* a couſened
fcholler,who verified the prouerbe,*that greateſt Clerks be not
euer the wiſeſt men,*with his fables of *Hales* and *Aſpricollis*. It is
pity his pretie ſtyle was not employed in a better ſubiect.For
verier idle fables in ſo good and pleaſing Latin, were neuer
written. Another is he that hath written the tales of *Nereus*,
Cardinall *Baronius* his oratoricall patron . In whom though
ſome things are very incredible, yet moſt things are ſuch as
many a good honeſt hearted Paſtor in our Church doth. He
prayed for ſicke folks,whoſe life by their friends was deſpai-
red, and they recouered; ſo might they haply haue done
without prayers. To tell theſe tales were but to waſte time.
Let the iudicious Reader repaire to the Authors, they ſhall
find them abundant in proofe of all that I haue ſaid : yet are
they fitter for a fires ſide in a Winters euening , then for a
ſtudie and deske in a Sommers morning. Of whom, and o-
thers like, I will ſay but as one of their owne ſaid of others,
and might beſt ſay of himſelfe: *Fronte ſunt plerique omnes,plus* Surius in com
quàm meretricia, & neſciunt erubeſcere : The moſt of them all breu.rerum in orbe geſtarū.
haue worſe then harlots foreheads, they cannot bluſh. Quid facie- Bellar.in Prēf.
mus hominibus iſtis, qui cauſam non quærunt tueri ſuam, niſi frau- lib.de Chriſto.
dibus & mendacijs ? What ſhall we do to thoſe men, who ſeeke no-
thing to defend their owne cauſe,but deceits and lyes? If *Maſſonus*
our aduerſary, their friend, did admoniſh his Chriſtian rea-
der, *Me in hoc & ſequentibus libris,authores multo inferiores ve-* In Benedict.2
teribus, atque impares citaturum: That in this & my following
bookes,I ſhall cite authors farre inferiour to the ancient,and
vnlike them: his Reader was not to heare *Tertullians, Hie-*
romes, Auguſtines, but *in compariſon of theſe,* certaine baſer fellowes,*whom following ages brought forth in degenerated ſtrength:*

Certainly we may well and vpon good reaſon call vpon all good Chriſtians to take heed of ſuch impoſtures, of whether paſt or preſent times, that haue infected the very aire with the filth and ſtinch of their dangerous and damnable lyes and abſurdities.

CHAP. XIIII.

When all is ſaid and done, it is neither the antiquitie of Scriptures, Councels, Fathers, or Hiſtories, nor the ſupply of Traditions, Conuenticles, Baſtard Fathers, or Legends, that can confine the Romane Catholickes within the limits and bounds of truth, for the triall of their religion; but all muſt be referred to the Catholicke Church: this muſt be vnderſtood for the Church of Rome, and this againe muſt be contracted into the Popes perſon, who muſt ſtand ſole Iudge in all matters of faith: and this muſt be the preſent Pope for the time being, or none other.

Phil.3.20.

He holy Catholicke Church being the ſpirituall Paradiſe of God vpon earth, where the Saints ſhould haue their conuerſation as in heauen; it hath pleaſed his diuine Maieſtie in his prouidence to water with a goodly fountaine, which hath deuided it ſelfe into theſe foure ancient riuers, of Scriptures, Councels, Fathers, and Hiſtories; reſeruing ſoueraigntie and ſufficiencie to the firſt, (as hath bene proued) but yet participating wholeſomneſſe in competencie to the reſt. This would haue pleaſed *Adam* well, if he had remained in his firſt integritie, and had held the poſſeſſion of that place wherein he was infeoffed by his glorious Creator. This would haue bene ſufficient to haue made the garden fruitfull both for pleaſure & profit, enough to haue made him happie for euer, had he not forfeited his hold, and cauſed ſeiſure into the Lords hands. *But man being in honour had no vnderſtanding, but became like the beaſts that periſh.* Thus hath it fared with their *dreſſers of this garden the Romane Catholicke Church:* they haue loſt the poſſeſſion, they

Supra cap 6.

Pſal.49.20.

are

are remoued out of this pleafant Paradife,*This enclofed garden,* Cant. 4. 12.
this fpring fhut vp, this fealed fountaine. And then no maruell,
that as fome writers tooke *Gange* in the fartheft *Afia*, and
Nilus in *Africke*, as if thofe had bene the riuers of *Paradife*:
fo thefe haue fearched in ftrange countries, by diuers
meanes, to find out *Traditions*, that haue more heads then
Nilus; and are farre more violent then *Gange*, and haue ioyned them with the new found lakes of *Conuenticles, baftard
Fathers, and Legends,* as if they were all riuers of the *Paradife* of
God.

2   But will they be contented with thefe, if they fhould be
allowed them? By no meanes without fuch conditions as
themfelues will propofe, and thofe are fuch as no true hearted
Chriftian will endure: Which is, to put our liues and our religion, which is dearer vnto vs then our liues, into the hands of
the Tyrant, that either thinketh, or pretendeth that he doth
God good feruice when he excommunicateth vs, or putteth Iohn 16. 2.
vs to death.

3   Admit their latter Conuenticles, as that of *Conftance*,
wherein three Popes were depofed, and one erected in their
places: *Quantum ad primas feffiones, &c.* As much as apperta- Bell. de Con-
ned to the firft feffions (faith *Bellarmine*) wherein it was defi- cil. l. 1. c. 7.
ned that the Councell was aboue the Pope, it is reiected by Supra, cap. 7.
the Councels of *Florence*, and the laft *Lateran.* But for the laft ,,
feffions, and thofe things which *Martin* the fift approued, ,,
they are receiued of all Catholickes. So much as is againft the ,,
Pope, that is refufed; that which he approueth, that is receiued,
though it be not cócluded by the Church. The like they hold
of all authoritie, be it what it will or may be, for age or youth,
it muft attend to be admitted into the Church, by him that
pretendeth the fole keeping of Saint *Peters* keyes. In fo much
that the Councels are no Councels, Fathers no Fathers, Hiftories no Hiftories, except the King of *Locufts* admit
them.

4   And that which is moft horrible to heare, and moft
fearefull to thinke, the Scriptures are no Scriptures, if not approued by him. Though he dominere with men, fhall he out-

Z 3   face

face God almightie? The authoritie of the Church is fo great,
that a man would thinke no mortall thing could be aboue it,

Stapl. princi-
piorum analy as *Stapleton* endeuoureth to demonftrate. *Eam Ecclefiæ autho-
ritatem effe,vt etiam non fcriptam doctrinam tradere queat; deindè
Scripturas interpretandi illam habere poteftatem, & maximam, &
infallibilem; quin & Scripturas quoque ipfas laxandi & confignan-
di facultatē, certoq, Canonicas ab Apocryphis ius decernendi penes
,, *illam effe.* The Church hath fuch authoritie that fhe may de-
,, liuer doctrine vnwritten, that fhe hath greateft and infallible
,, power to interpret Scriptures, yea and to fet at libertie, or
,, feale vp the Scriptures themfelues; and the difcerning the Ca-
,, nonicall from the Apocryphall, is alfo in her power. This
is more then enough, yet one blufheth not to fay fot the Pa-

Muri ciuit.
fund.2. pifts, *Calumnia eft,nos Ecclefiā fupra Scripturas euehere, nos Ec-*
clefiam Scripturæ iudicem facere: It is a flander to fay, that we
aduance the Church aboue the Scriptures, that we make the
Church Iudge of the Scriptures.

5   But may the Church hold this power when fhe hath
it? Nay,the Pope may enlarge or reftraine all this, at his owne
pleafure. Let this ferue as much as it may, if it will not, then
fteppeth in the Bifhop of Rome with his omnipotency. And

Intus quis? Tu
quis? Ego fū.
Quid quæris?
Vt intrem.
Fers aliquid?
Non. Sta fo-
ras. En fero.
Quid? Satis.
Intra. Extra de
tranfl.Epifc.c.
Quanto in
Gloff. at Rome all writers are receiued as dearely as their Clients.
Bring they nothing for them, let them ftand without ; bring they
ought, they may come in and welcome. Euer prouided vnder the
Popes protection. And no maruell, for he can of *nothing make*
fomething, (obferue the blafphemie; for who can do this but
God?) can call them into the Church that were neuer of it,
thruft out thofe that haue liued long in it. He can make hea-
thē Philofophers clafficall authors for the Catholike Church,
and make *Bertram* and fuch like more ancient then the beft
of theirs,Heretickes at his pleafure. Nay a Cardinall can do it
vnder the Popes elbow.

6   Cardinall *Bellarmine* or fome friend of his, to his honor, hath made Catalogues in his firft two volumes, of fuch

Tom.1. im-
preff. Lugdu-
ni.1587. authors as he hath alledged, wherof the firft containeth, *Tum*
vetuftiores, tum recentiores, Ecclefiæ Romanæ authores: Alter,
fectarios & fufpectæ fidei Scriptores: The older and the yonger
authors

authors of the Church of Rome, but the other the ſectaries and writers of ſuſpected credit. In the firſt volume, among the authors of the Romane Church, are *Ariſtotle, Homer, Iſocrates, Plato, Plutarch, &c.* all Grecians by nation and ſpeech; Philoſophers and Poets, Orators, Hiſtorians, not one Romane. Which ſeemeth ſtrange, for *Tullie, Virgil, Cæſar, &c.* were Romanes indeed, though perhaps not of their Church; but the Cardinals authors, were neither of the Church nor common wealth, *Yet authors for the Romane Church.* In the ſecond volume poore *Bertram*, of whom their *Index expurgatorius* is ſo ſolicitous to ſhift off, ſo ancient that it is aſhamed to caſt him out, ſo diſperſed that he cannot be called in : is put into the Catalogue of Hereticks and Sectaries, and *Ioannes Scotus*, with him, one ancienter then he was, and all becauſe 800 yeares ago they held that opinion of the Sacrament which we maintaine at this day. For they are all Here-ticks that ſpeake againſt them, in ſo much that I maruel how Saint *Peter* or eſpecially Saint *Paul*, hath eſcaped them. And thus they deale with all authoritie whatſoeuer.

Bellar. de Eu-char.ſacra. l.1. cap.1.

7 When they haue ſought heauen for Prophets, Apoſtles, Euangeliſts, Fathers, Martyrs, and Saints, of all times, they find not any that fauour their cauſe : therefore they vilifie and re-ject all their teſtimonie. Then they ſeeke Purgatorie, for Ab-bots, Priors, Friars of all faſhions, and Schoolemen of all fa-ctions. And yet theſe they dare not well truſt, or commit their cauſe vnto them, becauſe ſometimes they hit vpon a truth, and reproue the Pope as *Balaams Aſſe reproued the madneſſe of the Prophet*; and ſuch muſt be purged. *Then they* rake hell, for na-turall Philoſophers, curious Orators, laſciuious and lying Po-ets, to aſſiſt them; and though they be their helps in many things, yet in ſome things the Romaniſts are ſo abſurd, as na-ture* it ſelfe abhorreth them, ſo groſſe and palpable, that Rhe-torick can neither defend their paradoxes, nor proue their ab-ſurdities, ſo falſe and impudent, as the Poets can neither reach their ſcurrilities, nor match their fables. And therefore they muſt ſtraine a note aboue *Ela*, and fetch their witneſſes and iudges out of their owne den of thieues, from the beaſt with

*Numb.22.30 2.Pet.2.16. Plato and Virgil are their Authors for Purgatory. * Plutarch of Numa and Pythagoras.*

Z 4   ſeuen

feuen heads, or from the whore of *Babylon* that fitteth there-

Greg. de Va-
len. in analy.
lib.5. cap. 8.
in Rubrica.
on. That is in plaine tearmes,*Nec præteritam aliquam Traditio-
nem fine præfenti authoritate iudicem effe fufficientem omnium controuerfiarum fidei* : Neither any former Tradition without the
„ prefent authoritie, to be a fufficient iudge of all controuerfies
„ of faith.
„   8   When *Salmeron* had commended both Scriptures and
Traditions for triall, yet concludeth after a folemne place to
Tom.1.prole-
gom. 9. prim.
quinquagena.
can.1. cap.1.
cœl. Hier.
that effect out of *Dionyfius*: *Neque hæc funt fatis nifi accedat vn-
Etio & eruditio fpiritus Sancti, quem promifit Dominus manfurum
nobifcum in æternum, qui & in generalibus Synodis , & in Chrifti
vicario & Petri fucceffore refidens,omnes incidentes quæftiones,&
ortas de fide controuerfias , fuâ authoritate, terminet atque refol-
uat.* Neither are thefe fufficient,vnleffe there concurre the vnction and inftruction of the holy Spirit, whom the Lord promifed to remaine with vs for euer ; who being refident in generall Synods, and in Chrifts vicar & the fucceffor of *Peter* by
his authoritie determins and decides all incident queftions &
controuerfies arifing concerning faith.

9   So that in very truth, or at leaft in their meaning , neither from Angels nor holy men , neither from Scriptures nor
Councels,neither from Fathers nor ftories, neither from Traditions, nor new Conuenticles, neither from baftard Fathers,
nor golden Legends, neither from Friars or Schoolemen,nei-
ther from Chriftian or heathen, neither from old or new,nei-
ther from time paft , or time to come : but from the prefent
Church militant, and that not Catholick,or vniuerfally fpread
vpon the face of the earth , but abridged or confined to the
Church of Rome;they muft determine all controuerfies,inter-
pret all Scriptures, affoile all doubts, refolue all queftions, order all affaires, difpofe of all rights, eftablifh all truth vpon the
earth That all men may flatter and fay, *ais ? aio : negas? nego.* I
fay as you fay,I denie what you denie,I beleeue as the Church

Antoninus
par.3.fi.23.c.3
§. 2. Quære
plu. in not. p.
18.19.
beleeueth. For *nulli dubium eft quòd Ecclefia Apoftolica fit mater
omnium Ecclefiarum , à cuius nos regulis nullatenus conuenit de-
uiare; & ficut filius venit facere voluntatem Patris,fic vos implete
voluntatem matris veftræ quæ eft Ecclefia, cuius caput eft Romana
Ecclefia.*

Eccleſia. No man needeth doubt, but that the Apoſtolique „
Church is the mother of all Churches, from whoſe rules to „
erre, is not conuenient at any hand; and like as the Sonne „
comes to do the will of his Father, ſo fulfill you the will of „
your Mother the Church, whoſe head is the Roman Church, „
and the Pope the head of it. And ſo there is head vpon „
head, like top and top gallant. And then the Church muſt
hold what the Pope alone commands. So that he is the *baſis*
and groundworke of all truth; which how it may ſtand with
Religion, reaſon, probabilitie, or poſſibilitie, ſhall afterwards
appeare.

10 If this were true, or could euer be proued, I muſt confeſſe it were the moſt expedit courſe to end al controuerſies,
and to eſtabliſh as conſtant a peace, as is held by *Satan* and
all his diuels in hell. For what need we ſtudy the Scriptures,
ſearch the Councels, reade the Fathers, recollect the hiſtories, ſo long, and with ſo great contention, labour in reading, diſputing, writing of ſo many *queſtions* and controuerfies, if one man, whoſe perſon and place is knowne, can define and determine all as he liſt, and his word muſt ſtand as a
finall end to all men, in all matters, through all the world?
No maruell then if the Romaniſts be ſo eager to preſſe this
aboue all things, and to vrge it by all meanes againſt the Goſpell, that the Pope is all in all.

11 Neither may we wonder that Cardinall *Bellarmine*
maketh it the top and ſumme and ſubſtance of all our differences. *De quâ re agitur, cùm de primatu Pontificis agitur?*
breuiſſimè dicam, de ſummâ rei Chriſtianæ. Id enim quæritur, debe-
átne Eccleſia diutiùs conſiſtere, an verò diſſolui & concidere. What „
is queſtioned when we handle the matter of the Popes Pri- „
macie? I will anſwer ſhortly, euen of the ſumme of all Chri- „
ſtianitie. For this is the queſtion, whether the Church „
ſhould conſiſt any longer, or it ſhould be diſſolued and fall „
for euer. If he had ſaid of the Supremacie, the firſt part of „
his ſentence had ſome truth; for proue it, proue all. So is
it not by the Cardinals leaue with the Primacy. For the Pope
will be eaſily granted Prime, if he be a good Biſhop, but
not

Præf. in lib. de
Rom. Pont.

no in reme, be he neuer so good. But the Church stood, and may stand still, if he be neither : though in truth the Romish Court cannot if we deny him either. Doctor *Stapleton*

Princ.doct.l. 7.c.10.&l.10. c.11. saith, that neither Councels, *nor Fathers, nor any thing, but the Pope, is iudge of all controuersies*, and that he saith not onely once. And if a Councell be called, it is more then needs, rather of congruitie then of condignitie, rather for conuenience, then necessitie : So saith a Cardinall *Ioan. de Turre-cremat. Quanquam summus Pontifex pro singularitate principatus sui omnem legem condere & dare possit toti Ecclesiæ, iuxta caput, Sunt quidam, 25. quæst. 1. nihilominus sæpè (& hoc rationabiliter) patres*
,, *Ecclesiæ Synodaliter congregat, &c.* Although the great Bi-
,, shop for the singularitie of his principalitie, may make and
,, deliuer all law to all the whole Church, according to a Chap-
,, ter (in *Gracian*:) yet notwithstanding often (and that reasonably)
,, he gathers the Fathers of the Church Synodically. By which it is plaine, that he may choose whether he will call Councels or

Tho. Aquin. quodlibet 8. alleg. à Ioan. de Turre-cre- mat.(um.de Ecclesia.l.2. c.112. not, there is no great necessitie for it. *He can make and deliuer all law to the Churches.* And what need we more ado? yea another saith, *Magis standum est sententiæ Papæ quam de fide in iudicio profert, quàm quorūcunq, hominum sapientium, in Scripturarum opinionibus. Nam & Caiphas cum esset Pontifex licet nequam, prophetauit.* It is better resting vpon the sentence of the
,, Pope, which in his iudgement he deliuers, then the opinions
,, of whatsoeuer wise men in matters of Scripture. For euen
,, *Caiphas* when he was high Priest, though wicked, yet he
,, prophecied, and so did *Balaam.* And againe he saith, *Sic om-*

Idemibid. Agapto.PP.in c.Sic.distinct. 19. *nes Apostolicæ sanctiones accipiendæ sunt tanquam ipsius diuina voce Petri firmatæ:* So are all the Apostolicall sanctions to be receiued, as if they were confirmed by the Diuine voice of *Peter* himselfe.

12   And they are yet to this day more desperate in the maintenance of their Popes priuiledge then euer they were, though with sinne and shame enough. *Pernegamus contin-*

Greg. de Val. de idolatriâ. lib.4.cap.16. *gere posse vt Pontifex aliquid in rebus controuersis cum authoritate definiens (ad quod scilicet credendum obliget vniuersam Ecclesiam) Scripturæ sacræ repugnet. Sed illud asseueramus constantissimè*

ſimè hæreticos eſſe qui non credunt id Scriptura ſacræ conſentaneum
eſſe, quod ea ratione Pontifex definiat: For it cannot poſſibly »
be, that the Pope concluding any thing in controuerſie, by »
his authoritie (in that he binds the vniuerſal! Church to be- »
leeue) ſhould contradict the Scripture. But we conſtantly »
affirme them heretickes that beleeue it not agreable to the »
Scriptures, euen for this reaſon, becauſe the Pope concludes »
it. Yet for all this Pope *Vrbane* in that law doth ſomewhat limit himſelfe, that he may not make a law againſt that which
Chriſt or his Apoſtles, *or the holy Fathers that followed them*
haue definitiuely determined. Notwithſtanding the Gloſſe aſ-
keth, why not againſt the Apoſtle? ſeeing that Pope *Martin*
diſpenſed in Bigamie, and againſt a Canon of the Apoſtles, yea and
againſt the Lord alſo, who bids vs vow and pray; and yet he abſol-
ueth both from oath and vow. And I aske the ſame queſtion,
why not? *Seeing one Pope could diſpence with one King* to marry
his brothers wife; another Pope with another King to marry a ſecond wife, though his firſt liued; and a third with another King to marry his neece by conſanguinitie? and all
this for ought I ſee may be defended, (aſwel as the reſt) as the
Gloſſe ſaith. For againſt the Apoſtles if it concerne not an Article of faith, *and againſt the Goſpell by interpreting it, &c.* at his
pleaſure he may diſpenſe.

13   The Gloſſe hath yet a more ſubtill diſtinction. *Ga-* Extrau. 19. lib
ther hence, ſaith it, *that the prince of the Church & Chriſts Vicar*, 14. c. 4. Gloſſ.
may make a declaratiō vpon the Catholique faith, this may be tol- in verbo de-
lerable. *But he may alſo make an Article of faith: Si ſumatur Ar-* claramus.
ticulus non propriè, ſed largè: If you take an Article not properly ,
but largely, *for that we muſt beleeue.* With more ſubtile words, »
to ſmall purpoſe. So that we muſt beleeue what the Pope
commandeth. The tranſgreſſion whereof is as great a ſinne as
the violation of the Law of God. So the Gloſſe applying
that to the perſon of the Pope, which the text of the Law giueth to the word of God, ſaith in the Popes name , *Quicun-* Diſtinct. 50. c.
que præceptis noſtris non obedierit, peccatum idolatriæ & Paganita- Si qui ſunt.
tis incurret: Whoſoeuer obeyeth not our commandements, »
let him incurre the ſinne of idolatrie and Paganiſme. And »
what

what is this,but to make it as grosse a fault,not to beleeue the
Pope, as not to beleeue the Gospell of Iesus Christ the
Sonne of God? and then (as I said) what need any longer
dispute?

14 Though *Stapleton* and *Tutrecremata* in this case be direct
enough, yet *Gretzer* that defends the grossest Popery in the
grossest maner, disputes the case against a *Caluinist* in plainer
& more downright termes,thus.The *Caluinist*,as *Gretzer* cals
him,saith,*Per Ecclesiam intelligunt Papistæ , primò Patres,&c.*
The Papists vnderstand by the Church, first the Fathers, *then
the agreeing opinion of the Fathers;for if they consent not all, they
giue them not so great authoritie. Mentitur Caluinista,suósque fu-
mos & nebulas vendit:* The *Caluinist* lyes, (a foule mouth) and
sels his smoke and clouds to his Companions.*Per Ecclesiam
enim quando dicimus esse omnium controuersiarum fidei iudicem,in-
telligimus Pont.Romanum,qui pro tempore præsens nauiculam mili-
tantis Ecclesiæ moderatur,ac gubernãt,quíque viuâ voce,sententiã
suam , clarè,disertè & euidentèr adeuntibus & consulentibus ex-*
„ *plicat:* For by the Church,when we say she is the iudge of all
„ controuersies of Faith , we do vnderstand the Bishop of
„ Rome,which for his time,in person,doth guide and gouerne
„ the ship of the militant Church,and who by his owne mouth
„ deliuereth his opinion, clearely, plainly, euidently, to them
„ that come vnto him, and seeke his counsell. And againe, *In-
telligimus etiam nomine Ecclesiæ Pontificem pro tempore viuentem,
cum Concilio quod ipse conuocare & congregare potest. Et hunc
summi Pastoris, & aliorum præsulum cœtum, dicimus esse imme-
diatum, ordinarium, & visibilem controuersiarum, quæ de religi-*
„ *one existunt, Iudicem.* We vnderstand also by the name of the
„ Church,the Pope for the time being,with a Councell which
„ himselfe may call and assemble ; and this company of the
„ chiefe Pastor and other Prelates we affirme to be the im-
„ mediate ordinarie and visible iudge of controuersies, which
„ arise in religion. But what needs this latter of a Councell
with the Pope, with so much concourse and trouble , when
the Pope may do it alone,though no body be with him,as
they all hold?Yet farther, *Ais tertiò, interpretantur Ecclesiam*
                                                                Papam

Papam.Non abnuo.Quid tum?De eius ſententia eſt etiam quod du-
bitemus.Num iure? Quomodo certi eſſe poſſumus ipſum non errare?
Ex illis,Tibi dabo claues,&c.Quomodo ſciam iſta ae Papa dici?Ex
traditione Eccleſiaſtica, ex conſenſu maiorum, totiuſq; antiquitatis
ſuffragio,ex textu ipſo,ſi ad eius lectionem nulla adferatur peruica-
cia & antecepta perſuaſio. Denique velis nolis ex ipſius Papæ ſen-
*tentia & definitione,&c.*Thirdly,thou ſayeſt,they interpret the ,,
Church the Pope. I grant it: What then? We may doubt alſo ,,
of his ſentence. But whether iuſtly? How can we be certaine ,,
that he erres not? From that which he ſaith : I will giue thee Math.16.19.
the *keyes*,&c: The gates of hell ſhall not preuaile againſt it: ,,
Whatſoeuer thou bindeſt, whatſoeuer thou looſeſt: I haue ,,
prayed for thee that thy faith might not faile. But who ſhall Luk.22.32.
iudge of the ſence of this place? or how ſhall I know this is ,,
ſpoken of the Pope? Frō Eccleſiaſticall tradition,the conſent ,,
of our elders,the ſuffrage of all *Antiquitie*, out of the text it ,,
ſelfe, if there be brought no peruerſe obſtinacie, or a fore- Preiudicate
perſwaſion.To conclude,whether thou wilt or no,from the opinion.
Popes owne ſentence and determination. A man would ,,
thinke this were enough, the laſt would ſerue, what need
the reſt?

  15   The *Caluiniſt* yet obiects: *Abſurdum & indignum eſt* Ibid.
dicere,omnes Pontificum definitiones habere æqualem authoritatem
cum Scriptura ſacra: It is abſurd and vnworthy to be ſpoken, ,,
that all the determinations of the Popes be of equall autho- ,,
ritie with the holy Scriptures.*Abſurdum eſt, ſed in ſchola Cal-* ,,
uini,non Chriſti, loquendo de definitionibus fidei quantum ad infal-
libilitatem attinet,&c. It is abſurd indeed; but in the ſchoole
of *Caluin*,not of *Chriſt*,if you ſpeake of definitions of faith,
as much as appertaines to the infallibilitie thereof.

  16   This is a faire and full confeſſion of *Romes* doctrine,
that it is neither Scriptures, nor Councels, nor Fathers, nor
hiſtories, but the Church; and that not Rhetoricall, but Lo-
gicall, not with a broade hand, but with a clitcht fiſt, without any body,the head alone, the Pope himſelfe. *Neque ſa-* Greg.de Val.
cra Scriptura , neque etiam ſola Traditio (ſi ab ea ſepares præſen- Analyſ.l.5.c.1.
tem in Eccleſia authoritatem infallibilem ; ſic enim de Traditione
                                                        nunc

*nunc loquimur) est illa authoritas infallibilis, magistra fidei, & iu-
dex in omnibus quæstionibus. Talis igitur authoritas non est propria
alicuius, vel aliquot hominum, vita defunctorum. Quod si extat, tamen aliqua talis humana authoritas, vt probatum est, neque verò ea
est illorum hominum propria, qui iam præterierunt : restat vt viuat*
,, *semper inter fideles præsens.*Neither the holy Scripture, nor Tra-
,, dition alone (if thou separate from it the present infallible
,, authoritie in the Church, for so we now speake of Tradi-
,, tion) is that infallible authoritie, the mistris of faith, and
,, iudge in all questions. Therefore such authoritie is not pro-
,, per to any, one or more, departed this life. So that if there be
,, extant any such humane authoritie, as is proued, and is not
,, indeed proper to those men who are already passed, it re-
,, maineth it should liue present alwayes amongst the faith-
,, full.

Cap.2.
Cap.3.
Cap.4.

Cap.5.6.7.

Cap.8.

17 This he goeth about monstrously and profanely to
proue, by the *obscuritie of the Scriptures*, then *by their insuffici-
encie, then by reason,* as farre as I see, out of his owne rule, then
by the *exactest forme of a commonwealth, then out of Saint Peter,*
lastly by the maner *whereby God teacheth men,* as much to say,
by blasphemies, vanities, nullities, suppositions, surmises,
without feare or wit, grace or honestie. Yet he audaciously
proceedeth, *Sicut de authoritate ipsius Scripturæ necesse est, per
aliam certam regulam constare, ita etiam de authoritate Traditio-
nis, si ea quoque reuocetur in dubium. Non enim Traditio loquitur
etiam clarè & perspicuè de sese, vt neque ipsa Scriptura. Deinde
cum Traditio scriptis ferè Doctorum orthodoxorum in Ecclesia
conuersetur, quæstiones & dubia moueri possunt de sensu illius, sicut dubitatur sæpe de sensu & mente Doctorum, &c. hoc in loco,
velim vt ij qui sectis hodie addicti sunt, incipiant secum perpendere,
quantopere à recta fide aberrent: siquidem eam discere nolunt ex a-
liquâ authoritate præsente: cuius tamen solius vt probatum est, ab-
soluta & plena potestas est, in omnibus fidei quæstionibus iudicandi.*
,, As of the authoritie of the Scripture it selfe, it is necessarie it
,, should stand by some certaine rule, so likewise concerning
,, the authoritie of *Tradition,* if it be brought into question. For
,, *Tradition* speaketh not clearely and perspicuously of it selfe:

ſo neither the Scripture . To conclude, whereas *Tradition* „
is found in the writings of the orthodoxall Doctors in the „
Church, queſtions and doubts may ariſe of the ſence of it, as „
it is often doubted of the ſence and mind of the Doctors,&c. „
In this place I would that they who this day are addicted „
vnto ſects, would conſider with themſelues how much they „
erre from the true faith, in as much as they will not learne it „
from the preſent authoritie: which notwithſtanding alone, „
as is proued , hath an abſolute and full power of iudging in „
all queſtions of faith. *Cum authoritas illa,magiſtra fidei,apud ip-* Lib.6.Aſſertio
ſos Chriſti fideles perpetuò vigeat, non alibi vel quæri decet, vel in- prob.
ueniri poteſt, quàm apud veram Chriſti Eccleſiam, huc eſt, apud
congregationem verè fidelium. Ea verò congregatio non alia eſt
quàm cœtus eorum qui Rom.Pontifici pro tempore exiſtente parent.
Whereas that authority, the miſtris of faith,doth perpetually „
flouriſh amongſt the faithfull of Chriſt themſelues, it ought „
not to be ſoght for,nor elſewhere can it be found,then in the „
true Church of Chriſt, that is,in the congregatió of the truly „
faithfull. And that congregation is no other, then the aſſem- „
bly of thoſe who obey the Romane Biſhop exiſtant for the „
time. *Non in ſingulis,non in omnibus Chriſti fidelibus,——ſed reſi-* Cap.4.de Ec-
det illa ſumma Eccleſiæ authoritas in Chriſti Vicario.ſummo Ponti- clef.proprie-
fice,ſiue vnà cum Epiſcoporum Concilio , ſiue abſque Concilio res tatibus.
fidei definire velit: No: in euery particular, not in all the faith- „
full of Chriſt,but that prime authoritie of the Church,is reſi- „
dent in Chriſts Vicar,the chiefe Biſhop , whether he define „
matters of faith , aſſiſted with the Councell of Biſhops , or „
without the Councell. *Ipſa vna Paſtorem rectiſſimè agnoſcit,* Cap.9.
*eiuſq́; iudicio in controuerſiis acquieſcit:*Which onely moſt iuſtly „
acknowledgeth her Paſtor,in whoſe iudgement concerning „
controuerſies ſhe reſteth. „
 18 To this he applieth a ſpeech of Saint *Cyprian: Plebs* Cypr.l.4.epiſt
Sacerdoti adunata,& Paſtori ſuo grex adhærens : A people vni- 10.ad Flor.
ted to the Prieſt, and a flocke cleauing to the Paſtor. That Pap.
which the Father ſpeaketh of euery Paſtour and his owne
flocke, that *Valentia* appropriateth to the Biſhop of *Rome*
alone,with great iniurie to the reſt,while ouermuch is arro-
gated

Valé.l.7.aſſer.
probanda,

Ibid.c.vlt.
gated and vſurped by one. *Pontifex ipſe Romanus eſt in quo au-*
thoritas illa reſidet, quæ in Eccleſia extat ad iudicandum de omni-
bus omnino fidei controuerſiis. Tria igitur à nobis hactenùs probata
& defenſa ſunt, ex quibus certiſſimè concludimus Rom. Pont. ſu-
premâ in Eccleſia authoritate ad conſtituendum infallibiliter de re-
bus fidei & morum præditum eſſe. Secundo, non Petro ſolùm, ſed eius
etiam vſque in ſæculi finem legitimis ſucceſſoribus eam à Chriſto au-
thoritatem tribui. Tertiò, Romanos omnino Pontifices eſſe in eo ge-
nere legitimos D. Petri ſucceſſores. Quare manet profectò, Rom.
Pontificem pro tempore exiſtentem, eum eſſe, cui tanquam ſucceſſori
D. Petri vniuerſalis Eccleſiæ cura, quod ad fidem moreſ́q́, ſpectat,
commiſſa ſit, & in quo proinde de quæſtionibus omnibus fidei, decer-
„ *nendi authoritas, reſideat.* The Biſhop of *Rome* himſelfe is he
„ in whom that authoritie is reſident, which is extant in the
„ Church, for iudging of all controuerſies of faith. There are
„ therefore three things hitherto proued and defended of vs,
„ vpon which we certainly conclude: 1. The Romane Biſhop to
„ be endowed with ſupreme authority in infallible concluding
„ of things concerning faith and manners. Secondly, that au-
„ thoritie was giuen by Chriſt, not alone to *Peter*, but alſo to
„ his lawfull ſucceſſors, euen to the end of the world. Thirdly,
„ the Romane Biſhops all together in that kind are the lawful
„ ſucceſſors of Saint *Peter*. Whence indeed it remaineth, the
„ Romane Biſhop for the time extant, to be he, vnto whom, as
„ to Saint *Peters* ſucceſſor, the care of the vniuerſall Church, as
„ touching faith and manners, is committed : and in whom
„ alſo the authoritie doth reſide of diſcerning all queſtions of

Lib.8. aſſert.
prob. pag.66.
faith. *Quotieſcunque Rom. Pont. in fidei quæſtionibus definiendis, illa*
qua eſt præditus authoritate vtitur, ab omnibus fidelibus tanquam
doctrina fidei recipi, diuino præcepto debet ea ſententia, quam ille de-
cernit eſſe ſententiam fidei : toties autem ea ipſum authoritate vti
credendum eſt, quoties in controuerſiis fidei, vel per ſe, vel vnà cum
Epiſcoporum Concilio, ſic alterutram ſententiam determinat, vt ad
Ib.cap.3.p.70,
vbi plura.
eam recipiendam obligare velit vniuerſam Eccleſiam. Againe:
Siue Pontifex in definiendo ſtudium adhibeat, ſiue non adhibeat,
modo tamen controuerſiam definiet, infallibiliter certè definiet, at-
que adeò re ipſa vtetur authoritate ſibi à Chriſto conceſſa. As often

as

as the Biſhop of *Rome* practiſeth that authoritie he vſeth, „
the ſence he decerneth to be the ſentence of faith, ought by „
diuine precept, of all the faithfull to be receiued as a doctrine „
of faith. And it is to be beleeued, that he vſeth that authoritie „
as often as in controuerſies of faith, either by himſelf, or toge- „
ther with the Councell of the Biſhops, he ſo determineth ei- „
ther way that he would bind the vniuerſali Church to the re- „
ceiuing of it. Whether the Biſhop vſe or not vſe his beſt ende- „
uour, notwithſtanding he define the controuerſie after that „
manner, he queſtionleſſe ſhall infalliblie define it, and ſo in „
very deed, ſhall vſe the authoritie granted him from Chriſt. A „
man would thinke this were enough, if not too much.

19   The ſupereminent, I may iuſtly ſay, the omnipotent power, which the Canoniſts, and ſome ſchoole Diuines, attribute to the Pope in this caſe, is beyond and aboue all this
abominable in it ſelfe, incredible to them that cannot reade
it themſelues, and will not beleeue it on our reports. *His ful-* Extrau.r.Tit.
nes of power: His impoſſibility to erre: His ability to make of nothing I.c.2.Gloſ.
ſomething : That the Decretall Epiſtles are to be numbred with, De tranſl. E-
or taken for, the Canonicali Scriptures : and therefore are to be ac- ca.Quanto.
cepted as if they proceeded out of the diuine mouth of Peter. That Diſt.19.c.Sic
if the whole world ſhould ſentence againſt the Pope in any matter, omnes.
yet it ſeemes we muſt ſtand vnto the Popes determination: That 9 q.3. Nemo
none may iudge of his iudgement, much leſſe retract it: That if the eſt fil.
Pope be found negligent of his owne and his brethrens ſaluation, vn- Diſt.40. ſi Pa-
profitable and remiſſe in his affaires, and beſides be ſilent in all good- pa.
neſſe, and rather hurts himſelfe, and all others ; neuertheleſſe car- I thought the
rieth innumerable people with himſelfe in extreame ſlauery to hell, Pope had no
there to be puniſhed with himſelfe, with many ſtripes; yet let no mor- brothers but
tall man preſume to reproue his faults , becauſe he may iudge all all children.
men, and be iudged of no man, except he be deprehended out of the But in truth
faith: That truth cleaues to his chaire: That God would not haue it haue more
reſpected whether it be Iudas, or Peter, or Paul, but onely this, that brothers and
be ſit in the chaire of Peter, and that he is an Apoſtle, and the Le- ſiſters.
gate of Chriſt, is the thing he would haue regarded. With more Hoſius Conf.
and worſe to this purpoſe. *That he is our Lord God; can do all* Petroc. c.29.
things; might do what him liſted, yea euen vnlawfull things; and
A a   *is*

De fectis. 115.   *is more then God*, as *Zabarell* faith, that the Popes flatterers
Staple.art pi-   haue perfwaded. That he is, *Supremum in terris numen*,The
ftola.
Pope Gregorie   higheft Godhead in earth. To conclude, that innume-
the thirteenth   rable the like, or more extrauagant then thefe, are difper-
is called ter   fedly fcattered through the Canon Law, in the text and in
tius Apofto-   the Gloffe, among the Canonifts and other Popifh writers,
lorum, 5 E   is fo apparent they cannot deny it; nay they will not, but
uang.
impudently defend it to this day, moft wickedly and
profanely, and it cannot be but againft their owne confciences. Or elfe they excufe it, and qualifie it ridiculoufly,
rather to delude then fatisfie a doubtfull mind. By this infallibility of truth, *Iohn* the 22 could not define an vntruth, for
though his will was abfolute, and his purpofe refolute, yet
God would rather kill him, and preuent him by death,to faue

Analy.l.8.c.3.   the credit of that Sea,&c. as faith *Valentia*.

   20   But what need we fearch into this dungeon of darkneffe, the Popes Decrees or Canons? we haue it cleare by the
frefheft,and neweft writers of the Romane Church,that when
all is done the Pope muft be the laft refuge for triall of all
queftions and doubts; no wit but in his head, no truth but in
his breaft, no ftrength but in his hands, no reft but in his
chaire. Which although it be before proued fufficiently,yet

L.2.c. 10.   a word or two more will not be amiffe. *Infuetum non eft , vt*
veteres itidem damnentur errores, fi nocendo fiant noui , faith def-
,, perate *Gretzer*: It is not vnufuall, that old errors with their
,, authors fhould likewife be condemned, if by hurting they
,, be made new: and fo farre very well and truly. *We haue exam-*
,, *ple hereof in Gelafius the Pope, who tooke out of faithfull hands by*
,, *a law, Tertullian and Origen, and others very ancient.* Neither is
,, this amiffe if they will make no vfe of them themfelues. *This*
,, *right euer is, and was, and fhall be in the Church, to turne out that*
,, *carefully , which bringeth detriment to the flocke .* Yet neither is
,, this to be mifliked. *And if it be lawfull to banifh a whole booke,*
,, *it may be as lawfull, to profcribe a part whether great or little.* I
could grant this as reafonable, the one as the other, *Either by*
cutting it forth , or blotting , or fcraping, or fimply leauing it out,
and that for the readers profit. Here now are two groffe impo-
                                                                      ftures

ſtures and villanies, that vnder this coulour, they will corrupt
and depraue all the Fathers at their pleaſure, that no teſtimonie of *Antiquitie* after the Scriptures may be had : the other,
that none ſhall iudge what is true or falſe, right or wrong, to
be put out, or left in, but what their Synagogue will, or their
contracted Church (which is the Pope) pleaſeth.

21　So that the Pope may interpret the Scriptures, as himſelfe liketh, he may cancell Councels as he will, he may make
voide the Fathers in part or in all as him liſteth, no *Antiquitie*
or authoritie can confine him, nor Traditions tye him; and
then what ſtriuing with ſuch a mighty man ? *Sicinius* as tur-　Plutarch.
bulent as he was, yet durſt not meddle with *Craſſus. Fœnum in*
cornu gerit. Either he had too much money in his purſe, or too
much power in his hand to be dealt withall. He is more then a
curſt cow, he is a mad bull, and hath long hornes;no man that
hath wiſedome in his heart, or wit in his head, will meddle
with him, or at leaſt truſt him. He will engroſſe all our weapons into his owne hands, as the Philiſtines vſed the Iſraelites,　1.Sam. 13.19.
and worſe, not leauing vs ſo much as to mend our ſhares
wherewith we might plow the fallow ground of mens hearts
to ſow the good ſeed; nor ſharpen our hookes, wherewith
we might weed vp the cockle and tares which Antichriſt
hath ſowed in the night of darkneſſe and ignorance, while
men ſlept in ſecuritie, and attended not their owne ſaluation.

22　What need any more be ſaid hereof? Seeing it is not
onely before ſufficiently obſerued, what authority the Biſhop of Rome and his Antichriſtian Sea hath challenged
ouer the Scriptures of God, and all monuments of *Antiquitie*,
but it is alſo yet confeſſed and put in practiſe, that the Pope
preſent may make voide whatſoeuer his predeceſſors haue
concluded. His ſucceſſors no Pope can ſo confine within any
limits, but that he may make voide what himſelfe liketh not.　Extra de elect
This is directly written in the Canon law, and this is practiſed　& elect. po-
by the irregular Popes. *Innocentius* the third ſaith, *Nobis per*　teſtate c. In-
eum adempta non fuit diſpenſandi facultas, &c. The power of diſ-　notuit.
penſing is not (by our prædeceſſors) taken from vs, whereas that was　Prohibentis
not the intention of his prohibition, who could not in this behalfe　intentio.
A a 2　　　　　　　　　*worke*

worke any preiudice vnto his succeffors, who are to exercife the like,
Par in parem *yea the (ame power; whereas thofe who are equall haue no authori-*
imperium
non habet. *ty each aboue other.* This by practife is confirmed, as in many
things heretofore, fo lately in a matter of greateft moment,
which is the tranflation of the Scriptures. *Sixtus quintus* after
diuerfe editions and caftigations of the vulgar Latine tranflation according to the Decree of the *Trent* Conuenticle, fet
forth the fame old tranflation of the Bible, conferred with
ancient Copies, from diuers libraries, out of fundry Vniuerfities of moft nations; many things he amended with his owne
hand, had it printed by the Apoftolicall Printer, and repofed
in the Vatican library; difperfed ouer all countries, as well
on that fide the Alpes, as on this; commanded to be vfed, and
that onely, in all fchooles, preachings, and writings. Who
would not thinke that a thing of fo great moment, vpon fo
long deliberation, after fuch care and prouifion, by an vnerring Pope, for fuch publicke vfe, vpon fuch hazard, or helpe, of
Chriftian foules, fhould be done one once for all, and receiued
for euer, to the common bliffe or bane of the Church? Yet
euen this is altered, changed, almoft made voide, by *Clemens
octauus* another Pope, diuers, yea moft contrary in many
things; expofed and authorifed as the former was by his predeceffor, which more largely and more plainly is by Doctor
Bellum Papa- *Iames* moft wittily obferued. *Innocentius* words are verified in
le. our dayes by this example, *That no Pope can limit the power of
his fucceffor.*

23　And any Pope made derogate from, or vtterly abrogate the acts of his predeceffor. Which is no new thing, if we
remember the times and deeds of the Popes that followed,
Baleus ex as *Formofus, Stephanus, Romanus,* and others. Of which dayes
Stella. *Stella* iuftly complaineth, that *Omnis virtus, tam in capite quàm*
,, *in membris, ex hominum ignauiâ confumpta fuerit:* All vertue, as
,, well in the head, (which was the Pope) as in the members,
,, (which were his Clergie) was by the floth of men confumed.
Platin. in Ro- And of whom *Platina* faith, *Nihil aliud hij Pontificuli cogita-*
mano. *bant, quàm & nomen, & dignitatem maiorum fuorum extinguere,*
,, *&c.* Thefe pettie Popes thought vpon nothing elfe, but how
they

they might blot out the name and honour of their anceftors. „
Againft which bafeneffe he inueyeth moft bitterly vnto the
end of the ftorie of *Romanus*. And fpareth not to lay about him
before and after, giuing diuers Popes though not perhaps all,
yet many of them, part of their deferts. Howbeit thefe and
fuch as thefe, are the men muft haue the decifion of all controuerfies, the command ouer all confciences, the affurance of all
truth, the guidance of all the world, yea & as much worfe then
thefe, as the worft of thefe is worfe then their beft Popes, as
after fhall appeare.

24 Yet heare the impudencie of a fuperftitious (fhall I
fay) or a blafphemous man, for his Antichrift, againft God
and his Sonne Chrift, the Sauiour of the world. *Pro infallibili* Cufanus Epift
regulâ falutis noftræ Chriftus hanc tradidit poteftatem & autho- 2. ad Boëmos
ritatem &c. Chrift hath giuen to his Church this power and p.833.
authoritie for an infallible rule of our faluation, that when „
we ftand in the vnitie of that Church which cleaueth clofe „
to *Peters* chaire, by which he doth bind his fucceffors, euen „
the wicked, to Chrift the head; we cannot erre from the way „
of Saluation, although in the Church one goes one way *where is their*
and another another. You will fay perhaps, the Church of cor vnum
thefe dayes doth not fo walke in the rite of the Commu- via vna.
nion, as before thofe times, when moft holy men did both „
in word and worke confirme by the force of Chrifts precept, „
that the Sacrament was neceffarie in both kindes. Could the „
Church then erre? verily no. But if not, how is that, now „
adayes, not true, which was then affirmed by all mens opini- „
on: whereas this Church is not another then that? Certain- „
ly thou muft not let this moue thee, that at diuers times, now „
one rite, then another, is found in the facrifices, and alfo Sa- „
craments; yet the truth ftanding, and that the Scriptures are „
fitted to the time, and diuerfly vnderftood, fo that at one „
time they be expounded according to the current vniuer- „
fall rite, but that cuftome changed, the opinion may be „
changed.   „

24 Where then is *Antiquitie*, fo much commended, fo much
admired, fo often vrged? A new Pope may alter an old

Popes Decrees.This is nouelty,for *Antiquity*.A new cuſtome
may vndermine an old. This alſo is noueltie, for *Antiquitie*.
Yet this muſt ſtand for an infallible rule of Saluation , then
which nothing is more vncertaine. Yea though confirmed
by the force of Chriſts precept, yet may it be altered by the
Popes pleaſure , or cuſtomes inſtabilitie. Howſoeuer it be,
no man need be troubled, hold what men will, ſo they hold
Peters chaire faſt , they are ſafe from error, though they defend contradictories. What is this, but to turne all religion
out of the Church , and to ſet it on the weathercocke to be
whirled about with euery blaſt of falſe Doctrine? As time
may alter opinions in Religion in the ſame Church, (for the
Romaniſts will haue but one , and that theirs onely, or no
bodies) ſo may it alſo varie with places, but prouided alwayes the triple Crowne be not touched. *Animaduerten-*
dum, habendam eſſe rationem prouinciarum, nationum , gentium:

Azoriusinſtit.
Morall.2.c.13

” This is worth obſeruation,that conſideration muſt be had of
” prouinces,nations and kingdome.For it is wont alſo to come
” to paſſe,that the opinion which is common in one Countrie
” and kingdome, is not receiued in another. For in France
” there are ſome opinions taught with common conſent,
” which notwithſtanding in Spaine or Italy are refuted, and
” improued, almoſt of all men. As that the Croſſe ſhould not
” be worſhipped with the honour and veneration of *Lætria*,
” (that is, that worſhip which is due to God alone) but with
” ſome other inferiour worſhip, many writers in Germanie
” and France haue taught,but in Spaine with common conſent
” it is taught that the worſhip and honour due vnto God a-
lone is to be giuen to the Croſſe. And *Salmeron* ſaith,that
Eccleſia dicitur vna,non tempore, aut loco,aut gente; aut indiuiduis
quæ tranſeunt,ſed fidei confeſſione circa definita & propoſita omni-
bus ad credendum, quæ varia, vario tempore & diuerſis locis cre-

In Epiſtolas
B.Pauli lib.1.
part.3. diſp.1.

” *denda propoſuit pro variâ hominum capacitate:* The Church is
” ſaid to be one, not from the time,or place,or nation, or indi-
” uiduals which are tranſitorie,but from the confeſſion of faith
” concerning things defined, and propounded to be beleeued
” of all men: Which hath propoſed diuers things, at diuers
times,

times, in differerent places, to be beleeued, according to the ,,
diuers capacities of men.   ,,

25 If thefe men onely teach the religion of Chrift, at what
time, or in what place, may a man be fure to find the truth?
Can the Pope fit in his chaire and moderate the Church, and
reconcile, or rather maintain oppofite propofitions? They fay
the diuell wondred to fee two fhips faile contrarie wayes,
with one wind. But this is vfuall we fee in the Sea of Rome,
where they can croffe the very heauens with contradictions;
a monftrous wonder to men and Angels; yet the leffe wonder, becaufe we fee it moft common.

26 Thefe premifes confidered, I would gladly aske D. Suruay. l, 2. c.
Kellifons queftion with little alteration of his words, as the 6. §. 14.
cafe requireth: If one in England fhould doubt whether he
fhould worfhip the Croffe with the higheft, or with inferior
worfhip, (which is a queftion of great moment and confe-
quéce; for to giue leffe then due, is a profaneffe; to giue more,
is plaine idolatrie) whither may we fend him for refolution?
To France? there is one opinion: To Spaine? there is another.
To Germanie? they are one with France? To Italy? they are
indifferent. To the Church? it confifteth of thofe members,
as they conceipt, and they are principall parts of the whole.
To the Pope? who fits ftill like the idoll *Baal*, and is afleepe, 1. King. 18. 27
or otherwayes bufied, he meddles neither with the one opi-
nion nor other, but hath let it hang in fufpence thefe many
yeares, without determining any certaintie with either partie; which notwithftanding he may do, by their learning, with
a dafh of his pen, or a blaft of his mouth, for one peniworth
of inke, parchment, and lead.

27 The like may be faid of many other points, as of the
conception of the bleffed virgine *Marie*, or certaine fubtilties of fchoole Diuinitie, or other indifferent points of doctrine, not defined by the Church, but left to the free cen- Ibid. §. 15.
fure of euery man. For which there hath bene not onely contention in words, but bloudy blowes. Be the queftions of
leffe or greater moment, there is but one truth. And what is
not truth is error, and what is error is finne, and all fin ftin-

geth the confcience, and defileth the man, and without Gods mercy damneth the foule. If the Bifhop of Rome can determine all queftions of faith ; cannot erre in the higheft myfteries of Religion, is the worlds oracle and *Apollo* himfelfe, why fetteth he not peace in thefe things in his owne deare Spoufe? He will neither beleeue Scriptures, nor any other *Antiquitie* in thefe cafes. If he haue not the power they fpeake of, let him renounce it : if he hath it, let him exercife it, and compofe all difficulties, for the peace of his friends, and the ftopping of aduerfaries mouthes.

28   Forafmuch as I vnderftand, they haue no other reafon to make fuch a do for their vniuerfall Bifhop ouer the whole Church, but to determine controuerfies, reconcile contradictions, appeafe ftrifes, fatiffie confcience, that all men may goe one way of certaine truth towards heauen, where they would be. About this D. *Kellifon* maketh many words Suruay.lib.1. and vfeth many fimilitudes, *That euery kingdome muft haue a* c.6.   *King, euery dukedome a Duke, euery common-wealth a magiftrate, euery citie a maior or baliffe, euery army a generall, yea euery village almoft hath a conftable, euery family a good man of the houfe, and euery fchoole a fchoolmafter; and fhall not the Church of God, the focietie of the faithful and chofen feruants, haue a vifible head to direct it, and a Iudge to rule it by lawes, and to gouerne it by authoritie? &c.* God defend elfe: but *Rome* fhould haue her Bifhop, and *Alexandria* hers, and *Conftantinople* hers, and *Canterburie* hers, and *Yorke* hers, and euery kingdome, and prouince, and dioceffe haue their Bifhops. But muft all kingdomes haue one King ouer them, the other pettie Kings vnder him? And fo one Duke ouer all Dukes? one magiftrate ouer all common wealths? one maior or baliffe ouer all cities? one conftable ouer all villages? one goodman ouer all families? one fchoolmaifter ouer all fchoolmaifters? and all other but fubftitutes vnder that one, to be directed, commanded, impofed on whom he will, expofed to what he wil, depofed when he will, as the Pope challengeth ouer all Bifhops, Archbifhops, and Patriarkes, and now of late ouer all Kings and kingdomes of the world? This muft the Doctor
prefume

preſume or aſſume, or all his building falleth.

29 For the booke of God teacheth vs, that there was a Church at Epheſus, at Smyrna, at Thiatyra , at Philadelphia, ſeuen Churches in the leſſer *Aſia.* And the ſame booke doth teach vs, that there was a Church at Rome, another at Corinth, another at Philippi, and ſo of all other Churches euen vnto priuate families. That euerie of theſe Churches ſhould haue her Paſtor, euery Dioces his Biſhop, euerie Prouince his Archbiſhop, beſhrew him that will deny it for me. And what elſe doth all that the Doctor hath ſaid conclude? But that all the world ſhould haue one vniuerſall ouer all, can neuer be gathered by the bookes of God, by Councels, Fathers, ſtories, or drift of reaſon. It is neither conuenient, neceſſarie, nor poſſible.

30 That it hath no proofe of *Antiquitie*, is debated and proued by many, it is not my purpoſe to enlarge that diſpute. That it is not conuenient, is apparent; for then all truth ſhould be pinned to one mans ſleeue : and it is too much for any mortall man to manage. That it is not neceſſarie, there are as learned men diſperſed in diuers kingdomes, Churches, Vniuerſities, as is the Biſhop of *Rome*, or can be. And therefore he is not neceſſarie, where others, as good as he, or better, may be had. The promiſes pretended to be made vnto him, are meerly deluſory, to mock fooles, or delude children. That it is impoſſible, the diſtance of places, the multitude of ſuiters, the coaſt of the iourneys, the perils of ſeas, the diſcord of Princes, the varietie of cauſes concurring, as for the moſt they would, do ſufficiently argue it.

31 They might haue ſome probabilitie , if they would diuide al the world into foure Patriarchates, as now the earth is deuided, one for *Europe*, another for *Aſia*, a third for *Africa*, and why not a fourth for *America*, and a fift for *Magalanica*? Or why not as needfull to haue no more Kings? or but one generall King ouer all, as to haue but ſo many Patriarchs, or one Pope ouer all? All nations may be better gouerned by one poſitiue and perpetuall law, then one nation by many and mutable lawes. Make the Law of God the rule
vnto

vnto all Chriſtians, it mattereth not into how many king-doms, Prouinces or Dioceſſes they be deuided. The ſame law vnto them all is a perpetuall direction, whereunto in all diffi-culties there may be recurrence. But where mens lawes beare the ſway, they may be diuers, flexible, arbitrarie, ſome beneficiall, ſome incommodious; ſome iuſt, ſome iniurious;

Plutarch.in
Coriolano.

ſome regall, ſome tyrannicall; ſome inconuenient, ſome wic-ked; moſt diuers, many quite contraries; whereby the peace of the world may be broken, mens minds diſtracted, aliena-ted, inflamed to furie and armes. Or there may be a caſe of ſuch importance in matter of iuſtice, that in dangerous times it were good, nay, we ſee it beſt, in kingdomes to haue one head and gouernour that may command all, and haue ſu-preme authoritie of iuſtice in his hand, but neuer ſtretched ouer the world generally, much leſſe in matters of faith and religion.

32   In this caſe it might ſeeme to be much more reaſona-ble to haue one vniuerſall King (and others pettie kings vn-der him) to whom all theſe differences might be referred, then to haue but one Oecumenicall and vniuerſall Biſhop, where all are ſubiect but to one law, which all may vſe with-in their owne limits, without enuie, emulation, contradictió, or heart-burning one againſt another. If it be anſwered, that this law, by diuers men diſperſed into ſundry places, may be as diuerſly taken and interpreted; yet I know not, neither can I ſee reaſon, why a learned man in *France* may not be be-leeued, as wel as a learned man, and better then an vnlearned man in *Italy*, as many Popes haue bene: and as good in *En-*

Cypr.l.3.ep.13

gland as in *France*, in one kingdome as in another. *Ideo plures ſunt in Eccleſia Sacerdotes, vt vno hæreſin faciente, cæteri ſubueni-*
" *ant:* Therefore there are many Prieſts in the Church, that if
" one fall into hereſie, the reſt may helpe. As for the pretence of *Peters* Chaire, it is but a meere foppery to cozen the world withall; it may be repoſed for a dull relique with Pope *Ioanes* or her ſucceſſors ſtoole. *Non domus dominum, ſed dominus do-*

Hieron.
ſup, cap.4.

mum cohoneſtat: The houſe graceth not the maiſter, but the maiſter the houſe. *Non ſunt filij Sanctorum qui tenent loca San-*
ctorum,

Eiorum, ſed qui ſequuntur opera eorum : They are not ſonnes of „
the Saints,that hold their places,but that follow their works. „
There may be Popes of diuers affections or factions, ſome „
milde, ſome furious, ſome patient, ſome cholericke, many
Gibelines, (and what if a Guelfe ſhould get in, or proue a
wolfe when he is in?) ſome Franciſcans, ſome Dominicans,
perhaps hereafter Ieſuites.They will not be of one mind,and
therefore will neuer determine and conclude one thing. For
which cauſe we may iuſtly reſolue, that there is no ſtay for
Chriſtians in one vpon earth. We muſt ſet our mindes on
heauen, and our repoſe vpon the certain and infallible lawes
of God,or elſe we ſhall neuer find reſt vnto our ſoules.

CHAP. XV.

*Suppoſe there muſt be one ſuch vniuerſall Iudge in the Church, to
whoſe finall determination all controuerſies muſt be referred,(which
notwithſtanding is vnreaſonable and vnpoſſible) yet the Biſhop
of Rome,things ſtanding or rather falling,as they do,and
long haue done, cannot,may not be that vniuerſall Iudge,for many reaſons.*

Nfidels that neither worſhip nor know the Hilar.lib.1.'de
true God, conceited multitude of gods: yet Trinitate.
diſtributed the gouernment and chiefdome
of all, aboue others, vnto three. *Iupiter* had
the Eaſt, *Pluto* the Weſt, and *Neptune* the
Iſles of the Sea; as was thought of ſuch as
take them but for men-gods,that is,gods made of men. But Cicero de
they that deemed and dreamed they were gods indeed, al- natura Deorū
lotted *heauen* to *Iupiter*, the ſea to *Neptune*, the earth and in-
fernals to *Pluto*.Whether they thought them men or gods,
they neuer eſteemed any one of them of might or maieſtie
ſufficient to moderate the vniuerſal,as *Plutarch* remembreth Plutarch in
in the caſe of *Pompey* and *Caeſar* : Though *Among the gods* Pompey.
*themſelues all things by lot deuided are, And none of them intrudes
himſelfe within his neighbours ſhare* : yet they thought not the
Em-

Empire of *Rome* enough for them, though they were but two. Euen so the Romane Catholickes are so giuen to impropriations, and to ingroffe all into one hand, that the beft, who take their God to be but a man, yet giue him both the Eaft, and the Weft, and the Iles of the fea; as *Alexander* the fixt, who gaue the Weft, with the Iles thereof, to the King of *Spaine*; the Eaft, with her Iles, to the King of *Portugal*, (which were as truly his owne to beftow, as all the kingdomes of the

Math.4.

earth were his who led our Sauiour Chrift to the mountain.) This he could neuer haue done, if himfelfe had not bene infeoffed in them by the god of this world, as in his own right. For, *Nemo poteft plus iuris in alium transferre, quàm ipse ha-*

Sacra.cerem.
l.1.fol.36.fec.7
Poteft. habet
super omnes
poteftates tam
cœli quàm
terrę.Eugen.3

bet : No man can giue more right to another, then himfelfe hath. Therefore he claimed and held it by title of good Scriptures ill applied: *Dominabitur à mari vsque ad mare*: He shall rule from one fea to another. *Data eft mihi omnis poteftas in cœlo & in terra*: All power is giuen me in heauen and in earth.

Steph. Archie-
pifc.Patrac.

Pfal.37.

2 They that would haue their Maifter to be a god, giue him not onely the difpofing of Paradife, and *keyes* of heauen, as a porter or doore-keeper, as *Dauid*, though a King, defired to be; or as they make Saint *Peter* (that were bafe) but as a gouerner and commander ouer Angels and celeftial fpirits, yea and alfo the fea, as he nameth his feate, the earth, Purgatorie, and hell, as much as was euer attributed to all the heathen gods, more then euer was challenged by the true God. So potent, fo powerfull, fo monopolicall a deitie do they imagine their great Maifter to be, as if nothing were excepted or exempted from his omnipotent power in all the world.

3 He hath his lightenings and thunderbolts like *Iupiter*: his triple Crowne or trident Croffe, like *Neptunes* mace. He hath the riches of the earth, the command of Purgatorie, the power of hell it felfe, as *Pluto*. His flatterers and clawbackes offer him no leffe; his owne pride and prefumption hath challenged and admitted as much. God knowes it, and abhorres it; men fee it, and deteft it; the diuels obferue it, and reioyce

in

in it, becaufe it derogates from Gods kingdome, it de-
ftroyeth mens foules, enlargeth and aduanceth hell and damnation.

4 To this God on earth, or this earthie God, or this Vicar of the god of this world, the Romanifts flie as vnto their
onely oracle, to interpret all Scriptures, to authorize all Councels, to moderate all matters, to confirme and eftablifh all
truth, and fet their reft vpon him and none other. So Doctor
Kellifon in effect faith, *Seeing that after Saint Peters death, the* Suruey l. 1. c.
Church hath no leffe need of a vifible Paftor then before: as Chrift 6. §.9.
left him for his Vicegerent, fo in him did he appoint a continuall
fucceffion of his fucceffors; that the Church might alwayes be pro-
uided of a vifible Paftor. And therefore as Bifhops are the fucceffors
of other Apoftles, fo fome one muft fucceed Peter, and muft haue the
fuperiority ouer other Bifhops, which S. Peter had ouer the other
Apoftles; this we grant. And truly no man more likely to be this
man then the Bifhop of Rome, &c. And after againe, *Therefore fi-*
thence that S. Peter muft haue a fucceffor, and that needs muft be
one vifible Iudge vnder Chrift, to whom in all doubts we muft re-
paire, the Pope of Rome is likeft to be he, &c.

5 I will not examine the particular defects of this paffage,
as that there was *great need of a generall Paftor at all after Chrift:*
Or that Saint Peter had that vniuerfall charge: Or that Chrift left
him his Vicegerent. and in him appointed a continuall fucceffion of
his fucceffors: Or that Saint Peter had any fuperiority, or authori-
tie, iurifdiction or command ouer the other Apoftles, (in all which
the Doctor fheweth himfelfe a very impudent begger of principles which will neuer be granted; though he may be borne
with for begging, becaufe all his arguments are halt and
lame, and perhaps may beg by authority.) I onely alledge it
for this, that *the likely man for this charge, can be no man, but the*
Bifhop of Rome, or that the Pope is moft like to be he: which is
concluded by all the men of that man of finne, without all
likelihood or peraduenture.

6 But this was neuer held reafonable, it hath bene euer
for the moft part thought both improbable for argument, and
impoffible for demonftration, much more for practife.

                                                      To

To difpute of Saint *Peters* 28 prerogatiues which Cardinall
Bellar.de Rô. *Bellarmine* vrgeth; or the 15 blemifhes which by ours are layd
Pont.l.1.c.23. &c. cap.28. to his charge,maketh not to my purpofe,either for, or againft
it. We will lay no imputation vpon fo good and great an A-
poftle, which the word of God hath not difcouered : neither
will we amplifie, or aggrauate, any of his imperfections. We
will thanke God for his repentance,& pray the more feruent-
ly , left we fall into the fame temptation and fnares of Satan.
We will yeeld and attribute whatfoeuer the Scriptures giue
him,or due reuerence may afford vnto him.

2.Cor.11.5.   7 He was an Apoftle, fo were others ; and Saint *Paul* not
inferior *to the chiefe.* He was the firft in order, but not in pre-
heminence of power. He was the *chiefeft*, but for his age , as
Hieron.   Saint *Hierome* faith, not for his authority. He had a forward &
an excellent fpirit; yet he fhewed that he was but a man.
Chrift declared many fignes of his familiaritie and loue to-
wards him : yet was there a beloued difciple, peraduenture in
Math.20.20. our Sauiours affection before him. For he was his kinfman
Gal.1.19.   according to the flefh, he was *Iames* brother , and *Iames* was
Ioh.13.23.24. the brother of the Lord. He leaned on his breaft at his laft
fupper. He was intreated, and aduentured to aske a queftion ,
which no other difciple no not *Peter* durft,or at leaft did; and
Ioh.18.15.   receiued a kind anfwer. He followed Chrift neareft without
Ioh.19.26.27. deniall of his Maifter. He accompanied our Sauiour to his
croffe, had commended vnto him the mother of God , as his
efpeciall charge. She was to him as his mother, he to her as
her fonne, in fo much as a Popifh pamphlet hath this infcrip-
A Pamphlet tion concerning them , *Our Ladie hath a new fonne* ; he came
fo entituled. firft to the graue; he outliued all the Apoftles in the charge of
the Church.

8 Saint *Peter* was as the reft of the Apoftles, and they as
he : all receiuing the keyes of the kingdome of God : all ha-
Ioh. 20.22. uing part of the breath of the Sonne of God , when he breathed vpon them the holy Ghoft: *all pertaking the fame holy*
A&. 2.3.   *Ghoft, in the fhape of fierie tongues:* all equally fent by the fame
Prince, vnder the fame commiffion , with the fame inftru-
ctions, the fame prerogatiues,the fame indowments of grace,
in

in preaching and working miracles. *Go therefore, and teach all* Math.28.19. *nations, baptizing them in the name of the Father, and of the Son, and of the holy Ghoft. Teaching them to obferne all things whatfoeuer I command you. And thefe fignes fhallfollow.* The *titles* which Marke 16.17. he affumeth to himfelfe are, *The feruant and Apoftle of Iefus Chrift,* or an *Elder.* That which may be lawfu•ly added more, is, that he was not only the fpokefman, but alfo the penman of the holy *Spirit* of God. Yet of other Apoftles we may fay the fame.

9 Howbeit admit Saint *Peter* had not onely all the prerogatiues, that be, or euer haue bene pretended to be due vnto him alone, and aboue the reft, what is that to his fucceffors in his chaire, if they preferre not, profeffe not, his faith in holineffe, without which no man fhall euer fee God? much leffe Heb. 12.14. fhall he be accounted Chrifts *Vicegerent,* and the onely facred *Organ* of the holy Ghoft. Saint *Peter* himfelfe while he liued neuer practifed, no nor pretended fuch priuiledges as due vnto him, which his vfurping fucceffors do impudently claime from him. They claime from him that which he neuer had while he liued, could neuer leaue behind him when he died. His immediate fucceffors in number about threefcore, in time for the fpace of 600 yeares, neuer made challenge to that vnlimited title of vniuerfall, which lately hath bene vfurped with great craft and hypocrifie, and maintained with much tyrannie and bloud. Many of the firft Bifhops were martyred by infidels that knew not God. Thefe intruders into that feate, murther and maffacre all, that with true faith and a good confcience feeke to ftand approued in the fight of *Iefus Chrift.* In fo much, if euer Saint *Peter* fate in Rome, (as I will not call it now in queftion,) whatfoeuer is was then, it hath degenerated fince, for many hundred yeares together, and the pride of Rome gates might be abated with this deferued infcription:

O domus antiqua quàm difpari Domino dominaris?
O ancient *houfe,* which truth once bleft,
Of how lewd Lords art thou poffeft?

10 For neuer any in that Sea was worthy the honour and
authoritie

authoritie due to Saint *Peter.* In his time he was of eminent

Bel.de script.
Ecclesiast.
authoritie, together with Saint *Paul,* while they both liued in Rome, vntill they both(as some think)died together in one day and yeare, for the testimonie of Gods truth; and so might be sought vnto, as the worthy pillars of Gods Church for their time. Yet I see no reason, why either *Linus,* or *Cletus,* or *Anacletus,* or *Clemens,* should haue the like respect with *Iohn* the Euangelist, who seemeth to haue outliued them all. For he had his immediate commission from Christ, was a sacred writer of the Gospell, three Epistles, and that diuine *Reuelation* and prophesie of the State of Christs Church vnto the end

Hen. Henri-
ques.l.6. set.
de Poeniten-
tiæ sacram.l.
3.c.5.
of the world. *Vera sententia est, in solis Apostolis, & summo Pontifice qui est vniuersalis Christi Vicarius, & habet sedem Apostolicam; iurisdictio immediate concessa fuit iure diuino. Nec est probabilis opinio asserentium Apostolos accepisse iurisdictionem à Petro, præter Barnabam.* This is the true opinion (saith a fresh

,, Schooleman)that iurisdiction was immediatly granted by the
,, Law of God onely to the Apostles, and to the Pope, who is
,, Christs vniuersall Vicar, and holdeth the Apostolicall Chaire.
,, Neither is their opinion probable, who say, that the Apostles
,, receiued their iurisdiction from *Peter,* except *Barnabas.* Yet

Turrecrema-
ta.
Cardinall *Turrecremata* doth hold the contrary, with some other, as *Henriques* there alledgeth. And therefore howsoeuer those were excellent in their generations, yet certainly Saint *Iohn* had the Primacie, if any were, whiles he liued. I will not

Hierome.
presse Saint *Hieromes* authoritie, who preferred him in some cases, before Saint *Peter,*while they both liued; and that if S. *Peter* had any preference at all, it was for his age, rather then any other, respect. But there is no congruitie that any of Saint *Peters* successors, should ouertop this Apostle and Euangelist,

Gal.2.9.
whom Saint *Paul* ioyneth with *Cephas,* and *Iames,* as reputed with them a pillar of the Church. And therefore the edge of the Bishop of Romes authority was not set on that seate while Saint *Iohn* liued. And it may be well presumed, that if S. *Iohn* had come to Rome in their dayes, they would not haue challenged any Primacy ouer him in his person, or ouer his Church where and while he gouerned.

11   Rome

11 Rome then had not the ministeriall head, but *Ephe-sus*, during Saint *Iohns* life. If then Saint *Iohns* may be suppo-sed not to be Saint *Peters* equall, while he liued, (for which there is no reason, much lesse Scripture,) yet though not in seate, yet in honour, power and authoritie, Saint *Iohn* sate higher then any of Saint *Peters* successors; & so he succeeded *Peter* in the most excellēt things (if he may be said to succeed, which hath no ground.) Whereunto Cardinall *Bellarmine* seemeth willingly to condescend. *Fuit in illis Ecclesiæ primor-* De Rom. *dijs necessarium ad fidem toto orbe terrarum celeriter disseminan-* Pont.lib.1.c.9 *dam, &c.* In those beginnings of the Church for the sprea- ,, ding of the faith in the whole world, it was necessarie that ,, principall power and libertie should be granted to the first ,, Preachers and founders of Churches, but when the Apostles ,, were dead, the Apostolicall authoritie only remained in the successors of Saint *Peter.* From which his ingenuous con-fession there arise two ineuitable conclusions against Saint *Peters* primacy, and his successors supremacy.

12 For if all the Apostles while they liued had *summam po-testatem & libertatem*: highest power and libertie, then Saint *Peter* was but their equall, and they his: and so he had no Primacie whiles he liued, for other out-liued him. Much lesse had Saint *Peters* successors supremacie, while any of the Apostles liued. *For the Apostles must be dead, before the* Supra.c.14. *Apostolicall authoritie* could be planted in Saint *Peters* succes-sors. So that in the first hundred yeares, (for so long it is thought Saint *Iohn* liued, who deceassed last of al the *Apostles*) there was neither primacie nor supremacy belóged to the Bi-shops of Rome. And therfore for so long the Bishop of Rome was not the man to whom all interpretations of Scripture, and determinations of truth, did condignely belong. All which Saint *Cyprian* affirmed, not very long after, in the midst of the third hundred yeares, *Hoc erant vtique cæteri A-* De simp. *postoli, quod fuit Petrus, pari consortio præditi & honoris & pote-* Prelat. prope *statis, sed exordium ab vnitate proficiscitur, vt Ecclesia vna mon-* initium. *stretur.* That were the rest of the Apostles that *Peter* was, ,, indued with the like fellowship of honour and power. But ,,

the

,, the beginning proceeds from vnitie, that the Church may
,, be manifested to be but one. And Saint *Ambrose* not long af-

De incar. do-
minicæ sa-
cram.c.4.& 5.

ter him in the next age, *Petrus statim loci non immemor sui, primatum egit, primatum vtique confessionis, non honoris ; primatum
fidei, non ordinis: Peter*, not vnmindfull of his place, immedi-
,, atly exercised his primacie, that is, his primacie of confession,
,, not of nonour; his primacie of faith, and not of order. This
,, may be amplified by multitude of testimonies, for the
first 600 yeares. In all which time there appeared nothing
that maketh shew of supremacie in the seate of Rome. And
therefore in this case our aduersaries do but vainly brag of
Antiquitie.

13 Succeeding ages, wise for their owne aduantage,
tooke euery hyperbolicall speech, vttered by the Ancients, in
commendation of Saint *Peter*; euery reuerend tearme vsed
in a respectfull regard of the Bishop then gouerning : euery
title of honour giuen from an inferior Sea ; and set them on
the tenters and stretched them to most aduantage ; as if
euery word had his iust proportion of weight. And what in
curtesie was voluntarily offered, that was receiued and accepted as bounden dutie. And what was once gotten, was in-
creased by daily accesse : nothing remitted of that which
was giuen. And thus grew the Pope to his omnipotencie.
First a claime of superioritie, then a title of vniuersalitie, then
an vsurpation of powerfull regalitie, at last a possession of tyrannicall supremacie : which he holdeth and defendeth,
neither by booke, nor word, but by fire and sword, against
all people, and Princes, that are or are not made drunke
with the dregges of the whore of Babylons abhominations.

Coc.Sabell.
Ennead 8.1.6.
Platina in vi-
ta Benedict.2.
Papyr.Mass.

14 The best Bishops were chosen by the Clergie and
people of Rome. The second so chosen, but confirmed by
the Emperour. The third were elected by the Emperors a-
lone, without either Clergie or people. The last by the Cardinals without either Clergie, people, or Emperor. The first
ranke were chosen of the most holy and learned, without all
partialitie, and therefore were all good men, like the golden

den head of *Nebuchadnezzars* Image. The ſecond learned too, and good men many, as the ſiluer , but ere long degenerated into braſſe. The third declined in vertue and learning, as they climbed by ambition , and degenerated farther and farther from their progenitors, and became as iron, hardned againſt all reformation. And laſtly they ſo blended the temporall Monarchy with the Eccleſiaſticall Supremacie, as that nothing claue together, but brake forth into all diſorder, and became a meere ataxie and forlorne eſtate, as now it ſtandeth. A pompous Court, no preaching Church.

15 Wiſedome will perſwade men eaſily to yeeld much reſpeċt, and reuerence vnto the firſt ſort. Modeſty would induce vs to hold the ſecond ſort in due reputation. Diſcretion will aduiſe to examine the declining age , and make more preciſe triall of the ſpirits , whether they were of God or not. For before that time many falſe Prophets had ſeized vpon the world. But as for the laſt rank, there is no conſciéce they ſhould be obtruded vpon vs, there were no wiſedome to admit or accept them. For a worſe generation of moſt filthy Epicures, proud Prelates, cruell tyrants, there neuer was heard of in any ſucceſſion vpon the face of the earth : yet theſe muſt be the men, and none but theſe, in theſe dayes of ſinne; this not onely declining, but failing, yea this ending of this wilfull and wicked world , to whom we muſt reſort for reſolutions of all doubts. Wherein how fairely we ſhould be ſerued if we ſhould repoſe our faith vpon them, firſt reade, and then iudge.

16 Some of our aduerſaries haue bene ſo ingenuous as to confeſſe, that *Omnis homo errare poteſt in fide, etiam ſi Papa ſit:* All men may erre in faith, although he be the Pope, ſaith *Alfonſus de Caſtro.* This his poſition he fortifieth by examples of *Liberius* the Arian : *Anaſtaſius the Neſtorian : and Celeſtine that erred about the marriage of the faithfull, when one of them falls into hæreſie : a thing euident to all men. Wherein he erred not onely as a man, but as a Pope. That his definition or determination was in the old Decretall Epiſtles , which (ſaith he) ego ipſe vidi & legi, I my ſelfe haue ſeene and read. But that ſome ſay, he is* Aduerſus hæreſes. l. 1. c. 4.

De conuerſ. infid. cap. Laudabilem.

B 2   not

not Pope that obstinately erreth in faith, and vpon this affirme the Pope cannot be an hereticke: It is but to dally with words in a serious matter. For this is not the question, whether the same man may be a Pope, and an hereticke, but whether one that otherwise might haue erred in faith, by the power of his Papall dignitie, be made vnerrable? For I cannot thinke that any can be so impudent a flatterer of the Pope, that will yeeld him this prerogatiue, that he can neither erre nor be deceiued in the interpretation of the Scriptures. For seeing it is well knowne that diuers Popes haue bene so palpably vnlearned, that they haue bene vtterly ignorant of their Grammar, then how can they be able to expound the Scriptures? I must confesse that all these words are not to be found in all the editions of *Alphonsus:* but that this was his iudgment, is manifest by the editions of his works set forth in his life time. That now they are in some impressions left out, it is the shameles imposture of these impudent times, wherin nothing is left vnattempted, that may make for the furtherance of Antichrists kingdome. As he wrote it boldly (though it seemes not without blame,) so is it likely he had good examples and authoritie for it, else would he not haue deliuered a passage so preiudiciall to the Pope, the top of his spirituall kin, and vniuersall head of his owne Church.

     17 A particular example whereof by vndeniable authoritie, is *Benedict the ninth*, who whether he were but a youth, or springall, or beardlesse boy, as *Papirius Massonius* tearms him, or not aboue twelue or ten yeares old as *Glaber Rodulphus* writeth, & *Baronius* ingenuously acknowledgeth, rather the lesse then the more : certainely he could not well vnderstand his Grammar by that time; or if he did, he could not be reputed learned; or if he were more pregnant then was cōmon to a child of those years, yet not sufficient to interpret all Scriptures, assoile all questions, resolue all doubts, sit at the sterne, and guide the ship of the Church, with all the soules that are contained therein. *If there were any fault in bribing for his election, I thinke it was not to be attributed to him* (poore princocks lad) *but to his friends and kindred,* saith *Massonius*; which is his best excuse for the pretty or pettie child Pope.

Nondum pubes, impubes. Lib. 4. in Benedict 9. l. 5. c vlt. l. 4. c 5.

Et censebant omnes ij qui in tali tenera aetate dolo malo locum non esse iurif. consultorum disciplinae scire volent.

Pope. But it mattereth not much, *siue decennis, siue duodenis* In Plassæi *fuerit, tantæ functioni, in tantilla ætate parum aptus fuit.* Whether Myst.pag.332 he were ten, or whether he were twelue, in such a diminutiue ,, nonage, he was vnfit for so great a function, saith *Gretzer.* ,, This child was the head of the Church, the vniuersall oracle of the world, could neither erre himselfe, nor misleade others; might call Councels, determine causes, depose kings, command Angels, open and shut both hell and heauen, and in a word do whatsouer another Pope might do. Whose chaire belike can as well infuse learning into a child to serue the Romane turne, as it can make *Iudas* a good Apostle, or one as bad as *Iudas* a worthy Pope, for a need as good as *Peter.* As Cardinall *Hosius* hath said in the last Chapter. *Leui* offered Hosius. tithes in the loines of faithfull *Abraham*, but this Pope neuer paid any seruice to God in the loines of *Peter*, for he is vtterly worne out of his bloud or linage.

18 I neuer read that this example hath bene answered or excused, nor his entrance, life, death, or monstrous apparition in an vgly shape, defended; yet he liued and reigned, and raged and raued, and tumbled like *Behemoth* or *Leuiathan* in that dead sea of *Rome*, aboue twentie yeares. Let any reasonable man iudge, whether euer Christ spake to him in Saint *Peter*, *Feed my sheepe, feed my lambes, feed my sheepe.* Ioh 21. *The heire as long as he is a child, differeth nothing from a seruant,* Galat.4.1. *though he be Lord ouer all, but is vnder tutors and gouerners, vntill the time appointed of the father.* If the law of man, thus strengthened by the word of God, be thus prouident, not to commit a temporall estate into the hands of a child, though it fall vpon him by naturall and legall descent: shall we euer imagine that God will be lesse prouident for his Church and the saluation of mens soules, and commit it to a boy, to a child, to litle more then an infant? God threatened it as a plague by his Prophet, euen vnto a common wealth, that *children should* Esai.3.4. *rule ouer them.* A greater pestilence could neuer fall vnto the Church, Gods spirituall common wealth, (if *Rome* had bene such) then to haue a child both for years and vnderstanding, to haue the keyes and power of all in his weake and feeble

and

and wicked hands. It is monſtrous in nature, ſo *litle a head for ſo great a body.* It was a blemiſh in *Pericles*, that his head was a litle too big for his bodie, which the ſtatuaries couered with an helmet in al hisimages. But this litle head for ſo great a bodie, miſ-ſhapeth much more. I know not how this monſtroſitie may be ſhrowded or ſalued. How much wiſer was *Ariſtotle*, that would not haue a youth hearer of morall Philoſophie? Though this Pope was not ſo forward as *Iuuenis ætate*, a youth for yeares, yet his life ouertopt the moſt ancient in all impietie. If they ſay, that this is not without example, that great offices haue bene committed to litle children, as *Caius* and *Lucius*, *Auguſtus* ſons were made Conſuls at foureteene yeares old : yet they had a father that was Emperour to command them, the Pope had no father to ouerrule him. Theſe were foureteene, (vnfit for gouernment, I confeſſe) he but twelue, or rather ten, much more vnfit to manage the Eccleſiaſticall monarchie.

19   In ſuch a childs behalfe, what can be ſaid, either to excuſe him, or to blot out this ſtaine and blemiſh of that Romiſh ſynagogue? Or in ſuch a caſe, what helpe or ſtay for the vniuerſall Church? The anſwer may ſeeme eaſie, and that from a boy preacher, *Cornelius Muſſus*, who is ſaid himſelfe to haue preached with admiration and great confluence of hearers, when he was but twelue yeares old; a fit play-fellow for ſuch a yong Pope. Who ſaith, to helpe out his maiſter at a dead lift, *Dubitanti quomodo conſcientiæ errores, & ſcrupuli tolli poſſunt? Reſpondendum tibi fortè videretur, Conſule doctiores. At quoniam de more diſſentiunt, aliquibus affirmantibus, negantibus alijs nonnullis dubitantibus. Dico tibi ego: Quod prælatus conueniendus eſt, illiuſq́; conſcientiæ tua conſcientia committenda atque credenda. Caue autem ne dicas non audeo animam meam illius conſcientiæ committere. Non enim in manus hominis animam tuam poſuiſti, ſed in manus Dei. Tanquam Deo igitur, non tanquam homini illi pareas. Adeo enim tua illa obedientia placebit Altiſſimo, etiamſi ille indigniſſimus fuerit, vt ſtatim omnes ſcrupuli diuina gratia ſint receſſuri. Imo eo fructuoſior erit, quo ille fuerit indignior,* " *cui propter Deum ſubijci voluiſti.* To him that doubteth how

the

Sidenotes:

Plutarch.in Pericl.

In vita Auguſt

Sixt.Senenſ. Bibl.ſanct.l 4.

Cornel.Muſſ. in Rom. c.5. p.252.

the errors and fcruples of a confcience fhould be remoued? „
Perhaps it will be thought good to anfwer, Confult with the „
more learned.But becaufe ordinarily they difagree, fome af- „
firming, others denying, others doubting: I fay vnto thee, „
conforme thy felfe to the Prelate, thy confcience is to be „
committed and repofed vpon his confcience. Take heed left „
thou fay, I dare not commit my foule vnto his confcience: „
for thou haft not put thy foule into the hand of a man, but „
into the hand of God.Therefore fee thou obey him,as a god, „
not as a man. So this thy obedience fhall pleafe the moft „
High,although he were moft vnworthy. Thus forthwith all „
fcruples,by Gods grace,will depart.Yea fo much the better „
will it be for thee, by how much he was more vnworthy vn- „
to whom thou haft fubmitted thy felfe,for Gods fake.　　„

20　If he fpake this of euery Prelate, I cannot perceiue
what he differeth from a Pope. If he meane the Pope,all that
I haue faid is anfwered, but very ftrangely, if not madly;
which is in effe&, that it is more merit to beleeue this Pope-
lad, or any his like, then Saint *Gregorie* or Saint *Peter* either.
If this be not ftrange learning, ancient both writings and
writers are quite out of tune: which neuer thus make flefh
their arme, nor teach to put fuch confidence in man. Yet he
faith further: *Quem ergo pro Deo habemus, in his quæ Dei funt,*
quicquid ipfe dixerit, tanquam Deum audire debemus. Si certum
tibi fuerit illum contra Deum dicere,regulam habes,Obedire magis
oportet Deo quàm hominibus: At fi dubium tibi fit dicátne fecun-
dùm Deum vel non,ne follicitus fis, Prælato crede: illius culpa erit
fi peccabis. Whom we haue in the place of God in thofe „
things that pertaine to God, we ought to heare him as God, „
in whatfoeuer he fpeaketh. If it be for certaine,that what he „
affirmeth,is againft God, thou haft a rule, Rather obey God Act.5.29.
then men. But if it be doubtfull to thee, whether he fpeake „
according to God or not,be not folicitous:beleeue the Pre- „
late, it fhall be his fault if thou finne. By which the word of „
truth is made falfe: *Euery one fhall liue by his owne faith:* and *E-* Abac.2.4.
uery finners bloud fhall be vpon his owne head. He is in a fory cafe, Ezech.18.13.
that in matter of religion and confcience hath his beleefe fo

tied to an ignorant asses sleeue. But perhaps they haue a better answer.

21   The Romanists are not abashed to obiect vnto vs, that we made a woman head of our Church, when noble Queene *Elizabeth* reigned. Yea Cardinall *Bellarmine* is not ashamed to say and write, *Iam reipsa Caluinistis in Anglia, mulier quædam est summus Pontifex:* Now in very deed the Caluinists in England haue a woman Pope, or chiefe Bishop. Which is a monstrous lye. And therefore he hath mended it in his Recognitions, as the Fletcher mends his bolt: *Rectius dixissem, Protestantibus in Anglia mulierem esse caput Ecclesiæ:* I should haue said better, that the Protestants in England had a woman head of their Church. Which is a greater lye. Yet *Sanders* our countriman, that knew the contrary in his conscience, slanders worse, when he saith, that *The Queene of England doth exercise the priestly act of teaching and preaching in England, with no lesse authoritie then Christ himselfe or Moses euer did.* Their owne Prelates, the Popish Bishops, gaue that title of Head to King *Henrie* the eight. Which is written against by some of our partie, as an incompetent title for a mortall man. Her Highnesse *disclaimed it in her life time by word and deed, his Maiestie requireth it not,* that now most worthily reigneth. We giue him no more then Gods booke allowes him by word and example. His Maiestie asketh no more then King *Dauid, Iehosaphat, Hezechiah, Iosias,* the good Kings of *Iuda* enioyed, with contentment of their good subiects, and the approbation, yea and commendation of God himselfe.

22   But suppose we did let any vnpartiall man iudge, that hath more care to satisfie his conscience then to maintaine a faction, whether it were not better to rest on our most learned Kings iudgement in matters of faith, then an vnlearned Pope: yea vpon a most learned Queene, then a Lady-Pope, or a child of Niniueh, that scarce knew his right hand from his left? Are they not partiall in their owne conceits, that iudge vs wrongfully in that, wherein they condemne themselues most euidently?

23 This

[margin notes:]
De notis Ecclef.lib.4.c.9.

Pag.49.

Sand.vif.Monarch.l.6.c.4.

Iac.rex Apol. 281.

Ionas 4.

23 This monstrous defect his Cardinals, who are assistants in his Consistorie, must supplie. A miserable head the while, who hath his wit to seeke in others braines. A yong Pope may haue as yong Cardinals, as a yong *Reboboam* may haue yong Counsellors. *Clemens sextus quosdam nulla habita ætatis ratione,* Papir. Masson *& in his aliquot penè pueros creauit : vt Petrum Belfortium Ioan-* in Clemen, 6. *næ sororis filium, Vrbaniq, postea successorem,qui vicesimum ætatis annum nondum attigerat. Clemens* the 6 created some Cardinals, ,, hauing no consideration of their age, and amongst them some ,, almost children : as *Peter Belfortius* his sister *Ioanes* sonne, ,, and afterwards the successor of *Vrban,* who had not attained ,, the 20 yeare of his age. Doctor *Reinolds* brings good autho- Apolog. The ritie of all this in his quotations. *Ioannes Medices* a Cardinall sium. §.26. about 13 yeares of age, *Innocentius Montius,* no innocent, but a lasciuious youth. *Ferdinandus Medices* a boy about 13. O-*dettus Caustillioneus* about 11 yeares old, and *Alphonsus Lusi-tanus* at 7 yeares. I maruell that some were not created in their mothers wombe, (as the question is moued, whether a child may not be christened in his mothers belly:) or at least in their armes and sucking at their breasts. Were not a boy Pope well helped vp with such child Cardinals?

24 Yet he needs want no helpe, for he may call a Coun-cell of Bishops, and those can stop all gaps of error with the bushes of their braines, and set *Peters* ship straight, howsoe-uer the wind blow. But what if these may be children also, as many haue bene? As a certaine noble man at 18 yeares in our owne Countrie of England, *George Neuil,* after Archbishop of Yorke, before consecrated Bishop of Exeter vnder xx yeares; and diuers Bishops and Archbishops so farre from maturitie of iudgement, that they were scarce able to put on their owne clothes, nor worthy to carrie a good scholers bookes. For heare their owne friends speake, *Nam quotusquisque hodiè est* Nic. Cleman-*ad Pontificale culmen euectus qui sacras vel perfunctoriè literas le-* gis de corrup. *gerit, audierit, didicerit, imo qui sacrum codicem nisi tegumento* fol. 10. *tenus, vnquam attigerit, cum tamen in iureiurando illas in sua insti-tutione se nosse confirment ?* For who at this day is preferred to ,, the Pontificiall dignitie, which hath read, heard, or learned ,,
the

„ the holy Scriptures but slightly, yea who neuer touched the
„ holy Bible, but on the vtmost couer, who notwithstanding
„ professe to haue vnderstood it, by their oath in their insti-
„ tution.

    25   After that *Theodoricus de Niem* had at large discour-
sed, of the ignorance, carelesnesse, couetousnesse, and simony
of *Boniface* the 9; I will not say, he concludeth, (for he hath
much more of his prophane madnesse afterwards) but he hath

Lib. 2. cap. 12.
& præced.
sequen. cap.
this passage among many: *Pro certo baratrias & multas nouas
inuentiones dicti Bonifacij ad extorquendum pecunias indifferen-
tèr ab omnibus fiebant, vt vix aliquis per omnia scribere possit.
Tunc temporis vidisses etiam continuo valdè multos apostatas, di-
uersorum Ordinum mendicantium, in eadem vrbe discurrere, & a-
liquos effici armigeros ipsius Bonifacij, sed plurimos titulares Epis-
copos, ac plerosque sedis Apostolicæ capellanos, ad aliquam Ecclesiam titularem promouebat; itaque nonnulli qui heri, vt scurræ seu
histriones, aut dyscoli, per vicos & tabernas, aliaq; suspecta loca
per vrbem discurrebant, in publico hodie facti Episcopi, & Prælati,
sancta tractabant, nonnullis præmijs, nulla prius habita pœnitentia
seu absolutione, à censuris Ecclesiasticis, quas sic euagando per mun-
dum & apostatando, & peccata enormia committendo, damnabilitèr*
„ *incurrebant, &c.* Certainly such cogging cosenages and mani-
„ fold new inuentions of the aforesaid *Boniface*, to wrest mo-
„ ney, were indifferently practised of all, that scarce any man is
„ able to expresse them by writing. At the same time mightest
„ thou haue seene continually many apostates of the diuers
„ Orders of mendicants, to wander in the same Citie, and some
„ of them made pentioners of the same *Boniface*, but many titu-
„ lar Bishops and the most Chaplaines of the Apostolicke Sea,
„ which he had promoted to some titular Church. Whence
„ some that yesterday were ruffians, scoffers or stage-players,
„ and trewants that did loyter in the Citie, about the streets, Ta-
„ uerns, and suspected places, to day in publicke were made Bi-
„ shops and Prelates, performing the holy rites not without re-
„ ward, no penance before inflicted, nor absolution receiued
„ from Ecclesiasticall censures, which they had damnably in-
„ curred by such wandring through the world, and apostating,
and

and committing enormious offences,&c. The like teftimony Nicm.1 c.8.
giues *Otto* of *Vrbanus: Pro certo Pater nofter non Vrbanus, fed po-* Vrbanus,
tius, vt timeo, Turbanus dicetur, & multis erit aduerfitatibus in- Turbanus.
uolutus, & ruina mulhorum: Certainly our father may be called ,,
not *Vrbanus,courteous,*but rather as I feare *Turbanus,troublous,* ,,
who fhall be inwrapped in many aduerfities, and fhall be the ,,
ruine of many. This author liued in thofe times, was of the ,,
Court of Rome,followed the part of *Vrban* and his fucceffors,
againft the *Anti-Popes, toto illo tempore & poft, præfens in Rom.*
curia per 30 *annos vel circa, in obedientia quadam Urbani PP.6.*
fuccefforumq́,fuorum remanfi: I abode all that time& after, be- ,,
ing prefent in the Romane Court, by the fpace of 30 yeares or ,,
thereabout, in the attendance of Pope *Vrban* the 6, and his ,,
fucceffors. Is it likely the Pope cannot erre, turning vpon Cardinales
fuch hinges? cannot be furprifed hauing fuch watchmen? Epifcopi.

26   But you will perhaps yet reply, that though fome are
fuch, yet fo are not all. Some are aged and graue, fome wife
and learned, the moft part fuch as are able to communicate
their counfell to the head or members. Howbeit, may they
fpeake their minds freely and faue their oathes? (for they are
fworne to the Bifhop of Rome.) That may they not. *Ego N.*
Papatum Romanæ Ecclefiæ, I will defend the Papacie of the Romane Church, &c. Euery Bifhop that trauels to a Councell
hath his tongue as ftrait tied, as a theefe is pinioned when he
goes to the gallowes.Like *Romulus* his *Patricians* in older or Plut. in Rom,
oldeft Rome:*Who did meddle with nothing,but had only an hono-* ,,
rable name, and a robe,and were called to Councell onely for fafhion ,,
fake, not for their aduice and counfell: for when they were affembled ,,
they only heard the Kings pleafure & cómandemḗt,but they might ,,
not fpeake one word, and fo departed hauing no other preheminence ,,
ouer the commonwealth,fauing they firft knew what was cócluded. ,,
What elfe did the Bifhops in a Councell? They onely heard a
Maffe of the holy Ghoft, whom they expected not from heauen, but ftom Rome. They had honourable titles of Benefices without benefit,and they wore their robes,and affembled,
rather for fafhion then for their audience and counfell, atten-
ding the Popes pleafure and command.Onely in this they had
the

the preference of *Romulus Patricians*, that they might speake one word, which was, *Placet*, nothing else durst they speake but told the clocke. Thus *Romulus* cosened his Citizens, and so his successors the Bishop of Rome coseneth the whole world.

27 So that if the Pope will erre, he may; if he haue not sufficiencie in himselfe, little helpe may be expected from o-thers. Or suppose some of them would be bold enough to

Loquere vt te videam.

speake, yet are they such blind bayards, that they cannot see to speake, nor be seene by speaking. Yonger sonnes of noble houses obtained great Bishoprickes, rather for their aduance-ment then for their learning or merit, or for the good of Gods Church: to build great houses, not to preach or teach

Barthol . Fu-mus aurea ar-mil.verb. Be-neficium.

the Gospel of Iesus Christ. Although *Beneficia Ecclesiastica con-ferre pueris, non solũ inexcusabile, sed intolerabile videtur*: To be-stow Ecclesiasticall Benefices vpon children, is not onely vn-excusable, but also intollerable. All Histories are full of such examples. And I beleeue if many Bishops in *Italy* and *Spaine* and *France* too, were well examined, they would be found to haue greater liuings then learning, higher in honour then much in labour, fitter for ciuill then Ecclesiasticall employ-ments.

28 I will not vrge the Bishops of *Italy* with their igno-

Cl.Espencæus

rance and lacke of learning. Of whom *Espencæus* reporteth,
,, that they studied the Canon Law, they medled not with the
,, Scriptures, (and then no doubt they were like to proue good
,, Diuines:) for if they did but so much, they had some learning,
,, or at least shewed that they minded somewhat, that concerned
,, the Church gouernment at the least, according to the custome and fashion of their owne countrie, yet were vnfit to deter-mine matters of faith. Take but a taste of the learning of a Bi-shop or two in this land, who liued in the dayes of darknesse, when blindnesse was as good as sight. For *Argus* with his 100 eyes could see no more in a darke caue then *Polyphemus* with his one or no eye. But these, though the obiect had not bene intercepted, could not see, because the darknesse of blind ig-norance was in themselues, they had not so much as one eye to
see

to see the truth, were it in it selfe neuer so euident, bright and glorious. I know not how the strength of an obiect might bring sight to their eye, it is certaine the eye of their vnderstanding could cast no sight on the obiect.

An visus fit extramittendo, vel intro mittendo.

29 The *King of England* wrote to the Pope for the preferment of his Secretarie to the Bishopricke of *Duresme*. The colledge of Cardinals disswaded his acceptation, becaufe he was *Laicus indoctus, & Episcopatu indignus*: that is, a Lay man, vnlearned, and vnworthy a Bishopricke. Yet his Holinesse out of his great care and prouidence for that Church, answered, *Verè si Rex Anglia pro asino supplicasset, obtinuisset ad vota, pro hac vice* : Certainly if the king of England had intreated for an *Affe*, he should haue had his defire for this turne. Such a Bishop as *Marcus Lepidus* was a Consul, the verieft *Affe* in all Rome. *Lodouicus de Bello monte*, more noble for his houfe then reuerend for his learning, allied to the Kings of England and France, was confecrated Bifhop of the fame Sea. Which when he receiued at the hands of the Archbifhop of Yorke, he was so learned forfooth, that *Quamuis per multos dies inftructorem habuisset, legere nesciuit, & cum auriculantibus alijs, ad illud verbum Metropolitica, peruenisset, diuque anhelans pronunciare non posset, dixit in Gallico, Soit pour dict:* Although many dayes before he had an inftructor, yet he could not reade, and when with others prompting him, he was come to the word *Metropoliticall*, and panting a great while, he could not pronounce it, he said in French *let it ftand, for spoken.* At another time, when he did once giue Orders, and could not get out the word *in aenigmate, dixit circumftantibus. &c.* He faid to the by ftanders: *Par Saint Lowis, iln'eft pas curtoys, qui cefte parolle yci efcrit. By Saint Lewis he had no curtefie that wrote this word there.* Here wäted a Pope *Innocent*, who made voide the election of the Bifhop of *Penneffis, quod donum fcientia Pontifici conueniens non effet affequutus* : Becaufe he had not attained to vnderftanding fit for a Bifhop. Or an *Honorius 3. Qui Epifcopum Latinenfem adeo de illiteratura & infufficientia compertum, vt nec Grammaticam didiciffe, neque Donatum legiffe, fateretur a Pontificij executione & Ecclefia adminiftratione*

De Antiquitate Brittani. Ecclef. p. 262.

Plut. in Sylla. Ypodigma Neuftriæ per Tho. Walfingham. Ex catal. Epifcoporum Lindaffarn. vfque ad Richard Bury. Cl. Efpencæus in 1. ad Timoth. digreff. 9.

stratione penitus submouit : Who depoſed the Biſhop of Lati-
num both from the execution of his office, and all authoritie
in the Church, for that he was found to be of ſuch illitera-
ture, & inſufficiencie, that he confeſſed he had neuer learned
his Grammar, nor ſo much as read *Donatus*; and yet no doubt
worſe were admitted and ſuffered. What if the Pope ſhould
call ſuch Biſhops to a Councell? were there not good hope
of due conſideration of matters of faith ; and accordingly of
reformation in religion and manners? This hath bene the

Cardines,
Whence Car-
dinals.
Epiſcopi vi-
gilatores.
Ioₐ.1.6.
Parue puer
petulans didi-
ciſti ludere
pluma?
Iohn 2.15.

ſtate of the Church of *Rome in capite & in membris* , in head
and members. And if ſuch were the head and ſhoulders, what
were the feete ? If ſuch were the armes, what were the toes ?
If ſuch were the hinges, what were the haſpes ? If ſuch were
the watchmen, what were the ſleepers in that ſhip?

    30 The Pope a child, yea and better fed then taught. *Car-*
dinalls lads, called rather to receiue liuing then diſpenſe learning. Biſhops boyes, fitter to conſter *Cato* the interpret Scriptures, to ſcourge a top then to whip buyers and ſellers out of
the Temple. If they be men, yet ignorant, palpably ignorant,
knowing nothing themſelues, much leſſe able to inſtruct o-
thers. Then may it ſtand either with Gods prouidence to
prouide ſuch rulers for his true Church, except he ſend them
as ſometimes he ſends Kings in his anger, to plague the
Church? or may good Chriſtians relie and reſt vpon them, as
their laſt and beſt refuge in the dayes of ignorance or trouble? Of ſuch Popes yet they ſay (for they except none) *Vt ve-*

Ia. Naclātus in
Epheſ. c.2. p.
99.

rè nemini fidelium liceat dubitare penes illum , & ſupremam , &
omnem, reſidere poteſtatem Ecclefiæ Dei, qua non ſolum poſſit, quic-
quid ad ædificationem Ecclefiæ facere iudicauerit , & animarum
ſaluti conducere animaduerterit executioni committere, ſed & ſin-
gula Ecclefiæ membra , certis muneribus diſtribuere , poteſtatem
communicare, & non ſecus ac caput de quibuſcunque membris diſ-
,, *ponere.* So that truly it ſhall not be lawfull for any of the
,, faithfull to doubt , but that both the ſupreme and totall po-
,, wer of the Church of God reſides with him. By which not
,, onely he may put in execution, what euer he iudgeth may be
,, to the edification of the Church , and perceiueth to conduce

to the fauing of foules : but alfo to diſtribute euery member „ of the Church vnto their certaine functions, to communicate „ power to them, and difpofe of them , no otherwiſe then as „ the head of euery member. Which when he faid , he hath „ not done. For by the example of the Scribes and Pharifies, wicked Popes may fit in *Peters chaire.* And therefore concludes, that whatſoeuer he offereth , muſt be kiſt as if Saint *Peter* himſelfe had fent it. As not onely in the text, but in the marginall note for better obferuation is obferued: *Quæ traduntur à ſummo Pont. non ſecùs ſunt accipienda, ac ſi traderentur à Petro:* What is deliuered from the Pope, is to be no otherwife receiued , then as if it were deliuered from *Peter* himſelfe.

31 *Caiphas* fpake one true word, *That it was fit one ſhould* Iohn. 11. 51. *dye for the people, &c.* Therefore the truth was fo tied to *Moſes* chaire , that he could not erre, though moſt falſly he layd blaſphemy to our Sauiours charge, when he fpake that truth, which beleeued might haue faued the Prieſts foule. No not though he procured the death of the Sonne of God , and perfecuted his Apoſtles with higheſt extent of malice, and liued and died in deteſtation and perfecution of the Chriſtian faith. So the Romaniſts, becauſe they can now and then, in a vaunt, drop vs down a learned Pope, or a learned Cardinal, or a learned Biſhop, they will make the world beleeue that all are ſuch. Or if they be not in their perſon, they are in their office. If not before they be entred, yet as foone as they be fet and warme in their Chaire. It is a greater worke of Gods omnipotencie to make a good man of an ill, then to make a man of the ſlime of the the earth. To make a Pope is in the hands of the Cardinals, that are the fole electors; & they may chuſe a *Iudas*, or *Balaams* Aſſe, as they haue done many; but ſuch is the omnipotencie of the Chaire , that it can make the Pope good and inerrant *ipſo facto*, or *ex opere operato*, at a tricke or in a trice. Which may be as true, as that all *Midas* touched was turned into gold: or more truly, that all who looked on the *Gorgons* head, were turned into ſtones. I fee not, but that as one noble *Zopyrus* was vnto *Darius inſtar mille*

mille Babyloniorum: One loyall subiect before a thousand
enemies. So one learned Diuine before a thousand such

Muri ciuit. sanct.fund.11. Popes, such Cardinals, such Bishops. Our Aduersarie giues
this rule out of *Augustine: Insinuat aprè Augustinus inter dissen-*
tientes in religione Doctores illos esse audiendos qui fama celebritate,
,, *& populorum frequentia antecellunt: Augustine* doth fitly insi-
,, nuate, amongst Doctors disagreeing in religion, they are to
,, be heard, that exceed others in fame, and frequencie of peo-
,, ple. So if my selfe were in other Articles a Papist, and were
in doubt and would resolue my conscience, by one of mine
owne partie: I would rather aske a *Bellarmine*, or a *Baronius*,
or such like learned man, that were famous for knowledge,
and of honest and conscionable conuersation (if they
were such,) then the Pope, though he sit neuer so fast
in his Chaire, if he be lesse learned. This is Saint *Augustines*
rule.

32 Where God purposeth the end, he disposeth the means.
Numb.22.28 One *Asse* spake miraculously, and neuer more. *Caiphas* spake
prophetically, and that but once. So such a Pope may hit vp-
pon a truth by miracle, or for once; he can neuer bolt it out
by industry and learning for euer, or often. *Vnum præesse Ec-*
Confess.Pe-trocou.c.27. *clesiæ toti, adeo necessarium est, vt absque hoc Ecclesia vna esse non*
,, *possit*, saith Cardinall *Hosius*, That one should haue the go-
,, uernment of the whole Church, it is so necessarie, that with-
,, out it the Church cannot be one. Which is very true if he
could vnderstand it of Christ, who is indeed the vniuersall
shepheard of his owne fold, the chiefe corner stone of his
owne Church, vpon whom the Apostles are equally layd;
the onely gracious head of his holy members : as Saint *Am-*
Ex Socolo.de vera & falsa Ecclesi.l.3.c.14 *brose* speaketh: *Librum signatum illum propheticum non seniores,*
non potestates, non Angeli, non Archangeli aperire ausi sunt; soli
Christo explanandi prærogatiua seruata est; The propheticall
,, booke that was sealed, neither the Elders, nor Potestates, nor
,, Angels, nor Archangels durst open; the prerogatiue of ex-
,, plaining it, is reserued only vnto Christ. This sheapheard we
will follow whither soeuer he goeth. This corner stone we
will rest vpon wheresoeuer it be laid. By this head we wil be
directed,

directed; and to his meaning we will offer all obsequiousnes and obedience,whatsoeuer he commandeth.But if he meane of his Popes,yea with al their assistants,you haue heard what they haue bin,and you may guesse what they may be,and accordingly how to trust them.One iaw of an asse in a *Sampsons* hand,would slay a thousand such Philistines : one roaring of that Lion , would not onely terrifie many such Asses , but might make all the beasts of the Romane field tremble.

33 All that hath bene said notwithstanding, let vs imagine and suppose that the Pope and all his attendants may be as learned for knowledge, as profound in vnderstanding as were needfull,yet may he not himselfe be surprised with hereticall opinions , and so defend that which he himselfe fauoureth?Or may he not be wilfull,and refuse good counsell? or wicked,in following his owne wil ? May he not be proud, and disdaine the simplicitie of the Gospell ? May he not be couetous,and make sale of the truth ? May he not be lecherous, and ouerruled by women, yea harlots ? May he not be cholericke, and ouerswayed with anger ? May he not be lazie,and debothed by sloth?May he not be malicious,and seek for reuenge ? May he not be ambitious,and hunt after vaineglorie ? Are not all these things incident to mans nature ? Or haue there not bene Popes,many not onely spotted,but poisoned with these,shall I say infirmities, or rather most grosse and damnable sinnes,and that in a high measure? Haue they not liued long,and at last died in them? and reputed damned by the best friends of the Romane synagogue?

34 Auant with those shifting distinctions,*Error in manners,not in faith: in person,but not in office: as a priuate man,not as a Pope: before he was chosen,but not in his seate : in matter of fact, but not of faith: alone by himselfe, but not in a Councell: in his chamber, but not in his Consistory: by way of conference , but not conclusion:in a priuate letter,but not in a decretall Epistle : in his pallace, but not in the pulpit;* and this last I hold truest, if it be true, *he neuer comes there,* as for the most part it is most true. Why waking,but not sleeping; standing,but not sitting; talking,but not walking; dead,but not liuing ? These may feele

to be good coine in the darke, but they are seene to be counterfeit when they are brought vnto light. They are dallian-
ces, to delude children in vnderstanding, no necessarie distinctions to further the truth. Vnto them which haue their spirituall eyes enlightened to discerne the shifts of craftie men,
that seeke nothing else but to cosen the world, they appeare
as they are, to be but the quintessences of wit, extracted
through a Chymical retort of selfeconceit, committed to the
commendation of Montebankes, to amaze simple people,
whom no man of wisedome or spiritual prouidence wil trust.
Of which and many other cases betweene our aduersaries
and vs, we may well say as Cardinall _Bellarmine_ saith well in
another case: _Qui defendunt imagines adorari latriâ:_ They that
” defend images to be adored with the honor which onely be-
” longeth to God, are driuen to vse most subtill distincti-
” ons, which they scarcely vnderstand themselues, much lesse
” the vnskilfull people. So is it with the defenders of the Popes
inerring spirit, they are driuen to vse most subtill distinctions,
which themselues vnderstand not, much lesse the deceiued
and traduced people. And therefore there is no reason to let
loose that hold of proofe we haue : whereby we can directly
conuince, that many of their Popes haue bene damnable heretickes against the faith, most wicked of life in all their
conuersation : and therefore vnfit to be Iudges sole or paramount in the Church of God. It were well for them if they
were honest members. Such as pretend they cannot erre as
Popes, but may as priuate men; and so defend their false harts
by fond distinctions, may well be serued as _Metrodorus,_ who
being asked his opinion in a matter of weight by _Tigranes,_
answered, _As an Embassadour I say thus, but as a Counseller o-
therwise;_ who iustly lost his head for his labour.

35 That _Marcellinus_ a Pope sacrificed vnto idols, no
man, I wot of, denieth. Not Cardinall _Bellarmine,_ who im-
proueth his wit to the highest extent, either in denying all
the faults of the Bishops of _Rome_ flatly, or excusing them miserably and shamefully, or extenuating them craftily. One
saith, that he did it publikly, whereby _sapientia nautarum Ecclesia,_

Bellar.de ima. l.2.c.22.

Plutarch.in Lucullo.

Pont.Damas. Concil.Sinues. Epist.Nicol.1. ad Micha. Bellar.de Ro. Pont.l.4.c.8. Iacob.de Va-lent.in Ps.106.

clesia, quasi deuorata est : The wisedome of the Churches mari- Concil.Sinues.
ners, was in a sort deuoured. But this is nothing in Cardinall Volaterā.Pla-
Bellarmines iudgement : *Nec docuit contra fidem, nec fuit hære-* tina.
ticus, vel infidelis, nisi actu externo, ob metum mortis : He neither ,,
taught against the faith, neither was an hereticke, or infidell, ,,
saue onely in the externall act, for feare of death. Who doth ,,
apostate, but for feare, or profit, or honour? What mattereth
it what induceth him thereunto? If he committed idolatrie
in fact, he *offended litle ones. He had better haue had a milstone* Math. 18.6.
hanged about his necke, and be cast into the bottome of the sea. By
his example he taught idolatrie. Christ our Sauiours *triplex*
pasce, was *triplex doce*, triple feeding was triple teaching,
with word, with hospitalitie, with example. *Quos illuminaue-* Chrysost.in
ritis per verbum quasi lux, condiatis per exemplum vt sale: Whom Math.5.
you brighten with the word like light, those keepe sweete ,,
by your example like salt. When this salt hath lost its sauour, ,,
shall it be questioned, whether it should be cast on the dunghill? *Marcellinus* committed idolatrie. It is a question whether he fell from his Papacie. If he did not, then a Pope was
an Idolater. If he did, the Church of *Rome* hopt headlesse till
he died, or resigned, I will not say his triple Crowne, such
were geason in those daies, but his woodden Chalice. I could
wish he had liued a golden Priest. May we beleeue *Lactantius,*
he did more then teach, he did confirme idolatrie, which is De vera sapi-
more then simply to teach it. *Debet perfectus Doctor docere præ-* ent.c.24.
cipiendo & confirmare faciendo: A perfect Doctor should teach
by precepts, confirme (his doctrine) by example. What this
Pope taught by his precepts, I know not, I am sure he confir- Soit biē faict,
med nothing but idolatry by his example. Yet this was one of si biē faict:
that ranke that ruled the Romane Church, and who must be Old Queene
heard when all the world must hold its peace. This is well, if *mother of*
it be well. I would not trust such a Pope with my conscience. France.
Athan.epist.
   36   *Liberius* a Pope also submitted himselfe to the *Arrian* ad sol vit. ag.
Emperours wil, subscribed to that heresie, set his hand against Hieron. in
Athanasius, communicated with *Valens* and *Vrsacius* : he chronico.&
wrote Epistles, whereby he discouered his false heart. Yet catal scrip.
for all this he was not truly an hereticke. *He was driuen to all* Liberij.
            Cc 2   *this*

Bellar.de Ro
Pont.l.4.c.9.
Verè.

this against his will, compelled to it by the force of torments: that it was not his opinion, which threatnings and terrors wrested from him, but rather that which he vttered when his affections were better composed. What strange and vaine excuses are these? A good Rhetorician might excuse Saint *Peters* deniall better, *Iudas* his treason as well.

37   The time hath bene when the sonnes of *Rome* were plainer men, and not foreseeing the consequents of these foule acts of their Popes,that would follow to the preiudice of that vsurping sea, set downe stories truly and plainly, without either such impudent deniall,or friuolous & shamelesse excuses. But since the Romanists haue bene hunted like foxes to their vtmost shifts, they bend their wits to nothing else but to cast clouds ouer the truth, and to intercept all authoritie that may conuince the errors or wickednesse of their ancestors.

38   Who euer denied the storie of Pope *Ioane*, till many yeares after *Luther?* It passed currant with all writers,vntil it was vrged against the presumed,vninterrupted succession of that sea of *Antichrist* ; wherein she sate by fact and faction, by nature and function, a very whore of *Babylon* indeed. Whereof there is a cloud of vndeniable witnesses, with circumstances most pregnant to proue it. So were the stories of *Marcellinus, Liberius,*those idolatrous and hereticall Popes, with many others,obserued by the friends of *Rome.* Yet now they are Sainted, *Saint Marcellinus,*and *Saint Liberius* , with *Bellarmine,* Saint Idolater and Saint Hereticke. Fit Saints indeed to fil vp the Romane Kalendar with red letters.Of their fall we are certaine, of their repentance vncertaine. While they were Popes,they did that we lay to their charge ; and that sufficiently euinceth our assertion,that Popes erred concerning faith. Like ill maisters of Saint *Peters* ship, the one made shipwracke,the other let in a leake , which brought it into equal danger and damage.A Bishop of theirs set downe the matter with the euent thereof, and perill wherein the Church stood thereby, plainly, without such mincing of it, as is now vsed. *Facies Ecclesiæ incœpit hæretica prauitate deturpari in tantum, quod Romæ Liberius, & Hierosolymis Cyrillus, &*
Alexan-

Iacob.Peres
de Valentia
in Psal.106.

Alexandriæ Georgius raptim & procaciter Ecclesias regebant om-
nes hæretica fictione, & in tantū persequuti sunt Catholicos, vt hæc
persequutio omnes præteritas Tyrannorum persequutiones supera-
re videretur : The face of the Church began to be tainted with
hereticall prauitie. In so much that at Rome *Liberius*, at Hierusalem *Cyrillus*, at Alexandria *George*, did filchingly and shame- „
fully gouerne all Churches with hereticall dissembling, and „
so vehemently persecuted the Catholickes, that this persecu- „
tion seemed to surtop all passed persecutions of former ty- „
rants. He is a plaine tale. *Liberius* was not onely an hereticke, „
but he gouerned his Church with hereticall dissimulation, „
he persecuted the Catholickes worse then former tyrants. „
And a Cardinall as plaine as that Bishop saith, that *Fœ-* ^{Io. de Turre-}
lix was sent into banishment, & loco eius Liberius factus hæreticus, crem.l.2. cap.
substitutus est : And in his place *Liberius* being made an heri- 103.
ticke, was substituted. So that it seemeth he was put in as an
hereticke, into a banished Catholickes roome ; that he perse-
uered an hereticke and persecuted the Church, which is the
highest degree of malicious apostasie. There were no Iesuits
in the world in those dayes, the secrets of the Romane Court
were not then fully discouered. She was in peace: as the Laodi-
ceans, *She said she was rich and wanted nothing*; but now we see Reuel.3 17.
she was *bare and naked, and her filthinesse is discouered.*

39   The like may be said of *Anastasius* the second; who Pontific.in
communicated with knowne heretickes the Nestorians : was striken eius vita.
by Gods hand with a sudden and fearefull death. He is registred
by *Gratian* in the *Decrees* to be no better then a *Reprobate.* Distinct. 19.c.
More may be said of *Honorius the first, a Monothelite* ỹ denied Anastasius.
two wils in our Sauiour Christ, and thereby destroyed his two
natures. He was discouered by his owne letters, conuinced
and condemned by a Councell, accursed aliue and dead. A Concil.6.
matter of so pregnant proofe in all histories and monuments
of *Antiquitie*, and chiefly in the sixt Councell, as that nothing
was said against it in aboue 600 yeares after. Yet now that
paire of Cardinals, *Bellarmine* and *Baronius*, will haue *Hono-*
rius his own Epistles produced against him either to be counterfeited or corrupted, the Councell falsified, not in one
place, but many : with such bald reasons and impertinent cir-

Cc 3   cumstances,

cumſtances, and miſerable euaſions, as if a theefe in hot pur-
ſuite ſhould ſo loſe himſelfe in a wood, that he pines himſelfe to death, to eſcape hanging. So the Cardinals rather
ſhame themſelues, then ſubmit their error to iuſt cenſure.

Gerſon.ſer.de
Paſch. 40   What ſhall we ſay of *Iohn* the xxij, that denied vnto
Saints departed, the viſion of God vntill the day of iudgment?
That this was his opinion, it is not denied; that he made it
known to others will be granted,& that he would haue publiſhed it,& decreed it too,is more then probable,&was hindered more by others oppoſitions then perſwaſions, by force
then his owne will. Yet he muſt needs be excuſed. He might

De Rô. Pont.
l.4.c.14. doubt of it, without hereſie thinkes *Bellarmine*, becauſe this
queſtion was not then determined by the Church. Is it not
manifeſt by the Scriptures? What need other determination?
Or he brings one *Villan*, that ſaith, he reuoked his error before his death. See,he hath but one witneſſe, and he a *Villan*,
perhaps in deed as in name. Suppoſe all this true ; yet he liued
in a groſſe error, he could not extricate himſelfe out of the error by any infuſion of *Peters* chaire, nor perſwaſion of all
Chriſtendome beſides.The excommunication of him by *Phi-*
lip the French King, his endeuour to impoſe ſubſcription
thereunto, by all that ſhould take degrees, the oppoſition of
the Vniuerſitie of Paris, the caſhiering of that error by ſound
of trumpet, I leaue to the authors that report it. It is ſufficient
to perſwade me neuer to truſt him with my ſoule while I liue,
that could reſolue no better what ſhould become of his owne
when he was dead.

    41   *Iohn* the xxiij, that denied the reſurrection of the
dead, as it is among his articles obiected vnto him in the
Councell of *Conſtance*,where he was worthily depoſed, for a
moſt wicked, notorious, ſcandalous, perfidious, ſymoniacall,
diſhoneſt man.Words can hardly expreſſe his villanies.*Bellar-*
mine cannot deny them. Onely he excepteth againſt that one
opinion of the reſurrection, which he ſaith was among the
articles not proued; perhaps the foole ſaid it but in his heart,
becauſe he did ſo expreſſe it in his life. But *Platina* ſaith, *Qua-*
„ *dam contra fidem iudicata ſunt*: Some are iudged to be againſt
                     the

the faith. Yet for feare of the worſt, left this alſo ſhould be „
better diſcouered, *Bellarmine* ſaith plainly: *That Iohn the xxiij* De Rō. Pont.
*was not at all a certaine and vndoubted Pope, and therefore need*ſ l.4.c.14.
*not to be defended. For at that time there were three, that would
be counted for Popes, Gregory the* 12, *Benedict the* 13, *and Iohn
the* 23, *and it was hard to iudge which was the right and lawfull
Pope, when euery one had moſt learned Patrons,* (he is a happie
man that is the Popes Patron.) Of all theſe Popes Patrons I
would aske, whether there were at that time three Popes, as
there were three factions in Rome betweene *Pompey, Cæſar,* Plutarch in
and *Craſſus,* or the ſeditious in Ieruſalem? or one Pope, or no Craſſo.
Pope?

42　If three, then the Romane Synagogue was a monſter
as *Geryon* that had three bodies for one head, when to one
bodie ſhe had three heads. Will they ſay thus? If there were
two, then the Church was an Idoll, like *Ianus* with two faces.
If there was but one Pope of the three, there was more proba- Concil.Baſil.
bility for *Iohn,* then either of the other. *Iohn* was elected in
Bononia, by all the Cardinals. He was an Italian, whence for
the moſt part, the more part of Cardinals are. He had done
good temporall ſeruice for the Church, in procuring peace,
recouering lands. The world obeyed his ſummons. He came
in perſon to the Councell of Conſtance, though he ran away
diſguiſed, ſome ſay in womens clothes, like a coward or a ſlut.
He was depoſed with moſt ſolemnity, the other but as ſchiſ-
matickes againſt the Pope. He onely of the three ſtandeth in
moſt Hiſtories and Catalogues of Popes. All which duly conſidered, he was certainly the very Pope, if there were any at
all. If he were the Pope, then he erred in doctrine and life, for
he was depoſed for both. And being depoſed by the Councel,
it doth ratifie the authoritie of a Councell aboue the Pope.
If there was none Pope of the three, then during all that
ſchiſme, there was no miniſteriall head of their Church at all,
and then their Church was dead, without ſenſe or motion; or Principium
like Sir *Iohn Mandeuils* monſters, that had eyes in their ſenſus & mo-
ſhoulders, for lacke of heads. And then finally, their ſucceſſion tus à cerebro.
was intercepted and quite broken, wherewith they ſeeme

　　　　　prin-

principally to outface the Gospell of Christ. *Petrus Crespetius,* to salue the Popes credit, in stead of a plaister, maketh a greater wound, and inclineth to this, that when there were three Popes, there was none: *In summa. Quando Concily Constantiensis Patres tres Papas deposuerunt, noueris tempore schismatis quando nescitur quis sit verus Papa, (dubius Papa habetur pro non Papa, &c.) When the Fathers in the Councell of Constance deposed three Popes, know that in the time of schisme, when it was vnknowne who was the true Pope, (a Pope in doubt is reputed for no Pope) then the Councell might, and ought to exercise their power against such. Yet shall it not therefore be aboue the Pope, because these be not indeed truly Popes, therefore there was no Pope during that schisme.*

43   Cardinall *Bellarmine* hath a Catalogue of forty Popes, as he pretendeth, against whom exception hath bene taken in this kind of error or heresie. Out of which I haue excerpted these few, enough to cloy a strong stomacke. Of the rest as some were good, whom we reuerence and honour, so others may be somewhat better. Yet certainly very many are worse then will be easily beleeued. Some are therefore such as we loue and commend; others we rather reiect their counterfeit writings, then except against their persons in life or doctrine. Some such as we can neither credit for doctrine, nor like for their conuersation. This is the summe of this passage; seeing diuers Popes haue bene such, and for ought we know are, or may be such, can any man of indifferent iudgement, and care of his owne soule, commend or commit it to such keepers?

Luk.16.10.11   44   Such keepers? *He that is not faithfull in a little, who will trust him in much? And he that cannot dispense earthly, who will trust him with heauenly treasure?* He that knowes not how to obey God, can neuer be a fit gouernor of men. He that is not good to himselfe, can be good to no body. Can *Catiline* perswade peace, that studied nothing but mutinies and insurrections? Can *Nero* preach pittie that exercised all crueltie on his nearest and dearest friends, his Tutor, his mother? Can *Heliogabalus* teach temperance and chastitie, whose life was a monopolie monopoly of all gluttonous & lafciuious villanie? Worfe the thefe haue fome Popes bene ; and I verily beleeue this affertion cannot be contradicted with ftorie , *That neuer any fucceffion of Emperors, Kings or Prie(ts, among Iewes, Heathens, Tartarians, Perfians, Turkes , much leffe Chriftians , can fhew fo many fo monftroufly wicked , as the Sea of Rome in their Popes:* coniurers , forcerers, murtherers, poyfoners, affaffins, blafphemers, idolaters, Atheifts, adulterers, inceftuous, trucebreakers, warriers, proud , cruell toward the liuing and the dead, intractable, incorrigible, reprobated, damnable. Almoft al thefe abhominable vices compact together in fome one of them, many of thefe villanies in moft of them, fome or one at the leaft in euery one of them, that haue liued thefe laft 800 yeares.   I will not ftretch my line farther, though all before were not Saints.

45   To begin with Pope *Ioane,* that was a whore indeed, and fate in Babylon , and fo may truly and *catexochen* be called the whore of Babylon. Whofe ftorie though it be by *A bene diui-* fome Romanifts impudently, againft all hiftories denied, yet *fis ad bene* aboue thirtie vnfufpected perfons , in moft florifhing times *coniuncta.* of the Romane tyranny, writing it, they come too late with their new deuifed fhifts , to blot her out of the catalogues of Popes. She was one. *Siluefter* the feconda notorious coniurer, came to the Popedome by the helpe of the diuell ; to whom he gaue his body and foule for reward, as infeoffing himfelf & his fucceffors in fee to hold of fatan, & to be vicars of hell for euer. A fucceffion of fixe or feuen Popes from *Formofus* downward : what digging vp of carkaffes, demolition of tombs, iudging dead bones, as if it had bene a liuing man? what cutting off of fingers? cafting into Tyber ? what curfing and excommunicating ? what cancelling and making voide of Patents, of ordinations, of admiffions, of confecra- *Ext. de Ma-* tions, of holy orders, among them? To whom the words in *ior. & obedi-* the Prophet *Ieremie,* may be better applied then *Innocent* the *ent. c. Solitæ.* third applies them for the Popes omnipotent power. They *Ierem. 1.* did nothing but *roote vp, plucke downe, and deftroy,* whatfoeuer each other faid, or did.

46 Thefe

46 These may be accompted for a mixt kind of Popes, who contradicted one another in that which was *error mani-festus contra fidem*, a manifest error against the faith, and also shewed themselues to be of most cruell and malicious na-tures,in exercising of all reproachful and inhumane villanies vpon those whom they affected not. Among others whom *Bellarmine* laboreth to excuse in that fearefull and infamous faction, are *Stephanus* and *Sergius*, against whom he layeth the obiection thus: *Stephanus & Sergius non solùm iudicarunt Formosum, non fuisse verum Pontificem,sed etiam ordines sacros, quos ille contulerat, non fuisse ratos,qui est error manifestus contra*
,, *fidem*: They did not only iudge *Formosus* to be no true Pope,
,, but also the holy orders which he had conferred, to be void;
,, which is a manifest error against faith. For although *Formo-*
,, *sus* had not bene Pope,& had remained deposed & degraded
,, still; yet becaue he was sometime a true Bishop, and was
,, stil, concerning the character and power of his order (which
,, can by no meanes be taken away) it was an error in faith to
,, say, that holy orders collated by him, were no true holy or-
,, ders. Heare the Cardinals answer, & iudge whether he were
    awake, or asleepe, or opprested with the spirit of giddinesse
,, when he made it.*Respondeo*: I answer,saith he,That *Stephanus*
,, and *Sergius* made no Decree,by which they determined,that
,, those who were ordered by a degraded Bishop, and namely
,, by *Formosus* being degraded, should be ordered againe. But
,, *de facto*,indeed, or in fact, they did command them to be a-
,, gaine ordered.Which commandement proceeded not out
,, of ignorance or heresie , but from malice against *Formosus*.
,, For *Sigebert* in his Chronicle of the yeare 903, noteth,that
,, *Stephanus* the sixt did by force ordaine againe those, who by
,, *Formosus* had bene ordained, almost all crying out against it.
The obiection is for matter of faith , this is not denied, but excufed. It was not decreed: but it was acted; which is more then a Decree. For a Decree may come forth, and ne-uer be executed,as a man may receiue his sentence , and yet not be hanged. But if he be hanged without a Decree,there is iniustice in the doer, meere wrong to the sufferer. They
did

De Rom.
Pont.l.4.c.12.

did it not of ignorance or hereſie: as much to ſay, they did it wilfully, and againſt their conſcience. Ignorance might in ſome ſort craue pardon, and hereſie may be pitied, if it proceed from a miſinformed conſcience, which would reforme vpon better information. They did it vpon malice to the partie deceaſſed, not for loue of truth, or for iuſtice of the cauſe. But *ex odio*, out of hatred. This aggrauates their wickedneſſe; it neither leſſeneth their error, nor diminiſheth their ſinne. They erred ſhamefully, and ſinned damnably. Let any man iudge that hath but braine, whether they ſtand not exceedingly wel cleared and acquitted by the Cardinall? as white as an Ethiopian waſht in ſope.

47 *Gregorie* the ſeuenth, as *Benno* a Cardinall of his own time deſcribeth him, is rather a monſter then a man. Such poiſonings, coniurations, excommunications, iars in Rome, warres abroad, contentions with his owne Cardinals, outrages againſt the Emperors and ciuill ſtate, are ſtrange to heare. *Bellarmine* gainſayeth this ſtorie, and *Benno* his authoritie, without reaſon, by two conieſtures. The one forſooth, *It is ſo full of impudent lies, that ſome Lutheran was the author of the booke, and ſet it forth in Benno his name.* The other, *that if Benno wrote it, he ſet it forth but as an Idea or deſcription of an ill Pope vnder the name of Gregorie the ſeuenth, as Xenophon deſcribed a good Prince vnder the name of Cyrus.* This *Benno* was an archpresbyter of the Romane Church, and a Cardinal of the ſame. He liued in the ſame time of *Gregorie* the ſeuenth. When the authoritie cannot be caſt off with any probabilitie, then they conceipt it to be counterfeited by a *Lutheran*. The goodman had neuer ſought his wife in the ouen, if he had not bene there himſelfe. None ſo iealous ouer a chaſte wife, as an old adulterer. *Bellarmine* knowes that many writings haue bene obtruded vpon the Chriſtian world by the Romane faction, vnder the name of Fathers, that were neuer the workes of any learned or religious man. That they do themſelues they impute to others. It was not *Bennos* in the Cardinals iudgement: yet a very few lines before, he ſaith, that *Benno* was *iuratus hoſtis Gregorij ſeptimi, qui illo tempore ſcripſit, & vitam*
Gre-

De Rom. Pont. l.4.c.13.

Cacotopia. Eutopia.

Gregorij septimi scriptam reliquit: A sworne enemie of *Gregorie* the seuenth, liued in his time, and left his life written. How then did a *Lutheran* write it? or if himselfe did, then *Benno* was a *Lutheran*, and so *Lutherans* were older then *Martin Luthers* dayes.

48 For his conceit of an *Idea*, it is a meere *Idea* of his own braine. If *Benno* had intended any matter of fiction, & not of truth, he wold haue taken an indefinite *Gregory*, & not giuen him his number, liuing in his time. But as *Xenophon* described the office of a good King vnder the name of *Cyrus*, whose gouernment drew very neare vnto his description; so it is not like that *Benno* would haue taken such a name, of so good a Pope, as is pretended, & that vnder his nose, in his own daies, to make him the patterne of an il Pope. That many historians commend this Pope, it is no maruell. For he was a most violent defender of the priuiledges and honour of that Sea, which was counted the onely grace & glorie of Bishops in those times, and since: as if all had bene done for the good of the Church, which indeed was for to execute their malice, or enlarge their dominions, or to courbe Kings, or to protect wicked Priests, or to dispose of all Church liuings, or the like profitable or pleasurable considerations. And this got *Thomas* of Canterbury a place in the Calendar, and of a Traytor to be made a Martyr, and a shrined Saint.

49 I am weary with wading in this dead sea of desperate and damned Popes. I will onely name a few more, and conclude this Chapter. For to prosecute all would aske *Hercules* labour at *Augeus* stable. Take *Iohn* the xij or xiij. Liued there euer such a wicked villaine vpon the face of Gods earth? I will not speake of Christians, but of Infidels, and of them the worst, the very Cannibals? A dicer, a drunkard, a rioter, a blasphemer, an adulterer, a murtherer, what shall I say? a monster, a diuell incarnate. Yet *Bellarmine* for reuerence to his Holinesse, toucheth him but gently, and saith onely, that he was *Paparum omnium ferè teterrimus*: Almost the wickedest of all Popes. Verily, I thought him euer till now, the very worst. But I perceiue the Cardinall better
acquain-

acquainted with the Popes secrets, then I, either knew or
had read of worse then he. Which certainly could neuer be
any but *Beelzebub* himselfe. *Benedict* the ninth almost as bad
as he. *Innocent* the eight, aboue measure leud in all damnable Papir.Masson
adulteries, though not vncommended in his funeral Oration,
where he is much extolled for humanitie, courtesie, and holinesse of life. Which argued a flattering Preacher, but neuer
the honester Pope. For he had *nothos ex scelesto concubitu satos,*
bastards borne of most wicked copulation, whom he preferred with great wealth.

50 *Boniface* the eight, *Entred like a foxe, reigned like a*
Lion, died like a dog. Alexander the sixt, the shame of mankind,
in all poisonings, adulteries, incests, and such like papall ver- Papir.Masson
tues. *Paulus* the second, ignorant for learning, and wicked
for life. *Leo* the tenth, a hunter and a hawker. *Clement* the sixt,
an indifferent Pope in comparison of many, yet *à fœminei se-* Ibid.
xus delicijs ne Pontifex quidem abstinuit quem decumbentem in le-
cto, & morbo quo esse desijt, laborantem, solæ fœminæ consanguineo-
rum, vel affinium vxores earumq́, pedisequæ rexerunt : He abstai- „
ned not from the pleasures of women kind, no not when he „
was Pope: but as he lay in his bed, sicke of the disease where- „
of he died, onely women, the wiues of his kin by bloud or „
affinitie, and their waiting women, ruled the rost. He guided „
the Church, as *Themistocles* ruled *Athens,* by his wife and his Plutarc.The-
sonne: so he by his kinswomen and their maids: Or as *Cethe-* mist.
gus ruled *Rome,* and was ruled himselfe by *Præcia* his queane. Idem in Lu-
So did *Hildebrand* by *Matilda.* Some naught, some worse, cullo.
few good, or so much as tollerable in these times . As *Iulius*
the second and the third, in whose life one saith:

51 *Hæc narramus quia gesta sunt. Quod si Pontifices nolunt* Papir.Masson,
turpia & nefaria de se narrari, nihil huiusmodi faciant; at t cum fe-
cerint, non putent, ea ipsa ita latere, vt & sciri & posteris narrari
nequeant. Quanquan in Pontificibus nemo hodie sanctitatem requi-
rit, optimi putantur, si vel leuitèr boni sunt, vel minùs mali, quàm
cæteri mortales esse soleant. We report these things because „
they were done. But if the Popes will not haue their filthi- „
nesse and wickednes discouered, let them do no such things; „

or

,, or if they do, then let them not thinke that they can be kept
,, so secret, that they cannot be knowne and reported to poste-
,, ritie. Although no man at this day doth require holinsse in
,, Popes; they are thought excellent, when they are but scarce
,, good, or at least not so starke naught as other men vse to be.
This is written neither by a *Lutheran* nor *Caluinist*, as the
Romanists vse to call vs, but by a bird of their owne nest, a
child of their owne mother, a brat of their owne begetting.
Such is the force of truth, that it often breaketh forth from
the children of error, though thereby they shame themselues.

Habeat dum
Roma pudo-
rem. Iuuen.

Rome in heathenesse would blush at these shamefull enormities. Which if it be true, then what is become of the Popes
holinesse? that hath it not onely attributed vnto him in the
concrete, but in the abstract, as if he were holinesse it selfe;
aboue all the Saints in heauen, who are but *Sancti* · perhaps
God himselfe, to whom is sung, *Sanctus, sanctus, sanctus, Ho-*
ly, holy, holy; but the Pope, if you will, in all the degrees of
comparison, *Sanctus, sanctior, sanctissimus, Holy, more holy, and*
holiest of all. But no maruell, for what the Pope hath not by his
own merit, that he hath by the priuiledge of his predecessors.
Beleeue this that list, I shall neuer be perswaded, th t such
vnholy, godlesse, gracelesse, and deboshed villaines, can e-
uer be counted Christs Vicars, or Saint *Peters* successors : or
should euer be beleeued in matters of faith, or so much as

Psal.50,17.

take Gods word into their mouth, seeing they hate to be reformed.

    52   To conclude, if I, or any of our Church should write

Sueton.c.34.

of the Popes, *Eadem libertate, qua ipsi vixerunt,* as licenciously
as they haue liued , our very bookes would blush in the relation, and the readers would detest the obscenitie and bru-
tish beastlinesse of the very leaues, lines and letters, wherein
their wickednesse should be written and reuealed . If they
could repent, we would rather burie such works of darknesse
in the deepest dungeon of obliuion, then to dash their dung
in their owne faces, not onely to their euerlasting shame, but
also the nuisance and vexation of others, whose haires would
stand on end, and eares tingle, and hearts bleed, to see, heare,

and

and confider the more then monftrous fchifmes, herefies, i-
dolatries,adulteries,incefts, murthers,and otherinfinite mif-
chiefes and villanies of the Bifhops of *Rome*. But their owne
writers, beft acquainted with them, haue difcouered thefe
things vnto very loathing, to whom I leaue them.

CHAP. XVI.

If the ftate of the Romane Church were fuch as is faid in the head,
it was as ill at the leaft in the members , which caufed and increafed
ignorance and fuperftition: thefe gaue way to herefie indoctrine
and diffoluteneffe of life; and thence to that apoftafie from
faith, and ataxie in manners , which hath long
continued , and yet remaineth in that
Church to this day.

Lato was wont to fay, that, fuch as Princes
were in their Common weales, fuch were
their Citizens; which *Cicero* confeffeth to
be diuinely written. And the Wife man faith
in the Prouerbes, that, the wickeds reigne
is the peoples ruine. And as in naturall bo-
dies, fo in kingdomes, that difeafe is moft dangerous which
proceedeth from the head; as when *Herod* was troubled, all
Ierufalem was troubled with him : and for the moft part, the
whole world is compofed to the Kings example. Neither
do the examples of Gouernours only moue their inferiours,
but after a fort conftraine them; whence *Paul* to *Peter* the
chiefe of the Apoftles, moft wifely faid , *Cogis Gentes Iuda-*
zare,Thou compelleft the Gentiles to do like the Iewes. So
highly did he aggrauate his example, becaufe he was the
chiefe Paftor of the Church , that he feemed not onely to
perfwade, but to compell; but he forced not by the power
of doctrine, but by his example and conuerfation : as Saint
Hierome wrote in a certaine Epiftle to *Auftin* . As therefore
thofe which rule well are worthy of double honour; fo thofe
which rule ill, do incurre and deferue hardeft iudgement.
Thus

Simanca de
Dominijs té-
poralib.tit.23.
S.13.
Lib.1.Epiftol.
famil.
Prou.28.16.

Math.2.3.

Gal.2.14.

1.Tim.5,17.

Thus farre *Simanca* a Romane writer.

Cicero de Le-
gibus, lib.3. 2   Naturall men haue in effect said as much, to shame Christian Princes in Common wealth or Church, who de-stroy more by their ill example, then they benefit by their bountie. For, as by the vices of Nobles a whole citie is infe-cted; so by their continencie it is amended and corrected. For it is not so great an euill, that Princes sinne, (though it be a very great euill in it selfe) as it is for that there be many followers of Princes fashions: and therefore I am perswaded, that the change of Noblemens liues and diet, changeth also the manners of Citizens; by how much the more pernicious Princes do euil deserue of the States, for that they not onely bring forth sins themselues, but also disperse them into the whole Common wealth: neither onely are they vnprofita-ble, because themselues are corrupted, but also for that they infect others; and finally hurt more by their example then by their sin. Thus farre *Cicero*: and that not without as good reason as experience.

3   For if the sap be naught in the roote, the fruit will ne-uer be good in the branches. If the head be light, the feete will reele. If the braine be tainted, the nerues, tendons, and the whole strength of the body will be easily dissolued, and faile in all faculties of sense and motion. *Diruto fundamento, corruit ædificium*: Dig vp the foundation, downe fals the buil-ding.

4   The Pope is the roote of the Romane tree, that hath spread her branches broader then the Okes of *Basan*, or the Cedars of *Lebanon*; and ouerspread the earth, as the tree in *Nebuchadnezzars* dreame. How poisonous humours may this roote send into such dispersed boughes, enough to infect all the fruits thereof? The Pope is the giddie head of the Ro-mane body; if it be vnconstant, where shall the legs stand? The Pope is the very braine of the Romane state; if he be so deadly infatuated, how shall the ioynts and sinewes of that Church hang together? He is the foundation of *Maozims* temple; if he was so demolished, how should the walls, the battlements, the roofe be shaken? This was the very case

of

of that daughter of *Babylon wafted with miferie. Who* retained Pfal.137.8.
long *a name that fhe liued, and yet was dead,* yea *twice dead, and fit* Reuel.1.3.
to be pluckt vp by the rootes. Iude v. 12.

5   Her Popes were either impotent children, or impudent
men, ignorant, negligent, careleffe, prophane, fchifmatickes,
heretickes, proud, ambitious, violent, lecherous, fimoniacall,
couetous, cruell and murtherous, fuperftitious, idolatrous, and
more then all this, as before hath bene faid and proued. Her Supra cap.15.
Cardinals and Bifhops, whelps of the fame haire, as bad or
worfe, which is hard to fay. Then what were the inferior
Priefts and the rif-raffe of their Clergie? what were the miferable, wretched and forlorne people, committed vnto their
charge?

6   *If feauenty men of the Ancients of the houfe of Ifrael, and* Ezech.8.11.
Iaazaniah the fonne of Shaphan ftanding in the middeft of them,
with euery man his cenfer in his hand, and the vapour of their in-
cenfe afcending like a cloud: as if they would darken the light
of heauen: and if the Prophets of God *haue feene what thefe*
Ancients of Ifrael haue done in the darke, euery man in the houfe
of his Imagery: is it maruell though their women *commit grea-*
ter abhominations, and mourne (yearely) for *Tammuz* their Prophet, the Prophet of their Idols, or that the people fhould
commit yet greater *abhominations and worfhip the Sunne?* If all
they which fhould haue kept others in the feare and true feruice of God, were the ringleaders to all abhominations, and
examples of error and impietie, was it maruell that the women and people did degenerate? If the *Ancients of Rome,* their
Cardinals and Bifhops, and *Iaazaniah* their Pope in the middeft of them commit fuch fearefull and damnable both idolatrie and wickedneffe, out of their ignorance & vnexpertneffe
in the word of truth, may we wonder that either the inferior
Clergie, or the common people fhould vnderftand any thing,
but euen be led, as the 200 men that went out of *Ierufalem,*
belike neither knowing whither, nor what to do, *but went in* 2.Sam.15.11.
their fimplicitie knowing nothing, to become as they were, and
to do as they did, hauing neither better teaching, nor better
example?

Hieron. lib.3.
in cap.8.
Seniores.
Presbyteros.

7   For as Saint *Hierome* on this place: *When he saith there were 70 men, Elders of the house of Israel, who held their censers in their hands, he shewes there were many other Elders which did not this, yet were guiltie of other faults; and that one, by name Iaazanias, stood in the middest of them, was the Prince of their wickednesse and sacriledge, who omitting the religion of God, worshipped Idols. And in the Temple they worshipped not God, whose Temple it was, but the pictures on the walles. And it is well said, that Iaazanias the sonne of Shaphan, that is, of iudgement and condemnation, stood in the middest of the Elders: because both the chiefe, and they whose chieftaine he was, stood with a firme foote, neither did they wauer in euill, but most stoutly persisted therein, and the vapour of their cloud, and confusion, and tempest which rose out of the incense, did demonstrate the sacriledges of the Idolaters.* —— And after by application: *Quando videmus plebem pessimam congregatam, When we shall see a wretched people gathered together, of which it is written, I haue hated the congregation of the wicked, and their chieftaines, and their Prince, which is set ouer both people and Priest, we may say, that Iezonias standeth before his pictures, and euery one his censer in his hands, not worshipping the Maiestie of God, but their owne opinions, and that there ascendeth no sauour of sweet smell vnto God, but a stench vnto the Idols.* Nothing can be more significantly, either figured by the Iewes, or premonished by Saint *Ierome*, whereby the superstition and idolatry of the Bishop of Rome, his Clergie and people, may be set before the eyes of the deceiued world.

8   This is a righteous iudgement of God vpon the carelesse sonnes of men, which the Prophets foretold should be, and we and our fathers haue seene it come to passe: *Like people, like Priest.* In the purer times of the Church, the Pastors were diligent and painefull, but the people refused discipline, and fell into corruption of manners, and despised their guides, and said *desperatly;* (as the people in the Prophet *Ieremie*) *Surely we will walke after our owne imaginations, and do euery man after the stubburnnesse of his owne heart.* Then it pleased God to send them *Idol shepheards, blind guides, dumb dogs,* that fed themselues, and neglected their flocks. And this brought these

Esay 24. 2.
Hos. 4. 9.

Iere.18.12.

thofe miferable dayes, wherein the *people were deftroyed for* Hof.4.6.7.
*lacke of knowledge, and the Priefts that did refufe knowledge were
refufed of God, and becaufe they forfooke knowledge, God forfooke
their children, and as they increafed fo they finned,* and therefore
God would *turne their glory to their fhame.* This alfo is a perfect
patterne or modell of the eftate of the Romane Synagogue,
which long walked in darkneffe and in the fhadow of death,
and fell into manifold and moft manifeft errors in doctrine,
& vnholineffe of life, to the difhonor of God, & fcandalizing
of the name of Chrift among the children of vnbeleefe; So
that the very Turks and infidels may rife vp in iudgement a-
gainft thefe wicked and ignorant generations.

9 *Liuie* complaineth of the iniurie of times that had im- T. Liui, hifto-
plicated fo many errors, that the truth could hardly be found riæ ab vrbe
out, and aboue all he faith, that *Vrbs quingentis annis fcripto-* condita,l.1.
*ribus caruit: for fiue hundred yeares the Citie wanted writers:
which could celebrate the actions of thofe times and commit them
to memory.* The fame complaint may iuftly be made, and by
fome of our aduerfaries is confeffed to be true, that in the
nine hundredth yeare, and fome hundreds after, there was fuch
ignorance in the Church, fuch penurie of writers, as that their
Catholickes for thofe centuries, are cleane almoft emptie, efpecially for Diuines. The moft were Chroniclers and Hifto-
rians. *Saculo nonagefimo nullum fuit indoctius & infelicius, There* Bellar. de R 6.
was no age more vnlearned or vnhappie then the ninth, faid *Bellar-* Pont.l.4.c 12.
mine: and *Baronius* groanes vnder the fame yoke, and cals that
age, *for the afperitie, fterility of good, for the deformitie of euils a-
bounding, and penurie of writers, plumbeam & ferream*, as if it
were made of lead and iron. After fome few fhewed themfelues: and taking the times as they found them, being for
the moft part Monks or Friars, fome lamented the backfli-
ding of the Church; fome defended all that lay before them.
Thofe that found faults, were fuppreffed for heretickes. Thofe
which foothed and defended the Romane Sea, with all her
appurtenances, were either aduanced in earth to be Cardinals,
or fome great men, or after life canonized for Saints in Romes
Purgatory, or Paradife.

10 Then

1.Tim.6.20.

10 Then came in the throng of the Schoolemen, who mingling Diuinitie with Philofophie, and pretending *fcience falfly fo called*, brought in of themfelues, or obtruded what they found in the corrupted ftate of the Church, when Antichrift had full poffeffion, and peaceable fruition of all in his owne hands. Thefe as they were few in number, fo was their learning intricate and hard to be vnderftood, and paffed rather in their Schooles then in their pulpits; when the poore Priefts, yea and rich Bifhops too, by your leaue, were contented with their Maffe books, portuifes, and offices, and enquired no further. He was learned that vnderftood their *Manipulus Curatorum*, or their Legend, or Feftiuall, or could preach out of their *Sermones difcipuli*, or was able to reade his Seruice with true accents, or congruous Latine; which neither they that read it, nor the people that heard it, for the moft part, did vnderftand.

11 So that learning was vtterly decayed in the Clergie that liued not in the fchooles. And the what knowledge in the people, who vnderftood not fo much as their ten Commandements, their Beleefe, or the Lords prayer, in their owne tongue? In fo much, that to haue thefe, or the Epiftles and Gofpels, or any prayers in the vulgar tongue, was holden the new religion, and herefie. This being the ftate of thofe times when all the world was thus hoodwinkt & blind, what errors, what herefies, what finne, what wickedneffe, might not be impofed vpon, and practifed by fuch ignorant fots?

12 To proue this ignorance in Priefts or in people, or that groffe wickedneffe which was practifed in thofe darke and fuperftitious ages, by particulars, would perhaps moue *Heraclitus* to more teares then ordinarie in pitying the Romane captiues miferable bind madneffe, or *Democritus* to more profufe laughter, in deriding their groffe ignorance and ridiculous behauiour. I am fure writers of all forts in their times, fome lamented, as the grauer and beft hearted Diuines: fome merily, but verily taxed their impudent and licencious liues, as the beft witted Poets and Orators.

Petrarch.
Mantuan.
Mirandula.
Chaucer.

13 For

13 For the Cleargies ignorance, I will not fend my reader to _Henrie Stephens_ his Preparatiue to the Apology of _Herodotus_: nor to any of ours that write of that argument, or fo much as girded at them by the way, in any of their workes; nor for the wickednefse of thofe times to the complaints of any that may feeme partiall, or the accufations of any that may be thought malicious, nor to bruited tales of either, whereof the world is full; which are fitter for a fire in a winter euening, then for a difcourfe intended either for the conuerfion, or fatisfaction of Chriftian foules. For fuch, as they are infinite for number, fo are they almoft incredible for report, yet fitter for a booke of merry tales, then to take roome among more ferious matters. The neceffary confequence from the greater, much more greateft, to the leffe, or leaft, from head to foot, from firft to laft, is fufficient to euince all that may be faid in this paffage. If it were fo in the greene tree, what in the drie? If fuch were Popes, Cardinals and Bifhops, what were Parfons, Vicars, and Curates? And then what were the blind, wretched and mif-led people, who were not onely precifely kept from all light of truth, but alfo perfwaded, that _Ignorance was the mother of deuotion?_ The Canon law it felfe, with all Cafuifts and Queftionifts, doth not onely infinuate, but manifeftly demonftrate the groffe and palpable ignorance of Priefts, by their queftions, prouifions, preuentions of fuch abfurdities as would follow their difpenfations, executions, and adminiftrations of the word and Sacraments.

14 Heare a learned man, worfhipfull for his calling, and very much commended & refpected in his time, for his learning, _Iohn Gerfon_ Chancellor of Paris. _Quem è facerdotum numero mihi dabis non ignarū legis Chrifti?_ Whom canft thou giue me of the number of the Priefts, not ignorant of the Law of Chrift? And heare a Pope or a Cardinall: _Pudeat Italiæ facerdotes &c._ Let the Italian Priefts be afhamed, whom it is manifeft not once to haue read the new law; amongft the _Thabo-rites_, fcarce fhall you find a woman which is ignorant to anfwer concerning the new or the old Teftament. And heare

Io. Gerfon Tom. 1. ferm. coram Alexand. PP. in die Afcenfionis.

Æneas Sylui-us de dictis & factis Alphon. Regis. l. 1. c. 17.

a Preacher too, but of your owne, and famous in his time.

Nicol. Cle-
mangis de
corrupt. Ec-
clef. ftat fol. 5. *Non à ftudys, & fchola, fed ab aratro, &c.* They fwarmed from each part, not from their ftudies, or fchoole, but from the plough and feruile artes to the gouernment of parifhes, & other benefices, who vnderftood little more of Latine then of

Idem. Ibid.
fol. 13. the Arabicke tongue. And yet againe. *De literis verò & doctrina quid loqui attinet? &c.* But concerning letters and learning, what may be fpoken? when almoft all the Presbyters are without any vnderftanding, either of the things or vowels; we fee them fcarce able to reade diftinctly and fyllabically. Thefe ignorant Priefts were the moft defperate defenders of the Romane errors, they promoted, fummoned, accufed, witneffed, exclaimed againft euery one y angred them, & broght them to the fagot. Like mercenary fouldiers, who are ignorant of the caufe of war, whether it be iuft or vniuft, & therefore haue no pricke nor ftay of confcience, but for the moft wages they fight beft; and the more ignorant, the more confident, and defperate.

15 Adde vnto all thefe, that when the Antichriftian Rabbins had perfwaded the abfolute neceffitie of Baptifme, to their pettie Priefts, they were faine to make prouifion they Manip. cura-
torum cap. 2. did it not in *rofe water, nor in vrine, nor in the broth of flefh, if it be long boyled; nor for feare of the* Childs damnation, fhould in the perill of death, throw an Infant into a well, when they had nothing to draw water, rather then its foule fhould perifh; or whether, or how, a Child might be Chriftened in the mothers belly. This we may fuppofe proceeded out of practife. For as *good lawes proceed from euill manners,* fo thefe queftions were begotten by the Priefts abfurd actions. Againe, if a forry Prieft erred in a fyllable or letter, in the beginning of a word, it hindered the forme of Baptifme. But if in the latter end, it was good enough affe a Prieft and De confecrat.
dift. 4. c. Regulerunt. yet a M-affe Prieft baptized a Child, *in nomine Patria & filia, & fpirita fancta,* which in Latine hath no fence at all, neither can it be Englifhed, it is fo beyond all meafure abfurd, except a man fhould fay, *In the name of the Mother, the daughter, and the Neece* : there is nothing that founds *Father, Sonne and holy*

holy Ghost. Yet the Pope iudged this to be the true forme of Baptisme. If in setting downe the Popes names we should take their three or fower and twentie *Iohns*, and write for euery one *Ioanna* for *Ioannes*, our aduersaries would thinke we mockt their great Maister, & sought to slander all the Popes of that name, falsly, as we do taxe one in a matter of truth. This doubtlesse would anger them; that, certainly could not but offend God.

16 Thus did they patter their prayers, speaking gibbrish or Pedlers French rather then Latine, or any other common language: With what feeling? With what zeale? With what deuotion? could the Priests performe their diuine offices? or the people heare them? I am loth to blot my paper Mat.14.21. with many particulars. One when the the Gospels beganne to be published in English, read how Christ our Sauiour fed with fiue loaues and two fishes, 5000 men, besides women & little children, the people that had neuer heard it before, blest themselues and gaue signes of admiration, with crossing their foreheads. The Priest, fearing that the people thought this a great lye, to giue satisfaction, for feare of the world: he told them, it was not so great a matter as they made of it, for in those dayes when that was done, *Loaues were then as big as ouens were now*: were not this people well assoyled of so deepe a doubt? Another durst not so much as reade 5000, but read 500, and being asked why, answered, these be enough, no body will beleeue there were so many.

17 Another Priest in the first yeare of Queene *Elizabeth* that had turned to the safer side, when a child was brought to the font, and named *Ester*, askt whether it were a lad or a lasse: so skilfull was he in the storie of the Bible. *Stella* a Spanish Romanist, writeth of his owne knowledge, of a Preacher that would proue that *Maria* the blessed Virgines name, was foretold, many ages before in the holy Scriptures, when God called *the gathering of the water Maria*, which sig- Stella de mo-nifieth the Sea, and not *Marie*; and that the gathering of do conciona-waters, was the gathering of vertues. As if a man should take di, pag. 15. a *horse to ride on, for a hoarse in the throate*, or Gill a wench, for

a Gill of wine;nay,to a fcholler it is much worfe then this,for not onely the fence, but the very accent diftinguifheth them. And this was a man of great note and had many followers, as mine author reporteth. This were a fine argument, why the blefled Virgine fhould be called *Stella maris.Father Par-fous, who is Iohn Keltridge now.* Is not this worfe indeed, then you imagine in him? The fame author tels of more like thefe; fo do others, and thofe Romanifts too : by which they might learne, if they had grace, in what cafe the poore people were,that were kept in fuch a dungeon of darkeneffe

Math.15.14.   fo many hundred yeares: *The blind leading the blind, and both falling into the ditch.* Worfe then the Scribes and Pharifes,

Luk.11.52.   for they *kept the key of knowledge, and would neither enter them-felues, nor fuffer other that would.* For keeping prefuppofeth hauing; but thofe had no key of knowledge, and therefore *for lacke they perifhed* themfelues, and mifguided others , and yet could not be perfwaded they were blind.

Seneca ad Lu-cil.epift.51.   18 Such may be compared to *Harpafte, Seneca his wiues blind-foole, the burthen of his houfe,* as thofe Priefts were of the Church; who when fhe was ftarke blind,would not beleeue it, but thought the houfe darke wherein fhe was. *Incredibi-lem tibi narro rem, fed veram, nefcit fe effe coecam:* He accoun-ted it an incredible report,yet was it true, that fhe knew not

Barrhad.par.2 comment.in concord.E-uang. c.12.   fhe was blind. There were & are many Priefts like this foole, they are blind, and yet as the Scribes and Pharifes, they fay that they fee ; but who doubts of their blindneffe , though they thinke themfelues to haue *Linceus* eyes ? When God would chaftife his people, & plague them indeed, he threat-

Amos 8.11.   neth them with a *famine,not of bread, but of hearing the word of God.* If euer this plague lighted vpon any Church, it lighted

Math.5.13.14   vpon the Romane Church,whofe falt had loft its fauour, and whofe light was become darkneffe, euen the palpable dark-nes of Egypt. They were all very *Dolopians,* an idle people

Plutarch. in Cimon.   that liued without labor,by robbing of men,and murthering of foules.

19 To fpeake of the manners of both Priefts and people, would aske rather a volume then a Chapter. It is painfull to
fearch

fearch deepe wounds, loathfome to ranfacke filthy vlcers, and to rake vp the dead carkaffes, or bones, or afhes of their and our anceftors. Let that be the diftained honour of Popery, and thofe cruell Lions,and wolues, and Tygers, who were neuer fatiate with the bloud of Saints, nor could fuffer their bodies to be buried,or lye in their graues.Their Mona-fteries,their Cloifters, their Cels, their Nunneries, their Pil-grimages,their very Hermitages haue cried for the vēgeance of God vpon them in this land,for their vnnaturall and mon-ftrous lufts, befides adulteries, incefts, robbings, murthers, euen finnes againft nature; and it is executed, as our eyes haue feene. It remaineth for other nations that are defiled and corrupted with the fame finnes, that they be fubieƈt to the fame torments. For they haue long groaned vnder the fame burthen,are fubieƈt to the fame fins,and therefore may iuftly expeƈt the fame iudgements.

Formofus. Wicliff. Bucer. P.Fagius.

20 Take the teftimony of *Ferus*,a Frier, in thefe laft times of greateft oppofition, when men, if euer,fhould looke to themfelues, if it were but for fhame and feare to be feene and obferued of their aduerfaries. *Quis porrò etiam non videt infatiabilem auaritiam Ecclefiafticorum, Sacerdotum, Monacho-rum,& Epifcoporum,&c.* Furthermore, who alfo feeth not ,, the infatiable couetoufneffe of Ecclefiafticks,Priefts,Monks, ,, and Bifhops? I vnderftand thofe which feeke Ecclefiafticall ,, offices,and draw them vnto them,and yet for no other caufe ,, then for their temporall profit and gaine : or verily thofe ,, that conuert the things whereof they are but ftewards and ,, feruants, not vnto the honour of God, not to the faluation ,, of foules, neither vnto the vtilitie and benefit of the holy ,, Church, but onely to their owne profit. Yea they fell what ,, they fhould freely beftow,they feeke their owne out of that ,, which is none of theirs.Alfo in fpiritual and heauenly things, ,, they hunt for nothing but temporalities.We inuent not thefe ,, things,but we find them written, not in ours,but their owne friends bookes.

Ferus Domi-nica 11.poft Trinit.fer.5.

21 Of former ages let Saint *Bernard*, Saint *Huldericke* Bifhop of *Augufta*,let the Romane Chronicles of thofe times

in

in their feuerall places, let *Clemangis*, *Menot*,*Barelete*,and o-
ther Preachers of thofe times; let *Mantuan*,*Petrarch*,*Palin-
genius*, our *Chawcer*, the Poets of thofe ages, Bifhops, Ab-
bots, Monks, Friers, Panders and Painters, be asked of the
Popes Court, the open finnes of *Rome*,the fecret iniquities of
irreligious houfes,their deepe hypocrifie, their fained fanctti-
tie,their vaine fuperftition, their groffe idolatry, their damnable villany,in all fexes,in all forts,in all ages; and they will
crie with one voice,that faith and iuftce were departed from
the face of the earth. Among the people fuch vfuries, fuch
extortions,fuch cruelties, fuch murthers, fuch villanies; and
all fo common,as if the world had made no other profeffion
Newbridg,l.2 then to liue wickedly and damnably before God and men.
cap.16.ex luel For fuch fanctitie, vertues and holineffe of the Englifh Romane Clergie, that had committed robberies, rapes and
murthers, your Pope fainted. *Thomas* of *Canterburie* ftood
Sup.cap.15. againft his King, and came to his merited and iuft death; if
it had bene as lawfully executed, as it was well de-
ferued.

22 If it fhall be replied, that in thefe dayes and in the
light of religion, finnes of many thofe forts do likewife a-
bound: it cannot be denied. But now not fo frequently, nor
fo profeffedly, as heretofore, or in other kingdomes where
Popery is profeffed. We haue no ftewes of allowed bawde-
rie; no man that defendeth any groffe iniquitie, as their Cardinall *de Cafa* did. The difference is, we are not fo good as
we fhould be; they were for the moft part as ill as they could
be. There is an imperfection in our Church, a plaine defection in theirs.If our ftate be like Purgatory, theirs is as hell.
Our peoples knowledge may haply bring them from information of the will of God, to reformation of life and manners: they are like to proceed in their malice, and fo in their
danger, vntill Gods *light fhine in their darke places,and the ftar*
2.Pet.1.19. *appeare in their hearts.*Our doctrine of manners is certaine in
Scriptures; theirs variable and flexible,in the will of a finfull
man, who as he often changeth in perfon, fo may he change
in will and affections. One may take euill for good, another
good

good for euill: and then aske *Bellarmine* what the case of the
world would be, *Si Papa erraret, præcipiendo vitia, vel prohiben-* Bellar.de Ro-
do virtutes, teneretur Ecclesia credere vitia esse bona, & virtutes Pont.l.4.c.5.
*malas, nisi velit contra conscientiam peccare: If the Pope should erre,
in commanding vice and forbidding vertue, the Church were
bound to hold, that vices were good, and vertues euill, except she
would sinne against her conscience.* A monstrous and fearfull resolution, worthy deepe consideration, and euerlasting detestation.

CHAP. XVII.

*Whatsoeuer is pretended of the corruption and apostasie of the Ro-
mane Church in faith or manners, it is most certaine that the Romanes faith was once commended by the Apostle Saint Paul, and
was after continued found vnder the holy Martyrs, Bishops of
that sea. Shew when, how, the time, the meanes by which this
once holy Spouse of Christ fell from her first integritie,
to such error in faith, such leud-
nesse of life?*

Oft men delight themselues with the quiet
fruition of their owne countrey, accounting
it best, though there be many better; and some
so dote ouer the place of their birth, that they
mislike nothing there, can endure nothing
elsewhere. A bird would rather liue in fields a-
broad, in the coldest frost and snow, when she cannot find
a berry to saue her life, then pearch in a fine cage, and in a
warme house, with the best prouision may be made for her.
A miserable and miscreant *Indian*, would rather abide still, or
returne soone, though naked and sauage, into his owne countrey, then well clothed, and well, not onely fed, but feasted
in a ciuill kingdome. *Nescio qua natale Solum dulcedine cunctos,
Ducit: I know not how, each man doth loue his place of birth.* The
smoake of *Greece* was more pleasant to *Vlysses* then the fire
of *Troy*.

2 The

2 The Romanifts are thus tranfported and infatuated, thus delighted and enamoured on their Italian Court, the whore of *Babylon*, that they can find neither blemifhes in her body,nor wrinkles in her face, for which they may lothe and forfake her. As if their fhooes had growne with their feet, and their clothes with their backs, euer fince our Sauiour Chrifts time,as *Ludolphus* conceiteth our Sauiour Chrifts did. As if théirs were the onely country that flowed with milke and hony,the land of promife,the Paradife of pleafure. This makes them fo much dote on her, though wafted with defe&ions, and degenerated from her ancient beauty and integritie, that they will not endure to heare the voice crying *vnto them, Come out of her, left you partake of her plagues.* They will venture,rather to perifh in her defolation and de-ftru&ion,then admit to heare of amendment or reformation. They will not go forth of *Sodome* to be faued with *Lot*, they would rather be confumed with the Sodomites.They wil not enter the Arke with *Noah*,they choofe rather to perifh in the waters with the world. They will not be like *Abraham*,that left his country and his fathers houfe, and fought another country,a citie not made with hands,one aboue that abideth for euer,whofe author and finifher is God.

3 To iuftifie the integrity and aduance the glory of this country, all the Romanifts with tongues and pens, by word and by writing, feeke to defend, that fhe remaineth as faire as the firft day of her conuerfion and mariage vnto Chrift; as if yet her face were *fine ruga aut macula,* without wrinkle or fpot, as Saint *Paul* did, and Saint *Peter* might haue left it, at their dying day. This building they reare vpon this foundation : *Rome once had the true faith; and it cannot be proued,when, or how fhe fell from it, or it parted from her.* We had it, therefore we haue it,is no good reafon.Many an vnthrift that hath fold and confumed his lands,would giue a large fee to make this good. It is an old faid faw, *Was good,neuer loued the Frier.*One yeare in prefent poffeffion,wil do a man more good then the conceit of an hundred yeares paft,when the leafe is expired. *You haue a name that you liue, but are dead,* (faith the Angell

in

Deut.8.4.

De vita Chri-
fti,part.z.c.63.
pag.221.col.2

Apocal.18.4.

Gen.19.14.

Gen.7.

Heb.11.8.

Rom.1.8.
16.19.

Imò habui
Chreme.

Reu.3.1.

in the Reuelation.) Rome had but a name ſhe liued, ſhe was ſicke long, no maruell if ſhe be now dead, or at leaſt at deaths doore. *Infeliciſſimi infortunij genus fuiſſe felicem*: It is a moſt mi- ſerable infelicitie, to haue bene happie. *Romes faith was fa- mous*, not for that ſhe was a teacher of other nations, as ſome of the Romaniſts boaſt; but for that ſhe had receiued the Goſ- pell her ſelfe, as *Tollet* better *obſerueth. Famous for her owne conuerſion, not ſo then for others inſtruction. That *the faith was in Rome, we grant*: That it is their now we vtterly deny, our aduerſaries cannot proue, except it be in corners, priſons, or the Inquiſition houſe.

Boetius in Conſol.

Nos ſuimus Troes, fuit Ilium & in- gens, Gloria Teucrorum. Miſerum eſt fuiſſe.

* In Rom. 1.

   4   The faith was at Ieruſalem, at Antioch, where belee- uers were firſt called Chriſtians; at Corinth where Saint *Paul* was often, and long together; in all the leſſer Aſia, in Greece. The Romaniſts themſelues will deny that it is there now. Though it hath bene long, and is yet, in ſome places euen vn- der the Turkes perſecution, in many of theſe countries, leſſe corrupt then vnder the Papacy or Romane tyrannie. What can Rome pleade why ſhe might not fall from the faith, as well as other cities, other nations? They cannot plead Scrip- tures. Let them ſhew if they can, one, not onely ſentence, but word, that intituleth Rome, or the Biſhop thereof, to any pri- uiledge aboue other cities. I know nothing they haue to ſay for Rome, but that it was remembred by the Apoſtle, to haue receiued the faith, that they are commended for it, that they then kept it, that the Goſpell had bene there preached by Apoſtolicall authoritie, &c. Which can leaue no ſuch im- preſſion, as if it could neuer fall from the faith afterward. For if ſuch commendation were ſo operatiue and powerfull, the ſame Apoſtle giues commendations to the Theſſalonians, more in number, greater in force, amplified with ponderous circumſtances, of their true conuerſion, firme faith, worthy workes, all publiſhed and made famous to all the world; and yet they are now declined and their Sunne ſet: and why not the Romanes? Paralell all that *Campian* hath collected out of the Epiſtle to the Romans, with theſe and other places of his Epiſtles to the Theſſalonians; if theſe do not exceed thoſe,

1. Theſſ. 1. 6.

2. Theſſ. 1. 4.

let

let them haue the day.

    5   In the queſtion I haue in hand; whether Rome be a-
poſtated from their firſt faith? thus they proceed. Cardinall

Bellarmine.   *Bellarmine* ſaith, *In omni inſigni mutatione religionis, iſta ſex de-*
mōſtrari poſſunt: Author, Dogma, Tempus, Locus, Oppugnator, Cœ-
,, *tus exiguus vnde oritur.* In euery *notorious change of religion,* (if
,, he had ſaid in euery ſudden change, we would not haue ſtucke
,, with him,) *theſe ſixe things may be demonſtrated. The Author,*
,, *the Opinion, the Time, t he Place, the Oppoſite, ſome ſmall company*
,, *from whence it ariſeth.* Coſterus that teſtie Ieſuite, hath the ſame

Epiſtola ad   in effect in his Epiſtle dedicatory to his Apologie, but not
Apolog.   with ſo many circumſtances. *Vbi, quando, quomodo, & à quo*
,, *introducta ſit fidei mutandæ ratio? Where, when, how, and by whom*
,, *was this change of faith introduced?* Againe, *Campian* that diſloy-
all and our forlorne and forſaken countriman, exceedingly
Iudges 16.4.   pleaſeth himſelfe with this *Delilah* as fit for his mincing dalli-
Campian Ra-   ance. *Quando igitur hanc fidem tantopere celebratam Roma per-*
tio 7.   *didit? Quando eſſe deſiit, quod ante fuit? Quo tempore? Quo Pon-*
tifice? Qua via? Qua vi? Quibus incrementis? Vrbem & orbem
religio peruaſit aliena? When did Rome loſe this faith ſo much ce-
Doct. Kelliſon   *lebrated? When ceaſſed ſhe to be that which before ſhe was? In what*
hath the ſame   *time? Vnder what Biſhop? By what way? By what force? By what*
in effect.   *increaſe or augmentation, did this ſtrange religion ſeize vpon that*
Suruey l. 2, c. 1.   *Citie, and the world?* Whoſoeuer was the Grecians, this is the
p. 163.   Romans *Helena,* they are all enamoured vpon this minion. Anſwer this, the moſt is anſwered, if not all. *Gregorius de Valentia*
hangeth in the ſame ſtring, or is rather intangled in the ſame
ſnare, perhaps caught by *Campian,* for he magnifieth his con-
Greg. de Va-   ceit aboue meaſure; *Quo tempore, vel à quibus Eccleſiis pri-*
lentia. l. 6, c. 12   *mùm, poſt Apoſtolorum tempora, doctrina ea quam nunc Eccleſia*
Romana tenet, contra doctrinam Apoſtolicam introducta fuerit,
doceri non poteſt. Neque facere poſſum, quin hic propter loci oppor-
tunitatem, adſcribam pulcherrimam ac Spiritu Dei plenam, Cam-
piani noſtri non it a pridem fortiſſimi in Eccleſia Chriſti Martyris,
orationem, quæ figmentum ſectariorum de corruptâ doctrinâ in Ec-
cleſia Romana mirificè redarguit, de illis verbis, quando fidem tan-
,, *topere celebratam Roma perdidit.* It cannot be taught, in what
time,

time, or in what Churches after the Apoſtles time, that do- „
ctrine now maintained by the Church of Rome, was firſt „
brought in againſt the Apoſtolicall doctrine. Neither can I „
chooſe by reaſon of the opportunitie of the place, but ſet „
downe that oration, both excellent and full of the Spirit of „
God, of our *Campian*, yerwhiles a victorious Martyr in the „
Church of Chriſt, that wonderfully reproues that figment of „
the Sectaries concerning corrupted doctrine in the Church of „
Rome. Of thoſe words, When Rome forſooke that faith ſo „
much famouſed.

6 Firſt I ſay, that *Bellarmines* poſition of his ſixe circumſtances, *Campian* and *Coſterus* their queſtions are all abſurd,
and vnreaſonable to be demanded, eſpecially in euery particular: Secondly, that in moſt things of greateſt moment, we
can ſhew the change in their Synagogue, with all, or the moſt
part, of their owne conditions, to the iuſtification of our cauſe,
& condemnation of theirs. I could make a ſhort anſwer which
I can well proue. How fell the Romane Church? I will ſay for
certaine (as one of yours ſaith in another caſe, but moſt falſe-
ly:) *Hypocriſi, contemptu (Scripturarum,) conuitijs, ſcilicet nemo* Muri ciuit.
repente peſſimus euadit, & iſti gradibus quibuſdam per aſtutiam fund. 7.
ad nequitiam peruenerunt. By hypocriſie, contempt (of Scrip- „
tures) and railing. For no man aſcends ſuddenly to the height „
of villanie. And theſe by certaine ſteps haue proceeded by „
craft to wickedneſſe. But to proſecute my propoſed me- „
thod.

7 Is it not abſurd and vnreaſonable, to appoſe vs with
ſuch queſtions or demands, that may make as well for the i-
dolatry of the heathen againſt the Iewes, who certainly had
the Law, the Couenant, the Promiſes giuen and made vnto Rom. 9. 4.
them, from the onely true God creator of heauen and earth?
or for the Iewes againſt the Chriſtians, who notwithſtanding
haue the certaine truth? Nay, which would ſerue the preſent
Turkes and Infidels againſt the Romaniſts themſelues, for
their religion at this day? For what could hinder the Gentiles for making this plea againſt the Iewes? *Noah* had the
faith, he taught it to his ſonnes, they repleniſhed the world:

When,

When,where, how, did the faith faile in the ſtocke of *Iaphet*, more then in the linage of *Sem*? Did not the truth faile in *Na-*

Geneſ. 31. 53. *hor*, deſcended from *Sem*, before the Couenant was renewed with *Abraham*? for *Abraham* had the true God, *Nahor* had another; and therefore an Idolater. What monument remaineth in the world hereof, more then is writen in the Scrip-

Eccleſ. 7.12. tures of God? *Say not vnto them,why are the former dayes better then theſe. for thou doeſt not enquire wiſely of this thing.*

8 Or what could hinder the Iewes, to ſay to our bleſſed

Math.5. 23. Sauiour, who iuſtly taxed their manifold corruptions in do-
Mat.3.9.   ctrine and life;How,where,and when,&c. fell our Fathers in-
Ioh.8.33.9.28 to theſe defections? We know,and can proue that *Abraham* was our father; that *Moſes* receiued the Law from God, and deliuered it to our Anceſtors; that the Prophets of our nation in ſundry ages taught vs the truth from heauen ; that we haue

Malach.2.7. the receiued promiſes ; that the Prieſts lips ſhould preſerue
Pſal. 132. knowledge ; that Sion ſhould be Gods reſting place for euer,
Iere.7.23.31.1 and for the Arke of his ſtrength. That God Iehouah would be their God, and that they ſhould be his people. Finally, that

Rom.9. 4. they had the preheminence many wayes, as Saint *Paul* confeſſeth. In what Kings dayes? vnder which high Prieſt? by what fraud? by what force, left we the truth, which ſo many ages was continued to our Fathers, and deliuered vnto vs?

9 Grew all the Turkes defection at once? Or can any man tell how the Indians declined from that Saint *Thomas*

Moſcouits. taught them ? or other nations which yet ſauour of Chriſtian
Abiſſens. religion, but are farre from that which is contained in the Scriptures? and the farther from them , the more erronious. How came the Grecians ſo farre to decline in their faith from their firſt integritie; (who were elder brethren to the Romans) as not onely experience, but the Romaniſts owne confeſſion, and accuſation taxe them withall? Saint *Peter* and S. *Paul*, with other good and painfull miniſters of the Goſpell, preached in thoſe countries and cities:which though many of them are Chriſtians,yet are not in euery particular of the faith which thoſe Apoſtles and miniſters taught by word, (as with-

out

out queſtion we may be bold to affirme,) not by extant writing, as we are moſt certaine and ſure. If theſe queſtions or
expoſtulations would be derided and reiected as abſurd by a-
ny religion that is not onely better then other in ſuppoſition,
but diuers from other in oppoſition; why may not they be as
well caſt off by vs, who hold the truth of God, not as by preſcription of a few ages, or generations before vs, but as
drawne out of the cleare fountaine of liuing waters, the primarie and originall Scriptures of God? If they ſhall bring
vs ſome ſtations and times wherein there fell mutations in
the temporall ſtate, that is not to be applied to the ſtate of
Religion. Gods true worſhip long declining in many ages,
was puniſhed by tranſlation of the State & captiuity of the
people: defection in veritie was the cauſe of alteration of the
ciuill State, not this alteration the cauſe of defection, as after
ſhall appeare.

10 Antichriſts proceedings are called a myſtery, & a myſtery worketh not openly but ſeeretly; not at once, but by little
& little, and then getteth greateſt aduantage when it is leaſt
obſerued or ſuſpected: therefore *Bellarmine* ſubtilly inſer-
teth in his propoſition, *Inſignis, notable* : as if euery great mutation which we preſently finde with griefe, and feele with
paine of our hearts, were notorious in the firſt entrance or
beginning thereof. That which hath an obſcure and an vn-
ſenſible beginning at the firſt, may worke a ſenſible and notorious change in the end : and yet the wiſeſt ſhall not ſo
eaſily find out the firſt entrance, as the ſimpleſt may apparently ſee, and palpably feele the groſſe & dangerous euents
in the end. The banks of riuers are long wearing before a
manifeſt irruption and inundation of flouds. It hath fared
with the Court of Rome, as it did formerly with the common-wealth of Rome, *Too late they found that there is not ſo lit-* Plutarch in
tle a beginning of any thing, but continuance of time may make it vita Cæſaris.
ſtrong, when through contempt there is no impediment to hinder
the greatneſſe : So grew *Iulius Cæſar* by little and little, ſo the
Romane Pope and his Court by ſome and ſome.

11 The enuious man ſowed his tares in the night, when Mat.13.25.
                    E e   men

men were afleep,they grew vp in time, and became fo ranke, that they ouertopt the corne. So while men contented with their owne power and principalities, enioyed all things at their pleafure, and being fecure from oppofition, they ſtood ſtill at a gaze, and obſerued no likelihood of danger, and therefore made no reckoning of ſmall matters: vnder which careleſſe ignorance and idle gouernment, diuerſe things were brought into the Church, perhaps by the ſubtiltie of a few; admitted by the negligence of moſt and chiefeſt; foſtered and maintained by cuſtome; among the greater part grew to take ranke and deepe roote, hardly to be weeded out, and became ſo familiar,that they crept into Church Canons, and ſo were confirmed by law, as found and ſincere learning. A matter not vnuſuall in any State.

12   Confider with me how abſurd it is, that becauſe it is hard to find out the beginning and increment of euery particular hereſie in the Romane ſtate and Court, (for I may better call it ſo then a Church)therfore we muſt not beleeue what we ſee with our eyes, and what we feele with our hands, in theſe groſſe and ſuperſtitious abſurdities which are ingroſſed and enterteined by our aduerſaries againſt Gods truth, and would be obtruded and impoſed vpon vs, if we had not prudence and prouidence to foreſee them, good meanes and ſufficient power, to auoid them.

13   The Romane Synagogue is not onely *Spelunca la-* Lerna malo-
rum. *tronum, a denne of theeues,* but λϵϼυη χαχῶν, a very ſinke of euils and hereſies, *yea a mare mortuum, a dead ſea,* wherein this ſpirituall Sodome & Gomorrha are not ſunke,but ſwimme, and flouriſh, and abound with all error and iniquitie. How theſe fearefull euils were congeſted from a handfull to a heape; how they increaſed from an eb to a floud,it is hard to ſay directly, I confeſſe, yet not impoſſible to proue, as will appeare.They were not all throwne in the pit in one day, as 2.King.10.6. the 50 heads of *Egiptus* ſonnes, or as the 70 heads of *Ahabs* children, that were preſented at once to the King at the en- 2.Sam.15.1. trance of the gate. But as *Abſolom* who firſt vnder pretence of neglect of iuſtice in his Father, promiſe of more care therof

of in himſelfe, ſtole the peoples hearts; then pretended a ſacrifice, then prouided Counſellers; then drew the people
vnto him; at laſt made open rebellion, and proclaimed
himſelfe King. So haue the Popes aduanced their tyrannie.

14 Obſerue the alteration in naturall or artificiall bodies,
in ciuil and politicke States, whether publicke or domeſtick;
and euery dayes experience will ſufficiently inſtruct common ſenſe, that ſuch dangerous changes in the end haue proceeded out of neglected and contemptible paſſages at the
firſt, when they might haue bene eaſily preuented, that now
can hardly be reformed with any humane helpe.

15 I knew a child whom I ſee a man, my ſelfe a child,
now an old man. I know not how he or I came from child- Obrepit non intellecta ſe-
hood to manhood, from youth to age; therefore I may ob- nectus.Iuuen.
ſtinately deny him to be a man, or my ſelfe an old man. I behold a houſe ruinous, which in my yonger yeares I knew
new built; I muſt not confeſſe it to be in default, becauſe I
know not how it fell into decay. I haue ſeene a tree greene
and floriſhing, which is now not onely fruitleſſe but ſtarke
rotten; I muſt not beleeue it, becauſe I cannot tell when the
wind ſhakt it (when the lightening blaſted it, when the froſt
nipt it,) or when the worme bit it, as it did *Ionas* his gourd. Ionas 4.7.
Seeing is no leeuing with theſe men, they will take no witneſſe
of their owne eyes. I behold the Sunne ſetting in the Weſt,
that in the morning roſe in the Eaſt. But I may impudently
deny it, becauſe I cannot diſcerne how this noble Giant Pſal.19.5.
ran his courſe. As if a man could not erre, that hath bene once
in the way.

16 Is not this ſtrange? or is it not enough to a ſober man
in his right wits, that I can proue him a man that was a child,
the houſe to be ruinous that was once new builded; the tree
to be rotten that onc floriſhed; the Sunne to be in the Weſt,
that was in the Eaſt; a man to be in a wilderneſſe, that was
once in the way? The charitable Samaritane that found the
wounded man in the high way, neuer askt him who woun- Luke.10.33.
ded him, where, when, why, with what weapons he was hurt,

with

with what deuice he was entrapped: but fell to his beſt helps
for the preſent, & prouided for after. His wounds called for
remedy, his perill admitted no delay. To enquire theſe circumſtances which might argue folly in the Samaritan, griefe
to a pained poore man, and danger to his wounds , was not
onely needleſſe, but perillous. *Serò medicina paratur, Cum ma-*
la per longas inualuere moras.

 17 Me thinkes Saint *Auguſtine* fits by a like familiar ex-
Aug.Epiſt.29. ample, a very direct and ſubſtantiall anſwer to theſe queſtions. A man fals into a pit, and cals for helpe, he that ſhould
lend him his hand for preſent reliefe, falls to asking him this
queſtion, *Quo modo huc cecidiſti: How diaſt thou fall in here?* and
you wil, when? at which corner? who thruſt thee in? &c.
would not the diſtreſſed man beſhrow him in his heart? and
anſwer : *Obſecro cogita quomodo hinc me liberes , non quomodo*
,, *huc ceciderim quæras* : I pray Sir, aduiſe me how I may come
,, out, neuer aske me the queſtion, how I fell in , *Non quia la-*
tet miſeriæ principium , ergo pigreſcere debet miſericordiæ offi-
,, *cium*: Becauſe we know not the beginning of a mans
,, *miſerie , ſhall we therefore deferre or detract an office of*
mercie?

 18 How breed diſeaſes in mans body? what? to the
height and extremity at once trow you? Do not ill humours
fiiſt ingender , then increaſe, then inflame, at laſt breake
forth into ſuch dangerous maladies that menace death? Yet
by the Romaniſts learning, neither the Phiſitian that by his
skill knowes it, nor the patient that to his great griefe feels
it, muſt beleeue that the diſeaſe is dangerous, or is at all,
becauſe they both are certaine, there was once health, and
can giue no reaſon when the diſeaſe began, or by what
acceſſes and increaſings it proceeded to that deſperate
danger.

Plutarch.in
Publicola. 19 The vnholy religion of the Court of Rome, grew as
the holy Iſland in *the citie of Rome.* Sheaues of wheat that
,, grew in the field of *Mars*, were throwne into the riuer , and
,, not far off ſtayed, ſunke, and ſetled. Afterward the water
,, brought downe continually ſuch mudde and grauell, that it
euer

euer increaſed the heape more and more: in ſuch ſort, that „
the force of the ſtreame could not remoue it from thence,but „
rather ſoftly preſſing and driuing it together,did bind it,and „
harden it,and made it grow to a firme land. Thus this heape „
riſing in greatneſſe and ſoliditie, by reaſon that all which „
came downe the riuer ſtayed there, it grew in the end by „
time ſo farre, that it is called at this day, the holy Iſland of „
Rome: in which are goodly temples of diuers gods; and it is „
called in Latin, *Inter duos pontes*, betweene two bridges. So „
the wheate of Chriſts Goſpell once grew in *Rome*, but it being caſt into the riuer of contempt and negleƈt, ſunke and
ſetled in the bottome of obliuion,till with the mud and grauell of traditions and violent interpretations it increaſed to
a huge heape, which preſſed ſoftly by hypocriſie and pretences of deuotion,made it as cruſtie as the hardneſſe of heart or
a ſeared conſcience. Thus this vaſte and vndigeſted heape,
grew ſo much and ſo long, till it was called, The holy religion of *Rome*;where are built goodly Temples for idolatrous
worſhip, and may be iuſtly ſaid to be *inter duos pontes*, between the bridge of ceremonious Iewes and of ſuperſtitious
Gentiles, or their pretended traditions and the Popes tyrannie, which may truly be called the Brigs of dread. The
change and alteration which *Sylla* brought into the Com- Plutarch.in
monwealth, was thought ſtrange at the firſt among the peo- Sylla.
ple; but afterward men by proceſſe of time being vſed to it,
it was throughly eſtabliſhed,& men miſliked it not: ſo were
many alterations brought in by Popes, which at firſt were
repined at, but after grew into vſe, and obſerued with contentment. Becauſe Saint *Paul* and S. *Peter* left *Rome* Church
like a *Platoes* Commonwealth, therefore the Romaniſts will
not beleeue that it is degenerated in the diſordered and corrupt poſteritie of *Romulus*; as *Cicero* obſerued in *Cato* his o- Plutarch.in
uer ſeueritie.   Phocion.

20   True it is,that ſome diſeaſes ſuddenly follow ſurfets
of meate,drink, cold,wounds,poiſons,&c. So ſometime hereſies in particular Churches breake forth on a ſudden; and
the dangers perceiued as ſoone as they are felt, are the more

easily cured before further contagion and accidents indanger the life of faith. The more euidently the cause is perceiued, the more easily is the malady recouered. Popery poisoned not the Church with a hot venime that speedily killeth, but like the biting of a mad dog, that is scarce discerned till it be past cure; as experience proued in *Baldus* the great Ciuilian. Lingring diseases, and such vnsensible poisons are most dangerous. Heresies for the most part begin without obseruation, creepe on like a *Cancer*, and without contradiction or preuention, consume the truth. Is it now such a wonder to see an army surprised, while the Sentinels haue slept? I read of a woman that so accustomed her selfe by degrees to eate poison, that at last she could eate it and digest it without hurt, like naturall, ordinary and wholesome food. As it is said of a lyer, he may tell a lye so long, till he beleeue it himselfe; and so from telling and tatling, will sweare it to be true: so it fareth altogether with our Romanists, they haue so long vsed themselues to the poison of falshood and heresie, that they digest it as well or better then the Scriptures of God: and haue now lyed so impudently, so long, and so loud, that they beleeue legions of their Legendary lyes, tales to be truths, and fables to be stories, indeed fitter to be moralized like *Æsops* Fables, then entertained with any credit as matter of truth. And this is the lesse strange, because the *Spirit speaketh euidently, &c. that some shall giue heed to spirits of error and doctrines of diuels:* some that wil not obey, but *forsake the truth, shall be led through hypocrisie to beleeue lyes.*

21   Moreouer, we may truly say, and proue if need be, that the ancient Fathers saw not all dangers that befell the Church: some wrote not all they saw, or might haue written; some were so busied in matters of greatest moment, to oppose mightie aduersaries, that they neglected smaller matters, the danger whereof was not so present. But as they that haue the Lion in pursuite, heed not the whelpes, who notwithstanding in time may grow as dangerous as their sires: so those times foresaw not so much the danger of superstitions

Marginal notes:

Griuinus de Venenis, Ambr.Paraeus

2. Tim. 2. 17.

Forest. de Venenis.

1. Tim. 4. 1.

2. Thes. 2. 11.

tions new growing, as they manfully ouercame the moſt preſent and peſtiferous heretiks. Beſides,ſome of the Fathers ancient monuments are loſt,ſome infoiſted into their rooms, ſome caſtrated,ſome bombaſted, or ſome way or other ſophiſticated, as hath bene proued. Sup.cap.8.

22 Againe, ſome Fathers, though they ſaw and lamen- & 12. ted many ſuperſtitions crept into the Church in their owne dayes, yet durſt make no ſtrong oppoſition for ſome cauſes, or in reſpect of ſome perſons either waiward or turbulent: and this was Saint *Auguſtines* caſe, as himſelfe confeſſeth. Auguſt.ep.118 And finally, ſome of an honeſt *ſimplicitie* beleeued tales for truths, vpon the credit of them that told them, as one of Canus. their owne acknowledgeth.Though there were ſeuen thou- Aug. & Greg. ſand in *Iſrael* ſecret ones,that had not *bowed the knee to Baal,* out of Lucian. *not kiſſed him,*yet the Prophet *Hoſea* complaineth of *Ephraim:* Vt ſup.cap.4. *Strangers haue deuoured his ſtrength, and he knoweth not ; yea* B.Rhenan. ep. *gray haires are here and there vpon him, and yet he knoweth not.* ante Euſeb. Vpon which Saint *Hierome* ſaith, *Multo errauit tempore, &* Hoſea 7.9. *nihilominus ignorauit ſenectutem & vetuſtatem , de qua ſcriptum eſt, quòd veteratur & ſeneſcit, prope exterminium eſt : Ephraim ,, erred a long time,and yet was ignorant of his old and worne age : of ,, which it is written,That which waxeth old,and is ſuperannated, is ,, neare expulſion. Et ſi ad iuſtum virum & Eccleſiaſticum dicatur, Cani hominis ſapientia eius; quare non dicatur ad iniquum & hæreticum,Cani hominis ſtultitia eius ? If we may ſay vnto a iuſt and ,, Eccleſiaſticall man,Wiſedome is in gray haires; why may we not ſay ,, to a wicked and hereticall man,(be he a Pope if you will)There is ,, folly in gray haires ?* ,,

*Nemo repentè fuit turpiſſimus,accipient te Paulatim:
No man on ſudden is made extreme wicked,
His nature b'inches is brought to be crooked.*

As one of their owne before alledgeth it. Or a better Author Epiphan.l.3. more aptly to our caſe: *Singulæ res non ab initio omnia habue-* c.75. *runt, ſed progreſſu temporis,ea quæ ad neceſſariorum perfectionem requiruntur,parabantur :* Euery thing hath not it perfection ,, from the beginning , but by tract of time,things neceſſarily ,, required to perfection,are prouided.Which he exemplifieth ,, by *Moses* his beginnings and proceedings.

23　There are diuers cuſtomes crept into the Church, whereby the Laitie preſcribe againſt the Clergie in paiment of tithes; a ſmall rate for a tithe of great value. We know well enough, that tithes in their firſt inſtitution were payd in kind. Now we find in our experience, & feele to our loſſe, that this by cuſtome and preſcription is quite altered. Let the beſt Lawyers in Chriſtendome tell me when theſe cuſtomes began, in their ſeuerall times and diſtinct places. Or let them proue the Romaniſts argument good, *We had it, therefore we haue it*; I would promiſe them good fees.

24　If they ſay, ſome will appeare by writings and compoſitions; ſome crept in, we neither know when, by whom, nor how: ſo in matters of religion, we can ſufficiently proue, and therefore may eaſily grant, that originally all was well at *Rome*, Saint *Pauls* pen hath regiſtred it; and when many falſhoods and errors inuaded and tooke poſſeſſion of that Church, (as is ſaid) it is not impoſſible to diſcouer; and yet to proue each of theſe particular circumſtances in all and euery ſingular, goes beyond that themſelues can do in any point of our profeſſion and religion, if they were appoſed. Yet notwithſtanding, we as well diſcerne the Romaniſts errors to be blaſphemous againſt Gods glory, and ſcandalous to his Church, as we feele theſe cuſtomes to be preiudiciall to the Clergie and miniſtery of the Goſpell.

De Ro. Pont.
l. 2. cap. 5.
25　Cardinall *Bellarmine* himſelfe can ſay, when it will ſerue his turne, that *ſæpiſſimè accidit, vt conſtet de re, & non conſtet de modo, vel alia circumſtantia: It often fals, that the thing is manifeſt, though the maner or ſome other circumſtance cannot be proued.* The Cardinall will haue Saint *Peters* being at *Rome* granted without contradiction, though he can neither proue when he came thither, nor how long he there continued *reſident*, nor who ſaw him there. Our Sauiour Chriſts death is certaine that it was, but the time when it was, is diuerſly taken by many writers, whom the Cardinall nameth. We find and take a theefe in the houſe, with his fardle truſſed vp, and ready to be gone: what mattereth it when he came in, or where?

where? who helpt him? whether he crept in at a window, or brake through a wall, or vntiled the houſe, or pickt a locke? He is a theefe, he is taken, he may be hanged without all circumſtances but one, and that is, that which circumſtands his necke. If we apprehend the theefe, and attach the ſtolen goods, all other matters, if they be found, they ſerue not ſo much to the diſcouery, as to preuent the like villanie, by making all more ſure. We apprehended the Romane theeues in the houſe. We haue found their fardell of truths, which they haue ſtolne out; their error and hereſies they haue brought in; we proue the fact, what neede more circumſtances for them, but that one which they well deſerue? It was not as now it is: it is not as ſometimes it was, this is ſufficient.

26   Another friend of Rome, ſpeaking of inueſtitures, Catholicke Diuine.cap. §.16. ſaith, that *If we ſeeke the beginnings of inueſtitures, how, and when, and to whom they were firſt granted, we ſhall find the matter very vncertaine, &c. but rather crept in afterward, yea and rather taken, and vſurped to themſelues, by certaine Princes, by inuaſion and intruſion vpon the Church, priuatly firſt; and then more publickly afterward: & thereupon pretended by their ſucceſſors, rather then granted by ſpeciall gift, or conſent of the Pope at all.* Alter but the words, the caſe will not alter. This Catholicke Diuine hath anſwered them all, that euer propoſe theſe fancifull and idle queſtions. Or if you will, aske *Plutarch* when corruption of the people by bribes and banquetting entred into the old Romane common wealth, and he will directly anſwer, theſe curious and inquiſitiue men. *This peſtilence crept in by* Plutarch in Coriolano. *little and little, and did ſecretly win ground, ſtill continuing a long time in Rome before it was openly diſcouered. For no man can tell, who was the firſt that bought mens voyces with money, nor that corrupted the ſentence of the Iudges, but he knoweth that this tooke away all anthoritie,* and deſtroyed the common wealth. What ſhall let but that we may now ſay the ſame of the degenerated Romane Church? When it was we know not, but that it is Roma vno non eſt ædiſſcata die. we plainly ſee. Neither was Rome built in a day, nor Troy deſtroyed in a night. Antichriſt and the diuell do imitate

good

good things in fhew, yea and in proofe too, as Apes do men. When the Temple was built, there was not a toole heard, all in filence, & yet finifhed. So Antichrift who imitateth God as an Ape doth a man, in erecting his temple, did it in filence, by little and little: but vp it is we fee, and downe it fhall; for God is true. One ftate of gouernment hath in time degenerated into another, without found of trumpet, or clafhing of armor. And yet hath bene fenfibly felt, and enforced reformation. Rome was once built on feuen hils, their names are knowne; the whole Citie now ftandeth on the bankes of Tyber, and in *Mars* his field; a great and euident mutation, it cannot be de-

Campian. nied. But it would pofe, not onely that leafh of Iefuites, but
Bellarmine. three and threefcore to tell vs how it remoued, withall their
Cofterus. circumftances. There was a time when the Arian herefie was not, yet it crept into many Churches by fecret influences, till

Hieron. aduer. all the world wondered, and *lamented to fee it felfe an Arian:*
Luciferianos. Though the beginning thereof was knowne to many of the learned, yet the generall was corrupted, no man knew how: for they wondred at themfelues. So hath it befallen the Romane Church. But fhe wondreth not to fee her felfe leprous with herefie, and fallen away from the truth by apoftafie, and become enemie to the Gofpell.

27 In which cafe, let me aske in good earneft, can a man be neuer poore that hath bene rich, except all the world be acquainted how, and when, &c. he fell to decay? A bankrupt is perhaps difcouered on the fudden, but he declined long vnder a faire fhew. Or let me aske more ferioufly and appofitely,

Efay 1.21. with the Prophet: *How is the faithfull Citie become an harlot?* *It was full of iudgment, and iuftice lodged therein, but now there are murtherers.* As who fhould fay, though neither you nor I know *how*, yet God knowes *how*. I fee it is fo, fo may you if you be not blind. May not we rather aske our aduerfaries this queftion, vpõ the manifeft euidence of their prefent defection

Gal. 3. 1. and apoftafie, as S. *Paul* asked the Galathians? *O ye foolifh Galathians,* (or Papifts) *who hath bewitched you? Is it not a fhame to fow in the fpirit and reape in the flefh? to begin with the Gofpell and fal to the Law?* Were not this a wife anfwer of the Galathiãs, to
                                                                aske

aske another queſtion of the Apoſtle: *When, where, how, by whō, were we bewitched?*So it fareth with the Pontifical Synagogue; they are bewitched,they haue reapt in the fleſh,they are fallen from the Goſpell.

28 We may ſay with the Prophet, *Credidi, propterea loquutus ſum; I beleeued,and therefore I ſpake.*We ſee it, which is Pſal.116.10. more,& therefore we may ſay it, if need be we are ready to ſweare it: Rome is deceiued. If they aske when? we will anſwer, now. If they aske, where? we ſay, vnder the Popes noſe. If they aske how? we tell them,by their Clergies partly negligence, partly ignorance. If by whom? by Antichriſt that poſſeſſeth the *chaire of ſcorners.*If by what force? by fire & ſword, Pſal.1.1. wherewith they haue conſumed the bodies of many a Saint. By what way? by keeping the Scriptures in an vnknowne tongue : knowing all mens ſecrets by auricular confeſſion; by enioyning penance for euery thought conceiued againſt their proceedings ; by diſpenſation with Princes luſts, to currie their fauours; with many more in this kind which are eaſie to be diſcouered, but we need not all this adoe. If we can do this,as hath bene done often,and may be againe,that is,proue their errors preſent, it is ſufficient for vs, to conuince them thereof, though we ſought no further.

29 The Parents of him that was borne blind, anſwered well to this queſtion, *Is this your ſonne whom you ſay was borne* Iohn 9. 19. *blind? How doth he now ſee? We know that this is our ſonne , and* 20. *that he was borne blind, but by what meanes he now ſeeth,we know* 21. *not,or who hath opened his eyes cannot we tell.*If the like queſtion ſhould be asked concerning the Romane Synagogue now, but by the contrary: *Is this that ancient mother that was borne with cleare ſight? How is it now that ſhe is become blind? We know that this was a good woman, and in her birth, and many yeares after ſaw very well; but how ſhe became blind,or who put out her eyes we cannot tell.* We ſee that ſhe is blind,let her tell how her eyes were put out.

30 *When went the Spirit of the Lord from me* (ſaith *Zid-* 1.King.22.24. *chia the falſe Prophet* , when he ſmote *Michaia* on the cheeke) *to ſpeake vnto thee?* Here is the ſame queſtion, *Quando,*When?

God

God knoweth when, might the Prophet well say, but I know
that now thou doeſt prophecie lies in the name of the Lord. When
decayed the Greeke Empire? We know when the laſt *Paleo-*
Hiſtory of the *logus* with his imperiall Citie was taken,ſacked and deſolated
Turks. by the Turke. But this was the death of the Empire, not the
diſeaſe or decay thereof. This ſickneſſe was long growing
(as was often complained and lamented) partly by the enuie
of the Latines, partly by the policie of their oppoſites, partly
by their owne leuitie and pride, partly by ciuill and inteſtine
diſcord, partly by the moſt Emperours careleſneſſe and negligence, in not conferring helpe, partly by Chriſtian Princes
often breach of promiſe. Neither had the Popes malice and
couetouſneſſe the leaſt intereſt in this diſmall and diſaſtrous
Tragedie. It once flouriſhed, it is now faded, it is as certainly
fallen,as it is certaine it once ſtood. Is it not euen ſo with the
Romane Synagogue? We will confeſſe that it was once as a
bright ſtar in the right hand of the Son of God, or a precious
pearle in his glorious crowne. Now we ſee and lament, and
are ſorie we cannot helpe it:Angels are become diuels : Beth-
ell is turned into Bethauen: The virgine is become an harlot,
Ieruſalem the *ioy of the whole earth, is become a cage of vncleane
birds*, and an hiſſing to all that paſſe by her. *Nunc ſeges eſt vbi
Troia fuit. Now graſſe there growes, where Troy once ſtood. Babylon, that great Citie is fallen.* This is a wonder to all that ſee it,
incredible to thoſe that ſee it not,yet certaine in it ſelfe, as by
manifeſt demonſtration hath bene by many,and often proued,
and ſhall be by my ſelfe,if God vouchſafe me life to finiſh my
meditations.

31   Behold all the Apoſtolicall Churches,thoſe in Aſia,o-
thers in Greece, which began their defections euen in the A-
poſtles times, and declined from naught to worſe, till their
fatall and finall periods came vpon them. When they had filled full the meaſure of their ſinnes,then God powred on them
the full viole of his iudgements. This onely remaineth not
executed vpon the Church or Synagogue of Rome : but ſhall
in due time, according to the Prophecies that haue gone be-
2.Pet.3.9. fore, though hereafter comes not yet. For God will not *fore-
ſlacke*

slacke his promise, yet a little while and he that shall come, will come, Heb.10.37. *and will not tarrie.*

32 I hope we may fay, and I am perfwaded they liue that fhall fee the finall execution of this Prophefie: *The dayes of* Hofe 9.7. *vifitation are come, the dayes of recompence are come, Ifrael fhall know it. The Prophet is a foole, the fpirituall man is mad, for the multitude of thine iniquities.* Rome her felfe fhall confeffe it, that hath long diffembled it, that their great Patriarke hath bene a foole, and his Cleargie mad men, when her friends and merchants, cafting duft on their heads, *weeping and wayling fhall crie and fay: Alas, Alas, that great Citie, &c. For in one* Reu.18.19.20 *houre fhe is made defolate. O heauens reioyce of her, and you holy Apoftles and Prophets; for God hath punifhed her, to be auenged on her, for your fakes: When a mightie Angell fhall take that ftone like a mil-ftone, and caft it into the Sea, faying, with fuch violence fhall that great Citie Babylon be caft, and fhall be found no more.* Happy were fhe if in this her day fhe could fee her owne nakedneffe, but it is hid from her eyes.

33 *Iefus came to iudgement into this world, that they which fee* Iohn 9.29. *not might fee, and fuch as fee might be made blind.* And happy were many if they were indeed blind, for fo they fhould *haue no finne, but feeing they fay, they fee, therefore their finne re-* Ioh.Ibid.vlt. *maineth.* This is great obftinacy and hardneffe of heart, they fay they fee, and yet are blind; had they but eye-falue to recouer their fight but a little, they would behold with E-*lias* feruant the cloud afarre off, and preuent the tempeft that is like to ouertake them, in the great and finall defolation of Antichrift and all his power. They may not like *Thales* be fo rapt with contemplation of the high planets and ftarres, that they fall into a pit before they are aware. While they ftudie nothing but pedegree, and to blazon the nobilitie of their anceftors, they fee not the bafeneffe and fordiditie of their owne prefent eftate. But howfoeuer it was in elder times, high ouer vs, or farre beyond vs, that will neither affure vs of our prefent ftate to be fuch, nor faue our foules in the day of Chrift. We fee, and wifh, that they could fee, and had grace to acknowledge, that where *was beautie, there is* Efay 3.24. *bald-*

baldnesse, where was a girdle there is a rend. This as ingenuously confessed, as it hath *bene* most pregnantly proued, might be the repose of any honest true-hearted Christian man.

34 To conclude, many were *Abrahams* children by naturall, lawful, and lineall propagation, according to the flesh; but all these had not *Abraham* to their father by spirituall grace and faith: and when all is said and done, *this is* Rom.2.28.   *the onely circumcision of the heart, the praise whereof is not of men but of God.*

35 But let vs suppose this question to be as reasonable, as it is common; and grant that an answer is thereunto as due, as the Romanists deeme it, without exception. We will not refuse our aduersaries herein. That neuer too much commended Noble man, *the Lord du Plesseis*, hath preuented me in this labour, by a large and a learned discourse of the progresse and opposition of the Romane religion, *ab ouo ad malum*, I may English it from the best, to the worst times : wherein this question is most demonstratiuely debated, & his aduersaries directly conuinced. But his volume is not for euery mans hand, nor for euery mans purse. Therefore though I hold it impossible in a short Chapter, or indeed at all, to demonstrate their demands, answered in euery particular, with all their circumstances: (& if I could, perhaps it would be tedious to produce all instances;) yet in some few Articles controuerted betweene the Romanists and vs, and those of greatest moment, I will lay open and shew the beginnings, passages, increments and consummation (I hope I may as well presage their consumption,) of some of their doctrines, that the rest by them, may be discerned *tanquam ex vngue Leo*, as the Lion by his paw; and then let the skilfull painter guesse *Hercules* stature by the proportion of his foote.

Mysterium iniquitatis.

Aulus Gellius.

36 Howbeit let not our Romanists refuse to submit themselues to the same lawes and conditions which they so clamorously lay vpon vs. Can they shew euery of our positions in Religion (which they gainesay) to be of a newer spring

or

or growth, then from the Apoſtles times; when? where?
how? by whom? &c. they firſt began, and ſo proue them
nouelties, as we will proue theirs? If they cannot, they
do vs wrong to demand that of vs they cannot do themſelues in the like caſe. If they can, let them deſcend to
particulars, and we will either beleeue them, or ſhew good
reaſon why not. Let them plainly and directly ſhew when
the volume of the Scriptures of the old Teſtament began to
be bound within the Hebrue Canon, as we hold at this day?
we can tell when, and by what meanes many Apocryphall
writings were added vnto them, Let them tell vs what hereticke or falſe harlot preferred the Hebrue and Greeke
text of the old and new Teſtament, with the good Fathers of the primitiue Church? We confeſſe we do it, we
can proue the Romaniſts do not; let them ſeeke the regiſter Eſra.2.62.
of Genealogies, as *Ezra* did, and ſee whether hold with the
firſt and beſt *Antiquitie.*

Let them except againſt this concluſion of our doctrine,
We hold(or we accompt)that a man is iuſtified by faith without the Rom.3.28.
workes of the Law. This we hold without gloſſe, without cauillation. Tell vs who contradicted this firſt? where, or how
this was once true, and is now falſe? Was Romes doctrine,
now is not? If they can ſhew him that firſt oppoſed this, they
will find an hereticke indeed.

Let them confeſſe, who put the commandement into the
Decalogue, that forbiddeth the worſhip of Images? What
hereticke? what corrupted times? what infamous place?
by what cunning? by what force, was this impoſed vpon
our Church? Not onely the firſt written Law of God, but alſo the firſt religion eſtabliſhed in oldeſt Rome, euen among
Infidels, condemned ſuch worſhippe of Images as now
Rome hath vſurped, doing thoſe things openly which the
heathens were aſhamed to do in ſecret; who tooke it for a Plutarch in
ſacriledge, to preſent heauenly things by earthly, &c. Numa.

37 That Angels ſhould not be worſhipped, becauſe
they are fellowes with the *Apoſtles and Prophets .* That Ieſus Reuel.22.9.
Chriſt *is the onely Mediator, Aduocate and Interceſſor:* who only 1.Iohn.2.1.
ſitteth

Colloſſ.3.1.
Heb.12.2.

1.Tim.2.5.

Ioh.16.
Eſai.63.3.
Heb.9.12.

ſitteth at the right hand of God, *making interceſſion for vs; who when we ſinne is our Aduocate with the Father : who as truly as there is but one God , ſo is there but one Mediator betwixt God and man, the man Ieſus Chriſt :* who hath promiſed, that what-ſoeuer we aske of the *Father in his name, ſhall be giuen vnto vs. Who hath trodden the wine-preſſe alone , and of all nations there was not one with him. Who hath entred into the Sanctum ſancto-rum, the holy of holieſt, by the tabernacle of his fleſh, and hath pur-chaſed eternal redemption for vs.* Did *Martin Luther, Iohn Huſſe,* or *Iohn Wickliffe* inſoiſt theſe ſentences into the Bible? or who was the firſt that by idle diſtinctions and vaine ſophiſticati-ons , ſought to make void the fruite and comfort of theſe Scriptures ?

38 Let them ſhew when the ſame new deuice of mini-ſtring the Communion in both kinds to the people, now v-ſed in our Churches: or the ſame commending of Scriptures to all nations in their owne languages : or that there are but two wayes for ſoules after their departure out of this life : or that all ſinnes are mortall, and without Gods mercie would condemne vs for euer : or that no pardons ſhould be ſold for remiſſion of ſinnes, by the Pope : or that it is better to marry then to burne. Whereunto *Bellarmine* giueth as flat contradiction as the diuell did vnto God, when he told the woman ſhe ſhould *not die,* though ſhe eat the forbidden fruit.

Bellar.de Mo-
nach.l.2.c.30

Vtrumque eſt malum & nubere & vri: imò peius eſt nubere, quicquid reclament aduerſarij: How ſoeuer both be naught, yet the worſe is to marry, whatſoeuer our aduerſaries talke. Where he maketh Saint *Paul* his aduerſary, or at leaſt woun-deth him through our ſides, and in both oppoſeth the Spirit of God. The Romaniſts would be aſhamed to rip vp the be-ginnings of all theſe doctrines, they are too old for their lear-ning; we can tell them when theſe began , and ſo can they if they liſt. We can diſcouer when the contrary to theſe crept into the Church, ſo ne at one time, ſome at another, by often and frequent acceſſes growing to a great heape: as if *Rome* were the chiefe receptacle of all hereſies.

39 New we will ſhew how *Rome* departed from the
faith,

faith, and hath hearkened to the spirit of error, and doctrines 1.Tim.4.1.
of diuels. Wherein we must not expect that a sudden destruction fell vpon them, as the fury of *Pilate* vpon the Galile-
ans, or the tower of *Siloah* that fell on the Iewes in *Ierusalem*; Luk.13.1.
but one after another, as theeues creepe in at a window to
steale, by diuers means, by diuers men, at sundry times, & after sundry maners; for the most part with deep silence, sometimes with more ado; at all times with sinne against God, and
shame to their owne faces.

40   For the first three hundred yeares after Christ, though
there were hot contentions about the obseruation of Easter,
betweene the Romanes and the Grecians; and *Victor* Bishop
of *Rome* tooke more vpon him then he caried away without
iust reproofe of his compeeres, who wrote vnto him as to
their fellow, not as their Iudge. Yet in all this time, and in all
this controuersie, not one word of commanding or control-
ling supremacie, no not so much as perking primacie, which Primacie.
hitherto was not onely not borne out of a presumptuous Supremacie.
pen, but not begotten in an idle braine. All Epistles written
from Saint *Cyprian* to *Cornelius* and *Stephanus* Bishops of
Rome, are full of familiaritie and brotherly kindnesse, without all swelling titles of superioritie or subiection to or from
either partie.

41   In the fourth age, in the great and first general Councell of *Nice*, order was taken with the Patriarks of *Rome*, A- Concil.Nicē.1
lexandria and *Antioch*, that they should be conformed one Can.6.
to another, and enioy their equall rights each in his owne Parilis mos.
Prouince : so farre was the world then, from so much as a
thought of supremacie. About the end of this century, or
the beginning of the next, there was some hammering in
Rome about Primacie, which full faine the Bishops of that sea
would haue claimed, and did ; and withall a certaine superioritie also in this, that Appeales might be made to the sea
of *Rome*. This affaire, *Zozimus, Celestine* and *Boniface*, three
Bishops of *Rome* in a ranke, canuassed with all their wit and
industry, yea and aduenture, perhaps losse of their credits,
with all posteritie. They sought the consent of the Councell

of *Carthage*, where were gathered two hundred and feuen-
teene Bifhops (among whom Saint *Auguftine* was one,) for
the approbation of their pretended claime. To induce them
the rather,they alledged and vrged a Canon of the Councell
of *Nice*,wherein this fhould be ordained : (obferue that no
Scripture was yet diftorted or abufed to this purpofe.) The
African Fathers, for time but fourefcore yeares after at the
moft,for calling Bifhops,for learning renowmed in their places, in number many, in integritie without exception, making fearch from all the Eafterne Patriarks, for the true and
perfect copies of this pretended and fophifticated Councell,
could find no fuch at home or abroad, in publicke libraries
or in priuate ftudies, but all was meere collufion and impofture. And therefore thofe Romane Prelates were fo farre
from obtaining their purpofe, that the learned Bifhops in
all probabilitie, of purpofe made a Canon, directly to preuent this prefumptuous pride, and to fmother this perillous
monfter in the birth. They made Canons quite oppofite to
the Popes requeft, taking from them not onely the practife
of Appeales, but the very titles of fuperioritie. *No man in A-
frica* might appeale *ad tranfmarinas partes, to the parts beyond
the fea*: which was in plaine termes,to *Rome*.No man fhould
Concil. Afric. be called, *Summus Pontifex, Vniuerfalis Epifcopus, aut aliquid
tale*, *Chiefe Prelate or Pope,or Vniuerfal Bifhop*,no by his leaue,
not the Bifhop of *Rome*.

    42 In this paffage,we obferue a proud and prefumptu-
ous claime, enforced by many infinuations, and fome falfe
fuggeftions; but refifted, and in a maner flaine, (but that
Popes haue nine liues like a cat, who though they die faft
in their perfons,yet they hold faft in their fucceffion.) It lay
in this fwoune till the dayes of *Leo* the Great,a Pope of more
then ordinary learning. and great boldnefle of fpirit. Vpon
competition which the Patriarke of *Conftantinople* pretended
for the honour of new *Rome*, he ftickled hard by his letters
and his agents, to procure that which his predeceffors had
fought, but could neuer find; and do what he could, the
Councel of *Chalcedon*,the greateft by many,of the foure firft,
and

and the laſt of theſe beſt, gaue *Conſtantinople, paria iura, equall* right *with old Rome* : yet the elder to go before, for reuerence of the Cities antiquitie , not for any words ſpoken by our Sauiour to Saint *Peter.* No otherwiſe then as the *Epheſine* and *Conſtantinople* Councell had concluded before. *Sedi veteris Romæ Patres meritò primatum dederunt, quòd illa Ciuitas alijs imperaret* : *The Fathers worthily gaue the primacie to the Chaire of old Rome, becauſe that Citie ruled ouer others.* No reaſon from Diuinitie, but from bare, or at moſt, courteous ciuilitie. So that hitherunto, though a certaine ſupremacie was aimed at by the Popes, yet could they neuer hit the marke of their deſigne. The rather hindred therein by the riualitie of *Conſtantinople,* who wooed the ſame ſtrumpet, and ſtayed *Romes* adulterous luſt. Somewhat ſhe got, *ratione Imperialis Ciuitatis, by reaſon of the Imperiall Citie,* but no more then her ſiſter, or brother if you will, the Sea and Patriarke of *Conſtantinople,* who was equalled in all rights with her. With what mind Pope *Leo* wrote that which followeth , was beſt knowne to himſelfe : but well I am aſſured, that in this generall he wrote well : *Superbum nimis eſt & immoderatum vltra fines proprios tendere, & Antiquitate calcata, alienum ius velle præripere, &c.* It is an ouer proud and inordinate conceit, to breake ouer preſcribed bounds, and deſpiſing *Antiquitie,* to wreſt anothers right. *And that one mans dignitie ſhould increaſe, to impugne the primacie of ſo many Metropolitans :* and to wage a troubleſome warre againſt peaceable prouinces , and the ancient holy Councell of Nice, and to diſſolue the decrees of venerable Fathers, and to bring forth the conſent of certaine Biſhops, whereunto a long ſucceſſion of time hath denied effect. Apply this to whom you will, I am ſure it taketh hold of the Biſhop of *Rome,* for his ambitious vſurpation.

Leo ep.53. ad Pulcheriam Auguſtam de ambitu Anaſtolij.

43 Some time after ſucceeded *Pelagius* and *Gregorie* the Great, in the ſea of old *Rome,* when *Iohn* a proud Prelate and a turbulent, ſate at *Conſtantinople.* This fellow, as it ſeemeth, not contented with an equalitie, ſet vp his ladders of pride, and began to ſcale the ſea of *Rome* for ſuperioritie. Thoſe Biſhops of *Rome,* who were not taken with the ſweete baite

of earthly honour, by all meanes withftood him, not onely in his owne claime, but alfo in themfelues, in their predecef-fors, and in as much as in them lay, for their fucceffors for e-

Ex Regiftro,
l.4.
Epift.30.32.
38.39. & alijs.
Lib. epift.

uer. Saint *Gregorie* is full of moft vehement inuectiues, to the Emperour *Mauricius*, the Empereffe, to *Iohn* himfelfe, to o-ther Bifhops, againft the very titles of fuperioritie. For him-felfe, *Remouete ab auribus meis, Remoue from my eares this proud title.While you attribute too much vnto me, you derogate too much from your felues.* For his predeceffors, *Nemo deceſſorum mea-rum, None of my anceſters haue vſurped ſuch a profane title.* For his fucceffors, *Ego ſidentèr dico, quiſquis ſe vniuerſalem Epiſco-pum appellat, vel appellari deſiderat, in elatione ſua Antichriſtum* ,, *præcurrit: I ſpeake it confidently, whoſoeuer ſhall call himſelfe, or de-* ,, *ſire to be called vniuerſall Biſhop, in his pride he forerunneth An-* ,, *tichriſt.* Here is no illufion, no tergiuerfation, no diftinction of old ftampe, or new ftraine, that can help in this cafe. Thefe withftood it in others, renounced in themfelues, would not take it when it was offered, would preuent it in their fuccef-fion. And therefore vntill fixe hundred yeares after Chrift, though the leauen was layd, yet was not the batch made; the Church was not yet infected with the poifon of fupremacie: which afterward became the vtter bane therof. All this while fee, there was hewing and hammering about the title of fu-premacie and vniuerfalitie, but the intended Idoll was neuer perfected nor placed in open view to be adored, as fince it hath bene.

44   Not long after, this myfterie of iniquitie, in the dayes of *Phocas* the Emperor, that had murthered his Maifter *Man-ricius*, and vfurped his crowne, began to worke more ftrong-

Ioan.de Parif.
de poteſt.reg.
& Papal.c.13.

ly. For, *Bonifacius obtinuit à Phoca, vt R. Eccleſia eſſet caput omnium Eccleſiaru̅: Boniface* (Bifhop of Rome) *obtained of Pho-cas, that the Church of Rome ſhould be the head of all Churches.* The feed that was fowne before, and fprouted a little, as it ſhewed the leaft life, was euer troden downe, though not throughly weeded vp, by the renowmed Fathers in their fe-uerall times. But that wherewith the fwelling fea, which

Iud.

long hath fomed out her owne ſhame, had in her pride con-ceiued

ceiued in the hearts of ſome of her Biſhops, came now to the
trauell in the dayes of *Pelagius* and *Gregory*,was brought forth
into light in the dayes of that *Boniface*,grew vp and gathered
ſtrength in ſucceeding ages vnder *Gregory* the ſecond, *Con-*
ſtantine and *Zachary*, increaſing ſomewhat more and more in
euery Popes time,till *Sylueſter* the ſecond gaue full poſſeſſion,
by tradition of himſelfe body and ſoule to the diuell; then the
Pagiant began to be playd openly vpon the ſtage and Theater of the world, by *Gregory* the 7, who ſet it forth, not onely as a growne man, but as an ouergrowne monſter: and
ſtrengthened it with curſings, excommunications, interdi-
ctions, abſolution of ſubiects from dutifull obedience, expo-
ſing the Empire to rapine and deſolation. Which times conſidered or obſerued not, how the Pope like *Iulius Cæſar*, en-   Plut.in Cæſa-
terchangeably conquered the Emperours with the Romane   re.
weapons and ſouldiers, and won the Romans by the gold
and ſpoyle of the Empire. Finally, *Innocent* the third furniſhed
it, not onely with temporall armies againſt the Emperour *O-*
tho, but with two Prieſtly armies of infernall locuſts, the Dominicans and Franciſcans, who haue euer ſince ſupported the
Church of Lateran, as *Innocentius* dreamed. Theſe being almoſt rotten, and through their ambitious hypocriſie, neare
their ruine, the Ieſuites with their ſcience *falſely ſo called*, their
policies in States, inſinuating into Courts, their currying fauour with Princes(which *Claudius Eſpencæus* miſliketh vtter-   In 2.Tim. 2.
ly) their lying on all aduantages, their equiuocations and
mentall reſeruations, haue ingroſſed the opinion of the blind
deceiued world,to be as learned as the Scribes;and the Capuchins for ſeeming holineſſe, like Phariſes among the Iewes.
Theſe are Antichriſts hands and feete, the breath of his no-
ſthrils, and the life of his ſoule. The rooting out of theſe, will
be the confuſion of their grand Maiſter the Pope & his kingdome for euer. Finally, as the Schoolemen grew, ſo grew the
Popes errors: as the Canoniſts multiplied,ſo the Popes honour
and titles increaſed.He was come from Biſhop to Archbiſhop
& from Archbiſhop to Patriarke before:but to be *Papa* alone,
Summus Pontifex, Pontifex maximus, Optimus Maximus, San-
            Ff 3   *ctiſſimus,*

ctiſſimus, diuinum numen , Dominus Deus noſter. Pope alone, high Prieſt, chiefe Biſhop, greateſt and beſt, moſt holy, our Lord God; theſe titles came in by the ambition and flatterie of the Popes clawbacks, who depended on him, abhorrent from all *Antiquitie*, which in the firſt and beſt ages of the Church neuer knew them. Farther *Antiquitie* perhaps they may find for ſome of theſe among the Iewes and Gentiles, but neuer among the Chriſtians. And howſoeuer, *nomen Deorum*, the name of Gods (in the plurall number) was giuen to Angels and Saints of God; yet the name of God was neuer

Theodor.hiſt.
Eccleſi. l.5.c.
11. giuen to man or Angell, but to the bleſſed Trinitie properly and directly, metaphorically to the diuell, vſurpedly to the Biſhop of Rome alone. Herein any indifferent reader may find a beginning, a ſtation, a progreſſe, and proceeding of this greateſt myſterie of impietie, with all theſe Ieſuites circumſtances, reaſonably and ſufficiently deciphered and deſcribed.

Daniel 3. 45 The next great *Idol of abhomination*, bigger then *Nebuchadnezzers* image that was ſet vp to be worſhipped in the valley of Dura; or the great Coloſſus at the entrance of Rhodes hauen, is *Tranſſubſtantiation*, which was knowne neither by nature nor name in the primitiue times of the Church: no Father teaching it, no Councell confirming it, no Hiſtory recording it; but certaine emphaticall and patheticall, ſome metaphoricall and hyperbolicall ſpeeches of the Ancients were firſt deliuered by them, to moue affection and deuotion in the Communicants: which afterward through ignorance of times, were drawne into a literall and more groſſe ſence, and in time more gathered then was euer ſcattered, more ſuppoſed then was euer meant. Afterward it grew into queſtion, then into ſtrong oppoſition, and became a controuerſie; which will aske no better confutation, then to find the truth of a miracle; therefore I would craue in this controuerſie but one inſtance or exception in all the Scriptures or any approued author : *What miracle was euer wrought, whereby the ſenſes were not conuinced of the truth thereof? as when water was turned to wine, it diſiſted to be what it was,* and appeared *in colour, taſte, ſmell,* and comfort to be wine, and no *water.* So of others, which

which is not in this, nor euer was, nor will be found. *Berenga-rius* a learned man, and in all likelihood others with him against it: the Schoolemen and Friars difputed for it: the Councell of Lateran concluded it: Pope *Innocent* confirmed it: many a good Chriftian was burnt for it; and fo this myfterie of iniquitie was fulfilled.

46 This baftard as the former, was long begetting in obfcuritie; as the night was lengthened when *Iupiter* begat Ouid. *Hercules*; but it lay many yeares fuppreffed in the wombe before it came to the birth; then kept fecret, as *Saturns* fonnes in the mount Ida, till opportunitie came to make it knowne that the Councell receiued it into the Church, that the Pope admitted it, as an article of his doftrine. It was fwadled in the clouts of Schoolemens diftinftions and fophiftrie, it was clothed in the habite of fuperftitious deuotion, fed with the braines of idle imagination, protefted with the power of Church cenfures, graced with Papall Decrees and authoritie, fet vp in the Temple to be adored for an Idoll, and finally by the inftigation of the importunate and potent Clergie, defended by the materiall fword of Imperiall maieftie. Thefe two Idols, the Supremacie and Tranffubftantiation, vnder pretence of Eclefiafticall power, and lowly deuotion, haue exhaufted more bloud then all the other articles of the Romane Synagogue, more for qualitie, more for quantitie.

47 For the Supremacie Kings and Emperours haue bene excommunicated and depofed, their armies deftroyed their lands expofed to rapine and ruine, their perfons murthered, their pofteritie rooted out, their very foules (as farre as the Popes *brutum fulmen* could reach) by cenfures deuoted and accurfed as blacke as pitch, to euerlafting damnation. For other men of all ages and fexes, learned and vnlearned, men and boyes, women and girles, Cleargie and Laitie, the fuperior reuerend Prelates, the inferior painefull Minifters, haue bene confumed with the cruell torment of fire, and bene burnt vnto afhes, their bodies after death digged vp, and their bones burnt in the ftreets. *Alcides* ftrength was exercifed in taming monfters, thefe monfters are occupied in murthering men.

Acts and Monuments, all former ftories. Cranmer. Ridley. Latimer,&c.

Ff 4

Pſal.137.9.   men. Bleſſed ſhall he be that ſhall ſerue this child of *Babylon* alſo as its Proctors haue ſerued vs, yea happie ſhall he be that taketh this baſtard brood while it is yong, and daſheth its head againſt the ſtones:ſo ſhall it not need to be brought into after queſtion.

     48   Do we not know, that Saint *Paule* warned the Co-
Col.2.18.   loſſians, *Not to be deceiued through humilitie in worſhipping of Angels?* This afterward crept into the Church, brake into an
De Hæreſ.   open hereſie, cenſured by *Epiphanius* with the place where it began, though he doubt of the Author: Afterward put by
Ad Quodvult   Saint *Auguſtine* into his Catalogue of hereſies, and noted for
deum.hær.39.   no other error but *Cultus Angelorum*, *the worſhip of Angels*.
Hæreſ. 38.   And *Prateolus*,no flatterer of vs, chargeth them with nothing but, *cum adoratione Angelorum,vnde Angelici dicti*, the *adora-*
Angeliſts.   *tion of Angels*, *whence they were called Angeliſts*. Theſe being long buried after Saint *Paules* time,by the ſpace of about 200 yeares after our Sauiour Chriſts incarnation, reuiued vnder *Seuerus* the Emperour and *Victor* then Biſhop of Rome ; this is now Catholicke Romane doctrine, good and ſound, that Angels may be adored and worſhipped. It was an hereſie in the primitiue Church, it is none now at Rome; how can theſe new pretended Catholickes make that a verity by their vſage, which old Chriſtianity hath accompted an hereſie, with vt-moſt deteſtation ?

     49   What a little Babe was our Sauiours Maſſe (if he euer had any, as he neuer had) when it was no longer then is ſet down by the Euangeliſts and Apoſtles, with the bare words of inſtitution ? how little growne, when Saint *Peter* added but the Lords prayer?Suppoſe Saint *Iames* added ſomewhat, Saint *Baſill* a little, *Chryſoſtome* not nothing, yet theſe are
De inuentio-   now confeſſed counterfeits.But take *Polydor Virgils* collecti-
ne rerum, l. 5.   on of all the ſcraps, and patches of the Maſſe, and ſee what
GII.   a huge Maſſe, of ſo little a mite, is made. *Celeſtine* brought the *Introit*; *Damaſus* or *Pontianus*, the Prieſts confeſſion;*Gre-gorie* the Antiphona, and the *Kyrie*, with other accidents; *Teleſporus*, *Glory be to God on high*; *Gelaſius* the concluſions of the prayers ; *Saint Hierome the Epiſtle and Goſpell*; others other

other peeces and additaments. In proceſſe of time it grew
to be a huge monſter, ſo degenerating from *Ambroſe* , from
Gregorie, from all antecedent times & formes,that the Councell of Trent deemed it to be out of all order. *Pius Quintus*
turned the inſide thereof outward,and pruned and pernd it,
waſht it, ſwept it, like the maw of a venimous beaſt, full of
all filthy and poyſonous infection. And after all reformation, is left as deformed and vnlike the firſt ſimplicitie, as a
proud perking and vaine ſtrumpets apparell and geſture is
vnlike an ancient matrous modeſt and comely attire.

50   What was the hereſie of the *Collyridiani* ? Was it not
for adoring the bleſſed mother of God, the virgine *Marie*
aboue a creature ? for attributing more vnto her then God,
or true religion would allow?And could they giue her more
then the Romaniſts do at this day ? They make her Queene
of heauen, aſſumpted into the nature of the Godhead, as if
ſhe had authoritie ouer her Son, & he at her commandemēt.
She is made the mother of mercy,when Chriſt reſerueth on- _{D.Anton.hiſt.}
ly iuſtice for himſelfe; ſhe treadeth vpon the ſerpents head; part.3.Tit.
ſhe giues the booke , Chriſt giues the Lacons which are the ²³ c.3.
beads; as if ſhe taught men , Chriſt but children ; ſhe gaue Coſteri En-
ſtrong meate, Chriſt but milke: as in the fronts of diuerſe chirid.
bookes is pictured. How ſay you if ſhe be preferred by *Gre-*
gorius Valentia before her Sonne, and placed with two per- Greg. de Val.
ſons of the Trinitie, as if ſhe were the third, and the holy Laus Deo, &
Ghoſt quite left forth? This is it often , *Laus Deo Patri, nec* riæ,Deo:item
non beatiſſima virgini Maria, & eius filio Ieſu Chriſto, Praiſe to I.C. honor &
God the Father, and alſo to the moſt bleſſed virgine Marie, and to gloria:ad finē
her Sonne Ieſus Chriſt. Firſt God the Father, then(ſhall I ſay) lib.de Epiſ.&
God the mother(what intend they elſe?)the bleſſed mother, rentia.
and laſt her Sonne. The holy Ghoſt either wilfully caſt out, Laus Deo &
or careleſly neglected, or ill forgotten , or worſe forſaken, Beatiſſ. virg.
for he forſaketh them that forſake him. I know not how they Mariæ,ad fi-
can excuſe theſe things , they cannot exenuate them , they Indulgentijs
may not deny them. I can find no oddes betweene the old Sometimes the
hereticks & theſe, but that theſe are manifoldly more groſſe Virgin is after
and blaſphemous then euer they were. her Sonne.

51 Chaz-

51　*Chazinzary,* as in their owne tongue, *Staurolatræ* in the Greek, a branch from the ſtemme of the Armenian heretiques, had their name according to their doctrine, for yeelding diuine worſhip to the Croſſe of Chriſt, were anciently condemned heretickes. Who exhibite this honour more directly, more groſly, more palpably, more idolatrouſly then the Romaniſts do at this day? who not onely practiſe by the ignorant people, but teach and defend in open ſchooles, the worſhip of the Croſſe with that very *latriâ* or worſhip which themſelues confeſſe, belongs ſoly to the bleſſed Deitie, and the perſons in Trinitie; & not onely that very Croſſe wheron Chriſt died, but euery Croſſe of whatſoeuer matter, made vnto the ſimilitude thereof. For denying whereof one *Giles a Spaniard was burnt at Siuile* by the *Inquiſition, after he was condemned for an hereticke ſince the Councell of Trent, ob latriæ cultum Cruci denegatum : For that he denied diuine Worſhip to the Croſſe.*

52　The firſt forbidding of mariage in holy orders began long after the Apoſtles times, who were maried themſelues, for the moſt part. The prohibition entred not in all at once, but the prime motion was, that thoſe which were maried, ſhould not be receiued : then, that thoſe which were actually maried, ſhould be ſeparated from their wiues. This in the beginning touched but Biſhops & Prieſts, afterward Deacons, then Subdeacons and all. At firſt it was rather perſwaded, as of congruitie, afterward impoſed as of neceſſitie. Some countries were long freed, after others were enthralled; ſome ſtood out, and would not yeeld. Some Popes ſaw reaſon to take wiues from the Prieſts, others ſaw greater reaſons to reſtore them. It was but late ſince it came to this, that it were better for a Prieſt to hold many whores, then one lawfull wife : That a man who hath maried a widow, or ſucceſſiuely two wiues, is thereby made irregular, and can not be made Prieſt without a Papall diſpenſation ; and yet if a man after the deceaſſe of his lawfull wife, keepe queans, be they fewer or more, he may be made Prieſt without diſpenſation ; whereupon the Gloſſe confeſſeth, that whoredome hath

greater

Tho. Aquin.
p. 3. quæſt. 25.
art. 2.
Magiſtralem
Cononicum
Ægidium.
Velloſel. aduert. theolog. Schol. in
5. Tom. Hieron. ad 10.
quæſt.
Suarez 3. part
Tho. tom. 1.
diſp. 54. ſect. 4.
& 56. 2.

Autor. comment. in Epiſt.
ad Rom. nomine Ambro.

Pius 2.

Pigghius.

Gloſſ.

greater priuiledge,then honeſt mariage. *Polidore Virgil* out De inuentio-
of *Antiquitie* aſſigneth the times,and the Popes names,when ne rerum.
and by whom this thraldome was brought into the Church;
to whom I referre the reader.There ſeemeth by *Socrates,* y Socrates.
a motion was made hereof in the firſt Councel of Nice,& almoſt accorded againſt this mariage: but that *Paphnutius* by
alledging Scriptures,brought the Fathers into a right mind.
After this, *Siricius* was the firſt that impoſed ſingle life, and
that was on the brinke of 400 yeares after Chriſt. Which a
Romane eare ſhould not endure to heare, as Saint *Hierome* Ad Pamma-
ſpeaketh: yet did it remaine indifferent many yeares after chium.
that, vntill after a thouſand yeares, *Gregory* the ſeuenth a
moſt lecherous Pope, if hiſtorians giue him his due, partly
by ſeueritie of Canons, and partly by tyranny in perſecutions,enforced it, to the ouerthrow of chaſtitie and common honeſtie.

53   The ſecond doctrine of diuels, which is *abſtinence
from meates,which God hath created to be receiued wtth thankeſgi-
uing*,was not in the Apoſtles time,but by Saint *Paul* prophe-
ſied that it ſhould be: *When the bridegroome was taken away,* Mat.9.15.
the diſciples faſted in thoſe dayes, and out of all doubt the
Saints continued in faſting and prayers day and night,
vſed it as an eſpeciall furtherance of deuotion. Howbeit this
continued long without choiſe of meates, preciſe ſet daies
or times, diſtinction of fleſh or fiſh, or any apiſh imitation
of ſo holy an exerciſe, by ſupply of all delicate iunkets, in
ſtead of more groſſe diet. We can tell that *Montanus* was Prateolus ex
the firſt that preſcribed lawes for time and maner of faſting, Euſeb. &
and impoſed that with command, which before was volun- Niceph.
tary and permitted to publicke or priuate occaſions, as the
Church in generall, or the Saints in their particular were moued. *Manicheus* followed, and not onely manned out *Montanus* deuice,but added of his owne, and attributed vncleane-
neſſe to ſome meates in compariſon of other, and their Illu- Aug. ad quod
minates might eate what their nouices might not, or the vultdeum.
nouices what the Elders might not. That which heretickes
brought in, that ſuperſtition apprehended, policie maintained,

ned, tyranny inforced, and so it standeth at this day. The Romanists themselues know the times, the places, the persons, the opposites, withall other their circumstances in these things, and yet defend the same heresies in their words, and like false tradesmen, offer the same cloth, closer and hotter prest, with a faire glosse, but the same in substance, and impose their obseruations vpon mens consciences on the perill of their soules.

54 Our Sauiour Christ left two Sacraments in his Church to be vsed according to his ordinance vntill he returne vnto iudgement. These we haue held, and reuerently obserue. The Romanists haue found fiue more, how long did they seeke them? where did they find them? A thousand yeares was this Cockatrice in hatching, came out of hell iust at the loosing of Satan. For *Bellarmine* confesseth that the precise number of seuen Sacraments hath no further *Antiquitie* then 600 yeares. The first finder was *Peter Lombard*, his fellowes the Schoolemen, the foster fathers. This was neuer known to the ancient Fathers, neuer heard of in the primitiue Church, neuer thought of by the Spirit of God in the holy Scriptures. *Bellarmine* loues to be opposite to the Doctors of reformed Churches; they haue confined *Antiquitie* to the first sixe hundred yeares, and *Bellarmine* will proue by the last sixe hundred, which is old enough for his new religion.

De Sacramé-tis.l.2.c.25.

55 Let all our Romanists shew when Images were so much as spoken of before the first Councell of *Nice*, but in vtter condemnation and detestation of them? So writes *Clemens* if he be the man. So *Irenæus* writing of the *Carpocratians* and *Gnosticks*. So *Origen* against *Celsus*, who obiected that the *Christians* had then neither *Images*, nor *Altars*, nor *Temples*. Which *Origen* is so farre from denying to be true, that he saith plainly, *It cannot be possible, that any man should worship God and an image.* Not long after that Councell of *Nice*, the *Elibertine* Councell prouided precisely by a Canon, *Placuit picturas in Ecclesia esse non debere, ne quod colitur & adoratur in parietibus depingatur*: Our pleasure is, that there be no pictures in the Church, lest that which is worshipped and adored, should be painted

Lib.5. ad frat. dom. Aduers. hæref. l.1. c.24.lib.4.

painted vpon walls. It is ſtrange to conſider how *Bellarmine* Bellar.
firſt extenuateth the credit of this authoritie by the paucitie
of the Biſhops, and the obſcureneſſe of the place; then would
ſhift off their meaning, as if it were intended onely for pictures painted, and not for images grauen, (where he forgets
his ten commandements:) nay, his wit can fetch out an argu- *Gods comman-*
ment from thence to proue the antiquitie of Images; for if *dement greater*
then a Councel,
they had not bin before, they had not bin forbidden then. *forbids grauen*
Yea and for the authority of them, for a fault was reformed, *images.*
that they ſhould not be ſo baſely painted, but fairely carued.
This is the ſubſtance of *Bellarmines* diſpute, to illude this ancient Councell. Is it not more likely, that the Chriſtians before that time, in the dayes of perſecution had no images, becauſe they had no Churches? And that Churches then beginning to be built, ſome Chriſtians for ornament, others not ſo
well weaned from their heatheniſh faſhions, for imitation,
began to adorne them, as they thought, with ſuch deuices?
and that therefore the Fathers of the Councell made voide
what was either executed or intended, and ſought to preuent
what might follow thereof. Which is fortified by *Polydore* De inuēctione
Virgil, vpon the authoritie of Saint *Ierome,* who ſaith, that rerū.l.6.c.13.
Simulacra omnes fere veteres ſancti Patres damnarunt, ob metum
idolatriæ: Almoſt all the ancient holy Fathers haue condemned i-
mages, for feare of idolatrie. To deſcend vnto particular teſtimonies of the Fathers in following ages, were infinite and
tedious, and ſufficiently deliuered by thoſe that write of this
common place. We know how vehemently this queſtion
was ventilated from Eaſt to Weſt, in the more corrupted
times of the Church, not onely by ſcholaſticall arguments,
but by Imperiall violence, ſetting vp and plucking downe,
maintained and oppoſed, vntill in that partiall and vnlearned
ſecond Councell of *Nice* it was confirmed. Where it was diſputed by ridiculous reaſons, fearfull abuſe of Scriptures, abſurd and falſe forgeries, groſſe flatteries of the ſuperſtitious
Empereſſe, fained miracles, and finally by the ſtrong hand
of earthly power, againſt the diſtrict commandement of Almightie God, the perpetual current of Canonical Scriptures,
the

the writings and practife of the ancient Fathers. This Councell was repealed and made void, and pronounced to be no

By Carolus
Magnus.

Councell, in another Councell of *Frankford* . Many good
Chriftians fince haue fpent their bloud in oppofing this idolatry; and yet the Romanifts defend it as a chiefe article of
their corrupt faith.

56 Indulgences and pardons, for finnes paft, prefent, and
to come, were not in the primitiue Church, the ancient Councels were neuer of counfell with them, the old Fathers neuer fauoured, nor fo much as fauoured them. When inuaded
they the Church? I may fay, when the Popes began to be in-
folently proud, and bafely couetous. But a Catholicke Romane would rather heare a Catholicks opinion or two : *Po-*

De inuêtione
rerum, l. 8. c. 1.

lydore Virgil tels you , that *Cœperunt indulgentiæ poftquam ad*
Purgatorij cruciatus aliquandiu trepidatum eft: Indulgences began
after the paines of Purgatory were a while trembled at. But Bifhop *Fifher* the Popes martyr, and therefore true to his triple
crowne and dignitie, that fhould haue bene a Cardinall if his
hat had not wanted a head , and therefore well deferuing of
his maifter, anfwers the queftion when Indulgences began,

Fifher.

thus: *Ego refpondeo, non fatis certò conftare, à quo primùm Indul-*
gentiæ tradi cœperint. Apud prifcos, vel nulla, vel certè rariffima
fiebat mentio de Purgatorio. Quandiu nulla effet cura de Purgato-
rio, nemo quæfiuit indulgentias, nam ex illo pendet omnis indulgen-
tiarum æftimatio, fi tollas Purgatorium, quorfum indulgentijs o-
,, *pus erit? I anfwer* (faith he) *that it is not very certaine from whom*
,, *pardons tooke their beginning. Among the ancients there was either*
,, *none, or verily very litle mention of Purgatory. As long as there was*
,, *no care of Purgatory, no man fought for pardons , for vpon it de-*
,, *pends all the eftimation of pardons. If you take away Purgatorie,*
,, *what need of indulgences?* Here we find a double confeffion,
that both Purgatorie and pardons were of late inuention.

Plato.
Virgil.

Or if they will alledge their Doctors, *Plato* and *Virgil* for
the antiquitie of the one, or fome counterfeit decretall Epiftles of Popes for the others authoritie ; yet it was long ere
either crept into the Church , or were feared or beleeued of
Chriftians.

57 Com-

57 Communicating vnder one kind, and depriuing the people of halfe the Communion, or cofening them with an vnconſecrated cup, to bleare their eyes & ſtop their mouthes, was neuer dreamed of in the primitiue times of the Church. *Stephen Gardiner* cannot tell when it began, but he faith, that *Some thinke it ſprang onely from a certaine ſuperſtition and ſimpli- citie of the people.* The *Trent* traitors confeſſe it was inſtitu-ted and practiſed by our Sauiour Chriſt in both kinds. It continued ſo in the Primitiue Church; Saint *Cyprians* time allowed the Sacrament according to that firſt inſtitution. And before him *Iuſtinus Martyr.* All the Fathers with one conſent follow in the ſame mind. No man for a thouſand yeares gainſtood or gainſaid it. Firſt, it was neglected by the ignorant people, then filcht away by the Prieſts, then murmured at againe by thoſe that loſt it, then defended it was by thoſe that ſtole it, and the ſtronger part bare away the bucklers in theſe latter baſe conuenticles, and now it is fenced with fire and ſword. In which one caſe, ſee the ſtrange out-facing impudencie of a ſeruant to the man of ſinne and father of lyes, he ſerues two maiſters who boldly auoucheth that *Nemo fuit vnquam qui modo vel ſacras literas ſerio legerit, vel antiquitatis Eccleſiaſticæ aliquam notitiam habuerit, vel qui ſaltem ſobrio & quieto animo res ſacras tractauerit, qui vtriuſque ſpeciei vſum magnopere neceſſarium eſſe iudicarit:* There was neuer any ,, that had ſerioully read the Scriptures, or had any vnderſtan- ,, ding of Eccleſiaſticall antiquitie, or euer handled holy things ,, with a ſober and quiet mind, which euer iudged the vſe of ,, both kinds greatly neceſſary. An audacious ſpeech, not onely ,, againſt al antiquitie, but in truth moſt impudently auouched without authoritie, ſap or ſenſe.

58 Auricular confeſſion found ſome hole to creepe into the Church. It was ſoone abuſed, then diſclaimed and cried downe, then receiued and admitted againe: but was long practiſed as voluntary for good counſell, not coactiue to re-ceiue penance. Vſed for comfort to the weake, not to tyran-nize ouer mens conſciences: for ſome, whoſe ſpeciall caſe may require it, not for all, that need none of it.

59 What

In his diuels ſophiſt.

Socol. Annot. Cenſu.Orient.

Socra.l.5.c.19.
Soz.5.l.7.c.16
Niceph.l.12.
c.28.
Chryſoſt.de
Lazar.hom.4.
De Pœnitẽtia,
hom.5.& alijs
homilijs.

59   What shall I speake of praying to Saints, not onely as Mediators or intercessors, but as helpers and sauiours: not by their prayers to God, but their owne merits: not as Gods seruants, but his fellowes, nay perhaps his betters? If we consider their might and miracles, their Churches and Chappels, their oratories and offerings, the dayes feasts, and eues fasts dedicated to the Saints, you shall easily find many more then were euer consecrated to God the Father, Sonne and holy Ghost. Insomuch that there is great probabilitie, that if the Church of *Rome* had proceeded without stop, heauen would haue bene turned from the *Monarchicall* gouernment of one onely true God, into an *Aristocraticall* commonwealth of the Angels and great Saints, or into a democraticall confusion of all the Popes canonized creatures, beginning at *Nereus* the father of the gods in the Poets register, and ending at *Nereus* the last I know in the Romane Kalender.

60   Pilgrimages to these Saints and their shrines. As if God were not as neare them at home, as in a farre countrey. Or as if a Saint can heare vs better in *Spaine* or *Italy*, then in *Scotland* and *England*. Or as if nothing, but farre fetcht and deare bought, would serue their tooth, that is, of the new cut and last inuention. Let our aduersaries shew their beginning; we can tell when they were not so much as thought of in the Church of God. Will they set vs to seeke their Masses priuate and publicke, high and low, for rich and poore, for sicke and found, for liuing and dead, for kings and paisants, for reasonable creatures, and for hens, and for swine? Such penies such *Pater nosters*, such oblations such priests, such sacrifices such incense, as the diuell said to two yong Friers, when like slouens they mumbled their Mattens in their bed. And yet these be the onely *Antiques of the world*. We need not seeke them, let them find them themselues who would haue them; we know they are not in Gods treasurie, where is all good, new and old.

61   I could instance in many circumstances that concerne these principals. The equalling of the Apocryphals with the

Canonicall

Canonicall Scriptures.Their denying the vulgar to haue them in their owne tongues. Their impudent and sacrilegious deniall of the Scriptures to be sufficient vnto mans saluation. Their keeping their prayers darkned like *Ceres* seruice,or *Numa his* secrets,that the ignorant and vntaught people may not vnderstand their religion nor the reason of it. That the host must be reserued, caried about, sometimes on foote, sometimes on horsebacke, vpon a white palfrey,euer with a Canopie to keepe it from raines wet, or Sunnes burning. That it be adored with gaze of the eye, beating the breast, bowing the knee, prostrating the body, and all signes of reuerend and diuine worship that can be giuen by a mortall man,yea to the true and euerliuing God. That there is power in holy water, consecrated beades,waxe, candles, medals, Agnus deis, amulets, halowed crosses, palmes, and such like bables and childrens lacons, like the heathens holies: As *holy walls, holy virgins, holy bookes, holy lampe, holy relickes, holy band, holy dragon, holy race, holy banner, holy wars, holy dayes, holy fire, holy monuments, holy candle, holy ceremonies, holy cornell trees, and other holy things, holy games, euen to the holy geese*,the best keepers of their gods. These and more had the heathen, some of these and many more haue the Romanists, either from them, or of a newer erection: to pardon sinnes, to defend from enemies, to saue from shipwracke, to cast out diuels, to do almost any miracles. That some dayes are better then other, not onely for the vse, because they therein serue God,but for the very dedication though not instituted by God. That the Church should haue her fiue commandements, as duly and better obserued then God his ten. That women may baptize children, and Priests bells (a seruice good enough for Baals Priests.) That God the Father, and the holy Ghost may be pictured, and their pictures worshipped.That subiects might kill kings for heresie, if the greatest hereticke in the world, or Antichrist himselfe pronounce him so to be.That the Pope should forsake his Christian name, when he is first chosen, as if *ipso facto* he renounced his Christianity. Contrary to Saint *Peter,* who had a surname giuen him as added to his other, not his

Plutarch.

Plutarch.

Gg   pro-

proper name changed for pride and fingularitie , rather attributed by his Maifter,then vfurped by himfelfe.That the Pope hath both fwords, and power to depofe Princes. That his fupremacie admitteth no bounds nor limitatiō,but paffeth from foule to body, from goodneffe to goods , from fpirituall to temporall, from excommunications to depofitions and exterminations, and reacheth from earth to Purgatory , and from heauen to hell,and there I leaue him.

62 It would be tedious and troublefome to remember all. Thefe are more then a good many. Sufficient to fhew mine intention proued, and their requeft fatisfied, that of all things the Romanifts hold againft that truth which is maintained by the reformed Churches , we can proue thefe circumftances they required, in each of their particulars, although with reafonable and vnpartiall men we might eafily take a more expedite courfe.

63 For why may not all their queftions be thus anfwered? Whatfoeuer is not cōtained in the Scriptures, nor was practifed in the primitiue Church within 600 yeares, may be fufpected, examined, and if caufe fhall appeare, caft out of the
Hierome.
Church. For fuch things *Eadem facilitate reijciuntur qua admittuntur: Are with as great facility reiected, as admitted.* New
Iudg.16.12.
cords could not bind *Sampfon* wher he vfed his ftrength, thefe new deuices cannot bind the confcience of a conftant Chriftian , that knoweth the truth, and is contented to be ruled by it.

64 *Ezra* was a wife Scribe, and experienced in the law of *Mofes*, and endued with the fpirit of prophecie. A queftion
Ezra 2, 61.
grew, whether the fonnes of *Barzillai* were of the race of the Priefts? Did they bid *Ezra* proue when they came in ? or did *Ezra* bid them proue their lawfull defcent, or they fhould be thruft out, and fo were, and forbidden to eate of the moft ho-things? Our cafe is the fame. The Romanifts pretend and auouch all thefe doctrines to defcend from the Apoftles and primitiue Fathers.We deny it: who fhall proue ? Shall we difproue their pedegree? or fhall they proue their owne ? Becaufe we cannot deduce them from the line of Apoftolicall
doctrine,

doctrine, therefore we refuse them. Let them not tell vs now of their rotten worm-eaten chaire, or succeffion of Popes fo often interrupted: that is not our queftion. Let them proue their doctrine primitiue and moft ancient, we are willing to embrace it with hand and heart: otherwife we fay of as much as wherein they diffent from vs, that we know when none of it was in the Church of God, that all of it began after the writing of the new Teftament; that moft particulars of it hath both time, place, and perfons named, when, where, and by whom, they were brought in. That they came in, not like a true man by the doore, but like a theefe that Iohn 10. creepes in at the window, or breakes through a hole in the wall, to rob and to fteale the hearts and confciences of men, not at once, as a tempeft, but by little and little, like a foking raine, which wets to the skinne before it beates on the face.

65 Rome hath not bene fwallowed vp at once, in a few dayes with water, as the old world was drowned; nor confu- Gen. 7. med in an houre, as Sodome and Gomorrha was with fire and Gen. 19. brimftone: but at diuers times, and in fundry places, many crept in, men of corrupt minds, *and deftitute of truth; which thought that gaine was godlineffe. Who as Iannes and Iambres* 1. Tim.6.5. *withftood Mofes, fo thofe alfo refifted the truth, men of corrupt* 2.Tim.3.8.9. *minds, reprobate concerning the faith.* But fuch fhall preuaile no *longer, for their madneffe fhall be euident vnto all men, as theirs alfo was.* They foked into the hearts of the fimple, and diftilled their poyfon with fundry *deuices,* and then deliuered it to kings in the whores golden cup.

66 To conclude, that there is *infignis mutatio* in the Church of Rome, all good Chriftians may eafily fee, and lament ouer her as our Sauiour did ouer Ierufalem, that would Luke 19. not know the day of her vifitation. By what degrees fhe hath fallen thereinto, it is curiofitie to be ouer inquifitiue. It behoues her felfe to call for helpe in time of God and of good men. We will not ceaffe to pray that fhe may turne vnto the Lord, and he might heale her. For as yet though we haue cured her, fhe is not healed.

67　Rome was a Church,but fhe is a Court. She had good Bifhops that became martyrs for the teftimonie of the Gofpell; fhe hath wicked tyrants that make martyrs, and difpoile the Church of her fpirituall Patrimonie. She was a fpring of religion and vertues,fhe is a finke of fuperftition and iniquity. She was a worthy mother that nurfed children at the teats of the old and new Teftament. She is a cruell ftepmother that feeketh to poyfon and murther the deare children of her pretended husband. Cardinall *Bellarmine* confeffeth a time when Popes degenerated from their predeceffors integritie and in-

Bel. Chrono-log. circa an-num 1029. nocencie. *His temporibus, in quibus Romani Pontifices,&c. In thefe times wherein the Romane Bifhops began to degenerate from the pietie of their Anceftors, the Princes of this world flourifhed in holineffe.* So that howfoeuer or whatfoeuer they were at firft, they may be without abfurdity and are without all queftion moft erronious and wicked now. If *Peter* the teacher of the Iewes, and *Paule* the teacher of the Gentiles were their founders; yet their degenerated followers, as *Peters,*denying their Maifter, as *Saules,*perfecuting and making hauocke of the Congregation of God, are confounders of all religion and piety. If yet any aske how this might come to paffe, let them fearch the monuments of oldeft Rome, and they may behold the perfect picture of her vnhappie eftate,as in an embleme fet out to life.

68　*Romulus* iffued but from a fmall beginning, yet increafed to great power and ftrength, to the fupport of his fubiects, and the terror of his enemies. How did he rife? By warre and bloodfhed:How did he proceed? Aske the ftoric.

Plutarch in Romulo. *His power being growne great, his weake neighbours did fubmit thefelues vnto him,being glad to liue in peace by him. His ftronger neighbours were afraid of him, enuied much his greatneffe, and did hold it no policy to fuffer him thus to rife in defpite of the world, and would faine haue clipt his wings.* Howbeit he was not onely flufh or flig, but high flowne, before he was fo well obferued as that he might be eafily preuented or fuppreffed. But now all the Chriftian world may fee, and haue good caufe to mourne, that this brood of *Romulus* the Parricide
retaineth

retaineth yet the rauening qualitie of that wolues milke. Which though it could not ſhew it ſelfe in the poore cottage of his firſt education, with *Fauſtulus*, kept vnder by the feare of perſecuting Tyrants ; yet after ſet at libertie , and gathering ſtrength, he builded vp a Citie in bloud , and hath erected a Babylonicall Tower with fire and ſword, though to his own glory for the time, yet for his confuſion & condemnation in the end, *and without repentance, for euer.*

CHAP. XVIII.

By what principall meanes was the Apoſtaſie of the Romane Church begun, ſtrengthened, and ſo long continued?

Lthough moſt diſeaſes of the naturall body haue inſenſible beginnings, yet afterward they are felt and eaſily obſerued, in their increment, ſtate, and declination. So in politicke bodies , whether of Church or Common-wealth , ill humors ingender, it is Vt, ſupra 17. hard to know how; but when they increaſe , they are felt by the patient, and diſcerned by the Phyſition, and in deſpite of both they will hold a ſtate for a time , vntill by good meanes they be brought to decline: the while recouery ſtandeth euer doubtfull, ſometime deſperate. This hath bene the caſe of the Romane Church. Her diſeaſes had ſecret (as I may call them) influences and inſinuations, though felt by ſome, yet not attended by many. They increaſed to a deadly and deſperate ſickneſſe, neglected all counſell, refuſed all Phyſicke, caſt vp all cordials, whereof many a good Phyſition, or at leaſt the beſt Phyſition of our ſoules might ſay, *Curauimus Babilonem, & non eſt ſanata.* Babylon was long in Ierem. 51.9. cure, but neuer healed.

2 For the breeding and increment of the diſeaſe, the former Chapter hath diſcouered. Now it is worth the obſeruation, how that Synagogue ſtood like a *mare mortuum*, a dead

sea, though now and then a little agitated with the tongues and pennes of a few conscionable men in their generations; yet vnmoueable in the maine, as supported and maintained

Gen.11.4. by impregnable forts, that menaced heauen like the tower of Babell, and could neuer be demolished but by diuine prouidence from heauen, (for who could withstand *Nimrod* of Rome that mighty hunter?) when the outward face of the Church spake all but the language of Rome, as if Israels

Nehem.13. tongue had bene more then halfe turned into Ashdod, and could not speake Scripture language. Vntill it pleased God to turne the curse into a blessing, and to discouer the hidden and almost outworne Hebrue and Greeke tongues, the originals of the Diuine Scriptures, and to open the heart of

Exod 31.2. that *Bezaliel* or *Aholiab* that by Gods inspiration deuised printing, by which the Gospell was dispersed into diuers nations, in the dayes of reformation, as it was by the Apostles who spake all tongues, at the first teaching and information thereof.

3 In this discourse I must distinguish times; those of former ages from these present dayes. For they had not one shift to tenne, which are now found out and practised. For as in a kingdome of darknesse, there may be many a candle light, and shining, and yet the kingdome remaine darke, saue onely neare to that little light; and therefore lesse ado need to be made to preserue the darknesse. Ei-

Mat.5.15.
Mark.4.21. ther putting them out, or couering them vnder a bushell, or setting them vnder a bed, would serue the turne. But when the Sun casteth forth the brightnesse of his beams, and that all darknesse beginneth to be dispersed, then the children of darknesse begin to stirre, not onely to preserue the darknesse wherein they were, by opposition to the light, but also turne light it selfe into darknesse, or would if it were possible. The state of the Romane Church had a long night

Iohn.3.19. of darknesse, which continued the longer because men loued darknesse more then light, *For that their deeds were euill*. Now and then, and here and there, there was a *Beda*, or a *Bertram*, or a *Bernard*, or such like Bees that offred hony, and yet did

sting

sting the Romane Church, for their manners, and gaue some light in some particulars with their doctrine. Others more vehement, as *Iohn Wickliffe*, *Iohn Husse*, & *Hierome* of *Prage*, with many others needlesse to be named, (a few lights I confesse, in such a kingdome of darknesse) of whom some were kept vnder with little or no preferment, that their light might not shine abroad though it did appeare to some; but others were cleane put out, their bodies aliue, or their bones being dead, were burnt to ashes.

4   But the Romanists in our age are like fishes in a pond, from whom the water is drained. As long as they had water at will, though it were neuer so muddy, yet they were pleased well enough with their grosse element : but when the water is drawne from them, and they begin to be skanted, they leape, and they friske, and flappe with their tayles, though they are rather hurt then helped thereby. So they, as long as they liued in possession of their owne broken cisterns, and enioyed the contentment of their muddy waters, they stirred little. But since by the warmth and Sommer of the Gospel, their filthy ponds are almost drained, and they left to the open light, their Pope, their Cardinals, their Friars, their Iesuits, their agents of all sects and factions, leape, and friske, & tumble head ouer taile, from countrie to Court; from nation to nation : like the vncleane spirit that was cast forth, and sought seuen diuels worse then himselfe, that they may make the end of their Synagogue worse then the beginning. The dayes of *Paulus Quintus*, worse then the times of *Boniface* the third, that first vsurped the title vniuersall ; or *Gregorie* the seuenth, that first peremptorily & with effect excomunicated King or Emperor. *Ier. 2. 12.* *Mat. 12. 43.*

5   These latter times would aske large commentaries, to discouer and discourse of the Bishop of Romes profuse riot in this behalfe. I will in this Chapter confine my selfe vnto some few examples, wherein notwithstanding I wil not say much, but that which is necessary to my present purpose. Because this searcheth so neare the quicke, that it will aske a soft hand to touch it easily, or a quicke foot to trip ouer it lightly.   Gg 4   6 First

6 Firſt,the Biſhop of Rome wanting neither wit, wealth, nor friends, allured ſome diſtreſſed to ſhrowd themſelues vnder his protection,and therein exerciſed his wit,iuſt as *Romulus* did : vouchſafed helpe, by releeſe of men, munition, and money, to thoſe that ſhadowed themſelues vnder his wings; and therein he ſhewd his bountie,and found vent for part of his wealth.And he cōmonly banded his deuices,eſpecially for the time,til he grew a nown ſubſtantiue to ſtand by himſelfe, with the ſtronger partie. By the former meanes, and vpon this ſeruice he ſpent his friends. So *Boniface* holpe *Phocas* againſt *Mauricius* with his wit. *Iohn* the fourth redeemed captiues his countrymen from the Lombards, with his treaſure. Others built Churches and Monaſteries, tranſlated ſome Saints, and canonized others, whereby they got both admiration and vaine glory,obtained friends,and curried fauour with the Princes of the earth, and were applauded of the people as gracious benefactors.

7 Then they began to grant immunities to the Clergie; then got *Gaoles*,partly to protect Clerks from the iuſtice of ciuill power, partly to puniſh thoſe whom they would call heretickes : to iudge Metropolitans, forreine and farre diſtant;wherby they were forced either to make ſhew of loue, or to lay downe their ſhields, or take a broken pate. Others ſtudied to bring in muſicke to the Church, idle ceremonies into the Church ſeruice and Sacraments.Others gained priuiledges and exemptions for themſelues and their friends, ſeparated the Clergie from the people, as the elect from the profane: but in all things they were then carefull,

> *Populo vt placerent quas feciſſent fabulas:*
> *They indeuoured ſtill to make themſelues able,*
> *To pleaſe the vulgar with euery fable.*

By theſe means they held the world like tame fooles, with their hypocriſie; which were contented,becauſe they felt no ſenſible hurt, like cuſtomarie tenants, who careleſly neglect the encroching of their Lord vpon their ancient cuſtomes, till they feele the burthen they can neither beare nor caſt off, and endure thoſe loſſes which they can neither ſuſtaine nor recouer.   8 This

Plutarch.

Honor.1.

Eugenius.1.

8 This continued vntil Popes grew yet ſtronger,degene-
rating from the tollerable ſimplicitie,competent wealth,and
not many obliged friends in theſe times , vnto a craftie and
as reſolute praᶜtiſe of their greater growne wits , and a fulneſſe of treaſure,by cheating the ſuperſtitious; and finally to
a gathering of friends by faᶜtious partaking and ſtickling in
temporall affaires. But then they turned all both doctrine
and diſcipline of the Church to their beſt aduantage, feared
no expenſe, their treaſures were inexhauſtible: they purcha-
ſed friends with their vnrighteous Mammon, and by theſe Luke.
meanes bound vp the world in one bundle, and caried them
at their pleaſure on their owne backs. That part which wold
be eaſily caried,they kept ſtil to their ſeruice,and would giue
them diſpenſations for their faults, or priuiledges for their
benefit.That which was weary and would not be caried,they
either exterminated by the furie of excommunication,or vtterly conſumed with the fire of perſecution. By the former
they obtained the friendſhip of al deboſhed varlets,or ſtopped the mouthes of all hungrie Locuſts. By the other they
preuented or ſuppreſſed the iuſt executions of laws by Kings
and Emperours, or burnt vp the bodies of ſuch as eſpied and
publiſhed their errors and hereſies , with any the leaſt con-
tradiᶜtion or defeᶜtion. Like *Sylla* and *Lyſander*, they made Plutarch.in
lawes with fire and ſword, and forced men to obey them. Compar.Sylle
9 The full execution of theſe things (though the foun- & Liſandri.
dations were layed before) brake not forth into open violence till the days of *Hildebrand* and his followers. For albeit
many Popes before him had bene moſt hereticall in doᶜtrine
and deboſhed in life, yet it was kept more ſecret then in latter times, and was huſhed in a ſlumber at home , while the
church was lulled aſleep abroad.But in his time & after,they
made apert oppoſition with all violence,of excommunications,treaſons,poiſonings,murthers,ſecret conſpiracies, open
rebellings,depoſing of Princes, aſſoiling ſubieᶜts from their
oathes of obedience , whereby the greateſt Emperours , as
Henrie the fourth and fifth, and *Fredericke* the ſecond, were
made to apply to their bent,wait at their gates, to hold their
ſtir-

ſtirrop, and leade their palfrey, and ſtoupe to their lure, with diuers others, who loſt either their liuings or their liues, for gainſaying their vnholineſſe pleaſures, or gainſtanding their wils ; and this was a ſtrong band to tye the world faſt to the Popes backe. And although the Nobles and Potentates did groane vnder their burthen, and deteſted their owne ſlauery in the ſeruice of the Italian Prieſt, and hated him from their hearts, whom they feared in their ſubiection : yet they were faine either to ſubmit their lips to the ſlippers, and their necks to the feet of Antichriſt, or to flye and ſhift for their liues, as

*Quem metu-
unt oderunt.*

Ouid. Faſt. 3.

> *Quando metu rapitur tunica velata recincta,*
> *Currit vt auditis territa dama lupis.*

I can Engliſh it no better then thus, *Hee muſt needes runne whom the diuell driues.* Our owne Kings of this land, *Iohn,* and *Henrie* the ſecond, the one kiſſing *Pandulphus* the Popes Legats knee, the other going barefoote, and diſcipled at *Canterburie*: beſide *Chilperike* King of *France* quite depoſed by *Zacharies* either counſell, or conſent, or approbation when it was done, do ſufficiently proue that of the ſame Poet to be true,

> *Abſtulerat vires corporis ipſe timor:*
> *Feare made them ſmart, feare burſt their heart.*

Or of another more properly:

> *Latro rogat, res eſt imperioſa timor:*
> *The Pope doth aske, and feare performes the taske.*

10   When the Lions were faine to roare, not for ſtate but for feare, could all the beaſts of the field do any thing but tremble with them ? When the Captaines and Generals were thus ſurpriſed, what could the people do? If either Clergie or lay men, through either reuerence or conſcience did ſticke to their Princes, and ioyned to their partie, as they were bound by faith and true allegiance ; firſt they were aſſoyled from their oathes, that all falſe hearts might, if they would, take the aduantage thereof. The reſt had their Churches interdicted, their perſons excommunicated, their goods expoſed to rapine. If any would rebell, they were not onely animated, but aided therein. Buls to perſwade them: Buls to re-

ward them. Cursings vpon their enemies: blessings vpon
themselues. Angels commanded to assist them while they liued, to conuey their soules to heauen when they were dead.
This proud vsurpation kept the world in such awe, and withall so turmoiled the minds of men, and filled their hands
with weapons, that there was no thought of bookes. Most
men had no leisure to thinke of learning; and those that did,
either sung *Placebo*, or put vp their pipes, or they bought
their libertie of conscience at the deare rate of their bloud. *Plutarch. in*
Lysander spake more wisely then honestly, when he said, *Whē* *eius vita.*
the Lions skin will not serue, we must help it with the case of the fox.

11   As Antichrist obliged some vnto him by feare, so he
allured and bewitched others vnder pretence of friendship.
The principall meanes whereof, were those more then bountifull dispensations in incestuous or adulterous mariages betweene great personages, who were prohibited partly by his
owne law, but chiefly by the law of God. By which he
brought, not onely Nobles and Kings, but their succession
and kingdomes vnder his girdle, either to hold their States
from him, or to lose them for vnnaturall and incestuous generation. I will not speake of the dispensations in spirituall
kindred (as they call it) which is betweene Gossips that are
witnesses at childrens baptisme: this was but a net to catch
mony, and to drag it vnto the Popes bank. The consequence
thereof was not so dangerous to common wealths, as it was
preiudicial to priuate mens purses, perhaps sometimes a snare
to their consciences.

12   Neither will I stand vpon that dispensation of *Mar-*
tin the fift, which by some Papists testimony of no small note,
licensed a brother to hold mariage with his owne sister; as
not onely *Angelus de Clauasio*, whom *Gretzer* will haue to *Gretze. exam.*
mistake *Antoninus*: but also *Siluester Prierias*, and that with *Mysterij Pless*
the authoritie of the great *Archdeacon*, a *Goliah* in the Canon *4.3.pag.514.*
law, who saith plainly, *Reperitur Martinus quintus (vt Archi-* *part.3.cap.11.*
diaconus refert) dispensasse cum eo qui cum sua germana contra- *§.1.*
xerat & consummauerat: Martin the fift (as the Archdeacon ,,
reporteth) was found to dispense with one who had con- ,,
tracted

„ traƈted and conſummated mariage with his owne ſiſter.
Which ſeemeth to be likely, partly for the authoritie of many, partly for the eaſie miſtaking of *eius* for *ſua*,
not an inſolent ſoleciſme in thoſe dayes among otherwiſe
good Clerkes, as they were then eſteemed. But whether it
was his ſiſter, or the ſiſter of his queane, the Pope holding
Antonin.ibid. (and not incongruouſly with the Scriptures) that *Affinitas
contrahitur tam ex fornicatione, quàm ex legitimo matrimonio*, *in*
„ *quo caſu non poteſt Papa diſpenſare:* Affinitie is as well contra-
„ ƈted by fornication, as by lawfull mariage, in which caſe the
„ Pope cannot diſpenſe. And therefore the Popes, whether o-
uerſight or wilfull pleaſure, was moſt wicked, and againſt his
Bellar.de ſacr. owne limited authoritie, by his owne law. Neither will I
Matrim.l.1. vrge *Innocentius* the third, who diſpenſed with men to hold
c.18.
Extra. de di- their brothers wiues; nor of *Alexander* the ſixt, who diſ-
uortijs. cap. penſed in the ſecond degree, as *Caietan* reporteth; but you
Deus qui. ſhall heare of greater abhominations, both in faƈt and con-
ſequence.

13   In ſome caſes our aduerſaries will haue all ſpirituals
aboue all temporals, as the ſoule is more precious then the
bodie. And therefore the Pope is aboue the Emperour, and
vowes of ſpirituall mariages aboue promiſes in ciuill con-
traƈts; whence perhaps it is a more prodigious matter to
marry a Nunne, then to marry ones ſiſter. Yet *Celeſtine* the
third, to gratifie the King of *Aragon*, was contented to permit him to marry a Nun by diſpenſation, and in all probabilitie either his neare kinſwoman, or heire to a Crown, or elſe
how could it be good to procure peace in their kingdomes?
Math.Paris   14 Another ſtory there is in *Mathew Paris*, of *Simon Mout-*
out of M.Foxe *fort*, Earle of Leiceſter, who maried the Kings ſiſter, that
his Aƈts and was deuoted with a mantle and ring. And though the Monks
Monuments. murmured at it, for ought I reade, they could not amend it, for
De diuortijs & the Pope had diſpenſed with it. *Beza* doth not onely obſerue
repudijs.p.87. of former times, how by the Popes diſpenſations *Philip* the
„ ſecond, Duke of Burgundie in our fathers memory, married
„ his owne vncles wife, in affinitie his owne Aunt. How *Ferdi-*
„ *nand* King of Naples by the like authority maried his Aunt,
in

in confanguinitie, his fathers fifter; how *Immanuel* King of „
Portugall maried by the Popes Bull, two fifters : and Queene „
Catherine in his memory, was maried to two brothers : But „
of his owne knowledge telleth of certaine Noble men, of „
whom one by Romane approbation had maried two fifters, „
another the widow of his brother , the third of his Vncle. „
And withall ftorieth that thefe fought fuch libertie or rather
damnable licence from a Synod in the reformed Churches,
and could not obtaine it; but at Rome they were difmiffed
with leffe money in their purfes , no religion in their hearts,
with finne to cleaue by them all the dayes of their liues. In
which as they liued, fo they were like to die. And who cared
for it ?

15   Let fuch difpenfations paffe currant and without controlment for Kings and great States, that they may make inceftuous and adulterous mariages(whereof the pretended Catholicke Church hath not wanted examples)what obligation
vnto Antichrift ? what a confufion vnto glorious kingdomes
and monarchies,might this bring?For it muft moft neceffarily
follow, that euery fuch delinquent muft be illaqueated in this
ineuitable *Dilemma* : The fucceffion muft either fupport the
Popes authoritie, or elfe the kingdomes by Law & Diuinitie
are iuftly expofed to the lawfull heires. How happie had fuch
kings & nobles bene if God had vouchfafed them the choyce
of *Dauids* three plagues? for then they might find one that
might leaue them in the hand of God. But alas poore foules,
they muft either lofe earth or heauen, their kingdomes in this
world, or the kingdome of life and glory. They fhall neuer
dare to betake themfelues to Chrift , for feare of Antichrift
the father of their fornications. This hath bene a potent obligation to bind great perfonages and States, in the dungeon
of darkeneffe, and hell of Romifh fuperftition , from whence
though they would,yet they durft not then,they dare not now
extricate themfelues.

16   For pettie difpenfations,I will not blot my paper with
them : Onely to name them , will expofe them to fufficient
deteftation;That boyes may not onely be Paftors and Vicars,
but

but Bishops and Archbishops, if need require: but not without
a feeling to get money like mountaines, to fill vp their treasure, or powerfull friends to bandie with them, and support
their estate. How many homicides and murtherers were smo-
thered by monasteries, and vnholy sanctuaries? What prote-
ctions from the due course of law in punishing offences? What
preuentions, yea to commit some sinnes at ones pleasure, so he
passed not the bounds of his comission? Some had pardons for
sinnes to come, and that cost the pardoner his purse, for the
fellow that had the pardon robbed the Pardoner, and pleaded
his pardon, and saued himselfe harmelesse. I will not speake
for killing of men, I haue rather heard of them then seene any
dispensations or indulgences to that effect: but for keeping of
Concubines more or fewer, dissoluing of bonds, vowes, and
oathes, were infinite for number and value, not that they were
worth any thing, but because they cost much. These so obliged the common and loose people, who most needed
dispensations, that all the wicked and licentious of the world
flocked vnto them, and conspired with them, & rested among
them as in a denne of theeues.

17   The next obligation wherewith they so long kept
the world in the dungeon of *Malchiah*, where was nothing
but darknesse and dirt, was the oath enforced on the Bishops
to the man of sinne; the Priests to the Bishops: and all to such
slauish obedience vnto all the Popes pleasures, as that it was
like the sinne of witchcraft and sacriledge, to call any thing
into question that he exacted or imposed. The Laitie were
tethered with the same rope. They were also sworne as *Otho*
the Emperour to *Iohn* the Romane Prelate, from which particular they ground this generall : *Omnis potestas iurat fidelitatem
Papæ & obedientiam; recognoscens ab eo, omne quod habet.* Euery
power sweareth faith and obedience to the Pope, acknowledging that he holdeth from him, whatsoeuer he hath. And
» therefore when the Emperours *giue any thing to their Sea, as*
» *Constantine, it was not a gift, but a restitution.* Who durst displease
so great a landlord? nay who durst whisper against so dreadfull a tyrant?

Ierem.38.6.
Supra cap. 11.

Distinct. 63.c.
Tibi Domino
Bartho. Fium.
aurea Ar-
milla, verbo
Papæ. 7.

18 I may adde vnto thefe the ignorance both of Clergie and Laitie, whereof I haue fpoken before. Which was firft impofed by the Priefts themfelues, by keeping the Scriptures in an vnknowne tongue, afterward affected by the people, who liued fo long in darkneffe, that they knew no light: as thofe that were neuer out of hell, neuer thinke or expect any other heauen. The old world would not enter the Arke with *Noah*, Gen.7. 19. nor the wicked Sodomites leaue their Citie with *Lot*. But as they were bred in ignorance, fo were they brought vp in fuperftition, that they neither knew nor defired any other religion; like the people that dwelt neare the great Cataract or fall of *Nilus*, which fo deaffed & aftonifhed children as foone as they were borne, that they neuer heard it more, and liued as well pleafed with it as with a ftill aire. They could not beleeue that themfelues were blind, they mifdoubted all others, that they could not fee. They trufted their guides, and they had no eyes. They followed as they were led, though to their owne perdition. Some few among the many called, were fometimes chofen: who by a glimmering of the Gofpels brightnes, walked in the way of truth, and happily attained the end of their faith, to the fauing of their foules. But many perifhed in the gainfaying of *Corah*, and ioyned themfelues to the rebellious Iude 11. generation that prouoked God by their hatefull idolatrie euery day. How eafie is it to delude a child long with pinnes and points, glaffes and faire fhewes, and not onely entertaine them in their follie, but deceiue them to their hurt? But a man of vnderftanding may not be fo eafily circumuented. This was a fearefull and dangerous ftratagem deuifed certainly by the Prince of darkneffe, who detefteth the light himfelfe and in all others.

19 By thefe meanes the chiefe Maifters infinred ouer their blindfolded fcholers, of whom it may well be faid, as Saint *Hierome* writeth: *Nihil noui afferunt, qui in huiufmodi applaudente fibi perfidia fimplices quidem & indoctos decipiunt, fed Ecclefiafticos viros, qui in lege Dei die & nocte meditantur, decipere non valent.* They fpeake no new thing, who applauding ,, themfelues in their owne perfidioufneffe, deceiue verily the ,,

Ad Ctefiph5-tem cont. Pelag. c.1.

fimple

„ ſimple and vnlearned; but Ecclefiaſticall men, (men of vnder-
„ ſtanding) who are exercifed in the Law of God day and
„ night, cannot be deceiued. Happie were thofe Kings and Nobles, Prelats and Clergie, that could caſt off that vneafie yoke
and heauie burthen, which Antichriſt had layd on their necks
and backs. And happie were thofe people, that would take the
word of truth, life and light into their hands, and feeke themfelues the certaine way to their Fathers kingdome.

20 Auricular Confeſſion is another Iriſh wythe, to tye
vp blind Chriſtians in the bond of iniquitie, and the ſnares of
the diuell. For by this the fecrets of Princes were knowne,
and their counfels preuented; the peoples finnes were made
manifeſt to them, that prayed not for, but preyed vpon their
foules. Not onely the workes of their hands, but the thoughts
of their hearts were reuealed, or fuppreſſed, or puniſhed with
feuere penance. By this the Laitie became vaſſals to the Clergie: euery Prieſt knew his neighbours, both husbands and
wiues faults, and learned himfelfe the way to finne. What
could be more powerfull to keepe the world in awe? and not
onely to put their heads vnder their fathers girdles, but to
hold their nofes clofe to the grindleſtone, till they turned
their faces into plaine ſhooing-hornes. This to a pariſh Prieſt
made his offerings better then his tythes, and his tythes well
payd for feare of the worſt. Yet can they not tell vs, when this
cofening tricke firſt began. Some will haue it out of Paradife,
but it neuer was there; fome from the time of *Caine*, neither
cometh it from thence; fome vnder the Law in the time of *Iofuah*; fome in the new Teſtament by the authoritie of Saint
Iames: but it is beſt to fay, quoth the Gloſſe, that it came by a
certaine tradition of the vniuerfall Church, rather then out of
the old or new Teſtament. The cuſtome whereof is but onely
among the Latins, but not among the Grecians, who yet haue
receiued no fuch tradition. The oldeſt time that *Socrates, Sozomen* or *Nicephorus* aſſigne vnto this priuate confeſſion, was
the being of the Nouatian herefie, which began not till the
yeare 255, as *Prateolus* writeth. It laſted not in the Greeke
Church two hundred yeares, neither was it then as now it is
                 vfed

*De pœniten-
tia, dict. 5.c.in
pœnitentia in
Gloſſ.*

*Lib. 5.c.19.
Lib.7.c.16.
Lib. 12.c.28.
Lib. 12.c.9.
Hiſt.tripart. l.
9.c.35.*

vfed in the Romane Church.

21 Perhaps, when *Nectarius* did banifh it out out of Conftantinople, for that a Deacon had made it the inftrument of his villanie with a noble woman, it fled out of all Greece, and neuer returned thither to this day. It may feeme to haue bene a deuice drawne from the heathen idolatrous Priefts. For when *Lifander* came to confult with the Oracle in Samothrace, the Prieft bad him confefle the greateft finne that euer he did in his life. *Lifander* asked him, whether that counfell or command came from the Gods or from himfelfe? When he anfwered, from the Gods: Then get thee hence, quoth *Lifander*, if the Gods aske me, I will tell them. The Romane Priefts are as craftie to demand the difcouery of mens finnes to their aduantage: O that Chriftians were as wife as *Lifander* to confefle their finnes to God, out of the Priefts hearing. But as the Priefts are *Curiofum genus hominum ad cognofcendam vitam alienam, defidiofum ad corrigendam fuam*: A curious kind of men to pry into other mens liues, but „ moft flow or lazie in amending their owne; fo may we fay „ of the befotted people, they were paffing forward in obferuing their priefts counterfeit deuotion, but neuer had the vnderftanding to difcerne their impudent intrufion. *Diego Chaues*, king *Philip* the fecond of Spaine his confeffor or ghoftly Father, vnder this veile fometimes couered, and with this wind fometime blew abroad what he lifted to faue the Kings credit, for and againft *Perez*, about the murdering of *Efcouedo, Don Iohn* of Auftria his Secretary. Which one example if there were no more, may fufficiently informe Chriftians to beware of Popifh deuices, and efpecially the tricke of *Auricular confeffion.*

Plutarch.in Laconicis.

Auguft. Confeff.l.10.c.2.

The generall biftorie of Spaine.l.31. pag.1259.

22 I cannot difcourfe at large of euery fingular deuice the Romane Synagogue had, to flatter and feare thofe ignorant times withall; whereby they held the fimple in admiration of their Hierarchie, courbed the Nobles with the feuere execution of their cenfures, drew on the wicked and couetous by their fees and promifes; and deluded and gulled all men, by impoftures and fained miracles, by holy pretences

vnder hypocriticall diffimulation, walking of fpirits, dreams, vifions and reuelations, which being fwallowed and beleeued, were able to giue a defperate checke, if not a deadly mate, vnto the truth, among thofe that liued in darkneffe and in the fhadow of death.

23 The terror of Purgatory fire, with hope to be deliuered therefrom, was a bridle for fooles to hold them in feare, a fpur to the wicked, to run on in their madnes, in hope alfo that by mony or friends, they might be in time deliuered. But among, if not aboue all, their vnholy Inquifitions, with their loathfome and pitileffe imprifonments, fecret fmotherings, pinings, ftaruings, publicke fhamings vnder colour of penance, cruell and tyrannous tormentings with fword and fire, without all pittie or mercy, without refpect of age, fexe or calling, drew many, held more.

24 Finally what the wit of men could inuent, or the diuels in hell could fuggeft, or both with all their malice and power could execute, that was done to a very haire breadth for the promoting and fupporting of Antichrifts caufe and kingdome. It is hard to fay whether the Turkes haue learned of them, or they of the Turkes, to forbid fo much as difpute or queftioning of their fuperftition and religion without perill of death.

25 As *Dioclefian* fhut vp the fchooles of learning againft Chriftians, that by ignorance they might be difenabled to vnderftand and defend the truth: and *Iulian* the apoftata bereft Chriftians of their goods and eftates, that their pouertie might affoord them no means to countenance the truth; and thefe were moft cruell and perfecuting Tyrants: fo hath the Bifhop of Rome long done, playing both their parts in one perfon. He kept fron the people, yea from moft of the Clergie the key of knowledge, which fhould open the gates to grace and glory: & fo fcraped vp the wealth of the world, partly to the Romane Court, partly to the Clergies hands; partly to the indowments of Monafteries, partly to the fhrines of Saints, and all at Antichrifts commandement: that a few fauorites excepted, (whofe purfes or employments for the

the great Maifters aduantage, preferred them in greatneffe not in grace,) all the people labored vnder extreame pouertie, and either begd the Clergies almes, or were their retainers, or liued vnder them as their tenants, or were fome way at their deuotions, that they could not ftirre but with hazard of their eftates or reftraint of their libertie, or perhaps loffe of their liues. Flye they could not, but as the Prouerbe is, out of the frying pan into the fire. For moft kingdomes were couered with one cloud of darkneffe, and the Italian Monarch kept watch by night and ward by day, to turne all into Purgatory at the leaft, if not into hell at the worft. Few went to heauen but in a chariot of fire, or a riuer of bloud. They were fellowes either with the three children in the fornace, or with *Ionas* in the water, or with *Iob* in his pouertie, or with *Dauid* in aduerfitie, or with the Prophets, Apoftles and other holy men of God in one affliction and tribulation or another. No maruell then they held fo faft and continued fo long.

26 Thefe diuellifh deuifes haue continued the ftate of the Popedome, and the appertenances thereof; that is, error, fuperftition, herefie and idolatry fo many ages. Thefe are the feete of that chaire of peftilence, which hath fo faftened it felfe in the ground of the Church, that it hath pofed noble Emperours and Kings to remoue it. As the ftrong Lion which was deliuered from the fnare by the nibling of the weake moufe, could not be tyed vp againe by all the hunters in the field: fo the Pope aduanced by little & little, from his meane ftate, to that height of glory which he hath ouerlong poffeffed, and that by fimple and impotent Emperors, or ambitious and afpiring Princes, will not now fubmit his necke to the yoke againe, but tumbleth and fnuffeth like Leuia- Iob. than in the fea, or Behemoth on the land, he is made without feare euen of God or man. The abfent or ignorant haue longer time affoorded by law to make claime to their right, as children and fouldiers, then others. Men of yeares, and prefent at home, haue their termes bounded with a fhorter limitation. We may not maruell that the fimple deceiued people,

children

children in vnderſtanding,& men withdrawn by worldly employments from the ſerious meditation of ſpirituall and heauenly things,were ſo long kept from the right of their inheritance,eſpecially in thoſe dayes of darkneſſe,wherein many
(God wots) groaped after the light and could hardly find
it , and ſtroue to enter into the kingdome of heauen, and
were not admitted ; though ſome ſaw light at a little hole,
haply ſufficient to bring them into a land of comfort and
glory.

   27 The foure great Monarchies of the world continued
their times vntill their periods appointed by him by whom
Kings reigne,was come. They were each ſubdued by other,
rather by dint of ſword, and conqueſt of ambitious Kings,
then by any wearineſſe or deſire of change in the people,
who were contented to abide the gouernment whereun-
der ſometime they groaned , vntill they were changed
from one State to another , rather at the will of the
conquerors then their owne deſires. So hath it fared with
this tyrannicall Monarchy of the Church of Rome , and the
ſilly and ſimple people that were in elder times ſubiected
thereunto.Who felt not their owne ſickneſſe, and ſo ſought
for no remedie ; ſaw not their owne miſerie, and therefore
were not ſolicitous to procure their reliefe : knew nothing
but bondage,and therefore indeauored not to redeeme their
libertie. In which eſtate the world hath by ſo much the longer continued , by how much thoſe later ages added ſtronger helpe of policie , riches,and crueltie, vnto the malicious,
pride, or blind ſuperſtition of that man of ſinne. Which that
it ſtood ſo long without any ſtrong oppoſition, by theſe
meanes which are already deliuered, is manifeſt , not onely
by thoſe arguments which haue bene drawne from the condition of thoſe times : but alſo appeareth plainly by the
concourſe of people to the Goſpell , at the firſt breaking
forth of the light of it.

   28 For as in the times of the primitiue Church, at firſt,
there were a few ſcattered that were caught in Chriſts holy
net, who as they grew in number were perſecuted with ma-
                                                              lice,

lice, vnto the effufion of their bloud; and as they that made
profeffion of their faith were purfued to death by Imperiall
Edicts and cruell Proconfuls, and yet ftill *Sanguis Martyrum* Tertul.in A-
was *femen Ecclefia,* The bloud of the Martyrs was the feed of pol.
the Church:fo it befell the times of reformation in the dayes
ot Antichrift. At the firft appearing of light out of darkneffe,
fome ftartled at it, and wondered, a few difperfed began to
embrace and profeffe it. Prefent perfecution was raifed a-
gainft them; and then *Ligabantur, includebantur, cædebantur,* Auguft.de ciu
torquebantur, vrebantur, & multiplicabantur: They were fhac- Dei,l,22.c,6.
kled, imprifoned, beaten, tormented, burnt, and yet they in- „
creafed and multiplied. So ftrong is truth, that at laft it pre- „
uaileth.: the profeffors whereof may be *murthered, but neuer* Cypr.ep.3.l.1.
*ouercame,*Their vertues flourifhed in their very wounds. The
Samaritans fhewed that there was expectation before they
beleeued; the feed was long growing before it was white
vnto the harueft, but being ready to the fickle, it eafily yeel- Ioh.4,
deth to the reaper, and with litle ado is gathered. Therefore
a few words of the woman made them beleeue , brought
them forth of their citie, led them to Chrift to be more perfectly inftructed. So was it in the time of reformation, the
people were ripe, &c. This is fufficient to proue , that if the
light had fooner appeared, it would haue bene receiued with
gladneffe and ioy of heart; and that when it appeared , it
was entertained with great comfort and contentment. And
certainly nothing ftayeth the farther propagation thereof, in
the eye of man, but worldly policie and the Inquifitors crueltie; and yet it increafeth daily, and fo our hope is, it will do,
till our Sauiour come in the clouds , and puts an end to all
queftions, and gathereth his children into his kingdome.

29   There is but one queftion in this cafe, which may not
vnaptly be asked, and I hold it expedient that it be anfwered. There were fome learned men in the blindeft times: and
at this day they fwarme on the Romane partie, among the
Iefuites and other Orders, as all men may fee, and muft of neceffitie confeffe. How did thofe then not fee the light? How
do thefe now oppofe the truth? I would not be curious to
Hh 3   enter

enter into the ſecrets of Gods iudgement, in whoſe hands
are the hearts of Kings, who knoweth and diſcerneth betweene the veſſels of mercie and the veſſels of wrath, who
taketh compaſſion on whom he will, and whom he will he
hardeneth. Saint *Paul* obſerued the calling of God, that *not*

1.Cor.1.26. *many wiſe men after the fleſh, not many mightie, not many noble,*
are called: but God hath choſen the fooliſh things of the world to
confound the wiſe, and God hath choſen the weake things of the
world to confound the mightie things, and vile things of the world
and things which are deſpiſed, hath God choſen, and things which
are not, to bring to nought things that are, that no fleſh ſhould glorie
in his preſence. Why may not this ſtand for a ſufficient anſwer?

Math.16.17. *Fleſh and bloud reuealed not* that good confeſſion which Saint
Peter made; neither ſtandeth it with wit or learning, to com-

1.Cor.2.14. prehend or apprehend the things that are of God. The Sa-
Ioh.4. maritans beleeued at the word of a woman, without any mi-
Math.16.1. racle; the learned Scribes would haue a ſigne. Neither
after Chriſts preaching, nor for his diſputations, whereby
they were ſo confuted that they durſt aske him no more que-

Matth.22. ſtions; nor for his miracles wrought in his life, nor Gods
wonders ſhewed at his death, nor the ſouldiers report, that
he was raiſed from the dead, nor their knowledge in the law,
nor their skill in the Prophets, could perſwade or relaxe the
bent of their extreme malice. They would rather giue mo-

Matth.28. ney to the ſouldiers to tell a lye, then acknowledge a truth
which they could not gainſay. If our Sauiour touch the Ger-

Matth.8.34. geſens ſwine, though he deliuer a man poſſeſſed with a legion of diuels, they will deſire him to depart out of their
coaſts: but the Samaritans when they beleeued, deſired him
to abide with them. Of all this Saint *Chryſoſtome* giues a good

Chryſoſt. reaſon: *Nihil enim inuidiâ & liuore deterius, nihil inani gloria*
” *difficilius, quæ infinita corrumpere conſueuit bona:* For nothing is
” worſe then enuie and ſpite, nothing more difficult then vain-
” glorie, which is accuſtomed to corrupt infinite good things.

  30   There was neuer ſect (though there were many abſurd among the Philoſophers) which ſome or other embraced not: but all contemned the Iewes as the abſurdeſt generation

ration in the world. And as *Festus* said to *Agrippa*, that the Act.25.19.
mattters for which Saint *Paul* was accused, were questions
about their owne superstitions; as if Iewish religion had bin
but a meere superstition, as *Plutarch* reporteth that one in Plutarch.
Rome was accused for holding with the superstition of the
Iewes. Yet they and they onely were priuiledged many
wayes, and had the Law, the Prophets, the Temple, Rom.9 4.
the Sanctuary, seruice, and promises: *Non taliter fecit omni* Psal.147.20.
nationi, He dealt not so with any other nation, they had no
knowledge of his lawes. Were there not as learned Priests
in the dayes of the idolatrous Kings, *Manasses* and others,
that opposed the true Prophets of God, *Esay* then, and afterward *Ieremie*, and caused them to be persecuted? Who can
deny, but that the Scribes and Pharises, and Priests, were most
learned in their times, had the authoritie in their hands, and
were most respected and admired amongst the people? yet
were they greatest enemies vnto the truth, and in their malice against it, put to death the God of glorie. How did *Galen*
that great Physition, *Plutarch* that great Historian and Philosopher, with their wittiest Poets, condemne Christians, and
deride Christianitie, as an idle and vaine thing, start vp in later times, admitted by fooles onely, as the absurdest religion,
as the Athenians thought when Saint *Paul* preached Iesus Act.17.18.
and the resurrection?

31   That which Saint *Paul* foreprophesied of the later
times, and which we haue read of former, yet in comparison
of later ages, and see with our eyes vnto this day, may giue
any reasonable and indifferent man satisfaction in this behalfe. For as Antichrist himselfe should come *by the effectuall* 2.Thess.2.9.
working of Satan, with all power and signes, and lying wonders, and
in all deceiueablenesse of vnrighteousnesse among them that perish:
So his fellowes, *because they receiued not the loue of the truth*
that they might be saued, therefore God shall send them strong delu-
sions that they should beleeue lyes, that all they might be damned
which beleeue not the truth, but had pleasure in vnrighteousnesse.
Sic omnino errare meruerunt, qui Christum & Apostolos eius, non Aug. de con-
in sanctis codicibus, sed in pictis parietibus quaesierunt. Nec mirum sens.Euang.
l.1.c.10.

Hh 4   si

si à pingentibus, fingentes decepti sunt. So they vtterly deserued to erre, who sought not Christ and his Apostles in holy books, but on painted walls. Neither was it maruell if Painters deceiued Poets, and Poets Painters.

32   There neuer liued any since the time of our Sauiours appearing in the flesh, to whom this prophesie of the Apostle or sentence of that ancient and learned Father might be better applied then to the apostaticall sea of *Rome*, which flieth from Scriptures, as the sheepe were scattered when the shepheard was apprehended; as the Apostles fled when Christ was taken: which obscureth the passion of Christ by her owne merits, as the Sunne was eclipsed when Iesus gaue vp the ghost: who hath rent her selfe from the doctrine of the Prophets and Apostles, as the veile rent in sunder when Gods bloud was shed: which had their learning rather painted in brittle glasse windowes, then printed or written in S. *Pauls* parchments. Let this therefore deterre no honest heart from the truth of the Gospell, as if a multitude could not erre from it long without preiudice thereof; or as if the learned could not be blind in the light of the Gospell, which is often kept hidden from *the wise and men of vnderstanding, and yet opened vnto babes. It is so, O Father, because thy pleasure was such.*

Mat.26.31.

Luk.23.45.

Mat.27.51.

2.Tim.4.13.

Mat.11.25.

33   It is a question of the heathens, why God suffered the world to liue so long in darknesse, as if God had then newly bethought himselfe of sauing them, and had damned all their fathers? A speech better befitting a plaine Atheist, then a professed Christian. Their onely way is, that would be saued, to receiue the vndoubted truth of God reuealed in his word, and not be caried away in a cloud of darknesse with the blaze of the Catholicke Churches name, and an implicite faith, as if they were playing at blind Eddie. And not to thinke of their forefathers errors which are behind them, but *endeuour to looke on that which is before, and follow hard after the marke, for the price of the high calling of God in Christ Iesus. Let as many of vs therfore as be perfect, be thus minded: if any be otherwise minded, God shall reueale euen the same vnto you.* So do O Lord for thy mercies sake.

Phil.3.13.

CHAP.

CHAP. XIX.

If the Catholicke Romane Church were so declined, or rather
fallen away, and continued in that defection so long ; then
what became of our Ancestors, who liued and died
in those dayes of darknesse, are
they all condemned ?

Vr fathers honour should be deare vnto vs, for *their glorie is our crowne.* Such they may Pro.17 6. be, that it would proue impietie to thinke a-misse of them, ingratitude and villanie to speake euill of them. But as we are often taught, not to follow our fathers in that Zach.1. which is naught; so may we not commend, no nor yet so much as defend their errors in doctrine, or faults in côuersation. For this will be no glory to them, but certaine shame to vs. The way to expresse our duties to our Ancestors, is to silence their vices, as *Shem* and *Iaphet* their fathers nakednesse; to imitate Gen.9.23. their vertues, as *Isaacke* and *Iacob* their fathers faith : to looke that themselues eate not of the sowre grapes, wherewith their Iere.31.29. fathers teeth were set on edge; nor approue their fathers deeds in murthering the Prophets, by building vp their Math.23.29. tombes. For that is to rake out of their graue the fathers infamie, and to publish vnto the world their owne shame, that they were the sonnes of murtherers. Our fathers should be v-sed as the Apostles vsed the Ceremonies, they vouchsafed Aug. them an honourable buriall. They let them lie quietly in their sepulcher, and preached the Gospell as Christ had commanded. So may we giue our fathers a reuerend memoriall, and leaue them to the hopefull resurrection. But our selues must looke, that *being ioyned together in loue, we grow vp in all things* Ephes. 4.15. *in him that is our head Christ Iesus.* That hurteth not them. This profiteth vs. It is without doubt, that good sonnes haue issued from the loynes of wicked parents. What if those died in their sinnes, shall not these incline their hearts to righteous-nesse?

neſſe? He anſwered wiſely to one that vpbraided his parents ignobility; What if the meaneneſſe of my parentage be ſome blemiſh to me? I am ſure thou art an open ſhame to thine. Many gloried in the ignobility of their parents, or at leaſt would anſwer truly when they were askt the queſtion of their anceſtors, thinking it no ſhame, but an honour, to haue that glorie in themſelues, which others boaſted to be in their progenitors; as *Bion* to *Antigonus*, and *Soſtratus* to another, *Ob hoc debui magis laudari, & in admiratione eſſe, quòd à me genus initiū cœpit:* This deſerues in me praiſe and admiration, that the glory of my ſtocke began in my ſelfe. The like, but ſomewhat more bitter, made *Cicero* to *Saluſt.*

Lycoſt. ex Laert. l. 4. c. 7. Ex Antig. in Meliſſ. part. 2. ſer. 79.

2 Wherefore, when we are asked this ſcandalous queſtion, which the Papiſts, *Pelagius* and their chamberfellow *Porphyrie* Pagan, asked the ancient Chriſtians, we will anſwer with Saint *Hierome. Qua ratione clemens & miſericors Deus, &c.* How did it befall that the gentle and mercifull God, from *Adam* to *Moſes,* from *Moſes* to *Chriſt,* ſuffered all nations to ,, periſh in their ignorance of the Law and Commandements? Neither did Brittaine ſwarming with tyrants, nor the Scottiſh nations, and other barbarous countries, about the Ocean, ,, know *Moſes* and the Prophets. What need was it for him to ,, come in this laſt time, and not before ſuch innumerable multi- ,, tudes of men had periſhed? This is the very queſtion, now in ,, hand. How happened it that God ſhould ſo long ſuffer our ,, fathers to liue in ignorance and error, and appeare in this re- ,, formation at laſt, when ſo many thouſands haue bene dam- ,, ned? To which queſtion ſaith Saint *Hierome,* The bleſſed A- ,, poſtle writing to the Romans doth moſt prudently ventilate, ,, but yet confeſſing his owne ignorance, he leaueth it to Gods ,, knowledge. I pray thee vouchſafe to be ignorant alſo of that ,, thou askeſt. *Concede Deo potentiam ſui, nequaquam te indiget* ,, *defenſore:* Yeeld vnto God power of himſelfe, he needes not ,, thee to be his proctor.

Hieron. ad Cteſiph. ad- uerſ. Pelag. c. 4

Stoicæ, pro Scoticæ.

Aug.

3 Who can anſwer this queſtion but God, whoſe iudgements are often ſecret, but euer iuſt? As euery ſeruant to his Maiſter, ſo euery man ſtandeth or falleth to his owne Lord. In this

this cafe we may probably and charitably conceiue, either feare or hope : but by refolute demonſtration we can conclude and determine nothing. *He that fearcheth into Gods fecrets, ſhall be oppreſſed with his glorie.* There is no peeping into the Arke 1.Sam.6.19. of God without iuſt puniſhment. It is well if we can ſtand in the Courts of the Lords houfe, we muſt leaue his *Sanctum fanctorum* to himfelfe. The top of the mount may admit a *Mo-* Exod.19.20. *fes* or an *Aaron*, or a *Iofuah* not farre off, but let the people be 24.24.1. content to ſtay without the railes. What God reuealeth to *Mofes*, that they muſt do. Euery one hath his fitteſt taske in his owne ſtation. *Cætera relinquantur Deo:* All other things muſt be left vnto God: *Who ſheweth mercie on whom he will, and* Rom.9.21. *whom he will he hardeneth. Hath not the Potter power ouer the* Iere.18.6. *fame clay, to make veſſels of honour and diſhonour? What if God would, to ſhew his wrath, and to make his power knowne, ſuffer with long patience the veſſels of wrath prepared to deſtruction? and that he might declare the riches of his glory vpon the veſſels of mercie, which he hath prepared to his glorie?* As for vs, we haue our cautell *not to iudge leſt we be iudged, nor condemne leſt we be con-* Math.7.1. *demned.*

4 A raſh iudge may foone precipitate an vniuſt ſentence, and therefore in this cafe aboue many, *Procedendum eſt ad fententiam cum plumbeis pedibus:* We muſt proceed vnto ſentence with leaden feete. For befides that experience teacheth, that many men feeme Saints to vs who in Gods fight are diuels, yea and that the diuell himfelfe may be deceiued in this cafe, who is more acute then man, as he was in *Iob*; we alfo know God to be *a mercifull God, and gracious, ſlow to anger, and abun-* Exod.34.6.7. *dant in goodneſſe and truth, referuing mercie for thouſands, forgiuing iniquitie, and tranſgreſſion, and ſinne.* And againe, feeing with God *there is mercie, and with the Lord there is plenteous re-* Pfal. 130.7. *demption, his mercy is ouer all his works, and endureth for euer.* We 145. 9. may well be cautelous and propitious in our iudgement vpon 136. men of former times and ages, and leaue them to Gods fo louing, fo large, fo euerlaſting mercy.

5 Yet as God is not vniuſt to condemne the righteous with the wicked; fo is he not fo mercifull, as to faue the obſtinate

ftinate and irrepentant with the innocent or penitent.Neither may we fo iuftifie fome in our hope of Gods mercy, that we make way vnto all, be they neuer fo wicked. And therefore a measure muft be kept, & difcretion vfed in this behalfe. Who knoweth not that Chrifts flocke is but a *little flocke for number*, and as bafe for worldly reputation (*for not many mighty are called*,)& though *many are* outwardly called,yet *few are* (inwardly) *chofen* ? Was Gods mercy preiudiced when the whole world was drowned, and but *eight perfons onely* deliuered from the waters; not all of thefe eight from Gods fecret iudgement? What became of *Noahs* kindred? His father liued till within fiue yeares of the floud, and *Methufela* his grandfather till the fame yeare ; perhaps his brethren and fifters, or fome of them were drowned, if fome of them died before. There were but foure deliuered out of thofe wicked cities, that were confumed with fire and brimftone from heauen, and one of them was turned into a pillar of falt.But three then faued,and from them fprang wicked enemies of the Church of God,the Ammonites & the Moabites.I fay but three to many thoufands, & eight without doubt to many hundred thoufads.

6   If we refpect either length of time, or number of people,how long did God fuffer the Gentiles to remaine in darkneffe, & in the fhadow of death ? and how many of all nations were without all doubt condemned, becaufe they beleeued not in the name of the onely begotten Sonne of God? *Dearum cultores* (faith *Lactanctius*) *libenter errant & ftultitiæ fuæ fauent, à quibus fi rationem requiras perfuafionis eius, nullam poffunt reddere,fed ad maiorum iudicia confugiunt,quòd illi fapientes fuerint*. The Idolaters erre willingly, and fawne vpon their owne folley,of whom if you aske a reafon of their perfwafion, they can yeeld none, but flie to the iudgement of their Anceftors,becaufe they were wife men . A wife reafon. As if the wifedome of the world might not be foolifhneffe with God ; or as if their predeceffors could not erre, and for this error be condemned of God ? Change but a few words as the cafe requireth, and then confider whether the fame imputation of folly may not be applyed to him that now asketh this queftion.

Luke 12.34.
Math.20,16.
1.Cor.1.26.

Gen.7.13.

Gen.9. 25.

Gen. 19.26.

Iohn 3.18.
Lactan.de Iuftitia.

1.Cor.2. 14.

ftion. Our fathers, fay they, were wife men: what if they were? Saint *Paul* tels them, that *the wifedome of the world was foolifh-neffe with God, and while they thought themfelues wife, they be-came fooles,* and all their *fcience was falfly fo called.* Surely our fathers were faued, fay the ignorant. Are you fure? how do you know it? Our fathers were not damned. Be you fure of that? did you neuer heare what Saint *Auguftine* faith? *Mul-torum corpora veneramur in terris, quorum animæ cruciantur in infernis:* We reuerence the bodies of many in earth, whofe ,, foules are tormented in hell fire. So may we perhaps thinke ,, in our charitie thofe to be faued whom God knoweth moft certainly to be damned. *Iobs* friends condemned him as a great finner, becaufe he was fo fore punifhed: but God iuftified him againft the diuell, and them all, for the *moft righteous man in the land of Hus.* So many were perfecuted, and burnt in the fury of Antichrift, who were condemned of the ignorant world to be heretickes, and yet ferued God from their heart, and were the beft Chriftians.

　7　Saint *Iohn* the Baptift preuented this obiection of the Pharifes and Sadduces: *Thinke not to fay with your felues, we haue Abraham to our father,* for *I fay vnto you, God is able of thefe ftones to raife children vnto Abraham.* There is no boafting of our anceftors; if we be euill, neither fhall their euill hurt vs if we do well. The fathers may eate fowre grapes, and yet the childrens teeth be neuer fet on edge. Sinne ly-eth at the dore of him that commits it. It vexeth not the con-fcience of him that is free and faultleffe from it. How vehe-mently did the Iewes pleade with our Sauior, that they were *Abrahams feed?* So was *Ifmael* the baftard, and *Efau* the pro-fane. But the Sonne of God anfwereth, that he that *finneth is the feruant of finne.* He can claime no priuiledge in *Abraham* that hath not his faith; neither can any man be hurt by his fathers iniquitie, if himfelfe be righteous. The foule that fin-neth fhall dye the death. To enquire of our forefathers ei-ther faluation or condemnation, auaileth vs little. God hath done with our fathers, as it hath pleafed him. let vs looke to our felues that we may pleafe him. And this certainly is

the

Rom. 1. 22.
1. Tim. 6. 29.

Iob.

Mat. 3. 7.

1. 9.

Ezech. 18. 2.
Ierem. 31. 29.

Gen. 4. 7.

Ioh. 8. 33.

the safest way.

8 If you will aske this question, and will accept Saint *Augustines* answer, ye may soone take satisfaction. Our fathers receiued this of their fathers, saith *Crefconius* the heretticke; *sed errantes, ab errantibus*, saith Saint *Augustine.* We receiued this religion from our fathers, say the *Papists*, and our fathers learned it of theirs: but they erring one after another, and so the blind leading the blind, both fell into the ditch, and their paritie of error must needs bring equalitie of punishment. Or if it pleased God then to stay the stroke of condemnation in our forefathers, yet now the axe is layed to the *root of the tree, euery tree that bringeth not forth good fruit, shall be hewen downe and cast into the fire.* It is not vnlikely but that this is one of the hardest crusts, vpon the Iewes hearts vnto this day, that their fathers were perswaded that the body of Iesus was nor by the power of his Godhead raised from the dead, as Saint *Paul* reasoneth, but that his disciples came and stole him by night while the soldiers were asleep. An impudent and dangerous deuice in them that broached it, and insensible in it selfe (for they were asleep,) damnable certainly to them that beleeued it. Were not their children happy, if they would confesse their fathers iniquitie, and forsake their error? or were it such a sinne in them now, to condemne their fathers, if not in word for reuerence, yet by hearty conuersion and true repentance, in the sauing of their owne soules?

9 Who with any sap or taste of Christianitie, nay who but a plaine Atheist can but condemne the desperate respect, that *Rhatholdus* Duke or King of Thracia had vnto his forefathers? who vpon our question receiuing a plaine answer, renounced his saluation. For being perswaded to become a Christian and to be baptized, ready to receiue that sacrament with solemnitie, as he was entring the water, askt what was become of his ancestors, that were neuer baptized? The Archbishop answered, they were all condemned to hell, that beleeued not. Then saith he, *Ad inferos ire malo cum propinquis & amicis, neque tanti est mihi baptizari, vt ab illis seiungar.*

Margin notes:

Auguſt.

Mat.15.14.

Mat.3.10.

Rom.1.4.
Mat.28.13.

Sigebert.in Chron. ad an-num.718.
Antimachia-vellus de Po-lit.l.3. Theor. 7.
Legend.au-rea in vita Sancti Pela-giani.Bachor-tus K.of Frife

I

I wold rather go to hel with my kinſmen & friends, neither „
is baptiſme of ſuch eſtimation with me, that I will be parted „
from them. He would rather renounce Chriſtianitie then „
not liue in his progenitors infidelitie. He choſe rather to be
damned with his fathers and friends, then to be ſaued with
the people of God. A ſtory very remarkeable, and of great
vſe in theſe dayes, when men are ſo tyed to their forefathers
ſteps, that they will rather aduenture their ſoules vpon their
anceſtors faith then reſt vpon their owne knowledge, for aſſurance of their ſaluation. What knoweth any man whether
God was diſpleaſed with his fathers? *Turne vnto me, ſaith the* Zach. 1.2.3.
Lord of hoſts, and I will turne vnto you, ſaith the Lord of hoſts;
be not as your fathers to whom the former Prophets haue cried.
Your fathers where are they? and do the Prophets liue euer? As
if he ſhould ſay, God knowes where your fathers are, you
know not. God is our euerlaſting Father, vpon whoſe word
if we rely, we cannot erre; vpon whoſe promiſes if we depend, we cannot be deceiued.

10   Suppoſe the vnbeleeuing Iewes had asked our Sauiour the ſame queſtion: If they onely be ſaued that beleeue
thy doctrine, then what is become of our fathers? are they
all damned? If they be ſaued in that religion they profeſſed,
why not we profeſſing the ſame with them? Might not our
Sauior iuſtly anſwer, *Fulfill you alſo the meaſure of your fathers?* Mat.23.32.
As ſome of their fathers might be condemned, and them-
ſelues ſaued; ſo might their fathers be ſaued, and yet themſelues damned: yea though they did but that, and no more
then their fathers did. *If I had not come and ſpoken vnto them,* Iohn 15.22.
they had bene without ſinne, but now haue they no cloake for their
ſinne, ſaith our Sauiour. Their fathers, to whom Chriſt came
not (though he came for them,) becauſe the fulneſſe of time
was not then come, might and were, by the mercy of God,
and their faith in the Meſſias ſaued, though their children to
whom the light came, becauſe they loued darkneſſe more
then light, might iuſtly be condemned. For though they
ſaw the light, yet they receiued not that light that enlighte- Iohn 1.9.10.
neth euery man that hath light in this world: and therefore
were

were now without excufe. Many of them haply were as
Marke 10.47. blind as *Bartimæus*, yet they begged as heartily to haue their
eyes opened, confeffed their blindneffe, and defired to fee;
& this might be imputed vnto them for righteoufnes. Thefe
Iohn 9.41. like the Pharifies, fay they can fee, and yet are certainly ftarke
blind, and may perhaps be condemned, becaufe in their pride
Mat.13.17, they fay they can fee. Many *Prophets*, Kings & righteous men,
Luk. 10.24. defired to fee the things which the Iewes faw, and to heare
the things they heard, and yet neither faw nor heard them,
but notwithftanding departed the true feruants of God.
This is the reafon that our Sauiour faith, that *Iohn* the Baptift was greater then any of the Prophets, and that the leaft
in the kingdome of God is greater then *Iohn* Baptift. For
as greater meanes were by God vouchfafed, fo was more
knowledge by him required. Where the meanes were leffe,
God required leffe ; and where the meanes are more, there
more is expected, as in the difpofing and employments of
Mat.25. the talents. If our fathers vfed one talent well, they fhall
haue their reward. If we haue fiue, we muft not expect preferment if we neglect foure, and make vfe but of one. That
which would ferue our fathers turnes, will not ferue ours.
We cannot make the fame plea in the day of Chrift. As *Tully*
Offic.1, faid to his fonne, he muft abound in the precepts and learning of Philofophy, becaufe he was taught by a learned Maifter, and was brought vp in a famous Vniuerfitie. So doth
Chrift looke for in thefe dayes of light, that which he neuer
expected in the times of darkneffe. Their defires might in
mercy well be accepted. But except we bring more plentifull
fruit, then they did or could, we may be iuftly reiected.

11 Suppofe a father hath two fonnes : he fendeth one
vpon a iourney in the night, through hils and dales, woods
and wilderneffe, without guide to conduct him, or
meanes to inftruct him, prefixeth him a time to returne, and
that before day, howfoeuer his bufineffe doth proceed. If the
fonne keepe the way as neare as he can, obferue the time by
his father limited, though his paines feeme fruitleffe, yet his
father will eafily pardon his defect, pitie his paines, and reward

ward his diligence. The other sonne he sendeth in the open day, giueth him a guide for his direction; but he goeth wilfully out of his way, scorneth his guide, loytereth and gameth, and so returneth with his errand vndone. Shall not the father iustly punish the wicked wilfulnesse of such a leud and carelesse sonne? So verily it fareth with God, in the comparison betweene our ancestors and vs. It pleased God to send them in the night of feare, through the hils of pride in the Romane Church, and the dales of ignorance in the Pope and his Clergie; through the woods of darknesse in the schooles of Diuines, and the wildernesse of errors in the deceiued world. There they wandred the time of their pilgrimage, and returned when their father appointed. Why might not he shew mercy vpon their ignorance, who had so many impediments in their trauell? And why might not God reward their diligence, that laboured in loue to do their fathers will, but failed in the meanes of the exact performance thereof? But now our Father hath sent vs in the day light, and for doubt of the least cloud that might ouershadow vs, he hath giuen vs his word in all tongues, to be *a lanterne vnto our feete* Psal. 119.105. *and a light vnto our steps*; hath vouchsafed vs guides to direct vs, teachers to instruct vs. If we desperatly refuse the meanes, and follow our owne wilfull conceits, should we not iustly deserue our Fathers displeasure, and without hope of his fauour incurre the danger of damnation? By which it is plaine, that two may either omit the same dutie, or do the same fact, and yet both not punished with the same torment. Therefore no pleading our fathers forgiuenesse, to hearten or harden vs in our ignorance or wilfulnesse. God in his mercie may forgiue them, and yet we remaine without excuse.

12   Many good men might liue in the corruptest times, whose memory though it be not recorded vpon earth, yet their names may be registred in the booke of life. For the foundation of God *is sure, and hath this seale, The Lord know-* 2.Tim.2.19. *eth who are his: and let euery one that calleth on the name of the Lord, depart from iniquitie.* Here is Gods seale, which is secret,

I i   onely

onely knowne to himſelfe. Here are mens works, which are
apparent, and were ſeene in their times. We muſt leaue vnto
God that which is his, and depend on his mercy. Of that
which was before vs, let vs that follow iudge charitably; and
howſoeuer it hath fared with our forefathers, euer be labouring to do Gods will our ſelues. Me ſeemeth Saint *Auguſtine*
giueth great light, if not cleare ſatisfaction to this queſtion:

Auguſt.de præ
deſt.Sanct.c.9. *Cum nonnulli commemorantur in ſanctis Hebraicis libris iam ex
tempore Abrahæ, nec de ſtirpe carnis eius, nec ex populo Iſrael, nec
aduentitia ſocietate in populo Iſrael, qui tamen huius ſacramenti
participes fuerunt, cur non credamus etiam in cæteris hac atque il-*
,, *lac Gentibus, &c.* When many are mentioned in the holy He-
,, brew bookes, euen from the time of *Abraham*, neither of the
,, ſtocke of his fleſh, nor of the people of *Iſrael*, neither by any
,, neare ſocietie with the children of *Iſrael*, who were parta-
,, kers of this ſacrament: why may we not as well beleeue, that
,, here and there among the Gentiles diuers were, albeit we
,, find not that they are remembred in the ſame authorities?
*Ita ſalus religionis huius per quam ſolam veram, ſalus vera, vera-
citerq̃ promittitur, nulli vnquam defuit qui dignus fuit, & cui defuit dignus non fuit:* So the health of this religion, by which
,, truth onely is moſt truly promiſed, was neuer wanting to any
,, that was worthy; and to whom it was wanting, he was vn-
,, worthy. So from Chriſt to *Luther*, and from *Luther* to vs, and
ſtill at this day we may ſay truly, as we haue cauſe to remember it thankfully, *Nec prophetari deſtitit, nec qui in eum crede-*
,, *rent defuerunt:* Neither did God ceaſſe to teach, neither wan-
,, ted there ſuch as did learne and beleeue. God roſe early, and
Ierem.7.13.
Eſai.53.1. ſent his Prophets; ſome did receiue, ſome did contemne their
report, to weale or wo, to life or death.

Act.17.30. 13   Why ſhould men tender that which God regardeth
not? *The time of this ignorance God regarded not,* ſaith Saint
*Paul: but now he admoniſheth all men euery where to repent, be-
cauſe he hath appointed a day, in which he will iudge the world in
righteouſneſſe.* Howſoeuer it pleaſeth God to ſhew his mercy
or iuſtice to elder times, he admoniſheth vs now by his certaine word, by his maruellous works, to accept and embrace
                                                                    the

the truth which now ſhineth, and to accept it with reue-
rence, *not as the word of men, but as it is indeed the word of God.* 1. Theſſ. 2. 13.
Saint *Auguſtine* vpon that of Saint *Iohn, But now they haue no* Ioh. 15. 22.
cloke for their ſinne, asketh this queſtion, *Vtrum hij qui priuſ-* In Io. tract. 89.
quam Chriſtus veniret in Ecclefiam ad Gentes, & priuſquam E-
uangelium eius audirent, vita huius ſine prauenti ſunt, ſeu praueni-
untur, poſſunt habere hanc excufationem: Whether thoſe that „
were or are preuented by death before Chriſt came in his „
Church to the Gentiles, or before they heard the Goſpell, „
may haue this excufe, his anſwer is, *Poſſunt plane. Sed non ideo* „
poſſunt effugere damnationem, quicunque enim ſine lege peccaue-
runt, ſine lege peribunt: They may vſe the ſame excufe, yet can Rom. 2. 12.
they not thereby eſcape damnation, for they that ſinne with- „
out Law, ſhall periſh without Law. Make the ſame your fa- „
thers caſe (which God forbid we ſhould conclude of all)
yet are not you now thereby excufed. For his word is gone Pſal. 19. 14.
out into all the earth, and his truth vnto the ends of the
world. God hath giuen vnto vs his ſtatutes and his lawes; if Pſal. 147. 19 20
he hath not dealt ſo with other nations, or other times, it
was his iudgement toward them, we find and confeſſe his
mercy towards vs. Though your fathers tempted God, yet Pſal. 95. 8. 9.
harden not your hearts, but heare his voice this day. For this
is the day that the Lord hath made, we haue great caufe to Pſal. 118. 24.
reioyce in it. But as for our elders, let vs modeſtly ſpeake of
them, and in our charitie leaue them to the goodnes of God,
who is a ſafe keeper of all that haue put their truſt in his
mercie.

14 Moreouer we know, and are ſufficiently able to
proue, that the very Romane religion, was not that before
Luthers time, in many points fundamentall, which now it is.
For as before is obſerued, the Scriptures of God were neuer Sup. c. 6. & 10
refuſed in the triall of truth, vntill *Luther* had driuen the Romaniſts from any hold by them, and had confuted the moſt
points of Popery by them. But when they ſaw their errors
conuinced, they could neither yeeld vnto the Scriptures
their deſerued reuerence, nor ceaſſe to cauill as the Herodi-
ans, Scribes, Phariſes, and Saduces, when they were conuin- Matth. 22.

ced;

Matth. 4.

ced;nor runne away with the diuell,when they are by Gods
word confounded. But the Scriptures, and together with
them, all *Antiquitie*, muſt be not onely ſet aſide, as a thing
not neceſſary,but vtterly contemned and reiected as hurtfull
and dangerous. Though the Scriptures in our fathers dayes
were kept in ſilence and ſecrecie , yet they loſt not all their
honour, as now they haue in the Romane Church : which
hath bene ſufficiently proued. Dig downe but this foundation,the ſtrength of all religion faileth.And therfore in this,
our modernes ſeeming Chriſtians, are farre worſe then their
anceſters. For their fathers were ignorantly blind, they are
wilfully mad. The Popes omnipotencie was neuer defended
in butchering mens conſciences; maſſacring Chriſtians, and
murthering Kings , was not ſo much as named in former
times: but now ſuch things are taught, perſwaded and executed, that not onely Chriſtian eares ſhould abhorre it, but
we may iuſtly ſay with the Apoſtle in another caſe, they do
ſuch things euen in this particular, as are not named among
the Gentiles who knew not God.Traditions were neuer before theſe dayes of ſinne *compared with,much leſſe preferred before the Scriptures.*

Cicero.

　15 Equiuocation deteſted by the heathens, to whom
it was odious to ſay, *Iuraui linguà, mentem iniuratum gero*: I
ſweare with my tongue, but not with my heart. Firſt,ſince
the time of Chriſtianitie,practiſed profeſſedly by the Priſci-
lian heretickes,and deteſted of ancient and true hearted Catholickes, when was it impudently auowed , defended by
word, by writing , before theſe deſperate dayes? If weakneſſe or ignorance in Frier *Francis* vſed it to ſaue a life,
as in his Legends , yet he neuer learned the doctrine
thereof in any ancient Father , nor the practiſe from any
honeſt man . For to ſaue a body perhaps from the iuſtice of
law , he maketh ſhipwracke of a good conſcience, which
ſhould neuer do euill that good might come thereof. Not to
burthen my paper with ouerlarge diſcourſe of this damnable
doctrine, I will but deliuer what I haue out of one Romaniſt,
which is certainly the common opinion of them all;and leaue

it not to be farther difcuffed, but to be vtterly detefted and abhorred of all Chriftians. *Quotiefcunq, aliquis iure poteft,vel debet occultare aliquam veritatem, &c.* As often as any man can, or fhould keepe fecret any verity, by the fame right it is lawfull for him to vfe ambiguous and doubtfull words; ,, which when they are deliuered by reafon of their diuerfe fen- ,, ces, the truth may be couered without a lye. It might be ,, couered verily by the hearers taking of the words otherwife, ,, or in other fence then they are deliuered by the fpeaker. But ,, without a lye: becaufe that fence which is deliuered by the ,, fpeaker is alfo true, whereas the words are ambiguous and ,, haue diuers fences,and all true. Neither is this kind of deceipt ,, to be reputed a fault, or to be blamed: becaufe he that fpea- ,, keth the words is not bound to open the truth vnto his hea- ,, rers, but rather to hide it.Neither is he bound to fpeake in the ,, fence wherein the words are commonly taken, or may be ta- ,, ken of the hearers. But it is fufficient that the fence in which ,, the fpeaker deliuereth them be true,though it be diuers from ,, the common, and frõ that in which they are taken of the hea- ,, rers; let him looke to this left he lye. He doth illuftrate this ,, by examples as damnable as his doctrine. *Teftis qui contra or-* ,, *dinem iuris, &c.* A witneffe who againft the order of the Law ,, is compelled to giue his teftimonie in the true offence of his ,, brother, he may vfe doubtfull words,by which he may referue ,, to himfelfe one fence, but in deliuery deceiue the Iudge, ta- ,, king them in another fence. Alfo a guilty perfon without or- ,, der of law being asked,may do the like. And fo may a Con- ,, feffor, who by a tyrant may be commanded co reueale a con- ,, feffion,or a Clerke who fhould be cõpelled by a Iudge to giue ,, teftimony in caufe of bloud. For in thefe kinds of deceipts he ,, lyeth not, whereas his words are in fome fence true; neither ,, doth he deceiue his hearer, when he is not bound to open vn- ,, to him the truth, but rather to hide it. But he that heares de- ,, ceiues himfelfe taking them in another fence, to whom the ,, fpeaker is not bound to conforme himfelfe.Thus far *Hen-* ,, *riques*. Shew me fuch a difpute before the light of the Gof- pell fo bleared the eyes of the more then purblind Romanifts,

[marginal note:] Hen. Henriq. q. 62. art. 2. cont. 15. pag. 206. 1.

that they could endure no truth, no honeſtie, no ſincerity. Our forefathers were neuer acquainted with ſuch villanies; there were the no Ieſuits in the world. If *Solon* an heathen reproued *Theſpis* ſharply for lying on a ſtage, though it were but in ſport, would he not knocke his ſtaffe on the ground, nay about their eares now, and tell theſe Ieſuites, that lying in ſport would bring it in earneſt into all trafficke and commerce? Much more would he condemne ſuch religious lying, that is drawne into practiſe in matters of higheſt nature.

Plutarch in Solon.

16 In elder dayes it was no ſcandalous queſtion, to aske a ſicke man: *Credis, non proprijs meritis, ſed paſſionis Domini noſtri Ieſu Chriſti virtute & merito ad gloriam peruenire?* Doſt thou beleeue, not by thine owne merits, but by the merits and vertue of the paſſion of our Lord Ieſus Chriſt, to attaine vnto glorie? And againe, *Credis quod Dominus noſter Ieſus Chriſtus, pro noſtrâ ſalute mortuus ſit? & quòd ex proprijs meritis, vel alio* ,, *modo, nullus poſſit ſaluari niſi in merito paſſionis ipſius?* Doſt thou ,, beleeue that our Lord Ieſus Chriſt died for our ſinnes, and ,, that by his owne merits or any other meanes, no man ſhall be ,, ſaued, but in the merit of his paſſion? or finally was this concluſion denied? *Non erit deſperandum nec dubitandum de ſalute illius, qui ſupra poſitas petitiones corde crediderit, & ore confeſſus fuerit*: We may not deſpaire nor doubt of his ſaluation, who ,, beleeueth in his heart, and confeſſeth with his mouth, the ,, foreſaid propoſitions. This was Catholicke doctrine, and is ,, taken out of the Scriptures; was taught by the Clergie, was beleeued by the people, and is the very groundworke and foundation of our ſaluation in Chriſt. But this is not onely accurſed in the Councell of Trent, but alſo purged out of the booke, by *Quiroga*, and the Spaniſh Inquiſition, as hereticall and vnworthy to ſound in the eare of a Romane Catholicke on his death-bed; belike for feare he ſhould not attend the maiſter of error and blaſphemie vnto the kingdome of darkneſſe prouided for the diuell and his angels. I for my part make no doubt, but honeſt and deuout men, though in ſome points caried away with the ſway of time, ſo queſtioned,

Ordo Baptizandi, cum modo viſitandi, impreſ. venet. 1575.

Rom. 10. 9.

Index expurg. Hiſpan.

truly

truly anſwering, faithfully beleeuing, and ſo dying, might
be ſaued, and ſo without doubt in the moſt ignorant ages many were.

17   In the ſame manner they haue dealt with many ſen- In eodem In-
tences of the Fathers, vnder the colour of their Indices or ta- dice ſæpiſſ.
bles; when indeed they cenſure the very words of the text,
and paſſages in *Ferus*, and other of their owne writers, which
in truth are the gracious words of ancient Orthodoxe authors, whom they moſt deſperatly wound through the ſides
of their owne fellowes and friends. Their ſophiſticating of
Fathers in their new approued prints, their blotting out, and
putting in, and corrupting of all reuerend *Antiquitie*, was not
thought vpon in thoſe dayes. Therefore the Fathers being
more innocent in many things then their ſonnes, may haue
obtained the mercie of God, which may iuſtly be denied to
thoſe who willingly withhold the truth of God in vnrighte-
ouſneſſe, vpon whom the wrath of God ſhall be reuealed from Rom. 1.18.
heauen. So that we may conclude with good reaſon, many
of our Anceſtors who liued in the dayes of Romane darkneſſe,
might be receiued to mercy, and be ſaued in that viſible
Church, holding thoſe former poſitions and concluſions, and
ſo dying. Whereas now in the ſame Church, few or none can
be ſaued, who deſtroy theſe foundations, & build vnto themſelues a Babylonian tower, of all pride and preſumption, hereſie, villanie, and impietie.

18   We farther know, that there are twelue houres in the
day of a mans life, wherein ſome are called at the firſt, ſome at Math. 20.1.3.
the third, ſome at the ſixt or ninth, ſome at the eleuenth
houre; and yet by the mercie and bountie of that great houſe-
holder, euery one may receiue his penny. Though late repentance be ſeldome true, yet true repentance is neuer too late.
That of Saint *Auguſtine* is common in euery mans mouth: *Inter pontem & fontem inuenitur gratia* : Betweene the bridge
and the water grace is found. Yet he is a foole that aduentures his ſoule vpon ſo narrow a ſcantling. There is but
one example in Scriptures of this late repentance, which
is the theefe on the croſſe. One indeed left a true penitent Aug.

might defpaire; yet but one, left a wicked finner might prefume. But in cafe of error, out of all doubt, many a deuout
Chriftian liuing in the former dayes of darkneffe, hungring
and thirfting after righteoufneffe, holding the former foun-
Pfal. 19.12. dations, and heartily begging pardon for his fecret faults,(fecret to himfelfe, and therefore the more pardonable, but
knowne to God, from whofe eyes nothing is hid) may well
reft vnder our hope of his faluation. For neceffary ignorance
may moue much compaffion,when voluntary ignorance is an
Dan. 1.15. aggrauation of the fault. *Daniel* and the three children were
as chearefull and well liking when they were brought before
the King, though they fed on pulfe and dranke water, as they
that fared delicioufly with the Kings diet, yea and better too.
So haply many of our forefathers, that fared hard with
fuch food as they had, might be prefented vnto God with
more acceptation then they that fared better and proued
worfe.

    19   Chriftians muft liue by lawes, and not by examples.
A King vpon circumftances of the fact, in difcretion, or by
his royall power, in his fauour may pardon fome malefactors
in cafes for which many are worthily executed. Gods wifedome is not leffer, nor his power weaker, nor his fauour
flower to repentant finners. He may fhew mercy or execute
iudgement, what is this to vs? we muft be cautelous not to
iuftifie where God condemnes: *Caines* fonne had finned if
he had iuftified his father. We may not condemne where God
doth iuftifie; as *Dauid* and *Paule,* whom God in mercy pardoned.

    20   Wherefore let Chriftians, who haue a better triall
of their faith, and a more fure foundation of their hope, neuer depend vpon fo weake and idle a plea, as hath bene or
may be, and in truth is, infifted vpon, by the Iewes, Turkes,
Indians, Calecutians, and Infidels of all forts, euen to this
day. Some depend on the Law, and refufe the Gofpel as the
Iewes. Some worfhip God, and not Iefus Chrift whom he
hath fent, as Turkes. Some worfhip diuels, and are vtterly
without God in this world, as many forts of Infidels. We
                                      know

know this by the light of truth, and we feeke their conuerfion, or we fhould with our vttermoft trauels. May they not
all ftop our mouthes with the fame pitifull queftion of their
fathers damnation? and fo perfift in their fathers errors, and
abide the fame doome? They are obliged in nature as farre
as we, therfore their pitie may extend in this behalfe as farre
as ours.

21 Howbeit our anfwer of our fathers may be with great
hope, yea fome affurance, as hath bene proued. If they yeeld,
their very conuerfion pronounceth fentence againft their fathers, that they were condemned. And therefore if this may
ftand for a reafonable queftion, I cannot fee how euer there
fhould be hope to conuert Iewes, Turkes, or other infidels,
left their fact fhould condemne their fathers. But ô fooles &
flow of heart, that beleeue not the Scriptures, and the power Luke 24.25.
of God. Therefore do you erre becaufe you know them not, Mat. 22.29.
neither haue tafted the fweetneffe of Gods promifes, or the
bitterneffe of his curfes. You know not the day of your vi- Luke 19.42.
fitation, nor what belongeth vnto your peace: you wilfully
abandon the preaching which ingendreth faith, and receiue
not that word which is able to faue your foules. Wherein
if you were inftructed, you would learne with Saint *Au-* Aug. if his.
guftine, that ftarres haue fallen from heauen, and ftones and
rubbifh, duft and afhes hath bene aduanced to glory. The
very Angels that finned were not fpared; who pitieth their
damnation being iuft, and they remaining the enemies of
God? Neither fhall the faued fathers pitie their condemned
children, nor the faued children their condemned fathers,
in the day of Chrift, when loue fhall be moft inflamed in the
hearts of the faithfull. We may foolifhly pretend more charitie, but we come farre fhort of that we fhall then haue.
Then fhall all teares be wiped from our eyes, & all forrowes Reuel.
remoued from our hearts; our ioy fhall be full, without a-
batement; conftant, without alteration; ftrong, without
fhaking; true, without faining; when we fhall be like the Mat. 22.
Angels in heauen. This fhould and muft content vs, that
God hath concluded all vnder finne, that he may fhew mer- Rom. 3.

cy

Acts.13.

cy on all that appertaine vnto the election of grace, and shall be saued.

22 When *Abraham* was called out of the idolatrous house of his fathers, was he sollicitous to aske what became of his fathers, before he yeelded his obedience vnto God? I trow not. What if they perished in their vnbeleefe? What if the time of their ignorance were not regarded? What if by the infinite mercy of God some of them were pardoned? What if a few were conuerted? The best conclusion can be made, is, It was happy for *Abraham* that he by faith was saued. There were some very good Kings, that had as very wicked parents. Should the sonnes be so propitious to their fathers, as to damne themselues? So might *Iosiah* neuer haue

2.King.22.

rent his clothes, bene sorrowfull for the transgression of the Law, nor reformed the Church of God: for some of his progenitors were most wicked idolaters. The same might be the defence of any malefactors sonne. His father was a theefe, an adulterer, a traytor, an idolater; yet some such haue bene saued: therefore he will walke in his fathers steps, lest he might seeme to condemne him. Might he not say with our Ignorants, shall I condemne my father? if he were saued, why not I? This is folish pitie, and worse presumption.

Rom.5.20.
6.1.
Ezech.18.

What if Gods grace superabounded where mens sinnes abounded, shall we sinne that grace may abound? God forbid. The question is assoyled by God himselfe. *The soule that sinneth shall dye the death. The sinner that repenteth him of his sinne, shall liue.* When these were, or where these are, or who these be, or how the number of either shall be made vp, that God knoweth, it is not for vs to enquire. Euery one shall beare his owne burthen; and herein haue we great cause to glorifie God.

23 Wherefore, although we haue many causes to hope of Gods mercy toward our fathers, who might in their simplicitie hold sure the foundation, yet erre in the building: who would haue done better if there had bene tendered better meanes in their times, and perhaps loued that which they knew not, hauing an eye on Gods promises, & expectation

tion of the refurrection: yet there is no caufe to affoord the fame hope to their children, that haue forfaken the foundation, as before is proued, and build vpon the fand of mens Traditions and inuentions, which can neuer ftand out againft the tempeft of Gods wrath, nor couer in the day of vengeance.

24 But whatfoeuer our aduerfaries make their profelites beleeue of vs, that we reuile & damne all our fathers (which is an impudent vntruth, and may ftand but for a railing word againft their confcience) yet it may, and doth moft euidently appeare, that by their owne pofitions they are more cruell to their anceftors, then we are feuere; we more charitable, then they conniuent. For they hold moft peremptorily, that he that erreth in any one point of their religion, which they prefume to call Catholique, (but without caufe) fhall be damned. Whereeby they conclude, that no Father of the ancient Church, not the former Schoolemen of their owne, not themfelues who haue writen in our time, (who all or the moft part in fuch things erre each from other, and fo from the Church of Rome,) yea fome fince the Councell of Trent, fhall neuer be faued. Nay, I dare boldly fay, and can moft euidently proue, that there was neuer Patriarke, Prophet, Euangelift, Apoftle, or Martyr, faued, if Doctor *Kellifons* pofition be true. His words are: *That whofoeuer doth not hold all and euery point of the Catholicke faith entirely, fhall perifh eternally.* Which is very true as *Athanafius* deliuereth it, but moft damnably falfe as the Doctor abufeth it. For neuer any before Poperie beleeued all their religion.

(margin: D. Kellyfon. Idem. 3. con. uerf. all. Idem.)

25 That which the Father hath applied vnto the faith deliuered in that Creed, (which indeed is all Catholique and orthodoxall, but is not all the Catholique and orthodoxall faith,) that the Doctor applies not onely vnto the whole Catholique faith, wherof many particulars are not expreffed in that Creed, but vnto the Catholique Romane faith now held, as al his difcourfe pretendeth. And fo what is indefinitly fpoken, or rather with reftraint, and may admit qualification, is generally and abfolutely taken, without all exception.

Where-

Wherefore take it in *Athanafius* words, it is an holy fpeech, and a charitable:take it with the Doctors meaning,it is moft vngodly and mifchieuous. For certainly there was neuer any order of Gods Saints expreffed in the Scriptures, that euer held that monftrous religion that Rome now holdeth. Neither haue there bene any fince that time, whofe writings, in more or leffe,haue not manifeftly deflected from the Roman Church. How inhumane then is this Doctor, and with him all of his opinion, that hold they are all damned eternally, and therefore not to Purgatorie, where is hope of releafe, or

Schoppius de where is their *Beatitudo inchoata*, that is, where their happi-
Indulgentijs. neffe or bleffedneffe is begun:but to hel,where is no redemp-
cap.48. tion,which are not in euery point of their Catholique faith,
which is the Romane herefie?

26 We are not fo peremptorie, fo rigorous,fo comfort-
leffe, fo mercileffe. For although he that violateth one of
Iames. Gods commandements is guiltie of all; and he that erreth in one materiall point, may be iuftly condemned by the God of truth, as if he had erred in all ; yet I hope they will not fay, that all finnes fhall be alike damnable, and all errors alike vnpardonable. They will not compare a queftion about Purgatorie, which is a part of their Catholique religion, with an error about the Trinitie, which who holdeth may indeed be damned. This is too Stoicall, too aufteretere.

Vincentius. 27 How will fuch Romanifts take the cenfure of *Vincen-*
Lyrinenf. *tius Lyrinenfis* in this cafe? He can be content in reuerence & charitie to an ancient Father and a Martyr, to hope or rather affure the mercy of God vnto him. Who knoweth not, but that Saint *Cyprian* erred in a groffe abfurditie againft the Scriptures of God, in the matter of rebaptization? Yet he is acquitted by him, and he yeelds him a great part of Gods mercy.He feemeth to fay more: That a maifter teaching error may be faued, and the difciple learning the fame may be damned; whereby he warbleth the fame ftring that refolueth our queftion, and thereof yeeldeth this reafon.Becaufe one may teach error in his fimplicitie and ignorance, and fo

be

be pardoned: learners may erre of wilfulneffe and obftinacy, and die in their finnes.

28   In which cafe Saint *Cyprian* himfelfe may well, and doth fweetly fing the fong of *Dido*: *Non ignara mali miferis fuccurrere difco*: *The fenfe of mine owne fmart, breeds pitie in my heart.* He hath a long difcourfe to *Iubaianus* of this very mat- Cypr.ad Iu-ter, and giueth a very good refolution and determination baian. therein: *Fruftra quidem qui ratione vincuntur confuetudinem nobis opponunt,&c.*They verily deale but vainly,that when they ,, are ouercome with reafon, pretend cuftome, as if cuftome ,, were greater then truth: or as if that in fpirituall things, ,, were not to be followed, which by the holy Ghoft is better ,, reuealed.Of which he yeeldeth this reafon· *Ignofci enim potuit fimpliciter erranti,ficut de feipfo dicit eApoftolus Paulus, &c.* For ,, pardon may be granted to one that erreth of fimplicitie, as ,, the Apoftle *Paul* fpeaketh of himfelfe : I who at firft was a ,, blafphemer and a perfecutor, and iniurious, haue now ob- ,, tained mercy, becaufe I did it ignorantly. But after infpira- ,, tion and reuelation made, he that wittingly and willingly ,, perfeuereth in that wherein he erred,finneth without pardon ,, of his ignorance. For he leaneth vpon prefumption and ob- ,, ftinacie,when he is ouercome with reafon. Yet he procee- ,, deth farther,and maketh this obiection: *Sed dicit aliquis,quid ergo fiet de hijs,qui in praeteritum de haerefi ad Ecclefiam venientes, fine baptifmo admiffi funt?* Some man will fay,What then fhall ,, become of thofe who in times paft returned from herefie to ,, the Church,and were admitted without baptifme?Though ,, this be not our aduerfaries obiection in fo many words, yet the anfwer fatisfieth the queftion in fubftance for all. *Potens eft Deus, mifericordiâ fuâ indulgentiam dare,&c.* Our Lord is ,, powerfull in his mercy to giue pardon, and not to feparate ,, them from the benefits of his Church, who fimply were ad- ,, mitted into the Church, and died therein : yet notwithftan- ,, ding a man muft not alwayes erre, becaufe he hath once er- ,, red.Whereas it better befeemeth wife men,and fuch as feare ,, God, to obey the truth willingly, when it is once reuealed ,, and perceiued,and that without delay, rather then obftinatly ,, and

and peruerſly to ſtriue for hereticks againſt our bretnren and fellow Prieſts.

29　The Church may be likened to a houſe, wherein are veſſels of honour and veſſels of diſhonour : and wherein two may be in one bed, the one taken, the other forſaken; yea in one wombe, as in the wombe of *Rebecca*. And Chriſt our Sauiour foretold, that the time ſhould come, that *father ſhould be againſt ſonne, and ſonne againſt father; mother againſt daughter, and daughter againſt mother; the mother in law againſt the daughter in law, and the daughter in law againſt the mother in law.* In this houſe there is a husband, the great houſholder; a wife, as in times paſt *Iſrael* and his chiefe guides : ſo now, or rather before *Luthers* time, there was a viſible Hierarchie in theſe Weſt parts of the world. The children are all the particulars in this houſhold. The husband he keepes conſtant in his loue, till his wife playeth the harlot; he vrgeth repentance, and deferreth the diuorce; he departeth into another country to receiue a kingdome, taketh order for the gouernment of his wife and family vntill his returne. She continueth to play the harlot till her children eſpie it. They are iealous of their fathers honour, and humbly intreate reformation; as *Luther* did of Pope *Leo*, and a Councell to whom he appealed. She yet continueth in her ſpirituall fornications; and the more ſhe is intreated, the more ſhe is inflamed with inordinate luſt, as *Phædra* in the Tragedy, or *Ioſephs* miſtris in the Scripture, and increaſeth in her abhominations. In this caſe what ſhall the children do? Shall they become the mothers bawds? Shall they ſee her ſinne, and ſay nothing? Shall they perceiue their fathers glory ſtained daily, and ſuffer it? This were to bring their mothers ſinnes vpon their owne heads, and haue her bloud required at their hands. Her husband would be reconciled, if ſhe would amend; her children would returne as chickens vnder her wings, if ſhe would be reformed. This ſhe will not do. Therefore her husband writeth her a bill of diuorce, and her children worthily forſake her. They haue cauſe to complaine, and not ſhe.

30　Examine this, and apply it to Chriſt the Spouſe of the

ancient

Marginal notes:

Rom.9.21.
Luk.17.34.

Luk.12.53.

Seneca.
Geneſ.

ancient Romane Church, and the head and members of her
prefent Ecclefiafticall Hierarchy,and many of the both Clergie and people that faw and long with griefe endured their
leud mothers fornications and idolatries. And it may eafily
appeare, that many of the children that grieued at her in
their hearts, and mourned ouer her whoredomes in zeale of
their Fathers glory, and were fo weake they could not, or fo Thefeus.
fearfull they durft not either depart or venture their liues to Phædra.&
their mothers tyrannie, might right well be faued, as Hippolytus.
no partakers of the grofneffe of their mothers finnes, when
their mother might be damned with all her louers & bawds,
without pitie or mercy. In which cafe, neither doth Gods
promife faile vnto his beloued Spoufe that neuer played the
harlot, which is called the houfhold of faith,and children of
obedience, which was difperfed ouer the face of the earth:
and was neuer but by vaine prefumption confined vnto the
Citie of *Rome*, more then to any other Church where the
truth of Chrifts Gofpell was preached and profeffed. There
were vndoubtedly many children in houfe with that vngracious mother, which might be mercifully faued: and
there might be, and certainly were many iuftly condemned,
& that without all preiudice vnto their pofteritie.How doth
one *Schoppius* chop Logicke in this cafe, with an outcry a-
gainft all of our Religion,as if we held there were no Church
for many hundred yeares, and that therefore none could be
faued in all that time? *Ite nunc miferi & infœlices Lutherani,&*
magiftris veftris tam abfurda præcipientibus aufcultate: Go to now
you miferable and vnhappie Lutherans, and hearken to your mai-
fters, who teach you fuch abfurdities. If there were neuer any
Church, (what a ftrange and monftrous fuppofition is this,
by vs vtterly denied and condemned) *then no man could be fa-*
ued thefe fiue hundred yeares: then all Martyrs and Bifhops of the
Church were damned; then all Auguftines and Hieromes perifhed:
and it was falfe which Chrift promifed, that he would build his
Church vpon a rocke that could not be fhaken. This he. Admit his
fuppofition, which he can neuer challenge from vs, and all
this will follow, *No Church,no faluation: no Church, no father*

of

of the Church. But we fay, there was a Church, knowne onely to God; there was a Church confpicuous vnto the world. Though this Church were corrupt in many things, yet not in all, and to many in it God might and did fhew mercy, as hath bene faid.

31 In cenfuring our anceftors, we muft vfe truth, charitie and wifedome; which well obferued, we fhall hardly iudge amiffe. Truth, which will lay no more to their charge then we know them to be guiltie of, nor to aggrauate and make things worfe then indeed they were. Charitie to interpret all to the beft, that may admit an indifferent cenfure, or rather then faile, to hide fome blemifhes thereby, which is able to couer a multitude of finnes. And wifedome, to difcerne and diftinguifh times, perfons, places and meanes, that we neither fuffer the ballance of iuftice to be ouerfwayed with partialitie, nor ouerweeningly defend what is blameworthy, nor cenforioufly condemne what may either by difcretion be tollerated, or with meekneffe mollified, and by Gods mercy pardoned. There was a great and contagious plague in the Church of *Rome*, yet fome by Gods prouidence were not infected; fome that did partake the fickneffe, yet by Gods mercy efcaped. *Lazarus* went to heauen though ful full of fores. And many with one eye, or one foote, might fee and walke the way to heauen, better then thoufands that thought themfelues furnifhed with more then *Argus* eyes, and more feete to runne then a Dromedarie, or a Roebucke.

Luk.16.
Matth.

32 What need be faid more in this queftion? We are propitious and charitable vnto our forefathers: the Romanifts are barbarous and cruell to them they would feeme moft to affect. We leaue them vnder hope; they leaue them nothing but defpaire. We defend their caufe againft a wicked and peruerfe generation: they wound them with byblowes, while they feeme to be their friends. We defire to couer many faults vnder the wings of Gods mercy; they damne them for one fault to eternall condemnation. We will eafily grant with Saint *Auguftine*, that *Multi errore viam deferunt,*

De doctrin.
Chrift.l.1.c.36

deferunt, & tamen per agrum eò pergunt quò via ducit . But one
ſtep out of the Romane high way is holden to leade no whither but to hell; and yet Saint *Auguſtine* ſaith, Many come to ,,
the end whither the way leadeth,though they ſometimes find ,,
not the directeſt path that leadeth thereunto . But ô Lord ,,
thou knoweſt who are thine from euerlaſting . Thy loue to
our predeceſſors couered a multitude of ſinnes. Thy patience
and long ſuffering of vs, inuiteth vs to repentance . As in the
dayes of *Helias* ſeuen thouſand were reſerued that neuer bo-   1. Kings.
wed the knee to *Baall*; as after crucifying the Lord of life , a Rom. 11.5.
remnant was reſerued, according to the election of grace ; ſo
ſtill God can ſhew *bountifulneſſe and ſeueritie* to the veſſels of
mercy and wrath. It is not in the cenſure of men : it reſteth in
the meere mercy of God.In this let all men be ſilent,and God
onely ſpeake , who onely knoweth who belong vnto him.
And when all is ſaid and done , we can reach no further then
the Apoſtle S. *Paule* , who when he had diued into this depth
to the very bottome, and had ſoared into this myſterie aboue
the higheſt mountaine,yet found a depth whereinto he could
not ſearch , and an height whereto he could not reach . And
therefore creepeth with humilitie vnder Gods protection,
and in ſtead of a concluſion breaketh out into admiration,and
this patheticall exclamation: *O the deepneſſe of the riches ,* Rom.11.33.
both of the wiſedome and knowledge of God! How vnſearchable
are his iudgements, and his wayes paſt finding out? For who hath
knowne the mind of the Lord? Or who hath bene his Counſellor?
Or who hath giuen vnto him firſt, and he ſhall be recompenced? For
of him,and through him,and for him are all things : to him be glo-
rie for euer, Amen : and ſo I conclude this matter.

Kk   CHAP.

CHAP. XX.

How may an vnlearned true hearted Chriſtian Catholicke, in this
preſent Romane defeɛtion from the true Church and faith , and in
ſo great variety of opinions as are now ventilated in the Chriſtian
world , ſecure himſelfe and haue his conſcience ſatisfied with
comfort, that he is a member of the true, holy, anci-
ent, Catholicke and Apoſtolicke Church.

1.Tim. 2,4.

He loue of God herein appeareth, that he *would haue all men to be ſaued, & come vnto the knowledge of the truth* : wherein is deliuered, who of men, and by what meanes they ſhall be ſaued. Not all, without exception of any man, but of all men ſome, without exception of any kind of men. Which reſpecteth not onely nations, as Iewes and Gentiles, but alſo ages, ſexes, and conditions of men, old, yong, male, female, bond and free. The meanes of ſaluation is by the knowledge of the truth. For this *is eternall* John 17. 3. *life, to know God, and whom he hath ſent Ieſus Chriſt* . In the want of which knowledge no Chriſtian man can ſtand excu-ſed before God. For either he hath the meanes offered to his perſon, or the ſound of the Goſpell is gone out into all lands: Enough to leaue the ignorant without excuſe : Enough to giue knowledge of ſaluation to them that ſit in darkeneſſe Luke 1.79. and in the ſhadow of death, *and to guide their feete into the way of peace.*

2   Whereof our dayes may ſpeake, if euer any, that *The grace of God, which bringeth ſaluation vnto all men, hath appeared, and teacheth vs to denie vngodlineſſe, and worldly luſts, and that we ſhould liue ſoberly, and righteouſly, and godly in this preſent world, &c.* Here is likewiſe, all men, be they rich, be they poore, be they wiſe, be they ſimple, be they learned or be they vnlette-red, maiſters or ſeruants. *The grace of God* hath neuer *appea-red* vnto them , if they haue not learned as they haue bene taught, *to forſake vngodlineſſe,* which is ſuperſtition, idolatrie, and

and error in religion. And *worldly lusts*; that is, all prophane-
nesse, licenciousnesse and wickednesse in conuersation. The
fault is not in God, who hath manured his vineyard, but in Esay 5.4.
themselues, who haue refused or neglected so great saluation
offered. For the Lord hath not onely taught them to eschue
euill, but to do good. And to make them compleate Christians, he instructeth them to liue *soberly*, in their priuate selfe
cariage; *righteously*, with all men, with whom they conuerse;
and *godly* toward their Maker, Redeemer and Sanctifier,
whose religion they must hold in truth, professe without dissimulation, and continue in it vnto the end without tergiuersation, that they may be saued.

   3 This blessed saluation most men wish in their good
moodes; some men seeke in their better meditations; but few
men follow hard at the marke for the price of the high cal- Philip.3. 14.
ling, and will labour and trauell with patience in the race set Heb.12. 1.
before them, in the way of life, that leadeth thereunto. Some
neuer so much as desire to learne; some are euer learning, and 1. Tim.2.7.
yet neuer come to the knowledge of the truth; some attaine
vnto some measure of knowledge, but either mixe it with i-
dle superstition, or else scandalize it with vngracious conuersation. But those are worst, who *cùm in mala scientes ruunt*,
when they run to their damnation wilfully and with open
eyes, *yet they conceite that they husband excellently for them-*
selues; and therefore say and doubt not: Mihi sic vsus est, tibi vt o- Cicero de fi-
pus est facto, face: This is my fashion or custome, if thou canst nibus, lib. 5.
do better for thy selfe, do it. Which is not onely appliable to
the learnedder sort, that will not confesse they see, when they
do perceiue: but to such also of the common throng, who are
in the middest of light, and may see it, but will not; are where
they may heare the truth, and yet refuse it, and flie from
it, and sticke not to say without doubting, This I haue bene
vsed to do, I will do no otherwise; if you haue any better way,
walke in it.

   4 Such would be taught a better lesson, if they had grace
to learne it; which they may do from a heathen, if they will
be led but onely by the very light of nature. For euen it (saith

Cicero)

Idem de fin. *Cicero*) *hath ingendred in euery man a desire to find out the truth.*
lib. 2.   And therefore falshood may be called a very contradiction
to nature it selfe in its corruption, and an opposition to reason
not accompanied with religion. How much more should re-
ctified nature, reformed by regeneration, and led into a more
high contemplation and admiration of heauenly obiects a-
Colos. 3.1. boue, where Christ sitteth at the right hand of God his Father, search and labour without ceassing to be informed in the
truths of Christian religion, and therein neither spare trauell
nor cost, vntill vpon knowledge, and the conuincement of
vnderstanding, it may rest and resolue vpon certaine truth? In
which case the counsell of an aduersarie is not ill: *Animus vt*
Muri Ciuit. *de religionum probabilitate iudicet, &c.* A mind (or a man) that
fund. 11.   will iudge of the probabilitie of religions, *it is necessarie that*
he weigh the reasons and drifts of euery one, as if he were of none,
that he may wisely entertaine truth, in an incorrupt mind.

5 This can we neuer do, except with the Academicks we
Aug. de vtil. haue some doubts arise in our hearts, as Saint *Augustine* con-
credend.   fesseth of himselfe: as the Apostles had, when their hearts
Luke 24.32. burnt within them. Whereby we may be moued either to
make farther search by reading our selues, (if we be able) or
by asking questions of those that are more learned: but neuer to receiue satisfaction vpon bare words, or credit without
demonstration; neither to be so wedded to our owne wilfull
and vngrounded opinions, but that when our consciences are
conuinced, without further preiudice we yeeld vnto the truth.
When we see light, to delight in it; when we find the way, to
walke in it; and hold it no shame to returne from error to
truth, without all respect of faction or affection, rather see-
Math. 16.26. king to saue our soules, then to gaine the whole world.

6 Who were more enamoured vpon their owne opinions,
then the old Greeke Philosophers? famous for their learning,
followed by their schollers, applauded of the States wherein
they liued. Yet some trauelled to Egypt, and others to Iewrie,
Persia, Chaldæa, to obserue the secrets of Philosophie, and either to confirme the truth of their conceiued opinions, or to
learne a further truth, then by their owne wits, and in their
owne

owne countries they could attaine. Wherein they fhewed no
leuitie but great wifdome & conftancie, in the diligent fearch
of that, which by the light of nature feemed to them moft
precious; and fo alfo did *Lycurgus* fearch for lawes.   Plutarch.

7 And what a grace of God had it bene in them, and
what a benefite vnto pofteritie, if all the fathers had either
preuented or followed Saint *Auguftine* in their times, who
reuoked that in his age, which he wrote not foundly in his Aug.Retract.
youth? that when he was a Bifhop, which he wrote when he Confeffions.
was but a Presbyter? whofe Retractations, and Confeffions
may well be efteemed the beft bookes that euer he wrote.
Æneas Syluius, though with a worfe mind, difclaimed many
things when he was *Pius fecundus*, Bifhop of Rome: and
practifed cleane contrarie to his former pofitions. And after he had long run with the Hare, yet at laft held fo with the
hound, that he bit as fore as his forerunners, and for his aduantage held it no difparagement to alter his mind. Our
prefent and pregnant Cardinall *Bellarmine*, hath played Saint
Auguftines ape in this kind, though to litle purpofe, and with Bell.Retract.
leffe integrity, rather to counterfeit a part, then to act a reall
benefit for Gods Church.

8 Which makes me not a little wonder at the ignorant
folly and obftinate madneffe of many in this age, who are fo
peremptorie in their vngrounded refolutions, or rather wilfull obdurations, that they refufe to heare or reade any
thing that croffeth their preiudicate conceipts, or would
bleffe them in the way of truth. They are of a religion which
they call Catholique, but they neither know what religion
or Catholique is or meaneth. They pretend confcience, but
without all fcience, and continue *pura entia*, as one alluded to
the Priefts of his time, meer blocks & idols, that can neither
fee with their own eyes, nor wil heare with their own eares, Pfal.115.
nor may walke with their owne feet. But the beft they haue,
is but a blind fuperftitious zeale, and the moft they haue, is
but an obftinate will to do that wherein they are fetled. Like
Iron once faftened in a poft till it be ruftie, will neuer be
drawne forth, but with cleauing the wood or breaking the

pin. So thoſe who haue bene long nouſled in the ſuperſtitious blockiſhneſſe of the Roman Church, can neuer be ſeuered therefrom but with rending that Church, or burſting the heart of ſuch refractaries with the hammer of Gods potent word;and they were happy if that would do it:which it might do,if they would heare it.But they haue fed ſo long of poiſon, that it is become their beſt food; neither will they acknowledge blindneſſe in themſelues,but impute the darkneſſe to the houſe, yea rather then faile,to the very aire and the bright Sunne. And ſo *ſpeake euill of that they know not,*and corrupt themſelues *like beaſts in that they know.*

Forreſt,de venen.

Iude verſ.10.

9 Theſe can neuer be taught a better leſſon but by *Pythagoras* method. Firſt they muſt learne to forget that which they had receiued, & then haply they may admit that which might informe them better. Howbeit God hath giuen the ſame leſſon, & that in more excellēt maner.*Hearken O daughter, and conſider, and incline thine eare, forget alſo thine owne people and thy fathers houſe.* If the daughter would heare her heauenly Father, and conſider her owne weakneſſe, ſhe would ſoone forget the idolatrous houſe of her earthly father in Egypt,and take pleaſure in *Salomons* both pallace, and temple, though in a ſtraage land : and would with *Moſes* refuſe to be called the ſonne of *Pharoahs* daughter, and chuſe rather to ſuffer affliction with the people of God, or at leaſt would incline her eare with all obedience and readineſſe, and not returne to her Maiſters infidelitie,nor to corruption of life.

Pſal.45.10.

Heb.11.25.

Doway in Pſal.44.

10 But if I ſpeake of the vnlearned ſort of men or women in this land, the labour of forgetting is eaſily ſaued. For as a man cannot loſe that he neuer had, ſo cannot a man forget that which he neuer learned : which is the common caſe of the vulgar ſort. They neuer attained vnto knowledge in any religion; not in ours,and therfore they are ſo eaſily drawn away. Not in the Romane religion, wherein they are kept more ignorant, but are made withall more obſtinate. For as knowledge hath no greater enemies then the ignorant, ſo

falſe

falfe religion hath no more zealous patrons, then the wilful, who know leaft, and therefore make moft defperate aduentures. A generous horfe will not be fpurred to a dangerous downfall which he feeth; he will ftart backe, and fhew his diflike,and as the Prouerbe is,he will looke ere he leape: but a dull blinde iade may be led to his breaknecke with eafe, and will iob on without feare, as another Prouerbe faith, None fo bold as blind Bayard.This maketh many liue,and to be contented to dye, in a perfwafion whereof they haue no ground: a religion which they hang onely on the fleeue of him that teacheth it, or vpon fuch generalities wherewith the wifeft may be deceiued; or by fuch vngranted and begged principles, that their maifters can neuer euince by any demonftration, no nor fo much as perfwade with any probable reafon, but that they haue gotten credulous difciples to whom *ipfe dixit*, their bare word,muft be their beft warrant.

11 If any confcionable Romane Catholique, who hath a zeale to God, though not according to knowledge,(which I cannot but confeffe of many, and would be willing to witneffe it with fome,) fhould vpon fuch reafonable motiues as are premifed, aske how he might refolue to his beft fatiffaction,whether our Chriftian, or their Romane Catholique Church haue the certaine veritie? and how he may know it,that he might liue and dye in it? or to vfe Saint *Auguftines* words in this matter: *Primùm quærere cuinam religioni animas noftras purgandas inftaurandáfque tradamus* : As if we would now firft feeke to what religion we would commit our foules to be cleanfed and rectified, I would not bind him to *Ariftotles* exigent: *Oportet difcipulum credere*: The difciple muft beleeue his Maifter, as the Papifts do : for that ftandeth indifferent on both hands. One Maifter teacheth him one thing, another teacheth perhaps quite contrary. And fo it ftandeth with him whether to beleeue: rather according to his affection to the perfon, then the euidence of the truth. When we are asked what we beleeue,we muft anfwer, *The Scriptures,* and *nothing befide them.* But who fhall inter-

Rom.10.1.

De vilitate credendi. c.7.

Muri ciuit. fanct.fund.12.

Kk 4

interpret them? No better interpreter then the Scriptures themſelues. If we be further asked, what account we make of our teachers; we anſwer, According to their learning and credit in the Goſpell, and as they teach out of the Scriptures. This a Ieſuit derideth in all. Aske a prieſt the ſame queſtions: he careth for no Scriptures as is premiſed, but from School-men to Fathers, or Traditions, or finally to the Pope, who may be as ignorant as the verieſt ſot in the world. If our an-ſwers be ill, theirs are twentie times worſe. In which caſe what is to be done? how may an honeſt man repoſe himſelfe with contentment in his life, and comfort in his death, that he may be ſaued? Halt betweene both he may not, he muſt reſolue of one, and but of one; for there is but one faith, as there is but one Lord the obiect of that faith.

Epheſ.4.5.

12 To giue ſatisfaction in this ſcruple, it will aske an humble and diſcreet teacher, a deuout and ſober ſcholler. No quarrels muſt be pickt, no knots ſought in ruſhes, nei-ther falſe accuſations impoſed vpon the one ſide; no vaine ſuſ-pition or idle imagination, nor preiudicate opinion on the other ſide. But on both parties a reuerend feare of Gods Ma-ieſtie, a deſire of the truth, hunger and thirſt after righteouſ-neſſe, and a preferring of Gods glorie before any thing in this world, euen with *Moſes* and Saint *Paul*, before their own ſaluation. For which cauſe the Apoſtle requireth among other graces in a Miniſter, that he be apt to teach, as well without doubt in priuate conference, admonition, inſtructi-on, as with euidence of the Spirit in publike preaching of the Goſpell. The hearer muſt haue either, as the better tranſla-tions haue, *cor intelligens*, an vnderſtanding heart, or as the old vulgar hath, at leaſt *Cor docile*, a docible or tractable heart. For then they ſhall be taught of God. All which the Apo-ſtle compriſeth in one period: *The ſeruant of the Lord muſt not ſtriue: but be gentle toward all men apt to teach, ſuffering the euill. Inſtructing them with meekneſſe that are contrarie minded, prouing if God at any time wil giue them repentance, that they may acknow-ledge the truth, and come to amendment, out of that ſnare of the Diuell,*

Exod.32.32.
Rom.9.3.
1.Tim.3.2.

1.King.3.9.

Iohn 6.45.
2.Tim.2.24.

Diuell, of whom they are taken prisoners to do his will. The agent thus doing his dutie, and the patient his, it resteth that the teacher should be instant, in season and out of season, and neuer be weary of well doing: that the hearer keepe that he learneth as a treasure, not let it be dried vp as the mornings dew. Or as *Tiberius Cæsar*, who saw light in the night sudden- Plin.nat.hist. ly as soone as he awaked, as in the day, but by litle and litle lib.11.c.37. darknesse grew vpon him, and saw no more then when he was asleepe.

13 In which conference, poore soules must not be terri- fied with damnation, as children with boggards. For this is like a robber by the high way, that asketh money with a drawne sword, the point at the heart. Though he meane not to murther, yet a poore traueller will yeeld his purse, rather then venture his life. Neither must they be outfaced with an outward shew and ostentation of the Church, and pictures Speculum pro of their succession in glory, nor new beginnings in infancy; Christianis or our sufferings of martyrdome for conscience of the truth; seductis. their treasons and conspiracies, and due executions of lawes vpon them according to their deserts, with inducements of like qualitie, which are but *phalaræ*, and therefore do *fallere*; as trappings and toppings set out a iade to sale that is not worth his furniture. Neither with intricate and schoole di- stinctions, which the capacitie of the vnlearned can neuer vnderstand nor conceiue, more then that is read in an vn- knowne tongue, as hath bene obserued by Cardinall *Bellar-* Bellar. *mines* confession, such as themselues do not vnderstand. Which may dangerously perplexe, but neuer giue due satif- faction to a conscience that heartily seeks information. Nei- ther with generalities, which commonly implicate many de- ceits, and distill preiudice into the ignorant, against all par- ticulars that may be most pregnantly proued, and wherein heresie and error standeth, and so must be perswaded or con- futed.

14 All the heresies of *Simon Magus, Cerinthus, Ebion, Marcion, Arrius,* and others, were once new; yet they grew with the beginnings of the Gospell, and haue their equall

An-

Antiquitie with the prime of the Church. Theſe, as they haue their ſingular hereſies, ſo haue they bene particularly confuted by diuine authoritie: ſome of them immediatly from the Apoſtles mouthes while they liued; others, by their writings when they were dead. In thoſe times there was no ſuch ſuperlatiue and extrauagant power of the Biſhops of *Rome*, who as they liued vnder tyrannicall perſecution, ſo were they not reſpected but as other Patriarks. When peace by the mercy of God was granted to the Church, then Councels were called againſt emergent hereſies : which were neuer reiected vnder pretence of the Churches authoritie, but by the power of diuine Scriptures, as they were taken and interpreted by the moſt learned Fathers. That which is now moſt predominant, was not then once named for repoſe of conſcience. For the Fathers wrote, and the Councels concluded againſt all heretickes and their hereſies, onely by the Scriptures; as the ſole meanes left by diuine prouidence, and receiued by all that defended the truth. And when all is ſaid and done, we ſhall find it our beſt repoſe at this day.

15   Theſe impediments and rubbidge remoued, I would gladly lay my foundation vpon certaine and vndeniable Aphoriſmes, or Axiomes, or Theoremes, or rules, or grounds, or what you will call them : ſuch, as I verily beleeue, no man profeſſing Chriſtian Religion, will deny, or can ouerthrow. Of which, the firſt toucheth neareſt the glory of God, and the auiling of man. The ſecond in contrary reſpect, the honor and ſtate of the pretended Hierarchy of the Romane Church, or rather Court, with the profit and pleaſure that accrueth vnto the miniſters and officers thereof. The third, that tyrannie and policie, which hath and is yet vſed in that Synagogue in higheſt extent. Laſtly, the outward ſenſes and the affections, which are not to be pleaſed or tickled with delight and admiration. Which is indeed nothing elſe but a pin or naile of *Iaels* tent, brought with butter in a lordly diſh. In which ſeuerals, each hath its particular branches, which will fall into examination by a Chriſtian conſcience.

Iudg.4.19.
5.25.

16 **To**

16   To begin with the firft,I fay, that *The Religion which attributeth in all the paffages thereof moft glorie to God, leaft vnto man, that certainly muft be the true Religion. This doth our Reli-* gion, *not the Romanifts : therefore ours is the trueft Religion, not theirs.* If any man fhall except againft the firft propofition,he wanteth either wit or grace to conceiue or entertaine what belongeth to Gods glory. For we queftion not how far men may feeke Gods glory by one meanes,and fome by another. as *Iobs* friends againft him,and he againft them : they feeking Gods glory out of *Iobs* condemnation; *Iob* by iuftifying a-gainft them, not againft God, his owne integritie. But we fpeake of the bent and fcope of Religion,which aimeth only at Gods glory in all things , or detra&eth therefrom. That aduanceth man in his nature,in his wil, in his integritie,in his merit,more then he deferues,or fhould defire: or deie&s and cafts downe nature and will , and whatfoeuerproceedeth from them vnder the power,and wifedome,and prouidence, and difpofition of God, to approue or difproue what plea-feth or difliketh him. And this is the very fource and foun-taine of all the mercies of God deriued vnto man by Iefus Chrift.

The Romanifts clane contrary.

Iob.

17   For as the beginnings of all riuers and fountaines are from the fea; fo of all vertue,knowledge, and what goodnes foeuer,is from the Lord. And as all riuers returne to the fea, from whence they came; fo muft all thanks and glory be re-turned to God for all the good things he beftoweth vpon vs. Thus therefore we muft ioyne Saint *Paul* with Saint *Iames,* *Euery good giuing,and euery perfe& gift is from aboue, and cometh downe from the Father of lights*:therefore vnto him *that is able to do exceeding abundantly aboue all that we can aske or thinke, ac-cording to the power that worketh in vs,be praife in the Church by Chrift Iefus throughout all generations for euer, Amen. I am Iehouah,faith the Lord, this is my name, and my glorie will I not giue to another, no not to any other,*except his Sonne,who is the *brightneffe of his Fathers glorie , and the ingrauen forme of his perfon*; and therefore was bold to aske, *Father glorifie thy Son, that thy Sonne may alfo glorifie thee*: and was worthy to receiue

Bernard. in Cant.fer.13.

Ecclef.1.7. Ecclus.40.11.

Iam.1.17.

EpheC.3.20.

Efai.42.8.

Hieron.ib. Heb.1.2. Ioh.17.1.

this

Ioh.12.26.

this anſwer from heauen when he prayed, *Father glorifie thy Name: I haue glorified it, and will glorifie it againe.* And theſe were the onely ends of Chriſts coming, and ſuffering in the fleſh, to *glorifie God*, and ſaue ſinners. Therefore he proteſteth that he came *not to ſeeke his owne glorie, but the glorie of him that ſent him.*

Ioh.8.50.
7.18.

18 When one called our Sauiour Chriſt, *Good maiſter:* he anſwered, *There is none good but one, that is, God. Why calleſt thou me good?* Intimating thereby two things: the one, that himſelfe was God: the other, that if he had not bene God, that title of honour had not belonged, and therefore ſhould not be attributed vnto him. *Recte me appellabis bonum, ſi me noueris Deum. Nam cum me nihil aliud quàm hominem putas, quid me dicis bonum?* Thou ſhalt call me good, by good right ,, (ſaith Saint *Auguſtine*) if thou know me to be God: but if ,, thou takeſt me onely for a man, why calleſt thou me good? And *Chryſoſtome: Hac ratione laudem ſibi oblatam ab eo repulit, quia non quaſi Deum bonum, ſed quaſi hominem bonum eum dicebat:* For this cauſe Chriſt refuſed this honour that was offered, becauſe he called him not a good God, but a good man. And Saint *Ambroſe* continueth Chriſts ſpeech thus: *Quid me dicis bonum, quem negas Deum? quid bonum dicis, cum bonus nemo niſi vnus Deus? non ergo bonum negat, ſed Deum ſig-* ,, *nat.* Why calleſt thou me good, and denieſt me to be God? ,, why ſayeſt thou good, when there is none good but God? ,, therefore he denieth not himſelfe to be good, but affirmeth ,, himſelfe to be God. Wherefore as God is onely, truly, and indeed goodneſſe, the roote and fountaine of all good; ſo to him onely is to be referred all glorie, as the ſea and receipt thereof: which who ſo vſurpeth to himſelfe, he doth therein imitate *Lucifer*, that not contented with his owne eſtate wherein he was created, but affected the throne of God, puſt vp in his pride, he *aſcended an Angell, and came downe a diuell.* Which made all the religion of the Gentiles not onely vaine, but odious in the ſight of God: who though *they knew God, yet they glorified him not as God, neither were thankfull, but became vaine in their imaginations, hauing their fooliſh hearts full*

Matth.19.16.

Auguſt. cont.
Max. Arian.
l.3.c.23.

In opere imperf. hom.33.

In Luc. cap.18
lib.8.c 74.

Chryſoſt. in
Mat. hom.64.

Aug.

Rom.1.21.

of

of darkneße: and so gaue the glory of the *Creator to a crea*- Rom.1.21.
ture, and therein aboue meafure difhonoured God.

19   He that came from *Bofra, with his garments all red, and* Efa. 63.3.
*had troden the winepreße alone, and of all nations of the earth there
was none with him*, in the dayes of his flesh profeßed, that his
glorie was nothing, as he was inferiour to his Father. And therefore not onely his words bent all to glorifie God, but his Iohn 8.54.
works alfo: as of *Lazarus, This fickneße is not vnto death, but
for the glory of God, that the Sonne of God might be glorified thereby.* How fignificantly our Lord Iefus fpeaketh, when he attributeth all *glorie to God;* he faith *not that the Sonne of man, but* Iohn 11.4.
that the Sonne of God might be glorified. For though the fame
perfon was the Sonne of man that was the Sonne of God, yet
glorie belonged vnto him, not as he was the Sonne of man,
but as he was the Sonne of God. Therefore the Pharifes
counfell to him that was borne blind, and was recouered by
our Sauiour, was true, and good: *Giue glory vnto God;* though Iohn 9.24.
their motiue and reafon were wicked and malicious, *We know
that this man is a finner.* For if Chrift had bene a finner (as all
men are, excepting him, that was *in all things tempted like vs,* Heb. 4.15.
yet without finne) they had not erred. As in that, *who can far-
giue finnes but God onely?* Certainly the anfwer muft be,
that none can, but that Sonne of man that was the Sonne of
God. And therefore our Sauiour denieth not the propofition,
but excepteth againft it in their application to him, which had
a double nature in one perfon, that they knew not. And when
he taught that moft excellent prayer, he beginneth it with
Our Father, & concludeth it, *For thine is the kingdome, the power* Math.6.13.
and the glory for euer. And fo hath the religious and deuout
wifdome of the Church militant ordered, that all glorie fhall
be afcribed vnto the holy, bleßed & glorious Trinitie. *Glory be
to the Father, and to the Sonne, and to the holy Ghoft.* Vnto the
imitation of the Church triumphant, and thofe foure and
twenty Elders, *Who caft their crownes at his feete that fitteth vp-* Reuel.4.10.11.
*pon the throne, and before the Lambe, faying, Thou art worthie
O Lord to receiue honour, and glory, and power:* and they giue
this reafon, *For thou haft created all things, and for thy wils fake,*
                                                            they

they are, and haue bene created. It was the ſong of the Angell,&

Luke 2. 14. hoſt from heauen: *Glory be to God on high.* And it was the dit-
Reuel. 5.11. tie *of many Angels in heauen, that were round about the throne and about the beaſts, and the Elders ,* and there were *thouſand thouſands ſaying with a loud voyce: Worthy is the Lambe that was killed,to receiue power, and riches, and wiſedome, and ſtrength,and honour, and glory, and praiſe .* And together with them all *the creatures which are in heauen , and on the earth, and vnder the earth, and in the ſea, and all that are in them ,* he heard ſaying, *Praiſe, and honour, and glory, and power vnto him that ſitteth vp-pon the throne, and vnto the Lambe for euermore. Pacem meam do vobis, non gloriam meam do vobis :* Chriſt ſaid to his Apoſtles, *My peace I giue vnto you ,* but neuer to any , I giue you my glorie.

Super Cantic.
ſer.13. 20 Which Saint *Bernard* obſerueth elegantly vpon that of the Angels, *Glorie be to God on high, and in earth peace:* the An-gels diſtinguiſh , what *God reſerueth to himſelfe , and what he vouchſafeth to impart vnto men. He reſerueth glorie for himſelfe, he giueth peace to men; take thankefully what he giueth , and leaue to him what he reſerueth . Abiuro gloriam prorſus ne fortè ſi v-ſurpauero non conceſſum , prodam meritò & oblatum :* I vtterly abiure all glorie,leſt while I vſurpe that thou haſt not vouch-ſafed , I loſe that which thou haſt offered. This may be truly aſſigned the cauſe,why God hath bene pleaſed to produce all his wondrous workes by ſmall , and in the ſight of man, baſe meanes, and weakeſt inſtruments , *That no fleſh might glorie in his preſence,*but that he that will glorie *might glorie in the Lord.*
Bern. in ſer-
mon Epiſtola
123. For *Solus gloriam meretur qui facit mirabilia ſolus ,* He onely ſhould haue the glorie,who onely doth great wonders,which might be exemplified by many particulars, as in *Moſes,* in *Io-ſuah,*in *Sangar,* in *Gedeon,* in *Iephta,*in *Sampſon,*and *Dauid,*and aboue all, which one hath made the greateſt miracle , euen a-
De mirabili-
bus. boue the reſurrection of Chriſt, that ſo few, ſo meane , ſo vn-vnlearned poore fiſher-men , and others of as low eſtates cr meaner vocations, could perſwade the reſurrection of the dead vnto ſo many, whoſe fartheſt capacity before was but onely nature and reaſon, from which nothing is more abhorrent.

rent. These were instruments of wonders; but God hath the glorie.

21 Seeing therefore that praise, and glorie, and giuing of thankes, *are alwayes to be offered vp for all things vnto God in* Ephes. 5.20. *the name of our Lord Iesus Christ:* seeing God himselfe requireth it, and his glorious Sonne both taught it, and practized it; seeing it is the voyce of Saints and Angels in heauen; both of the regenerate, and very naturall men in earth; seeing it hath the consent of all creatures, the beasts of the field, the birds of Psal. 8. the aire, the fishes of the sea, *which in their kind bow their knees,* Psal. 148. and glorifie God their Creator, as a dutie and seruice belon- Phil. 2, 10. ging onely vnto him: it must necessarily follow, that whosoeuer, and whatsoeuer religion detracteth glorie from God, and attributes it to any the works of Gods hands, much more to the works of mens hands, that man is a lyer, and slayeth his owne soule; that religion is false, and hatefull vnto God, both to be abandoned of all that feare God, and loue his Gospell, which is the power of God to saluation to all that beleeue. Rom. 1.16. For God himselfe hath said, *I will giue my glorie to none other.* *He is proud,* saith Saint *Bernard,* that saith, *Though thou giue it* In natali Do- *not, yet will I vsurpe it.* It is the ouerthrow of all, when mortall mini. serm. 4. men are not pleased with the Angelicall diuision: Glory be to God, peace to men; while they vsurpe glorie, they disturbe peace. Wherefore let all the world acknowledge in their hearts, and confesse with their tongues without cauill, distinction, or tergiuersation, as he that was admitted into the secrets of heauen: *To him now that is of power to establish you accor-* Rom. 16.26. *ding to my Gospell, and preaching of Iesus Christ, &c. euen to him* *that is able to keepe vs that we fall not, and to present vs faultlesse* *before the presence of his glorie with ioy; to God onely wise, our* *Sauiour, be glorie and maiestie, and dominion, and power, both now* *and for euer, Amen.*

22 If this be the infallible truth of God, with the vniuersall consent of all his creatures, as without all doubt it is; then though an Apostle, or an *Angell from heauen shall preach any o-* Gal. 1.8. *ther doctrine, let him be accursed.* Accursed the bringer, and accursed the receiuer. For where there is like Priest like people

in

in their error or ſinne, there ſhall be the like iudgement in their condemnation and torment. For which cauſe euery one is bound to looke to one, for euery ones bloud ſhall be vpon his owne head. This is the very caſe betweene the reformed Churches and the Court of Rome. We in all our doctrines giue God the glorie; they in moſt of their poſitions detract from Gods glorie. We debaſe and vilifie all things in our ſelues: they arrogate and aſſume that which is none of theirs, and rob God of his glorie. But wo worth ſuch blind leaders of the blind, who are poore and yet proud, naked and not aſhamed, who feele not that the further they are from the fire, the colder they waxe; who perceiue not that the more remote they are from the light, the blinder they are; who conſider not that the more they detract from the glorie of God, the more ignominious and inglorious they are, and do nothing elſe but ſome out their owne ſhame. Yet the fire remaineth hot, the light cleare, and God euer glorified, in and by his Saints.

23   He that toucheth the leaſt ſparke of Gods glorie, toucheth the apple of Gods eye, and therefore Saint *Bernard* calles it Chriſts *Noli me tangere*: Touch me not. He that fetcheth the leaſt bit of this ſacrifice from Gods altar, though he be *Iouis ales*, the Eagle her ſelfe, will ſet her neſt on fire. Now the queſtion is whether partie is guiltie of this ſacriledge, and high treaſon againſt God, which cannot be diſcerned but by particulars. For in the generall we agree, that all glorie belongeth to God, to vs nothing but ſhame and confuſion of our faces, and therefore we both claime this poſition as proper to our ſelues, each denieth it vnto other. Wherefore we will inſtance in a few particulars. Let the iudicious Reader cenſure.

24   I will begin with the ſcepter of Gods kingdome, which is a right ſcepter: euen the Scriptures, which are the written word of God. Our Church attributeth vnto them all ſufficiency for Chriſtian inſtruction, both for faith & manners. They hold them imperfect, inſufficient; a great indignitie to the glorie of God, his lawes, his laſt will and teſtament, ſuggeſted by the holy Ghoſt, penned by the Prophets and Apoſtles,

Marginal notes:
Supra cap. 2.
Iud. verſe 13.
In feſto omnium Sanctorum, ſerm. 5.
Daniel 9. 7.
Pſal. 45. 6.
Supra cap. 6.

ſtles, ſealed with the bloud of ſo many Martyrs, whereby all
the hereſies of the Primitiue Church, and many ſucceeding a-
ges, and all heretickes were confuted, all errors from age to
age, from generation to generation, were ſuppreſſed, without
any appeale to other Tradit·on, to Church or Pope, vntill
theſe later euill dayes, when the Romaniſts not onely ſee, but
feele their caſe by the Scriptures deſperate. And therefore
they hold it as a note intollerable, neither to the purpoſe nor
truly ſet in the margine of *Iuſtine Martyr*, by *Langius*, *Quòd ad
Scripturam ſacram omnia ſint referenda in diſputationibus Eccleſiaſticis*: That in Theologicall diſputations all things are to be
referred to the holy Scripture. This is purged as an error, but
with a worſe derogation to the word of light and life. But of
this odious and hateful paſſage, there hath bene enough ſpoken before, in the Chapters of Scriptures and Traditions: Supra.cap.6,
where is alſo at large remembred, that they not onely taxe cap.10,
them with inſufficiencie, but in ſuch contemptible and baſe
termes, that a modeſt man would not ſo vilifie *Tullies* offices,
or *Ariſtotles* Ethickes, that onely intreat of good manners
and ciuill honeſtie, no not *Æſops* Fables, and their Moralities.

25   We alſo offer theſe holy Scriptures in thoſe natiue
tongues wherein they were penned and deliuered to the
Church. They will haue a doubtfull, vncertaine, and in compariſon a barbarous tranſlation, pretended indeed to be the
old or Italian tranſlation, corrected by Saint *Hierome*, conferred with the allegations of the· Fathers diſperſed in their
works. Whereas it is vncertaine whether the old Italian
of which Saint *Auguſtine* ſpeakes, was all one; I am ſure Saint
Auguſtine in his works followeth it not in many places that
I haue of purpoſe obſerued : wherein is found ſuch varietie
betweene the Louain tranſlation, *Sixtus* the fift and *Clement*
the eight, by Maiſter *Iames* now worthily Doctor in Diuinitie, a diligent ſearcher, and carefull obſeruer of true *Antiquitie*, as that they not onely differ from many other, but are at Bellum Pa-
irreconciliable warre among themſelues, to their vtter ſhame pale.
ad perpetuam rei memoriam.

26 And whatſoeuer pretence is made, that there was no ſmall paines taken in conference with the Hebrue & Greek fountaines and the Fathers commentaries, yet how little is performed any skilfull Linguiſt wil eaſily diſcerne; and how both *Pagnines, Arias Montanus* paines, and *Poſſeuines* deſires haue bene accepted and ſatisfied, appeareth partly in that nothing is done therein vnto this day, and partly in that there is little likelihood euer any good will be done hereaf-
Analyſ.l.8.c.5 ter. Eſpecially whereas *Gregorius de Valentia* hath bene ſo bold as to preſtolate and forepriſe any ſuch motion. *Porrò* ,, *ex dictis intelligitur, &c. Moreouer by that which hath bene ſaid,* ,, *it is to be vnderſtood, that thoſe authors are not by any meanes to* ,, *be heard, who yet after the Councell of Trent do contend that the* ,, *vulgar Edition may be amended by the Hebrue and Greeke books,* ,, *as by the fountaines (as they ſay) in ſome places, as concerning the* ,, *very ſence or ſentence. Non licet hoc facere, quin potiùs Græci &* Hebraici Codices ſicubi à noſtra editione diſſideant, per noſtram cor-
,, *rigendi & emendandi ſunt &c.* This may not be. But rather ,, the Greeke and Hebrue books, if they be any where diffe-
,, ring from our Edition, ſhould be corrected and amended by ,, it. *For this the Church by a peculiar deciſion hath approued in all* ,, *things, and not them, though it hath not reiected them, but where* ,, *perhaps they croſſe this our edition.* Is not this a faire peece of worke? as if they would turne the world vpſide downe, and put the ſteeple into the Bell, and the Bell into the clapper, beggars an horſebacke, and Lordings lackey: for what is this elſe, when they preferre the riuer before the ſpring, the worke before the rule; the tranſlation before the originall? Which hath ſcarſe bene heard of among profane authors, much leſſe ſhold it be thought vpon in the diuine Scriptures.

27 Let any intelligent Chriſtian conſider in this caſe, whether we are rather to truſt that euidence which is brought out of ſtrangers and enemies hands, and extorted from them by due right and title, in deſpite of them, who for ought we know, agree with neither of vs: or that which our aduerſaries offer vs of their owne tranſlation and edition, out of their one cells or Vatican library, cor-
re&ted

rected or rather corrupted with their owne hands, printed by their sworne seruants, diuulged by their owne authoritie, impofed by their predominant tyrannie. In this certainly God is exceedingly difhonored, and mens wits and authoritie ouerprized and aduanced.

28   The fecrefing and hiding of this word of Scripture vnder the veile, or rather the cruft of an vnknowne tongue, is alfo a great hinderance to Gods glorie. For our Sauiour commanded, that *What I tell in the darkneffe, that fpeake ye* Math.10.27. *in the light, and that you heare in the eare, that preach ye on the houfes. For there is nothing hid that fhall not be opened: neither* Mark.4.22 *is there a fecret, but that it fhall come to light.* This is the will and commandement of the bleffed Sonne of God. How then is God difhonored in keeping that fecret which he would haue open? to appropriate that to priuate, which God wold haue to the common vfe of his whole Church ? where Saint *Paul* would rather himfelfe *fpeake fiue words with his vnder-* 1.Cor. 14.19. *ftanding, that he might inftruct others, then ten thoufand in an vnknowne tongue.* A great difproportion, fiue to ten thoufand. Yet thefe men that pretend the inftruction of others, would rather haue ten hundred thoufand in an vnknowne tongue, then one in a knowne; left the people fhould fee how God is difhonored, and be iealous of his glory.

29   When *M. L. Drufus* purpofed to build an houfe, Velleius Paand his workman promifed to build it fo that it fhould ftand terculus. remote from all fight, free from arbiters, and that no man fhould fo much as looke into it: Nay, faith *Drufus*, if you haue any skill, build my houfe fo, that whatfoeuer I do, all men may fee it. Howfoeuer the world would account *Drufus* wife or foolifh, there is no man but would thinke him honeft and iuft, that durft expofe his priuate conuerfation to all mens view. Faithfull *Abraham looked for a citie, whofe builder* Heb.11.10. *and maker is God.* He prouided himfelfe of workmen, not like falfe Apoftles, who were *operarij fubdoli,* craftie worke- 2.Cor.11.13. men, much leffe *operarij iniquitatis,* workers of iniquitie, *nor mali operarij, euil workers,* but fuch workmen that *need not to be* Phil.3.2. *afhamed.* There is nothing faid or done in this citie or houfe, Luke 13.27. 2.Tim.2.15.

whereof the Maiſter or workmen need to be aſhamed. There was in the Law a ſecret or holy place, whither no man might enter but the Prieſt onely: there is no ſuch reſeruation in **Ierem.31.34.** the Goſpell; from the leaſt to the greateſt, they ſhould know the Lord.

30 The firſt glorious reuelation of the Sonne of God was vnto poore ſhepheards. The Gentiles made fire and wa-ter common. This is the fire of Gods altar, the water of life; ſhall the children of God be debarred of it, without the diſ-honor of their Father, who maketh them large allowance, but that the niggardiſe and miſerable wretchedneſſe of the ſtewards will not affoord it? It may ſeeme a very ſtratageme of the diuel, which he euer hath oppoſed vnto the wiſedome of God. For it hath pleaſed God to write his word in tables, and to cauſe it to be written in bookes, to be read openly to the people: wherein he hath reuealed his whole will. But the diuell hath his ſecret ceremonies, and darke ſeruices of *Veſta*, of *Venus*, of *Bacchus*, which may not be knowne to **Plutarch.** the world. So *Pythagoras, Numa, Lycurgus*, the fathers of ſu-perſtition. What was the reaſon of both? In Gods booke all things were true, holy, pure, righteous, it could abide and endure the light: but their ſeruices and writings were ob-ſcure, falſe, vaine, ridiculous, if men had ſeene them they would haue abhorred them. This is the ods of Gods Scrip-tures and our Seruice in a knowne tongue, the diuels ſecrets and their Maſſes in an vnknowne tongue. Laſciuious Poets and phantaſticall fictions of braine-ſicke fellowes, would be kept from the people, which rather breed corruption of **1.Cor.15.33.** maners then edification in truth; for euil words corupt good manners: but to keepe the light from the children of light, muſt needs be a great diſhonor vnto the Lord of light. Op-poſe not voluntarily and wilfully a cloud of darkneſſe vnto the brightneſſe of the Sunne: ſeeing God hath affoorded it, let it ſhine in perfect beautie. For this is glorious to God, and comfortable to all men. Thoſe who are contrarie min-ded God will iudge.

31 Therefore we complaine, that the prayers of the
Church

Church,which fhould be publicke, are alfo made priuate by
their couering of them vnder the fame bufhell. The Maffe,
and all their Seruice is vtterly darkened from the peoples
vnderftanding,who returne from the Church as *Lycurgus* ci-   Plutarch.
tizens from ther dinner;they might not vtter one word they
heard there,no more could the people bring one word from
the Popifh Seruice. If the Priefts had bene as ill fed as the
people was ill taught, their bellies would haue bene as litle,
as the peoples ignorance was great.

   32   Their additions of humane and vncertaine writings,
& equalling of them to the word of God that hath bene euer
vndoubted, is alfo a great blemifh vnto Gods glory. As if
Gods defeƐs muft be fupplied by mans abundance : and as
if the fountaine of all wifedome had bene exhaufted, and
muft be filled againe with gutters, or broken cifternes of
mens wits and writings. Perhaps, nay out of doubt, in this
cafe our aduerfaries will obieƐ vnto vs, that we difhonour
God rather in detraƐing of thofe Apocryphals, then they in
adding them,or rather continuing them in the Canon,which
we reieƐ.Let this deceiue no man. All the old Church,in all
their Catalogues of the old Teftament, admit no more then
we do for Canonicall Scriptures. The other are afcited, and
iniurioufly annexed, yea inferted into the Canon of the authenticall Scriptures, for aduantage, againft all ancient au-
thoritie.Which *Iames Gretzer*, the moft virulent writer that
euer fet pen to paper,excufeth in the Fathers, rather then denieth it of them,it is fo euident. They refufe them,he confeffeth,as well as we. But forfooth, they do it not,*contumaciter*   Defenf.Bellar.
& pertinaditèr aduerfus Conciliorum generalium fanctiones, with   cap.10. lib.1.
contumacie and pertinacie againft the Decrees of generall
Councels.They be honeft men and good Fathers for leading;
but by the Romanifts learning,we are hereticks for following : they good Catholicks forfaking them, but we fcarce
Chriftians for the fame.

   33   If *vnanimis confenfus Patrum*,the vniforme confent of
Fathers be in any thing controuerted betweene the Roma-
nifts and vs, it is in this ; and therefore *Gretzers* diftinƐions   Ibid.

of *Hebrew,and Church Canons,of doubted and vndoubted,*is doltiſh and idle, forged of late to excuſe a fault, neuer before found . For all the moſt ancient Fathers are for vs. Neither were theſe euer canonized or canoned by any ancient and approued Councell,as before is obſerued,vntill that conuenticle of *Trent* (which is a very midden or muckheape of all the groſſeſt errors and hereſies of the Romane Church) did determine it. I might iuſtly taxe them with the Decrees of *Gratian,*the Decretals of Popes,the traditions of the Church, which are all equalled, againſt pietie and conſcience , with the Scriptures, in all which they wilfully derogate from the glorie of God ; but thereof ſufficient hath bene ſaid before.

34   I might eaſily illuſtrate and enlarge my ſelfe in the ſame kind, by ſundry particulars beſide ; which if I ſhould amplifie but a litle, they would ſurcharge this Chapter with ouerlength:I will onely oppoſe a few things,and that ſhortly, that any conſcience tendering Gods glorie, ſhall eaſily yeeld,that we ſtand on the firmer ground,and are built vpon a ſurer foundation, which is principally to be conſidered for the ſafetie of the building. Ours deliuered in the Scriptures, without all gloſing ; theirs entertained in their Schooles, with intricate diſtinctions,ſuch as the people can neuer comprehend.

35   We hold this concluſion, *A man is iuſtified by faith without the workes of the Law.* This, with all the ancienteſt Fathers,we take to be faith, not alone or ſolitary, without *holineſſe,without which no man ſhall ſee God:* but onely without any merit or deſert of ours: *And to be found in him, not hauing our owne righteouſneſſe which is of the Law, but that which is through the faith of Chriſt ,the righteouſneſſe which cometh of God through faith.* Theſe words are direct, they containe in this point the faith of the old Romanes,which Saint *Paul* taught them,and reſted vpon himſelfe. Here needs no gloſſe, no *meritum congrui* or *condigni,*neither congruitie nor condignitie, nor *opera antecedentia* or *ſubſequentia* going before or following after iuſtification ; *no firſt and ſecond iuſtice.* God hath the glorie,

Rom.3.28.

Heb.12.14.

Philip.3.9.

man

man hath the shame.

36 *Bellarmine* confesseth it *the safest way.* No learned Pa- Bellar. de Iu-
pist (as I am perswaded) dareth make any other plea before stif.l.5.c.7.tu-
God on his deathbed, when he is to stand as he falleth, either tissimum.
to the Lord by faith in his mercie, or from the Lord with
confidence in his owne merits. This is heresie at *Rome*; they
haue *merita operum,* and *opera merentur,* merits of works, and
works do merit. Though Christ bids vs say, *When we haue* Luk.17.10.
done all we can , yet we are vnprofitable seruants: yet they will
haue God vniust, if he *giue vs not saluation for our workes: which* Rhemists.
he ought to render as duly, as hell fire for our ill workes: yea, which
is more, they can do works of supererogation, and make vp
a treasure of one mans works for another, when a man hath
deserued more then will serue his owne turne; which that
no man may or should presume, *Bellarmine* proueth by an ineuitable Dilemma : *Vel habet homo vera merita, vel non habet:* Bellar. de Iu-
si non habet, periculose fallitur, seque ipse seducit, dum in falsis me- stif.l.5.c.7.
ritis confidit. Istæ enim sunt fallaces diuitiæ apud S. Bernardum,
quæ veras impediunt. Si verò habet, nihil perdit ex eo quòd ipse ea
non intuetur, & in solo Deo confidit. Either a man hath true me- „
rits, or he hath not : if he haue not, he is dangerously decei- „
ued, and seduceth himselfe, while he trusteth in false merits. „
For these are but deceitfull riches with Saint *Bernard,* which „
hinder true (riches.) If he haue, he loseth nothing by this, „
that he respecteth not them, but trusteth onely in God. „

37 How dishonorable is it to God, to haue a base wret- Gen.18.27.
ched sinfull creature, verier dust and ashes then *Abraham,* a Psal 22.6.
vilder worme then *Dauid,* a more wretched man then Saint Rom.7 24.
Paul, who confessed himselfe of all sinners the chiefe, stand 1.Tim.1.15.
out in the face of his omnipotent Creator, and presuming to
approach vnto his chaire of iustice, and pleade his owne righteousnesse, his owne merits, his owne deseruings for himselfe
and others? How glorious will it be to God, for the oldest
Patriarks, the diuinest Prophets, the sincerest righteous men,
the most blessed Apostles, Euangelists, Martyrs, to stand at
the footstoole of his Maiesties mercies seate, acknowledging
their sinnes, begging of pardon, crying for helpe, renouncing

them-

themſelues, appealing to his promiſes, embracing his mercies, bewailing their vnworthineſſe, proclaiming his goodneſſe, and by faith laying hold on their bleſſed Sauiour for the forgiueneſſe of their ſinnes, and ſauing of their ſoules? Let theſe Phariſes approch as neare vnto the throne of Gods iuſtice as they dare, with preſumption of their works; I will ſtand afar off, and knocke my breaſt with the Publican, and ſay, *Lord be mercifull to me a ſinner.*

Luk.18,13.

38 How glorious is it to God, that his word be like himſelfe, abſolute, and without imperfection? that his commandements ſhould haue that height, that depth, that length, that breadth, which might become ſuch a pure and powerfull maieſtie to giue? ſo compleate and iuſt, as might fit ſo excellent a creature who anſwered the image of God, to receiue? Such commandements did our glorious God deliuer, as wherein ſhined the glory of his iuſtice, not of his mercie: manifeſting what man was bound vnto, and what he might haue eaſily fulfilled if he had remained in his integritie; and thereby concluding all mankind after *Adams* fall *vnder ſin,* both *Iewes and Gentiles,* as the Apoſtle Saint *Paul* proueth to the old Romanes. And not onely theſe ten Commandements of Gods morall law, but *the whole Scripture hath concluded all vnder ſin, that the promiſe of faith by Ieſus Chriſt, ſhould be giuen to them that beleeue.*

Rom.3.9.

Gal.3.22.

39 This is not a paſſage like an interlocutory ſentence, but it is a concluſion, *tanquam res iudicata,* a iudgement paſſed, that expecteth nothing but execution; a definitiue ſentence, not in any ſmall trifle, but for *ſinne, the reward whereof is death,* not on ſome, but on all that are concluded vnder ſin, without exception. To this end, without all doubt, that the glorie of Gods mercie might appeare by faith in *Ieſus Chriſt,* which is not ſold and bought, no nor yet deſerued, but *giuen;* and what is freer then gift? and that not vnto all that are concluded vnder ſinne by the Law, but to them *that beleeue?* Yet our aduerſaries make this Law of God eaſie to be fulfilled, euen in the ſtate of corruption; wherein all *Adams* children are inuolued, excepting Ieſus Chriſt that knew no ſinne. Pretending

Rom.6.23.

tending that becaufe our Sauiour hath faid, *That his yoke is* Math.11.29. *easie, and his burthen is light*: and for that Saint *Iohn* faith, *His* 1.Iohn 5.3. *Commandements are not heauie*, therefore all the commandements of God are eafie and light, and portable enough. Not vnderftanding, that this is not meant as the commandements are in themfelues, or as the performance is exacted by God in the feueritie and rigor of his iuftice which muft be fatisfied, but as they are made vnto vs, that are in Chrift Iefus, and as God conformeth our hearts to the willing obedience vnto his Law. Which though as it proceedeth from vs, be full of imperfection, yet by the fupply of Chrifts obedience, who hath layd his fhoulder to our burthen, it is accepted as moft Colof. 1. 12. perfect obedience without fpot or wrincle. If this will not be accepted as a fufficient anfwer out of my pen, let Saint *Hie-* *rome* fpeake it, or rather Saint *Paule* in him. *Poffibilia (inquit* Hieron. ad *Pelagius Papifta) mandata dedit Deus. Ecquis hoc negat ? Sed* Ctefiph. c.4. *quomodo hæc intelligenda fit fententia, vas electionis apertiffimè do-* *cet: ait enim, Quod erat impoffibile legi, in quo infirmabatur per* *carnem: Deus Filium fuum mittens, in fimilitudine carnis peccati,* *de peccato, condemnauit peccatum, in carne.* A Papifticall Pela- „ gian will fay, that God hath giuen poffible Commande- „ ments. And who denies it ? but how this is to be vnderftood, „ *that veffell of election* fheweth plainly. For he faith, That which Rom. 8.13. was impoffible to the Law, in that it was weake according „ to the flefh, God fending his Sonne in the fimilitude of finfull „ flefh, condemned finne in the flefh. This is neither Pelagia- „ nifme nor Papiftrie.

40 I will in this cafe but deliuer a prefumptuous affertion of a Papift, and confute it by an vndeniable experience of an ancient Father, which I thinke will giue fatisfaction to an honeft heart. No doubt his fellow Iefuites, who haue fued to haue him Sainted, haue no leffe eftimation of their brother *Gonzaga* then he had of his owne integritie. Cardinall *Bel-* Gonzaga. *larmine* before a publicke Notary affirmed, that he verily Ceparius in e-thought him to be without mortall finne in all his life, but ius vita.l.3.c.2 was fure from feuen yeares. He could find *no veniall finne* Item fol.220. *in himfelfe* : this feemed to grieue him that he could not find it.

Fumus armil-
la in verb cir-
cumstantia,
nu. 2.
it. He neuer then needed to go to confeſſion; for he needed not to confeſſe veniall ſinnes, he could not confeſſe mortall. Which whether it were more pride in him to be ſo perſwaded, or peruerſeneſſe, ſo to murmure againſt that, which (if it had bene true) was ſo good for him, ſuch a mercy from God; let his compeers iudge; whatſoeuer they thinke, I will neuer defend it nor beleeue it. If *inuidentia fraternæ gratiæ*, be by the ſchoolemen made a ſinne againſt the holy Ghoſt, why not this, *inuidentia propriæ gratiæ*, againſt himſelfe? as it is counted a more haynous ſinne to kill a mans ſelfe, then to ſlay another.

Tho. Aquin. 2
2.q.14.art.2.
Lombard.l.2.
diſt.43.c.For-
taſſe.

41   Saint *Hierome* makes this a plaine Pelagian hereſie, and confutes it with many arguments. Among other paſſages to this purpoſe he ſaith: When the Pelagians had fooliſhly anſwered, ſeeking with a new *tricke to illude the truth*, that forſooth they meant not that any preſent, or paſt could fulfill the Law, but yet *there might be ſuch*: *Egregij Doctores dicunt eſſe poſſe, quod nunquam fuiſſe demonſtrant*: Trim Doctors, that ſay a thing may be, which themſelues demonſtrate neuer was. Againe, *Facilia dicis Dei eſſe mandata, & tamen nullum proferre potes, qui vniuerſa compleuerit*: Thou ſayeſt the commandements of God are caſie, and yet thou canſt produce no man that euer fulfilled them all. He proceedeth with his ineuitable *dilemma* by way of queſtion: Are they *eaſie or hard? if eaſie, bring me the man that hath fulfilled them*. Perhaps *Bellarmine* will find *Gonzaga* a Ieſuite: but neither *Peter*, nor *Paul*, *Iames*, nor *Iohn*, Prophet, nor Apoſtle. But if they be difficult, with what face *canſt thou ſay, they are eaſie, when no man euer fulfilled them?* And therefore yet ſaith in the following dialogues againſt the ſame heretickes, *Noli ponere in cœlum os tuum, vt per eſſe, & eſſe poſſe, ſtultorum illudas auribus; quis enim tibi concedet, poſſe hominem facere, quod nullus vnquam hominum potuerit? Gonzaga*, ſet not thy mouth againſt heauen, with thy, it is, or it may be, to deceiue the eares of fooles; for who will grant, that a man can do that which neuer man could? and thou *Gonzaga* canſt neuer be perfect, *niſi imperfectum te eſſe noueris*, except thou know thy ſelfe to be imperfect. But if the Romaniſts will

Hieron. ad
Cteſiphon.

Idem in dia-
log. aduerſ.
Pelag.l.1.c.2.

not

not be taught by the euident Scriptures, and the conſent of the moſt of the Fathers: as the ſluggard is ſent to the Ant or Piſmire, to learne prouidence, ſo will I ſend him to a heathen, or rather Saint *Hierome* himſelfe doth it, euen to *Horace* a Poet: *Nam vitijs nemo ſine naſcitur, optimus ille, qui minimis* Iuuen. *vrgetur,*

> *No man without faults was ere borne or bred,*
> *H'is beſt, to feweſt that can be miſ-led.*

42   With this ſpeech I had thought to haue ended this paſſage, but that Saint *Auguſtine* offereth this ſentence, as a ſword to cut the throate of this preſumption: *Vnuſquiſque,* Auguſt. de ci-*(quamuis laudabiliter viuens) cedit in quibuſdam carnali concu-* uitate Dei.l.1. *piſcentiæ, & ſi non ad facinorum immanitatem, & gurgitem flagi-* c.9. *tiorum, atque impietatis abominationem, ad aliqua tamen peccata* Reade his *vel rara, vel tanto crebriora, quantum minora;* Euery man whole booke (though he liue laudably) yeelds in ſome things to carnall de perfectio-concupiſcence, and if not vnto the height of villanies, and to „ ne iuſtitiæ. the gulfe of wickedneſſe, and the abhomination of impietie, „ yet vnto ſome ſinnes though ſeldome, yet by ſo much the of- „ tener, by how much the leſſer. And ſo may a ſhip be as well „ ſunke in the ſand as ſplitted at a rocke, if God enter into iudgement with him: in whoſe ſight no man liuing can be iu- Pſal.143.3. ſtified.

43   Who can more derogate from Gods glorie then he that attributeth vnto man the freedome of his will, euen in the ſtate of nature? God by his Spirit doth plainly tell vs, *that we cannot ſo much as thinke a good thought, as of our ſelues,* but 2.Cor. 3.5. *all our ſufficiencie is of God.* For it is *God that giueth vs the will* Philip.2, 13. *and the deed, not of ours, but of his good pleaſure.* Were it not a great credit for the Maiſter of a ſhip, if euery marriner ſhould take vpon him to ſit at the helme and guide the ſhip as well as he? Certainly, it is aboue meaſure diſhonourable vnto God to take that power into our owne libertie, from him, that hath all reſting in his owne hands. The hearts of Kings Pro. 21.1. are in the hands of God, much more of all the inferiour ſort. And *what haue we that we haue not receiued? If we haue receiued,* 1.Cor. 4.7. *why do we boaſt, as if we had not receiued?* Saint *Paule* himſelfe
could

could find no man,no nor thing, *that could deliuer him from the body of death, but onely the grace of God in Chriſt Ieſus our Lord.* They arrogate therefore exceedingly vnto themſelues,and derogate from the ſtrength of God, who attribute that vnto the weakeneſſe of man, which belongeth onely to the will and direction of almighty God that is aboue nature.

Rom. 7.24.

44 We haue the expreſſe charge of our glorious Creator, *To call vpon him in the day of trouble and he will heare vs, that we might glorifie him:* And *Thou ſhalt worſhip the Lord thy God, aud him onely ſhalt thou ſerue.* We haue the call of the Sonne of God, *Come vnto me all ye that labour and are heauie loaden, and I will refreſh you. How ſhall we call on him in whom we do not beleeue?* But we beleeue in none but in the bleſſed Trinitie. Therefore we are to call vpon none other. We haue but one God, *and one mediator betweene God and man, the man Ieſus Chriſt.* As but one God, ſo but one mediator. *If we ſinne, we haue an Aduocate with the Father, euen Chriſt the righteous, who is the propitiation for our ſinnes. Who ſitteth at the right hand of God, and maketh continuall interceſſion for vs, and the holy Ghoſt intreateth for vs.* God challengeth all this to himſelfe, and to his bleſſed Sonne, with our Sanctifier which is the holy Ghoſt. What euaſion is left that modeſty and an honeſt heart can pretend? For her is *innocation, adoration, ſeruice, mediation, aduocation, interceſſion,* and all for God. No Angels either required any of theſe, or accepted them when they were offered. No Patriarke, Prophet, no righteous man, no Apoſtle, or holy Martyr euer practiſed otherwiſe in this caſe, but as we teach and deſire to performe. Our aduerſaries diſclaime Scriptures in this behalfe. The people are neuer able to vnderſtand their nice diſtinctions, and euaſions of *latria, dulia, and hyperdulia, of mediator of redemption, and interceſſion.* We ſee what is forbidden,we find what is commanded.God knoweth what is beſt for vs,moſt glorious to him ; wherein we ought to reſt.

Pſal. 50.15.

Math. 11.28.

Rom. 10.14.

1. Iohn 2.1.

Rom. 8.

45 It is but idle to tell vs, that the glorie which they giue vnto Gods Saints, he taketh and accepteth as done vnto himſelfe. Theſe are the parts of Gods worſhip, which he hath

appro-

appropriated to his diuine nature : he will impart it to none other : neither may we pretend the prayers of the liuing Saints one for another, seeing the question is of Saints departed this life. We make holy vse of that which God commandeth or permitteth, we detest that which God refuseth and reiecteth. He that prayeth vnto God, by Iesus Christ, through the sanctifying of the holy Ghost, is sure that he prayeth not amisse. All other adorations, prayers, supplication,&c. tendered to the Saints or any creature, cannot be denyed to be doubtfull, if not damnable. Therefore it is most comfortable to men, most glorious to God, that we call vppon him, who ought to be feared, and glorified for euer.

46 Can any man be so simple in knowledge, or hardened in impudency, as to deny that all the Scriptures of God, with that distinct and district commandement against Images, stand for vs against our aduersaries? To omit other texts of Scriptures, together with the consent of all the truest and first *Antiquitie* of the primitiue Church : the very words of the text, without all glosse, are so plaine, written in so great characters, that he that runnes may reade them. *Thou shalt not make to thy selfe any grauen Image, nor the likenesse* Exod.20.4. *of any thing that is in heauen aboue, or in the earth beneath; thou* Deut.5.6. *shalt not bow downe to them, nor worship them. Making* to any religious vse, to our selues, without Gods commandement, as in the Cherubins : *of things in heauen aboue,* neither of God himselfe, or Angels, nor yet the fowles in the aire, not in the earth or vnder it, beasts, fishes, or creeping things, *neither bow downe vnto them,* wherein all outward reuerence is forbidden: *nor worship them,* wherein all inward deuotion is denied vnto them.

47 All which notwithstanding, the Popish Church makes them to *religious* vses. They make them by their own authoritie, without all allowance of God. They make Images of God the Father, like an old man; of God the Sonne, in sundry shapes, old and yong; like a graue man preaching, or a little child playing in his Mothers lap. It may be to the imitation

Plutarch in Theſ.

tation of the *Athenians*, who had a litle God, called *Calcodus*. Or rather renewing the remembrance of that wicked time,& thoſe blaſphemous hereſies which Saint *Baſil* complaineth

Baſil.epiſt.70. of and lamenteth: *Magnus apud illos Deus eſt & paruus:* They haue a great God and a little, and liuing in the cradle, and dying on the Croſſe. The holy Ghoſt like a Doue, the bleſſed Trinitie like *Gerion* with three faces to one body, as he had three bodies to one face. Angels like men with wings. Saint *Iohn* with an Eagle, and Saint *Hugh* with a Gooſe, or a Swan at moſt. Saint *Hierome* with a Lion, and Saint *Antonie* with a pigge; and perhaps theſe birds and beaſts were worſhipped as well as their Maiſters that ſtood by them. By this deuice of painting, picturing and imagerie, they could giue the bleſſed Virgine prerogatiue to be conceiued without ſinne,

In the common Legend, and in many pictures. by her fathers and mothers kiſſing onely; as if ſhe had not bene begotten according to the common order of nature. A greater miracle to be ſo begotten then to be borne of a virgine. She commonly pictured with a triple crowne, when the *Trinitie* is bare headed; and ſhe ſometime a faire Imperiall crowne, and her Sonne with none; ſhe giuing books, her Son but beads; ſhe treading on the ſerpents head, he playing in his mothers lap; ſhe as vertue in the middeſt and moſt excellent, ſitting betweene God the Father and her Sonne, the holy Ghoſt like a bird, fluttering ouer her head. With infinite more ſuch blaſphemous conceipts, whereby a moſt vile contempt is ingendred of the glorious Deitie, in the heads and hearts of ſilly people, when they behold it deiected to ſo baſe a comprehenſion, the creature worſhipped with or aboue the Creator, who is onely bleſſed for euer.

Supra cap.17.

48 Moreouer, the woodden Croſſe of Chriſt is taught to be worſhipped with diuine worſhip, onely proper to God by their owne learning. And that becauſe it either touched

Tho. Aquinas part.3.art. 4. quæſt.25. the body, or was ſprinkled with the bloud of Chriſt, or for the ſimilitude of his expanſion. And yet they teach that neither the body of Chriſt ſeparated from the diuinitie, nor the bloud ſeparated from the body, is to be adored with that

worſhip

worfhip which they allow vnto the Croffe. If any Romane
Catholique will vouchfafe to reade this paffage, I dare appeale to his owne confcience, yea to one of a thoufand, yea
ten thoufand, yea millions of thoufands, whether he do vnderftand the diftinctions of *Typus* & *prototypus*, of *latria, dou-
lia*, and *hyperdoulia*; and I wot not what the like, wherewith
they aftonifh poore Chriftians, and with men of vnderftanding fhame themfelues. The worft in all this cafe that they
can obiect vnto vs, is but that wherewith the Poet derided
Gods people for lacke of Images:	Iuuenal.
 Et puras nubes, & cœli numen adorant:
 On clouds they onely call,
 And heauenly God withall.

 49 In this vaine, fuperftitious, and idolatrous worfhip,
they difhonor God, who is not to be worfhipped but in fpi- Iohn 4.
rit and truth, which our Church doth both teach and practife, and therfore giueth glorie to God in all thefe premifes.
The Romanifts difglorifie God in all thefe particulars, and
thereby fcandalize the Chriftian Religion both with Iewes
and Turks, befide other infidels who are foftered in the fame
idolatrie by fo wicked an example. Not one of thefe points,
but in the letter our aduerfaries hold, and that I know,
deny not but that all theirs may hold them fafely. All this
notwithftanding is queftionable, doubtful; and may be, for
any thing a fimple Chriftian can vnderftand, dangerous and
pernicious. Therefore to an vnlearned Chriftian ours is the
beft and fafeft. I will conclude this with a paffage of one of
their owne friends, whofe true confeffion may ftand againft
our aduerfaries for a certaine euiction of their groffe, dangerous, and intollerable Idolatrie. *Multi Chriftiani in re bo-* Lodouic.Vi-
na plerumquò errant, quòd diuos, diuáfque non aliter venerantur ues in Aug.de
quam Deum: Nec video in multis, quid fit difcrimen inter eo- l.8.c.vlt.
rum opinionem de Sanctis, quàm id quod Gentiles putabant de Dijs
fuis: Many Chriftians offend for the moft part in a good cafe,
who worfhip their he Saints and fhe Saints no otherwife
then they worfhip God himfelfe; neither do I fee in many
things what difference there is between their opinion of the
              Saints,

„ Saints , and that which the Gentiles thought of their Gods.
Neither are theſe words purged by the Romane Cenſures.

50 My ſecond conſideration, is honor, profit or pleaſure,
vnto the chiefe leaders and guides; as Prieſts and Church officers, which I would frame thus. *That religion which brin-*
geth and continueth moſt honour, and pleaſure to the Clergie ; that
is moſt ſuſpitious vnto the Laitie; and ſo contrary : *that is their*
religion, not ours. Therefore their religion is ſuſpitious , and
not ours. Although ſomewhat hath bene ſaid of the firſt propoſition in the fourth Chapter among Cardinall *Bellarmines*
notes of his Church; where it is proued that proſperity is not
ſo much as a probable marke thereof; yet a word or two as
the caſe requireth. In conſideration wherof, if we ſhall turne
backe to the obſeruations of former times, we ſhall find that
though the Patriarks were eminent in their generations, yet
nothing in compariſon of the nations round about them.
They liued in diuers ſeates , in famines , and perils, in exile,
and bondage, and grieuous oppreſſions , that any man may
euidently behold rather extraordinary diuine prouidence in
their protection, then any ſtately being to procure countenance in the world.

51 Vnder the Law, the Prieſts & Leuites were wel prouided for to liue among their brethren, but no ſupereminen-
cy in any thing but the immediate ſeruice of God, which was
not lawfull for any other Tribe to execute. The high Prieſt
himſelfe was ſubiect to the ciuill Magiſtrate, was by him ordered, and might vpon due deſert be depoſed, as *Abiathar*
was. They did ſlay the ſacrifices, preſerued the fires, cleanſed
the Tabernacle, and layd it vpon their ſhoulders when it remoued. They did neuer ouertop the Nobles, but held themſelues to Gods ſeruice, with all humilitie. The Leuites were
ſcattered among the tribes for the peoples good, not their
own benefite. They are coupled with the poore & the ſtran-
ger , that ſhall be partakers and be fed with the firſt fruits
of the peoples increaſe. Their reſpect was giuen vnto them
rather for their goodneſſe then their greatneſſe. They neuer
aſſumed any title which God gaue them not; they neuer
encroched

encroched authoritie which God allowed them not, nor v-
surped any thing but what Gods Law affoorded them.

52 In the new Teſtament our Sauiour taſted nothing
but diſhonour, want, and griefe; he promiſed no better to
his Apoſtles; they enioyed no other while they liued; they
left no order after them to aduance the Preachers of the
Goſpell vnto high eſtates. It was long in the Primitiue
Church before the thought of Ambition came into the Biſhops of *Romes* hearts. They were vnder the rod of Gods
correction, vnder the hands of wicked tyrants that did ſhed
their bloud without pitie or mercie. Then there was no talking of Pope aboue Emperour, nor Cardinals compared, if
not preferred before Kings; with the reſidue of the Eccleſiaſticall Hierarchie, which our bleſſed Sauiour neuer taught,
when by word he forbad them to be as Princes; nor yet by Mat.20.26.
example, when he waſhed his Apoſtles feete; and was fol- Ioh.13.4.
lowed by the poore people, when the great ones deſpiſed Mat.11.5.
him.

53 Their treaſures in the primitiue times were vertues,
learning, and deuotion; their pleaſures were paines, in preaching of the word, in labouring night and day, in patient
ſuffering of many perſecutions; yea in dying for the name of
the Lord Ieſus. In this Saint *Paul* gloried, when he ſaid, *God* Gal.6.14.
forbid that I ſhould reioyce in any thing but in the croſſe of our
Lord Ieſus Chriſt, whereby the world is crucified vnto me, and I
vnto the world. And herein the Apoſtles reioyced, that they
were thought worthy to ſuffer *perſecution for the name of* Act.5.41.
Chriſt. There was no glorying in triple Crownes, in Cardinals hats, in Archbiſhops Palles, in Biſhops Miters, in Croſſes
or Croſiers, no talke of *Peters* keyes or *Pauls* ſword. But *Sil-* Act.3.6.
uer and gold haue I none, was Saint *Peters* word. Shew me a
Pope theſe thouſand yeares that could ſay ſo, and ſpeake
truly; or need ſay ſo, except he was driuen to neceſſitie by
his owne wilfulneſſe, and the faction of his Cardinals, as *Bo-*
niface the eight, though he called himſelfe *Mundi Dominum,*
Lord of the world, that would change Gods *bleſſing and his,*
for meate and drinke, as *Eſau* ſold his birthright for a meſſe of

pottage : yet this was not for pouertie, but vpon ſtraight
ſiege; for, as the ſtorie ſaith, there was more treaſure found
in his Pallace, and his three Cardinals, and the Marquis,
then all the Kings of the world were able to make for one
yeare.

54   If this be the ſtate of the Romane Church, as well or
rather as ill in her head as members, it is no maruell if the
belly haue no eares, and that they cannot hearken to the *Fa-*
ble of the Goſpell, as Pope *Leo* the tenth called it, with ſo great
loſſe. But if they were kept at the pittance which the fourth
Councell of *Carthage* allowed them, perhaps they would be
the more eaſily intreated. There were then no Biſhops Pal-
laces, but *Hoſpitiolum non longè ab Eccleſia* , a litle hoſtill or a
lodging neare the Church: and *Vt Epiſcopus vilem ſupellecti-*
lem, & menſam, & victum pauperem habeat, & dignitatis ſuæ au-
thoritatem, fide & vitæ meritis quærat : That a Biſhop ſhould
,, haue but meane houſhold ſtuffe, a poore table and diet, and
,, ſhould ſeeke the reputation of his worth by the deſert of his
,, faith and life. And this is inſerted in their Decrees. If experience teach vs, that a Prince will betake himſelfe to Antichriſt for a Dukedome, or a King for the acceſſe of a kingdome, we may not wonder that ſome Popes haue bequea-
thed themſelues to the diuell, as *Siluſter* the ſecond, for a
Popedome; and that *Paulus quintus* will beare him company
rather then loſe his triple Crowne ; and the Captaine will
want no followers, in ſo glorious, ſo pleaſurable, and ſo profitable an expedition.

55 When *Peter* warmed his hands he denied his Maiſter.
A warme kitchin is a great preſeruatiue of the Romane Clergie. *Probus* the Emperour was ſlaine by his ſouldiers, becauſe
when he had brought the world to peace, he ſaid, *Breui fu-*
turum, vt legionibus atque præſidys nihil eſſet opus : He hoped
that ſhortly he ſhould need no more ſouldiers. I beleeue, if
the Pope ſhould but ſay ſo of his Monks and Friers, the Ieſuites would take it as they did the abſolution of the
French King at the hands of *Sixtus quintus,* who liued not
long after, & for that cauſe, as the Secular Prieſts report. It is
not

Bale.

Can.14.

Can.15.
Diſtinct 41. E-
piſc.

Dux Nuren-
burg.

not the precious ſtones of *Aarons* garments, nor of the cele- Iacob.Reihin, muri ciuit. ſanctæ.
ſtiall *Hieruſalem*, as is pretended, but of *Paris* and *Gulicke*,
with their appertenances, that make Nobles ſudden Proſe-
lites and Apoſtataes, who were otherwiſe taught before, all
the dayes of their liues.

56 No more is it the old Teſtament or the new, that
the Romane Clergie reſpect, but their owne emoluments
and profits. Perhaps they may helpe the crie, with the rude
multitude,*Great is Diana of the Epheſians*, and ſo pretend a
religion,though it be idolatrous ; but the matter that moues
them to ſtand out,rather *pro focis* then *pro aris*, rather for their
chimneys then their Churches, is the reaſon of *Demetrius* to
the Craftſmen, *Sirs, you know that by this craft we haue our* Act.19.25.
goods. And it would be long ere we ſhould find one among
their Prieſts that would forſake all to follow Chriſt, or ſell
all to buy that precious pearle that our Sauiour ſpeaketh of.
This would be *durus ſermo*, a hard ſaying, for they haue great Ioh. 6.60.
riches. I would take him for a true conuert, that would ſo Mat.19.22.
conuert as Chriſt teacheth. *Demas* would find more companions then Saint *Matthew* or *Zachæus:* and the Pope would Mat.9.9.
haue more Chaplains then our Sauiour Chriſt diſciples. It is Luk.19.6.
no wonder to ſee men loue rather the praiſe of men then the
praiſe of God,and to be honoured in this world, howſoeuer
they ſhift for heauen. *Pride,fulneſſe of bread,and idleneſſe,*were Ezech.16.49.
three of the foure ſinnes that reigned in *Sodome* till it was
deſtroyed. Voluptuouſneſſe, vainglory and couetouſneſſe, Mat.4.
were the three temptations wherewith the diuell aſſayled
our Sauiour himſelfe. Theſe ſinnes as they may be paralelled
in themſelues, ſo certainly they are vnder other termes, the
very ſame that vnto this day predominate in the Church of
Rome, Honour,profit,pleaſure. From whence (as out of the
Troian horſe) iſſue infinite armies and ſwarmes of the Romane Clergie, that care not whom they ruine and ranſacke,
in reuenge of their faire *Helen* the whore of *Babylon*, who
cauſeth the very Kings of the earth to fall downe and worſhip her for theſe precious ſtones, more deare vnto them
then the beautifull walls of the celeſtiall *Ieruſalem*.

Mm 2   57 To

57 To apply this generall in each particular vnto the Romane Courtly Church, though it were eaſie becauſe it is plaine, yet would it be troubleſome, they are ſo many. A few for illuſtration may ſerue, by which the reſt may be ſcantled; for example, their honour in their ingroſſed titles, in their incroched preference, in their ſupereminent authoritie, vnlimited iuriſdiction, and vnbounded ſoueraigntie appeareth, not onely as by a cloud of witneſſes, but as a ſea of Iurers, that will depoſe and giue verdict againſt them before that iuſt Iudge of quicke and dead. The great Maiſter, who hath

De notis Eccleſ.l.4.c.8.

bene contented with the name of *Preſbyter*, as *Irenæus* called *Victor*, *Anicetus*, *Pius*, *Teleſphorus*, and *Xiſtus*, as Cardinall *Bellarmine* confeſſeth, diſdaineth the title of Archbiſhop or Patriarch, which were his firſt names. The very name of *Papa*, which in the originall ſignifieth a father, or as it may be taken, and is by ſome, *Pater patrum*, Father of fathers; or rather now *Papé*, an Interiection of wonder, ſince he is become *Stupor mundi*, the dread monſter of the world; or perhaps

Aul. Perſius Sat. 6.

Popa, (and ſo *Pope* from him that cut the throate of the ſacrifice, as he doth of good Chriſtians that profeſſe the truth againſt his idolatry:) is ſcorned as nothing, except *Sanctiſſimus* be put vnto it. Which hath bene as due to many of them, as vnto their father paramount the diuell himſelfe. Or which better agreeth with him, as he hath embraced all things into his owne reach, *Oecumenicus*, vniuerſall, or *Optimus maximus*,

Extraua.Ioan. 22. de verb. ſignif.cap.4. Gloſſa in fine.

which is yet more, or *Diuinam numen*, a diuine Godhead; or in plaine termes, *Dominus Deus noſter Papa*, Our Lord God the Pope: which is taken for a title ſo due, that a Pope is not aſhamed to pleade it againſt an Emperour : that he may not be iudged by humane iudgement, becauſe forſooth it is euident he hath by an Emperour bene called a God. Which titles if they were offered vnto him by a few flatterers and Poets, it might be taken rather as a ieſt, or at moſt a faſhion, or a fault in them, without iuſt imputation of pride in him, though it be much to ſuffer it. But their ſageſt Canoniſts, their greateſt Diuines, giue theſe titles in their Prefaces in their bookes, he refuſeth them not, and they haue bene

ordinarily

ordinarily ſet in the Canon lawes. Himſelfe accepteth them
aſſumeth them, challengeth them as due and appropriate vnto
himſelfe.

58 One Croſſe of wood which our Sauiour caried on his
backe, was ſufficient to beare his title ouer his head, *Ieſus of* Mat.27.37.
Nazareth King of the Iewes. But if it ſhould be written behind, and before, from top to bottome, in the leaſt character,
it could not containe the Popes titles. And therefore belike
it is that he hath a triple Croſſe of gold caried before him
vpon another mans ſhoulder, as well to ſignifie the multitude
of his titles, as to certifie the world, that he beareth not one
Croſſe himſelfe, but layeth vpon other mens backes a
triple Croſſe of moſt couetous and inſatiable exactions, moſt
thundering and fearefull excommunications, moſt dreadfull
and damnable murtherings of peoples by vniuſt warres, of
Princes, by moſt ſecret and wicked ſtratagemes, conſpiracies
and treaſons, and ſaith in his heart,

> *Flectere ſi nequeam ſuperos, Acheronta mouebo.*
> *If Gods will not be mou'd to my deſire,*
> *Ile fetch the Diuels out of hell fire.*

59 To deſcend by all their degrees in their Eccleſiaſticall
Hierarchie were ſuperfluous, they haue bene publiſhed by o-
thers, and are now notorious vnto the world. *Billye Watſon*
the tumbling Prieſt, who fetcht a friske that broke his necke,
thought it much ſcorne that an Eſquire ſhould take place of
him or of his fellowes; nay euery Prieſt was as good as any
Knight. According to which foundation if we ſhould aſcend
vnto the Popes throne, we ſhould find no place in earth, but
muſt be enforced to ſeate him with the Prince and powers
that rule in the aire. But this is nothing if we conſider the
neight of their titles indeed.

60 For though Cardinall *Bellarmine* will proue that the Bellar.de
Pope cannot be Antichriſt, becauſe he is called the Vicar of Rom. Pont.
Chriſt, who is God to be bleſſed for euer; for that Antichriſt l.3.cap.14.
muſt exalt himſelfe aboue all that is called God : yet by this,
if there were no other argument, it is moſt apparent that he
doth not ſeate himſelfe vnder Chriſt as his Vicar, but challengeth

geth the ſame Conſiſtorie, and claimes ſucceſſion not onely from *Peter* as from Chriſts Vicar, but as from Chriſts owne ſucceſſor: who is *eiuſdem loci, dignitatis, & authoritatis*, with his predeceſſor, as *Feſtus* was, who ſucceeded *Felix*, not as his ſubſtitute, but as his equall, and then in place his better. So is Saint *Peter* called. *Ipſe Chriſtus primùm denominatione ſucceſſorem inſtituit.* Firſt Chriſt himſelfe by name appointed his ſucceſſor, *ſaying to Saint Peter, Feed my ſheepe . Inſtituit*, he did inſtitute or appoint. He did not ſubſtitute or ſubordinate, *ſucceſſorem, a ſucceſſor, not a Vicar, or Vicegerent*, which afterward in the ſame Chapter he calleth him, yet not a *Vicar of Chriſt, but Vicegerens Dei , Vicar of God.*

61 In which caſe though ſome be cautelous to vſe this title of ſucceſſor, either not at all, or very ſparefully, yet there is that dares enforce it moſt deſperatly euen to this day. *Qui ſuccedit loco Chriſti, ſupremum caput in tota Eccleſia, illi debita eſt ſuprema regni & Sacerdoty Monarchia. Sed talis eſt Petri ſucceſſor: therefore the ſeauenth reaſon which it ſelfe proueth ſingularly an abſolute Monarchie*, which is this : He that *ſucceedeth in the place of Chriſt*, the chiefe head of the whole Church , to him pertaineth the ſupreame monarchie both of kingdome and prieſthood : But ſuch a one is the ſucceſſor of *Peter*. What monſtrous diſhonor is this vnto God , that a ſinfull ſeruant, and a vile varlet, ſhall be made ſucceſſor, and ſo equall with his bleſſed Sonne the Lord Ieſus? The ſonne in minoritie differeth not from a ſeruant , but is vnder tutors and gouernors. But now our Sauiour hath taken his power into his owne hands, he is by this time of full age to manage his owne affaires with the ſcepter of his owne word, and by the direction of his owne Spirit. He hath no tutor nor gouernor , though they yet paint him like a child. Neither hath any man an heire in the ſame inheritance , nor a ſucceſſor in the ſame iuriſdiction while he liueth to enioy, reſideth to gouerne in his owne perſon. Therefore howſoeuer the Pope may be ſucceſſor to *Peter* who is deceaſſed, yet can he not be heire or ſucceſſor to our Sauiour Chriſt, who liueth and reigneth for euer , and is with his Church to the end of the world.

Marginal notes:
Act. 24. 27.
Sacrar. cerem l.1. cap. 2.
Bozius de téporali Eccleſ. Monarchia. l. 1. c. 7.
Mat. 28. 20.

62 But

62 But behold and obſerue , *Aliud ex alio malum* , One monſter begetting another. If we ſhould make an Arithmeti-call or Geometricall proportion,& calculate it as their gloſſe doth between the Pope and an the Emperour, which is found to be an exceſſiue number,&an vnmeaſurable diſtance;a man would thinke that the Pope might well be as much leſſe then Chriſt as the Emperor is beneath the Pope. But if we gather a concluſion out of the Romane premiſes,we ſhall find Chriſt as farre below the Pope, as the deepeſt center of the earth is from the higheſt top of the moſt glorious heauens.Such is the greateſt creature in compariſon of the Creator , yea *all nations* Eſay 40.15. *as the drop of a bucket, or the duſt of a ballance.* But ſuch is the vnlearnedeſt, the drunkeneſt, the baſeſt Prieſt of the Romane Church , who is ordinarily ſtiled *Creator Creatoris:* The Serm.diſci-creator of his creator. If the Prieſt create Chriſt , then is puli.Serm.111 he more excellent, and glorious then Chriſt, in as much as he that buildeth the houſe, is more excellent and glorious then Heb.3.3. the houſe. As if it were nothing (as in the alledged ſermon) to preferre euery bald and pild Prieſt *before Kings and Princes,* equalling them with Angels,and with the virgine *Marie,* but making them creators of their creator , a moſt monſtrous blaſphemie, which is not onely auouched by that rude Mai-ſter,but *conficere corpus Domini,*to make the body of the Lord is an vſuall phraſe in the Romane language. In which caſe it may be a queſtion, whether the lay man be not better then the Prieſt,who hath power to eate that which the Prieſt doth make. But herein ſtandeth the priuiledge of the Prieſt aboue him. The Prieſt can make his god , and eate him, and licke his owne fingers like no ill Cooke : the lay man can but eate him,when the Prieſt hath made him into paſte.I muſt confeſſe theſe are dreadfull inferences , but yet ſuch as neceſſarily fol-low vpon their abſurd premiſes, according to the old ſaying, *Vno abſurdo dato, mille ſequuntur,*a man may build a thouſand abſurdities vpon one. And this may ſuffice for their honors, whether of titles or rather prerogatiues,which they chalenge in their malignant Church , ſo baſphemous againſt God, ſo proud in themſelues , ſo iniurious vnto others , as cannot be

ſpoken without iuſt indignation. From whence we may gather, that all hereſies haue ſprong out of this ſource or fountaine in the opinion of a Father Ieſuite. *Pride is the mother, and*

pride hath begotten all hereſies. Therefore the proud Pope as
the father, his proud Cleargie as the mother, haue begotten
and brought, and nouriſhed and foſtered all hereſies.

*This pride God hath puniſhed in heauen, hath puniſhed in Para-
diſe, will puniſh in the earth, and what elſe ſhall burne in hell
then pride, and ſelfe-will, which ſubmitteth not, nor reſigneth her
ſelfe to God.*

　　63　If they ſhall obiect, that we reſerue honorable titles and
ample authoritie, &c. in our Church, we deny not, but that we
haue ſome names, either expreſſed in the Scriptures, as Biſhops, Doctors, Presbyters, Paſtors, and Deacons; or not abhorrent from the Scriptures, as Archbiſhops, Deanes, and
Archdeacons, yet neither are theſe adorned with Croſſes,
Croſiers, Palles, and Miters, for pompous ſhew : neither is
their authoritie and iuriſdiction other then the word of God
will allow. That there were ſubordinate degrees in the Apoſtles times, and in the primitiue Church, it is to me out of queſtion. For that the Diſciples were leſſe then the Apoſtles, and
the Apoſtles did that out of their power which none o-
ther did vndertake to do but themſelues, or by their autho-

ritie, as appeareth by the choice of *Matthias* : *calling the multitude* about the choice of the ſeuen Deacons, and aſſembling that Councell the firſt and beſt that euer was, as it is

cleare by theſe particulars; Saint *Paules* viſiting the new conuerted Churches, ordaining of Elders, taking order for gouernment, determining exurgent controuerſies in a Synod, his

giuing power to *Timothy* and *Titus* to gouerne the Church in
their owne perſons, and to appoint others in places defectiue.
Their laying on of hands ſometime by themſelues, as the A-

poſtle ſaith, *By laying on of my hands;* and *lay thy hands on no man
ſuddenly;* & ſometime with other, *as laying on of hands of the company of the Elderſhip.* This ſubordination we haue and hold
vnder ſome other names. But concerning doctrine and authoritie, it is in effect all one. Some callings ceaſſed, ſome

　　　　　　　　　　　　　　　　　　　　　　　con-

continued, according to Gods ordinance, and the Churches need.

64 Their honors and estates they acknowledge to haue proceeded from the bounty and deuotion of noble and religious Kings, to whose successors they stand obliged, and will rest thankfull vnto this day. And their ciuil authoritie in correction of faults is likewise from kingly commissiō. We haue had Archbishops, and Bishops, who haue renounced their honour, and layed downe their liues for the testimony of Gods truth. Not to defend their liberties, which bred licentiousnesse in the inferiour Clergie, nor to protect malefactors from the ciuill power, as *Anselme* and *Thomas Becket* did. Ours preach, teach, do the works of Euangelists, and deserue their titles by their diligent preaching and vertuous deserts; are for the most part men of maturest iudgement, and fittest for gouernment. How far your titular Cardinals, and Bishop, and Priests, & Pope himselfe come short of this, many of your own faction haue complained, perished soules haue felt, and all the world points at as at the shame and vtmost infamy of your religion. Which you may see in *speculo in* a golden glasse, when bawds and Cooks, and boyes were made Priests for mony.

Iuel.
Aureum Speculum in Antologia.

65 For their wealth and riches, it is beyond all measure or meane. *Crœsus* and *Crassus* were but beggers in comparison of some Cardinals; not *Salomon* in all his royaltie and riches to the moderne Popes. Except perhaps they be as *Adrian* the fourth, an English man, who complained, *Incude & malleo dilatauit me Deus*: As if God had clouen him with a beetle or maule, and wedges, and so protested: *Sit ditissimus qui electus est, sequenti die pauper erit & infinitis creditoribus tenebitur obligatus.* Let the Pope be neuer so rich when he is chosen, the next day he shall be poore, and stand bound to infinite creditors. A rich Cardinall, and a poore Pope; and here was no simony. And yet he seemeth to comfort himselfe in this, that he came not to his throne as some did whom he toucheth in a mysterie. *Ambire ad summum Pontificem, & non sine fraterno sanguine ad illud etiam ascendere, & Romulo succedere*

Anton. part.3
Tit.22.c.8.

Vincent.in speculo Historiali.l.27.
c.3.

„ *re in parricidys* , *non Petro in ouibus paſcendis.* To aſpire vnto
„ the Popedome, and aſcend not without the effuſion of ones
„ brothers blood, is to ſucceed *Romulus* in his parricide , not
„ *Peter* in feeding the ſheepe. His ſolace ſeemes to be, that
though he vſed ill meanes, yet others vſed worſe. He by ſi-
mony, they by murther. And perhaps he had reference to the
time of *Gregorie* the ſeuenth, who is ſhreudly tainted by ſtories for Italian tricks , in ſending his predeceſſors by that
floud of blood. For he reigned within 80 yeares after him, and
might liue neare or in his time. To this compaſſing of the
Popedome , he alludeth betweene *ſede* and *cæde.* As if they
ſucceded not *Peter* in *ſede,* but *Romulus* in *cæde.* Which thogh
in pronunciation they are all one, in deed they differ as much
as ſeate, and ſlaughter, and concludes with an alluſion vnto
a peece of his title, and thereby taxeth the Romanes couetouſneſſe. *Bene ergo dicitur, non tam nuncupatiuè , quàm etiam
ſubſtantiuè, ſummus Pontifex, ſeruus ſeruorum: ſeruiat enim ſer-
uis auaritiæ, i. Romanis, neceſſe eſt vt niſi ſeruierit fiat aut ex-Pont.*
„ *aut ex-Romanus.* It is well therefore ſaid, not onely by way of
„ nuncupatiō, but in very ſubſtance, that the Pope is *the ſeruant*
„ *of ſeruants.* For he muſt either ſerue the ſlaues of Couetouſ-
„ neſſe, that is, the Romanes ; or if he ſerue them not, he ſhall
„ be no Pope, or no Romane. Belike he paid very deare that ſo
complaineth of his bargaine. But a little time would ſerue
to gather vp his crumbs in that profitable ſeate , where they
ſoone proue ſtall-fed , as *Cæſar* that was in debt , and went
poore into Gawle, but returned with infinite riches and treaſure to Rome.

66   Howbeit ſuppoſe they had more wealth then they
haue, we would not enuie it them, if they came honeſtly by
it. That which principally in this caſe brings their religion
into ſuſpition, is, that their very acts of that ſeruice which
they pretend is done to the glorie of God , and their very
opinions are gainfull; which cannot be ſaid of any one act
or opinion of our religion. For albeit we haue the reuerſions,
and almoſt ſcraps of thoſe ſpoiles which the Romane Clergie left vnto ſucceeding ages, out of that infinite wealth
which

Bale, ex alijs hiſt.
Prateolus in catal.

Ibid.

Plutarch.

which they enioyed in lands, tithes, offerings, mortuaries in kind, and fuch like; yet thefe they haue where they rule, befides ten times more, and that for opinions which a man muft hold vpon paine of life, or libertie at leaft : and that for fuch acts or feruices belonging to God, which fhould be performed of meere charitie and dutie, as they are Paftors of charges committed vnto them.

67 As Maffes, holden with them the chiefe feruice of God, yet to be purchafed with money or lands; and their facrifices in them for quicke and dead, either by fingles or fewes, by trentals or fardels, from the maifter of the houfe to very horfes in the ftable, and fwine in the ftye, and hens in the coupe, efpecially belike if they be country hens, for they are religious, that might be benefited by them. In fo much that the contentious need not ftudy from whence their Maffe is deriued, from *Maffah, à mittendo,* or *dimittendo,* or from *Mefon,* becaufe the Prieft playes the cookes part, that dreffeth and eateth all himfelfe; or from *Mefenterium,* as it were the skin that couers the very intrailes of their deuotion. Plaine Latin or Englifh may ferue well enough. *Dicitur Miffa à maffà*: it is called the Maffe, becaufe it is a groffe maffe of idolatry, and bringeth in a huge maffe of wealth to the Priefts purfes, who are euer digging in that barren ground, as *Pompeys* fouldiers, when they had found a maffe of treafure, and could hardly be withdrawne from digging though they loft their labour, as thefe Maffe-priefts do daily. Which agreeth well with the prophefie of *Daniel,* that in ftead of God, fhould be worfhipped *the god Mauzzim,* that is, of power and riches; for thefe *Mauzzim* or Maffes are not honored onely with gold, and with filuer, and precious ftones, and pleafant things on their altars and Priefts backs, but alfo for gold and for filuer, with which they filled their purfes and enriched themfelues. Adde vnto this, Purgatorie aboue meafure gainfull: Pardons of all prices, and for all purpofes, for rich, for poore, and for meaner fort. Pilgrims from one countrey to another, from one Saint to another, with iewels and treafures more fumptuous then Kings, *tefte Loretta & Compoftella,*

Marginal notes: Saint Antonies Pig. Alan. de Eucharift. Sacrific c. 32. Plin. nat. hift. lib. 10. cap. 41. — Plutarch. in Pompey. — Dan. 11. 38. — Loretta. Compoftella.

poſtella. Their offerings, from a great mans chaine to a beggers red herring or his egge. As I knew an old man, that proteſted he firſt miſliked the Romiſh religion for that he ſaw rich men that gaue fat offerings, brought to the bleſſed Virgin or the Crucifixe, coſtly attired and curiouſly painted; but the poore that brought offerings of ſmall value, to a picture of baſer ſtuffe and meaner aſpect. Satisfaction for ſinnes built ſo many Monaſteries and Cels for Monks and Nunnes, that they became a burthen to the earth.

68 Annates, reſeruations, preuentions, for appeales, for palles, for faculties, for diſpenſations in mariages among ſpirituall kindred, a meare purſe-net to catch Conies; in legall affinitie, in naturall conſanguinitie, for keeping concubines, for curteſans and ſtewes, for eating fleſh in forbidden times, for whitemeats in lent, for canonizing Saints, for all kind of mortall ſinnes, from murthering a mans father, to the ſtealing of a point; with many more trickes and deuices daily practiſed by them, reproued by vs, confeſſed by ſome of Romes more moderate and temperate ſonnes, yet neuer amended, but where wiſedome, truth and loue out of a good

1. Tim.1.5.

conſcience and faith and vnfained, hath ſlipt the coller, and haue eſcaped out of Babylon the mother of fornications and fearefull abhominations. Theſe things no honeſt eare can heare without horror, nor Chriſtian heart think on without indignation; which may bring their whole religion into iuſt ſuſpition, if not into deteſtation, and vtter and finall condemnation. Is not this a great prouocation to the great Prieſt of Rome his Cardinals, his Biſhops, his Prieſts, regulars and ſeculars, of all ſorts and factions, to ſtand not onely ſtifly, but ſtoutly, for the defence of ſuch treaſures, ſo eaſily gotten? when many obiect their liues to vtmoſt danger for

Plutarch.

leſſe profite, as theeues and robbers. When *Brutus* the Romane would adde courage vnto his ſoldiers in campe againſt *Octauius Cæſar* and *Anthony*, he made them rich armours, the moſt of ſiluer and gilt; gaue them great gifts, and promiſed more, if they would acquite themſelues like men. A powerfull policie indeed; for he thought it an *encouragement, which*

maketh

maketh them fight like diuels, that loue to get, or be afraid to loſe,
&c. This is the drift of the Romane Captaine and Biſhop at
this day, and his Cleargie too, they will fight like diuels rather then they will loſe the poſſeſſion of that they haue, or
be depriued of their hope of getting more: not onely the fa- Veſpaſian.
uour of gaine out of any thing is ſweet, but alſo the hauing
and handling of wealth, is a powerfull prouocation to ſtand
out in the defence thereof.

69 I will not amplifie their pleaſures with many words,
or enforce them with violent exaggerations. They are ſuch,
ſo many, ſo great, that they match, if they do not ouertop
Princes and Kings of the earth. Their diet delicious, their
apparell ſumptuous, their ſites amenous, walkes ſpacious,
their gardens pleaſant, their vineyards and orchards fruitfull
& profitable; their houſes without, magnificent, within gor-
geous, their attendance gallant and Courtlike , their fauorites and followers, *Sans* number. Beſides their eaſie acceſſe
vnto their neighbours wiues, by reaſon of their auricular
confeſſion, and cloſe conueyances to paſſe wenches to religious beds, ſome of the monuments whereof remaine in this
land vnto this day. I haue heard of a Pariſh, where after the *Baron Sauile*
coming of a luſtie red headed Popiſh prieſt to be the Parſon, *auouched it*
moſt of the children borne after his coming were red hea- *vpon good in-*
ded, not one to be ſeene before. Either there was *fortis imagi-* *telligence to a*
natio, or foule play. The ſame may be ſaid of Abbot *Wibrey* *neare kinſman*
of the Prieſts,
grandfather to Cardinall *Allan*, though another bare the *and as I remē-*
name. But theſe things, all that haue written of the liues of *ber, of his name*
Popes, of popiſh Votaries, of the ſwarmes of the Frierly and
Monkiſh brood, haue diſcourſed and diſcouered *ad nauſeam,*
to very loathing. The ſuruey of Abbeys regiſters at their ſup-
preſſion in this land, vnder their owne confeſſions, the skuls
and bones of drowned infants, not onely in the fiſhpond
that *Huldericus* the Biſhop of *Auguſta* ſpeaketh of, where Epiſt. Hulder.
were found thouſands; but alſo of moſt Abbeys in this kingdome do ſufficiently diſcouer theſe works of darkneſſe. And
not to ranſacke all ſecrets that in this caſe might be reuealed , which could not but offend chaſte eares to heare, and
                                                        modeſt

Archbiſhop of Mentz,an Engliſh man.

modeſt eyes to reade; let the letter of *Bomface* be obſerued, who without all bitterneſſe wrote a religious Epiſtle vnto *Ethelbald* King of *Mercia*, to admoniſh him of his laſciuious life, and his Nobles by his example with holy Nunnes, or rather vnholy votarıes, that liued in pleaſure with them. What was there for honour, profit or pleaſure,of offices, reuenues,huntings,hawkings,and all kind of royalties,which the Clergie had not equall with, if not aboue the temporall Lords of the land? Whom had they not vnder their girdles? with whom did they not dare to conteſt? Fearefull things haue bene written of thee thou Citie of pride.

70 Neither can theſe maiſters of miſrule ſtop this gap with a few ſimple Friers of their ſtraiter Orders,who perhaps macerate their bodies and chaſtiſe their carkaſſes with faſtings,hard lyings,or whippings, and ſuch like ſeuere diſcipline.For theſe, as they are fewer in number, ſo they are not learnedeſt for knowledge,nor wiſeſt for vnderſtãding.Some ſcrupulous poore ſoules that deſire to do for the beſt, but know no better, and therefore thinke by theſe bodily exerciſes which profit litle in compariſon of better, to merit both for themſelues and others, walke in this narrow way of their owne direction, without Gods approbation; like Portugals,of whom it is ſaid, that they are *Pocos,ſotos,deuotos,*a few deuout, ſots. But beſides that it may be ſaid vnto the beſt of theſe, *Who required theſe things at your hands?* the baſe hypocriſie of ſome, hath bene made manifeſt by many, euen of their owne children, vnto the view of all men. Not to ſpeake of their more free Orders of ancient Monks,the Ieſuites haue gotten a greater freedome,to flouriſh with more gallant ſhew vnto the world,and may in their outroades,and compaſſing the world, enioy the pleaſutes of ſinne, without impeachment of waſte. In ſo much that *Gonzagaes* friends thought it a good policie, to withdraw him from his *chips betweene his ſheets,his whippings with chaines of iron, and wearing ſpurres,* not on his heeles,but at his ſides to pricke him,which might ſhorten his life,or keepe him from ſleepe,like a Nightingale, and ſuch like voluntary crueltie vpon his owne carkaſſe,

1.Tim.4.8.

Purchas.

Ceparius de vita Gonzag.

kasse, to the Order of Iesuites, who would not suffer him to exercise vpon himselfe so great seueritie. An easier burthen were fitter for a tyred iade.

71   These were for the most part senselesse sots, not vnlike Saint *Francis*, who would beg lice to put on his own clothes, His Legend. and would preach to birds and beasts, and call them brothers and sisters: as his brother wolfe. What some in this kind haue done in secret it matteret not, perhaps not halfe so much as their friends report. A sober man would neuer dreame they could be so mad as their followers make them. But take the face of their outward Hierarchy, and there was neuer State or Kingdome or Empire flourished more then that which depended on the Romane Priestly Monarchs Court, and those who shrowded themselues vnder the shadow of his wings. But make the best of these their voluntarie worships and humiliations, what do they whereby they may iustifie the truth of religion ? Do not the Infidels of the East and West Indies perform not only as much, but a great deale more in this kind in the seruice of their abhominable Idols ? which of the true Prophets of God euer lanced themselues with kniues, as *Baals* Prophets did ? If Rome will boast of their Monasteries ; the Pagans haue more : if their diuersities of sects, these haue more: if their watchings, fastings, frequent prayers, night risings, whippings, lying on the ground, shauing of heads and beard, going bare foore, their Hermits, their votaries, their pretended chastitie, in all these the very heathenish Idolaters Purchas Asiæ go farre before them, and beyond them too. For they would lib.5.c.11. put themselues to death with most exquisite and horrible torments in their Idol seruice. What haue these Romanists done which the Greeke and Romane Philosophers haue not done in this kind of austeritie? Which of them euer attained vnto the Indian Gymnosophists, who made no bones to burne themselues aliue, aud to glorie therein? As *Caluanus* that burnt himselfe in a golden chaire before *Alexander* and his Nobles neare vnto *Babylon*. Such things may breed admiration with the ignorant, detestation with men of vnderstanding. They haue a shew of voluntary worship in not sparing the flesh,

flesh, but these with their deuices are damnable before God. Perhaps we haue fewer outward shewes or rules of mortification then our aduersaries, deuised by our selues : but what hath Gods booke commanded, wherein we come behind them? This is so far from being an argument to proue truth, that it draweth nearer to the fashions and manners of the heathenish infidels and idolaters, then it doth vnto the Prophets and Apostles, or the Saints of God in the primitiue Church.

72 To conclude, it was necessary this should be so : for otherwise neither were the Pope Antichrist, nor that sea the whore of *Babylon*, nor *Rome* with her seuen hils, the beast with seuen heads, which in her honor, profits and pleasures, hath bene long written, and is now read and interpreted by many a learned *Daniel*, who haue vnderstanding to iudge according to the *iudgement of God*, as he did the writing that *Baltazar* saw on the wall. The spirituall *Babylon hath glorified her selfe, and liued in pleasure : she hath said in her heart, I sit being a Queene, and am no widow, and shall see no mourning. The Kings of the earth haue liued in pleasure with her. Her ware was gold and siluer, and precious stones, and of pearles, and of fine linnen, and of purple, and of silke, and of skarlet, and of all maner of Thyne wood, and of all vessels of Iuorie, and of all vessels of most precious wood, and of brasse, and of iron, and of marble, and of Cinamon, and of odours, and of ointments, and of Frankincense, and wine, and oile, and fine floure, and wheate, and beasts, and sheepe, and horses, and chariots, and seruants, and soules of men.* What greater glorie? what greater riches? what greater pleasures? Such hath *Rome* and her Clergie long enioyed, and yet doth, where the gracious wisdome of religious Kings and States do not courbe their insolence, and stay them with bit and bridle *(sicut equus & mulus, in quibus non est intellectus :* like horse and mule, that haue no vnderstanding,) *lest they fall vpon vs* and them too.

73 Our Religion challengeth none of these, no not one of them. Our Prelats haue their offices and callings from God, their authoritie limited by his word, their gouernment
moderated

Dan.5.26.
Reuel.18.7.

ver.9.
ver.12.

ver.13.

Psal.32.9.

moderated by iust Canons and lawes; their censures Ecclesiasticall, applied rather to the reformation of manners, teaching of faith, and sauing of soules, then violence to bodies, rapacitie of goods, & preiudicing the saluatiō of men, which is the only practise of the Roman Prelacie. Our Bishops temporall estates and honors they receiue from Kings, for which they do them homage and fealtie, as becommeth good subiects. They enter to nothing vnder pretence of *Peters* keyes, they claime nothing vnder colour of *Pauls* sword. Our religion, as before is obserued, hath not one opinion or act, that euer I felt or knew beneficiall vnto any clergie man. We are contented with the poore remainders that your Popish Prelates & Monasteries left vs to gleane vpon after their spoile; our tithes are gleabs in part, not in whole. But not one tricke to fetch or filch in a penny of profite. As for pleasures, we haue none superfluous, but such as become Christian libertie, and that modestie which beseemeth the Ministers of the Gospell. If any out-ray, they are either punished by the Canons, or should be, and the more pittie they are not; or incurre infamie among the religious people, or are detested of their brethren, that grieue at their wicked conuersation, or idle deboshment. Their frequent preachings, that are as they should be, and we desire; the gracious gouernment, often opposed by the popular disorder; the profane oppositions of the ignorant & irreligious, and in many places popish multitudes; their paines in their studies, their watchings in meditations; some writing of matter of deuotion, some in points in controuersie, and such like exercises of their callings, will preserue conscionable and carefull Ministers that are resident vpon their charges and keepe hospitalitie, from surfetting of pleasures. For others I can say little; they haue better leisure, if they would imploy it, to answer for themselues. Yet this I dare say, they are no Puritans, nor troublers of the Church more then of their studies, as the Papists euery where are, and would be more, if the Law or power were in their owne hands.

74 My third consideration is of Tyranny and policy thus:

*That religion which is begun, and continued with tyranny and poli-
cie, is the worſe religion; that which is begun and continued by
meekeneſſe and euident ſimplicitie of truth, that is the better religion. The firſt is Romes, the later owers; therefore their religion
is the worſe, ours is the better.* Shall I need to fortifie the firſt
propoſitions, which are as certaine as Mathematicall de-
monſtrations? Is it not plaine in the oppoſition of *Cain* and
Abel? Doth not Saint *Auguſtine* build the Citie of God in
the bloud of the one; the citie of Satan in the murther of the
other? The ſonne of the bond woman perſecuted the ſonne
of the free. And *Eſaw* the profane, made *Iacob* in his ſimplicitie, flie his owne countrey, and leaue his fathers houſe, and
liue in ſeruice many a yeare. Did not *Pharaoh* and the Egyp-
tians with great crueltie maintaine their moſt groſſe idolatrie, and keepe vnder the Iſraelites, the onely true worſhippers and elected people of God?

    75   The Church was deliuered out of captiuitie, with
ſignes and wonders, with a mightie hand, and outſtretched
arme: but Gods Saints, *Moſes* and *Aaron,* ſhed not one drop
of bloud; all reuenge was left in the hand of God. Throughout the whole Scriptures, the Church was euer defendant, or
patient. The law was publiſhed with thunder, & lightening,
and fearefull noiſe from heauen; no violence was offered to
vrge it, or to enforce it, no politique or quaint diuice to allure or perſwade it. This would haue bene rather a preiudice
then a furtherance vnto a worke of God, if an arme of fleſh
or the wit of man, had concurred with Gods power and wiſedome. The temple was built without noyſe of hammer or
iron toole: much more the ſpiritual temple without armor or
weapons. *Though we liue in the fleſh, yet we warre not after the
fleſh : The weapons of our warfare are not carnall, but mightie
through God, to caſt downe ſtrong holds.* Neither did the A-
poſtle circumuent them by craft & guile whom he conuerted,
but preached with power and the euidence of the Spirit, de-
liuering with ſimplicity of words the high myſteries of godlineſſe. It is abhorrent from faith to be enforced, *Perſuaderi
poteſt, impelli non poteſt.* It may be perſwaded, it cannot be compelled.   76. Though

Marginal notes: Gen.4. De ciuitate Dei. Gen.21.9. Galat.4.29. Gen.29 1. Exod.1,11. Heb.12. Cor.10.3.4.

76 Though our Sauiour be called a Lyon of the tribe of *Iuda,* it was as the defender of the faith, not a deuourer of the faithfull. And therefore he is called the Lambe of Ged, fitter to be slaine himselfe then to kill others. Some of the heathen, as *Plinius Secundus* & others, though they liked not Christian religion, yet they pitied Christians, abhorred the crueltie of their fellow Idolaters;& he labored by his letters to the Emperor to procure the beleeuers peace. When our Sauiour chose his Apostles, he neither flattered them with faire words, nor terrified them with threatenings;he neither brandished a sword,nor fawned with faire speeches:but told them plainly whereunto to trust, and that was, not t offer, but to suffer persecution for the name of Christ. For God forbid that Christians subiects should either defend themselues with earthly weapons, *fire* or *sword,* or should be grieued to suffer where they should be tried. It is more *lawfull in this religion to be killed then to kill.* I will conclude this generall with *Tullie,* who maketh the same paire to concurre like *Symeon* and *Leuie* brethren in euill, to worke and effect mischiefe: *Cùm duobus modis fiat iniuria, aut vi, aut fraude* : Whereas there are two wayes of doing wrong, either force, or fraud ; fraud seemeth to be taken from the Foxe, force from the Lion, but both should be farre from a man : yet of all iniustice there is none more deadly then theirs, who when they deceiue most, would fainest seeme honest men. For as *Themistocles* told the Andrians, he had brought vnto them two gods; *Loue* and *Feare :* and they answered that they had two goddesses to confront them, *Pouertie* and *Impossibilitie:* so the man of Rome hath these as his two gods, *Tyrannie* and *Policie,* against which the Saints and seruants of God had nothing to oppose but *Faith* and *Patience,* which in part haue, and in time will vtterly ouerthrow these Romane gods, and their profane worshippers.

Mat. 10. 16.
Tertul. Apol.
c. 39.

Cicero.

Plutarch in Themisto.

77 These are the Romane Catholiques vp and down, who haue inuaded by force of armes, and terrified by the thundrings of Excommunications, Christian kings and nations, furiously ramping and roaring like Lyons; who haue vnder-

mined

mined and ſurpriſed, not onely States, but conſciences of credulous Chriſtians, and ſo drowned them in bloud of Maſſacres, or enwrapt them in the nets of ſpecious and plauſible
perſwaſions, that either they die, or are deceiued. The Turks
were neuer more infeſt & cruell to their bordering enemies,
then theſe counterfeit Catholiques haue bene to true and
tried Chriſtians. They pretend loue and feare, but they haue
neither loue of men nor feare of God. The Pope hath Sy-
nagogues for Iewes in his chiefeſt cities, and perhaps vpon
ſuite would not denie Turks to haue their Moſques or Moſ-
quitaes to worſhip their *Mahomet*. Both Iewes and Turkes,
liue and traffique with him and his in peace & contentment,
without hazard or dread of his deadly Inquiſition. But he
dares not ſuffer any man to bring into his kingdome of darkneſſe, one ſparke of the light of Chriſts Goſpel, leſt it ſhould
grow to a greater fire of zeale, that would burne vp all ſuperſtition and idolatrie before it, and melt the triple Crowne

Seneca.

vpon his head, and make him wilde like *Hercules furens*.
Such as profeſſe the Goſpel are either murthered with exqui-
ſite torments, or ſubuerted by ſubtill deceipts. They are vn-

2.Sam.13.

to Chriſt as *Abſalom* to his father, by policie: vnder pretence
of a ſheepſhearing he will gather his brethren together, and
then wil ſlay *Ammon* with the ſword; or nearer vnder colour
of religiõ, he wil draw ſimple harted men to a ſacrifice, & then
proclaime himſelfe King, and perſecute his father with open
rebellion. This hath euer bene the practiſe of the man of
Rome, that ſinfull man, that man of ſinne. Which though
it may be exemplified by many paſſages of the Popes & Papiſts practiſes, yet by none more liuely, then the famous infamous Maſſacre of France, eſpecially in Paris, where the
Peeres of the land were called to ſolemnize a mariage, and
to honour a royall feaſt, this was the Foxes ſubtiltie; but all
true Chriſtians, without reſpect of honour, age, or learning,
were moſt villanouſly murthered, againſt all faith and promiſe; and this was the Lyons crueltie: but all proceeded from the Popes Hollowneſſe, and his helliſh
League.

78   If I should repeate the cruelties executed, and the policies plotted from the cradle wherein the pride of the Romane sea was first rockt by vsurpation of the title *Vniuer-sall*, it would offer vnto all spectators, vpon the theater of times, the acts of the Romane Popes and their greatest and deareft children, as vpon a stage, the tragicall rampings, and ragings, and rendings of roaring Lions, or the comicall cosinages, sleights, and cunning deuices of craftie foxes. *Phocas* his bloudy hand layd the first foundation of the Romane supremacie, as *Romulus* of his parricidall citie; when after he had murthered his maister *Mauritius*, he gaue to *Boniface* that vnlimited title of Vniuersal, either to reward his seruice, or to bind his affection. Shortly afterward followed contentions about elections, stickling betweene the East and West Emperours, the one quite ouerthrowne, the other remoued out of Italy; then claime to certaine Signiories and kingdomes. And these robberies intitled with the specious name of Saint *Peters* Patrimonies: the Popes by craft vndermining, or by poifon extinguishing one another. Which rage reached not onely to the death-bed but to the graue, with digging vp bones, dismembring dead carkasses, derogating from their persons, abrogating their acts, disanulling their ordinations, disgracing their fauourites, and degrading the Prelates by their predecessors preferred. *From Formosus many Popes following. Platina.*

79   Then they grew able to make partie against any Emperour that gainstood their enormities, to excommunicate them, depose and disthrone them, assoile their subiects of their oathes, interdict their lands, expose them to rapine; to raise the sonne against the father; to combine with the Turk or Saracene to surprise the Christian Emperour. And were these tragedies acted without infinite effufion of bloud, and exercise of vtmost tyrannie vpon the obiects of their indignation? To these may be added the schifmes among Popes, sometime two, sometime three at once, distracting the amazed Christian world into parts and followers; one king with his kingdome taking part with the one, another with another, till a third or fourth came, and deuoured the factious. *Platina. Bale, &c*

N n 3   All

All this was not without bloud. Neither hath the Popes Court bene cleane without bloud when the great Maiſter was offended with his ſeruants; the Pope againſt the Cardinals,and they againſt him : when noſes and eares were cut off, their heads hung ouer the walls of the Caſtle *Angelo*,no Angelicall,but rather a diabolicall tower: when Tiber receiued them by pokefuls. All this ſheweth nothing but bloud, moſt fearful and diſaſtrous,ſo much as to enter into the heart

Plutarch.in Marcello.

with any thought of religion ; ſo like is new Rome vnto the oldeſt , when it might be called the temple of *Mars* fighting.

So   If thus among themſelues, with their founders, fellowes and beſt friends , what haue they done to their oppoſites,to Gods Saints,whom they haue called heretickes ? not that they were ſo indeed, but that they traduced them to be ſuch, becauſe they ranne not into the ſame exceſſe of ſuperſtition and idolatry with them . This brings to mind the ſauage and more then beſtiall crueltie ſhewed to Cabriers, Merondall,and the poore people of Lyons, with many other ſcattered in other nations,from the aſhes of *Wicklifes* ſo long buried bones,vnto the conſumption of many godly,learned, honorable and moſt reuerend perſonages,who ſuffered moſt patiently the torment of fire for the profeſſion of Ieſus Chriſt and his truth reuealed in his word in the dayes of Queene

The ſixe articles.

Marie. Who hatcht, brought forth and enforced that ſcorpion ſcourge or whip with ſixe ſtrings,that is,thoſe ſixe articles,that turned men,women and children *ad materiam primam*, to duſt and aſhes,whereof they came, but the bloudie

Gardiner. Boner.

Clergie,that well perceiued their idolatry to be diſcouered ? Who condemned and deliuered vp the bodies of as many as profeſſed religion in ſinceritie, into the inforced hands of the ſecular powers , to be moſt barbarouſly burnt, but the

Matth.10.

bloudy Biſhops, who thought they did God good ſeruice when they put the Saints to death ? In which caſe thouſands of particulars may be inforced, which the very Turks and other Idolaters would bluſh to heare that they were done againſt their deadlieſt enemies.

81 I know but two things they can anfwer to all this that hath bene faid : the one is, they will confeffe the deed, and defend it to be well done : the other is recrimination;we haue done or do the like our felues.The former argueth their impudencie in defending a villanie : the other the lying fpirit of Satan,that inuents vntruths,if not to quench(which all the water in the fea cannot do) yet to qualifie their owne vngodly and graceleffe defignes, by laying to our charge that which they can neuer proue.

82 If they will defend an act of fo great confequence to be lawfull and iuft,they muft haue either commandements of God, or multiplied examples of the faithfull,or direct deductions from Scriptures,or authorities of old Councels, or proofes from ancient Fathers, or report of antique hiftories, or vfe of the primitiue Church, which commanded,or abetted, or exercifed, or maintained, or reported the like to be done,or to haue bene done lawfully; or elfe the liues of men fhould be more precious in their fight.If they will pleade the executions done vpon the enemies of Ifrael, vpon idolaters, vpon *Baals* priefts, let them fhew fuch immediate commandements of God, fuch propheticall fpirits as *Elias* had, or at leaft fuch infidelitie or idolatrie in ours, as they committed that were fo executed. If we fhould enforce thefe examples againft our aduerfaries, they would take hold on them, becaufe they worfhip not God as he hath commanded. But whatfoeuer we are,we are neither infidels nor idolaters, not fo much as by imputation from them that are our deadlieft aduerfaries.If they fay,we be heretiques,we denie it,nor fhal they be euer able to proue it . Let them proue that we are blafphemous Arrians or Anabaptifts,heretiques in one point or other, in thefe dayes of light ; and we will vndergo, not onely their cenfure for our correction, but their fentence of condemnation to our confufion, which our felues in thefe euill dayes haue iuftly exercifed againft fome incorrigible perfons in this and other countries, as they haue well deferued.

83 What the Imperiall lawes prouided for the correction

of the Arian or other hereticks, it proceeded out of a zeale according vnto knowledge, a wiſedome for the peace of the Church and commonwealth; becauſe they were turbulent and ſeditious, as the Papiſts are at this day. But neuer was there true Catholicke Biſhop, that ſo dipt the leaſt of his fingers in bloud, as they haue. Shew me a *Gardiner* or a *Boner* in the primitiue Church. They would haue them brought to heare, that they might be conuerted, not murthered in their ſins that they might be damned. *Intrent, vt nolentes au-*

Auguſt.

                diant,volentes credant : Let them enter, that they may heare
                though againſt their wils, that they may beleeue with a good
                will. *Chryſoſtome* with his golden mouth and pen, hath giuen

Hom. de na-
tura humana.

                a golden rule : *Dogmata impia & quæ ab hæreticis profecta ar-*
                guere & anathematizare oportet, hominibus autem parcendum, &
                pro ſalute orandum : We ſhould reproue and accurſe the wic-
                ked poſitions, and what elſe proceeds from heretickes, but
                we ſhould ſpare the men, and pray for their ſaluation. Or ſay
the worſt; they are not fit to go abroad, for feare of hurting and infection; impriſon them, confine them, baniſh them : ſay more, they are vnworthy to liue. Take away their liues with pitie, delight not in their torments without all mercy, which is the ſhame of Rome and her potent patrons. Neuer good Chriſtian, nor honeſt man, either ſo applied Scripture, or ſo perſwaded crueltie as *Baronius*, when he aduiſed the Pope to *kill and eate* the Venetians.

    84 Their recrimination, that we vſe the like, or as they pretend, greater tyrannie to them then they to vs, is an impious ſlander, and queſtionleſſe againſt their owne conſciences. They cannot truly ſay or probably proue, that one Roman Catholike hath bene executed with capitall puniſhment ſince the truth of Chriſts Goſpell, which is the religion we profeſſe, hath bene by authoritie of law publiſhed and eſtabliſhed in this land; I ſay not one. For firſt, in King *Edwards* dayes, who reigned longer then Queene *Marie*, there was not one put to death for his profeſſion of Religion. The De-

Stow.
Holinſhead.

uonſhire, Northern, and Norfolke rebels, after an ouert inſurrection, and the cruell murther of ſundrie innocent perſons,

sons, either becaufe they profeffed the truth, or did the King feruice, or becaufe they were Gentlemen, were in fome of their Chieftains punifhed by death: but fuch as profeffed the fame religion and liued peaceably, loft not a ioynt of their little fingers. *Gardiner* and *Boner* were for a time bound vp as Satan was, left they fhould corrupt their flockes. But they liued to be loofed, as Satan out of his infernall pit, to perfecute the Saints and feruants of God.

85   But in the fhorter time of (fhall I fay) Queene *Maries* reigne, or the Popes and his Romane Clergies reigne, (for alas fhee was a deuout woman, and of a milder nature,) a moft reuerend Archbifhop, the firft that euer we reade of, was tormented by fire, and foure that were or had bene reuerend Bifhops; befides Doctors and other Clergie men a good fort; of the Gentrie and other Laitie a great number, and thefe with others, without reuerence of age, eftate, fexe, or any circumftance that might moue pitie in *Nero, Dioclefian,* or *Iulian* the Apoftata. In which cafe we will not fpeake of the Dukes and other Nobles or Knights, which rofe in armes againft that Queene. We hold no rebels Martyrs, as the Romanifts do both Earles of Northumberland, and others who rofe in open rebellion or confpiracy againft our noble, religious, and vertuous late Queene *Elizabeth*. In whofe peaceable and happy dayes, with thefe of our prefent gracious, mightie and glorious King *Iames*, now threefcore yeares compleate, there haue not fo many by halfe bene executed, for any caufe whatfoeuer, that fo much as may be drawne to matter of faith, as were in that time for religion, and no other caufe layd to their charge, or fo much as pretended againft them but religion onely.

86   For thofe popifh Bifhops before named, and diuers others in that famous Queenes reigne, they had faire imprifonment, and large maintenance, fome with Archbifhops or Bifhops, others in their owne houfes, fome in prifons; but all at that eafe, that many a better Chriftian then the beft of them, might then and would yet vnder the Roman tyrannie, fell all that they haue to liue as they did in all things, except
their

their reſtraint. They held all points of the Romane faith, yet were they neuer queſtioned for their life. All the firſt eleuen yeares of Queene *Elizabeths* happie reigne, vntill the rebellion in the North was moued from Rome by Roman Prieſts, few or none of the Laitie were ſo much as abridged of their libertie; but all enioyed their conſcience and liued in peace, for the moſt part, by more then a good many. Then lawes began to be made for preuention of the like, and ſuppreſſing of ſuch as might kindle a new fire.

87 Such mulcts as haue bene impoſed, haue bene gently to many remitted, in part or in whole. They who haue payd their fines haue bene well able to ſpare them, and to liue richly without them. And I haue heard a Recuſant taxe our gouernmēt of hard dealing with Catholikes, for that he was valued to ten pounds *per annum* in the ſubſidie, whē I was my ſelfe at aboue foureſcore; and yet he had more in poſſeſſion & neare poſſibilitie, then I had inmy beſt value three or foure times. Which when he heard, it ſeemed for the time to ſoften his complaint of perſecution. And I would know of our preſent Recuſants, that haue one part of three at the leaſt of their liuing left vnto them, and the whole valued at ſo low a rate, that vpon examination it will ſcarce proue that the King for his two parts hath the tenth part of their liuing, perhaps not the twentieth; whether their caſe for all their religion, which is oppoſite to ours, and blaſphemous againſt God, be not as good in the iuſt ſeueritie of our ſtatute Lawes, (not but that all our Non-conformitants are moſt deſeruedly puniſhed) as the vnreformed Miniſters, that hold the ſame religion with vs in *toto*, and varie but in matters of Ceremonies: who are depriued of their benefices, and iuſtly diſenabled to the exerciſe of their miniſterie, if they ſubmit not themſelues to the preſent laudable gouernment of our Church; both receiuing chaſtiſement, not for their opinions they hold, but for their diſobedience to the State and Church; whereunto they are both refractarie. Whereby it is cleare that the penalties are not impoſed for matter of religion, but for diſobedience to the lawes of the land, whereunto all are obnoxious, as well

Pro-

Proteftant as Papift.

88 The greater perfonages are ouer-rated perhaps with twentie pounds a moneth, as is faid, they are very well able to fpare it. The meaner fort with twelue pence for euery Sunday. So is euery Proteftant that is but negligent in frequenting the Church, fubiect to the fame penaltie. And where the ftatute is carefully executed, more Proteftants are leuied vppon, then the rankeft Papifts. If in this cafe we compare, they indifferently enioy the Lawes of the kingdome with vs, notwithftanding our difference in opinions. And therefore haue no iuft caufe of complaint, that they fuffer for their religion, more then others on whom the Law taketh hold, though of the eftablifhed religion. Certainly no pecuniary mulct may feeme grieuous to them that could be faciate with nothing but bloud. Who would not giue any price for the redemptiō of his life? Wifdome will aduife, that it is better *the King take their goods into his hand to repreffe them, then to fuffer them to be rich that may rebell againft him*: as *Caius Minutius* aduifed the Senate againft *Tarquine* the Proud.

Iob 1.

Plutarch in Publicola.

89 But what fay we to the Iefuites and Priefts that are fent from the Seminaries? Thefe are drawne, hanged and quartered ; their refetters and entertainers are executed with death. For what? Will you fay for religion? If you do, it is falfe. Who amongft them all haue bene examined, or indited, or arraigned, vpon any pofition controuerted betweene them and vs, in the booke of Articles or our Apologie, as for Tranffubftantiation, Reall prefence, referuation, or adoration of that Roman Idol? for worfhipping of Images, inuocating Saints, the Maffe, Purgatorie, Merits, Freewill, or any the like ? Not one, no not one. How many in England heretofore, and yet to this day, haue and do hold all the groffeft and moft hereticall opinions that are held in Rome it felfe, and yet are neuer called into queftion for life or limbe ? Queene *Maries* Priefts, that faid Maffe and ferued the turne for all Acts of the Church Seruice, were perhaps fome of them imprifoned, not one of them that I haue heard of euer executed. Neither certainly are the Iefuites and Seminarie

Priefts

Prieſts put to death for their profeſſion of the Romane faith.

90 Wherefore are they then tyed vp and ſlaughtered? In a word, for plaine treaſon. Yea, ſaith the Romaniſt, treaſon indeed, but of your owne making. And how elſe? or why not? Might not *Salomon* confine the perſon of *Shimei* that curſed his father, (a Beniamite, and therefore dangerous to his Crowne) to the citie of Ieruſalem, or not to paſſe ouer the brooke Cedron vpon paine of death? And did not his diſobedience iuſtly draw the ſeuerity of iuſtice vpon his owne head? Might he not haue liued long enough within the chiefe citie of the kingdome, with his eſtate, at his pleaſure, without controlment? The ſame we ſay of that curſing and rebellious brood of *Balaams* of-ſpring. Our Princes, our Clergie, our Nobles, our Commons, haue found by good experience that this generation is dangerous to our State, offenſiue to the Crowne imperiall of this land. They haue bene made inſtruments of rebellion in Ireland, in England, after the Popes tyrannous and blaſphemous Bull had bellowed the direfull and irefull ſentence of excommunication againſt that noble Queene.

1.King.2.36. (margin)

Sanders.
Felton.
Story.
Ballard, &c. (margin)

91 Her Maieſtie for her lands ſafetie, her ſubiects ſecuritie, her owne indemnitie, exaſperated her blunter lawes, and ſet an edge on them. She confined her ſubiects to her owne dominions; made a law that who ſo being a naturall ſubiect borne ſhould forſake her allegiance, or depart her kingdome without leaue, and then ſubmitted himſelfe to forreine iuriſdiction, and returned home without detecting himſelfe to ſome Iuſtice of Peace within three dayes, ſhould be holden for a traitor. What word of religion, or that toucheth their ſoules? They may liue in the land, profeſſing the Roman faith, and no traitors. They may continue long out of the land, and yet no traitors. They may returne into their countrey (not being baniſhed,) and vpon their ſubmiſſion incurre no perill of death. Suppoſe that a Miniſter ſhould depart this land, and in forrein parts be ſeduced, and betake himſelfe to the Biſhop of Rome, as in the ſtatute is contained,

and

and returne into the land without fubmiffion, and yet vpon good aduice returne to all his former for ne of faith. Yet the Lawes take hold on him, he may iuftly die the death; it is the Kings mercy if he be pardoned. Or if a Iefuite or a Prieft after his apprehenfion be conuerted to euery article of our faith, yet his pardon ftandeth not in his conuerfion, but on the Kings clemency and mercy.

92 If any will except and fay, all be not fo turbulent and dangerous to the State as is pretended, and therefore at leaft they might be fpared: I anfwer, that little foxes cannot do fo much hurt as their fires, yet are we willed to take and kill Cant.2.15. them by the direction of God. And we haue good caufe not onely to be iealous ouer the beft of them, but to prouide that we may preuent them. For, if not onely the Prouerbe, *Seldome comes the better*, but ouer patiently long tried experience findeth, that later times do bring forth *progeniem vitiofiorem*, a more viperous generation: then when we haue found the learnedeft and deuouteft both Iefuites and Priefts, plaine confpirators and traytors in the higheft degree, yea and euen then when the feculars iuftified themfelues, and proclaimed to the world their owne integritie, and the Iefuites trechery, why fhould we truft any? If fome fall not into the fame exceffe of villanie, it is not for lacke of will, but of wit to execute their diuellifh deuices, or of power to performe their grand-maifters infolent inftructions. And therefore according to the approued grammar rule, I fee no caufe why that which belongs vnto one thing, fhould not be put into the fame cafe. Neither can a common Law fo occurre vnto all particulars, but that it may faften as well vpon the leffer as the greater offenders.

93 But for ought I can conceiue, fuppofing we did as they fay, that is, punifh them with death for their religion, I fee no reafon but we may lawfully do it, I meane vpon their owne grounds. For if heretickes may be burnt, or muft be, as themfelues hold, and vpon that foundation they murther vs; I would gladly know, why we may not put Priefts to death for their not onely herefies, but open idolatries, as well as
they

they did vs and ours, vnder pretence of hereſie. If either partie be ſuch in truth as they are with them , then they make it
no queſtion but the tranſgreſſors ſhould die. If the caſe ſtand
doubtfull whether be in the right , it will equally incline to
vs as to them. And why may not we receiue the Prophets
Pſal.137.8.9. bleſſing without fearing the Popes curſe ? *O daughter of Ba-*
bel, worthy to be deſtroyed, bleſſed ſhall he be that rewardeth thee
as thou haſt ſerued vs. Bleſſed ſhall he be that taketh and daſheth thy
children againſt the ſtones.

94   Their policie is as potent , if not more virulent then
their tyrannie. For as by the one they terrified the people
from the truth , ſo by the other they led them into helliſh
error blindfold , not knowing whither they went, or what
they did : and ſo were induced in their ignorance to loue and
embrace that which, had they knowne, they would haue abhorred from their heart. Of this kind was the couering of the
Scriptures vnder the veile of an vnknowne tongue , which
kept the world in ignorance ; their auricular Confeſſion that
kept all men in feare, not of God, but of the Prieſts: their Merits, by which they built Monaſteries, and pampred their bellies : Pilgrimages , by which they enriched their Church-
men, and made them powerfull. Pardons, whereby the Popes
treaſurie was increaſed , leauing the duty of preaching to a
few begging Friars, and interpoſing then ſelues in Princes
affaires, as the men that onely managed the gouernment of
the world. Not to ſpeake of their creeping inſinuations into
the fauour of Princes, their ſubtill extortions vnder pretence
of fighting againſt Saracens and Turkes, for recouery of the
holy land , and of the holy ſepulcher ; their exhauſting of
kingdomes with all kind of exactions, as if Rome were as inſatiable as hell it ſelfe. By theſe meanes they got their riches,
increaſed their power , eſtabliſhed their errors , and turned
deuotion to ſuperſtition, truth to falſhood, charity to hypocriſie, ſimplicitie to deepe reaching policie, zeale to fire,
and finally perſwaſion and teaching, to plaine treacherie and
ſubtiltie. And this is the ſtate of the Romane Church to
this day.

95 Vnto all this may be added their inhibitions of all
our bookes, so much as to be read by one of their Proselytes,
yea by their Diuines, Doctors, Bifhops, Archbifhops; or to Archbifhop
call into doubt, or to aske a queftion of their Roman faith, of Spolado.
vnder paine of feuere Penance, to be impofed by their firft
Ghoftly father to whom they fhall confeffe it, not without terror of the Inquifition if he doubt long. Their falfe and
fearefull corruption of Fathers, yea and their owne writers,
a thing vnheard of in ancient times; a ftratagem fitter for
Iewes, Turkes and Infidels, then for fuch as profeffe themfelues the onely Catholickes of the world; but indeed
they haue but *a forme of godlineffe, and yet deny the power* 2.Timoth. 3.
thereof.

96 If the ciuill Law, do not onely lay a great pecuniarie Cod. de fe-
mulct vpon the violation of *fepulchers*, or demolifhers of the pulchro vio-
tombes of the dead, but alfo condemne it to infamie, to ba- lato.
nifhment, to flauery, becaufe they feeme to commit a double Iniofulam de-
villanie; *Nam & fepultos fpoliant deftruendo, & viuos polluunt* relegantur ad
fabricando; for they fpoile the dead, by plucking downe (their metalla.
monuments,) and defile the liuing, by building (to profane Cod. eodem,
vfes:) what fhall we fay to thefe feeming religious Romans leg. 4. qui fe-
in comparifon of thefe ciuill though heathen Romans? thofe pulc.
ancients, fo carefull to preferue, perhaps the vaine pompe, at
the beft, the friendly memory of well deferuing men? thefe
nouellants, fo lafciuious in corrupting the integrity, defacing
the truth, difcarding of old, infoyfting of new writings? If
thofe violaters of fepulchers were worthy punifhment by
purfe, by infamie, by deportation, by flauery, as an offence
neare to facriledge; thefe corrupters of the Fathers wri- Proximum
tings, the monuments of their faith, the glory of the ancient facrilegio in
Churches, the inftructions of future ages, what punifhment pergit auda-
in earth can be great enough for them? They are referued to cia.
the iudgement of God in that great day, except they repent
them of this great finne. For they haue dealt with thefe famous riuers, as their anceflers did with the fountaines of liuings waters; they committed two euils, they forfooke Iere. 2. 13.
them, and digged vnto themfelues broken pits that would
hold

hold no water:Theſe haue cómitted alſo two euils,they haue
diſhonoured their forefathers in corrupting their writings,
and they haue abuſed their poſteritie in deſtroying their
faith. I omit their trickes to coſin and delude the ſimple people, with the rolling of eyes, mouing their lips, beckning the
hand,ſweating,weeping,and ſpeaking of Images,that hazar-
Plutarch.   ded many a poore Chriſtian ſoule , miſtruſted and found to
be a coſinage among the heathens.

97 Theſe haue bene their ouert policies , which they
haue not onely executed,but defended as good, lawfull, and
religious. But if I ſhould ranſacke the hiſtories of their owne
writers, for the particular tricks and policies of the Romane
Popes, their Cardinals & Clergie, either among themſelues
in compaſſing their ambitious promotions; or againſt Emperors, Kings and States, to reuenge or currie fauor, it were
to leape into the Ocean at Mexico , with hope to ſwim and
land at Lisbon.All the Hiſtories that haue written any thing
of the Papacy, and the occurrents of the Roman Clergie, are
ſo full that they cannot be exhauſted, and written in ſo great
letters,that he that runs may reade them.I appeale to *Mathew
Paris*,*Platina*, *Sabellicus*, *Papirius Maſſonius*, *Guicciardine*, yea
to *Baronius*, though he be paſſing partiall for his great maiſters honour.

98 Neuer was there tyrannicall State on the face of the
earth ſupported with greater or the like policies. It may be
very well thought and with good probability, that *Nicolas
Machianell* had a modell of the papall gouernment purtrayed
before him, when he enlarged his Atheiſticall Commentaries of the managing ciuill States in all his bookes. What he
wrote was but a warbling deſcant vpon a ſure plaine ſong, as
the Nightingale vpon the Cuckoe : & his books but a diſcouery in writing of that which was practiſed in Popiſh Churches and common wealths. For he knew no other , except he
were acquainted with the Turkes,or the kingdome of Beelzebub. Poyſonings in the hoaſt their dreadfulleſt ſacrament;
tumbling ſtones from vaults , fearefull rumbling in the
nights, walking of ſpirits , counterfeit voyces to perſwade
                                                          the

the resignation of a Popedome , no small bit to be easily dif-
gorged. Yet these things haue bene acted, and by them great
designes effected , to the enriching and aduancement of
the Romane sea , and vtter subuersion of Christian Religion.

99 Our aduersaries cannot deny these premises, they are so
pregnant, so euident. If they would ingenuously confesse them
and be sory for them, they might find some conniuencie from
their opposites , and haply fauour and mercie at the hands of
God. But they must first put off the chaines of darknesse, and
adorne their necks with the halters of submission. They not 1.King.20.31
onely approue in their thoughts , but would proue with their
pennes, and with their pikes too, if they durst , that all these
tyrannies were but due executions of iustice , and these policies but honest carriage of their great affaires , and so couer Plutarch. in
foule facts with faire words. But now they haue in these e- Pericl.
uill and malicious dayes, deuised a tyranny neuer heard of before, a policie neuer thought of in former ages.

100 The time hath bene when Princes persecuted the
Church , but now Priests tyrannise ouer Princes. Their ancestors saw the day when a heathen would not lye, nor deceiue, Regulus.
to saue his life : now the pretended preachers of truth, are become teachers of the art of lying. Saint *Hierome* layeth to ones
charg, that he hath *voluntatem mentiendi*, but not *artem fingen*- Hieron. ad-
di : A will to lye, but no art or cunning in counterfetting: but uersus Ruffin.
these haue both the will and the tricke of it. Murthering of Balthaz.Sirac
Kings, equiuocating for aduantage, are broached as the *vlti-*
mum refugium, the last refuge of the Romane Synagogue. In
which case if there were but one that murthered the Prince of
Orange ; or an other *Iames Clement* frier Iacobine, that had
stabd *Henrie* the third King of France: or one *Iohn Chatell*
a yong Iesuite that attempted, or a *Riualiacke* that acted the
murther of the late French king: or one *Garnet* a Iesuite, or one
Gerard a Priest, or one *Catesby*, or a *Percy* forlorne gentleman,
and such like , out of malice ingendred in themselues , or
motions from other ; Assasins that had plotted and perpetra-
ted those cruell and vnnaturall acts , against Princes, Kings,
O o   whole

whole States, they might be colourably excuſed, that they were mad: or commended as zealous, or their facts qualified and extenuated by circumſtances; or their deſperate ſtate pitied; or their facts turned vpon their ownes heads, and be adiudged by their owne fellowes to be worthy of condigne puniſhment for their raſh attempts and exorbitant executions: whereby the eyes of the ſimple might be bleared, as if it were farre from the Popes Holineſſe, or the Clergies deuotion, to haue any ſuch thing done, no more then the Iewiſh Prieſts would put Chriſt to death.

Sixtus Quin-
tus Orat. 101 But that which goeth beyond all extent of impudencie, and extenuateth the Cannibals crueltie, and the Cretans lying, is the Romaniſts teaching, and defending, and practiſing and praiſing of all Dionyſian cruelties, and Bartholomean maſſacres, all Machiauellian treacheries, coggings, lyings, ſophiſtications, diſſimulations, ſurreptions, falſifications of faith and promiſe, euaſions, mentall reſeruations, equiuocations in priuate and publique, vpon word and oath, in friendly queſtioning, and in iudiciall examining: That if they cannot breake looſe by violence like Lyons, yet they will eſcape by craft, like Foxes, making no conſcience of any thing that wil ſtand them in ſtead *ad bonum ordinis*, to the benefit of their profeſſion. For it is now nothing for a Cardinall *Como* to abſolue a traiterous *Parrie* to murther his noble Queene and beſt benefactor, and to binde him to the execution by receipt of their Sacrament. Nothing for a Ieſuiticall *Weſton*, or prouinciall *Garnet*, to illude all queſtions of State by equiuocating vpon oath. Theſe are but priuate mens errors and ſlips, to reuenge their conceiued wrongs, to compaſſe their deſired liberties, to obtaine a name, as he that burnt the temple of *Diana*; or perhaps of blind zeale, as thinking they did God good ſeruice; of whom our Sauiour long ſince foretold, and whoſe condemnation ſleepeth not.

102 But vpon long ſtudy, mature deliberation, frequent conſultation, and approbation of Superiours, very many not Lawyers only, but profeſſed Diuines; not Seculars only, who may ſeeme to ſauour of the world, but Regulars, who pretend
the

the abrenunciation of the world; not in priuate writings, which may be eaſily ſuppreſſed, but in print, to the view of all the world; not in contemptible pamphlets, but in great diſperſed volumes; ñot as ciuill diſcourſes, but as religious treatiſes and matters of faith, propoſe & defend, that it is law-full for the Pope to depoſe Kings; meritorious for ſubiects to riſe againſt them, to take armes againſt them, to murther them.

Bull. Gregor.
13. Domino.
Kiriculhini
in Hibernia.

103   And as for lying and equiuocating, it is made an art, it is defended, commended, pretended to be proued by Scriptures, by the example of our Sauiour Chriſt himſelfe; and from their Legend, by Saint *Francis* the ſire of his hypo-criticall order. I am verily perſwaded, that if any of our honeſt Papiſts, (if there be an honeſt man among them) or a deuout one, that made any conſcience at all of ſinne, if he could be ſuffered to reade our bookes, and to know theſe villanies, he would deteſt their whole religion, and ſay of a truth, The di-uel is in them of their profeſſion. What would theſe do if they had *Gyges* ring? Would they preferre *honeſtum* before *vtile*, honeſty before profit?

Cicero offic.

104   Concerning the reuelation, and publication of that true religion, which was taught by our Sauiour Chriſt, com-mitted to writing by the Euangeliſts and Apoſtles, profeſſed vnto the effuſion of bloud in the primitiue Church, neglected at firſt, afterward perſecuted by the Romane Synagogue: and about three hundred yeares ſince, found as the Law by *Hil-chia*, that was hidden in a wall, and againe publiſhed, and made manifeſt in diuers nations, England, France and Bohe-mia, and now profeſſed vnder protection of noble Kings and States, defenders and maintainers of the faith: we may iuſtly ſay, and euidently proue, that it was proclaimed in peace, with-out any violence, preached in loue without any policie. God would neither haue the power of the mightie, nor the autho-ritie of the Nobles, nor the drifts and deuices of the prudent, but he brought ſtrength out of weakneſſe, wiſedome out of follie, and things that are, out of things that were not; that no fleſh might boaſt, but *that all glory might* redound to himſelfe.

1.Cor.1.27.

    Chriſts

Mat.10.16.   Chriſts diſciples were ſheep among wolues,they were deuoured, they worried not.The primitiue Fathers and Biſhops of
Rome ſuffered all violence, crueltie and tyrannie; they offered
no wrong. The beleeuing world was wonne, and ouercome
by the fooliſhneſſe of Preaching,not by the policie of States-
men.

    105 Such as was the information,ſuch hath bene the refor-
mation of the ſame religion , begun by contemptible men,
proceeded in by the ſimple,long continued by ſuffering,neuer
hauing warre offenſiue , but onely defenſiue, when they haue
taken the wall at their backes , and could flie no farther;
and onely not ſuffered their perſecutors to cut their throates,
but either put off their blowes, or betook them to their heels,
to ſaue their liues. So ſometime in Germanie : yet rather for
their liberties then religion , ſome free Eſtates haue refuſed
and reſiſted the yoke. So ſome few in France betake themſelues to the field , leſt they ſhould be murthered in their
houſes,or the ſtreets, as in the horrible maſſacre at Paris,euen
till Sequana was died with bloud.

    106 What policie vſed the poore men of Lions ? the pro-
feſſors of Merondoll, and Cabriers ? They went like ſheepe
to the ſlaughter, they were killed and increaſed; out of their
bloud there iſſued a noble offſpring of beloued Saints ,
true profeſſors of the Goſpell of Ieſus Chriſt. What craft was
found in *Iohn Wicklife* our countriman and his ſcholers? They
preached and taught not like the Scribes and Phariſes, nor as
the Schoolmen and Canoniſts, their owne wittie deuices, and
pretended traditions,but according to the extant and written
word of God. Thoſe which followed them were burnt,or o-
therwiſe ſlaine by the brood of Antichriſt, that yet could neuer ſince quench the diuine flame which they inkindled in
the hearts of beleeuers, & ſhall neuer be obſcured, or at leaſt
put out while the world laſteth. *Iohn Huſſe* and *Hierome* of
Prage came like ſimple ſcholers to the Councel of Conſtance,
were there intercepted againſt the Emperors ſafe conduct,
and burnt as hereticks,when they were better Chriſtians then
their beſt perſecutors. Whether was the policie, in them that
beleeued

leeued their aduersaries word to the losse of their liues, or in them that falsified their promise, to the shame of their religion.

107 *Luther* a poore Friar came forth of his cloyster, and opposed the Popes pardons, by plaine preaching and disputation, without policie or inuasion. He had no weapons but for a spirituall warfare, whereby notwithstanding he threw downe strong holds. *His girdle was veritie, his brestplate was* Ephes.6.14. *righteousnesse, his shooes were the preparation of the Gospell of peace, his shield was faith, his helmet was saluation, his sword was of the Spirit, which is the word of God,* whereunto were ioyned *prayers and supplications,* by him, and for him, and by the whole Church of the Saints. When the Emperor, the Pope, and almost all the States in Christendome detested him, conspired against him, sought to stop his mouth, to stay his pen, to shorten his life; without strength or policie he was preserued, and liued maugre and in despite of them all, vnder the mighty hand of Gods mercifull protection, vntill his great climactericall yeare, the fatall period of most excellent men, and gaue vp the ghost in his bed in peace; his friends about him; with confession of his faith, bewailing of his sinnes, renouncing his owne merits, calling for Gods mercy. Wherein God shewed his might in his defence, when his enemies had spit their malice for his destruction: and that which is said of him may be said of others, who were euer persecuted, but neuer offered violence. As *Phauorinus* the Philosopher wondred at three things in himselfe: *That being a French man he spake Greeke well; being an Eunuch he was suspected of adulterie, and hating the Emperor Adrian so extremely, yet died in his bed:* So *Luther* may moue maruell vnto all that duly consider his estate, he was *bred and brought vp a Friar, and yet found out the truth; he liued in chast mariage, yet accused of inconstancie; he hated the Pope extremely, and the Pope him, yet he liued to be old, and died in his bed.*

108 Now let vs consider the authoritie by which the reformed religion was published, established, and maintained. And we shall find, that as the teachers were such as hath bene

said,fo the inftruments which God raifed in the ciuill Eftate, to ftrengthen the Gofpell with their ftatutes and municipall lawes,were fuch as that no glory can be attributed vnto man, but all afcribed vnto God; who by his direct prouidence was both the beginner and finifher of this fo excellent a worke.God would not haue King *Henry* the feuenth,left the glory might be attributed to his wifedome and policy ; not King *Henry* the eight , left the honour might be giuen to his valour and mightineffe: but God referued it for a young *Io-fias* , a child,King *Edward* the fixt; and for a *Debora*,a woman, a Virgine Queene *Elizabeth*,who maugre the Pope,the Spaniard,the vnholy League,the diuell and all his angels,held it out their dayes, and all this without fword or fhield , without killing of Kings or poyfoning of Princes: without periury,without treachery,without villany: and haue now left it to a potent hand,our moft noble,learned,and religious King, from whom they fhall neuer wreft the leaft line of Chrifts Gofpell,more then *Hercules* club out of his clofed fift.

109   And that which in this cafe is a matter moft remarkable,that noble Queene (of whom pofterity will glory to the worlds end,) held out our faith with iuft fupport of lawes, and efcaped all the wicked plots and practifes of the Papifts, that by many deuices fought the fhortening of her dayes; yet died in her full age , euen that period which the Spirit of God fet downe for the age of man in the dayes of
Pfal.90.10. *Mofes* the man of God,threefcore and ten,and neuer loft one drop of bloud: whereas *Henry* the fourth of France, a potent King, wife and rich , yet referuing his purpofes more clofe, and practifing his policies with a little earthly wit, perhaps to compaffe peace vnto the Gofpell (for ought is knowne,) loft not onely a tooth by *Shatels* ftroake, but alfo his life by *Riualiaks* ftab;monftrous villanies on fo glorious a King,who fhould not haue bene touched,much leffe murthered,efpecially by Papifts,of whõ he had well deferued: to teach mortall men to be carefull how to cary themfelues in Gods matters,
Prou.21.30. that they may learne of wife *Salomon,* that as there is *no wifedome,no vnderftanding,no counfell againft the Lord*:fo will he not
bring

bring good things to passe but by good meanes, lest he shold lose the glory of his owne worke; that he may euer truly say, *I the Lord haue done these things.* As for vs we haue found by good experience, that *they haue taken counsell together, and it* Esay 8. 10. *hath bene brought to nought; they haue pronounced Decrees, but they haue not stood, for God hath bene with vs.*

110   The fourth and last consideration I propose vnto indifferent Christians that would faine be saued, and yet know not in what way, is this: *That religion which most pleaseth the senses, the naturall and outward man, that is the vnlikeliest religion to be true and pleasing vnto God. But such is the religion of Rome, not of England; therefore that is the vnlikeliest, and least pleasing to God.* The ground of this argument is drawne from the inexhaustible fountaine of all wisedome and knowledge, who saith, *The houre cometh and now is, when the true worshippers shall* Iohn 4.23.24. *worship the Father in spirit and in truth, for the Father requireth euen such to worship him. God is a spirit, and they that worship him, must worship him in spirit and in truth.* Which, what other meaning hath, it then that the multitude of the legall ceremonies should ceasse, and that God in the kingdome of grace would be worshipped without such ceremonies, of place, time, shewes, sacrifices, offerings, incense, musicke, whereby the senses of a rude people were exercised and drawne vnto an outward seruice of God, yet to moue their meditations to better things to come.

111   Therefore the Law is called a *carnall commandement,* Heb. 7.16. opposed to the *power of endlesse life. A shadow of things to come,* Coloss. 2.17. *the body whereof is Christ; the rudiments of the world,* impotent Ibid. verse 8. *and beggarly rudiments, and not after Christ,* which kept the Is- Gal. 4.3.9. raelites in a kind of bondage, as an *heire yet a child,* and therefore not *differing from a seruant.* Which the author of the Commentaries vpon the Romans, bearing the name of Saint Ambros. in *Ambrose,* expresseth thus: *Quantum distat seruus à Domino,* Rom. 1. *tantum distat lex ab Euangelio, non quòd lex mala sit, sed quòd Euangelium melius.* The Law differs as much from the Gospell ” as a seruant from his maister, not because the Law is euill, but ” because the Gospell is better. That was a good seruant, but ”

O o 4   this

this is a better maister. Reade the Law, it is full of ceremonies; some of greater moment, as their Sacraments; some of lesse, as their sprinklings, and washings, and such like. But reade the Gospels, and all the writings of the Apostles, and you shall find onely two Sacraments, *Pauca pro multis, eáque factu facillima, & intellectu augustissima, & obseruatione castissima.* "Few for many, and those easie for performance, and high "for mysterie, and for obseruation most chaste, *as is Baptisme,* "*and the celebration of the body and bloud of the Lord:* but very few, or no other ceremonies to be continued in the Church, but are all left to *decency, order and edification,* without precise prescript of any. Prayers with pure hands, praises from repenting hearts, reformation of our liues, obedience to the commandements of God, mortification of our earthly bodies, and subduing them to the Law of Christ; charity towards our neighbours, sobriety in our selues, faith towards God; are the best sacrifices and ceremonies that our blessed Sauiour hath left vnto his Church, other I know none.

112 For this cause Saint *Paule* feared the Corinthians, lest their *minds should be corrupt from the simplicitie that was in Christ*; and his owne reioycing was this, *The testimonie of a good conscience in simplicitie and godly purenesse, not in fleshly wisedome, &c.* Euer harping vpon this string, that the Seruice of God after Christs *consummatu est,* should not stand in shewes and shadowes, or in things delighting the outward man, but in the plaine euidence of the Spirit which giueth life, not in the letter which killeth: which our blessed Sauiour againe affirmeth; *It is the spirit that quickneth, the flesh profiteth nothing, the words that I speake vnto you are spirit and life.* At this all the Prophets of God aimed, to bring the people of the Iewes from the carnall shew to the spirituall substance of Gods Commandements, euen in this matter of ceremonies: as our Sauiour reformed the mistaking of the morall Law, by giuing it a more spirituall vnderstanding then the letter of it selfe did seeme to affoord.

113 Therefore the Prophet *Dauid* in the person of God saith, *I will not reproue thee for thy sacrifices and burnt offrings,*

that

August. de
doct. Christ.
l.3.c.9.

3.Cor. 14.

2.Cor. 11.3.

2.Cor.1.12.

Iohn 6.63.

Math.5.

Psal. 50. 8.
ver. 14.

that haue not bene alway before me, &c. Offer vnto God praife, *and pay thy vowes, and call vpon me in the day of trouble, and I will deliuer thee, and thou fhalt glorifie me.* Here is a fpirituall fa-crifice fubftituted and required in ftead of a carnall, as better pleafing vnto God, and more profitable vnto them. Therefore againe the fame Prophet after his greateft finnes which re-quired higheft propitiation, and the beft meanes to procure Gods fauour, renounced all facrifices but fpirituall; as, *Thou* Pfal. 51.16.17. *defireft no facrifice, elfe would I giue it thee, but thou delighteft not in burnt offrings. The facrifice of God is a contrite fpirit, a contrite and a broken heart, O Lord, thou wilt not defpife.* The Prophet *Efay* likewife fingeth the fame note, in his firft and laft Chap- Efa.1.11.66.3 ter; and the Prophets *Amos* & *Micheas,* make vp the confort. Amos.5.21.
If God then when the Law was not yet abrogated by the có-   Mich.6.6.7. ming and death of Chrift, fo farre preferred fpirituall before carnall facrifices, how much more now when Chrift hath cancelled the Law, and faftened it on his croffe, and hath called vs vnto a more gracious and glorious liber-tie, to ferue him in *holineffe and righteoufneffe all the dayes of* Luke 1. *our liues?*

114   Let vs proceed according to this ground, in triall of the truth, and let the more fpirituall feruice of God beare not onely the bel, but the Church away. That is ours without all queftion, we need not proue it, our aduerfaries will not deny it. But as for them, they haue glorious fights of candles and ta-pers, not onely at midnight, but at noone day : the fhining of gold and filuer on their Priefts backes, paintings & guildings of their images, curious caruings, and embofments of hifto-ries : Their women Saints fet forth in exquifite beautie, their necks & breafts naked, their apparell fet out with pearles and precious ftones, their goldilockes hanging about their eares, and what not meretricious fhewes befides? fitter to ingender luft then moue deuotion. *Lycurgus* was afraid of this in a com- Plutarch Ly-mon Town-hall. Their he Saints fome on horfeback, fome on curg. foote, fome with armour, fome naked; fome like gyants, fome like dwarfs : with fuch varietie for delight, to dazell the eyes of filly people, as if it were a very ftage play, or May-game, or

a ſhew of antickes. Beſides the conforming and pourtraying of the inuiſible, immortall, and all-glorious Lord God, like an old man, and the bleſſed Trinitie like a monſter with three faces in one head; which can neuer conuey a religious thought to a profane or deuout heart: it rather withdraweth from the meditation of heauen to earth, from ſpirituall contemplations, to carnall and groſſe ſpeculations, not to be imagined or thought of in the ſeruice of God. To theſe may be added, their croſſes, their banners, their carpets, their veſtments, their miters, their croſiers, their gloues, their canopies, their pixes, their triple Crowne, with all gallant pompe and ſhew, with their *Corpus Chriſti* playes, deteſted of their owne friends, and ſuch deuices fitter to coſin the idolatrous Indians, then to edifie honeſt and gracious hearted Chriſtians.

Lodouic.
Viues in
Auguſt. de
Ciuita. Dei.
lib. 8. c. 27.

115 This made their eyes full of all ſpirituall adulteries, and vtterly withdrew them from the ſweet, ghoſtly and comfortable meditation of Gods Maieſtie, in the creation of the world, of Chriſts mercie in our redemption by his bloud: of the worke of the holy Ghoſt, in the ſanctification of our liues. We haue no ſuch allurements of our eyes, but lift them vp to heauen, where Chriſt ſitteth on the right hand of God his Father; we ſet not our mindes vpon things of the earth: we haue no other pourtraiture of our Sauiour, but ſuch as Saint *Paul* exhibited and preſented to the Galathians, by preaching and writing, to *whom Ieſus Chriſt was before deſcribed in their ſight, and among them crucified*. I maruell this hath not bene by ſome Papiſts taken for painting, or caruing of Crucifixes, ſet out to the bodily eyes of the Galathians.

Col. 3. 1.
Acts. 7.

Gal. 3. 1.

116 As they haue theſe glaſſes to deceiue mens eyes, ſo haue they ſounds to deceiue their eares; fitter to delight vaine curioſitie, then to promote the glory of God, to the edification of his Church. Bels bleſſed, if not chriſtened, to ſtirre vp deuotion forſooth, to allay tempeſts, to coniure diuels, to further ſoules to go on merily in their iourneyes to Purgatorie, as the luſtie forehorſe of a ſtrong teame. Their Organs and curious Church-muſicke, which could paſſe no further then the eare which heard it, or perhaps to delight the heart a little

for

for the time, like musitians that sing to their instruments some pleasant tune without a dittie. The people sate but like a *Chorus* in a play, seeing antiques, and hearing melody, but neither knew what was piped or harped, what was sung, or what was said.   1.Cor.14.7.

117 We retaine Church-musicke, we confesse, but so, as that it needeth not any reformation. They haue it, and abuse it; we retaine it, and vse it, and desire it may not be abused; so did they ill, and so may we do well: we tie no holinesse vnto such things, as if the Seruice of the Church were lesse acceptable to God, or lesse comfortable to the people, in countrie villages where such things are not, neither well may be, then in Cathedrall Churches, where they are laudably retained, and may be continued to Gods glory; where if any thing were amisse, it might be easily reformed, as indeed it hath alreadie bene in the 49 Iniunction. Therefore our vse may be well endured, when their abuse missoundeth to their owne friends eares.

118 In which case as the sonnes of Rome haue complained, so haue the fathers of our Church reformed their meretricious musicke. *William Lindan* first a Deane, then a Bishop, by his owne experience, not onely sawe and heard, but inueyed against such musicke in the Popish Cathedrall Churches: *Psalmistarum locum inuadunt isti musici, non tantum vt de Choro eyicianter, dignissimi.* It is ouer long to write the Latine, in plaine English, it is this: The place of Psalmists is inuaded or vsurped by these *musicians, who are most worthy to be thrust out of the Quire, not onely for the wickednesse of their life, wherein they are eueriwhere euer moueable, & for their tunes of vnshamefast loue-songs, or of vnworthy warres, mixed with the holy praises of God, but also for their theatricall or stage-*like rather confusion of *sounds, then any religious modulation of piety & deuotion, which they are knowne to ingender eueriwhere in godly minds. For now musicians by their singing, do not so excite the mindes of their hearers to the seruice of pietie, and the desire of heauenly things, (as they call them) as auert & estrange them from it: for I know my self to haue bene sometime hearing those diuine praises, when I hearkened*

Lindan. Panopl.l.4.c.78.

ned

„ *ned moſt attentiuely, what haply was ſung , and verily I could not*
„ *vnderſtand one word ; ſo were all things ſhuffled with repetitions of*
„ *ſillables, and confuſion of voices, &c.* How can we ſpeake more,
or ſay worſe of this their abuſe ? Yet himſelfe ſpeaketh ſomewhat worſe, *Non eſſe muſicam, ſed inconditam nebulonũ laſciuiã,*
„ *templis exturbandam:* That ſuch their ſinging is not muſick, but
„ an vnſauorie wantonneſſe of knaues, to be thruſt out of the
„ Church. Whereat my ſelfe notwithſtanding ſomewhat mar-

All is one in the popiſh Church, ſuch confuſed ſinging of Seruice, or to haue it in a ſtrang tong. 1.Cor.14.26. uell, whereas but for the Deane himſelfe, and a few of the Church, it was all one, whether it were prickſong or play ſong. For it was in Latine which the people vnderſtood not. And to ſay the truth, I can not ſee how one can ſpeak againſt the one, and not againſt the other, as it is in their Church. For whether tends to edification, which the Apoſtle would haue be all in all? *Let all things be done to edificatio*, no maruel then that he diſ-graced that which miniſtreth no grace vnto the hearers. *Eraſmus* calls it a *confuſed ſound of voices*, & a diſſenting from Saint *Paul. Polydore Virgil, Franciſcus Petrarcha,* and others found fault with it in their times, by like inuections.

Q.Iniunct.49   119   This hath bene reformed by the late noble Queens Iniunctions, where we may learne, how this fault ſhould be re-ctified, & reduced to that forme, which may beſt ſerue to edi-fication. There ſhould be diſtinct *ſongs , ſo vſed in all parts of the common prayers of the Church , that the ſame may be as plain-ly vnderſtood , as if it were read without ſinging.* And no other, *except an hymme before and after morning and euening prayers, in more curious muſicke , for comforting ſuch as delight therein.* If there ſhould be ſuperſtitious ringing, or ſuch laſciuious ſin-ging as is in the Roman Church, it is inquirable in viſitations, and puniſhable by the Ordinaries. And therefore we hold this golden rule of the Apoſtle, both in praying and praiſing God:
1.Cor.14.15. *I will pray with the ſpirit, and I will pray with the vnderſtanding alſo : I will ſing with the ſpirit , and I will ſing with the vnderſtan-ding alſo.*

    120   To pleaſe the ſenſe of ſmelling, they haue their fran-kincenſe , their perfumes, their cenſings of dumme Images; as harlots perfume themſelues and their chambers , to allure
                 their

their louers vnto flefhly fornication, fo thefe to entice fimple fooles vnto their fpirituall adulteries. Which is as pleafant to God as the *Incenfe brought from Sheba, and fweete Cala-* Iere.6.20. *mus from a farre countrey, or the fmell in Ifraels folemne affemblies,* Amos 5.21. *or the fweete balles or Pomanders* of the mincing daughters of Efay 3.16. Sion, which the Prophets reproued, and God doth deteft. And therefore God may well, and will certainly aske them, *Who required thefe things at your hands?* The Iewes vfed per- Efay 1.12. fumes as they were commanded by God; the Gentiles vfed perfumes to their Idols by the inftigation of the diuell, and Cicer. de offto their ftatues as *Tullie* faith; but in the new Teftament, not fic.l.3. ad eas one fillable to command it as neceffary, or require it as need- thus & cere. full: but of the woman that fpent her fweet odors on the head of our Sauiour, which asketh no imitation of vs, more then the finners wafhing Chrifts feete with her teares, and wiping them with the haires of her head. Which all Chriftians are obliged vnto in fpirit, but not in outward action. And therefore of this vanitie, we fay *We haue no fuch cuftome, neither* 1.Cor. 11.16. *had the* (Primitiue) *Church of God.*

121 For tafting, they haue not onely their maundies and feaftings in their Churches, with al variety of curious iunkets and delicate wines, as if they had no houfes to eate and 1.Cor. 11. 22. drinke in, and muft defile the Church of God: but can make a religion of it, and improue it to merit to abftaine from one flefh and eate of another. But the confecrated wine in the 1.Cor. 15.39. cup at the holy Communion, may not be tafted of the people. To eate the daintieft fifh for the groffeft flefh, as if it were an acceptable fafting in the fight of God, is holden moft holy; to eate frefh Salmō, Bret, Congre, or Mulets, in ftead of beefe and mutton, is great deuotion. And more meritorious it is, to faft with fucket, marmelad, all curious fruits, roots, candied and condited, then to feaft or fatisfie hunger, with butter or milke, or cheefe, or a ruftie red herring on a good friday. You may not touch, nor tafte, nor handle fome meats at Coloff.2.21. fome times, becaufe it is a law of the Church, without fufpition of hereticall prauitie. But you may breake Gods fabboth, fweare not onely vainly, but falfly too, and commit
forni-

fornication , and what not in the breach of Gods commandements?and neuer be called into queſtion,farther then walking to a Confeſſor , doing a ſhort penance, and to it againe
like a perfect Roman Catholicke.Theſe we are ſure are tranſ-
greſſions of Gods morall & euer binding Law.The other are

Coloſſ.2.22.   at the beſt, but after the *commandements and doctrines* of men,
and at worſt, as Saint *Paule* elſewhere tearmes them, *doctrines*

1.Tim.4.1.2. *of diuels, proceeding from ſpirits of error , ſpeaking lies through hy-*
pocriſie, and vſed by men *hauing their conſciences burned with an*
hote iron. Of whom I would aske , in their owne religions,
whether the Chriſtian Friars that eate nothing but fiſh, be
better then all other orders that abſtaine but in Aduent and
Lent and other ordinarie dayes? I thinke they do not ſo
eſteeme them themſelues : which notwithſtanding they
ſhould, if it be ſo good as they make it, to eate fiſh for fleſh.
Howbeit this plant, let it taſte neuer ſo pleaſant to the Ro-

Math.15.13.   man palate, ſhall be rooted out alſo, becauſe it was neuer of
Pſal.34.8.   Chriſts heauenly Fathers planting. As for vs, *We deſire to taſte*
and ſee how ſweet and gracious the Lord is , bleſſed are they that
put their truſt in him.

     122 Finally,their feeling is alſo allured by kiſſing the Pax
at Church doore, and the croſſe at the high altar. Beſides his
holileſſe pantophle, vpon the Popes bleſſing, and curſed
feete. Onely the people may not touch holy things with
their hands, for that is reſerued for the annointed,and the an-
nointers the Prieſts alone , as a priuiledge onely belonging

Vaux his Ca-   vnto them.Who in their extreme vnction not onely annoint
tech.   the eyes & the eares of men & women,& the places moſt apt
to concupiſcence or neare vnto them : but alſo in exorciſmes,
the place of conception muſt be preſerued onely for the
Prieſts ſpeculation and worſe,&c.It is a ſhame to name thoſe

Eph.5.12.   things which theſe haue done in ſecret, that neuer in pulpit
handled the word of life.But the profane people (for ſo they
account them who haue not their crownes ſhauen, nor haue
receiued the marke of the beaſt) may not ſo much as touch
the Popes merchandiſe, not their chalice, not their holy veſſels or veſtments , except they be permitted to kiſſe the
                          hemme

hemme of the Prieſts garment, not to cure any of a bloudie Math.9.20, iſſue, but to infect many with a plague of the Roman leproſie. Chriſt our Sauiour by touching cured, and cleanſed all kinds of diſeaſes; theſe will touch many, but they cure none. And they touched thoſe whom it was not good for them to I.Cor.7.I. touch. I know not how to deliuer their wickedneſſe in better termes. We haue no ſuch allurements in our religion, all our profeſſion is cleane without ſuch whoriſh trickes, defilement of the fleſh; we teach not to touch any vncleane thing whereby we may be defiled in body or ſoule, but to lift vp pure hands vnto God as the Apoſtle exhorteth. And ſo we I.Tim. 2. 8. deſire to approue our ſelues in the ſight of God and man, as workmen that need not to be aſhamed.   2.Tim.2.15.

123   Theſe ſenſible or rather ſenſuall inducements and allurings, may eaſily and do often draw men, as children that are vnexpert in the word of truth, and are carried away with Heb. 5.13. euery blaſt of vaine doctrine, *by the deceit of men, and with craf-* Eph. 4. 14. *tineſſe, whereby they lie in waite to deceiue,* vnto their owne perdition. For they haue a ſhew of voluntary worſhip and ſer- Coloſſ. 2.23. uice of God, and draw diſciples more frequent and faſt then the euidence of Gods truth deliuered by the plaineneſſe and ſimplicitie of preaching. As we ſee profane and godleſſe men, preferre a play before a Sermon, and will rather giue money for a good place on a ſtage, then receiue or accept a ſtation at a religious exerciſe; whereof there is no other reaſon but this, that nature is much more apt to admit and accept euill then good, and to pleaſe the outward, then the inward man. As a ſicke man whoſe taſte by choler is diſtempered, taketh ſweet for ſoure, and ſoure for ſweet, loatheth medicine, and luſteth for meates moſt hurtfull for his diſeaſe: ſo thoſe who are ſoule-ſicke through ignorance and want of faith, take ſuperſtition for religion, loathe the onely ſoueraigne ſalue of their ſoules, and entertaine any thing that pleaſeth their preſent fancie and appetite, though it increaſe their diſeaſe to their condemnation.

124   This appeareth not onely in the Iſraelites, prefer- ring the onions, garlicke and fleſh-pots of Egypt, before the Numb.11.5, manna

Exod.32.6. manna of heauen; but their viſible golden calfe, before the
inuiſible God of heauen: and their dancing to it, before their
deuotions to him. Neither may this ſeeme ſtrange, if we
1.Cor.2.14. conſider how abhorrent nature is in conceiuing the things
that are of God. Looke on the wiſeſt heathen Philoſophers,
who diued as deepe into the ſecrets of nature as naturall eyes could poſſibly diſcerne; yet in the knowledge or
worſhip of the true God erring as farre as the Eaſt is from
the Weſt, or earth from heauen. Was it not as ſtrange the
Dan.3.1. Chaldeans ſhould worſhip a golden image, a thing without
ſenſe or motion, with ſolemnitie of aſſiſtance, and pro-
clamation, muſicke, and what not? being ſo wiſe and powerfull a people, that they had encroched almoſt the world
into their victorious hands? or that the Perſians who conquered them, ſhould worſhip fire, which if it were not ſupplied with fewell, would die before their faces? or the Egyp-
tians, a wiſe people, and in idolatrie deuout, that worſhipped
an Oxe, a Cat, a Crocodile? The like may be ſaid of the Grecians and Romans, as wiſe, as learned, as victorious nations, as
Cicer.Tuſcul. Hiſtories report of; yea and for morall conuerſation many of
Q.l.5. them ſo vertuous, that they ſhame many Chriſtians? As that
De natura ignorant Chriſtians ſhould be led; or learned vnſanctified
deorum,l.3. Chriſtians leade vnto the vaine ſuperſtitions of their times, &
beleeue that, and ſupport it with reaſon and ſyllogiſticall diſpute, which is abhorrent from the Scriptures which they wilfully forſake? It is no new thing, neither vnforetold by the
Spirit of God, that they who will not obey the truth ſhall
2.Theſ.2. 10. *beleeue lies*. They that ſhut their eyes againſt the light, when
11. they open them ſhall be dazeled, and not be able to enioy the
vſe and benefit of it.

 125 Theſe foundations thus layed, and weighed with
due conſideration, let an honeſt and vnpartiall Chriſtian
iudge, whether our religion as it is profeſſed in the reformed Churches, be the ſafer, the ſounder, the plainer, the ho-
lier, and more ſpirituall in all reſpects, then that of the Roman Synagogue. We deſire no man to beleeue leſſe or more,
as neceſſary to ſaluation, then what we can proue out of the
written

written and vndoubted word of God. They will loade the
people with traditions,for number infinite,for burthen most
intollerable, not onely not agreeable,but quite contrary vnto the Scriptures ; which can neuer giue any the least satisfaction to an vnlearned man, and therefore are confessed to
be vnneedfull for such a one,yea for any to beleeue. So saith
Andradius,that had the very quintessence of the Trent Coun- Defenf.Con-
cell distilled into him : *Quæ non literis, sed sola traditione inno-* cil.Trid.l.2.
tescunt, ignorari possunt, sine dispendio salutis : Those things ,,
which are published not in the Scriptures, but onely by tra- ,,
dition, may be vnknowne without preiudice of saluation. ,,
Then certainly any Christian may be saued by the reformed
religion,though he know none of the Romane opinions, because all ours is written , all or verily the most part of their
religion dependeth vpon traditions vnwritten,whereof men
may be ignorant without preiudice to their saluation.

126   To call vpon God onely *in the name of Christ*,is writ- Math.4.10.
ten ; to call vpon *Angels* or *Saints*, is a confessed tradition. Ioh.16.23.
Ours must be beleeued,or else we be infidels ; theirs may be
vnknowne, and neuer the further from saluation. We say
that Christ our Sauiour is our Mediator, Aduocate and In- 1.Tim.2.5.
tercessor; this must be beleeued, or else we perish : to haue 1.Ioh.2.1.
more mediators,aduocates or intercessors,is a confessed tradition; if a man be ignorant hereof,yet he may be saued. We
affirme that as there are two wayes in our life,the broad and Mat.7.13.
the narrow; so are there two places after death, hell and heauen; this is plainly written : our aduersaries make a third and
a fourth , the one to last till doomes day, that is Purgatorie,
which then shall be emptied : the other *Limbus puerorum*,
which is the place for infāts vnbaptized, & for ought I know
must continue for euer. For in their learning they shall neuer
attaine vnto the vision of God,as the Saints shall. All these
are confessed traditions , therefore if they do neuer know
them,they are neuer t'e further from saluation.

127   The same may be exemplified in the Masse,in prayer
for the dead, in *Peters* primacie, in reseruation, circumgesta-
tion,and adoration of the Sacrament; in all their ceremonies

of oile, ſalt, ſpittle, croſſings, geſtures and geſticulations, and as I ſaid, almoſt in euery particular that ſtandeth in queſtion betweene them and vs. For ours we haue the direct word of God; for theirs they haue onely tradition, whereof a good Catholicke may be ignorant, *ſine diſpendio ſalutis*, without preiudice of ſaluation. Then if any Romane Catholicke embrace our doctrine, he may be ſaued; for it mattereth not whether he know his owne religion, as much as it differeth from ours, or not, becauſe his hangeth all vpon tradition.

128　From this poſition of *Andradius*, there ariſe two dangerous conſequences, and fearfull to themſelues and to all Chriſtianitie. For that the Popes and the ſea of Romes ſupremacie, is a tradition not written, they cannot denie, becauſe that it is written they can neuer proue. Then if men had neuer knowne it, they had bene neuer the worſe, and for profeſſing it, they are neuer the better. Then is it not as they would make it, *de neceſſitate ſalutis*, of the neceſſitie of ſaluation, to beleeue that the Romane Biſhop is the vniuerſall Biſhop, or that Rome is the mother of all Churches. Which being granted, as it is, by *Andradius* his rule, and ſtandeth with good reaſon and Scriptures; then all Popery falleth to the ground. We need no ſharper axe to cut downe that poiſonous tree, no better ſluce to draine the Church from the puddle of all hereſies. Yet a greater imputation of blaſphemie to be layd on that Synagogue, will follow hereof: *Traditions*, ſaith *Andradius*, *need not be knowne, or may be vnknowne, ſine diſpendio ſalutis*, without preiudice of ſaluation. But the Scriptures, ſaith his fellowes, are no Scriptures, but as we receiue them by tradition: therefore we may chuſe whether we will euer take knowledge of the Scriptures, and yet neuertheleſſe be ſaued. Which indeed they hold, as hath bene proued before, to the great diſhonour of almightie God, and the vtter ſubuerſion of many a Chriſtian ſoule. What ſhall we ſay to baptizing of children? to the myſtery of the Trinitie, and other high points of faith, which ſome of them haue ſaid, are not to be proued by Scriptures, but by tradition? Therefore by Romane diuinitie theſe may be vnknowne without

Vbi ſuprà.

Chap.6.

without preiudice of a Christians saluation.

129 What may I then say to my beloued countrymen, who yet pleafe themfelues in that more then Cimerian or E-gyptian darkneffe of Rome? and are led from twilight to midnight, from darkneffe to blindnes, from one abhomina-tion to another, though not of wilfull and factious obftinacie perhaps, but rather of a deuout, yet ignorant zeale? but onely exhort them at the laft to open their eyes, and behold the way of truth, which is now laid broad before them, to heare, to fee, to handle the word of life, and to trie the fpirits, whe-ther they be of God or not; to depart from Rome, which is neuer in all the Scriptures called, or named or fo much as by any probable inference or infinuation inferred to be the *mo-ther Church,* or hath any prerogatiue aboue other Churches; no not fo much as fpoken in commendation thereof more, or fo much as the Theffalonians, as hath bene proued. But vnder the name and title of Babylon, it is called the mother of *fornications* and all abhominations. Which cannot be taken for the ftate of the Romane citie vnder the perfecuting Em-perours, as the Romane leaders would make the world be-leeue; but for that Church of Rome, which from a chafte fpoufe, is degenerated to be a proftituted harlot, and hath committed fornication, and fpread abroad the infamy of her wicked whoredomes vnto all that paffe by her. Which is cleare by this, that the Gentiles haue neuer fpirituall adultery laid vnto their charge, becaufe they were not efpoufed vnto God. But the Iewes before Chrifts coming, and the Church after his coming, are faid to become adulterers and adulte-reffes, when they fall from their firft loue, and betake them-felues vnto idolatries, errors, herefies, and fuch like wayes of perdition, whereby they forfake their God that hath taken them for a chafte fpoufe vnto himfelfe.

1. Iohn 1.1.
1. Iohn 4.1.

1. Theff. 1.5.

130 Come forth therefore from this Babylon: flie from Rome as *Iofeph* from his alluring miftris, left being partakers of her errors and finnes, you be alfo partakers of her plagues and deftruction. And who fhall be able to auoide or endure them? You haue light offered, it hath long appeared: fit not

Reu. 18. 4.
Gen. 39. 13.

Luk.1.74.   ſtill in the valley of darkneſſe the ſhadow of death, but craue of God to direct your feete into the way of peace. You are called to libertie, that is, not to licenciouſneſſe, as your Romane teachers would perſwade you; but to a Chriſtian freedome of conſcience, wherein being deliuered from your enemies, you may ſerue God without your perils or feare, in truth, holineſſe and righteouſneſſe. Take no longer pleaſure in your bondage. Take your euidences into your hands, view them, peruſe them, reſt vpon them, and you ſhall liue, and be ſaued by them. Accept this mercie of God ſo louingly offered, you ſhall enioy that glory which is ſo faithfully and liberally promiſed. For this is the end of that faith which the

1.Pet.1.9.   Apoſtles taught, and we now preach vnto you, euen the *ſauing of your ſoules*.

     131 Vpon all the premiſes of this whole precedent book, which ſtandeth for all, not onely certaine antiquitie of Scriptures, but for all probable antiquitie of Councels, Fathers, and Hiſtories, againſt all Nouelties; I will conclude euen in the words of an aduerſarie, by him partially miſapplied to his

Muri ciuit. ſanct. fund. 11.   partie: *Nullum eſt erroris periculum in tam trita via: There is no feare of error in ſo beaten a way (as we propoſe:) but ſuppoſe there be, which cannot be, yet is he worthy of pardon: neither can his error be damnable, that followes (the Scriptures of God,) ſo many Councels, Fathers and Martyrs. If a man erre with theſe guides, not he which followeth, but Gods prouidence (which is horrible to thinke) is to be accuſed, which prouided (not Scriptures, if this were true, but) falſe teachers, ſo long a time, for the whole world.* We reioyce and praiſe God for his prouidence, who hath left vs all theſe ſound and certain meanes of our ſaluation, which how to make the Romaniſts partakers of, we know not, becauſe they will not heare. For the ſame is their preiudice a-

Ioh.1.46.   gainſt our religion, which was Nathanaels againſt *Philips* report: *Can any good thing come out of Nazareth?* Can there be any good found in the Proteſtants Church? We anſwer with *Philip, Come and ſee.* So ſhall you find as *Nathanael* found Chriſt our Sauiour, & the truth of God reuealed in his word, which the Romane Court ſhall neuer be able finally to gainſtand.   **132** But

132 But what if ſome be ſo wilfull and obſtinate, that all this light notwithſtanding, they will not ſee the truth, nor come to our Church with all this inuitation? I would be loth to deuiſe any cruell weapons to fall vpon them, as *Doeg* a-gainſt the Prieſts, or any ſudden maſſacre, as *Elias* or *Iehu* vpon the Prophets of Baal: but I could gladly ſet an edge, and ſharpen thoſe wholeſome lawes which are eſtabliſhed againſt them, with due execution; becauſe they waxe proud & bold, and dare ſay that we haue no lawes to execute them, but our late Parliaments which make new lawes againſt the old religion. We haue already by many books yet vnanſwe-red, proued the moſt points of Poperie to be plaine hereſie; and therefore Papiſts to be notorious heretickes: and then aske themſelues, and *Simanca* an author of their owne will tell you how heretickes ſhould be ſerued.

Simanca in Enchirid. c. 1.

CHAP. XXI.

Seeing our Aduerſaries will haue no other witneſſes but domeſticall, againſt whom we may iuſtly except: no other Iudge but the Biſhop of Rome their obliged friend, our capitall enemie; often igno-rant, vniuſt, and wicked, and therefore partiall and incompetent; we vpon ſo iuſt cauſe appeale, from Babylon to Ieruſalem, from Trent to Nice, from Romes new Conſiſtorie in earth, to Gods Tri-bunall in heauen; from that pretended Vicar, to God the Father, and to Ieſus Chriſt his Sonne, the iuſt Iudge of quicke and dead, with the holy Ghoſt the ſanctifier of the Elect, for a faithfull and finall ſentence, whether Proteſtants or Papiſts haue and hold the truth of God in their Religion.

Ow ancient, frequent and neceſſarie the vſe of Appeales is, no man is ignorant. For *it pre-uenteth or correcteth the ignorance or iniquitie of Iudges,* ſaith *Vlpian* the Ciuilian. *Hippodo-nus* prouided for his Citizens this wholſome remedie, that there ſhould be *Conſeſſus, cuius ſumma eſſet poteſtas, ad quem referri oporteret res, quæ minus bene iudicatæ viderentur:* A Councell, which ſhould haue ſupreme power,

F. de Apellat. l. 1.

Ariſtot. Polit. lib. 3. c. 6.

power, whither matters, not well determined, might be re-
F.ibid.l.Serui. ferred. A maiſter may take the benefit of it for his ſeruant, or
a ſeruant for himſelfe, *Si ſententiam triſtem paſſus eſt*, if his ſen-
Plutarch.in
Publicola. tence be ouer rigorous. And therefore it is much more to
be allowed vnto free men, that haue equall right in the ſame
Ext.de reſcrip gouernment. The cauſe muſt be the feare or feeling of grie-
tis c.Sciſcitatus uances & iniuſtice paſt or to come; becauſe the Iudge is either ignorant, and ſo vnable to diſcerne the truth; or partiall,
and therefore not likely to giue ſentence for the truth. It muſt
Barth.Fumus
de Appel.§.2.
2.q.6.c.Cum
omnis.
Tho.Aquin.
2.2.quæſt.69.
art.9. be alſo from an inferiour to a ſuperiour Iudge. Thus vpon
confidence of a good cauſe, a man with a good conſcience
may appeale, ſaith the Popes Angelicall Doctor. In proſecution of ſuch Appeales, many circumſtances are required, as
in the ſeuerall titles, in the Digeſts and Code of the Ciuil law,
and the Decretals and Decrees of the Law, and in the Sum-
miſts and other Doctors at large is diſcuſſed, which are not
needfull here to be repeated.

2   This remedy ſo naturall, ſo legall, ſo conſcionable, I
will now vſe againſt our aduerſaries, in our iuſt cauſe, from
their Iudges vniuſt and wicked ſentence, whereby as much
as in them and their great Biſhop lieth, our cauſe is preiudiced, our credits empaired, and our perſons condemned vnto
temporall, our ſoules vnto eternall condemnation. This is a
fearfull ſentence, to be pronounced heretickes, to be excommunicated and cut off from the bleſſed body of the Sonne
of God, and that without cauſe proued; and therefore we
appeale.

3   To enlarge the cauſes of this our Appeale, I need not
by law. It is ſufficient we haue already felt, and haue good
cauſe yet to feare manifold, vnſufferable and intollerable
grieuances, from that ignorant, paſſionate, partiall, and vnrighteous Iudge, to whoſe onely Conſiſtory our aduerſaries
Muri ciuit.
ſanctæ, fun-
dam.11. would draw vs, that is, from the Biſhop of Rome: *Index vt of-*
ficio recte fungatur, à ſtudio partium, & fauore liber ſit neceſſe eſt:
That a Iudge may do his office as he ſhould, he muſt be free
from partialitie and fauour to either partie, by any meanes.
Therefore the Pope can neuer be our Iudge, who hateth vs,

fauours

fauours his owne friends our mortall enemies, and maketh
theirs his owne cafe. From him therefore aboue all others,
we haue great caufe to appeale. In which cafe *Robert Gro-* Baleus in vita
fthèad that learned Bifhop of Lincolne brake the ice for vs Innocentij 4.
almoft foure hundred yeares ago, who vpon iuft caufe of
grieuance appealed from Pope *Innocent* the fourth to Iefus
Chrift: and vpon very fhort fummons the Pope was cited
by the ftroke of death,before that high tribunall of the great
Iudge. But Saint *Paul* is a better prefident and warrant vnto
vs; when *Feftus* asked him whether he would go vp to Ieru- Act.25 9.
falem, and there be iudged of thofe things whereof he was
accufed? hauing good caufe to fufpect his aduerfaries of fub-
ornation or violence,the place where he had fuffered wrong, Act.23.14.
the Iudge who fought fauour of the Iewes; he appealed vn- Act.21.30.
to *Cæfar* the then fupreme Iudge vpon the earth. Euen fo it Act.25.11.
fareth with vs : we are accufed of the Romane Catholicks for
hereticks: we are cited to Rome to be tried before him that
would curry fauour with our aduerfaries,& curry our coates
for their fakes.The place is vnto vs dàgerous,the high Priefts
will fuborne falfe witneffes againft vs, we haue no hope of
equall triall or iuft fentence, we haue many reafons to fufpect and feare ouer hard meafure from fuch a Iudge; therefore we appeale, not to the Pope, for he is principall partie
in the action, and if he finne in his fentence, he may grant
himfelfe pardon, and abfolue himfelfe from his penance:
though in his Doctors opinion it were better he gaue facul- Hen.Henriq.
tie to his ghoftly father to difpenfe with him both in penan- de Indulgent.
ces enioyned,and in vowes intended. May we not appeale lib.7.c.3.
from the Pope to fuch his ghoftly father? We dare not truft
him,they might be and may be lightly,efpecially lately, falfe
harlots both

    4 From whom, to whom, or from which, to what fhall
we appeale? Shal we prouoke to any or to all Chriftian kings
and the Emperour? Our aduerfaries will tell vs, that is from Extra.de Ma-
the hall to the kitchin.The Pope is the Sunne, the Emperour ior.& Obedi-
is the Moone, then Kings are but *inter minora fidera*, among ent.cap.Solite
the leffer ftarres.His Holineffe is the head,they the feete; he

ſpirituall, they temporall, or rather in compariſon carnall.
There lieth no appeale from ſo high a floud of pride, to ſo
low an ebbe of debaſement. Who can endure it? It might
well ſtand from the ſonnes to the father,but from the father
to the ſonnes, that were _hyſteronproteron,_ the cart before the
horſe,except they will vrge vs with _Fabius Maximus_ his ſon,
who when he was Conſull, commanded his father to light
from his horſe,and come on foote, while he ſate in his chaire
of ſtate.

Plutarch.in
Fabio.

5 Shal we appeale from the Pope to his Cardinals,whom
he calleth brethren, and may not call them ſonnes, for that
is a word of debaſement, fitter for Kings and Emperours:
nay,were they his brethren indeed by nature or fellowſhip,
as indeed they be in malice and crueltie, yet _Par in parem po-_
teſtatem non habet, that were no iuſt appeale to a brother of
the ſame conſiſtory, when but from a brother. But what do
we talke of them? they are his creatures,he makes them. He
that can aduance them by ſhipfooles in his Romane ſea, can
emptie them by ſackfuls into the riuer Tiber. They are his
ſeruants,or rather his flattering ſlaues; he doth but call them
brethren of courteſie, not of condignitie, becauſe he is ſo
pleaſed, not becauſe they deſerue it, howſoeuer they deſire
it. Yea they are nearer and dearer then brethren, for _they are_
part of his bodie and of his owne bowels.

Extra.de re-
ſcript cap.11.
Ad audientiā
in Gloſſ.

Gigas de læſa
Maieſt.l.1.
Rub.4.q.5.
nu.6.

Vide Præfat.
ad Conſenſ.
Ieſ.& Chriſt.
682.

6 Shall we appeale to the Scriptures? Thoſe are with the
Romaniſts,but _Protagoras_ principles, _Sphinges_riddles,gooſe-
quils, a dead letter, a dumbe Iudge: which is all true, or elſe
they are moſt wicked and damnable blaſphemers. If we flie
from the tribunall of Rome, _Wherein can the Scriptures benefit_
an hereticke? Ad tanta ſuperbia monſtroſiſſimum faſtigium ducit,
falſarum hodie religionum fundamentum, de ſola Scriptura,&c.
That foundation of falſe religions at this day,to trie by onely
Scripture,hath brought men to that moſt moſtrous height of
pride.No talking of Scriptures with Romaniſts,except a man
would _caſt his ſtomacke, or turne his braine_; ſo do they vilifie
and blaſpheme them, as the old heretickes did in the time of
Tertullian. At a word,our aduerſaries appeale as eagerly from
theſe

Muri ciuit.
fundam.1.
Ibid.fundam.
12.

De Præſcrip.
aduerſ.hæreſ.

these to the Pope, as we do from the Pope to them. They will neuer suffer vs to prouoke thither, they hold them ouer-partiall on our part, they are all for vs. They will not be allowed as witnesses without manifold exceptions, much lesse as Iudges.

7   Shall we appeale to a generall Councell? That is but from the head to the members, from the landlord to his tenants, from the lord paramount to his liege subiects. This they refuse and refute as a grosse absurditie: sometimes indeed ventilated in the world, in the time of schisme, yet by the learnedest that then liued: but not dogmatically concluded, though by fact executed, by the deposition of three *Antichrists*, and substitution of one in their places, and that without the Roman Conclaue. Yet now the contrary opinion predominateth: The Pope is aboue the Councell; hecalleth it onely; he begins it, he onely inspires it, he ends it, he doth what he will in it, and with it; and without him it can do nothing. A Councell is the Church dilated, the Pope is the Church contracted,he can do what he lift without it,& therefore to it there can lie no Appeale from him.

8   What will they say to the Scriptures as they are expounded by the moft ancient Fathers of the primitiue Church?Neither will they grant this. For all Fathers are the Popes children, he is *Papa, pater Patrum*,the father of Fathers. *Non habet in Ecclesia vllos patres sed omnes filios*: The Pope hath no fathers in the Church, but all sonnes; not in the Church indeed, but in hell he hath. *Iames Gretzer* hath disclaimed this before. All ancient writers are at their great Maifters commandement. If he say the right hand is the left, and the left the right, he muft be beleeued, whatfoeuer any other speaketh or writeth to the contrary. How then, or whither? To the Bifhop of Romes person?That is, *identica praedicatio* from him,to himfelfe;and in his perfon he may erre.Therefore to his office?Therein he may erre in matters of fact, though not in queftions of faith. Then in articles of faith? But not at all times, nor in all places, but in his chaire, and at a Chapter, not when he speaketh interlocutorily, but resolueth definitiuely. But in this cafe, nay in euery
of

Bellar.de R 6. Pont.l.2.c.27.

Supra cap.8

of theſe caſes he hath erred, ignorantly, obſtinately, wilfully; if he ſhould do otherwiſe, it were againſt himſelfe, and what Iudge will condemne his owne cauſe? Then no appealing to the Fathers, by them ſelues, or in him.

9 Seeing there is nothing left in earth, no perſon, no place, but either we or our aduerſaries, do, or may, in our opinions except againſt it: whither ſhall we appeale? to heauen? The Pope claimeth power of heauen, as well as of earth and hell. Shall we prouoke to the Angels? they alſo are at the great monarke of Romes command: himſelfe is *diuinum numen*, which is more then an Angell, as Maiſter *Stapleton* ſtileth him. Shall we ſeeke the fauour of Saints? the Pope claimeth the onely right of their canonization. No more a Saint without the Popes leaue, then a god without the Senate of Romes admittance. Is there no place where Chriſts *vnica columba*, his onely doue may reſt her foote, but this rotten and ſtincking carkaſſe, and filthy dunghill, Rome and her Biſhop? Not in earth, not among creatures, ſay the Romaniſts.

(margin note: Tibi data eſt omnis poteſtas. Anton. in ſumma. part. 3. tit. 22. c. 5. Cant.)

10 We will appeale to the holy Ghoſt. *Campian* maketh a ieſt of this, and in the learning of Rome he is appropriated to the Popes chaire: and if *Tertullian* call the holy Ghoſt Gods Vicar in earth, our aduerſaries giue the ſame title to their man of ſinne, and a greater to them is he, in equall, or higher, not in ſubordinate authoritie to the holy Ghoſt.

(margin note: Rat. 1. De Præſcrip. aduer. hære- ſes. Breuiarium Rom. refor.)

11 May we appeale to our Sauiour Chriſts Vicar? Firſt S. *Peter* himſelfe to whom they are not afraid to ſay; *In fine mundi Iudex eris ſæculi*: In the day of doome thou ſhall be iudge of the world. *A vicario non appellatur ad eum qui dedit vicarium, ſed ad ſuperiorem ipſius dantis*: We may not appeale from the Vicar to him that made him his Vicar, but to ſome ſuperior Iudge aboue him that ſo made him: but Saint *Peter* and the Biſhop of Rome are more, for they muſt be *Chriſts ſucceſſors*. Now we are at a nonplus: who will find vs a *plus vltra* beyond *Hercules* pillars? There is none aboue thee, ô Lord Ieſu Chriſt: as thou art *Alpha*, ſo art thou *Omega*, as the firſt ſo the laſt, and who can number thy generations? Whither ſhall we appeale from thy preſence? Shall we ſay from Chriſt the ſonne

(margin note: Cathed. Petri. Ianuarij 18. F. quis, à quo appellatur.)

(margin note: Vt ſupra. Pſal. 86. 8. Math. 28. 18. Reuel. 1. 11. Eſay 53. 8. Pſal. 139. 7.)

of

of man, in respect whereof all power *was giuen him in heauen* Math.28.18.
and in earth, to man the Sonne of God wherein he is equall to Iohn 17.2.
his Father, and created the world? Let it be granted by con- Philip.2,6.
cession or in imagination. Yet are we not hereby aduantaged, Hebr. 1. 2.
if our aduersaries are to be beleeued. For if the eternall Sonne
of God, be *Dominus Deus*, the Lord God of the Christians, so Extrauag. Io.
call they the Bishop of Rome *Dominus Deus noster*, The Lord 22.c.4. glossa
God of the Roman Catholickes. But we will haue him not in fine.
onely in the communion of properties, but in both natures
conioyned in one person. The Roman Bishop is that also; for
Margarinus de la Bigne applyeth all that place to *Pope Gregorie* Epistola dedi.
13. which is written of our Sauiour, the Lord Iesus Christ the ad Greg. 13.
Sonne of God, in the Epistle to the Hebrewes: *For we haue not* Hebr. 4.14.
an high Priest, which cannot be touched with the feeling of our in- Supra.
firmities, but was in all things tempted in like sort; and *let vs there-* Ad thronum
fore go boldly vnto the throne of grace, that we may receiue mer- gratiæ tuæ vt
cy, and find grace to helpe in time of need; as before hath bene al- misericordiã
ready obserued. consequar, &
inueniam a-

12 May we appeale to God the Father of our Lord *Iesu* pud te gratiã
Christ? The Romanists paint him like an old man with a gray in tempore
beard; they will yeeld wisedome vnto old yeares, and vnder- opportuno.
standing to gray haires, and therefore preferre him before his Iob 12. 12.
blessed Sonne, whom they yet picture like a little babe. And
aske an old superstitious popish woman, and she will tell you
there is no reason but the mother should be better then her
own childe and therefore our blessed Ladie must be preferred
before her Sonne; whence it is, that some who thought them- Offici B.Ma-
selues wiser then old wiues, could say, *By the right of a mother* riæ Breuiaria.
command thy Sonne. If this right be in the mother, much more
is there in the Father. Will they then admit our appeale vnto
the Father? That may not be, for *Dei & Papæ est idem Consisto-* Hostensis de
rium: God and the Pope haue but one Consistorie. And that elect.& elect.
impudent Antichrist our capitall enemie, is ordinarily stiled potestate.c.4.
Vicarius Dei, the Vicar of God, (the Vicar of hell sooner:) per- Non pueri
haps they thinke Christ the Sonne too meane, because he hath hominis, sed
some mixture of earth with heauen, of Manhood with God- veri Dei vi-
head (pardon the speech, their wicked doctrine and absurd, cem gerit in
terris.
presseth

preſſeth the occaſion:) and therefore they will haue him the Vicar of God, as well, percaſe rather then of Chriſt. Then lyeth there no appeale to God from his Vicar, as is before ſuppoſed, and in the Roman learning proued.

13   Neither can they excuſe theſe more then monſtrous, blaſphemous, and idolatrous attributes vnto the Pope, as giuen in the time of dunſerie, or by Canoniſts, or Gloſers, the notorious flatterers then of that ſacred Sea; but they are yet continued, offered and accepted in the time ſince the Councell of Trent, when all things were promiſed ſhould be reformed.

De antiquo iure Romanorum in præfat.   *Carolus Sigonius* doth not onely call *Pius quartus ſalutis authorem,* which I know not better to interpret then the *Author of ſaluation:* but alſo that his *autoritas* is *diuina,* he hath *diuine authoritie,* and is *quaſi propitium numen aliquod,*as a certaine diuine Godhead. Another more apertly, more blaſphemouſly, and yet more ridiculouſly withall a great deale, *Schoppius* would needs dedicate his booke to *Clement* the 8, and that

1.Cor.3.7. Præfat. ad Clement 8. de Indulgentijs.   chiefly to be bleſſed of him. *For not he that watereth is any thing, but he that bleſſeth and giueth increaſe, euen God. Tu autem Deus es à ſummo Deo conſtitutus, & noui quòd benedictus ſit cui benedixeris, & maledictus in quem maledicta conieceris:* But “ thou art God appointed by the great God, and I know that he “ is bleſſed whom thou bleſſeſt, & he is accurſed againſt whom

Numbers 22.   thou caſteſt thy curſes: Where firſt he moſt plainly calleth the Pope a God, moſt blaſphemouſly applieth one Scripture to proue him a God, and moſt ridiculouſly abuſeth another, in entitling the Pope his Patron, with that which *Balac* the ſon of *Zippor,*gaue to *Balaam* the ſonne of *Beor* that wicked Prophet, when he would haue the people of God curſed. May not

Pareus.   a man write vnder this, as one did vnder *Adrians* inſcription, vpon his hoſpitall at Louan? *Traicctum me plantauit, Louanium me rigauit, Cæſar incrementum dedit;* one wrote vnder, *ErgoDeus nihil fecit:*this flatterer belike will neither haue God plant nor water, and the Pope muſt giue increaſe; there God needs do nothing, as indeed he hath nothing to do with the Popes pardons or doctrine.

14   All this notwithſtanding we muſt and will appeale, but

but whither ? Seeing they haue left vs neither heauen, nor earth, God, nor man, but onely the god of this world, and the man of sinne, to whom they will admit our Appeale: let them appeale while they will, *à superis ad Acheronta,* from heauer to hell, from *Iehouah* the God of Israel and his holy word, to Beelzebub the *god of Eccron* and his impostures. Let them vse armes of flesh and carnall weapons, and bring with them all these *powers and principalities, and spirituall enemies in heauenly* Ephes. 6.13. *places* (as the Apostle describeth thē) yet our trust shall be in the name of the Lord our God. For he being on our side, we need Psal. 23.4. not feare what man can do vnto vs. If he iustifie vs, no man Rom. 8.33. can condemne vs; we will not feare though ten thousands rise Psal. 3.6. vp against vs, and compasse vs on euery side: for the Lord sustaineth vs. An honest cause can neuer quaile before a iust Iudge. In confidence whereof we appeale from earth to heauen: from Roman Babylon below, to the new Hierusalem which is aboue: from the man of sinne, to him who is Sonne of man, and the Sonne of God without sinne: from earthly consistories, to the tribunall of Gods eternall Maiestie; from the father of lies who ruleth in the children of vnbeleefe and disobedience, to the Father of lights and of spirits, who is a God, blessed for euer and euer. Amen.

15 Howbeit it may be our aduersaries, though they cannot except against our iust cause of Appeale, nor flatly deny the authority of that Iudge to whom we appeale, yet they will alledge, that the cause being a matter not of iustice, and but of mercie, it belongeth not vnto God to meddle with it, much lesse to determine it. For as in the learned Poets who distinguish the nature of gods, they designe the woods to *Faunus* & his Satyrs; the riuers to *Nereus* and his Nereiades; and the one intermedled not, nor intruded into the iurisdiction of the other: Or more familiarly, as when by the Popes policie the Empire was ill deuided, (which was before well vnited) into the East and West, the one interposed not himselfe in the affaires of the other, nor inuaded his kingdome: So, seeing they can proue out of moth-eaten Legends, and our blessed Ladies most deuoted Chaplaines, that God hath bene pleased to

deuest

deueſt himſelfe of that throne of mercy whereunto guilty perſons might appeale , and hath reſerued onely iuſtice to him
ſelfe; and therefore this caſe belongeth not vnto the iuſt God,
who muſt giue ſentence according to right, but vnto the mother of mercy, who will pardon any ſinnes done againſt God,
for a loaſe caſt at the beggars head that askt it in her name; or
will ſet vp a light in hell to anger the diuell, for ones ſake that
neuer did good deed but offered vnto her one taper : or with
her beads will weigh downe the ballance wherein a wicked
ſoule had bene found too light if ſhe had not pitied his dolefull eſtate,and thereby ſent away the diuels that pleaded for it,
dreadfully howling.

16   For _this Empreſſe is of ſo great authoritie in the heauenly_
palace, that paſsing ouer all intermediate Saints ,it is lawfull to ap-
peale vnto her in euery grieuance. For although by the courſe of the
ciuill law, due order ſhould be kept in appeales, yet notwithſtanding
herein is obſerued the ſtyle of the Canon law, whereby omitting all
meanes (in the way) we may appeale vnto the Pope. Therefore eue-
ry man may appeale vnto her; whence we may ſay that of her,which
is written c.ad Romanam,2.q.6.where it is ſaid,Vnto her muſt all
that are oppreſſed appeale and runne as vnto a mother, from whoſe
breaſts they may be nouriſhed, by whoſe authoritie defended , and
from their oppreſſions deliuered. For a mother neither can , nor
ought to forget her owne child. Therefore let euery one confidently
appeale vnto her, whether he be oppreſſed with the diuell , or of any
_tyrant,or of his own body,or of Gods iuſtice._Of which mine author
exemplifieth the firſt three by one _Theophilus_ , that gaue himſelfe to the diuell vnder his hand-writing ; and by Saint _Baſil_,
who prayed againſt _Iulian_ the Apoſtata, and at whoſe re-
queſt our Ladie ſent one _Mercurie_ (belike the old meſſenger
of the gods)and lent him an horſe and a lance, with which he
killed the tyrant: and _Marie Egyptiaca_, who by her ouercame
concupiſcence; (and then of the fourth faith) _Licet ad ipſam ap-_
pellare ſi quis à Dei iuſtitia ſe grauari ſentit : It is lawfull to appeale vnto her , if any man be oppreſſed with the iuſtice of
God, which was ſignified, _Heſter_ 5. where it is ſaid,_That when_
King Aſſuerus was angry with the Iewes, _Queene_ _Heſter_ came to
appeaſe

Mariale Bar-
nard. de Bu-
ſto. part.3.ſer.
3.fol.96.
F. de appellat.
Recip.l. Im-
peratores.
Extra. de ap-
pellat. cap.Si
duobus.

A diuina iuſti-
tia.

appeafe him: to whom the King faid, Though thou aske halfe of my kingdome it fhall be giuen vnto thee. Therefore this Empreffe did prefigure the Empreffe of heauen, with whom Deus regnum fuum diuifit, God deuided his kingdome. *Cum enim Deus habeat iuftitiam & mifericordiam, iuftitiam fibi in hoc mundo exercendam retinuit, & mifericordiam matri conceffit : & ideo fi quis fentit fe grauari à foro iuftitiæ Dei, appellet ad forum mifericordiæ matris eius:* For whereas God hath iuftice and mercy, he hath referued iuftice to be exercifed by himfelfe in this world, and granted mercie to his mother; and therefore if any man be grieued or vexed in the court of iuftice, he may appeale to the court of his mothers mercy. Is not this ftrange learning? Yet it is fortified with a worthy example by another, and the teftimony of the diuell alfo : for when a young man had renounced the moft High for the diuels helpe, it was no bargaine except he would alfo forfake the mother of the Higheft. *Illa eft enim quæ maxima damna nobis infert. Quos enim filius per iuftitiam perdit, mater per mifericordiam & indulgentiam adducit.* She bringeth greateft loffe to vs. For whom her fonne deftroyes by his iuftice, thofe fhe relieueth by her mercy and pardon. And by their learning fhe can giue leaue to a Monke to commit adultery, if he falute her altar, and faft for her fake vpon the Saturday, fhe will faue groffe finners from damnation: the Romanifts haue more pro-ued her affection toward them in his kind; which being fo we dare not truft it.

De B. Virgine exempla poft term. difcipuli ,, ,, ,, ,, Ibid. A me licentiã accipiebat. Supra cap. 20.

17   When a fimple or ignorant Roman Catholicke reades or heares this, he will either vtterly deny it as neuer written by a Catholicke; or difclaime it, as ouer impudent, fhamelefle and blafphemous : or he will appeale vnto his learned teachers, whether any fuch thing be written; or if it be, how it may ftand with the glory of God who hath faid, *that he will impart his honor to none other*, as before is euidently proued. They muft of neceffitie anfwer, either that there is no fuch thing written in their bookes, and then they moft impudently lye. Or they muft fay it is written by fome outworne dunfe and obfcure fellow, that was neuer acknowledged for a clafficall author; and then they lye as falfly : for *Barnardine* is entituled *venerabilis*

Efay 42. 8.

venerabilis & eruditiſſimus, venerable and moſt learned: he did dedicate his book to *Alexander the ſixt* then Biſhop of Rome, which ſeemeth to haue bene thrice printed, if not oftener; as I haue ſeene *annis* 1511. 1515. and very lately, 1607. with this commendation to the ſale in the title thereof: *Quod quidem peregregium opus, non ſolùm verbi Dei concionatoribus & parochis, ſed & omnibus ſacræ theologiæ ſtudioſis, ſummam afferet v-* "*tilitatem:* Which excellent worke verily will bring great pro- "fite, not onely to the Preachers of the word of God, and pariſh "prieſts, but to all ſtudents of Diuinitie. Or they will ſay, it is but one Doctors opinion, and ſo priuate, which they are not bound to defend, (then why do they ſo often print it, and neuer correct it?) Which is alſo falſe, for many haue the ſame blaſphemie beſide *Burnt Barnard.* Or they muſt ſtand to it like a Ieſuite, that with an odde diſtinction will defend that the Crow is white, becauſe there is ſomewhat blacker; which not one of ten thouſand of the people, nay ſcarſe any among themſelues can vnderſtand, or dare expreſſe their meaning in plaine tearmes. And ſo are the ſimple people betrayed, and made beleeue that the creature is as much aboue the Creator, as mercy exceedeth iudgement; the ſame in effect may be ſaid of the other author, as abſurd and blaſphemous as he is.

18 Howſoeuer our aduerſe Catholicke Romanes would perhaps wiſh in their vaine hopes, that an Appeale might in our caſe be made vnto her, yet neither dare we tender an Appeale to the mother, and paſſe by the Sonne; or to the wife, and refuſe the husband; or to the aduocatrix, as the ſoberer Papiſts will haue her at the moſt, and leaue the Iudge; or finally to a meere creature though neuer ſo holy and excellent, and forſake the Creator who is bleſſed for euer, not among women as the holy Virgine, but aboue all things in heauen and earth. Neither if we ſhould appeale vnto her, would ſhe preſume to admit it, ſeeing nothing is more deare vnto her then the honor of her Sonne, who is her Sauiour, and ſhe his handmaid, he her maker, & ſhe his workmanſhip. Aske her, and ſhe will not ſay, do what I bid you, but, *Whatſoeuer he ſaith vnto you do it.* For it is he, and he onely, that can not onely turne our water into wine; but can waſh away our ſinnes with the water of life, and cheare

Similes habent labra lactucas. *Like booke like patron.*

In moſt of his Legends.

Iudicium & miſericordiã cantabo.

Luke 1.47.

Iohn 2. 5.

cheare our hearts with the fruite of the vine in his Fathers
kingdome. Therefore to the bleſſed Virgine, though by the
ſuperſtitious ſhe be ſeated aboue the Sonne, we may not appeale.

19 Conſidering all the precedent difficulties,after a ſhort
repetition of the reſt of all thoſe places and perſons,from
which and from whom our aduerſaries do peremptorily de-
barre vs,or our ſelues can by no meanes be induced to truſt;
I will in deſpite of Rome and Antichriſt, lay my Appeale
to that place and perſon, whither with ſafetie we may haue
acceſſe,and with whom we are ſure to find no iniuſtice.

20   Shall I name hell?This is the kingdome of darkneſſe,
wherein the higheſt throne of the Romane Antichriſt is aduanced; thither are many Popes and Cardinals already gone
before, and are infranchiſed as chiefe princes to that monarchie,or rather popular confuſion. Their Legends teach,that
their Saints can coſin the diuell, and force him to teach the S.Barnard.
Pſalmes,which euery day ſaid,will ſaue the ſoule of him that
ſayes them. That another caught the diuell by the noſe with Dunſtane.
a paire of tongs or pincers, in deſpite of his face,and would
not let him depart without licence, (many a better man
would haue bene glad to be rid of him with leſſe intreatie.)
Another could make him hold his candle till his finger burnt,
that he roared againe : as if Saint *Dominicks* candle burnt a- Dominicke.
boue the fire and brimſtone of hell, wherein the diuell and
his angels are tormented.Beſides,they can exorcize and coniure the diuels when they liſt. They haue holy water to appeaſe him , though in this the diuell was deceiued by *Me-* Melanĉh.
lanĉthon; or croſſes to terrifie him,which we haue not. They
will equiuocate for him , and he will lye downeright for
them;I trow he was preſident of the holy League:and of him
the Pope holdeth all the kingdomes of the earth, as in fee.
Chriſt our Sauiour refuſed them himſelfe,he neuer beſtowed
them on any other: his kingdome was not of this world;and Ioh.18.
therefore Rome hath forſaken him,and hath betaken her ſelf
to the prince of this world, that ruleth in the aire, and ouerruleth and reigneth in the children of diſobedience. Though

our aduerſaries would full faine haue vs, yet we will not appeale to that place or that Iudge.

21   What ſhall we ſay to Purgatorie? That is the Popes peculiar, all the ſoules there are his owne priſoners; the intollerableneſſe of their torment, and the hope of his pardon, wil eaſily draw all voices to his partie. We dare not put our fingers into that fiame, which is equall with the paines of hell, ſaue onely for perpetuitie. The Pope onely built this manſion, and ſet vp this kingdome . Our powerfull Creator, in whom we haue our greateſt, yea onely confidence, neuer made it, he knowes it not; neither meane we to come there: neither that place nor the perſons therein are competent iudges, we dare not commit our ſelues or our owne cauſe vnto them : and if we would admit the place , yet we know not where it is, nor can they themſelues agree where it may be found.

22   Their *Limbus puerorum* can affoord vs no iudge; they are but children, yea infants that died before baptiſme; they neither caried skill with them whē they went thither, neither are they permitted the viſion of God, or comfort of light, or conference with the more learned Saints; therefore they remaine ignorant and know nothing, they cannot diſcerne, much leſſe determine.

23   *Limbus Patrum* was emptied at the coming of Chriſt, neither Patriark, nor Prophet, nor righteous man remaineth there . The Romanes can find no tenants for that Lordſhip, and therefore in deſpite of Philoſophie, there is *vacuitie*.

Vacua remanet.

24   The fiſt ſubterranean place, where good ſoules are, which needed no purgation, and were not fitted *for the bleſſed viſion*, though it ſeeme not improbable to Cardinall *Bellarmine*, becauſe to venerable *Beda* it ſeemed a very probable *viſion*; yet for that all the Schoolemen hold but foure places, he dares not aſſeuere it, and reſolue vpon it, wherein me ſeemeth he need not to be very ſcrupulous. For *Limbus Patrum*, although it was a kind of priſon for the time, yet it was but *quaſi carcer quidam ſenatorius atque honorarius*, as the Cardinall ſaith of his newfound nothing, for ought I know, or he can

Bellar.de Purg.l.2.c.6, Idem ibid.

proue,

proue, a certaine noble and *honorable prison*, (rather like the Tower of London then Bishop *Bonners* cole-house:) and so perhaps was *quoddam quasi pratum florentissimum, lucidissimū, odoratum, amœnum, in quo degebant animæ, sed tamen ibi manebant, quia nondum idoneæ erant visioni beatæ:* As it were, a certaine ,, medow, most flourishing, most lightsome, odoriferous, plea- ,, sant, like the old Poets *Elisij campt*, which were pleasant fields, ,, where the soules conuersed, and yet stayed there, becaufe ,, as yet they were not fit for the vision of God. Why may not ,, *Bedaes* or *Bellarmines* fift place be the Schoolemens fourth place, and so no place added, nor any left emptie, but an old repaired, and new tenants put into possession? How weake a foundation will superstition build vpon?

25   Let vs repeate, not *ab ouo ad malum*, from the egge to the apple; but *à nido ad malum*, from the very neast of the Popes infancie, to the very top of his blasphemy and mischiefe; and we shall see how either in his owne right and proprietie, or by his forgery and vsurpation, he hath so forestalled and ingrossed all into his owne hands and power, as that no man, not endued with light and wisedome from aboue, can find either place and person, whither or to whom he may appeale. The Pope as in his owne right hath hell, Purgatory, with their members and appurtenances, or lims, if you will, both of children and fathers. We are rid of them and their inhabitants. From thence the Church was poisoned; they are worse then Scorpions, they can sting to death, but neuer cure to recouery He claimeth all the earth both in temporall and spirituall, ciuill and Ecclesiasticall gouernment. He possesseth as much as is not ours : he entitleth himselfe to that which we enioy, as infranchised into Gods inheritance. His owne he holdeth as his vassals, vs he reputeth as his enemies: we may not be tried by him and his; he will not be iudged by vs and ours. For they are indeed our malicious and sworne enemies, we are their opposites and aduersaries for Christs sake: therefore neither earth nor earthly men, nor places in the aire or vnder the earth, can affoord vs either place of iudgement,

or iuſt iudge in their or our perſwaſion.

26 Heauen alſo is vſurped by the Romane Biſhop, whereunto he pretendeth title in fee taile to himſelfe, and to his heires male, though once the Salicke law was coſined in Pope *Ioane.* We haue heard how there he commandeth Angels, indenizeth and canonizeth Saints, tieth God the holy Ghoſt to his chaire, keepeth God the Sonne either in a boxe ouer the altar, or laking and playing with beades in his mothers lap, or ouerruled by her importunitie, if not by her authoritie. He hath God the Father but his equall at moſt, if he be not his better; for he can bind where God looſeth, and looſe where God bindeth; he can make Gods truth error, and the diuels error truth. And finally, the bleſſed Virgin (whom I name laſt, as in their going proceſſion, becauſe they eſteeme her moſt) I cannot admit; or at leaſt their Lady, whom they not onely blaſpheme, as is before noted, and God in her, but alſo make her a midwife, with the help of Angels, at the birth of an Abbeſſes baſtard, and drudge to Saint *Bettrice* while ſhe wandred a whoring, and bawd to them both, while ſhe kept their counſell, couered their ſinne, ſmothered their ſhame, and preuented their puniſhment. Fearfull things to be ſpoken or thought of the Saints of God, yea the mother of God.

Diſcipulus de miraculis B. Mariæ.

27 They haue neuer done railing vpon vs, as if we derogated from that bleſſed Virgine Chriſts mothers honour; which is moſt falſe, and with great impudencie laid to the charge of our Church. But we may ſay to the king of Locuſts, as *Elias* the Prophet to *Abab* the tyrant, *Not I, but thou and thy houſe:* It is not we, but the Pope and his ſynagogue that trouble the ſeruice of God, ſometime playing and dallying with the Saints, ſometimes mocking them, blaſpheming them, and yet moſt ſacrilegiouſly diſhonouring God for their ſakes: and indeed ſinning and ſhaming themſelues with their open and impious idolatry and blaſphemy.

1. King. 18. 17.

28 May I not proceed and tender this Appeale to the bleſſed and glorious Trinitie? They for the moſt part yeeld that we are orthodoxe in the truth hereof, and we will be

content

content to yeeld them their part in the same truth. Yet herein haue they not left vs without scruple. For what if a Pope
hath said, that Saint *Peter* was taken in *Consortium indiuidua* Leo Epistola
Trinitatis? Is it not to proue himselfe to be admitted into the 89.
same fellowship of the indiuisible Trinitie? *Peter* would not,
the Pope should not, so blaspheme. Me thinks that the superexcellent honour of that most glorious maiestie should also
be much impeached, not onely by those monstrous pictures
and resemblances, mentioned in the last Chapter before, but
also by giuing almost all the attributes belonging to the e-
uerlasting Deitie, vnto their Lady; and that of mercy, euen a-
boue that God who gaue his Sonne; that God, that gaue himselfe; that God that inspired Chrifts humanitie, and proceeded from the Father and the Sonne; one God, three persons, to be euerlastingly glorified for euer. Amen. Which certainly they do most sacrilegiously, when they not onely
make the blessed Virgine Chrifts fellow, which is more then Catharinus in
should be, but when they attribute onely iustice to God, all Concil. Tri-
mercy to their Ladie, as hath bene said. When they take all Bonauentura.
the Psalmes of *Dauid*, which he most diuinely directed onely to the glory of God, and turne them, and wrest them to
their Ladie, foysting in *Domina* for *Dominus, Ladie* for *Lord*.
And among the rest, if not aboue all other blasphemies, when
they are not abashed to take that which our Sauiour applyed
to his owne person, *The Lord said vnto my Lord, sit thou on my* Psal.110.1.
right hand, till I make thine enemies thy footstoole; and whereby
he put his aduersaries to such a foyle, that after *no man durst* Math.22.46.
aske him any moe questions; and giue it to their Ladie, *Dixit*
Dominus Domina mea, sede mater mea à dextris meis: whereby
they do not onely misapply the Scripture, but, whereas here
is God the Father speaking to God his Sonne, the Sonne is
put into the Fathers place, the mother into the Sons roome,
and God the Father vtterly excluded, as if it appertained not
vnto him.

29   Let the quintessence of any quaint Roman Iesuiticall wit, presse out any better meaning of this blasphemous
passage out of the Seraphicall Doctors, if not illiterall, yet

vndi-

vndiuine words, if he can. I professe that I cannot. But it may
be as the Prophet said in his excesse, all men are lyers; so the
wisest of our aduersaries may confesse, that these haue bene
excessiue lyers. In hope whereof, notwithstanding all exceptions and aduantages they haue giuen vnto vs, we will now
at the last tender our Appeale.

Psal. 116. 11.

   30   Seeing the whore of Babylon, who hath openly and
without shame committed fornication with the Kings of the
earth, that is, the Romane Synagogue, hath entred action
and commenced suite against the gracious & chaste spouse of
Christ, because she will not partake in her spirituall adulteries, which are plaine idolatries: and hath preferred her libell, full of malicious slanders and lyes, which neither as yet
she hath, nor euer shall be able to proue; bringeth none but
her own priuate, pretended and corrupted euidences, against
such common principles, vnrazed, vndefaced, not questioned
for their truth, on either partie, as by vs are auouched; and
produceth no witnesses but domesticall, and such as are sub-
orned to say what she listeth, against faithfull, true, legall witnesses, as against whom no iust exception can be taken: will
haue no place for consistoricall proceeding, but Rome the
seate of the most deadly & direfull enemie of Christs Spouse,
against the tribunall of the euer blessed Sonne of God: No
iudge but Antichrist the man of sinne; now openly reuealed vnto the whole world of Gods Church, against the glorious Iudge of quicke and dead: no assistants, but Cardinals
and Bishops of her owne making, sworne to her obedience,
liuing by her pensions, honoured by her titles, against the
foure Euangelists, and foure and twenty Elders, the Prophets
and Apostles that stand about the throne of God: No hearers, but the silly ignorant people that scarce know their
right hand from their left, or some factious and preiudicate
gentles, who vpon priuate obligation of pardons, dispensations or the like, are readie to clap a *plaudite*, and reioyce at
euery word she speaketh against the communion of Saints, in
heauen and in earth, who behold the glory of God in the
face of Iesus Christ, and know the truth of God as it is reuealed

Reuel. 17.

Reuel. 4

led in his holy word: Therefore this holy Spouse appealeth vpon so iust causes, for these so many grieuances, to the Lord of heauen and earth, his blessed Sonne her Sauiour Iesus Christ, and the holy Ghost the sanctifier of his elect, in this manner:

31 *In the name of God, Amen.* Before you all publicke persons, Kings, Princes, and Magistrates, with Bishops, Deanes, Doctors, and learned men, and many other witnesses worthy credit, now present and liuing in this world; we the true and faithfull Ministers of the Gospell of Iesus Christ, called lawfully to be the publicke Preachers of the same Gospell, as Preachers in the name of our holy mother the militant Church, part of the vniuersall communion of all Saints, do say and alledge, and vnder our hand-writing with a mind and purpose to appeale and prouoke, and principally of the nullities, or nullity in law, do alledge: That whereas the late and present Bishops of Rome, the pretended Vicars of God and his Sonne Christ, (who is heire of all things, by whom the world was made, the lawfully appointed Iudge of quicke & dead) and so carying himselfe to be, in a certaine pretended cause of heresie and defamation, which before them the said Popes, betweene the whore of Babylon of the Church malignant, the pretenced actor or plaintife of the one partie, and our holy mother and mistris, the true Spouse of Christ on the other partie, hath long bene questioned and hung vndecided and vndetermined, and (sauing their reuerence) without all right and reason proceeded, and manifestly fauouring the cause and person of the said whore, haue giuen a sentence in the late Councell or Conuenticle of Trent, and in his owne vnlawfull Consistory, (if it may be called a sentence) in her behalfe: which they haue reduced into writing, read and published, at the instance, request, and sinister suggestion of the said whore, all order of law vtterly neglected and despised, to the great preiudice, infamy, losse and grieuance of our said holy mother and mistris. Whereupon we the said Ministers and Preachers well perceiuing and vnderstanding, that both our said mother and mistris, and we her Ministers and Prea-

Heb. 1. 1.

Qq 4   chers

chers on her behalfe, and for her fake, are by the premiſed
grieuances, iniuſtice, nullities, and other enormities, vniuſtly
and intollerably vexed and wronged: and fearing and mi-
ſtruſting to ſuſtaine more grieuance and vexation in time to
come, from the ſaid pretenced and partiall ſentence and definition, as vnduly and vniuſtly giuen, and from the publication thereof; we directly appeale vnto the good, iuſt, mercifull, glorious, omnipotent and onely wiſe God, and his onely
begotten Sonne our Lord and Sauiour Ieſus Chriſt, in that
high Court of his iuſt iudgement, when he ſhall iudge this
world with equitie, and his people with truth. And we re-

Apoſtolos.   quire meſſengers, or at leaſt effectuall letters teſtimoniall,
once, againe, and the third time, inſtantly, more inſtantly, and
moſt inſtantly, for vs and our ſaid mother and miſtris, from
you all Kings, Princes, and magiſtrates of the earth, to be
made, giuen & deliuered vnto vs, or our ſaid miſtris. And here
we proteſt that we will ſtand to, and proſecute this our Appeale with the aduenture of our eſtates, bloud and liues, in
the ſight of heauen and earth, Angels and men, before the
throne of the Ancient of dayes, and the Lamb, and the whole
hoaſt of the euerliuing and euerlaſting God, vnto whom
we moſt humbly tender this our hearty and humble petition.

Pſal. 43. 1.   32 Iudge vs, ô God, and defend our cauſe, againſt the
vnmercifull people (of Rome,) deliuer vs from the wicked
and deceitfull man of ſinne: for thou art the God of our
ſtrength: put vs not away, let vs not go mourning, while the
enemy oppreſſeth vs. For whom haue we in heauen but thee?

Pſal. 73. 25.   and we deſire none in the earth with thee. Send the light and
thy truth, let them leade vs, and let them bring vs to thy ho-

Pſal. 9. 19.   ly mountaine and to thy tabernacles. Vp Lord, let not man
preuaile, let the (Papiſts) be iudged in thy ſight: put them
in feare, ô Lord, that they may know themſelues to be but
men: cut off their flattering lips, and their tongues that ſpeake

Pſal. 12. 3. 8.   proud things. When theſe wicked ones are exalted, it is a

Pſal. 17. 3.   ſhame for the ſonnes of men. Vp Lord, diſappoint them, caſt
them downe, and deliuer our ſoules by thy ſword, which is

Pſal. 59. 5.   thy holy and written word. Awake, ô thou Lord God of
hoaſts,

hoasts,ô God of Israel,awake to visite all the heathen,be not mercifull to them that sinne maliciously : yet slay them not, left thy people forget it,but scatter them abroad by thy power, and put them downe ô Lord our shield. For the sinne of their mouth,and the words of their lips,let them be taken in their pride: and for their periury and lies which they speake, consume them in thy wrath, consume them that they be no more, and let them know that God ruleth in Iacob,and vnto the ends of the world. Breake their teeth (ô God) in their mouthes, breake the iawes of the yong Lions, ô Lord,hold not thy tongue,ô God of our praise:for the mouth of the wicked (Romanists) and the mouth of deceit are opened vpon vs, they haue spoken of vs with a lying tongue. They haue compassed vs about with words of hatred, and fought againft vs without a caufe. For our friendship they are our e-nemies,but we will giue our selues vnto prayer. They haue rewarded vs euill for good, and hatred for our loue. Turne their hearts ô Lord, if they belong to thy election of grace, and be ordained vnto euerlasting life, that thou mayeft take mercie vpon them: but rather then they may hurt thy little flocke,and lay wafte thy dwelling place,or supplant the foot-fteps of thine annointed,let them be couered with shame and dishonour, let them fall in slippery places,and let the Angell of the Lord scatter them.O daughter of Babylon wafted with mifery, blessed shall he be that rewardeth thee as thou haft serued vs ; yea happie shall he be that taketh thy yong children,and dasheth their heads againft the ftones. But help vs, ô Lord God of our saluation, saue vs according to thy mer-cie. Though our enemies curfe vs, yet ô Lord bleffe vs, and let the light of thy countenance shine vpon vs.Be fauourable vnto vs, ô Lord, be fauourable to thy people which serue thee in truth,according to thy holy word. Leade vs ô Lord in thy righteoufneffe, becaufe of our enemies, make our wayes plaine before our face. O let the malice of the wicked come to an end, but guide thou the iuft : for the righteous God trieth the hearts & reines.Haue mercie vpon vs ô Lord, confider our trouble which we fuffer of them, thou that lif-

Pfal.25.

Pfal.58.6.

Pfal.137.

Pfal.5.4.

Pfal 7.9.

Pfal.9.13.

teft

Pſal.17. teſt vs vp from the gates of death. Heare the right ô Lord, and let our ſentence come forth from thy preſence, and let thine eyes behold equitie. Shew thy maruellous mercies, thou that art the Sauiour of all that truſt in thee, from ſuch as refiſt thy right hand. Shew vs thy wayes ô Lord, and teach

Pſal.25. vs thy paths, leade vs forth in thy truth, and teach vs, for thou art the God of our ſaluation. Remember thy tender mercies, for they haue bin euer of old, and thy louing kindneſſes, for they haue bin for euer. And finally, this one thing haue we de-

Pſal.27. ſired, which we will require, that we may dwell in thy houſe all the dayes of our life, to behold the beauty of the Lord, and to viſite his temple. Which if in thy mercy thou ſhalt vouchſafe vnto vs, then will we ſing of thy power, and will praiſe thy mercy in the morning. Yea ſeuen times a day will

Pſal.63.4. we praiſe thee, and call vpon thy Name. We will magnifie
Pſal.57.7. thee all the days of our life. For our heart is prepared ô Lord, our heart is prepared, we will ſing and giue praiſe. And we

Pſal.50.15. will call vpon thee in the day of trouble, that thou maiſt heare
23. vs, and that we may glorifie thee. For they that offer thee praiſe, ſhall honour thee: and to them that diſpoſe their way aright, thou wilt ſhew the ſaluation of God. Yea we will

Pſal.9.1. praiſe thee ô Lord with our whole heart, we will ſpeake of
Pſal.18.46. all thy wondrous works. Let the Lord liue, and bleſſed be
Pſal.21.13. our ſtrength; and let the God of our ſaluation be exalted, ſo will we ſing and praiſe thy power. O God be mercifull vnto

Pſal.67.1. vs and bleſſe vs, and ſhew vs the light of thy countenance, and be gracious vnto vs: that thy wayes may be knowne vpon earth, thy ſauing health among all nations. That with one heart, and one voice, and one ſoule we may glorifie thy bleſſed Name, and ſay, *Come Lord Ieſu, come quickly.* End theſe dayes of ſinne, compoſe all controuerſies, trample vpon the head of thine enemies, and let thoſe that feare thy Name, ſay alway, *All honour, and glorie, and praiſe, and power be aſcribed to him that ſitteth vpon the throne, and to the Lambe, and to the holy Spirit pro- ceeding from them both, for e- uermore, Amen.*

Errata.

Page 5. line 11. for Example, reade Epiſtle. p.29.l.9.eò. r. eos. p.31.l.5. ha-
uen.r.heauen. p.3 2.l.11.enled.r. entitled.l.12.their.r.other.p.45.in marg.mun.
r.mur. p. 51.l.30.breath.r. breach.p.67.l.29.dedere.r.ebedire. p. 68. l. 24.r.with
his owne hands.p. 100.l.6.r.of the true Church.p.143 l. 7.r. Biſhops ſeeme. p.
160.l.24.afces.r.faces.p.170.l.30.receiued.r.reuerend.p.174.l.4. diſplacet.r. diſ-
plicet. p. 199.l.vlt. Nullus. r. Nullius. p.202.l.11.48.r. 58.p.226.l.23.eſſet.r.eſſe.
p.229 l.10. vſuall.r.vnuſuall.l 17. præſcribe. r.proſcribe.l.34.of.r. againſt.p.236.
l.27.firſt.r.fift.p.239.l.12.aſſutü.r aſſutum.p.257.l.27.thing.r.hinge.p.263.l.vlt.
thing.r.things. p.293.l.18.can.r cannot.p.312. l. 34.our.r.one p.316.l.5.old.r.
owne.p.317.l.2.Gyriſonians.r.Gryſonnians.p. 321.l.19.Anachtus. r. Anacletus.p.
325.l.vlt. deſcribed.r.deſcried. p.330.l.3. ferrei.r.ferreæ.l.36. liues.r.lies.p.347.
l.14.pray.r.pay.p.3 ; 6.l.27.made.r.may.p.361.l.26.coaſt.r.coſt.p.383.l.25 Of.
r.Or.p.389.l.10.He.r.Here.p.403.l.22.Catholickes.r.Catalogues. p.543. l.33.
Caluanus.r.Calanus.